WESTERN CIVILIZATION VOLUME II

Early Modern through the Twentieth Century

Ninth Edition

Editor

William Hughes

Essex Community College

William Hughes is a professor of history at Essex Community College in Baltimore County, Maryland. He received his B.A. from Franklin and Marshall College and his M.A. from the Pennsylvania State University. He continued graduate studies at the American University and the Pennsylvania State University. Professor Hughes is interested in cultural history, particularly the role of film and television in shaping and recording history. He researched this subject as a Younger Humanist Fellow of the National Endowment for the Humanities, and he was a participant in the Image as Artifact project of the American Historical Association, serving twice as a panelist at annual meetings. He is author of the chapter on film as evidence in *The Historian and Film* (Cambridge University Press) and has written articles, essays, and reviews for *The Journal of American History, The New Republic, The Nation, Film and History, American Film, The Dictionary of Literary Biography: American Screenwriters* and *The Dictionary of American Biography.* Professor Hughes also serves as an associate editor for *American National Biography,* a twenty-volume reference work to be issued by Oxford University Press.

A Library of Information from the Public Press

Dushkin/McGraw·Hill

Sluice Dock, Guilford, Connecticut 06437

The Annual Editions Series

ANNUAL EDITIONS is a series of over 65 volumes designed to provide the reader with convenient, low-cost access to a wide range of current, carefully selected articles from some of the most important magazines, newspapers, and journals published today. ANNUAL EDITIONS are updated on an annual basis through a continuous monitoring of over 300 periodical sources. All ANNUAL EDITIONS have a number of features that are designed to make them particularly useful, including topic guides, annotated tables of contents, unit overviews, and indexes. For the teacher using ANNUAL EDITIONS in the classroom, an Instructor's Resource Guide with test questions is available for each volume.

VOLUMES AVAILABLE

Abnormal Psychology
Adolescent Psychology
Africa
Aging
American Foreign Policy
American Government
American History, Pre-Civil War
American History, Post-Civil War
American Public Policy
Anthropology
Archaeology
Biopsychology
Business Ethics
Child Growth and Development
China
Comparative Politics
Computers in Education
Computers in Society
Criminal Justice
Criminology
Developing World
Deviant Behavior
Drugs, Society, and Behavior
Dying, Death, and Bereavement
Early Childhood Education
Economics
Educating Exceptional Children
Education
Educational Psychology
Environment
Geography
Global Issues
Health
Human Development
Human Resources
Human Sexuality
India and South Asia
International Business
Japan and the Pacific Rim
Latin America
Life Management
Macroeconomics
Management
Marketing
Marriage and Family
Mass Media
Microeconomics
Middle East and the Islamic World
Multicultural Education
Nutrition
Personal Growth and Behavior
Physical Anthropology
Psychology
Public Administration
Race and Ethnic Relations
Russia, the Eurasian Republics, and Central/Eastern Europe
Social Problems
Social Psychology
Sociology
State and Local Government
Urban Society
Western Civilization, Pre-Reformation
Western Civilization, Post-Reformation
Western Europe
World History, Pre-Modern
World History, Modern
World Politics

AE

Cataloging in Publication Data
Main entry under title: Annual Editions: Western civilization, vol. II: Early Modern through the Twentieth Century. 9/E.
1. Civilization—Periodicals. 2. World history—Periodicals. I. Hughes, William, *comp.* II. Title: Western civilization, vol. II: Early Modern through the Twentieth Century.
901.9'05 82–645823 ISBN 0–697–36318–X

Ninth Edition

Printed in the United States of America

Printed on Recycled Paper

Editors/Advisory Board

Members of the Advisory Board are instrumental in the final selection of articles for each edition of ANNUAL EDITIONS. Their review of articles for content, level, currentness, and appropriateness provides critical direction to the editor and staff. We think that you will find their careful consideration well reflected in this volume.

To the Reader

In publishing ANNUAL EDITIONS we recognize the enormous role played by the magazines, newspapers, and journals of the *public press* in providing current, first-rate educational information in a broad spectrum of interest areas. Many of these articles are appropriate for students, researchers, and professionals seeking accurate, current material to help bridge the gap between principles and theories and the real world. These articles, however, become more useful for study when those of lasting value are carefully *collected, organized, indexed,* and *reproduced* in a *low-cost format,* which provides easy and permanent access when the material is needed. That is the role played by ANNUAL EDITIONS. Under the direction of each volume's *academic editor,* who is an expert in the subject area, and with the guidance of an *Advisory Board,* each year we seek to provide in each ANNUAL EDITION a current, well-balanced, carefully selected collection of the best of the public press for your study and enjoyment. We think that you will find this volume useful, and we hope that you will take a moment to let us know what you think.

What exactly are we attempting to do when we set out to study the history of Western civilization?

The traditional course in Western civilization was often a chronological survey of sequential stages in the development of European institutions and ideas, with a cursory look at Near Eastern antecedents and a side glance at the Americas and other places where Westernization has occurred. Typically it moved from the Greeks to the Romans to the medieval period and on to the modern era, itemizing the distinctive characteristics of each stage, as well as each period's relation to preceding and succeeding developments. Of course, in a survey so broad (usually advancing from Adam to the atom in two brief semesters) a certain superficiality was inevitable. Key events whizzed by as if viewed in a cyclorama; often there was little opportunity to absorb and digest the complex ideas that have shaped our culture.

It is tempting to excuse these shortcomings as unavoidable. But to present a course on Western civilization that leaves students with only a jumble of events, names, dates, and places is to miss a marvelous opportunity. For the great promise of such a broad course of study is that it enables students to explore great turning points or shifts in the development of Western culture. Close analysis of these moments enables students to understand the dynamics of continuity and change over time. At best, the course can provide a coherent view of the Western tradition and even its interactions with non-Western cultures. It also offers opportunities for students to compare varied historical forms of authority, religion, and economic organization, to assess the great contests over the meaning of truth and reality that have sometimes divided Western culture, and even to reflect on the price of progress.

Of course, to focus exclusively on Western civilization can lead us to ignore non-Western peoples and cultures or else to perceive them in ways that some have labeled "Eurocentric." But contemporary courses in the history of Western civilization are rarely, if ever, mere exercises in European triumphalism. Indeed, they offer an opportunity to subject the Western tradition to critical scrutiny, to assess its accomplishments *and* its shortcomings. Few of us who teach the course would argue that Western history is the only history that contemporary students should know. Yet it should be an essential part of what they learn, for it is impossible to understand the modern world without some grounding in the basic patterns of the Western tradition.

As students become attuned to the distinctive traits of the West, they can develop a sense of the dynamism of history. They can begin to understand how ideas relate to social structures and social forces. They may come to appreciate the nature and significance of conceptual innovation and recognize how values often infuse inquiry. More specifically, they can trace the evolution of Western ideas about such essential matters as nature, humankind, authority, the gods, even history itself; that is, they learn *how* the West developed its distinctive character. And, as historian Reed Dasenbrock has observed, in an age that seeks greater multicultural understanding there is much to be learned from "the fundamental multiculturalism of Western culture, the fact that it has been constructed out of a fusion of disparate and often conflicting cultural traditions." Of course, the articles collected in this volume cannot deal with all these matters, but by providing an alternative to the synthetic summaries of most textbooks, they can help students better understand the diverse traditions and processes that we label Western civilization.

This book is like our history—unfinished, always in process. It will be revised biennially. Comments and criticism are welcome from all who use this book. To that end a postpaid article rating form is included at the back of the book. Please feel free to recommend articles that might improve the next edition. With your assistance, this anthology will continue to improve.

William Hughes
Editor

Contents

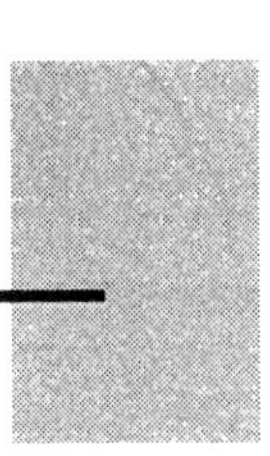

UNIT 1

The Age of Power

Six selections trace the evolution of political power in early modern times. Topics include the European state system, the emergence of British power, and the influence of John Locke on liberty.

The concepts in bold italics are developed in the article. For further expansion please refer to the Topic Guide and the Index.

UNIT 2

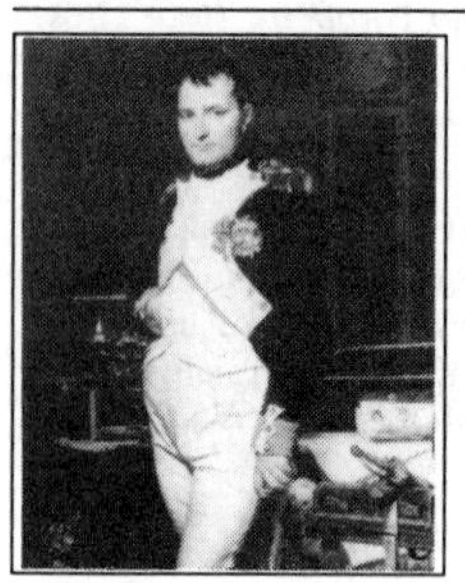

Rationalism, Enlightenment, and Revolution

Eight articles discuss the impact of science, politics, music, economic thought, changing social attitudes, and the rights of women on the Age of Enlightenment.

UNIT 3

Industry, Ideology, Nation-Building, and Imperialism: The Nineteenth Century

Seven articles focus on the nineteenth century in the Western world. Topics include the working class, the Industrial Revolution, the opening of the Far East, and the expansion of Europe.

UNIT 4

Modernism, Statism, and Total War: The Twentieth Century

Eleven selections discuss the evolution of the modern Western world, the world wars, the Nazi state, the effects of Europe's loss of economic and political dominance in world affairs.

UNIT 5

Conclusion: The Human Prospect

Eight articles examine how politics, war, economics, and culture affect the prospects of humankind.

The concepts in bold italics are developed in the article. For further expansion please refer to the Topic Guide and the Index.

Topic Guide

This topic guide suggests how the selections in this book relate to topics of traditional concern to students and professionals involved with the study of Western civilization. It is useful for locating articles that relate to each other for reading and research. The guide is arranged alphabetically according to topic. Articles may, of course, treat topics that do not appear in the topic guide. In turn, entries in the topic guide do not necessarily constitute a comprehensive listing of all the contents of each selection.

TOPIC AREA	TREATED IN
Art/Architecture	22. When Cubism Met the Decorative Arts in France
Business	4. High Price of Sugar 16. Samuel Smiles
Cities	3. Golden Age: Innovation in Dutch Cities 9. Madrid: City of the Enlightenment 21. Sarah Bernhardt's Paris
Cold War	28. Looking Back: The Cold War in Retrospect 29. How the Bomb Saved Soviet Physics 31. Future That Never Came
Colonialism	18. After Centuries of Japanese Isolation, a Fateful Meeting of East and West
Culture	20. Life and Resurrection of Alexandre Dumas 30. Other Camus 34. *Real* Clash
Democracy	8. The Pursuit of Happiness
Economics	38. Poor and the Rich
Enlightenment	8. Pursuit of Happiness 9. Madrid: City of the Enlightenment 12. Passion of Antoine Lavoisier 14. First Feminist
Fascism	25. Remembering Mussolini 26. Women and the Nazi State
Ideology	6. Locke and Liberty 15. Engels in Manchester 16. Samuel Smiles 32. End of the Twentieth Century
Industrial Revolution	15. Engels in Manchester
Labor	15. Engels in Manchester
Middle Class	6. Locke and Liberty 16. Samuel Smiles
Middle East	24. How the Modern Middle East Map Came to Be Drawn 33. Jihad vs. McWorld
Modernization	33. Jihad vs. McWorld 40. Whither Western Civilization?
Nationalism	17. Giuseppe Garibaldi 32. End of the Twentieth Century
Nation-State	1. Emergence of the Great Powers 2. War, Money, and the English State 36. Nation-State Is Dead. Long Live the Nation-State
Philosophy	6. Locke and Liberty
Politics/Authority	1. Emergence of the Great Powers 5. Cardinal Mazarin 13. Napoleon Takes Charge 25. Remembering Mussolini 32. End of the Twentieth Century
Religion	33. Jihad vs. McWorld 35. Europe's Muslims
Revolution	11. French Revolution in the Minds of Men 12. Passion of Antoine Lavoisier
Science	7. Newton's Madness 29. How the Bomb Saved Soviet Physics

The Age of Power

The early modern period (c. 1450–c. 1700) was a time of profound change for Western civilization. During this epoch the medieval frame of reference gave way to a recognizably modern orientation. The old order had been simply, but rigidly, structured. There was little social or geographical mobility. Europe was relatively backward and isolated from much of the world. The economy was dominated by self-sufficient agriculture. Trade and cities did not flourish. There were few rewards for technological innovation. A person's life seemed more attuned to reve-

UNIT 1

lation than to reason and science. The Church both inspired and delimited intellectual and artistic expression. Most people were prepared to subordinate their concerns to those of a higher order—whether religious or social. Carlo Cipolla, a distinguished European historian, has given us an interesting capsulization of the waning order: "People were few in number, small in size, and lived short lives. Socially they were divided among those who fought and hunted, those who prayed and learned, and those who worked. Those who fought did it often to rob. Those who prayed and learned, learned little and prayed much and superstitiously. Those who worked were the great majority and were considered the lowest group of all" (*Clocks and Culture*, Norton, 1978).

That constricted world gradually gave way to the modern world. There is no absolute date that marks the separation, but elements of modernity were evident throughout Western civilization by the eighteenth century. In this context the late medieval, Renaissance, and Reformation periods were transitional. They linked the medieval to the modern. But what were the elements of this emergent modernity? Beginning with the economic foundation, an economy based on money and commerce overlaid the traditional agrarian system, thus creating a more fluid society. Urban life became increasingly important, allowing greater scope for personal expression. Modernity involved a state of mind, as well. Europeans of the early modern period were conscious that their way of life was different from that of their forebears. In addition, these moderns developed a different sense of time—for urban people, clock time superseded the natural rhythms of the changing seasons and the familiar cycle of planting and harvesting. As for the life of the mind, humanism, rationalism, and science began to take precedence over tradition—though not without a struggle. Protestantism presented yet another challenge to orthodoxy. And, as economic and political institutions evolved, new attitudes about power and authority emerged.

The early modern period is often called the Age of Power, primarily because the modern state, with its power to tax, conscript, subsidize, and coerce, was taking shape. Its growth was facilitated by the changing economic order, which made it possible for governments to acquire money in unprecedented amounts—to hire civil servants, raise armies, protect and encourage national enterprise, and expand their power to the national boundaries and beyond.

Power, in various early modern manifestations, is the subject of the articles assembled in this unit. The first unit essay, "The Emergence of the Great Powers," surveys the shifting international balance of power during the seventeenth and eighteenth centuries. "War, Money, and the English State" explores relations among economy, society, and state in one country. "A Golden Age: Innovation in Dutch Cities, 1648–1720" shows how the economic power of the Dutch was translated into cultural influence. "The High Price of Sugar" describes the triangular trade and how the drive for profits and economic power transformed Western civilization into an Atlantic culture that combined European, American, and African elements. The article "Cardinal Mazarin" considers whether that influential royal adviser misused his power, as contemporary opponents and modern historians have charged. Finally, "Locke and Liberty" covers the philosopher's attempts to formulate a "modern" philosophy of politics, one resting on liberty and property.

Looking Ahead: Challenge Questions

How did the modern international order evolve?

How could modern states, such as England, afford such heavy investments in their military establishments?

How did the rise of the modern state apparatus affect warfare?

What were Cardinal Mazarin's contributions to the development of state power in early modern France?

What were the long-term consequences of the triangular trade?

What is it about John Locke's ideas that make them "modern"?

The Emergence of the Great Powers

Gordon A. Craig and
Alexander L. George

I

Although the term *great power* was used in a treaty for the first time only in 1815, it had been part of the general political vocabulary since the middle of the eighteenth century and was generally understood to mean Great Britain, France, Austria, Prussia, and Russia. This would not have been true in the year 1600, when the term itself would have meant nothing and a ranking of the European states in terms of political weight and influence would not have included three of the countries just mentioned. In 1600, Russia, for instance, was a remote and ineffectual land, separated from Europe by the large territory that was called Poland-Lithuania with whose rulers it waged periodic territorial conflicts, as it did with the Ottoman Turks to the south; Prussia did not exist in its later sense but, as the Electorate of Brandenburg, lived a purely German existence, like Bavaria or Wurttemberg, with no European significance; and Great Britain, a country of some commercial importance, was not accorded primary political significance, although it had, in 1588, demonstrated its will and its capacity for self-defense in repelling the Spanish Armada. In 1600, it is fair to say that, politically, the strongest center in Europe was the old Holy Roman Empire, with its capital in Vienna and its alliances with Spain (one of the most formidable military powers in Europe) and the Catholic states of southern Germany—an empire inspired by a militant Catholicism that dreamed of restoring Charles V's claims of universal dominion. In comparison with Austria and Spain, France seemed destined to play a minor role in European politics, because of the state of internal anarchy and religious strife that followed the murder of Henri IV in 1610.

Why did this situation not persist? Or, to put it another way, why was the European system transformed so radically that the empire became an insignificant political force and the continent came in the eighteenth century to be dominated by Great Britain, France, Austria, Prussia, and Russia? The answer, of course, is war, or, rather more precisely, wars—a long series of religious and dynastic conflicts which raged intermittently from 1618 until 1721 and changed the rank order of European states by exhausting some and exalting others. As if bent upon supplying materials for the nineteenth-century Darwinians, the states mentioned above proved themselves in the grinding struggle of the seventeenth century to be the fittest, the ones best organized to meet the demands of protracted international competition.

The process of transformation began with the Thirty Years War, which stretched from 1618 to 1648. It is sometimes called the last of the religious wars, a description that is justified by the fact that it was motivated originally by the desire of the House of Habsburg and its Jesuit advisers to restore the Protestant parts of the empire to the true faith and because, in thirty years of fighting, the religious motive gave way to political considerations and, in the spreading of the conflict from its German center to embrace all of Europe, some governments, notably France, waged war against their own coreligionists for material reasons. For the states that initiated this wasting conflict, which before it was over had reduced the population of central Europe by at least a third, the war was an unmitigated disaster. The House of Habsburg was so debilitated by it that it lost the control it had formerly possessed over the German states, which meant that they became sovereign in their own right and that the empire now became a mere adjunct of the Austrian crown lands. Austria was, moreover, so weakened by the exertions and losses of that war that in the period after 1648 it had the greatest difficulty in protecting its eastern possessions from the depredations of the Turks and in 1683 was threatened with capture of Vienna by a Turkish army. Until this threat was contained, Austria ceased to be a potent factor in European affairs. At the same time, its strongest ally, Spain, had thrown away an infantry once judged to be the best in Europe in battles like that at Nordlingen in 1634, one of those victories that bleed a nation white. Spain's decline began not with the failure of the Armada, but with the terrible losses suffered in Germany and the Netherlands during the Thirty Years War.

In contrast, the states that profited from the war were the Netherlands, which completed the winning of its independence from Spain in the course of the war and became a commercial and financial center of major importance; the kingdom of Sweden, which under the leadership of Gustavus Adolphus, the Lion of the North, plunged into the conflict in 1630 and emerged as the strongest power in the Baltic region; and France, which entered the war formally in 1635 and came out of it as the most powerful state in western Europe.

It is perhaps no accident that these particular states were so successful, for they were excellent examples of the process that historians have described as the emergence of the modern state, the three principal characteristics of which were effective armed forces, an able bureaucracy, and a theory of state that restrained dynastic exuberance and defined political interest in practical terms. The seventeenth century saw the emergence of what came to be called *raison d'état* or *ragione di stato*—the idea that the state was more than its ruler and more than the expression of his wishes; that it transcended crown and land, prince and people; that it had its particular set of interests and a particular set of necessities based upon them; and that the art of government lay in recognizing those interests and necessities and acting in accordance with them, even if this might violate ordinary religious or ethical standards. The effective state must have the kind of servants who would interpret *raison d'état* wisely and the kind of material and physical resources necessary to implement it. In the first part of the seventeenth century, the Dutch, under leaders like Maurice of Nassau and Jan de Witt, the Swedes, under Gustavus Adolphus and Oxenstierna, and the French, under the inspired ministry of Richelieu, developed the administration and the forces and theoretical skills that exemplify this ideal of modern statehood. That they survived the rigors of the Thirty Years War was not an accident, but rather the result of the fact that they never lost sight of their objectives and never sought objectives that were in excess of their capabilities. Gustavus Adolphus doubtless brought his country into the Thirty Years War to save the cause of Protestantism when it was at a low ebb, but he never for a moment forgot the imperatives of national interest that impelled him to see the war also as a means of winning Swedish supremacy along the shore of the Baltic Sea. Cardinal Richelieu has been called the greatest public servant France ever had, but that title, as Sir George Clark has drily remarked, "was not achieved without many acts little fitting the character of a churchman." It was his clear recognition of France's needs and his absolute unconditionality in pursuing them that made him the most respected statesman of his age.

The Thirty Years War, then, brought a sensible change in the balance of forces in Europe, gravely weakening Austria, starting the irreversible decline of Spain, and bringing to the fore the most modern, best organized, and, if you will, most rationally motivated states: the Netherlands, Sweden, and France. This, however, was a somewhat misleading result, and the Netherlands was soon to yield its commercial and naval primacy to Great Britain (which had been paralyzed by civil conflict during the Thirty Years War), while Sweden, under a less rational ruler, was to throw its great gains away.

The gains made by France were more substantial, so much so that in the second half of the century, in the heyday of Louis XIV, they became oppressive. For that ruler was intoxicated by the power that Richelieu and his successor Mazarin had brought to France, and he wished to enhance it. As he wrote in his memoirs:

> The love of glory assuredly takes precedence over all other [passions] in my soul. . . . The hot blood of my youth and the violent desire I had to heighten my reputation instilled in me a strong passion for action. . . . *La Gloire,* when all is said and done, is not a mistress that one can ever neglect; nor can one be ever worthy of her slightest favors if one does not constantly long for fresh ones.

No one can say that Louis XIV was a man of small ambition. He dreamed in universal terms and sought to realize those dreams by a combination of diplomatic and military means. He maintained alliances with the Swedes in the north and the Turks in the south and thus prevented Russian interference while he placed his own candidate, Jan Sobieski, on the throne of Poland. His Turkish connection he used also to harry the eastern frontiers of Austria, and if he did not incite Kara Mustafa's expedition against Vienna in 1683, he knew of it. Austria's distractions enabled him to dabble freely in German politics. Bavaria and the Palatinate were bound to the French court by marriage, and almost all of the other German princes accepted subsidies at one time or another from France. It did not seem unlikely on one occasion that Louis would put himself or his son forward as candidate for Holy Roman emperor. The same method of infiltration was practiced in Italy, Portugal, and Spain, where the young king married a French princess and French ambassadors exerted so much influence in internal affairs that they succeeded in discrediting the strongest antagonist to French influence, Don Juan of Austria, the victor over the Turks at the battle of Lepanto. In addition to all of this, Louis sought to undermine the independence of the Netherlands and gave the English king Charles II a pension in order to reduce the possibility of British interference as he did so.

French influence was so great in Europe in the second half of the seventeenth century that it threatened the independent development of other nations. This was particularly true, the German historian Leopold von Ranke was to write in the nineteenth century, because it

> was supported by a preeminence in literature. Italian literature had already run its course, English literature had not yet risen to general significance, and German literature did not exist at that time. French literature, light, brilliant and animated, in strictly regulated but charming form, intelligible to everyone and yet of individual, national character was beginning to dominate Europe. . . . [It] completely corresponded to the state and helped the latter to attain its supremacy, Paris was the capital of Europe. She wielded a dominion as did no other city, over language, over custom, and particularly over the world of fashion and the ruling classes. Here was the center of the community of Europe.

The effect upon the cultural independence of other parts of Europe—and one cannot separate cultural independence from political will—was devastating. In Germany, the dependence upon French example was almost abject, and the writer Moscherosch commented bitterly about "our little Germans who trot to the French and have no heart of their own, no speech of their own; but French opinion is their opinion, French speech, food, drink, morals and deportment their speech, food, drink, morals and deportment whether they are good or bad."

But this kind of dominance was bound to invite resistance on the part of others, and out of that resistance combinations and alliances were bound to take place. And this indeed happened. In Ranke's words, "The concept of the European balance of power was developed in order that the union of many other states might resist the pretensions of the 'exorbitant' court, as it was called." This is a statement worth noting. The principle of the balance of power had been practiced in Machiavelli's time in the intermittent warfare between the city states of the Italian peninsula. Now it was being deliberately invoked as a principle of European statecraft, as a safeguard against universal domination. We shall have occasion to note the evolution and elaboration of this term in the eighteenth century and in the nineteenth, when it became one of the basic principles of the European system.

Opposition to France's universal pretensions centered first upon the Dutch, who were threatened most directly in a territorial sense by the French, and their gifted ruler, William III. But for their opposition to be successful, the Dutch needed strong allies, and they did not get them until the English had severed the connection that had existed between England and France under the later Stuarts and until Austria had modernized its administration and armed forces, contained the threat from the east, and regained the ability to play a role in the politics of central and western Europe. The Glorious Revolution of 1688 and the assumption of the English throne by the Dutch king moved England solidly into the anti-French camp. The repulse of the Turks at the gates of Vienna in 1683 marked the turning point in Austrian fortunes, and the brilliant campaigns of Eugene of Savoy in the subsequent period, which culminated in the smashing victory over the Turks at Zenta and the suppression of the Rakoczi revolt in Hungary, freed Austrian energies for collaboration in the containment of France. The last years of Louis XIV, therefore, were the years of the brilliant partnership of Henry Churchill, Duke of Marlborough, and Eugene of Savoy, a team that defeated a supposedly invulnerable French army at Blenheim in 1704, Ramillies in 1706, Oudenarde in 1708, and the bloody confrontation at Malplaquet in 1709.

These battles laid the basis for the Peace of Utrecht of 1713–1715, by which France was forced to recognize the results of the revolution in England, renounce the idea of a union of the French and Spanish thrones, surrender the Spanish Netherlands to Austria, raze the fortifications at Dunkirk, and hand important territories in America over to Great Britain. The broader significance of the settlement was that it restored an equilibrium of forces to western Europe and marked the return of Austria and the emergence of Britain as its supports. Indeed, the Peace of Utrecht was the first European treaty that specifically mentioned the balance of power. In the letters patent that accompanied Article VI of the treaty between Queen Anne and King Louis XIV, the French ruler noted that the Spanish renunciation of all rights to the throne of France was actuated by the hope of "obtaining a general Peace and securing the Tranquillity of *Europe* by a Ballance of Power," and the king of Spain acknowledged the importance of "the Maxim of securing for ever the universal Good and Quiet of Europe, by an equal Weight of Power, so that many being united in one, the Ballance of the Equality desired, might not turn to the Advantage of one, and the Danger and Hazard of the rest."

Meanwhile, in northern Europe, France's ally Sweden was forced to yield its primacy to the rising powers of Russia and Prussia. This was due in part to the drain on Swedish resources caused by its participation in France's wars against the Dutch; but essentially the decline was caused, in the first instance, by the fact that Sweden had too many rivals for the position of supremacy in the Baltic area and, in the second, by the lack of perspective and restraint that characterized the policy of Gustavus Adolphus's most gifted successor, Charles XII. Sweden's most formidable rivals were Denmark, Poland, which in 1699 acquired an ambitious and unscrupulous new king in the person of Augustus the Strong of Saxony, and Russia, ruled since 1683 by a young and vigorous leader who was to gain the name Peter the Great. In 1700, Peter and Augustus made a pact to attack and despoil Sweden and persuaded Frederick of Denmark to join them in this enterprise. The Danes and the Saxons immediately invaded Sweden and to their considerable dismay were routed and driven from the country by armies led by the eighteen-year-old ruler, Charles XII. The Danes capitulated at once, and Charles without pause threw his army across the Baltic, fell upon Russian forces that were advancing on Narva, and, although his own forces were outnumbered five to one, dispersed, captured, or killed an army of forty thousand Russians. But brilliant victories are often the foundation of greater defeats. Charles now resolved to punish Augustus and plunged into the morass of Polish politics. It was his undoing. While he strove to control an intractable situation, an undertaking that occupied him for seven years, Peter was carrying through the reforms that were to bring Russia from its oriental past into the modern world. When his army was reorganized, he began a systematic conquest of the Swedish Baltic possessions. Charles responded, not with an attempt to retake those areas, but with an invasion of Russia—and this, like other later invasions, was defeated by winter and famine and ultimately by a lost battle, that of Pultawa in 1709, which broke the power of Sweden and marked the emergence of Russia as its successor.

Sweden had another rival which was also gathering its forces in these years. This was Prussia. At the beginning of the seventeenth century, it had, as the Electorate of Brandenburg, been a mere collection of territories, mostly centered upon Berlin, but with bits and pieces on the Rhine and in East Prussia, and was rich neither in population nor resources. Its rulers, the Hohenzollerns, found it difficult to administer these lands or, in time of trouble, defend them; and during the Thirty Years War, Brandenburg was overrun with foreign armies and its population and substance depleted by famine and pestilence. Things did not begin to change until 1640, when Frederick William, the so-called Great Elector, assumed the throne. An uncompromising realist, he saw that if he was to have security in a dangerous world, he would have to create what he considered to be the sinews of independence: a centralized state with an efficient bureaucracy and a strong army. The last was the key to the whole. As he wrote in his political testament, "A ruler is treated with no consideration if he does not have troops of his own. It is these, thank God! that have made me *considerable* since the time I began to have them"—and in the course of his reign, after purging his force of unruly and incompetent elements, Frederick William rapidly built an efficient force of thirty thousand men, so efficient indeed that in 1675, during the Franco-Swedish war against the Dutch, it came to the aid of the Dutch by defeating the Swedes at Fehrbellin and subsequently driving them out of Pomerania. It was to administer this army that Frederick William laid the foundations of the soon famous Prussian bureaucracy; it was to support it that he encouraged the growth of a native textile industry; it was with its aid that he smashed the recalcitrant provincial diets and centralized the state. And finally it was this army that, by its participation after the Great Elector's death in the wars against Louis XIV and its steadiness under fire at Ramillies and Malplaquet, induced the European powers to recognize his successor Frederick I as king of Prussia.

Under Frederick, an extravagant and thoughtless man, the new kingdom threatened to outrun its resources. But the ruler who assumed the throne in 1715, Frederick William I, resumed the work begun by the Great Elector, restored Prussia's financial stability, and completed the centralization and modernization of the state apparatus by elaborating a body of law and statute that clarified rights and responsibilities for all subjects. He nationalized the officer corps of the army, improved its dress and weapons, wrote its first handbook of field regulations, prescribing manual exercises and tactical evolutions, and rapidly increased its size. When Frederick William took the throne after the lax rule of his predecessor, there were rumors of an impending coup by his neighbors, like that attempted against Sweden in 1700. That kind of talk soon died away as the king's work proceeded, and it is easy to see why. In the course of his reign, he increased the size of his military establishment to eighty-three thousand men, a figure that made Prussia's army the fourth largest in Europe, although the state ranked only tenth from the standpoint of territory and thirteenth in population.

Before the eighteenth century was far advanced, then, the threat of French universal dominance had been defeated, a balance of power existed in western Europe, and two new powers had emerged as partners of the older established ones. It was generally recognized that in terms of power and influence, the leading states in Europe were Britain, France, Austria, Russia, and probably Prussia. The doubts on the last score were soon to be removed; and these five powers were to be the ones that dominated European and world politics until 1914.

II

Something should be said at this point about diplomacy, for it was in the seventeenth and eighteenth centuries that it assumed its modern form. The use of envoys and emissaries to convey messages from one ruler to another probably goes back to the beginning of history; there are heralds in the *Iliad* and, in the second letter to the Church of Corinth, the Apostle Paul describes himself as an ambassador. But modern diplomacy as we know it had its origins in the Italian city states of the Renaissance period, and particularly in the republic of Venice and the states of Milan and Tuscany. In the fourteenth and fifteenth centuries, Venice was a great commercial power whose prosperity depended upon shrewd calculation of risks, accurate reports upon conditions in foreign markets, and effective negotiation. Because it did so, Venice developed the first systemized diplomatic service known to history, a network of agents who pursued the interests of the republic with fidelity, with a realistic appraisal of risks, with freedom from sentimentality and illusion.

From Venice the new practice of systematic diplomacy was passed on to the states of central Italy which, because they were situated in a political arena that was characterized by incessant rivalry and coalition warfare, were always vulnerable to external threats and consequently put an even greater premium than the Venetians upon accurate information and skillful negotiation. The mainland cities soon considered diplomacy so useful that they began to establish permanent embassies abroad, a practice instituted by Milan and Mantua in the fifteenth century, while their political thinkers (like the Florentine Machiavelli) reflected upon the principles best calculated to make diplomacy effective and tried to codify rules of procedure and diplomatic immunity. This last development facilitated the transmission of the shared experience of the Italian cities to the rising nation states of the west that soon dwarfed Florence and Venice in magnitude and strength. Thus, when the great powers emerged in the seventeenth century, they already possessed a highly developed system of diplomacy based upon long experience. The employment of occasional missions to foreign courts had given way to the practice of maintaining permanent missions. While the ambassadors abroad represented their princes and communicated with them directly, their reports were studied in, and they received their instructions from, permanent, organized bureaus which were the first foreign offices. France led the way in this and was followed by most other states, and the establishment of a Foreign Ministry on the French model was one of Peter the Great's important reforms. The emergence of a single individual who was charged with the coordination of all foreign business and who represented his sovereign in the conduct of foreign affairs came a bit later, but by the beginning of the eighteenth century, the major powers all had such officials, who came to be known as foreign ministers or secretaries of state for foreign affairs.

From earliest times, an aura of intrigue, conspiracy, and disingenuousness surrounded the person of the diplomat, and we have all heard the famous quip of Sir Henry Wotton, ambassador of James I to the court of Venice, who said that an ambassador was "an honest man sent to lie abroad for the good of his country." Moralists were always worried by this unsavory reputation, which they feared was deserved, and they sought to reform it by exhortation. In the fifteenth century, Bernard du Rosier, provost and later archbishop of Toulouse, wrote a treatise in which he argued that the business of an ambassador is peace, that ambassadors must labor for the common good, and that they should never be sent to stir up wars or internal dissensions; and in the nineteenth century, Sir Robert Peel the younger was to define diplomacy in general as "the great engine used by civilized society for the purpose of maintaining peace."

The realists always opposed this ethical emphasis. In the fifteenth century, in one of the first treatises on ambassadorial functions, Ermalao Barbaro wrote: "The first duty of an ambassador is exactly the same as that of any other servant of government: that is, to do, say, advise and think whatever may best serve the preservation and aggrandizement of his own state."

Seventeenth-century theorists were inclined to Barbaro's view. This was certainly the position of Abram de Wicquefort, who coined the definition of the diplomat as "an honorable spy," and who, in his own career, demonstrated that he did not take the adjectival qualification very seriously. A subject of Holland by birth, Wicquefort at various times in his checkered career performed diplomatic services for the courts of Brandenburg, Luneburg, and France as well as for his own country, and he had no scruples about serving as a double agent, a practice that eventually led to his imprisonment in a Dutch jail. It was here that he wrote his treatise *L'Ambassadeur et ses fonctions,* a work that was both an amusing commentary on the political morals of the baroque age and an incisive analysis of the art and practice of diplomacy.

Wicquefort was not abashed by the peccadilloes of his colleagues, which varied from financial peculation and sins of the flesh to crimes of violence. He took the line that in a corrupt age, one could not expect that embassies would be oases of virtue. Morality was, in any case, an irrelevant consideration in diplomacy; a country could afford to be served by bad men, but not by incompetent ones. Competence began with a clear understanding on the diplomat's part of the nature of his job and a willingness to accept the fact that it had nothing to do with personal gratification or self-aggrandizement. The ambassador's principal function, Wicquefort wrote, "consisted in maintaining effective communication between the two Princes, in delivering letters that his master writes to the Prince at whose court he resides, in soliciting answers to them, . . . in protecting his Master's subjects and conserving his interests." He must have the charm and cultivation that would enable him to ingratiate himself at the court to which he was accredited and the adroitness needed to ferret out information that would reveal threats to his master's interests or opportunities for advancing them. He must possess the ability to gauge the temperament and intelligence of those with whom he had to deal and to use this knowledge profitably in negotiation. "Ministers are but men and as such have their weaknesses, that is to say, their passions and interests, which the ambassador ought to know if he wishes to do honor to himself and his Master."

In pursuing this intelligence, the qualities he should cultivate most assiduously were *prudence* and *modération.* The former Wicquefort equated with caution and reflection, and also with the gifts of silence and indirection, the art of "making it appear that one is not interested in the things one desires the most." The diplomat who possessed prudence did not have to resort to mendacity or deceit or to *tromperies* or *artifices,* which were usually, in any case, counterproductive. *Modération* was the ability to curb one's temper and remain cool and phlegmatic in moments of tension. "Those spirits who are compounded of sulphur and saltpeter, whom the slightest spark can set afire, are easily capable of compromising affairs by their excitability, because it is so easy to put them in a rage or drive them to a fury, so that they don't know what they are doing." Diplomacy is a cold and rational business, in short, not to be practiced by the moralist, or the enthusiast, or the man with a low boiling point.

The same point was made in the most famous of the eighteenth-century essays on diplomacy, François de Callières's *On the Manner of Negotiating with Princes* (1716), in which persons interested in the career of diplomacy were advised to consider whether they were born with "the qualities necessary for success." These, the author wrote, included an observant mind, a spirit of application which refuses to be distracted by pleasures or frivolous amusements, a sound judgment which takes the measure of things, as they are, and which goes straight to its goal by the shortest and most neutral paths without wandering into useless refinements and subtleties which as a rule only succeed in repelling those with whom one is dealing.

Important also were the kind of penetration that is useful in discovering the thoughts of men, a fertility in expedients when difficulties arise, an equable humor and a patient temperament, and easy and agreeable manners. Above all, Callières observed, in a probably not unconscious echo of Wicquefort's insistence upon moderation, the diplomat must

> have sufficient control over himself to resist the longing to speak before he has really thought what he shall say. He should not endeavour to gain the reputation of being able to reply immediately and without premeditation to every proposition which is made, and he should take a special care not to fall into the error of one famous foreign ambassador of our time who so loved an argument that each time he warmed up in controversy he revealed important secrets in order to support his opinion.

In his treatment of the art of negotiation, Callières drew from a wealth of experience to which Wicquefort could not pretend, for he was one of Louis XIV's most gifted diplomats and ended his career as head of the French delegation during the negotiations at Ryswick in 1697. It is interesting, in light of the heavy reliance upon lawyers in contemporary United States diplomacy (one thinks of President Eisenhower's secretary of state and President Reagan's national security adviser) and of the modern practice of negotiating in large gatherings, that Callières had no confidence in either of these preferences. The legal mind, he felt, was at once too narrow, too intent upon hair-splitting, and too contentious to be useful in a field where success, in the last analysis, was best assured by agreements that provided mutuality of advantage. As for large conferences—"vast concourses of ambassadors and envoys"—his view was that they were generally too clumsy to achieve anything very useful. Most successful conferences were the result of careful preliminary work by small groups of negotiators who hammered out the essential bases of agreement and secured approval for them from their governments before handing them over, for formal purposes, to the *omnium-gatherums* that were later celebrated in the history books.

Perhaps the most distinctive feature of Callières's treatise was the passion with which he argued that a nation's foreign relations should be conducted by persons trained for the task.

> Diplomacy is a profession by itself which deserves the same preparation and assiduity of attention that men give to other recognized professions. . . . The diplomatic genius is born, not made. But there are many qualities which may be developed with practice, and the greatest part of the necessary knowledge can only be acquired, by constant application to the subject. In this sense, diplomacy is certainly a profession itself capable of occupying a man's whole career, and those who think to embark upon a diplomatic mission as a pleasant diversion from their common task only prepare disappointment for themselves and disaster for the cause which they serve.

These words represented not only a personal view but an acknowledgment of the requirements of the age. The states that emerged as recognizedly great powers in the course of the seventeenth and eighteenth centuries were the states that had modernized their governmental structure, mobilized their economic and other resources in a rational manner, built up effective and disciplined military establishments, and elaborated a professional civil service that administered state business in accordance with the principles of *raison d'état.* An indispensable part of that civil service was the Foreign Office and the diplomatic corps, which had the important task of formulating the foreign policy that protected and advanced the state's vital interests and of seeing that it was carried out.

BIBLIOGRAPHICAL ESSAY

For the general state of international relations before the eighteenth century, the following are useful: Marvin R. O'Connell, *The Counter-Reformation, 1559–1610* (New York, 1974); Carl J. Friedrich, *The Age of the Baroque, 1610–1660* (New York, 1952), a brilliant volume; C. V. Wedgwood, The *Thirty Years War* (London, 1938, and later editions); Frederick L. Nussbaum, *The Triumph of Science and* Reason, *1660–1685*

(New York, 1953); and John B. Wolf, *The Emergence of the Great Powers, 1685–1715* (New York, 1951). On Austrian policy in the seventeenth century, see especially Max Braubach, *Prinz Eugen von Savoyen,* 5 vols. (Vienna, 1963–1965); on Prussian, Otto Hintze, *Die Hohenzollern und ihr Werk* (Berlin, 1915) and, brief but useful, Sidney B. Fay, *The Rise of Brandenburg-Prussia* (New York, 1937). A classical essay on great-power politics in the early modern period is Leopold von Ranke, *Die grossen Mächte,* which can be found in English translation in the appendix of Theodore von Laue, *Leopold Ranke: The Formative Years* (Princeton, 1950). The standard work on *raison d'état* is Friedrich Meinecke, *Die Idee der Staatsräsan,* 3rd ed. (Munich, 1963), translated by Douglas Scoff as *Machiavellianism* (New Haven, 1957).

On the origins and development of diplomacy, see D. P. Heatley, *Diplomacy and the Study of International Relations* (Oxford, 1919); Leon van der Essen, *La Diplomatie: Ses origines et son organisation* (Brussels, 1953); Ragnar Numelin, *Les origines de la diplomatie,* trans. from the Swedish by Jean-Louis Perret (Paris, 1943); and especially Heinrich Wildner, *Die Technik der Diplomatie: L'Art de négocier* (Vienna, 1959). Highly readable is Harold Nicolson, *Diplomacy,* 2nd ed. (London, 1950). An interesting comparative study is Adda B. Bozeman, *Politics and Culture in International History* (Princeton, 1960).

There is no modern edition of *L'amhassadeur et ses fonctions par Monsieur de Wicquefort* (Cologne, 1690); but Callières's classic of 1776 can be found: François de Callières, *On the Manner of Negotiating with Princes,* trans. A. F. Whyte (London, 1919, and later editions).

War, Money, and the English State

John Brewer

INTRODUCTION

'The hand that signed the paper felled a city;
Five sovereign fingers taxed the breath,
Doubled the globe of dead and halved a country;
These five kings did a King to death.'
Dylan Thomas,
Collected Poems, 1934–1952

From its modest beginnings as a peripheral power—a minor, infrequent almost inconsequential participant in the great wars that ravaged sixteenth and seventeenth-century Europe—Britain emerged in the late seventeenth and early eighteenth centuries as the military *Wunderkind* of the age. Dutch admirals learned to fear and then admire its navies, French generals reluctantly conferred respect on its officers and men, and Spanish governors trembled for the safety of their colonies and the sanctity of their trade. European armies, most notably those of Austria, Prussia and the minor German states, marched if not to the beat of British drums then to the colour of English money. Under the early Stuarts England had cut a puny military figure; by the reign of George III, Britain had become one of the heaviest weights in the balance of power in Europe. She had also acquired an empire of ample proportions and prodigious wealth. New England merchants, Southern planters, Caribbean slaves and Indian sepoys were subject to her authority. No sea was safe from British traders; even the Pacific and the Orient were beginning to feel the British presence. Thornhill's Painted Hall at the Naval Hospital at Greenwich (1717–25), with its extravagant depiction of Britain's military power, contained its share of wish fulfilment, but the allegorical presence of the four continents was not misleading: Britain was on the threshold of becoming a transcontinental power.

The extent of this transformation depends, of course, on the extent of the period one chooses. The change from the 1660s to the 1760s seems greater than those either from the 1650s to the 1750s or from the 1680s to the 1780s. The loss of the first British empire was even swifter than its acquisition. But we need to think not in decades but in larger epochs. The transformation of Britain into a major power in two or three generations is all the more striking when compared to the strategic and military history of the previous two hundred years. Ponder the question of how many English victories over continental powers you can name between the battles of Agincourt (1415) and Blenheim (1704). The most famous English soldier in the era between Henry v and Cromwell, Sir Philip Sidney, died at Zutphen (1586) in a futile action during a disastrous campaign. Nor will the obvious naval victories compensate for the poor showing of the nation's armies. Before the late seventeenth century spectacular naval victories never amounted to control of the oceans. Drake may have singed the King of Spain's beard, but he was incapable of cutting his throat. Aptly enough the *Sovereign of the Seas,* the pride of the seventeenth-century royal navy, had to be reduced in size because her three decks made her so unmanageable. Her effectiveness could not equal her pretensions. Only in 1763 did Britannia truly rule the waves, and by then she also controlled a lot more land.

There are several ways in which to explain this remarkable achievement. The most popular is implicitly patriotic and explicitly military, emphasizing the collective qualities of British redcoats and Jack Tars and the individual heroism of their leaders. To the former are normally ascribed those saturnine and English qualities of doggedness, tight-lipped determination and obduracy (though for some reason sailors are usually depicted as much less grim than soldiers), while to their officers are reserved those mercurial qualities of quick-wittedness, imagination and energy. Both, in their due proportion, are deemed valiant and brave. Seen in this light the history of Britain's military and strategic prowess resembles a gallery of eighteenth-century portraits in which the subjects, successful army and naval officers dressed in military regalia and touting swords, telescopes, maps and charts, occupy the foreground, while in the distance we observe some violent action fought by undifferentiated humankind. Marlborough, Cobham, Cumberland, Wolfe, Hawke, Anson, Vernon, Hervey and Rodney provide an exhibition of heroes, many of whom command more admiration today than they did in their own lifetimes.

Such an approach is not without its merits. For, though its rhetoric sometimes smacks of the *Boys' Own Paper* and tales of derring-do, it usually attends to the details of warfare—tactics and the conduct of battles—which, together with those quirks of fate which fascinated Tolstoy and infuriated Clausewitz, make up the substance of war and so often determine its outcome. Yet such accounts often lack a larger context. They are seen as part of the history of 'battles', or, in a more expansive version, of strategy, but remain disconcertingly separate from the overall history of a particular era.

A second interpretation of Britain's rise to power rejects the sanguinary glamour of battles and tactics, preferring to emphasize the economic and commercial roots of Britain's strategic advantage. There are at least two versions of the argument that Britain's aggrandizement was impelled by the powerful forces of commercial capitalism, the desire to increase profits and accumulate wealth. One is discreetly celebratory, the other overtly critical. The former points to Britain's commercial prowess and economic growth: the increase in output, the strength of her agricultural base, the abilities of overseas traders, the skills of her merchant marine and the wealth of her people. The latter draws our attention to the victims of British expansion: the costs incurred by the slaves, indentured servants and native peoples whose fate was inextricably bound up with the acquisition of new lands and the development of commodity markets.

At their worst these histories invoke 'the invisible hand' of the market as *the* explanation for all forms of behaviour, neglecting the complexities of culture and power. In their pessimistic version they can also reduce economic relations to an unmediated account of oppression and resistance. But the insights they offer are salutary. They remind us of the global context of Britain's newly acquired status and of the vital part—epitomized by the privatized imperialism of the East India Company—played by private initiative in the growth of wealth and empire. They underline the importance of economic and social resources—capital and labour, wealth and manpower—in enabling nations to become great powers. And some of this literature, especially the most eloquent and passionate writings, point to the stark contrast between the view from the metropolis and from its periphery. Englishmen may have prided themselves on their liberties and the rule of law, and praised the growth of commerce as a civilizing process, but authority was exercised very differently—often brutally and barbarously—in those distant lands and over those subject peoples which occupied the frontiers of commercial development.

Military heroics, economic growth and the global expansion of British enterprise all contributed to the changing international status of Britain. But to a very large degree they were accompanied by and depended upon a number of altogether less dramatic developments. Victory in battle relied in the first instance upon an adequate supply of men and munitions, which, in turn, depended upon sufficient money and proper organization—what modern military men call 'logistics' and sociologists dub 'infrastructure'. As seventeenth and eighteenth-century commentators knew, no amount of commercial skill, merchant shipping or national prosperity could secure the domination of trade routes or the protection of bases and colonies. These required troops and a navy, which in turn, required money and proper organization. Otherwise Britain might have fallen victim of what was recognized in the eighteenth century as the Dutch disease, a malady that prevented a nation enjoying unequalled individual prosperity and extraordinary commercial sophistication from remaining a state of great influence and power. Substantial economic resources were necessary to acquire the status of a major power; they were not, however, enough. Great states required both the economic wherewithal and the organizational means to deploy resources in the cause of national aggrandizement.

In the eighteenth century, clerks, as a group, remained virtually anonymous, but they transcribed an enormous amount of business records. The clerks knew more about what was transpiring in England than many of the politicians.

To illuminate the accomplishment of generals and admirals and cast light on the economy and commerce is, perhaps, to obscure or put unnecessarily into the shade those changes in government which made Britain's success possible. It is the aim of the following chapters to expose the hidden sinews which animated the British body politic, rendering it capable of those feats of strength which so impressed its allies and enemies. Though my account is very much concerned with war, it deals with bookkeeping not battles, with ink-stained fingers rather than bloody arms. Its focus is upon administration, on logistics and, above all, on the raising of money. Its heroes, if any there are, are clerks in offices. And its perspective is neither global nor from the periphery, but from Whitehall and Westminster, very much at the centre of the core.

Administrations thrive on routine. They abhor the stock in trade of the dramatist and the historian—change, disruption, violent action—aspiring to a ubiquity of sameness. Theirs is not only the quotidian: each day should be the same. But every administration creates friction in its attempt to impose order and structure on the entropic enterprise of collaborative human endeavour. It is precisely this tension between the desire for order and routine and the actualities of public conduct that creates the drama and conflict administrations are so eager to contain. The struggle for power and control may not have been fought out in the bright, sanguinary colours of battle nor on the large canvas of several continents but, no matter how contained or muted it might appear, its effects were far-reaching. The ability of government administrators to establish the routine by which revenues were collected, money raised and supply requisitioned could make the difference between victory and humiliation.

At the seat of dullness were the clerks. These pale and shadowy figures have never received their due. The eighteenth century saw an unprecedented expansion in the number of transcribers, copyists and record-keepers. A quick glance at the business accounts, financial records and government documents of this period attests to the prodigies of penmanship performed by men and women unaided by any mechanical means of duplication. Yet these clerks have no history. No group can ever have written so much and yet remained so anonymous. This is partly attributable to the difficulties of reconstructing their lives, but it is also the consequence of snobbery. The English revere the ownership of land and the tasks of manual labour; they have little time for pen-pushers, either clerical or intellectual.

What the clerks transcribed in the service of government—tax accounts, inventories of supplies, financial statutes, tables of revenue and trade, rules governing the borrowing of money and the purchase of equipment and supplies—is also not immediately accessible, for it requires a certain amount of technical knowledge. Modern readers, living in the era of the small investor and of media ever-attendant to the fate of stock-markets and rates of exchange, may have a better grasp of public and private finance than those eighteenth-century backbench MPs who seemed incapable of understanding any money matter which could not be compared to the running of a landed estate. But they nevertheless confront a system, if such it can be called, whose technical complexities were considerable and whose practices, though superficially similar to those of today had their own distinctive logic.

Yet, for all these difficulties of tedium and technicalities (problems I hope to dispel), the chief reason why financiers and administrators have not received their fair share of attention, except in the most technical of scholarship, is because their importance does not accord with the conventional wisdom about the English/British state. It has long been a source of self-congratulation to the British liberal tradition that Britain was wise and politic enough to avoid the enormities of a 'strong state'. This view could scarcely be more fashionable in the present political climate, which seems intent on repudiating the political objectives and dismantling the administrative apparatus of the post-1945 era. Seen from the liberal perspective, the state intervention that was typical of British politics between 1945 and 1979 looks like a temporary diversion from the mainstream of the British political tradition. The eighteenth century on the other hand, exemplifies the weakness of central government. It is portrayed as a period when the powers of central government were devolved on the localities and diluted by a spoils system which provided income and office for the scions of the landed classes.

But there is another picture we can paint of the same era, the one depicted in this book. The late seventeenth and eighteenth centuries saw an astonishing transformation in British government, one which put muscle on the bones of the British body politic, increasing its endurance, strength and reach. Britain was able to shoulder an ever-more ponderous burden of military commitments thanks to a radical increase in taxation, the development of public deficit finance (a national debt) on an unprecedented scale, and the growth of a sizable public administration devoted to organizing the fiscal and military activities of the state. As a result the state cut a substantial figure, becoming the largest single actor in the economy. This was no minor adjustment in the scope and priorities of government; it was a major commitment of resources. Taxes rose to levels as high as any of those in Europe, matching those of many modern, underdeveloped states. Borrowing reached such heights that if eighteenth-century Britain had gone to the modern International Monetary Fund for a loan it would certainly have been shown the door. The creation of what I call 'the fiscal-military state' was the most important transformation in English government between the domestic reforms of the Tudors and the major administrative changes in the first half of the nineteenth century.

How are we to reconcile this view of an exceptionally active state with the liberal interpretation? Or are the two positions entirely incompatible? We should first notice that we are discussing two rather different aspects of government. States are Janus-faced: they look in, to the societies they rule, and out, to those other states with which they are so often locked in conflict. In the former instance the business of the state is usually that of maintaining public order and exercising public justice ('law and order'); government also probably takes responsibility for various forms of economic and social regulation. In the latter case, states compete with each other, employing either the peaceful means of diplomacy or the violent means of war. The liberal focus on the British state has resolutely concentrated its gaze on relations with the domestic polity. I want to draw attention to the state's international role, to its actions as a military and diplomatic power.

Perhaps, then, this is the answer to our conundrum. The British government was able to act effectively against its international enemies but was weak in its dealings with its own subjects. This dichotomy is neat, but raises more questions than it answers.

Political commentators in early modern Europe were haunted by the fear that changes in the character of warfare, particularly the emergence of large standing armies controlled by rulers, would enable monarchs and autocrats not only to subjugate their foes but to enslave their subjects. Liberty and the institutions which guaranteed such freedoms, notably parliaments and estates, could be swept away by brute force. Clearly seventeenth-century analysts—rather like twentieth-century sociologists—were sceptical of the view that a state's international standing and activities could be sharply separated from its power over civil society. They were right to be sceptical. Admittedly, before the mid-seventeenth century the chief beneficiaries of the growth of standing armies were not rulers but private entrepreneurs: money-lending and tax-gathering syndicates, military enterprisers who specialized in raising and leading troops. It was also possible to wage war by using conquest and tribute rather than domestic resources to fund hostilities. But by the mid-seventeenth century rulers were gaining control of the forces that marched in their name, and self-sustaining warfare—the technique used by the Swedes in the seventeenth century and the Prussians in the eighteenth—was increasingly recognized as a hazardous, short-term solution because it could brook no check or setback. In the last resort states had to depend on domestic resources, in the form of money and men, and these were increasing under the direct control of monarchs and rulers.

The British were no exception. Indeed, judged by the criteria of the ability to take pounds out of people's pockets and to put soldiers in the field and sailors on the high seas, Britain was one of Europe's most powerful states, one which had acquired prodigious powers over its subjects. Whatever the situation when it came to the administration of law and order, in the fiscal-military sphere the state gained a hold as never before. This grip did not, however, become the stranglehold of autocracy, which raises, of course, the question of why Britain was able to enjoy the fruits of military prowess without the misfortunes of a *dirigiste* or despotic regime.

Before being seduced into that orgy of self-congratulation to which British historians are prone, we need to enter at least one qualification to the view that the British regime, for all its military effectiveness, was characterized by lightness of touch. The heavy-handedness of British rule increased the farther it extended beyond the metropolis. This may seem paradoxical, for British authority was much weaker outside England than within it. But it was for precisely this reason that the formal powers of British rule were so much greater farther afield. Coercive powers were required where tacit compliance was less assured. Subjects' rights were not the same on the banks of the Ohio, in Spanish Town or Dublin Castle as they were in London.

Yet, even in the metropolis, it was felt that liberties were under threat. Though the liberal view characterizes the eighteenth-century British state as conspicuous for its absence, this was not what most eighteenth-century commentators believed. They were obsessed by its growing presence. This anxiety is easy to understand. In the aftermath of the Glorious Revolution of 1688 the balance of political forces shifted decisively against those who had opposed or sought to limit Britain's role in international conflict. Britain plunged into a major, protracted struggle with Louis XIV's France.

The proponents of small government and limited warfare did not, however, surrender without a fight. On the contrary, they dug themselves in for a long struggle and, protected by the well-built fortifications of English constitutionalism, were able to conduct an effective war of containment. They fought to restrict the domestic effects of the fiscal-military state. And, although theirs was necessarily only a rearguard action, they enjoyed some success. The powers of the army over the civilian population were severely restricted, efforts to use civilian officers as a general 'police' rather than as tax gatherers were checked, and the bureaucracy's growth limited to those circumstances necessary for its successful operation.

The intensity of the struggle over the British state—about how it should be structured and what it should be allowed to do—is the most eloquent testimony that government had indeed undergone a radical transformation. But the protestations of those who opposed standing armies and big government were more than the mere symptoms of an important change; they became an integral part of Britain's institutional transformation. The war against the state helped to shape the changing contours of government: limited its scope, restricted its ambit and, through parliamentary scrutiny, rendered its institutions both more public and accountable.

Yet, paradoxically, this success made the fiscal-military state stronger rather than weaker, more effective rather than more impotent. Public scrutiny reduced speculation, parliamentary consent lent greater legitimacy to government action. Limited in scope, the state's powers were nevertheless exercised with telling effect.

This irony can best be understood if we reflect on what tend to be our rather naive and uncritical assumptions about what is meant by a 'strong' or 'weak' state. Too often strength is equated with size. But a large state apparatus is no necessary indication of a government's ability to perform such tasks as the collection of revenue or the maintenance of public order. Indeed, the opposite may prove true. In the hive that was the early modern European state there were often as many drones as workers; frequently as many sinecures as efficient offices. In short, big government is not always effective government.

A second solecism is that which fails to distinguish between what a state is entitled to do and what it can actually accomplish. To use the terminology of one distinguished social scientist, a regime may be strong in 'despotic power', entitled to dispense with its subjects' goods and liberties without legal restraint, but it may be weak in 'infrastructural power', lacking the organization to put its despotic power into effect. Conversely a state may be weak in 'despotic power' with strict limits on what it is entitled to do, but it may be strong on 'infrastructural power' capable of performing its limited tasks to telling effect.

Most of the British military action was out of sight. The effects of war, however, were felt on the economy of the home front.

To this distinction we need to add a consideration of the question of authority. The effective exercise of power is never merely a matter of logistics, a question of whether or not a state has the requisite bureaucracy or military cadres. States are not just centres of power; they are also sources of authority whose effectiveness depends on the degree of legitimacy that both regimes and their actions are able to command. Broadly speaking the less legitimacy, the greater the 'friction' produced by the conduct of the state and the more resources it has to devote to achieve the same effect.

The British fiscal-military state, as it emerged from the political and military battles that marked the struggle with Louis XIV, lacked many of the features we normally associate with a 'strong state', yet therein lay its effectiveness. The constraints on power meant that when it was exercised, it was exercised fully. As long as the fiscal-military state did not cross the bulwarks erected to protect civil society from militarization it was given its due. Yet it was watched with perpetual vigilance by those who, no matter how much they lauded its effectiveness against foreign foes, were deeply afraid of its intrusion into civil society.

The desire to restrict the political and military effects of war on the English polity, together with the almost total absence of hostilities on English soil, can give the impression that eighteenth-century wars were of little domestic consequence. Military action, after all, occurred far away beyond the horizon: in continental Europe (where foreign soldiers fought and died on Britain's behalf), in the colonies and on the quarterdecks of British battleships. Most of the military action was out of sight. It was not, however, out of mind. For the effects of war were never purely strategic, nor were they confined to the scene of battle. They were felt on the home front, particularly on the economy.

War was an economic as well as military activity: its causes, conduct and consequences as much a matter of money as martial prowess. Nowhere in eighteenth-century Europe was this better understood than in Britain. As Casanova, visiting London shortly after the Seven Years War, discovered in his conversations with Augustus Hervey, the captor of Havana, the British viewed war as far more than a matter of honour. It was also a question of property and profit. The progress of hostilities was followed by many members of the public with an assiduity worthy of Tristram Shandy's Uncle Toby, but their interest was not in tactics or siege warfare but in the economic repercussions of war.

These were difficult to measure then and remain so today. Nevertheless most eighteenth-century commentators were sure that fluctuations in the fortunes of war and the conduct of peace affected the everyday conduct of economic life. Similarly they argued that the longer-term changes in the nature of government—the emergence of the fiscal-military state—had altered the balance of social forces in Britain by penalizing the landed classes, creating a new class of financier and laying a heavy burden of taxes on the ordinary consumer. For more than a generation the state was seen as one of the major agents of social and economic change.

These developments were not watched idly by interested parties. Changes in government produced new organizations in society at large. Special interest groups were formed. These new organisms, the offspring of a new environment created by an expanding state, sought to flourish, in evolutionary fashion, at the expense of other new species. Lobbies, trade organizations, groups of merchants and financiers fought or combined with one another to take advantage of the protection afforded by the greatest of economic creatures, the state. They struggled for access to the corridors of power, for information that would enable them to thwart, create or affect policy, and for the support of those parliamentarians who could hold the fiscal juggernaut in check. As their tactics grew more sophisticated they learned to transcend their sectionalism and to appeal beyond their self-interested ranks to the public at large. By the second half of the eighteenth century some of them had learned the value of parasitism, making the state, as Adam Smith pointed out, their host if not their hostage.

In this, narrowly defined commercial and trading interests were following a pattern that can be observed throughout the eighteenth century. When the fiscal-military state first emerged it enjoyed considerable autonomy and excited much hostility and confusion. But gradually a variety of social groups and interests reached an accommodation with it. Some, notably the 'landed interest', were much more successful than others in taking advantage of new circumstances, but none could afford the luxury of ignoring the remarkable changes in the British state which were the early eighteenth century's most distinctive feature. . . .

A Golden Age: Innovation in Dutch Cities, 1648–1720

Jonathan Israel describes how the genius of the seventeenth-century Netherlands lay not just in painting but in blazing a trail in civic pride and technological improvements for the rest of Europe.

Jonathan Israel

Jonathan Israel is Professor of Dutch History and Institutions at University College, London and author of The Dutch Republic: Its Rise, Greatness and Fall, 1477–1806, *published by Oxford University Press (1995).*

Between April and June 1648 the most elaborate and impressive celebrations which had thus far ever been held in the northern Netherlands—parades, pageants, thanksgiving services, open-air theatrical performances, a series of bonfire and fire-work displays, sumptuous militia and regent banquets—were held in Amsterdam and most other Dutch cities. The reason for this unprecedented outlay, disruption of normal activity and quest to impress and involve the general public was the final ratification of the Peace of Münster (April 1648). This not only ended the Eighty Years' War in the Low Countries, one of the greatest struggles of Europe of early modern times, but marked the successful conclusion of decades of effort to establish and consolidate the Dutch Republic as a free and independent state on territory formerly ruled by the king of Spain.

That this was no small achievement can be seen from the fact that the United Provinces, as the Republic was officially called, was the only new state—as well as new type of state—created by means of a people's revolution against the power of monarchs in the early modern era before the 1770s, when the North Americans embarked on their great struggle (on occasion with the Dutch example in mind) against the British crown.

At the same time, these celebrations were the Dutch contribution to a wider set of festivities held all across northern and central Europe to mark the end of the unprecedentedly destructive Thirty Years' War. As such, the festivities of 1648, both in their Dutch and wider European context, were a psychological turning-point between a dreadfully bleak era of struggle and dislocation, and the deep pessimism and gloom which had resulted, and a more hopeful era; one of rebuilding and reconstruction. Many of the cities of Germany had been severely damaged by the war, as well as the slump and disease which had come in its wake; while even those which had not been, such as Hamburg and Bremen, had nevertheless shared in the general sense of fear and uncertainty and, like Copenhagen, tended to avoid all major new city extensions and building projects for the duration of the conflict, except only for large-scale improvements to city fortifications.

With the Thirty and Eighty Years' Wars simultaneously out of the way, city governments could now think about reconstructing their war-torn cities and, in the case of the Scandinavian capitals and flourishing Hamburg, embark on those ambitious projects and city extensions which it had seemed prudent to postpone whilst the fighting and disruption continued. Furthermore, since at that time the Dutch Republic was economically and culturally the most dynamic and flourishing country in Europe, it was entirely natural that many of these cities whether or not they had been devastated, especially those in the Protestant north, should look to the Dutch Republic for most of the ideas, designs, methods and technology which was to shape their general renovation and reconstruction during the second half of the seventeenth century and (particularly in the case of St Petersburg, Russia's window on the West) at the beginning of the eighteenth.

However, if we are to grasp how it was possible for such a small country as the Dutch provinces to have exerted such an immense influence over urban development in northern Europe, an influence which was, in most respects, far greater than that of Britain or France down to around 1720, it is by no means sufficient just to point to the general readiness for renovation and refurbishment, or to the special dynamism of the Dutch economy at that time. The phenomenon is more complex than that. For the Dutch cities were themselves then entering a major new phase of expansion and renewal, shaped by a dazzling array of innovations and new techniques and, more than anything else, it is this which gave them their special relevance

This article first appeared in *History Today,* March 1995, pp. 14-20.

and immense influence over such a considerable period.

If French influence in Europe in the late seventeenth century and early eighteenth century emanated, above all, from the court of Louis XIV, Dutch influence did not emanate from any arm of the Dutch state. Invariably, we find that it was not the Dutch Republic as such which appealed but specifically the Dutch cities, especially—but by no means only—Amsterdam. Over recent decades the Dutch Republic had proved remarkably effective politically, militarily and not least, in its financial operations. Yet this had been achieved without the new state intruding on the local autonomy of the cities. Somehow a remarkable balance had been struck between civic (and other local) particularism, on the one hand, and the 'Generality', as the Dutch then termed their federal institutions, on the other. Since the main cities and the provinces (each with its own local assembly) had been the backbone of the Revolt against Spain, this had indeed been a *sine que non* for the successful establishment of a Dutch state, and is what ensured that it would also be an entirely new type of state. For even in 1648 there was not yet a fully-fledged Dutch national identity. That was only to emerge more or less in its modern form at the end of the eighteenth century.

Most Dutchmen, like most Germans and Italians at the time, identified most strongly, and felt their principal political allegiance to, their city or locality rather than to the country as a whole. But they shared not just in the collective experience of the Revolt against Spain but, linked to this, an intense pride in the 'freedom' which they had won, the new political, religious and social context which they had created in which civic and local autonomy was combined with what we would call a federal, overarching, state. Of course, they can hardly have grasped that they had forged the world's first real federal republic—Switzerland being an earlier but only partial step towards genuine federalism. They can not have known that theirs would also be the only real federal republic until the American Revolution created the United States of America, but that this would one day (since Germany adopted the federal model after the Second World War) become possibly the most important type of state in the western world. But ordinary Dutchmen and Dutch women did vaguely grasp that they had achieved something altogether exceptional and remarkable which they referred to as their 'freedom'.

By 1648, the impact of the Dutch cities on the European urban scene was already very considerable and had been growing, especially since the 1590s. The seemingly miraculous expansion of Dutch commerce and shipping which had begun to take over the 'rich trades' of the world in the 1590s, elbowing all rivals aside, had reached such a point that it had aroused intense envy and resentment in almost every part of Europe and not least in England. Moreover, by 1648 those parts of Europe—especially Scandinavia, northern Germany and the Baltic—which were particularly susceptible to Dutch cultural influences were already so steeped in Dutch methods, styles and ways of doing things that everything else had been pushed into the background. When Hamburg and Copenhagen rebuilt their city fortifications during the second decade of the century they did so using Dutch engineers and Dutch designs.

If Christian IV (1588–1648) was the greatest builder and art collector in the history of the Danish-Norwegian monarchy, it is equally evident from the architects, engineers and artists he employed (who were nearly all Dutch) and the designs and styles he adopted, that the imposing cultural framework he created was essentially an extension of the Dutch Golden Age. Yet, notwithstanding this vast impact of Dutch commerce and shipping, and of Holland's art, architecture and engineering (particularly drainage, harbours and fortifications), those aspects of Dutch culture which were to have the greatest impact on urban development, refurbishment and planning after 1648, were only just beginning to be noticed.

The chief reason why the Dutch had not yet begun even potentially to make their real impact in the sphere of urban improvements, health care, town planning and public services is that the Dutch cities too, like those of Germany and Scandinavia, had since around 1620 been systematically postponing major new investment in buildings and city extensions. Just as Amsterdam needed a new and larger city hall long before 1648 but work on the new edifice began only in that year, and Leiden put up with old and delapidated gate-houses, only replacing them with magnificent new structures after 1648, so all big projects were put off. But once the Eighty and Thirty Years' Wars were finally over, the accumulation of grandiose and ambitious schemes led to a frenetic burst of building and refurbishment throughout the length and breadth of Holland. Not only were numerous large public buildings erected in the 1650s and 1660s, far more than in the previous three decades, but those cities which achieved an impressive measure of growth between 1648 and 1672, especially Amsterdam, Leiden, Rotterdam, The Hague and also Haarlem (see Table below) also laid out whole new urban quarters, constructed new canals and roads, and planned new housing as part of integrated urban development schemes. Delft too, though it grew much less than some others, had to be extensively rebuilt following the great gunpowder explosion of 1654 which devastated the city centre. Even Utrecht, a city quite stagnant compared with the Holland towns, seeing the ambitious projects of the others, drew up far-reaching plans, hoping by means of investing in redevelopment to attract more immigrants and activity.

However, the integrated reality of Dutch city planning and improvements

Table: The Demographic Expansion of the Ten Largest Dutch Cities (estimates)

City	1570	1600	1632	1647	1672	1700
Amsterdam	30,000	60,000	116,000	140,000	200,000	200,000
Leiden	15,000	26,000	54,000	60,000	72,000	63,000
Haarlem	15,000	30,000	42,000	45,000	50,000	40,000
Rotterdam	8,000	12,000	20,000	30,000	45,000	45,000
The Hague	5,000	10,000	16,000	18,000	30,000	30,000
Middelburg	10,000	20,000	28,000	30,000	30,000	30,000
Utrecht	26,000	–	–	30,000	–	30,000
Delft	14,000	17,500	21,000	21,000	24,000	19,000
Dordrecht	10,800	15,000	18,000	20,000	20,000	20,000
Gouda	9,000	13,000	15,000	15,000	20,000	20,000

after 1648 could not be emulated elsewhere in its entirety because many features of the Dutch urban scene were highly specific to Holland and Zeeland. Thus numerous foreign travellers of the period remarked that Amsterdam was much cleaner and less cluttered than London or Hamburg. But one of the main reasons for this was that the city government banned the use of horse-drawn coaches and wagons in the city, insisting that goods, supplies and furniture be moved by water and digging new canals and improving old ones to facilitate such traffic. This was perfectly feasible also in other Holland and Zeeland towns, but hardly practice elsewhere.

Another feature which could not be imitated elsewhere were the regular passenger services between towns by means of horse-drawn passenger barges, with departures several times daily between the main towns, working according to a published schedule, a phenomenon which has been brilliantly researched by the American historian Jan de Vries. Furthermore, not only these but also many other Dutch urban improvements of the period could only be effectively implemented because of the almost absolute power of the city governments within their cities and jurisdictions. Although they had to pay some attention to opinion within their city, the regents who staffed the city governments could otherwise raise money through municipal taxation of one sort or another, and decide what went on in their city, largely as they saw fit. If a city government wished to implement an ambitious and costly urban plan there was no question of this being opposed by any authority or body outside. In this respect, Swiss and some German Imperial Free Cities enjoyed a comparable freedom of action but cities under monarchs, such as London, Paris, Copenhagen or Stockholm, did not. Monarchs had their own agendas and priorities and, in most cases, a considerable sway over resources.

Franz Hals' 1664 painting—'Lady Governors of the Old Men's Home': social provision and public works were an important expression of Dutch civic governance.

Making the world go round; Berckheyde's portrayal of the Amsterdam Bourse.

But what other European cities, including London, could and did do, some sooner, some later, was to adopt in full, or in part, such individual urban improvements and innovations introduced by the Dutch cities as did not need specifically Dutch conditions for their implementation. A classic instance of such successful borrowing was the adoption of the Dutch system of public street lighting. Europe's first proper system of public street-lighting was planned, in conjunction with members of the Amsterdam city government, by the artist-inventor Jan van der Heyden (1637–1712). Van der Heyden designed a street-lamp manufactured of metal and glass with shielded airholes able to let out smoke without letting in the wind. The lamps burnt through the night on a mixture of plant oils with wicks of twisted Cypriot cotton.

Besides the considerable cost, the plans to light up the whole of Amsterdam at night presented appreciable problems. But the burgomasters and regents decided to go ahead, motivated by a desire further to improve orderliness in the city, and reduce crime, as well as the incidence of drunkards falling into

The Lion of Holland; this 1648 engraving shows up both the importance of a civic and a socially-mixed contribution to the province's identity and prosperity.

the canals at night and drowning. The plans were finalised and approved in 1669. By January 1670, the entire city was lit up after dark—what an amazing sight it must have been—by 1,800 public lamps (increased to 2,000 before long) affixed to posts or the walls of public buildings. The lampposts were placed 125 to 150 feet apart, Van der Heyden having calculated that maximum lighting efficiency with minimum wastage of oil and equipment was achieved with that spacing. One hundred public lamplighters were recruited who each re-filled, lit and, in the morning, extinguished, twenty of the lanterns. It took about fifteen minutes to light up the whole city. By 1681, another 600 public lamps had been added to the original 2,000. The advantages of lighting up the city at night were so obvious that first other Dutch cities, and then cities outside the United Provinces began to follow Amsterdam's example. Dordrecht installed the new system in 1674. Having ordered the equipment from Amsterdam, both Berlin and Cologne installed hundreds of Dutch lampposts and lit up their cities in 1682.

VOC warehouses and shipbuilding wharves underlining the maritime contribution to the Dutch profile in Europe after 1648.

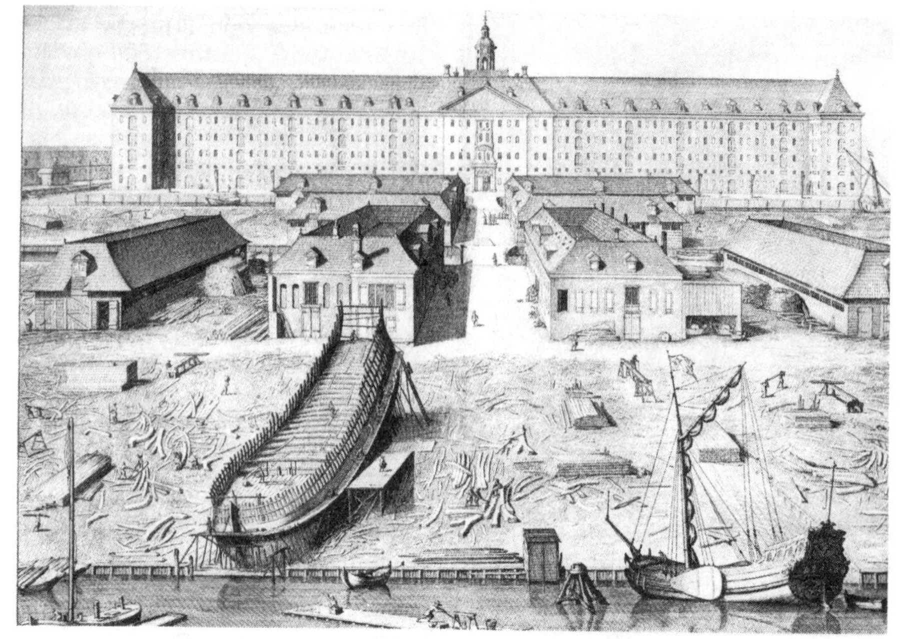

Another urban improvement which was widely imitated in late seventeenth-century Europe was Amsterdam's remarkable new fire-fighting service. Here again the technology involved was devised by Van der Heyden. But the key to success was the ability of the city government, having seen the potential of his innovations, to back them with funds and a sophisticated civic organisation. Although Van der Heyden was not the first Dutch expert to contrive a pump able to throw up a continuous jet of water from the canals, he produced improved pumps and was the first to join them to (leather) hoses. After being put in charge of the city's fire-fighting service, in 1672, he created an organisation the key element in which was the distribution of quantities of pumps and hoses around the city and their storage in special depots; and the assigning of able-bodied guild members in each quarter to take charge of the equipment and to ensure that it was promptly rushed to the scene and used in the event of fire. The sight of the new water pumps and hoses in action greatly impressed contemporaries, the effect being heightened by Van der Heyden's dramatic and well-publicised illustrations of fire-fighting scenes. One astonished English visitor described the hoses as being 'as big as a man's thigh which by the assistance of pumps, at which they labour continually for three or four hours, throw up water to the tops of the highest houses and force it three hundred paces over the tiling'.

Naturally, other northern cities were quick to see the value of the Dutch pumps and hoses and, albeit with a few years' time lag, proceeded to adopt similar systems based on the Dutch equipment. The revised civic fire regulations published in Hamburg in 1695, for example, are clearly based on the Amsterdam example, the central element being the storage of pumps and hoses in designated depots around the city and the assignment of responsibility, in each city quarter, for the maintenance and use of the equipment. Cologne obtained its pumps from Amsterdam; probably Hamburg did too.

One of the most crucial of the Dutch urban improvements of the mid-seventeenth century and one which was widely imitated, especially in Germany, Switzerland and Scandinavia, was the setting up in Amsterdam of a civic medical board called the *collegium medicum* consisting of three university-trained physicians and two prominent apothecaries to inspect, supervise, license and register medical practice in the city. Earlier there had been only the most rudimentary supervision over who practiced medicine, what medicines were sold in apothecaries' shops, how far the ingredients of medicines matched what was on the labels, and over how much was charged for medicines and medical supplies.

When the system of control was first introduced by the Amsterdam city government, by city edict of March 23rd, 1639, the chief concern seems to have been to curb the abuses going on in apothecaries' shops, especially the selling of impure or bogus medicines and wide discrepancies in charges. The edict laid down that the physicians of the collegium were to visit and inspect all the apothecaries' shops in the city 'two or three times per year', without prior notice, and verify what was being sold. At the same time, the city published a list of authorised prices for medicines to which apothecaries were expected to adhere and it was laid down that apothecaries and their assistants would only be permitted to practice in the city if they satisfied the collegium that they had adequate knowledge and expertise. Other Dutch cities followed and, soon, so did various German and Swiss cities. The city of Bremen published a new civic health *Ordnung,* based on the Amsterdam example, as early as 1644, the two main elements of which were the setting up of a system for regular inspection of apothecaries' shops by the city physician and the drawing up of a list of authorised prices for drugs and medicines. The Baltic city of Rostock adopted the system in 1659. In Stockholm, a *collegium medicum,* modelled on the Amsterdam example, was introduced in 1663.

Invisible earnings; alongside a canal, the Amsterdam Exchange Bank, created in 1609 to enable merchants to settle mutual debts.

While the original emphasis was mainly on supervision of apothecaries, the Dutch system of regulating civic health care gradually evolved during the middle and late decades of the seventeenth century becoming more comprehensive as well as more sophisticated. Notable additions to the original conception include the Amsterdam city law of May 1668, laying down that 'no one shall be allowed to practice as a midwife in the city unless she has first been examined by the *inspecteurs* of the collegium . . . and obtained a certificate of expertise' and the by-law of 1675, stipulating as a necessary qualification for obtaining a license to practice as a midwife, from the *inspecteurs,* to have worked as an assistant to a qualified midwife for a minimum of four years.

The Dutch city governments of this period, eager as they were to attract immigrants and increase the populations of their cities, made a serious and sustained effort, and with some success, to improve living conditions and health care. At the same time, they vied with each other in erecting imposing public buildings—hospitals and orphanages, as well as town halls, gate-houses and churches—beautification and splendour being essential aspects of the urban development schemes which they so intensively devised and debated. As the English physician Walter Harris remarked, in 1699, Holland contained 'a greater number of large, populous and considerable towns, than possibly are to be found so near together in any other part of the universe' so that, together with the great ease of passenger traffic between these cities, ordinary folk as well as the more sophisticated, were constantly appraising and making comparisons between them. If, as William Bromley remarked in his *Several Years' Travels,* the new Amsterdam city hall was 'the most magnificent structure of its kind in Europe', this is precisely what the Amsterdam city fathers had intended.

With both practical and aesthetic considerations firmly in mind, nothing appealed to the Dutch city governments of this period more than opportunities to combine public utility with beautification. A development which gave them precisely such an opportunity was the arrival in the middle decades of the century of new types of very large public clocks which (especially after the 1650s) also kept time much more accurately than the clocks of the past. In their drive to embellish Leiden, the city government there developed a veritable mania for affixing such clocks to the city's public buildings, including one, manufactured at The Hague, which was installed on the octagonal tower of their handsome new church (the Marekerk) in 1648. Another was placed at the top of the imposing new White Gate (built in 1650), near where the passenger barges loaded and unloaded the travelling public so as to facilitate punctuality in barge departures.

A typical feature of the new town hall of Maastricht built in the years 1659–64 to designs by Pieter Post (1608–69), one of the leading exponents of Dutch classicist architecture, were spaces assigned both inside and outside the structure for public clocks. The clocks, which were manufactured in Amsterdam, were installed a few years later. Needless to say the fashion caught on also outside the borders of the United Provinces. Dutch-style public clocks were affixed to several of the principal church-towers of Hamburg as early as the 1660s and 1670s.

The expansion of the Dutch economy, and of the Dutch cities, ended abruptly with the Anglo-French attack on the United Provinces in 1672. In that year Louis XIV invaded the Republic and occupied its eastern provinces while the French army, combined with the English and French fleets, delivered a blow to Dutch commerce and industry from which they were never fully to recover. After 1672, it was unquestionably England which was the most dynamic and the fastest-growing commercial economy in the western world. Nevertheless, it is important to note that at that time there were in Britain no large cities other than London (albeit as large as Amsterdam and the six next largest Dutch cities combined) which was by all accounts a somewhat disorderly and chaotic place compared with the Dutch cities.

Moreover, despite their stagnation after 1672, the Dutch cities were at that time sufficiently far ahead of England in technological innovations, health care and urban planning to retain something of an edge not only down to the end of the seventeenth century but even for a decade or two into the eighteenth. It was not until after around 1720 that Britain can be said to have overtaken the Dutch Republic in terms of technological sophistication.

Consequently, despite the emergence of England as the world's most dynamic economic and colonial power after 1672, it was still the Dutch cities, rather than the British, which were the main model for urban planning and improvements in northern Europe for another half a century.

FOR FURTHER READING:

C. A. Davids, 'Technological Change and the economic Expansion of the Dutch Republic' in C. A. Davids and L. Noordegraaf (eds.) *The Dutch Economy in the Golden Age* (Amsterdam, 1993); J. I. Israel, *Dutch Primacy in World Trade, 1585–1740* (Oxford, 1989); L. S. Multhauf, 'The Light of Lamp-lanterns: Street Lighting in 17th-century Amsterdam', *Technology and Culture* 26 (1985); J. L. Price, *Holland and the Dutch Republic in the Seventeenth Century* (Oxford, 1994); C. D. Strien, *British Travellers in Holland during the Stuart Period* (Leiden, 1993); Jan de Vries, *Barges and Capitalism: Passenger Transportation in the Dutch Economy (1632–1839)* (Wageningen, 1978).

The High Price of Sugar

To satisfy Europe's fondness for sweets, West Indian planters turned to Africa for plantation labor

Susan Miller

Right from the start, Columbus had a plan: to establish a sugar industry on Hispaniola much like the ones back home on the Canary and Madeira islands. So on his second voyage to the New World, he brought along several stalks of sugar cane. The Spanish hidalgos couldn't be bothered with the broiling, backbreaking task of growing and making the sweetener, so they forced the locals to do it for them. When the Indians started dropping from disease, the Spaniards turned to Africa. By the mid-16th century a nascent sugar industry completely dependent on black slave labor had taken hold in the Spanish Caribbean. The dramatic change on Hispaniola prompted a Spanish historian to write: "There are so many Negroes in this island, as a result of the sugar factories, that the land seems an effigy or an image of Ethiopia itself." Thus began a relationship between sugar production and African slavery that was to dominate Caribbean life for nearly four centuries.

This relationship had already existed in the Old World for hundreds of years. The first reference to sugar dates back to 350 B.C., with the report that people in India were eating rice pudding with milk and sugar and sipping drinks flavored with the sweetener. A little later, in 327 B.C., Alexander the Great's general, Nearchus, sailing from the mouth of the Indus River to the Euphrates, asserted that "a reed in India brings forth honey without the help of bees, from which an intoxicating drink is made though the plant bears no fruit." But not until about A.D. 500 is there unmistakable written evidence of sugar *making;* the technology didn't spread westward until the Moorish invasion of Europe in the seventh century. Sugar, according to anthropologist Sidney Mintz, followed the Koran.

The first Africans were enslaved soon afterward. Mintz reports that a slave revolt involving thousands of East African laborers took place in the Tigris-Euphrates delta as early as the mid-ninth century. Slavery grew more important as European crusaders seized the sugar plantations of the eastern Mediterranean from their Arab predecessors. By the 15th century, African slaves supplied the labor for the Spanish and Portuguese plantations on the Atlantic islands off the coast of Africa. To the Spanish way of thinking, then, African slaves were the logical solution to the labor shortages in the New World.

While Spaniards in the Caribbean were the first to produce and export sugar, their pioneering efforts were soon outstripped by developments on the American mainland. Sugar cane prospered in the Spanish territories of Mexico, Paraguay and Peru. By 1526, the Portuguese had begun shipping sugar from Brazil to Lisbon in commercial quantities.

By the end of the 17th century, the British had also established stakes in the Caribbean, and slavery became an integral part of their newly settled colonies almost from the start. Dutch traders, who had a foothold in Brazil, first introduced sugar making to English colonists on the island of Barbados in the 1630s. From humble beginnings, the British sugar industry spread north to the Leeward Islands, where it soon wrought a social, economic and political transformation so sweeping and rapid that historians have called it the Sugar Revolution. "England fought the most, conquered the most colonies, imported the most slaves and went furthest and fastest in creating a plantation system," writes Mintz in "Sweetness and Power." In 1655, when Britain conquered Jamaica—an island nearly 30 times the size of Barbados—she came to dominate the north European sugar trade.

The sugar industry was a messy business. Planters, clearing huge tracts of forested land, devastated the environment. In 1690, trees covered more than two thirds of the British colony of Antigua. By 1751 planters had stripped every acre suitable for cultivation. Antiguan John Luffman, writing in 1786, observed that even the largest hills were "clothed with the luxuriant verdure of the sugar cane to their very summits." The rapid deforestation only heightened the region's propensity for drought and erosion.

It was also extremely lucrative. In the 18th century, Antigua rivaled Barbados as one of the leading producers in the Caribbean, although neither could compete with Jamaica or French Saint Domingue (Haiti). "Barbados, in one period, and Antigua, in another, were producing more wealth than the entire North American continent," says Conrad Goodwin, an anthropologist who (along with geographer Lydia Pulsipher) has spent more than a decade excavating and studying sugar plantations on Antigua and the neighboring island of Montserrat.

The production of sugar—from holing, planting and harvesting to crushing, boiling and curing—depended on a large work force. To meet the demand for labor, Antiguan planters imported tens of thousands of slaves from Africa. In 1678 there were 2,308 whites and 2,172 blacks on the island. By the mid-18th century, Antigua's population had grown to nearly 40,000, and blacks outnumbered whites 10 to 1. David Barry Gaspar, an historian at Duke University, speculates that the ratio of blacks to whites would have been even higher if thousands hadn't commit-

From *Newsweek*, Columbus Special Issue, Fall/Winter 1991, pp. 70-72, 74.

ted suicide or died as the result of accidents, disease, poor diet, hard labor and mistreatment at the hands of their masters. "Because of the general oppressive environment of slavery, the slave population was not self-reproducing," says Gaspar. Their ranks had to be constantly replenished with imports from Africa.

A slave's life was grim beyond our capacity to imagine and sometimes beyond their capacity to endure. The workday was endless, and beatings were common for the smallest infraction. Mary Prince, a slave who lived on a number of different Caribbean islands in the early 19th century, describes her treatment by one particularly cruel owner: "To strip me naked—to hang me up by the wrists and lay my flesh open with the cow-skin, was an ordinary punishment for even a slight offence."

The conditions on plantations drove some slaves to suicide and infanticide. Others fought back with insubordination, malingering and feigned illnesses. Running away was virtually impossible since by the mid-18th century the forests had been cleared and most of the smaller islands afforded no place to hide. But, as recent scholars have begun to see, the slaves were often resourceful in adapting to their plight. "I'm not saying that slavery wasn't bad, because it was," says Pulsipher. "But slaves were not just victims. We should give them credit for being able to seize a bad situation and make the best of it."

On most plantations slaves managed to carve out a degree of autonomy by insisting on certain rights, such as a weekly day off and the right to sell, at Sunday market, food they had grown in their own gardens. "One of the forms of both accommodation and resistance, especially on Montserrat, was through these slave gardens up in the hills," says Goodwin. "Because they could escape white eyes, these gardens had connotations of freedom and self-worth. But the gardens were also advantageous to slave owners because they relieved them of some of the responsibility of supplying food to slaves."

Sunday, market day, had little religious significance for slaves who, at least in the early years, didn't attend church. Because slavery did not square with their religious teachings, Anglican planters had little interest in converting their labor force. It was not until the late 1700s, when the Moravians and Methodists arrived and opened their doors to slaves, that Sunday became important as a day of worship. In the meantime, they quietly practiced the religious traditions they had brought over from Africa. Islam had some influence, but it's not known how much.

But even after the introduction of Christianity, Sunday remained one of the few days that slaves found free time to enjoy themselves. John Luffman offered this description of a musical afternoon. "Negroes are very fond of the discordant notes of the banjar and the hollow sound of the toombah . . . The banjar is the invention of and was brought here by the African Negroes, who are most expert in the performance thereon, which are principally their own country tunes. To this music I have seen 100 or more dancing at a time . . . The principal dancing time is on Sunday afternoons, when the great market is over. In fact, Sunday is their day of trade, their day of relaxation, their day of pleasure, and may be called the Negroes' holiday."

Slaves seized an opportunity that was given them by the western European calendar and, quickly and entrepreneurially, started the markets. "Slaves used this time to socialize, reaffirm cultural links, meet their mates and sell whatever it was they had for sale: the baskets they'd woven, the food they'd made or the vegetables they'd grown. It was a time to improve their economic status, in small but significant ways."

In excavating Galways Plantation on Montserrat, Pulsipher and Goodwin unearthed an unusual abundance of artifacts from the plantation's slave village, including imported porcelain dishes, clay pipes, buttons, clothing fasteners, beads and coins. "These people were into a material culture," says Pulsipher. "Our theory is that their wealth was a result of their gardens up on the hillsides." Judging by the artifacts, Goodwin suspects slaves on Galways Plantation possessed maybe twice the material wealth of slaves on typical plantations in the southern United States.

In other parts of the Caribbean, however, slaves were not so fortunate. On Antigua, slaves had trouble finding space to plant their gardens because nearly every acre was in cane. Despite laws ordering slave owners to provide plantations with provision grounds, many wouldn't spare the land to ensure that slaves were adequately fed.

Throughout the Caribbean, sugar plantations were a curious blend of farming and factory work because so much of the industrial processing of the sugar was carried out on the spot. Mintz has dubbed the plantations "precocious cases of industrialization," and even the planters themselves recognized their industrial elements. In "An Essay Upon Plantership," Samuel Martin, an Antiguan planter writing in 1773, described the plantation as a machine with many moving parts: if one part broke, the machine broke. "Even that early, labor was very important, filling many cogs in the machine," says Goodwin.

The "sugar" cycle began in August or September, when the laborers prepared the fields for planting. Slaves, wielding hoes under a mercilessly hot sun, dug holes about five or six inches deep and about five feet square, into which they placed cane cuttings, covered them with a layer of mold and prayed for rain. The slaves tended the new cane shoots as they grew; the crop was harvested, one field at a time, 15 months later.

When it came to the harvest, timing was everything. As soon as the sugar cane was ripe it had to be cut and ground, often within 24 hours to keep it from spoiling. Black overseers, called drivers, would stand behind a line of slaves, crack their whips and give the order to start cutting. From the break of dawn until after dusk, the slaves toiled in the hot, sticky fields—cutting the cane, gathering up the stalks, stripping off the leaves and loading the 100-pound bundles onto ox carts bound for the mill. The pace was so frenzied that pregnant women were sometimes obliged to give birth in the field and then continue working.

For the slaves who fed the mill, the work was less physically demanding but posed different dangers. The feeders, as they were called, were liable, especially when tired, to get their fingers caught between the vertical rollers that crushed the cane. A watchman stood ready with a hatchet to sever an arm before it could be drawn into the machine. As terrible as this must have been, the alternative was worse. The rollers couldn't be stopped by flipping a switch. "If the limb wasn't chopped off, the slave would be crushed to death," says Goodwin.

The boilermen had a less exacting but hotter and heavier task. Juice from the sugar cane would enter the boiling house by a pipe that ran from the mill, and workers would siphon it into a great copper basin. After several hours of boiling and skimming, the slaves would ladle the steamy liquid into a number of successively smaller coppers until it was ready to crystallize. The sugar was then cooled, packed into barrels and rolled into the curing room. Holes were drilled in the bottoms of the barrels, allowing the molasses to drain into separate containers.

Laboring in temperatures above 100 degrees, the boilermen often worked through the night, and the darkness increased the likelihood of serious burns from the scalding, sugary liquid. But because their job required a high degree of knowledge and skill, the boilermen were among the most valued slaves on the plantation.

Slaves used the molasses and skimmings from the boiling house to make rum. Water, molasses, yeast and lees were combined in a fermenting cistern and left for a week to 10 days. The fermented liquid was distilled into rum and decanted in wooden barrels. The rum, as well as sugar and molasses, was stored in a warehouse until a ship arrived to carry it either to Europe or to one of the North American colonies.

In the 17th century, there emerged two so-called triangles of trade. The first and most famous of these linked Europe to Africa and the West Indies. European goods, such as trinkets, arms, gunpowder and gin, were exchanged for slaves in West Africa. The slaves were shipped to the West Indies and sold for sugar, coffee, indigo and other tropical products, which were then sent to the European mother country. The second triangle wasn't vital to world trade until the mid-18th century. In this scenario, New England merchants shipped rum to Africa, exchanged the rum for slaves and sailed to the West Indies, where they sold the slaves, bought molasses for rum-making and returned home.

As several scholars have pointed out, trade was not limited to these two triangles; more often than not, it moved in several directions. "Some of the trade did actually flow in legal channels as it was supposed to do, within a single imperial system," notes Philip D. Curtin, author of "The Rise and Fall of the Plantation Complex." "Much of it flowed outside those channels."

The sugar industry—so prosperous for nearly two centuries—had started to decline by the mid-19th century. Several factors contributed to its downward spiral: emancipation of the slaves, falling sugar prices and the development of alternative sweeteners. Still, on some islands—Puerto Rico, Barbados, Cuba and the Dominican Republic—sugar remains the main export today. On Antigua, the only reminders of the sugar heyday are the ruins of countless plantations, the Cavalier rum factory (which must import its molasses from the Dominican Republic) and a population that traces its roots to Africa. On Antigua, as with so many islands, one monoculture has simply been exchanged for another: tourism is now virtually the only industry.

Despite the changes wrought by 500 years of contact with the Old World, the people of the West Indies have managed to build a vibrant culture, mixing European elements with those of Africa and the Americas. In the British West Indies, for example, cricket has long been the most popular sport. Before a recent match between Montserrat and Antigua, the Montserratian team, which hadn't won a game all season, performed an old African rite to increase its chances: rising at dawn, they gathered on the playing field and started dancing . . . to drive away the evil spirits.

Cardinal Mazarin

Sidelined by historians, compared unfavourably with his predecessor Richelieu, the man who steered France through the years of Louis XIV's minority has had a poor press. But is the criticism justified? Richard Wilkinson thinks not.

Richard Wilkinson

Richard Wilkinson teaches history at Marlborough College, Wiltshire, and is the author of France and the Cardinals *(Hodder and Stoughton, 1995).*

'Richelieu I respected, much though I disliked him; Mazarin I neither liked nor respected'. Such was the verdict of Paul de Retz. Although this ambitious trouble-maker's opinions should be treated with caution, his contemporaries agreed that whereas Richelieu was '*le grand cardinal*', Mazarin was at best a stop-gap, a second-rater. Historians have been more generous, yet have found Mazarin enigmatic and forbidding. While studies of Richelieu roll off the press, Mazarin has been cold-shouldered. Geoffrey Treasure's *Mazarin,* which came out last year, is the first biography in English since Hassall's *Heroes of the Nations* study of 1904. Nor have French writers shown much greater interest.

Yet Mazarin's career was astonishing. Born Guilio Mazarini in Rome on July 14th, 1602, he came from an aristocratic, but impoverished, background. As a papal diplomat from 1634 to 1636 Mazarin impressed France's chief minister Cardinal Richelieu, who adopted him as one of his 'creatures'. Thanks to French influence Mazarin became a cardinal in 1641. When in 1643 Louis XIII followed Richelieu to the grave, the boy king Louis XIV's mother, Anne of Austria, made Mazarin chief minister, a position he was to hold for eighteen years—exactly the same 'innings' as Richelieu. And what momentous years they were.

Mazarin settled with the Habsburg powers at Westphalia (1648)—which ended the Thirty Years War—and the Pyrenees (1659). At home he guided France through the political and social crisis known as the Fronde (1648–53). Fronde means sling—the weapon used by Paris urchins against the rich. But there was nothing trivial or childish about this rebellion, the most serious challenge to the French crown's authority between the sixteenth-century religious wars and the revolution of 1789. After the Frondeurs had been defeated Mazarin devoted himself to the training of the young king, Louis XIV. Louis showed respect for his mentor by postponing his personal rule until Mazarin died on March 9th, 1661.

But contemporaries did not agree with Louis XIV. The one cause which united the socially and politically divided Frondeurs was contempt for Mazarin. For instance, in March 1652 the *Parlement* of Paris demanded Mazarin's exile:

> Cardinal Mazarin has shown, by seeking to continue the war [against Spain], that he does not care about the future: he has used all his efforts to do this, exhausting our soldiers and our money. We now see that he has caused so much disorder that we have both a foreign and a civil war.

The nobles hated Mazarin for usurping their rightful place in the crown's service. He was, they claimed, 'a foreigner from a very squalid background'. The common people shouted: 'No Mazarin, no mercy, kill, kill, kill'. Above all Mazarin was pilloried in the *Mazarinades,* the scurrilous rhymes and pamphlets which circulated in Paris during the Fronde. Mazarin was accused of vanity, hypocrisy, sodomy, the seduction of the queen, financial corruption, the deliberate prolongation of the war and inability to pronounce French. The poor man could do nothing right.

Where does the truth lie? The *Mazarinades* were both cause and product of a campaign to denigrate the chief minister who became the victim of the most effective character assassination in history. But the researches of the last thirty years have left historians with no excuse to be brainwashed. While Mazarin himself has been ignored by biographers, perception of the social, economic and political world in which he moved has been transformed. Thanks to Bayard, Castan, Dethan, Goubert, Mousnier and Porchnev in France, and Bonney, Briggs, Kettering, Mettam, Moote, Parker and Ranum in England and America, Mazarin can now be seen in context. How does he emerge from this enhanced perception? What was his rôle in the emergence of France as a great power? What was his contribution to the social and political development of France? Was the Fronde his fault or did his skill enable the crown to recover from a crisis which no-one could have prevented? What was his legacy to Louis XIV—and to France?

It is wrong to separate Mazarin's conduct of diplomacy from developments within France, for his domestic policy was indeed foreign policy-led. His failure to achieve a speedy end to the wars against the Habsburg powers allowed the Fronde to happen. The domestic situation which Mazarin inherited in 1643 was so fraught that he should have wound up France's foreign commitments as soon as possible. Instead, the war in Germany lasted until summer 1648, by which time the Fronde had begun. The contemporary allegation that Mazarin deliberately prolonged the wars to make himself indispensable is unfair. Yet there is something in the charge that he fluffed promising opportunities of ending the war, for instance after Condé's victories at Rocroi (1643) and Lens (1648), when the Habsburgs offered to negotiate. Obviously Mazarin had to avoid the appearance of a sell-out, for a 'soft' treaty would have made France's herculean sacrifices seem in vain. But he bungled his foreign and diplomatic policy, failing to recognise that a quick settlement in Germany was vital. Again, his over-clever, greedy pursuit of the Spanish Netherlands in 1648 provoked the Spanish and the Dutch to sign a treaty behind France's back which enabled Spain to continue the war for another decade.

To be fair, Mazarin's persistence and resourcefulness eventually brought results. He financed the armies and appointed the leaders who won the victories which brought the Habsburgs to the negotiating table. Mazarin's 'creature' Le Tellier raised and equipped the armies which Condé and Turenne led with such élan. The treaties which ensured the domination of Western Europe by France were the products of Mazarin's painstaking diplomacy. At Westphalia France's possession of Metz, Toul, Verdun and Breisach was confirmed, in addition to strategic control of Alsace. The Treaty of the Pyrenees awarded France Artois in the north, Rousillon in the south, valuable fortresses in the east and an advantageous marriage settlement between the French king and Maria Theresa, Philip IV's daughter. Mazarin thus dealt Louis XIV a strong hand.

Though Mazarin lacked the vision of Richelieu, who founded France's navy and overseas empire, he dominated Europe. He created the League of the Rhine, a coalition of west German principalities under French protection. Mazarin masterminded the Treaty of Oliva (1659) which brought peace in the Baltic. He supported the empire in its conflict with the Turks. His greatest coup was his alliance with Protestant, republican England—in its way even more daring and provocative to Catholic orthodoxy than Richelieu's alliance with Gustavus Adolphus. In the event Oliver Cromwell proved a more co-operative and reliable ally than the Swedish king. The Anglo-French victory at the Dunes (1658) finally brought Spain to her knees.

Recent research has thrown new light on the problems encountered by Mazarin in achieving a satisfactory peace settlement. David Parrott has stressed the ineffectiveness of the armies created by Richelieu, while Bonney and Ranum show what a nightmare France's financial problems presented. Indeed, Mazarin inherited an almost unwinnable war, in which both sides' armies blun-

The marriage of Louis XIV and the Spanish Infanta Marie Teresa, June 1660. The architects of the alliance—Mazarin and Anne of Austria—hover deferentially in the wings, stage left.

dered around on each others' frontiers, committing atrocities but incapable of winning victories. From 1648 onwards Mazarin fought the Spaniards with one arm pinned behind his back, as he encountered ever-increasing challenges to his authority at home. Treasure describes the ill-health which Mazarin suffered while he negotiated the complex Treaty of the Pyrenees and Louis XIV's marriage settlement. For the last months of his life he was carried on a litter, his body tortured by suppurating sores. He could only watch Louis' marriage procession through Paris from a first floor window. While contemporaries blamed Mazarin for not achieving peace sooner, in truth he only just lived long enough to see it happen.

If Mazarin bequeathed a strong hand to Louis XIV at considerable personal cost, the damage to the French people was horrendous: national bankruptcy, mass starvation and disease, large-scale civil war. To what extent was Mazarin to blame for this suffering? One point should be made straightaway. Mazarin inherited not only a war that was going badly, but an impossible situation at home. Richelieu's hand-to-mouth taxation and finance caused immense problems which could only end in catastrophe. Indeed, Richelieu got out in the nick of time. When Talleyrand died in 1832 King Louis Philippe exclaimed, 'I wonder why he has done that'. Similar flippancy about Richelieu's gruesomely prolonged and painful death might seem tasteless. Yet by dying when he did, *le Grand Armand* certainly escaped the consequences of his inept policies, leaving Mazarin to pick up the bill.

Even so, by overplaying a weak hand Richelieu's successors made a dire situation worse. Treasure thinks that Anne of Austria may have called the shots rather than Mazarin. This may be so, for Mazarin was preoccupied with diplomacy and war. The high-handed defiance of opponents which caused the Fronde suggests the proud, not very intelligent Habsburg princess rather than the wily Italian. But Mazarin too was a gambler. Anne of Austria and her chief minister conferred continually, for theirs was a close relationship, based on trust and affection. Both were strangers in a land whose politics they misunderstood. They incurred disaster together.

The problem was money. Richelieu had tackled it with short-term measures which put off the day of reckoning. He borrowed at high rates of interest, mortgaging future revenue. He invented sinecures which he sold for cash. By his death France was burdened with 40,000 office holders, most of them surplus to the requirements of administration. Richelieu extracted ever-mounting taxation by 'fiscal terrorism', that is to say, the use of troops. Starvation, suffering and resentment mounted. 'I do not understand finance', Richelieu claimed, disingenuously shrugging off responsibility. In fact he understood finance well enough to make his own fortune while France starved. With open eyes be accepted the risks of national bankruptcy since victory abroad would solve all problems. But victory proved a mirage.

Mazarin, who also protested his ignorance of finance, continued Richelieu's 'policies': more borrowing, more taxation, more sale of office and the employment of harassed finance ministers who could be thrown to the wolves. But Mazarin compounded the problem in two ways. First, he had no idea how to control public opinion. Richelieu adopted a sophisticated approach to propaganda, producing publications such as the *Gazette* which presented the government in the best possible light. Anne and Mazarin, however, displayed little flair or sensitivity when marketing the government's image. Secondly, Mazarin made mistakes which Richelieu would have avoided. He alienated the office holders, even though they had everything to gain from the government's success and stability. The Fronde occurred in summer 1648 when the entire judicial and financial machinery of government went on strike.

Anne and Mazarin turned a protest into a revolt by appealing to force. Throughout the Fronde there are echoes of England. The kidnapping of Broussel in August 1648 parallels Charles I's attempted arrest of the five Members of Parliament in January 1642. Both abortive coups had disastrous results. In the aftermath both governments left their capitals with little alternative but to appeal to arms.

Pierre Broussel was an unlikely hero. Elderly, austere, impractical, he was a member of the Paris Parlement, that exclusive club of snobbish and selfish lawyers. But unlike most of his fellow *robins* (members of the robe, as opposed to the sword nobility) Broussel was incorruptible, philanthropic and poor. By arresting this eccentric lawyer, Anne and Mazarin turned him into a cult figure and united the Parlement and the people of Paris. Because patronage linked the robins with the sword nobility, there emerged a formidable coalition which defied the government's attempt to besiege Paris. By the humiliating peace of Reuil (March 1649) the crown's tax-collecting machinery was dismantled and the claims of the Parlement to control finance were conceded. Such a settlement was a significant defeat for the regent and her cardinal.

In January 1650 Anne and Mazarin plunged the rest of France into civil war by imprisoning three princes of the blood, Condé, Conti and Longueville. This provocative measure was the climax of Mazarin's efforts to wriggle out of the Reuil settlement and defeat his aristocratic opponents' claims to patronage and power. Ranum defends the move: 'It was either arrest the princes or totally capitulate to Condé and give him control of the Council of State and the power to appoint governors'. Whether the alternatives were quite so stark, the coup blew up in the government's face.

During the next year Mazarin fought for his political life, on battlefields, by touring the provinces and towns of France and through patronage. His enemy Condé was imprisoned in remote fortresses where he read history and watered his plants. In the short term Mazarin lost. In February 1651 he personally released the princes at Le Havre and went into exile. Moote thinks that Mazarin had lost his nerve, Treasure that he was exhausted. Frightened, humiliated, baffled, Mazarin nevertheless appreciated that the cleverest step he could take in order to advance the crown's cause was to go. It is amazing that he ever came back given the song circulating in Paris:

> If he returns, whatever shall we do?
> We could cut off his private parts.
> But the king says: 'Don't do that,
> Mama still needs them'.

Mazarin did come back. In fact he twice went into exile and twice returned, on each occasion with a bodyguard of several hundred troops.

The crown survived the Fronde because Anne and Mazarin learnt from their mistakes. Mazarin mastered patronage, dominating both the capital and provinces such as Guyenne where his broker, Oppède, outsmarted Condé. Left to itself the Fronde fell apart. The agreement which united the Frondeurs in 1648 proved to be exceptional. For the widespread hatred of Mazarin was overtaken by universal hatred of soldiers. Irresponsible military violence was personified by Condé. In July 1652 his troops disgraced themselves in Paris, forcing their way into the city, roughing up a priest who tried to restrain them, taking the Hotel de Ville by storm when a hundred Parisians were slaughtered and setting up a puppet government. The French preferred to be exploited by Mazarin rather than be murdered or raped by Condé.

In addition, Mazarin was lucky. Set against the misfortune of inheriting Richelieu's mess was a series of fortunate deaths. Just as Richelieu's and Louis XIII's deaths had given Anne and Mazarin their chance, so Mazarin's rivals, Chateauneuf and Chavigny, died conveniently. These men apart, the Frondeurs failed to produce an alternative to Mazarin. No Pym, no Cromwell emerged: Broussel was a lightweight, de Retz (a combination of Mr Pooter and Mr Toad) was ludicrously blind to his own defects, Condé was insufferable. Mazarin was lucky too in retaining Anne's unwavering support. His greatest good fortune was that the Frondeurs totally lacked credibility as loyal subjects of a boy-king whose advisers they wished to replace. Louis wrong-footed them by making it clear where his own preferences lay.

But the Fronde cast a long shadow. While the civil war ended in 1653 with the capture of Bordeaux, violence continued throughout the 1650s: nobles revolted in nine out of France's thirteen provinces, while peasants lynched tax-collectors. Paris witnessed the so-called religious Fronde in which the *curés* defied the government by remaining loyal to de Retz, now their archbishop, and by distributing subversive tracts. Harvests were poor, trade in the doldrums, the government bankrupt. According to Colbert, at the cardinal's death in 1661 the debt stood at 451 million livres. In short, Mazarin can only claim a limited recovery by the crown from the Fronde, for he left what Parker calls 'a mass of unresolved problems'.

Indeed, the state of France in Mazarin's last years increases one's respect for Louis XIV. To be sure, nature had been kind to Louis. He had good looks, a tough constitution and a retentive mind. Furthermore, France worshipped her king and longed to be royally governed. Yet Louis was to demonstrate skills which his predecessors lacked. He was cheerful and urbane where his father had been morose and uncouth, he was as ruthless as Richelieu without incurring hatred, he was as devious as Mazarin without provoking contempt. Treasure calls the young king 'Mazarin's masterpiece', in recognition of the excellent training in kingship which the young man received from the old cardinal. This is fair comment. But Louis would need all his kingly qualities to govern France in the aftermath of the Fronde.

In the meantime Mazarin, basking in the admiration of the king and the love of the queen mother, reaped the rewards which he had always believed he deserved. During the summer of 1648 he had written:

> You must admit that it requires a commitment to the very limit and an extraordinary zeal to redouble one's efforts in public service—as I do—when one is treated so badly and when it is possible to say without vanity that my efforts are beginning to bear fruit.

Mazarin's whingeing was understandable, for while his 'efforts in the public service' were bearing fruit at Westphalia, he was traduced by the *Mazarinades,* and soon he would have to run for his life. But now all that was behind him, and in his last years Mazarin accumulated jewellery, pictures, sculptures, benefices and cash; he shamelessly and ostentatiously enriched himself. One of Ethelred the Unready's earls was called Streona, 'the accumulator'. Such a nickname would have suited Mazarin. There is an unforgettable story of Mazarin in his last illness lovingly surveying his pictures and his jewellery and murmuring, '*Il faut quitter tout cela*' ('I shall have to leave all this behind'). Whereas the exceptionally acquisitive Richelieu left 22 million livres at his death, Mazarin left 39 million. The French never forgave him.

Beggars in the 17th-century French countryside—economic instability combined with very real need provided a potent backcloth of discontent beside which Mazarin's apparent indifference to the poor could be used against him.

Did Mazarin deserve the abuse which his critics hurled at him? Much of it was outrageous, the product of envy and xenophobia. Mazarin was basically a tolerant, good-natured man of the world, devoid of malice or rancour. The only Frondeur he treated vindictively was de Retz (perhaps because de Retz so blatantly coveted Mazarin's job). In general Mazarin murdered the French language rather than Frenchmen. If he always won at cards and probably cheated, he spent his winnings on presents for his friends. For Mazarin liked to be liked. He was deeply hurt by the *Mazarinades* ('My nieces are now my daughters', he remarked sadly.) Perhaps his unconcealed extravagance was his way of getting back at his critics. The *arriviste* had arrived whether they liked it or not. Winner takes all!

The contemporary perception that when Mazarin succeeded Richelieu sleaze replaced style was correct. For his conduct of both public and private business was indisputably corrupt. So was his predecessor's, but Richelieu operated behind a propaganda smokescreen and with discretion. Richelieu would never have tried to bribe the austere advocate-general Omar Talon with an abbey for his brother—which Talon indignantly rejected. Geoffrey Treasure finds Mazarin's greed unattractive, though he suggests that insecure people who have narrowly survived catastrophe often behave like that. In Mazarin's world a bank account in Geneva was a sensible insurance—as he discovered when he went into exile. The truth is that public men usually had their snouts in the trough—but Mazarin's was a little further in than most.

In fact Mazarin's corruption is a secondary issue, though more important than his alleged marriage to Anne of Austria—conceivably possible as the cardinal remained in minor orders. The primary questions are, did Mazarin do a good job, were his priorities correct, did he achieve his objectives?

Arguably, Mazarin did an excellent job. He played his part well in the Bourbon programme. There is an identifiable consistency in the policies pursued by the first three Bourbon kings and their ministers. Domestic reforms such as the overhaul of taxation or the revitalisation of trade and agriculture were sacrificed to the single-minded pursuit of victory abroad. The population of France was subjected to increasing taxation, violently extracted and unjustly assessed, to enable France to wrest the domination of Europe from the Habsburg powers. In this story Mazarin played a crucial link role between the dynamic Richelieu and the masterful Louis XIV. As a resourceful and constructive minister Mazarin compares well with Richelieu. There were certainly two great cardinals, not one. Indeed, there is justice in Goubert's claim that Mazarin 'rather than his predecessor or his successor forms the pivot or the central bond of the seventeenth century'.

Whether the French people—especially the peasants who formed the majority of the population of France—benefited from this programme is another matter. While it might seem inordinately whiggish to pose such a question, it was in fact implied by contemporaries. Just as Richelieu's critics opposed the wars which caused such suffering, so the Frondeurs blamed Mazarin for failing to make a compromise peace. The Parlement of Paris expressed sympathy for the sufferings of the poor and achieved a temporary reduction of the *taille* by twenty per cent, while in the 1660s Colbert proved that taxation could be raised honestly and efficiently. Fénélon and Vaubon were to condemn Louis XIV's warmongering extravagance, perceiving that 'avoid encirclement' was code for 'French domination of Europe'. Yet the policy of war backed by fiscal terrorism continued. The defenceless, inarticulate taxpayers paid the bill.

In the face of this immense mass suffering modern historians argue that France 'had no choice' but to fight. So we have admiration for Richelieu's 'statesmanship', Bluche's hero-worship of Louis XIV and Hatton's special pleading for the Sun King's foreign policy. Treasure's biography of Mazarin is more balanced. He stresses that Mazarin inherited a programme which he was required to complete and that he served a dynasty rather than 'France' or 'Frenchmen'. Still, the question tugs: did it have to happen like that?

Mazarin's greatness lay in his ability to manoeuvre within the Bourbon programme. His considerable achievements reflect his political dexterity. He learnt from his mistakes. He developed a keen sense of the possible. He perceived that the salvation of the monarchy would be achieved not by absolutist authoritarianism but by persuading the rich and powerful that they had more to gain than lose from co-operation with the crown. Against this achievement must be set Mazarin's refusal to make the speedy termination of the wars an urgent priority and his failure to empathise with the poor, to reform French agriculture or tackle the monstrous injustice of government taxation. There is no evidence that he recognised the case for reform or that there were alternatives to the Bourbon programme. Nor did he encourage his pupil, the young king, to question this programme.

Did Mazarin ever have second thoughts? It is hard to say. Even Geoffrey Treasure still finds him an elusive figure. Perhaps his touching and humble dying words ('the hour of mercy, the hour of mercy') indicate a certain unease. Perhaps he realised that if Louis XIV was indeed his masterpiece, he had much to answer for. Nevertheless Louis was to recognise on his own deathbed fifty-four years later that the pupil would have done well to have adopted his master's patient pragmatism.

FOR FURTHER READING:

The books by all the historians mentioned in this article are to be recommended. In particular: Orest Ranum, *The Fronde*, (New York, 1993); Richard Bonney, *Political Change Under Richelieu and Mazarin,* (Oxford 1978) and *The King's Debts,* (Oxford 1981); Sharon Kettering, *Patrons, Brokers and Clients in Seventeenth Century France,* (Oxford, 1986); Geoffrey Treasure, *Mazarin,* (Routledge, 1995); George Dethan, *The Young Mazarin,* (Thames and Hudson, 1977); *Robin Briggs, Early Modern France 1560–1715,* (Oxford, 1977).

Locke and Liberty

As an articulate champion of liberty and toleration, of common sense and healthy measure in all things, England's John Locke (1632–1704) became in many respects the guiding spirit for America's Founding Fathers. His perception that personal freedom requires the private ownership of property remains a cornerstone of American political thought. Nonetheless, Locke is a hazy figure to most Americans. . . . Here,* Maurice Cranston *reviews the man's life and work.

Maurice Cranston

Maurice Cranston, 65, a former Wilson Center Guest Scholar, is professor of political science at the London School of Economics. Born in London, he was educated in England at St. Catherine's College and Oxford. His books include John Stuart Mill *(1965),* Jean-Jacques, The Early Life and Work of Jean-Jacques Rousseau, 1712–54 *(1982), and the reissued* John Locke: A Biography.

Among the philosophers of the modern world, John Locke has always been held in especially high regard in America. His influence on the Founding Fathers exceeded that of any other thinker. And the characteristically American attitude toward politics—indeed, toward life—can still be thought of as "Lockean," with its deep attachment to the rule of law, to equal rights to life, liberty, and property, to work and enterprise, to religious toleration, to science, progress, and pragmatism.

Like the Founders, Locke had participated in a revolution—the bloodless Glorious Revolution of 1688–89, in which the English overthrew the despotic King James II to install the constitutional monarchy of William and Mary and confirm Parliament's supremacy. Locke had justified that rebellion in his writings with arguments against "unjust and unlawful force," arguments that were cited as no less powerful in the American Colonies during the 1770s.

Earlier philosophers had theories about justice, order, authority, and peace. Locke was the first to build a system around *liberty.*

Locke's chief works—*An Essay Concerning Human Understanding, Two Treatises of Government,* and his first *Letter Concerning Toleration,* all published in London in 1689–90—spoke in terms that Thomas Jefferson, James Madison, and other Americans recognized. Men were created equal by God and endowed by Him with natural rights; the earth was given by God to men to cultivate by their own endeavors, so that each could earn a right to property ("the chief end" of society) by the application of his labor to the improvement of nature. In the New World, Locke's message received a warmer welcome than in crowded, feudal Europe.

The practical men who led the American Revolution and wrote the Constitution and the Bill of Rights recognized Locke as a Christian, like themselves, who had discarded nonessential dogmas and yet retained a pious faith in the Creator and in the Puritan virtues of probity and industry. Other European philosophers influenced the Framers' thinking: Montesquieu (1689–1755) contributed a republican element and Jean-Jacques Rousseau (1712–78) a democratic element, neither present in the constitutional-monarchist system of Locke. But the French philosophers, though they worked in a field prepared by Locke, did not have his hold on the American mind.

But who *was* John Locke?

Paintings, including a 1672 portrait by John Greenhill that Locke admired, show a tall, lean, and handsome man with a dimpled chin and large, dark, languorous eyes. He had asthma; one of his teachers, the great medical scientist Thomas Sydenham, urged him to rest much to conserve the "needful heat." A contemporary at Oxford called him a "turbulent spirit, clamorous and never contented," who could be "prating and troublesome." The earl of Shaftesbury, his long-time patron, thought him a "genius."

So, apparently, did Locke. His self-esteem shows in the understated Latin epitaph he wrote for himself before he died at age 73. The plaque at the Essex church where he was buried describes him as merely a scholar "contented with his modest lot," who "devoted his studies wholly to the pursuit of truth."

Locke was never a candid man. He had an almost Gothic love of mystery. A Tory spy once wrote that at Oxford Locke "lives a very cunning unintelligible life"; he was often absent, but "no one knows whither he goes." In his letters and notebooks, he used ciphers and a shorthand system modified for purposes of concealment. Yet a picture emerges from these and other sources: Locke was one of the most adept, compelling, and idiosyncratic "new men" to rise in what he called "this great Bedlam," 17th-century England.

John Locke was born on August 29, 1632, at Wrington in Somerset in the west of England, where modern commerce first began to challenge the old medieval order. His grandfather, Nicholas Locke, was a successful clothier. His less prosperous father, John Locke, was a lawyer and clerk to the local magistrates. His mother came from a family of tanners; she was 35 when her first child, the future philosopher, was born; her husband was only 26. The baby was baptized by Samuel Crook, a leading Puritan intellectual, and brought up in an atmosphere of Calvinist austerity and discipline.

England was Bedlam partly because of

From *The Wilson Quarterly,* Winter 1986, pp. 82-93.

tension between the arrogant, authoritarian, and High Anglican King Charles and the increasingly assertive and Puritan House of Commons. In 1642, when Locke was 10 years old, the Civil War began between the Royalist forces (the Cavaliers) and the Parliamentary army (the Roundheads). The struggle was religious and social as well as political. The ultimately victorious Parliamentarians tended to be drawn not from the traditionalists of the Church of England and the leaders of feudal society, but from the Calvinists and Puritans, men from England's "new class" of rising merchants.

Among these were Locke's Devonshire cousins, named King, who rose swiftly from the trade of grocers to that of lawyers, and then via Parliament to the nobility itself. Young John, too, would benefit from England's great upheaval.

During the Civil War, his father was made a captain of Parliamentary Horse by Alexander Popham, a rich local magistrate turned Roundhead colonel. Popham became fond of his captain's son. When Westminster, the country's best boarding school, was taken over by Parliament, Popham found a place there for the boy.

That was the *first* stroke of fortune that would assist Locke's rise from the lower- to the upper-middle class—a group whose aspirations he may have reflected when, as a political philosopher, he gave the right to property first priority among the rights of man.

At Westminster, Locke was influenced by headmaster Richard Busby, a Royalist whom the Parliamentary governors had imprudently allowed to remain in charge of the school. By the time Locke won a scholarship to Oxford's premier college, Christ Church, which he entered at age 20, he was well ready to react against the rule of the Puritan "saints" at the university.* By 27, Locke had become a right-wing monarchist; by 1661, when he was 29, and the Restoration had put the deposed king's son Charles II on the throne, Locke's political views were close to those of the conservative thinker of the previous generation, Thomas Hobbes.

In a pamphlet Locke wrote at that time, he said that no one had more "veneration for authority than I." Having been born in a political "storm" that had "lasted almost hitherto," he had been led by the calm that the Restoration brought to value "obedience."

By his early 30s, Locke was less interested in politics than in medicine, a new subject at Oxford. During the summer of 1666, he chanced to perform a small medical service for a student's father, Anthony Ashley Cooper, the future earl of Shaftesbury and leader of the Whig party, champion of the rights of Parliament over the Crown.† Even then Shaftesbury, a wealthy Presbyterian, was a vocal political "liberal," the chief foe of measures designed by the Anglican majority to curb the freedom of religious Nonconformists. If Locke had not already come over to Shaftesbury's views, the earl must soon have pulled him across the last few hurdles.

At 35, Locke went to live at Shaftesbury's London house as his physician. After he saved the earl from the threat of a cyst of the liver, Shaftesbury decided that Locke was too talented to be spending his time on medicine alone, and work of other kinds was found for him. Thus began Locke's 15-year association with a powerful patron.

Gradually, Locke discovered his true gifts. First he became a philosopher. At Oxford he had been bored with the medieval Aristotelian philosophy still taught there. Reading French rationalist René Descartes first opened his eyes to the "new philosophy" that was providing the underpinnings of modern empirical science. Discussions with Shaftesbury and other friends led him to begin writing early drafts of the *Essay Concerning Human Understanding,* his masterpiece on epistemology, the study of how we know what we know.

Shaftesbury, short, ugly, and vain, shared Locke's interest in philosophy and science. He was pragmatic: Though anti-Catholic, he thought that religious toleration would help unite the nation, the better to pursue the kind of commercial imperialism that was proving so profitable for the seafaring Dutch.

Charles II, though he favored toleration primarily for the sake of Catholic recusants, agreed with Shaftesbury. In 1672, the king made Shaftesbury his chief minister, lord high chancellor. But the two soon fell out. Shaftesbury came to believe that England's main rival in trade and her potential enemy was not Holland but France, while Charles II remained strongly pro-French. Ousted as the king's minister, Shaftesbury became his leading adversary.

Later, when Charles II refused to deny his brother, a professed Catholic, the right to succeed him as James II, Shaftesbury tried to get the House of Commons to make the succession illegal. The people, he said, had a right to say who should rule. When Charles resisted, Shaftesbury called on his allies to rebel. The plot was nipped, and in 1682 the earl fled to Holland, where he soon died.

Locke, too, went to Amsterdam. One year later he was expelled *in absentia* from his "studentship" at Oxford by the king's command. The next summer, after Charles II's death and James's accession to the throne, the duke of Monmouth led a failed rebellion against the new king. Locke, named by the government as one of Monmouth's agents in Holland, went into hiding as "Dr. van der Linden."

Locke's friends in Holland included many of those who plotted with the Dutch prince William of Orange to topple James II, who was indeed deposed in 1688. We do not know how deeply Locke was involved, only that he returned to London in 1689 with William's wife Mary, the new English queen.

These were the events behind Locke's most famous works.

By the time the *Two Treatises of Government* appeared, Englishmen had come round to Shaftesbury's view: They justified deposing James II not just because he advanced Catholicism, but also because he had tried to be an absolute monarch like France's Louis XIV. In his preface, Locke said that he hoped the *Two Treatises* would help "justify the title of King William to rule us." But he did most of the writing when Charles II was king. Then, the question of whether a people had the right to rebel against their ruler was not a backward-looking moral issue but a forward-looking moral challenge.

Thomas Hobbes wrote *Leviathan* (1651) to provide new reasons for men to obey kings. In the *Two Treatises,* Locke used Hobbes's "social contract" to justify revolt against despots.

*The Oxford routine was still medieval. Undergraduates had to rise at 5:00 A.M. to attend chapel, and do four hours' work in Hall before supper at noon. Conversations with tutors, and among students in Hall, had to be in Latin. Students had to hear at least two sermons a day, and visit their tutors nightly "to hear private prayers and to give an account of the time spent that day."

† The name Whig seems to have come from *Whiggamore,* a term for "horse thief" used by 17th-century Anglicans or "Tories" to express scorn for Scottish Presbyterians.

Locke's 'Shattered and Giddy' England

The tremors that rocked John Locke's times echo in his letters. England's fissures—between Crown and Parliament, Anglicans and Dissenters, aristocrats and achievers, rich and poor—had left a "shattered and giddy nation," he wrote at age 27. Few men "enjoy the privilege of being sober."

During the century before Locke's birth in 1632, England's population almost doubled, topping five million in 1540. But with growth came several woes: rising prices, falling "real" wages, and poor harvests and frequent famines caused by a miniature global ice age that lasted from about 1550 to 1700. While England was a naval power, as the 1588 defeat of the Spanish Armada had shown, the Dutch were far ahead in turning maritime prowess to profit.

BUT BUSINESS WAS becoming important: Retail shops created by a new breed of merchant began to replace the old market fairs. Abroad, firms chartered by the Crown traded English woolens and African slaves for West Indian molasses and sugar and American fish and timber; the East India Company (est. 1600) dealt in textiles and tea. Commerce had not (yet) remade England; if Locke's home county, Somerset, prospered from new industries (notably clothing), it was also plagued by such poverty that people, wrote one chronicler, "hanged themselves from want." But, slowly, medieval England was becoming the mercantile nation that, by the 18th century, would create the British Empire.

Authority was eroding. The Roman Catholic Church's supremacy had been broken by the Protestantism that had arrived via Martin Luther's Germany and Huldrych Zwingli's and John Calvin's Switzerland, and by King Henry VIII'S 1534 creation of the Church of England. And while the peerage was still dominant, the expanding landed gentry and the new commercial class now had to be heard. By the early 17th century, as historian Lawrence Stone has noted, "respectful subservience [to aristocracy] was breaking down."

King Charles I (1625–49), was besieged by troubles. Suspected by his Protestant subjects of "popish" leanings, he waged an unpopular war in Europe and, later, failed to secure Parliament's support in his effort to quash rebellion in Scotland, leading to the Civil War in 1542. The pro-Parliament Roundheads tended to be Calvinists (Presbyterians), Puritans, or Protestant Nonconformists—the rising merchants and the gentry. The royalist Cavaliers were High Church or Catholic aristocrats. The 1648 triumph of the Parliamentary Army under (among others) the ardent Puritan, Oliver Cromwell, was to an extent a victory—and not the final one—of the "new" middle-class England. Soon after, the English did what most Europeans then considered unthinkable: They beheaded their king and established a commonwealth.

Within five years, Cromwell assumed absolute power. His Protectorate was austere. Fancy dress, amusements such as alehouses and horseraces, and lively arts such as theater were discouraged. The Puritan zealots who controlled Oxford, wrote one of Locke's contemporaries, enjoyed "laughing at a man in a cassock or canonical coat." They would "tipple" in their chambers, but would not enter taverns or permit such diversions as "Maypoles, Morrises [folk dances], Whitsun ales, nay, scarce wakes." So unpopular were Puritan efforts to impose moral discipline that most Englishmen joined Locke in hailing the Restoration of Charles II in 1660. But the monarchy would never be the same. After Charles's successor, James II, was deposed, William and Mary became England's first constitutional monarchs. Merriment returned to everyday life. At Oxford, nearly 400 taverns flourished, as did, said one critic, "easy manners, unmorality, loose language, disrespect."

WHILE PROTESTANTISM—particularly Puritanism—played a large role in 17th-century politics, its influence went further. In the arts, it infused the epic poem *Paradise Lost* (1667), John Milton's eloquent attempt to "justify God's ways to man." In science, the mental traits fostered by Protestantism—independence, individualism, skepticism of authority—were central.

Early in the century Francis Bacon had called for close scrutiny of the natural world, for the adoption of the experimental method, and for an inductive style of reasoning. Among those who heeded him were Isaac Newton, Robert Boyle, and William Harvey, the pioneering anatomist. All helped dispose of scholasticism, the medieval system of inquiry that proceeded, in Aristotelian style, by deduction from untestable assumptions. The "new science" that they espoused encouraged a radical reconsideration of all areas of thought—in political theory, in economics, and in philosophy itself. It was, of course, an upheaval to which Locke himself made vital contributions.

Hobbes's social contract united men, whom he viewed as natural enemies, in a civil society with a common purpose. Locke did not see men as enemies. He took a Christian view. He argued that men were subject, even in a state of nature, to natural law, which was ultimately God's law made known to men through the voice of reason.

Hobbes's theory had simplicity: Either you are ruled or you are not ruled, either you have obedience or you have liberty, either you have security and fetters or you have chaos and danger. Neither condition is ideal, said Hobbes, but the worst government was better than none at all.

The Lockean analysis was less pessimistic.

Locke believed that men could be both ruled and free. While subject to natural law, men also had natural rights—notably rights to life, liberty, and property. These rights were retained when men contracted to form political societies. Instead of surrendering their freedom to a sovereign, as Hobbes suggested, men had merely *entrusted* power to a ruler. In return for justice and mutual security, they had agreed to obey their rulers, on condition that their natural rights were respected. Natural rights, being derived from natural law, were rooted in something higher than the edicts of princes, namely the edicts of God. They were "inalienable."

Locke's "right to revolution"—to reject a ruler who failed to respect natural rights—thus derived not only from the social contract but also from the supremacy of God's law to man's. People who might have misunderstood, or been unimpressed by, the social contract in abstract philosophy could appreciate the principle that God's law is higher than that of kings. And while Locke based his politics on religion, his was not the astringent faith of the Catholics or of Calvin, but that watered-down Christianity later known as Modernism.*

Locke's writing during his stay in Holland included a travel journal. It revealed how he would visit some great cathedral or chateau, but then take an interest only in working out the exact dimensions. He detested ceremonies and show, which he thought irrational and wasteful, and was pleased to find that one of the best Dutch universities had nondescript architecture. It proved "that knowledge depends not on the stateliness of buildings, etc."

"Knowledge" is the key word. Locke's philistinism was no aberration. He wanted to get away from the imagination, from the vague glamour of medieval things, from unthinking adherence to tradition, from enthusiasm, mysticism, and glory; away from all private, visionary insights and down to the plain, demonstrable facts. This was central to his mission as a philosopher and reformer. His antipathy to poetry and imaginative artists was coupled with scorn for ivory-tower scholars who talk "with but one sort of men and read but one sort of books." They "canton out to themselves a little Goshen in the intellectual world where the light shines. . . . but will not venture out into the great ocean of knowledge."

Locke's venturing made him a polymath, but he was in no sense a smatterer. True, his expertness was not equal in all the subjects he chose to study. Compared to his friends, chemist Robert Boyle and Sir Isaac Newton, the great physicist, he was an amateurish scientist. His knowledge of the Scriptures was questionable. Although he wrote influential essays on monetary policy, he could not appreciate the subtlety of other economists. But what was important in Locke's case was not his versatility, but that each department of knowledge was related in his mind to all the others.

In the *Essay Concerning Human Understanding,* Locke says in the opening "Epistle" that in an age of such "master builders" as Boyle, Sydenham, and "the incomparable Mr. Newton" it is "ambition enough to be employed as an under-laborer in clearing the ground a little and removing some of the rubbish that lies in the way of knowledge." Locke did much more than that: The *Essay* provides the first modern philosophy of science.

A recurrent word in the work is a Cartesian one, "idea." Locke's usage is curious. He does not merely say that we have ideas in our minds when we think; he says that we have ideas in our minds when we see, hear, smell, taste, or feel. The core of his epistemology is the notion that we perceive not *things* but ideas that are derived in part from objects in the external world, yet also depend to some extent on our own minds for their existence.

The *Essay* attacks the established view that certain ideas are innate. Locke's belief is that we are born in total ignorance, and that even our theoretical ideas of identity, quantity, and substance are derived from experience. A child gets ideas of black and white, of sweet and bitter, *before* he gets an idea of abstract principles, such as identity or impossibility. "The senses at first let in particular ideas, and furnish the yet empty cabinet." Then the mind abstracts theoretical ideas, and so "comes to be furnished with ideas and language, the materials about which to exercise its discursive faculty."

In Locke's account, man is imprisoned in a sort of diving bell. He receives some signals from without and some from within his apparatus, but having no means of knowing which if any come from outside, he cannot test the signals' authenticity. Thus man cannot have any certain knowledge of the external world. He must settle for *probable* knowledge.

Locke's general philosophy has obvious implications for a theory of morals. The traditional view was that some sort of moral knowledge was innate. Locke thought otherwise. What God had given men was a faculty of reason and a sentiment of self-love. Reason combined with self-love produced morality. Reason could discern the principles of ethics, or natural law, and self-love should lead men to obey them.

Locke wrote in one of his notebooks that "it is a man's proper business to seek happiness and avoid misery. Happiness consists in what delights and contents the mind, misery is what disturbs, discomposes or torments it." He would "make it my business to seek satisfaction and delight and avoid uneasiness and disquiet." But he knew that "if I prefer a short pleasure to a lasting one, it is plain I cross my own happiness."

For Locke, in other words, Christian ethics was natural ethics. The teaching of the New Testament was a means to an end—happiness in this life and the next. The reason for doing what the Gospel demanded about loving one's neighbor, etc., was not just that Jesus said it. By doing these things one promoted one's happiness; men were impelled by their natural self-love to desire it.

Wrongdoing was thus for Locke a sign of ignorance or folly. People did not always realize that long-term happiness could usually only he bought at the cost of short-term pleasure. If people were prudent and reflective, not moved by the winds of impulse and emotion, they would have what they most desired.

The preface to the English edition of the first *Letter Concerning Toleration* says, "Absolute Liberty, just and true Liberty, equal and impartial Liberty is the thing we stand in need of." Many people assumed these words to be Locke's; Lord King, a relative, made them an epigraph in a Locke biography. In fact, they were the words of the translator of Locke's original Latin, William Popple.

Locke did *not* believe in absolute liberty, any more than he believed in absolute knowledge. He thought the way to achieve as much as possible of both was to face the fact that they were limited and then to see what the limitations were. As he did with knowledge in the *Essay,* Locke focused on the liberty that men cannot have, to show the liberty they can achieve. The limits are set by the need to protect the life, property, and freedom of each individual from others, and from the society's common enemies. No other limits need be borne, or *should* be.

*Locke rejected original sin. He maintained in *The Reasonableness of Christianity* (1695) that Christ had come into the world not to redeem wrongdoing man, but to bring immortality to the righteous. Locke, a professed Anglican, here argued like a Unitarian, though he felt that word conjured up the unpopular image of a skeptical dissenter.

Locke set men on the road to the greatest possible liberty by the method he used to set them on the road to the greatest knowledge—teaching the impossibility of the absolute.

Locke guarded his anonymity with elaborate care. The *Essay,* which made him famous throughout Europe in his own time, was one of the few works that appeared under his own name. Most were published anonymously. When an English translation of the first *Letter Concerning Toleration* was issued in London, Locke protested that it had happened "without my privity."

Some of his secrecy stemmed from his days of hiding in Holland, some was for fun, some plainly neurotic. Some added a needed touch of romance to his relations with his women friends.

While Locke never married, he sought female affection and courted a formidable lot of professors' bluestocking daughters. Once, when he was 27, his father wrote to him of a Somerset widow who was "young, childless, handsome, with £200 per annum and £1,000 in her purse," but Locke would not settle down. His closest relationship with *any* person developed in 1682, when Locke, then 50, met Damaris Cudworth, the 24-year-old daughter of a Cambridge philosopher. They exchanged verses and love letters (signed "Philander" and "Philoclea"); he called her his "governess," a role that he was oddly fond of inviting his women friends to assume. Yet no union resulted, although the two were to remain close, even years after she married a nobleman and became Lady Masham.

Locke, as he wrote to an old friend, considered "marriage and death so very nearly the same thing."

Locke was careful with money. His detailed accounts show that during his 30s he had a modest income of about £240 a year from rental property in Somerset, in addition to stipends from Christ Church and profits from investments.* Once, when going abroad, he asked an uncle not to let his tenants know, "for perhaps that may make them more slack to pay their rents."

Locke's attentiveness to important people brought him not only lodgings—he had no home, being always the guest of various admirers—but job offers as well. He was once the Crown's secretary of presentations, a £300-a-year job involving ecclesiastical matters. He refused an ambassadorship in Germany, saying that the duties there more befitted someone who could "drink his share" than "the soberest man" in England. Shaftesbury made him secretary of the Lords Proprietors of Carolina, in which role he advertised for settlers (people who could behave "peaceably" and not use their "liberty" for "licentiousness") and helped write a constitution for the colony.†

In his mid-60s, Locke became the dominant member of a new Board of Trade. Though the post paid £1,000 a year, Locke complained to a friend: "What have I to do with the bustle of public affairs while sliding under the burdens of age and infirmity?"

Among other things, Locke's board made linen-making the "general trade" of Ireland (partly to keep the Irish out of England's wool business). When pauperism became an issue, Locke argued that the problem was not "scarcity of provision or want of employment," but indiscipline and "corruption of manners, virtue, and industry." He urged (unsuccessfully) new laws for the "suppression of begging drones." Healthy men between 14 and 50 caught seeking alms should serve three years on navy ships "under strict discipline at soldier's pay." Boys and girls under 14 should be "soundly whipped."

Lady Masham explained that Locke was "compassionate," but "his charity was always directed to encourage working, laborious, industrious people, and not to relieve idle beggars, to whom he never gave anything." He thought them wastrels, and "waste of anything he could not bear to see."

Locke was 68 before he retired, to the Masham country house, to spend his last years writing a commentary on the New Testament.

Although Locke has sometimes been dismissed as an ideologue of the age of bourgeois revolutions, he is in many respects the 17th-century thinker whose teaching is most relevant to the concerns of our own time. During the 19th century, that great age of nationalism and imperialism, Locke's individualism seemed narrow and dated. But in the presence of the kind of despotic and totalitarian regimes that have emerged during the 20th century, Locke's defense of the rights of man has taken on a new immediacy. During World War I, Woodrow Wilson looked to Locke to justify the use of force against tyranny. When World War II posed an even more intense challenge to democracy, Winston Churchill proclaimed the aim of victory in Lockean terms, as "the enthronement of human rights."

Numerous declarations and covenants of human rights have since expressed the principles through which the West has sought to formulate its demand for freedom under law. That is something we have claimed not only for our fellow citizens, but (as Locke did) for all men—not an ideal of perfect justice, but a minimal standard to which any government can fairly be called upon to conform. We no longer expect every nation to govern itself as democratically as we do ourselves, but we do demand that they all respect human rights, and we can still look to Locke for the classic formulation of the philosophy that informs that demand.

Modern opinion has often sought to add to assertions of the rights of individuals, pleas for the rights of groups, economic, ethnic, racial, regional, or whatever. But again, that was anticipated by Locke when he argued for the toleration of dissidents and minorities. In his time, religious persecution was at issue; in ours it is political. But persecution as such has not changed its character, and the case for toleration that Locke worked out 300 years ago is no less pertinent today than it was then. It is, if anything, more urgent, since progress has made persecution more common, efficient, and cruel.

The "storm" of change in which Locke was born continues. So, remarkably, does the value of his ideas on how to deal with change, maintaining the maximum liberty and justice for all.

---

*Though no plunger, Locke did speculate with some success (as Shaftesbury had) in the slave trade and in sugar plantations in the Bahamas. He wrote at least some books for money, among them a volume on French grape and olive cultivation (something good has "come out of France"). The estate he left, worth close to £20,000, was no fortune, but not a pittance either.

† Rejecting a "numerous democracy," the document prescribed legislative power balanced between citizenry and a local aristocracy; freemen had to "acknowledge a God." Locke received membership in the Carolina aristocracy and some land, But the colonists, who began arriving in 1659, repudiated the Lords Proprietors; the aristocracy was never created, and Locke's land appears to have yielded no rent.

Rationalism, Enlightenment, and Revolution

This unit explores facets of the Age of Reason (the seventeenth century) and the Enlightenment (the eighteenth century). These two phases of the Western tradition had much in common. Both placed their faith in science and reason, both believed in progress, and both were skeptical about much of the cultural baggage inherited from earlier periods. Yet each century marked a distinctive stage in the spread of rationalism. In the seventeenth century, a few advanced thinkers (John Locke and René Descartes, for example) attempted to resolve the major philosophical problems of knowledge—that is, to develop a theoretical basis for the new rationalism. The eighteenth century saw in the works of Immanuel Kant and David Hume a continuation of that theoretical enterprise. But there was a new development as well: Voltaire, Denis Diderot, and others campaigned to popularize science, reason, the principles of criticism, and the spirit of toleration. Increasingly, the critical attitudes engendered by rationalism and empiricism in the seventeenth century were brought to bear upon familiar beliefs and practices in the eighteenth century.

Several articles in this unit show the advance of critical reason. Science, the model for many of the new intellectual attitudes, is addressed in "Newton's Madness." "The First Feminist" reviews Mary Wollstonecraft's life and her arguments for "enlightened" treatment of women. "Madrid: City of the Enlightenment" locates the new developments in an unlikely place—a stronghold of Catholicism and the baroque, while "The Pursuit of Happiness" demonstrates how the ideals of the French Enlightenment resurfaced across the Atlantic.

The new attitudes often were troublesome, even revolutionary. During the seventeenth and eighteenth centuries no tradition seemed safe from criticism. Even the Bible was scrutinized for contradictions and faulty logic. Universities and salons became intellectual battlegrounds where advocates of the ancient classics (only recently restored and returned to favor by Renaissance humanists) confronted the stalwarts of modernity. But the struggle went beyond a mere battle of the books. Powerful religious and political institutions were subjected to the test of reason and were usually found wanting. The goal was to reorganize society on a rational or enlightened basis and to develop a new morality based on reason, not authority.

Of course, rationalism was not confined to the seventeenth and eighteenth centuries, as any reader of Aristotle or St. Thomas Aquinas can attest. Nor did the influence of the irrational disappear during the Age of Reason. The period, after all, witnessed a great European witch craze and a millenarian movement in England. And those who doubt that atavistic attitudes could surface among the rationalists need only explore Sir Isaac Newton's interest in alchemy and Blaise Pascal's mysticism.

As for the Enlightenment, many have questioned how deeply its ideals and reforms penetrated eighteenth-century society. On occasion, social change produced unanticipated consequences, as we see in Marcus Rediker's article about women pirates. Sometimes the lower orders stubbornly resisted the enlightened legislation passed on their behalf. And at the level of high politics, we are hardly surprised to learn that the so-called "enlightened despots" of the continent stopped short of instituting reforms that might have diminished their authority. Or else they manipulated education and the arts in order to enhance their own power. Nor did modern rationalism cause the great powers to rein in their ambitions, as the international rivalries of the period demonstrate.

And while the doctrines of the Enlightenment may be enshrined in the noblest expressions of the French Revolution, that great upheaval also witnessed mass executions and systematic efforts to suppress freedom of expression. The excesses of the Revolution are exemplified by the senseless execution of France's most brilliant scientist (see Stephen Jay Gould's article, "The Passion of Antoine Lavoisier"). In "Napoleon Takes Charge," James Shosenberg shows how the chaotic conditions of revolution could foster upward mobility for opportunists. The long-range impact of the Revolution is treated in "The French Revolution in the Minds of Men," where Maurice Cranston writes about the upheaval as it "became inflated or distorted in the minds of later partisans."

Historians differ about the possible links between the Enlightenment and the French Revolution. And even in the eighteenth century many thinkers questioned the ideals of the Enlightenment. But, as Herbert Muller has written in *The Uses of the Past* (Oxford University Press, 1957), it "not only diffused knowledge but set public standards of truth. Its principles were aboveboard, freely accessible to all men, and not dependent upon intuitive, mystical, or received truth."

In our century, with its mass atrocities, world wars, and nuclear weapons, it is difficult to sustain the Enlightenment's faith in reason. But even before our recent disillusionment, rationalism provoked a powerful reaction—Romanticism. In contrast to the rationalists, romantics trusted emotions and distrusted intellect; they viewed nature not so much as a repository of scientific laws, but as a source of inspiration and beauty; they were preoccupied with self-discovery, not social reform; and often they drew upon the medieval experience for their images and models. True, the dream of reason has survived the Romantic rebellion and the excesses of our era. It lives on in our modern programs of mass education and social uplift, which is to say that it is embodied in contemporary liberalism and that its prospects are precarious.

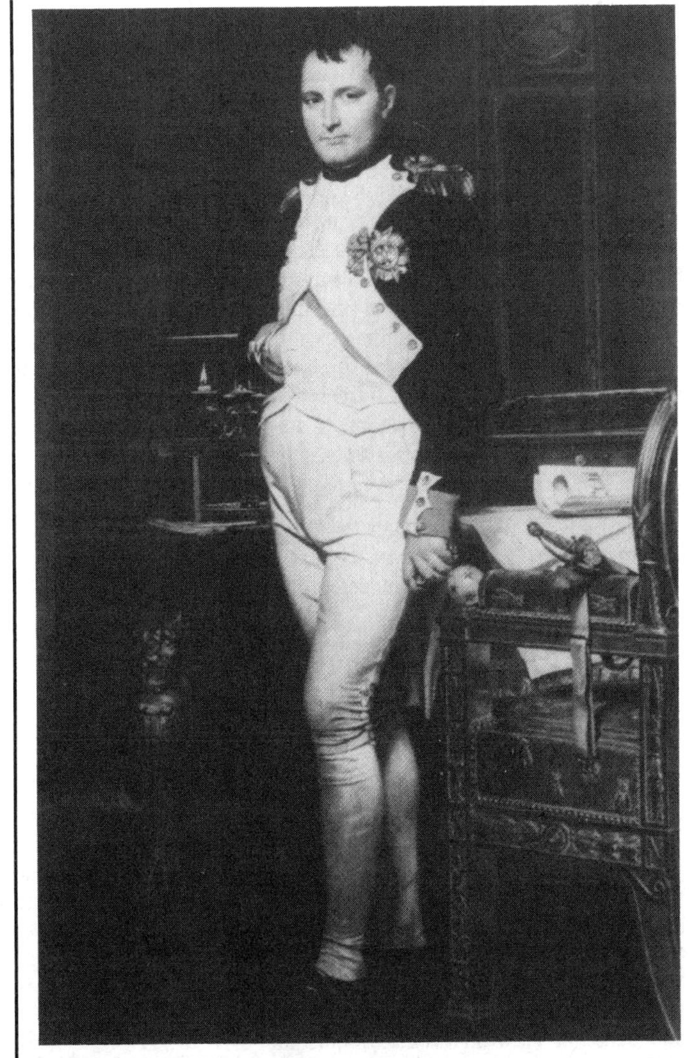

Looking Ahead: Challenge Questions

Discuss the effects of rationalism on the lives of ordinary seventeenth- and eighteenth-century Europeans.

In what ways did the Enlightenment influence American culture?

How did the new views of human nature affect eighteenth-century attitudes about womanhood?

Describe how and why France's greatest scientist was victimized by the French Revolution.

How did the French Revolution facilitate the rise of Napoleon to prominence and power?

Does Mary Wollstonecraft's feminism compare to today's version? Why or why not?

Newton's Madness

Madness in great ones must not unwatched go.
—Shakespeare *Hamlet*

We are all born mad. Some remain so.
—Samuel Beckett, *Waiting for Godot*

Harold L. Klawans, M.D.

Sir Isaac Newton is one of the few scientists in the history of Western civilization whose reputation is universal and whose name is synonymous with genius. Newton, Aristotle, Einstein—I doubt if there are many others. Newton lived from 1642 to 1727. Today he is considered to have been a natural philosopher. He was actually a physicist and mathematician and, with the possible exception of Albert Einstein, he may well have been the most original and influential theorist in the history of science. His list of accomplishments is impressive:

1. The coinvention of calculus. Working independently, Newton and Gottfried Wilhelm Leibniz both "invented," or discovered, calculus.
2. The discovery of the three laws of mechanics (Newton's laws) which transformed the entire field of physics.
3. The formulation of the law of gravity.
4. The discovery of the composition of white light.
5. The formulation of a theory of planetary motion.

The list does not end there, but my purpose here is not to investigate the mind of Sir Isaac Newton and the influence of that mind on Western civilization. Rather, it is to explore the nature and cause of Newton's madness and its effect on Newton the man and Newton the scientist. For Newton became mad. Not permanently deranged, but twice during his life, he suffered periods of prolonged abnormal behavior, bordering on psychosis. His madness was of his own doing, and it was a malady that did not leave him unscathed.

The first episode of his madness lasted through most of 1677 and 1678, while the second began in 1693. The former is not as well documented in contemporary records, for it came at a time in his career when he was not yet a public figure. Newton's symptoms of "madness" began at about the time of his first scientific publication concerning his theory of the composition of white light. Newton himself considered this work to be "the oddest if not the most considerable detection which has hitherto been made in operations of Nature." His paper was not immediately accepted by the entire scientific community and Newton's reactions to the criticisms of this work were not the logical reactions of a finely tuned genius. Newton scholar Richard S. Westfall studied these responses and suggested that Newton's behavior showed definite signs of abnormality. Westfall was particularly struck by Newton's correspondence with a critic named John Lucas:

> The correspondence dragged on until 1678, when a final shriek of rage from Newton, apparently accompanied by a complete nervous breakdown, was followed by silence. The death of his mother the following year completed his isolation. For six years he withdrew from intellectual commerce, except when others initiated a correspondence, which he always broke off as soon as possible.

It was not until 1684 that Newton once again began to seek the company of others and to interact with fellow scientists.

Although most studies of Newton's life have passed over this first instance of altered behavior, it is generally acknowledged in both the historical and scientific communities that in the years 1692 and 1693, Newton underwent a period of severe emotional and mental disturbance. This entire episode has always had about it something of an air of mystery. The first biography of Newton, published in London and Paris in 1728, the year after Newton's death, was written by a Frenchman named Bernard Le Bovier de Fontenelle, who was the permanent secretary of the Academie Royale des Sciences. Le Bovier de Fontenelle based his work largely on information and material given to him by John Conduitt. Conduitt was married to Newton's niece and had spent many years and much energy collecting materials for a projected biography of Newton that he intended to write but that he never undertook. Whatever he gave to Fontenelle contained no reference to any mental disorder suffered by Newton. Either Conduitt was ignorant of this episode or he knew of it but decided to suppress it—the latter being far more likely. Fontenelle's biography was widely read and, since it was based on contemporary source material, it became the primary foundation of virtually all subsequent studies of Newton's life. For the next hundred years, no biographies even hinted at the possibility of a mental illness.

In 1820, this viewpoint began to change. In that year, the French astronomer Jean Baptiste Biot wrote a sketch of Newton for the *Biographie Universelle,* in which he stated that in 1693, Newton suffered what Biot termed a "derangement of the intellect," during which his "reason" was abnormal.

Much of the proof that this "derangement of the intellect" actually took place became readily available only in 1961 when Volume 3 of Newton's correspondence, covering the years 1688 through 1694, was finally published. Most accounts of Newton's illness have dated its onset to late 1693. However, a careful study of his correspondence reveals definite signs of emotional stress beginning at least eighteen months earlier. On January 26, 1692, Newton, who was then living in Cambridge, complained to John Locke that his old and hitherto completely loyal friend, Charles Montague, had been false to him, and that he, Newton, was "done with him." The same distrust is revealed in other letters written at the same time.

Whether the conflicts that Newton experienced in his relationship with Montague, Locke, and others were real or imaginary, we have no way of proving, but since numerous relationships were similarly affected at the same time, the odds are that the problem originated in Newton's mind or behavior. For the next eighteen months, the letters reveal nothing out of the ordinary.

Beginning on May 30, 1693, there is a period of three and a half months of silence, during which we have no record of any letter either received or written by Newton. The silence was finally interrupted by correspondence in which he exhibited the peculiar sensitivity that had been present during the early months of the previous years, but in a far more intensified form. Newton sent the following strange letter to the famous diarist Samuel Pepys on September 13, 1693:

> Sir,
>
> Some time after Mr. Millington had delivered your message, he pressed me to see you the next time I went to London. I was averse; but upon his pressing consented, before I considered what I did, for I am extremely troubled at the embroilment I am in, and have neither ate nor slept well this twelve month, nor have my former consistency of mind. I never designed to get anything by your interest, nor by King James's favour, but am now sensible that I must withdraw from your acquaintance, and see neither you nor the rest of my friends any more, if I may but leave them quietly. I beg your pardon for saying I would see you again, and rest your most humble and most obedient servant,
>
> Is. Newton

The same year, Newton wrote to Locke: "being of the opinion that you endeavoured to embroil me with women and by other means I was so much affected with it as that when one told me that you were sickly and would not live I answered twere better you were dead. I desire you to forgive me this uncharitableness." Both Pepys and Locke recognized that Newton's mind was deranged, and in other letters it is clear that his memory was also impaired.

These symptoms are reminiscent of those of his first episode of madness, which also resulted in Newton's withdrawing from society: suspiciousness of others, accusations, and withdrawal.

What, in fact, caused these two breakdowns?

Did Newton have a recurring psychosis—such as manic depressive affective disorder—with two separate and distinct psychotic breaks? Or were there specific factors in his life that precipitated each of these periods of psychological maladjustment?

Most of Newton's twentieth-century biographers have focused on the latter and have suggested a staggering number of hypotheses to explain the precipitation of one or the other of these episodes:

1. The shock of his mother's death. This hypothesis is all very Freudian. Unfortunately, Mrs. Newton died in 1679, too late to account for the first episode and too early for the second.
2. A fire that destroyed some important papers.
3. Failure to obtain a desired administrative post in London.
4. Exhaustion following the writing of his *Principia.*
5. Religious fervor.
6. Local problems with the university at Cambridge.

The list goes on and on. I will attempt neither to document them all nor to refute them one by one. Instead, I will invoke what I sometimes call "Baker's law." Baker's law is a law that I have propounded out of one of A. B. Baker's irrascible bedside pronouncements. A. B. Baker, one of the leading figures of American neurology in the middle third of this century, was primarily responsible for the founding of the American Academy of Neurology, which has, in fewer than forty years, become the leading force in American and world neurology, and one of the founders of *Neurology,* the first American medical journal dedicated solely to the field. He was also the chairman of neurology at the University of Minnesota, where I began my formal training in neurology.

Abe Baker was a clinician who shot from the hip. During a typical teaching session, one of my fellow first-year residents was presenting a patient who had a confusional psychosis. After telling Abe about the entire medical history of this patient and the results of the physical examination, this poor, unsuspecting resident then began to recount the patient's psychiatric history. Abe would have none of it. He exploded. A psychiatric history is a waste of time, he said. No neurologist should ever take one. Everybody has psychiatric problems. The whole world is crazy, so are all its inhabitants. The question is not if a patient has a psychiatric problem. The question is whether the patient has a neurologic problem that can account for his or her behavior. That is a neurologic question and has to be evaluated on neurologic grounds, not on psychiatric ones. A psychiatric history is irrelevant.

Thus, Baker's law: The entire neurologic issue is whether the patient has a neurologic disease or not. All else is mere commentary.

Did Newton have a neurologic problem that could account for his psychosis? If he did, his mother's death is irrelevant. If not, then his mother's death is a subject for psychiatrists to debate.

What evidence is there that Newton could have had a neurologic disorder? From his correspondence, a list of his signs and symptoms, both neurologic and psychiatric, can easily be compiled. They include

1. Severe insomnia
2. Extreme sensitivity in personal relations
3. Loss of appetite
4. Delusions of persecution
5. Memory difficulties
6. Some overall decrease in mental acuity

This is certainly the type of behavioral manifestation that can be seen in a variety of diffuse processes that cause mild (neurologically speaking) alteration in the function of both hemispheres of the brain. It is a neurologic rule of thumb that generalized behavioral symptoms such as these are usually related to diffuse or generalized dysfunction of the entire brain, that is, both halves, rather than just disease in a single location. Diseases that affect a single site in the brain, in contrast, cause symptoms that are related specifically to the normal function carried out by that location: weakness, speech difficulty, and loss of vision.

Because behaviors like memory, concentration, intellect, and judgment are not localized in one spot, they are more likely to become deranged in mild diffuse diseases that insult the brain generally without singling out any one specific locus.

A neurologic cause is, therefore, plausible as an explanation for Newton's odd behavior. But what cause? In recent years, two separate scientific reports have suggested that Newton's madness was caused by chronic mercury poisoning and that the poisoning was self-induced, a product of Newton's interest in alchemy.

Two English scientists named Spargo and Pounds conducted a careful examination of the records of Newton's chemical experiments. Newton had shown an interest in alchemy and chemistry and had even purchased a variety of apparatuses and chemicals as early as 1669. His last dated chemical experiments were carried out in February 1696, not long before he left Cambridge and moved to London. During his many years in Cambridge, Newton carried out several hundred chemical experiments, of which only a small number were specifically dated. However, from those that are dated, it is clear that Newton ran many of his experiments shortly before the first signs of each of his episodes of "madness." Newton made use of a wide variety of materials in his chemical research, including nonmetallic materials, such as sulfur, "sal armoniak" (ammonium chloride), and sulfuric and nitric acids, and metals, such as antimony, mercury, iron, tin, bismuth, lead, "arsnick," and copper, as well as many of their ores. Metals tended to play a prominent role in virtually all Newton's experiments, and mercury in particular was a major component in many of his studies.

In many of his experiments, Newton heated metals, their ores, or their salts to convert them into a volatile form. He would often heat these substances in open vessels, breathing in the fumes and tasting the formed products. Some of these experiments were simple and took little time, while others were complex and extended over many hours or, in a few cases, even days. While conducting research, Newton regularly slept in his laboratory by the same fire, which did not go out for weeks on end. Since most of the volatized metal fumes would have settled back into the fire only to be volatilized again, this clearly exposed him to an additional risk of metallic poisoning.

Newton conducted a number of alchemical experiments in December 1692 and January 1693, in which he used antimony, antimony ore, and a "mercurial water of lead," which was probably a lead amalgam. In these experiments a saltlike substance appeared in the neck of the retort. After reporting the taste of this substance under two conditions, he then continued: "I held it to ye side of ye flame of candle and it did not take flame as [sulphur] would do but yet fumed away and ye fumes made the side of ye flame look blue."

Information about Newton's working habits in chemistry is also found in the recollections of his assistant, Humphrey Newton:

> He very rarely went to bed till two or three of the clock, sometimes not until five or six, lying about four or five hours, especially at spring or the fall of the leaf, at which time he would employ about six weeks in his laboratory, the fire scarcely going out either night or day, he sitting up, one night as I did another, till he had finished his chemical experiments, in the performance of which he was the most accurate, strict, exact. What his aim might be I was not able to penetrate into, but his pains, his diligence at those set times made me think he aimed at something beyond the reach of human art or industry.
>
> About six weeks at spring, and six in the fall, the fire in the laboratory scarcely went out, which was well furnished with chemical materials as bodies, receivers, heads, crucibles, etc., which was *(sic)* made very little use of, the crucibles excepted, in which he fused his metals: he would sometimes, tho' seldom, look into an old mouldy book which lay in his elaboratory, I think it was titled Agricola de metallis, the transmuting of metals being his chief design.

Tasting mercury compounds and breathing the fumes of its various salts is highly hazardous. Metallic fumes are one of the most efficient ways of introducing an excessive amount of a metal into the body, since they enter the lungs and are quickly absorbed. It was at this point that Newton began to suffer from poor digestion and insomnia. It is even possible that Newton himself identified the cause of his symptoms as exposure to the quicksilver (mercury) vapors. After all, its effects had been known to alchemical writers for centuries before Newton, and Newton was quite familiar with their writings. In the following passage, Newton hints at the correct diagnosis of his malady:

> The last winter by sleeping too often by my fire I got into an ill habit of sleeping and a distemper which this summer has been epidemical put me further out of order, so that when I wrote to you I had not slept an hour a night for a fortnight together and for five nights together not a wink. I remember I wrote to you but what I said of your book I remember not. if you please to send me a transcript of that passage I will give you an account of it if I can.

Obviously, Newton was exposed to metallic mercury in 1692–93. Was that also the case in 1676? The answer is yes. The experiments he performed in connection with his study of "optiks" often involved significant exposure to mercury vapors, and during the period 1676–79 he also began a period of intense study of alchemy.

The exposure is proved. Newton was at risk for mercury poisoning. But does mercury poisoning cause madness?

In his 1964 textbook on mercury poisoning, *The Toxicity of Mercury and Its Compounds* (Amsterdam: Elsevier), Peter Bidstrup supplied the following description of chronic mercury poisoning: "Nervous irritability, tendency to blush easily, and a history—often best obtained from friends or members of the family—of change of temperament, a tendency to avoid meeting friends and unexplained outbursts of temper."

This description certainly reminds us of Newton. Of course, the initial symptoms of mercury poisoning differ from patient to patient. In 1893, the great English neurologist William R. Gowers investigated the syndrome of chronic mercury poisoning and pointed out that it often begins with irritability and difficulty with concentration, followed by insomnia and finally by hallucinations and maniacal excitement. There is frequently a compelling, overwhelming timidness; a shyness of strangers; an embarrassment about the illness; discouragement and apathy about all aspects of life (but not despair); a loss of self-confidence; a loss of joie de vivre progressing to depression; and finally, a loss of memory.

The key to suspecting that a patient undergoing such a personality change has a neurologic disorder is the appearance of neurologic signs and symptoms. In mercury poisoning, the most common of these is a tremor.

And Newton had a tremor: His handwriting in 1692–93 became tremulous, while before and afterward, it was firm and precise.

We are now two-thirds of the way to diagnosis.

1. Newton had sufficient exposure.
2. Newton had a clinical picture that is consistent with mercury poisoning, including neurologic findings.

But what good is a hypothesis unless it can be tested? Not much. It is the last step that is critical in reaching a diagnosis. Is there any way to prove that Newton actually had a toxic amount of mercury in his body?

Spargo and Pounds did just that. Today, we often diagnose mercury poisoning by measuring the amount of mercury present in the urine, the blood, or the hair. Obviously, the first two cannot be evaluated for Newton, but Spargo and Pounds were able to locate several locks of his hair. In them they found clear evidence of excessive amounts of mercury.

Abe was right: Baker's law at work. The diagnosis could have been made on neurologic grounds, without the need of taking a psychiatric history.

What happened to Newton following his second episode of madness?

In 1696, Newton moved to London and became master of the mint, leaving Cambridge—and alchemy—behind him. During his London years, he enjoyed both power and worldly success. His position at the mint assured a comfortable social and economic status, and he was an active and able administrator. After the death of Robert Hooke, the great microscopist, in 1703, Newton was elected president of the Royal Society and was annually reelected to this post until his death. In 1704, he published his second major work, the *Opticks,* based entirely on work completed decades before. In 1705, he was knighted by Queen Anne who, according to Conduitt, believed that it was her good fortune to have lived at the same time as, and to have known, so great a man. In London, "he reigned as the most famous man of his age, of Europe, and—as his powers gradually waned and his affability increased—perhaps of all time, so it seemed to his contemporaries" (Conduitt). In the more than 30 years that he lived in London, after leaving Cambridge, his illness (insomnia, loss of appetite, loss of memory, melancholia, delusions of persecution, and possibly trembling of the hands, as seen in his writing) appears to have been for the most part forgotten. But he never recovered his former level of function, spoke little in company, and was rather languid in his look and manner.

Although his creative years had passed, Newton continued to exercise a profound influence on the development of science. In effect, the Royal Society was his instrument, and he played it to his personal advantage. His tenure as president has been described as tyrannical and autocratic, and his control over the lives and careers of younger disciples was all but absolute. Newton could not abide contradiction or controversy and marshaled all the forces at his command in his various disputes. In his battle with Leibniz over who had priority in the discovery of calculus, Newton enlisted younger men to fight his war of words, while behind the lines he secretly directed charge and countercharge. In the end, the actions of the society were little more than extensions of Newton's will, and until his death he dominated all science without rival.

Looking over his entire career, it seems likely that his two episodes of mercury poisoning left their scars. His recovery was probably not complete, and Newton was left less overwhelmingly brilliant than he had once been, and tainted by a paranoid, hypersensitive streak.

This cannot be proved, nor can it be disproved.

But it fits the facts.

To me the most impressive part of this tale is not the fact that Newton developed mercury poisoning; after all, his exposure to mercury was significant. Nor is it the fact that scientific sleuthing done two hundred years after Newton's death has been able to find evidence that he did indeed suffer from mental aberrations due to his mercury exposure. It is the fact that despite these episodes of prolonged toxicity to his brain, he still retained sufficient intellectual capacity to remain the greatest intellect of his age.

AUTHOR'S NOTE

The fact that mercury poisoning causes madness has long been suspected, and by the late nineteenth century it was part of general medical knowledge. In those times mercury was used in the felt-hat industry as a "carrot" or stiffening agent, and the most characteristic symptom of its workers was a tremor called "Hatters" shakes in the United Kingdom and Danbury Shakes in the United States. Since this condition was often accompanied by mental aberrations, Lewis Carroll based his character the Mad Hatter in *Alice in Wonderland* on a hatter whose madness was caused by mercury poisoning.

The two scientific articles that identified mercury poisoning as the cause of Newton's madness are these:

1. I. W. Johnson and M. L. Wolbarsht, "Mercury Poisoning: A Probable Cause of Isaac Newton's Physical and Mental Ills." *Notes Records of the Royal Society of London* 34 (1979): 1–9.
2. P. E. Spargo and C. A. Pounds, "Newton's 'Derangement of the Intellect': A New Light on an Old Problem." *Notes Records of the Royal Society of London* 34 (1979): 11–32.

The scientific analysis given here is based primarily on their discoveries. (The quotations from Newton's correspondence come from these secondary sources.) The best discussion of Newton's first mental crisis was presented by Robert F. Westfall (*Isis* 57 [1966]: 299–307).

A. B. Baker died in 1988. An obituary summarizing his contributions to neurology was published in *Neurology* (38 [1988]: 456). It makes no mention of Baker's law.

The Pursuit of Happiness

Most Americans take it for granted as a natural extension of "life" and "liberty." But as the author shows, the pursuit of happiness is an idea that has long been debated—and whose meaning is still up for grabs.

Robert Darnton

Robert Darnton is Shelby Cullom Davis Professor of European History at Princeton University. He is the author of, among other books, The Literary Underground of the Old Regime *(1982) and* The Forbidden Best Sellers of Pre-Revolutionary France *(1995).*

The idea of happiness has become so deeply embedded in American culture that it sometimes disappears from sight. It is everywhere and nowhere, an implicit assumption that colors a world view, hardly an idea at all. But an idea it very much is, and, if seen from the perspective of the history of ideas, it has a long and impressive pedigree.

It appears among the ancients in the philosophies of Plato and Aristotle and especially in the thought of the Epicureans and Stoics. The Epicureans incorporated the concept of happiness into a general philosophy of pleasure and pain, which led to an ethics of rational self-interest. The Stoics linked it to withdrawal from the dangerous hurly-burly of civic life and contentment in the minimal pleasures of life in Arcadian retreats. "Happy is he who, far away from business, like the race of men of old, tills his ancestral fields with his own oxen, unbound by any interest to pay," said Horace in the first century B.C. One could find similar sentiments scattered throughout the Augustan poetry and Ciceronian rhetoric of the Romans.

Not, however, among the early Christians. Before his death in 604 A.D., Saint Augustine characterized life on this side of the City of God as the pursuit of vanity through a vale of tears. His message corresponded to the human condition as it was experienced by most people for the next thousand years, when men and women worked the fields in a state of semislavery, ate little more than bread and broth, and died young. Theirs was an existence best summed up by Thomas Hobbes's description of life in the state of nature: "solitary, poor, nasty, brutish, and short."

By the 15th century, however, philosophers were facing a revived notion of pleasure—earthly as in Boccaccio and refined as in the court of the Medici. To be sure, the classical revival was snuffed out in Florence by Savonarola's bonfire of vanities in 1497 and in Rome by the troops of Charles V during the sack of 1527. The reformations and religious wars made happiness as a consummation to be desired this side of the grave look more unlikely than ever.

But in the Age of Enlightenment the idea of happiness revived once again, attached to other notions such as progress and prosperity. The Enlightenment philosophers took happiness to be the end of man's life as an individual and of society's existence as a collectivity. The most radical of them, Diderot, Rousseau, Helvétius, and d'Holbach, built the concept of happiness into a modernized Epicureanism, reinforced with a strong civic consciousness.

Having reached this point, philosophy in the 19th and 20th centuries could not turn back, despite the countercurrents of pessimism stirred up by figures such as Nietzsche and Freud. Jeremy Bentham's rallying cry, "the greatest happiness of the greatest number," actually was formulated by two philosophes of the Enlightenment, Francis Hutcheson in Scotland and Cesare Beccaria in Italy. Bentham worked it into a philosophy of enlightened self-interest derived from Epicurus and Lucretius and adapted to the reform politics of Britain. For Karl Marx, the prophet of socialist happiness, liberal reforms could never reconcile individual and collective interests, because class interests stood in the way. Instead, Marx imagined happiness as a historical state to be reached at the end of a dialectical process by society as a whole.

Such, in a snapshot, is how a history of the idea of happiness might look if seen at a very great distance, like the earth photographed from the moon. But from such a perspective, everything blurs into everything else. What would notions of happiness look like if seen up close? I would like to examine two such views located at what I have identified as the great turning point in the history of happiness, the Age of Enlightenment. More precisely, I want to explore two famous phrases: "We must cultivate our garden," offered by Voltaire as the conclusion to *Candide* (1759), and the right to "the pursuit of Happiness" proclaimed by Jefferson in the American Declaration of Independence. The effort, I hope, will shed light on that curiously quicksilver phenomenon known as "the American way of life."

The last line of *Candide,* "We must cultivate our garden," is the final remark in a philosophical discourse that accompanies a fast-moving, picaresque plot. Spoken by the chastened protagonist, it is meant to answer a question. But what was that question? None of the characters in the final chapter of the book ask Candide anything. They chatter past one another as they have done throughout the entire story. The question is provided by the story itself. In pursuing his true love, Cunegonde, from one adventure to another, Candide is pursuing happiness. How can happiness be found? That is the question posed by the novel, as by the entire French Enlightenment, and the answer can be reformulated as "Happiness lies in the cultivation of our garden."

Of the many glosses on the text, four stand out: Stoic withdrawal (by shutting themselves up in the garden, Candide and his companions turn their backs on politics); pastoral utopianism (the little society supports itself by farming, cutting itself off from commercial capitalism); secular salvation through work (everyone in the group labors hard, thereby staving off poverty, boredom and vice); and cultural *engagement* (cultivation means commitment to the cause of civilization). There is something to be said for each of these interpretations. Each fits the context of Voltaire's concerns in 1758 as he composed *Candide:* his quarrel with Frederick II; the horrors of the Seven Years War; the even more horrible disaster of the Lisbon earthquake; Voltaire's debate over the problem of evil with the followers of Leibniz and Wolff; and his recent decision to retire as a country gentleman to Les Délices, where he worked hard at creating a garden of his own.

The garden motif also summons up the Christian utopia of Eden, a favorite target of Voltaire in his youth. As a freethinking man about town in Regency Paris, he celebrated the pleasures of high society or "le monde" and derided Christian asceticism. Thus, in his youthful credo, "Le Mondain," he mocked the barbarity of our mythical ancestors in a weedy, unkempt Garden. He pictured Adam as an ape-man dragging his knuckles on the ground and Eve as a foul-smelling slut with dirt under her fingernails. Instead of Eden, Voltaire celebrated the world of wit and beauty enjoyed by the rich and the well-born in "le monde." Happiness was not to be found in paradise but in Paris, not in the afterlife but in the here and now. "Terrestial paradise is where I am," concluded "Le Mondain." It was an Epicurean credo, flung in the face of the church, and it captured the spirit of salon society in the early 18th century. But it had nothing to say to most of humanity, which lived in misery outside the salons.

By 1758, Voltaire had seen more of the world. But he did not cease to delight in the good things of life. The last chapter of *Candide* includes a description of the hospitality offered by a philosophic Turk, whose little farm provides a model for Candide's: exquisite sorbet, a fine selection of fruits and nuts, "mocca coffee which was not mixed with the bad coffee of Batavia" (Voltaire was a coffee addict), courteous service by the two daughters of the host, and intelligent conversation. Candide had received the same kind of hospitality, though on a grander scale, from the philosopher-king of Eldorado, the utopian society described in the middle of the novel. Voltaire himself offered it to visitors at Les Délices and later at Ferney. What distinguished this kind of good life from the Epicureanism advocated by the young Voltaire in "Le Mondain"?

The setting, for one thing. Candide settled his community at the eastern edge of European civilization, just as Voltaire established his estate at the eastern boundary of France, far from Paris and far from politics. "I never inform myself about what is going on in Constantinople," the philosophic Turk tells Candide. Of course, Voltaire worked hard to keep himself informed about intrigues in the French capital, but he had cut himself off from court life. He had withdrawn from "le monde," and he had changed his tone. A new note of anger and darkness crept into all his writing after he fled from Frederick II and Berlin. He found himself increasingly confronted with unhappiness—and, worse, evil.

Consider one of the unhappiest moments in Voltaire's life. It occurred in 1730. His beloved mistress, the great actress Adrienne Lecouvreur, suddenly died after playing the lead in his tragedy, *Oedipe.* Voltaire had sat by her bed in her last agony, and he may well have witnessed the unceremonious disposal of her corpse. Death struck Adrienne Lecouvreur before she had time to renounce her profession and receive Extreme Unction. As actors and actresses were excluded from the rites of the church, her body could not be buried in hallowed ground. Therefore, it was dumped in a ditch and covered with quicklime to speed its decomposition.

This obscene act obsessed Voltaire right up to the moment of his own death, when he feared that his body would receive the same treatment. It appears in some of his most impassioned poetry, in the *Lettres philosophiques,* and even in *Candide.* In chapter 22, Candide visits Paris and is told the story in all its horror. He then remarks: "That [was] very impolite." Not what we would expect by way of a comment on a barbarism that had set a lover's blood to boil.

But Voltaire filled the word "politeness" with a passion that may escape the 20th-century eye. The first characteristic Candide noticed among the inhabitants of the utopian society of Eldorado was their "extreme politeness." He marveled at their good manners, elegant clothing, sumptuous housing, exquisite food, sophisticated conversation, refined taste, and superb wit. The king of Eldorado epitomized those qualities. Like the philosophic Turk at the end of the book, he "received them with all imaginable grace and invited them politely to supper." Utopia is above all a "société polie" or "policée," which amounts to the same thing.

The 18th-century notion of "police" could be translated roughly as rational administration. It belonged (conceptually, not etymologically) to a series of interlocking terms—*poli, policé, politique*—that extend from culture to politics. For Voltaire, the cultural system of the Old Regime shaded off into a power system, and the code of polite society belonged to the politics of enlightened absolutism.

The interpenetration of culture and politics is the main theme of Voltaire's most ambitious treatise, *Le Siècle de Louis XIV* (1751). This was a crucial work for 18th-century writers, a book that defined the literary system of the Old Regime and that created literary history in France. In it, Voltaire effectively argued that all history is literary history. Kings, queens, and generals do not count in the long run, although they attract most of the attention of their contemporaries and occupy a good deal of Voltaire's narrative. What matters above all is civilization. So, of the four "happy" ages in the history of mankind, the happiest of all was the age of Louis XIV, when French literature reached its zenith and the politeness ("la politesse et l'esprit de société") of the French court set a standard for all of Europe.

By civilization, Voltaire meant the moving force in history, a combination of aesthetic and social elements, manners and mores ("moeurs"), which pushes society toward the ideal of Eldorado, a state in which men are perfectly "polis" and "policés." So Voltaire understood politesse as power, and he saw an essential connection between classical French literature and the absolutism of the French state under Louis XIV. This argument underlies the key episodes of *Le Siècle de Louis XIV.* Louis masters the French language by studying the works of Corneille, he controls the court by staging plays, and he dominates the kingdom by turning the court itself into an exemplary theatre. That idea may be a cliché now, but Voltaire invented it. He saw power as performance: the acting out of a cultural code. This code spread from Versailles to Paris, to the provinces, and to the rest of Europe. Voltaire does not deny the importance of armies, but he interprets the supremacy of Louis XIV as ultimately a matter of cultural hegemony. The script for his court tour de force was written by Molière, whom Voltaire describes both as a "philosophe" and as "the legislator of the code of conduct in polite society" ("le legislateur des bienséances du monde.")

However anachronistic and inaccurate, this view of history conveys something more than the chase after the good things in life in "Le Mondain." It conveys direction, purpose, power—somethlng akin to the "civilizing process" of Norbert Elias. It also demotes kings and puts philosophes in their place as the true masters of history, and it makes the historical process look progressive—uneven, to be sure, but one in which barbarism retreats before the forces of politeness.

Candide finally joins those forces. He becomes a philosophe—not a false philosopher, like his tutor Pangloss, but a true one, who opts for engagement instead of withdrawal. His pursuit of happiness, in the person of Cunegonde, does not lead to a happy ending. When he finally marries her, she has become ugly and disagreeable. But the pursuit has taught him to commit himself to something more substantial: polite society, or the process of civilization.

The pursuit of Happiness" is even more familiar to Americans than "We must cultivate our garden" is to the French. It is the most memorable phrase in the American Declaration of Independence, the rhetorical climax to Thomas Jefferson's enunciation of natural rights and revolutionary theory: "We hold these truths to be self-evident, that all men are created equal, that they are endowed by their Creator with certain inalienable Rights, that among these are Life, Liberty, and the pursuit of Happiness." What did Jefferson mean by "the pursuit of Happiness?" And what does his meaning have to do with a subject that belongs to the history of mentalities—namely, "the American way of life"?

Analysts of political discourse often determine meaning by showing what is not said as well as what is said. "Life, liberty, and property" was the standard formula in the political debates of the English-speaking world during the 17th and 18th centuries. In substituting "the pursuit of Happiness" for property, the Declaration of Independence deviated significantly from other founding charters—the Petition of Right and the Declaration of Rights connected with the English revolutions of 1640 and 1688, for example, and the declarations of the American Stamp Act Congress of 1765 as well as the First Continental Congress of 1774. If "the pursuit of Happiness" is to be viewed as a speech act, its meaning must consist, at least in part, in an implicit comparison with the right of property. By omitting property from his phrasing, did Jefferson reveal himself to be a secret socialist? Can Americans cite him today in order to legitimate demands for social welfare legislation and to oppose the advocates of minimal, laissez-faire government?

Before tearing Jefferson out of the 18th century and plunging him into the midst of our own ideological quarrels, it would be wise to ask how "happiness" resonated in the context of his time. As a philosophically minded lawyer, he had a thorough knowledge of the natural law tradition, which went back to Plato and Aristotle and was formulated for the law students of his generation by Locke, Pufendorf, Burlamaqui, and Blackstone. The most important of these was Locke. (Jefferson had a personal distaste for Blackstone's *Commentaries.)* In fact, Locke was so important that many scholars have considered him the grandfather of the American Declaration of Independence, which advanced a contractual theory of government that seemed to come straight out of his *Second Treatise on Civil Government* (1690).

The *Second Treatise* certainly provides grounds for asserting a right to revolution if the government violates its contractual obligations to the citizenry. But a right to happiness? Locke kept to the usual trinity—"life, liberty, and property." In his *Essay Concerning Human Understanding* (1690), however, he stretched "property" into "lives, liberties, and estates," and then went on to talk of "that property which men have in their persons as well as goods." In doing so, he shifted ground from law to psychology. Property in one's person implied the liberty to develop the self, and self-development for Locke was an epistemological process. It took place when men combined and reflected on sensations, the primary signals of pleasure and pain, according to the procedure described in the *Essay.* Thus, the sensationalism of Locke's epistemology could be combined with the natural rights of his political theory in a way that would open the road to the right to happiness. In short, Locke, too, was a philosopher of happiness. He said so himself: "As therefore the highest perfection of intellectual nature lies in a careful and constant pursuit of true and solid happiness, so the care of ourselves that we mistake not imaginary for real happiness is the necessary foundation of our liberty."

But Jefferson did not need to combine passages from the two John Lockes, the Locke of the *Second Treatise* and the Locke of the *Essay Concerning Human Understanding,* because the work had already been done for him by his friend George Mason. Mason was the one who did the most to stretch "property" into "happiness" in the philosophical deliberations of Virginia's radical squierarchy. Like Jefferson, Mason had a library packed with the works of philosophers, ancient and modern, in Gunston Hall, his country estate. Having worked through this material while participating in the agitation over the Stamp Act, Mason drafted a series of manifestos about representative government and natural rights. He discussed them with like-minded country gentlemen—George Washington, Thomas Jefferson, James Madison, Patrick Henry—around dinner tables and through correspondence. He debated them in free-holder meetings, held in the brick courthouse of Fairfax County, in 1774 and 1775.

Then, in May 1776, the Virginians met at Williamsburg and declared themselves independent of Great Britain. Mason provided the philosophic justification for this revolutionary step by drafting a "Declaration of Rights," which included the phrase: "All men are created equally free and independent, and have certain inherent natural rights . . . among which are the enjoyment of life and liberty, with the means of acquiring and possessing property, and pursuing and obtaining happiness and safety." Mason's wording runs exactly parallel to the famous phrase that Jefferson wrote into the Declaration of Independence a month later. It suggests that happiness is not opposed to property but is an extension of it.

Jefferson made no pretense to originality. He described his statement of principles as the mere "common sense of the subject." And a half-century later, when he discussed the Declaration of Independence in a letter to James Madison, he explained further: "Neither aiming at originality of principle or sentiment, nor yet copied from any particular and previous writing, it was intended to be an expression of the American mind."

Common sense and "the American mind"—we are entering territory the French call "the history of mentalities," and which I would prefer to describe as anthropological history. The American anthropologist Clifford Geertz has analyzed common sense as a "cultural system"—that is, as an admixture of attitudes, values, and cognitive schemata that ordinary people use to make sense of the world. Ordinary people, not philosophers. True, Jefferson, Madison, Mason, and their crowd look like American-style philosophes. And when compared with today's statesmen, they look like giants. But they were also Virginia farmers who inhabited a common-sense world of tobacco plantations, Georgian manor houses, Episcopal churches, county courts, taverns, horse races, and (let us not forget it) slavery. The plantations kept them separated from one another in semiautonomous units ordered according to patriarchal principles. The churches and courthouses drew them together in settings that reinforced the social hierarchy. The taverns and horse races gave them a chance to vent their passions and strut their status. And the slavery indicated the limitations of statements such as "all men are created equal."

This contradiction did not weigh too heavily with men who thought of themselves as successors to the slave-holding patricians of Augustan Rome. Their libraries confirmed the message of their larders. The classicism of their education echoed the classical architecture of their houses. Cicero and Seneca rang true, because they conformed with the values of order and hierarchy given off by the everyday surroundings in Virginia. So did Locke, the spokesman of a Whig aristocracy aligned against an alien, absolutist monarchy. In short, the philosophizing fit the social environment, not as an ideological afterthought but as the reflective gentleman's way of making sense of what his common sense already proclaimed. "Sense" in this respect belonged to what Max Weber called "Sinnzusammenhang," or "elective affinities": it was a way of ordering reality.

How did the Virginians describe reality in more casual moments, when they were not composing theoretical manifestos? Here is Jefferson again, writing from his country estate in 1810:

> I am retired to Monticello, where, in the bosom of my family, and surrounded by my books, I enjoy a repose to which I have been long a stranger. My mornings are devoted to correspondence. From breakfast to dinner, I am in my shops, my garden, or on horseback among my farms; from dinner to dark, I give to society and recreation with my neighbors and friends; and from candle light to early bedtime, I read. My health is perfect; and my strength considerably reinforced by the activity of the course I pursue. . . . I talk of ploughs and harrows, of seeding and harvesting, with my neighbors, and of politics too, if they choose, with as little reserve as the rest of my fellow citizens, and feel, at length, the blessing of being free to say and do what I please.

This is happiness, something embedded in the daily course of life. It is an American way of life—but closer to Horace and Virgil than to the America of Madison Avenue and Wall Street.

Also, it should be added, the Horatian glow dimmed during the next 16 years, a period when Monticello nearly collapsed into bankruptcy and its master felt increasingly alienated from the Jacksonian variety of politics, a speculative surge of capitalism, and an evangelical revival of religion. By cultivating his garden in Monticello, Jefferson withdrew from the world—unlike Voltaire, who used Ferney as a fortress for conquering it.

If Jefferson himself found an increasing disparity between his ideals of the 1770s and the realities of the 1820s, how did Americans see any continuity at all between his way of life and theirs during the next century-and-a-half? Horatian Jeffersonianism and industrial capitalism seem so far apart that one would think they have nothing in common. Yet they are bound together by a common thread: the pursuit of happiness.

As the intellectual historian Howard Mumford Jones has shown, that theme provides one of the leitmotifs of American jurisprudence. If, as the Declaration of Independence proclaims, I have a right to happiness, shouldn't the courts enforce it? Unfortunately, the Declaration of Independence did not become part of constitutional law, except as it was rewritten in the form of the Bill of Rights, and the Bill of Rights does not mention happiness. The state constitutions, however, do. Two-thirds of them have adopted some variant of Jefferson's phrase. So for more than a century Americans have gone to court, suing their authorities and one another over a right they believe belongs to them by fundamental law. They have claimed the right to happiness in order to set up massage parlors, sell contraceptives, and smoke opium. They have rarely succeeded, but their attempts indicate the prevalence of a general attitude—that the pursuit of happiness is a basic ingredient of the American way of life.

Of course, a great deal besides constitutional law went into this cultural pattern. The open frontier, the availability of land, the gold rush, the seemingly endless opportunities for getting rich and getting ahead—all oriented values around the notion of happiness in the 19th century. In each case, happiness appeared as something to be pursued, not something showered down from heaven; and the pursuit often led westward. In this respect, the Jeffersonian ideal also provided a jumping-off point, because the agrarian, yeoman democracy favored by Jefferson provided the ideological impulse for the conquest of the frontier. In the Northwest Territory Act and the Louisiana Purchase, Jefferson himself tried to shape the settlement of the West in a way that would perpetuate the society of farmer-philosophes he had known in Virginia. Horace Greeley and other publicists echoed this idea when they proclaimed, "Go West, young man!"

The real impulse, however, was money, money and land, the chance to get rich quick. The gold rush precipitated a general *Drang nach Westen.* Ever since 1848, it has seemed that the whole country has tried to move to California. I am exaggerating, of course, because the great waves of immigrants who were carried across the Atlantic during the late 19th and early 20th centuries generally washed onto the East Coast and emptied themselves in the slums between Boston and Baltimore. Many of the poor from Kiev and Naples never got farther west than the East Side of Manhattan, although their descendants usually crossed the Hudson and settled in the suburbs of New Jersey—not exactly in Jeffersonian freeholds but on their own plots of land, in houses with gardens and white picket fences, which turned into the new version of the American dream. To such people, America really was the land of opportunity, even if it took two generations to extricate themselves from the slums, even if suburbia was a far cry from the Oregon Trail.

Thus did the Jeffersonian vision become transformed into the American dream, a vision that was basically materialistic but that inflamed imaginations throughout the Old World, where millions struggled to get out and to get ahead. The dream is still alive today, although the immigrants generally come from Latin America and settle in Miami, Houston, and Los Angeles. But its realization remains an elusive goal to many African Americans, whose ancestors—who did the work on Jefferson's plantation—were legally excluded from its pursuit and who provided a living witness to the tragic flaw in the American dream.

That did not prevent the dream from gathering more force in the second half of the 20th century. Technology seemed to bring happiness within the reach of nearly everyone, because it provided the means of controlling the environment, of enjoying pleasure and mitigating pain. The point may be so obvious that we cannot see it, because we have become insulated from the pains of everyday life that existed in the age of Jefferson. If I may provide a homely example, I would cite George Washington's teeth. Washington had terrible teeth. He lost them, one by one, and finally acquired a full set of false teeth, made of bone, lead, and gold. The "Father of Our Country" and the toothache—it seems incongruous, but having read thousands of letters from the 18th century, I often think of the dread of rotting teeth, the horror of the itinerant tooth puller, the sheer pain in jaws everywhere in the early modern world. Dentistry may not look like a particularly noble calling, but it has weighed heavier than many professions in the hedonistic calculus we have inherited from Epicurus and Jeremy Bentham.

To dentistry, add medicine in general, vaccination, public hygiene, contraception, insurance, retirement benefits, unemployment compensation, lightning rods, central heating, air conditioning . . . the list could go on forever, because it leads through the endless array of goods we associate with the so-called consumer society and the services we expect of the "welfare state." I know that these are hard times for millions of Americans and that my remarks may sound hollow. But I have spent so much time in the 18th century that I cannot fail to be impressed with how much control man has gained over his environment in the 19th and 20th centuries.

The pursuit of happiness in America has spilled over from science and technology into popular culture, a favorite subject for historians of mentality. The most exotic varieties bloom in southern California: hot tubs, "perfect" waves, "deep" massage, fat farms, love clinics, and therapy of every conceivable kind, not to mention the happy endings that still prevail in Hollywood. This kind of popular culture can easily be caricatured, but it cannot be dismissed easily, because it has spread throughout the country and now the world. One encounters the face of "Joe Happy"—a circle with a smile in it—everywhere: pasted on windows, pinned in buttonholes, even, I have found, dotting the i's in students' papers. Along with the current greeting—"have a nice day"—it expresses the thumbs-up, bright-eyed and bushy-tailed form of public behavior that can be so annoying to Europeans, who prefer the limp handshake, the down-at-the-mouth Gauloise, and the café slouch as a style of self-presentation.

Of course, many other strains run through the patterns of culture in everyday America, and many run counter to the pursuit of happiness. In order to situate the motif of happiness within the pattern as a whole, it is important to keep three considerations in mind. First, America has always contained a vocal minority of cockeyed pessimists. The American jeremiad arrived on the *Mayflower,* along with sermonizing about the "City on a Hill," or colony of saints. While Thomas Jefferson expanded on Locke, Jonathan Edwards defined happiness as follows:

> The sight of hell torments will exalt the happiness of the saints forever. It will not only make them more sensible of the greatness and

> freeness of the grace of God in their happiness; but it will really make their happiness the greater, as it will make them more sensible of their own happiness; it will give them a more lively relish of it.

Americans have been avid consumers of anti-utopian literature: *1984, Animal Farm, Brave New World,* and dark varieties of science fiction. They also have produced a vast amount of pessimistic literature, from Hawthorne and Melville to T. S. Eliot, Kurt Vonnegut, and John Updike. The Civil War, the closing of the frontier, the Great Depression, the Beat generation, and the antiwar activists of the 1960s represented so many stages of disillusionment with the American dream. Most young people today feel they live in a world of limited resources rather than unlimited opportunity. Public opinion polls indicate that they do not expect to do better than their parents. If they no longer worry about a nuclear catastrophe and the Cold War, they sense economic contraction and ecological disaster everywhere. In the face of the AIDS epidemic, many of them feel angry—at the government and at the world in general, for AIDS represents the ultimate denial of the pursuit of happiness as a way of life.

Second, those who continue to believe in happiness as an end often pursue it with an earnestness that looks self-contradictory. They take up extreme forms of asceticism. They diet, they jog, they lift weights, they deprive themselves of tobacco, meat, butter, and all the pleasures that Falstaff categorized under the rubric "cakes and ale." To what end? To live forever? Aging has now become a major industry in America, and the American way of life has evolved into the American way of death—that is, the subculture of funeral "homes" and pastoral cemeteries that dress death up so prettily as to deny it. But most of America's worldly ascetics have transformed the old Protestant ethic into a new cult of the self. *Self* magazine, the "me generation," and the appeals to building a better body and developing a more assertive or better-balanced personality all express a general egoism that looks like the opposite of the Stoical and Puritanical varieties of self-discipline practiced by the Founding Fathers.

Egocentric asceticism brings us to the third point, John Kenneth Galbraith's characterization of the American way of life as "private wealth and public squalor." Despite food stamps and Social Security, the welfare state never made much headway in the United States. True, the national parks and some of the state systems of higher education opened the door to happiness for many millions. But the consumer culture (we do not have a national sales tax) and the cult of rugged individualism (we do not stand in line at bus stops) stood in the way of state-sponsored projects to assure a minimal degree of happiness for the entire population.

Roosevelt's New Deal, launched to the tune of "Happy Days Are Here Again," provided no answer to the problems of poverty and racism. Those problems continue to fester at the center of our cities, while individuals pursue their personal welfare in the private enclosures of our suburbs. It is, I believe, a national disgrace, but it is also a general problem—one that goes back to the opposition between the private and the public varieties of happiness that were incarnated in Voltaire and Rousseau, and back even further to the Epicureans and the traditions of antiquity. While remaining rooted in the Jeffersonian tradition, the American pursuit of happiness shares promises and problems that have characterized Western civilization in general.

What to make of it all? The leitmotifs in patterns of culture do not lead to bottom lines, so I will not try to end with a firm conclusion. Instead, let me cite two examples of the pursuit of happiness I recently came upon. The first expresses the technical, commercial, and individualistic strain. Dr. Raymond West announced a couple of years ago that "happiness is a warm stethoscope," and offered a new invention to an astonished world: a stethoscope warmer, which would make health checkups more pleasurable and abolish forever the unpleasurable sensation of "ice-cubes on the back."

The second example is less trivial. It expresses the collective end of the American republic as it was originally defined by Thomas Jefferson, and it comes from the inaugural address President Clinton delivered in January 1993:

> When our founders boldly declared America's independence to the world and our purposes to the Almighty, they knew that America, to endure, would have to change. Not change for change's sake, but change to preserve America's ideals—life, liberty, the pursuit of happiness.

Noble words. But Clinton would do well to think of Washington as well as Jefferson—Washington the statesman and Washington the victim of tooth decay. Imagine Washington sitting down to a banquet in Candide's garden. If we are ever to bring together the two ways of pursuing happiness, the individual and the social, we should follow Washington's example, set our jaws firmly, grit our teeth, tuck in, and dedicate ourselves to the public welfare. Such, at least, is the view of one American at a moment when the welfare state looks as beleaguered as Monticello.

This essay is adapted from a lecture given in Tokyo on October 6, 1993, to celebrate the opening of the Japanese Institute for Advanced Study, and draws heavily from the following works: Robert Mauzi, L'idée du bonheur dans la littérature et la pensée françaises au XVIIIe siècle *(1979); Howard Mumford Jones,* The Pursuit of Happiness *(1953); Ursula M. von Eckardt,* The Pursuit of Happiness in the Democratic Creed *(1959); and Rhys Isaac,* The Transformation of Virginia 1740–1790 *(1982).*

Madrid: City of the Enlightenment

Charles C. Noel illustrates how the remodelling of the Spanish capital reflected the new philosophical and cultural concerns of her rulers in the 'Age of Reason'.

Charles C. Noel

Charles C. Noel *was until recently Senior Lecturer in History at Thames Valley University. He has contributed several articles to books on Eighteenth-century Europe including* Enlightened Absolutism. Reform and Reformers in later Eighteenth-century Central Europe, *ed. H. M. Scott (Macmillan, 1990).*

In 1785 Tomas López, Royal Geographer to King Charles III and Spain's foremost cartographer, published his *Plano Geométrico de Madrid.* It was a particularly fine map of the Spanish capital and a typical product of later eighteenth-century enlightened European thought: elegant and accurate, at once both stylish and scientific.

Only in its optimism did it mislead its users, for López drew onto it buildings which were as yet unfinished or still being planned. His map embodied the achievement of surveyors, architects and geographers who during the 1750s and 1760s had carefully studied Madrid's topography, mapped its 506 streets and squares, and enumerated its 7,500 houses, monasteries, hospitals and other dwellings.

That López should include on his map uncompleted structures is not surprising. Since the accession of Charles III (1759–88) to the throne of Spain and its extensive and increasingly prosperous overseas empire, much of Madrid had been turned into a dusty construction site. Yet 'interior Madrid'—the densely populated town which lay within the modest city wall—had not been transformed. Impressive monumental structures had indeed been erected and certain urban improvements effected which impressed both the ministers who had implemented them and foreign visitors who described them in enthusiastic terms.

But the baroque inner Madrid of the sixteenth and seventeenth centuries remained largely unchanged. Instead, the crown and Madrid's municipal government had concentrated their efforts on the peripheral city. This lay beyond the heavily built-up neighbourhoods and just inside or immediately outside the city wall. From the banks of the puny River Manzanares on the west, around many of the poor districts of the south and, above all, on the long eastern side of the city, wide, straight, well-paved roads were laid. They were lined with double or treble rows of trees, beautified with fountains and statues and enhanced with fine new gates in the city wall. These *paseos*—de la Florida, de Atocha, del Prado and de Recoletos—were intended as much for strollers as for vehicles and transformed, if not interior Madrid, then at least the approaches to it.

The paseos were built to accomplish several objectives: to beautify Madrid and make it a more magnificent capital, worthier of its king and empire; to afford comfortable, safe, decent and well-ordered open spaces in which Madrid's citizens would gather and entertain themselves; and to provide an appropriately handsome setting for some of the most prominent new institutions of the Enlightenment in Madrid.

The Paseo del Prado and its northern extension, the Paseo de Recoletos, were especially singled out to fulfil the latter aim. Thereby the paseos were destined to give physical form to some of the foremost aims of Spain's enlightened reformers. By examining the Paseo del Prado-Paseo de Recoletos and the cultures—intellectual, artistic and political—out of which it arose, it is possible to understand much of the Spanish Enlightenment as well as its impact on the capital itself.

Madrid had only been Spain's capital since 1561 when Philip II made what had been a town of purely secondary importance the political centre of his empire. During the following two centuries its population expanded almost without interruption until, according to the census of 1797, it reached a total of some 200,000, similar to the Berlin and Vienna of those years, but far behind Paris or London—the capitals of Spain's imperial rivals.

Despite its demographic growth, it remained throughout the old regime period a court city, dominated by the king's household and government and their interests, as well as by the courtiers and other nobles and commoners attracted by the prospect of jobs, pensions, good marriages and high status.

Together, the crown, nobility and church owned more than half Madrid's land and buildings, and commanded its economy. The latter thrived on the receipt of taxes, rental income and feudal dues which flowed in from all over Spain and America. In such an economy the commercial middle classes had little to offer save the merchandising of necessities for the poor and luxury goods for the aristocratic and bureaucratic élites.

Large scale manufacture—except for a few royal factories producing porcelains, tapestries and similar luxuries—was virtually unknown and the poor generally found work as servants or badly paid unskilled workers and street vendors. Poverty was widespread, as were the problems of begging and vagrancy, petty crime, prostitution and street violence to which it contributed. Moreover, the second half of the century, particularly the years after 1785, witnessed an aggravation of the condition of the poor and a notable increase in their numbers. The threat this implied to order inspired some of the most significant of the reforms undertaken under Charles III.

The maintenance of order, implementation of justice, the crucial supervision of supplies of bread, wine, oil and other staples and the upkeep of Madrid's public spaces fell to the municipal government acting under the supervision of the king and his ministers. The king appointed the chief municipal executive, the *corregidor,* and most of the city's police and judges.

Throughout the old regime period, however, these essentially royal officials had to share power with the ancient oligarchy of aldermen—*regidores*—mostly hereditary, sometimes having purchased or rented their office, frequently corrupt, habitually inefficient and sometimes absent from their post for months or years at a time. They were normally rich merchants or noblemen and were naturally the object of considerable criticism and attempts at reform in this period.

Thus, new offices were created by the crown, most notably in 1768 the *alchaldes de barrio* (neighbourhood magistrates) to undermine traditional oligarchical power and more effectively co-operate with the crown in imposing further reform.

Still, even with the co-operation of an outstanding royal servant like José Antonio Armona, corregidor from 1777 to 1792, municipal government remained at best unwieldy, at worst riven by factionalism and rivalries between competing authorities. Only by steadily prodding or bribing it was the crown normally able to enlist the municipality on the side of reform and renovation of the city itself.

That renovation and beautification were needed was widely understood by mid-century, at least among foreign observers and conscientious natives. Madrid's physical aspect was notoriously disappointing and many travellers were dismayed by the filthy, insalubrious, unlighted and unpaved streets. Joseph Baretti, the Anglo-Italian man of letters who visited Madrid in 1760, was so appalled by the stench that he fled the city after only a few days' stay.

The Enlightenment was as varied and multifaceted in Spain as in most other European societies, the ideas and programmes of enlightened reformers moulded by differing social and cultural conditions.

Other visitors from more sophisticated capitals noticed the lack of attractive facilities for public socialising as poor *Madrileños* gathered with friends in the streets and the rich largely stayed secluded behind closed doors. Visitors almost always remarked on the absence of monumental buildings, grand squares and imposing vistas, and found ugly and mean the architecture of nearly all private houses and mansions. Even great churches, in this cathedral-less city, were few.

Not surprisingly, when Charles III—who had lived in Italy since 1731 as Duke of Parma and, from 1734 to 1759, as the first Bourbon king of Naples—arrived in his capital for the first time since he left it as a young boy, he was depressed by almost all that he saw. His determination to impose change provided a major impetus for the coming reforms.

Yet, monumentality was not entirely absent when Charles arrived in 1759. The huge, Italianate baroque New Palace, perched high above the Manzanares on Madrid's western edge and the sprawling Buen Retiro Palace and gardens on its eastern extremity, were worthy of any capital. The two palaces were linked by the series of great ceremonial streets running east to west bisecting the baroque Madrid of the Habsburg kings. Alcalá, Mayor and San Jerónimo Streets and the Puerta del Sol which linked them had since the sixteenth century been the venue of the great processions which marked early modern monarchical authority and ecclesiastical power.

These streets, lined with churches, convents and aristocratic mansions, most of them architecturally undistinguished and the fine renaissance City Hall, were virtually the best Madrid had to offer. To Charles III and his ministers they seemed unworthy of the greatness of the Spanish imperial monarchy. Equally significant, they seemed to reinforce too strongly the presence of the church in an era in which enlightened thought set out to undermine baroque religiosity and clerical influence in secular life.

The Enlightenment was as varied and multifaceted in Spain as in most other European societies, the ideas and programmes of enlightened reformers moulded by differing social and cultural conditions. Although Madrid was its capital, it flourished in a number of provincial cities like Barcelona, Cadiz, Zaragoza and Seville. Yet, despite variations, certain themes brought the reformers together. Enlightened thinkers naturally prized reason and critical thought, optimistically enthused about the power of science, practical knowledge and modern technologies. They, even clerics, as they often were in Spain, favoured a somewhat more secular society and a more restricted role for a streamlined church, purified of its baroque excesses.

The gates to an improved society would be opened with the keys of science and reason as well as that of political economy, and economists, both Spanish and foreign, were perhaps the greatest heroes of the 'Caroline Enlightenment'. This was so in part because of the rightly-held belief that Spain's economic backwardness held back its culture and restricted its international role. A wealthier Spain would be stronger but also socially more united, more humane, more orderly. With their moral fervour, enlightened thinkers tended to stress the need for self-discipline, hard work, the values of education and purified élite and popular cultures, shorn of hedonism and frivolities.

The latter trait was most apparent in the widespread campaign for 'good taste' in all the arts, from architecture to poetry and strongly affected the physical improvement of Madrid. But the characteristics which most typified Enlightenment reform in Spain were—apart from the heavy emphasis many thinkers placed on aesthetic values and the mission of the arts as means of improvement—the impetus it received from Charles III and most of his ministers and the significant role played by some noblemen. Among the latter were both titled aristocrats like the grandee Pedro de Alcántara, Duke of Medina Sidonia, or Juan Pablo de Aragon, Duke of Villahermosa, and untitled *hidalgos* like Gaspar Melchor de Jovellanos, a brilliant lawyer, economist and outstanding man of letters.

Predictably, numerous and frequently determined antagonists opposed many reform programmes and found in the Inquisition a degree of support. But the latter institution had, by the 1760s, lost much of its bite. Indeed, both Spaniards and foreigners often remarked on the ease with which Inquisitorial restrictions were bypassed while inquisitors themselves, especially in Madrid, were sometimes cultivated as sympathisers of moderate enlightenment.

Only during the reaction of the 1790s against the excesses of the French Revolution did most progressive thinkers find themselves effectively hedged in by the ministers and inquisitors of the new king, Charles IV (1788–1808).

Under Charles III, however, the king and his family, his ministers, sundry aristocrats in Madrid and elsewhere, many clerics and royal officials and some men and women of the professional and commercial middle classes harboured reformist ideas and patronised broadly enlightened artists and writers. As Madrid was the centre of courtly, political and artistic Spain, it inevitably shone above other cities and benefited most from the presence of its relatively sophisticated and cosmopolitan élite.

New institutions, like the Madrid Economic Society founded in 1775, and the Royal San Fernando Academy of Fine Arts set up in 1751, were created to foment reform in Madrid and serve as models for provincial cities. Older institutions, like the Royal Spanish Academy were made the seat of reformist thinking.

Salons—*tertulias*—grew and flourished, particularly from the late 1740s to the 1790s. The liveliest of them were hosted by men and women of wealth and distinction, usually aristocrats or senior government officials, but including even a few clerics like the Benedictine monk Martin Sarmiento, who gathered artistic and intellectual friends about him in his monastic cell.

High food prices and the shortage of necessities could easily spark riots in eighteenth-century Spain.

Such official and informal institutions encouraged several important phenomena. One was a gradual transformation of sociability in the capital. Gatherings of cultivated friends, strongly influenced by French and Italian manners, helped open out the previously secluded Madrid middle class or aristocratic household. It was in part, as with so much enlightened behaviour, a question of style and fashion, of imitating the foreigner, of learning from travel or reading imported novels and seeing French plays.

Another closely related phenomenon was the appearance for the first time of a number of talented, well-educated women at the centre of Madrid's cultural life. As hostesses, as members of the various royal academies, as participants in the growing polemic of the 1780s and 1790s regarding the role of women—and, rarely, as scholars, scientists and journalists—a few women exercised a powerful role.

The Ladies' Committee—*Junta de Damas*—of the Madrid Economic Society, established in 1787, was a notably conspicuous meeting place for such women. They were normally aristocrats who invested time, talent and money in educational, public health, industrial and other projects and research.

A few, like the duchess of Osuna—Maria Josefa Alonso Pimentel, very rich and in her own right duchess of Benavente—and Maria Francisca de Sales Portocarrero, Countess of Montijo, grandmother of the empress Eugenie, stood out in employing their wealth and intelligence to create a special world uniting taste and ideas. The duchess' famous villa and garden outside Madrid, the Alameda de Osuna, combined paintings by Goya and others, architecture and landscape design to conjure up an extraordinary marriage between fantasy and Enlightenment in her 'garden of ideas'.

This culture of the wealthy, enlightened élite, so heavily gallicised and secular-minded, was increasingly alienated from the ordinary people of Madrid, as well as the more traditionalist middle and upper ranks who chose to play no role in enlightened society. By the early 1760s, the reformers, aware of the widening cultural gap, began to target popular culture for change. Behind their aesthetic concern lay the ever present fear of disorder and violence, the constant threat of the capital's masses against Bourbon authority.

High food prices and the shortage of necessities could easily spark riots, as they did in the spring of 1766. The so-called Esquilache uprising, named after the Sicilian-born minister who was a principal target of the crowd's anger, spread from Madrid to many cities across Spain. It badly frightened the king and his ministers and helped inspire a series of innovations in policing and municipal administration in Madrid. Their apparent success led the crown to impose similar reforms on most municipalities.

Esquilache's successor as Charles' chief adviser on most internal matters was Pedro Pablo Abarca de Bolea, Count of Aranda, a rich and well-travelled grandee and army general. Aranda, an energetic and resourceful reformer, made the reordering of Madrid a principal aim. He was minded to tread carefully, however, for some earlier reforms—the imposition of dress controls against the traditional long cape and uncocked hat, both ever popular amongst Madrid's working people—had helped provoke the 1766 riots. Yet, with the cooperation of several ministerial colleagues, in particular the Marquis of Grimaldi and Pedro Rodriguez Campomanes, Aranda and his successor, the Count of Floridablanca, were able to make some significant changes to the culture and physical aspect of the city.

The king's control of the city was enhanced by doubling the size of Madrid's garrison; by imposing the *alcaldes de barrio,* who took police supervision into every household, at least in principle; and by establishing the General Superintendency of Police in 1782. But the fist of Bourbon authoritarianism was also clothed in the velvet of paternalism, with other reforms that aimed to win the co-operation of Madrileños or educate them into new ways consistent with the intentions of enlightenment.

The posts of deputy of the people and procurator were established for Madrid and other cities and were intended to serve the interests of the ordinary male subjects who elected them as well, of course, as those of the crown. Programmes from the early 1760s to pave and light the city's streets and remove the human and animal waste which had traditionally befouled them, were extended and implemented. The Manzanares was canalised and the Municipal Charity Committee, devised by Armona, was so successful that Charles III ordered similar bodies to be set up elsewhere. Free primary schools, essentially vocational, were established in each neighbourhood. Their task was as much to instill the values of Christian obedience, decent language and deportment and a sense of order and diligence, as to teach the three Rs and other skills.

The free schools, intended for the children of the poor, were a small part of the complex enlightenment campaign for the reform of sociability and manners among both the masses and the propertied élite. Frenchified 'civility'—a word whose meaning was at the time being invented—would be exported from the *tertulias* to Madrid's taverns, streets and middle-class sitting rooms.

The repeated attempts to put an end to bullfighting failed, but the encouragement and reform of the theatre in Madrid was more successful. The latter was a project which attracted the enthusiastic support of some of Spain's finest thinkers who, like Jovellanos, believed refined and conscientious neo-classical drama would help produce good citizens. Aranda, who also promoted masked balls open to the fee-paying public, ordered new theaters built and old ones revamped to make them safer, more attractive, and more suitable to dramas of 'good taste'. Aranda, Jovellanos and the king himself would have agreed with the Duke of Medina Sidonia when the latter wrote that with such entertainments available 'the power of the clergy diminishes ever more.'

Enlightened thinkers in eighteenth-century Madrid experienced relatively restrained success in transforming Spanish culture due to constraints of funds, lack of political will, and opposition from traditionalists.

They and other enthusiasts agreed, too, that social and cultural reform should be expressed in bricks and mortar. Enlightened intellectuals tended to accept that the arts, particularly painting and architecture, were crucial vehicles of change and from the 1750s the Academy of Fine Arts brought together artists and intellectuals. From the court too, issued plentiful and discerning patronage, as Charles III, Charles IV and several Bourbon princes invested much time and money encouraging refined baroque and neo-classical painters and architects.

Many others followed suit and the neo-classical language of painters such as Anton Raphael Mengs and the architects Ventura Rodriguez and Juan de Villanueva, designer of the Prado Museum, provided the predominant vocabulary of taste among the enlightened. Goya, too, was their ally, despite his rejection of neoclassicism in most of its varied forms.

Charles III, who had added numerous important buildings to Naples and nearby towns during his years as king there, sought from his first months in Spain to enhance his new capital. He revised building regulations, requiring owners to construct more imposing houses and churches and new projects to be vetted by the Academy of Fine Arts. He had a number of Madrid's most attractive and substantial buildings erected: the Customs House—now the Ministry of Finance—the Post Office in Puerta del Sol, the Royal College of Medicine and Surgery amongst them. Other projects originated by his predecessors were continued, often on a truly magnificent scale. Such was the Saint Charles General Hospital—now the Centro de Arte Reina Sofia—whose vastly ambitious scale made it financially impossible to complete as originally planned.

While interior Madrid was thus made more imposing, its periphery was effectively transformed by its new paseos. Though originally conceived earlier in the century, they were built mainly after 1760. They were a belt of groves and gardens, both celebratory and utilitarian, encouraging both aesthetic delight and intellectual improvement. They daily attracted many citizens who strolled, rode, lounged and took refreshments amongst their trees, fountains and pavilions. Grandees had new mansions built nearby—the grand neoclassical palaces of the Albas, Villahermosas and Berwicks included—and they were immortalised in tapestries designed by Goya. They embodied in urban space many of the aesthetic cultural and social aims of enlightened thinkers.

This was true above all of the Paseo del Prado. There, along its entire length and from the 1760s into the early nineteenth century, one structure after another was planned and built to express enlightenment programmes: the General Hospital and adjacent College of Surgery and opposite them the Astronomical Observatory dominated its southern end. To the north were the new Botanical Garden, the Museum of Sciences—now the Prado Museum—the great fountains of Neptune and Cybels and the magnificent Puerta de Alcalá.

They were intended to help transform Madrid's culture and Spanish society, combining beauty and sociability with science. The paseos and their buildings were also overwhelmingly secular, with only one major new church among them. Thus the paseos symbolised the optimistic hopes of the best enlightened thinkers.

Not all these hopes were, however, achieved. Even among the most enthusiastic reformers there was, from the mid-1780s, an understanding that much of their labour had been futile, that much remained yet to be changed and that their own energies might not suffice. The physical improvements imposed on Madrid were largely successful. Travellers describing the capital in the 1770s and 1780s were impressed by its well lit, clean and impeccably paved streets; by the Paseo del Prado, which became one of Europe's finest thoroughfares; and by most of the structures Charles III had had built.

They were less impressed by the mediocre cultural level they found, even at times among the aristocratic élite. According to the English traveller, Joseph Townsend, a cleric and scientist, Madrid's public libraries went largely unused, museums almost empty of visitors and free science lectures sparsely attended. Salon conversation was too often vapid, intellectual attainment too frequently shallow.

Lack of interest among the educated, opposition from traditionalists, limitations of funds, talent and perhaps of political will, help explain the relatively restrained success enlightened thinkers enjoyed in truly transforming Madrid's culture. In this, too, the Paseo del Prado may stand as a symbol, with its ambitious and unfinished General Hospital and the Botanical Garden, beautifully designed according to the best scientific standards, allowed to fall to ruin in the disturbed days of Madrid's nineteenth century.

FOR FURTHER READING:

Richard Herr, *The Eighteenth-Century Revolution in Spain* (Princeton, 1958); David Ringrose, *Madrid and the Spanish Economy 1560–1850* (Berkeley, 1983); Carmen Martin Gaite, *Love customs in Eighteenth-Century Spain* (Berkeley, 1991); Juan Remón Menéndez 'The Alameda of the duchess of Osuna: a garden of ideas,' *Journal of Garden History,* vol. 13, num. 4 (1993); Joan Sherwood, *Poverty in Eighteenth-Century Spain: the Women and Children of the Inclusa* (Toronto, 1988); Nigel Glendinning, 'Goya's Patrons,' *Apollo, 114* (October, 1981).

When Women Pirates Sailed the Seas

During the early 18th century, the heyday of Anglo-American piracy, two women, Anne Bonny and Mary Read, joined the crew of Calico Jack Rackam, a notorious Caribbean pirate. As historian Marcus Rediker relates, their choice was not unique. It placed them in the company of others of their gender—sailors, soldiers, adventurers— who "seized liberty" from society by disguising themselves as men.

Illustrations Courtesy of Marcus Rediker

Mary Read

Marcus Rediker

Marcus Rediker is associate professor of history at the University of Pittsburgh. He is the author of the award-winning book, Between the Devil and the Deep Blue Sea: Merchant Seamen, Pirates, and the Anglo-American Maritime World, 1700–1750 *(1987). He is currently working with Peter Linebaugh on* The Many-Headed Hydra: The Atlantic Working Class in the 17th and 18th Centuries. *A longer, footnoted version of this essay will appear in* Iron Men and Wooden Women: Gender and Maritime History *(Johns Hopkins Univ. Press), edited by Margaret Creighton and Lisa Norling.*

In late 1720 Jamaica's most powerful men gathered at a court of admiralty in St. Jago de la Vega for a series of show trials. Governor Nicholas Lawes, members of his Executive Council, the chief justice of the Grand Court, and a throng of minor officials and ship captains confirmed by their concentrated presence the gravity of the occasion. They had recently complained of "our Coasts being infested by those Hell-hounds the Pirates" and they were not alone. Pirates were attacking and plundering merchant shipping throughout the British Empire and beyond. The great men came to see a gang of pirates "swing to the four winds" upon the gallows. They would not be disappointed.

Eighteen members of Calico Jack Rackam's crew had already been convicted and sentenced to hang, three of them, including Rackam himself, afterward to dangle and decay in chains at

From *The Wilson Quarterly,* Autumn 1993, pp. 102-110. © 1993 by Marcus Rediker. Reprinted by permission of the author.

Plumb Point, Bush Key, and Gun Key as moral instruction to the seamen who passed their way. Once shipmates, now gallows mates, they were meant, according to *The Tryals of Captain Jack Rackam,* a contemporary account of the proceedings, to be "a Publick Example, and to terrify others from such-like evil Practices."

Two other pirates were also convicted, brought before the judge, and asked "if either of them had any Thing to say why Sentence of Death should not pass upon them, in like manner as had been done to all the rest." These two unusual pirates, in response, "pleaded their Bellies, being Quick with Child, and pray'd that Execution might be staid." The court then "passed Sentence, as in Cases of Pyracy, but ordered them back, till a proper Jury should be appointed to enquire into the Matter." The jury inquired, discovered that they were indeed women, pregnant ones at that, and gave respite to these two particular "hell-hounds" named Anne Bonny and Mary Read.

Much of what is known about these extraordinary women appeared originally in *A General History of the Pyrates,* written by a Captain Charles Johnson and published in two volumes in 1724 and 1728. Captain Johnson (who may or may not have been Daniel Defoe) made Bonny and Read leading figures in his study, boasting on the title page that the first volume contained "The remarkable Actions and Adventures of the two female Pyrates, Mary Read and Anne Bonny." Johnson's book proved a huge success. Translated into Dutch, French, and German, published and republished in London, Dublin, Amsterdam, Paris, Utrecht, and elsewhere, it carried the tales of the women pirates to readers around the world. Their stories were doubtless told and retold on countless ships and docks, and in the bars and brothels of the sailor towns of the Atlantic.

Mary Read was born an illegitimate child outside London; her mother's husband, who had died at sea, was not her father. In order to get support from the husband's family, Mary's mother dressed her to resemble the recently deceased son she had borne by her husband. Mary grew "bold and strong" and developed, reported Johnson, "a roving Mind." She apparently liked her male identity and decided by the time she was 15 or 16 to become a sailor, enlisting aboard a man-of-war, then signing up as a soldier, fighting with "a great deal of Bravery" in both infantry and cavalry units in Flanders. She fell in love with a fellow soldier, "a handsome young Fellow," allowed him to discover her secret, and soon married him. But he proved less hardy than she, and before long he died. Mary once again picked up the soldier's gun, this time serving in the Netherlands. At war's end she sailed on a Dutch ship for the West Indies, only to be captured by pirates. Before long she threw in her lot with the freebooters, plundering ships and exhibiting great boldness. When her new lover one day fell afoul of a pirate much more rugged than himself and was challenged to go ashore and fight a duel "at sword and pistol," Mary saved the situation. She picked a fight with the same rugged pirate, scheduled her own duel two hours before the one to involve her lover, and killed the man "upon the spot."

Anne Bonny was also born an illegitimate child (in Ireland), and to hide this fact she too was raised in disguise, her father pretending that she was the child of a relative entrusted to his care. Her father eventually took her with

Anne Bonny

Ann Mills

him to Charleston, South Carolina, where he became a merchant and planter. Anne grew into a woman of "fierce and couragious temper." Once, "when a young Fellow would have lain with her against her Will, she beat him so, that he lay ill of it a considerable time." Ever the rebel, Anne soon forsook her father and his wealth to marry "a young Fellow, who belong'd to the Sea, and was not worth a Groat." She ran away with him to the Caribbean, where she dressed "in Men's Cloaths" and joined a band of pirates that included Mary Read and, more important, Calico Jack Rackam, who soon became the object of Anne's affections. Their romance too came to a sudden end one day when she and her mates fell into battle with a British vessel sent to capture them. When the ships came to close quarters, "none kept the Deck except Mary Read and Anne Bonny, and one more;" the rest of the pirates scuttled down into the hold in cowardice. Exasperated and disgusted, Mary Read fired a pistol at them, "killing one, and wounding others." Later, as Calico Jack was about to be hanged, Anne said that "she was sorry to see him there, but if he had fought like a Man, he need not have been hang'd like a Dog."

Of the existence of two women pirates by the names of Anne Bonny and Mary Read there can be no doubt, for they were mentioned in a variety of historical sources, all independent of *A General History of the Pyrates.* A rare official pamphlet, *The Tryals of Captain John Rackam and other Pirates,* paints Anne Bonny and Mary Read as fierce, swashbuckling women, genuine pirates in every sense. One of the witnesses against Bonny and Read, Dorothy Thomas, had been captured and made prisoner by Rackam's crew. She claimed that the women "wore Mens Jackets, and long Trouzers, and Handkerchiefs tied about their Heads, and that each of them had a Machet[e] and Pistol in their Hands." Moreover, they at one point "cursed and swore at the men," their fellow pirates, "to murther the Deponent." "[T]hey should kill her to prevent her coming against them" in court, as was indeed now happening before their very eyes. Bonny and Read were at the time dressed as men, but they did not fool Thomas: "the Reason of her knowing and believing them to be Women was, by the largeness of their Breasts."

Other captives testified that Bonny and Read "were very active on Board, and willing to do any Thing." When Rackam and crew "saw any vessel, gave Chase or Attack'd," Bonny and Read "wore men's Cloaths," but "at other Times," presumably times free of armed confrontation, "they wore Women's Cloaths." According to these witnesses, the women "did not seem to be kept, or detain'd by Force," taking part in piracy "of their own Free-Will and Consent." A captured master of a merchant vessel added that they "were both very profligate, cursing, and swearing much, and very ready and willing to do any Thing on board."

Historians in recent years have discovered that these two bold women pirates were not entirely unusual cases. Women had long gone to sea, and in many capacities—as passengers, servants, wives, prostitutes, laundresses, cooks, and occasionally as sailors, serving aboard naval, merchant, whaling, privateering, and pirate vessels. They also made their way into armies. An anonymous writer insisted in 1762 that there were so many women in the British army that they deserved their own separate battalions, not unlike the women warriors who fought for the African kingdom of Dahomey during the same period.

Bonny and Read were part of a deeply rooted underground tradition of female cross-dressing, pan-European in its dimensions but especially strong in early modern England, the Netherlands, and Germany. Like other female cross-dressers, they were young, single, and of humble origin; their illegitimate births were not an uncommon characteristic. They had, in other words, little or nothing to lose, and a society that offered few opportunities for women to break out of their sharply defined positions had little to offer them. Bonny and Read perfectly exemplify what historians Rudolf M. Dekker and Lotte C. van de Pol have identified as the two main reasons why women suited up as men: Read did it largely to escape poverty, while Bonny, turning her back on her father's fortune, followed her instincts for love and adventure.

Other famous women in the cross-dressing tradition include Mrs. Christian Davies, who, dressed as a man, chased her dragooned husband from Dublin to the European continent during the early 1700s, survived numerous battles, wounds, and capture by the French, and returned to England and military honors bestowed by Queen Anne. Hannah Snell's picaresque life as a soldier and sailor during the 1740s and '50s was chronicled in the *Gentlemen's Magazine,* the *Scots Magazine,* and in books long and short, in English and Dutch. Ann Mills, according to an 1820 English account, went to sea "as a common sailor" in 1740 and distinguished herself in hand-to-hand combat against "a French enemy." She "cut off the head of her opponent, as a trophy of victory."

Women such as these were celebrated around the Atlantic world in popular ballads sung and heard by common men and women. Soldiers, sailors, dockworkers, farm laborers, washerwomen, servants, and others sang of the glories of "warrior women" at the fairs, on the wharves, around the street corners, and amid the throngs at hangings and other public events. Anne Bonny and Mary Read came of age in an era when female warrior ballads soared to the peak of their popularity—even if some of the women celebrated in those songs did not, like Bonny and Read, commit mayhem on the high seas.

So the two women rigged themselves out in men's clothes and gained entry into the always rough, sometimes brutal world of maritime labor, into the very line of work long thought to "make a man" of anyone who entered. Cross-dressing was necessary because women were not, as a rule, allowed to serve on the crew of deep-sea vessels of any kind. One reason for this division was the sheer physical strength and stamina required for shipboard labor—loading and unloading cargo (using pulleys and tackle), setting heavy canvas sails, and operating the ship's pump to eliminate the water that oozed through the seams of chronically leaky vessels. Some women, obviously, did the work and did it well, earning the abiding respect of their fellow workers. But not everyone—certainly not every man—was equal to its demands. It was simply too strenuous, too hard on the body, leaving in its wake lameness, hernia, a grotesque array of mutilations, and often premature death.

A second and perhaps more important reason for the segregation of the sexes was the widespread belief that women and indeed any reminder of sexuality were inimical to work and social order aboard ship. Officers of the British Royal Navy, for example, ruthlessly punished all homosexual practice throughout the 18th century, thinking it subversive of discipline and good order. Many merchants and captains believed with minister John Flavel that the death of "the Lusts" among sailors was "the most *Probable* Means to give *Life* to your Trade." Some version of this view apparently commanded acceptance at all levels of the ship's hierarchy. Many sailors saw women as objects of fantasy and adoration but also as the cause of bad luck or as dangerous sources of conflict, as potential breaches in the male order of seagoing solidarity. Early modern seafarers seem to have agreed that some kind of sexual repression was necessary to do the work of the ship.

The assumption was strong enough to command at least some assent from pirates, who were otherwise well known for organizing their ships in ways dramatically different from those of the merchant shipping industry and the navy. Pirate Bartholomew Roberts and his crew, contemporaries of Rackam, drew up articles of conduct specifying that "No Boy or Woman to be allowed amongst them." Another article stated that, should a woman passenger be taken captive, "they put a Centinel immediately over her to prevent ill Consequences from so dangerous an Instrument of Division and Quarrel." William Snelgrave, a slave trader held captive by pirates off the west coast of Africa in 1719, explained: "It is a rule amongst the Pirates, not to allow Women to be on board their Ships, when in the Harbour. And if they should Take a Prize at Sea, that has any Women on board, no one dares, on pain of death, to force them against their Inclinations. This being a good political Rule to prevent disturbances amongst them, it is strictly observed."

Black Bart Roberts was more straight-laced than other pirate captains (he banned gambling among his crew, this too to reduce conflict), so it may be unwise to hold up his example as typical. But while a few pirate ships willingly took women on board, such exceptions were rare, and they existed only because exceptional women such as Bonny and Read created them.

The harsh reality of working women's lives, which could encourage physical strength, toughness, independence, fearlessness, and a capacity for surviving by one's wits, made it possible for some women to disguise themselves and enter worlds dominated by men; the same reality then assured that such women would be familiar enough within early working-class culture to be celebrated. Bonny and Read represented not the typical, but the strongest side of popular womanhood.

Their strength was a matter of mind as well as body. Captain Johnson reports the testimony of their shipmates, who stated that in "times of Action, no Person amongst [the pirates] was more resolute, or ready to board or undertake any Thing that was hazardous" than Bonny and Read, not least because they had, by the time they sailed beneath the Jolly Roger, already endured all manner of hazard.

Bonny and Read were well prepared to adopt the ways of the sailor and even the pirate. They cursed and swore like any good sailor. They carried their pistols and machetes like those well schooled in the ways of war. That they eventually wore women's clothes among the pirate crew, as some witnesses observed, is evidence of the acceptance they won, despite their gender.

Courage was traditionally seen as a masculine virtue, but Mary Read and Anne Bonny proved that women might possess it in abundance. As evidence Captain Johnson quoted Read's response to one of her captives, who asked if she feared "dying an ignominious Death, if she should be caught alive":

> She answer'd, that as to hanging, she thought it no great Hardship, for, were it not for that, every cowardly Fellow would turn Pyrate, and so infest the Seas, that Men of Courage must starve: That if it was put to the Choice of the Pyrates, they would not have the Punishment less than Death, the Fear of which kept some dastardly Rogues honest; that many of those . . . would then rob at Sea, and the Ocean would be crowded with Rogues . . . so that the Trade, in a little Time, would not be worth following.

Bonny and Read added an entirely new dimension to the subversive appeal of piracy by seizing what was regarded as male "liberty." In so doing they were not merely tolerated by their male compatriots, for they clearly exercised considerable leadership aboard their vessel. Although not formally elected by their fellow pirates to posts of command, they nonetheless led by example—in fighting duels, in keeping the deck in time of engagement, and in being part of the group designated to board prizes, a right always reserved to the most daring and respected members of the crew.

Did Anne Bonny and Mary Read, in the end, make their mark upon the world? Did their daring make a difference? Did they leave a legacy? Dianne Dugaw, associate professor of

English at the University of Oregon, Eugene, has argued that the popular genre of ballads about warrior women such as Bonny and Read was largely suffocated in the early 19th century by a new bourgeois ideal of womanhood. Warrior women, when they appeared in this new milieu, were comical, grotesque, and absurd since they lacked the now-essential female traits of delicacy, constraint, and frailty. The earlier "gender-conflating ideal" became largely unthinkable. The warrior woman, in culture if not in actual fact, had been tamed.

But the stubborn fact remains: Even though Bonny and Read did not transform the popular conception of gender, even though they apparently did not see their own exploits as a symbolic blow for rights and equality for all women, their very lives and subsequent popularity nonetheless undercut the gender stereotypes of their time and offered a powerful alternative image of womanhood for the future. The frequent reprinting of their tales in the romantic literature of the 18th, 19th, and 20th centuries captured the imaginations of many girls and young women who, even if they were not about to imitate the pirates' lawless ways, felt imprisoned by the 19th century's ideology of femininity and domesticity. Feminists used the examples of female soldiers and sailors to disprove dominant theories that stressed women's physical and mental incapacity.

Anne Bonny and Mary Read also had an impact on what are now considered higher forms of literature. They were, after all, real-life versions of Moll Flanders, the heroine of Daniel Defoe's 1721 novel of the same name. The three had no small amount in common. All were illegitimate children, poor at birth and for years thereafter. All were what Defoe called "the offspring of debauchery and vice." Moll and Anne were born of mothers who carried them in the womb while in prison. All three found themselves on the wrong side of the law, charged with capital crimes against property, facing "the steps and the string," popular slang for the gallows. All experienced homelessness and transiency, including trips across the great Atlantic. All recognized the importance of disguise, the need to be able to appear in "several shapes." Moll Flanders, too, cross-dressed: Her governess and partner in crime "laid a new contrivance for my going abroad, and this was to dress me up in men's clothes, and so put me into a new kind of practice."

Delacroix's *Le 28 julliet: la Liberté guidant le peuple*

Moll Flanders suggests the truth of Christopher Hill's observation that "the early novel takes its life from motion." The novel, he continues, "doesn't grow only out of the respectable bourgeois household. It also encompasses the picaro, the vagabond, the itinerant, the pirate—outcasts from the stable world of good householders—those who cannot or will not adapt." Thus for John Bunyan, author of *Pilgrim's Progress,* as for Defoe and other novelists such as Samuel Richardson, Henry Fielding, and Tobias George Smollett, the experiences of the teeming, often dispossessed masses in motion—people like Anne Bonny and Mary Read—were the raw materials of the imagination. The often desperate activity of working-class women and men in the age of nascent capitalism helped generate one of the world's most important and durable literary forms, which indeed is inconceivable apart from them.

Anne Bonny and Mary Read may have influenced posterity in yet another, more indirect way, through an illustration by an unknown artist used as the frontispiece of the Dutch translation of Captain Charles Johnson's *General History of the Pyrates.* It featured a bare-breasted woman militant, armed with a sword and a torch, surging forward beneath the Jolly Roger. In the background at the left hangs a gibbet with 10 executed pirates dangling; at the right is a ship in flames. Trampled underfoot are an unidentifiable document, perhaps a map or legal decree; a capsizing ship with a broken mainmast; a woman still clutching the scales of justice, and a man, possibly a soldier, who appears to have his hands bound behind his back. Hovering at the right is a mythic figure, perhaps Aeolus, Greek god of the winds, who adds his part to the tempestuous scene. Bringing up the rear of the chaos is a small sea monster, a figure commonly drawn by early modern mapmakers to adorn the aquatic parts of the globe.

The illustration is an allegory of piracy, the central image of which is female, armed, violent, riotous, criminal, and destructive of property—in short, the very picture of anarchy. It seem almost certain that Bonny and Read, the two real-life pirates who lived, as their narrative claimed, by "Fire or Sword," inspired the illustrator to depict insurgent piracy in the allegorical form of a militant, marauding woman holding fire in one hand, a sword in the other.

This allegory is strikingly similar to Eugene Delacroix's famous painting, *Le 28 julliet: la Liberté guidant le peuple.* Compositionally, both works feature a central female figure, armed, bare-breasted, and dressed in a Roman tunic, looking back as she propels herself forward, upward, over and above a mass of bodies strewn below. The humble social status of each woman is indicated by the bulk, muscle, and obvious strength of her physique. (Parisian critics in 1831 were scandalized by the "dirty" Liberty, whom they denounced as a whore, a fishwife, a part of the "rabble.") Moreover, flags and conflagrations help to frame each work: the Jolly Roger and a burning ship at the right give way to the French tricolor and a burning building in almost identical locations. An armed youth, a street urchin, stands in for the wind maker. Where the rotting corpses of pirates once hung now mass "the people." Two soldiers, both apparently dead, lie in the forefront.

There are differences: Liberty now has a musket with bayonet rather than a sword and torch. She leads but now takes her inspiration from the living rather than the dead. "The people" in arms have replaced "the people"—as a ship's crew was commonly called in the 18th century—who are hanging by the neck in the Dutch illustration. More important, Delacroix has softened and idealized the female body and face, replacing anger and anguish with a tranquil, if determined, solemnity. His critics notwithstanding, Delacroix has also turned a partially naked woman into a partially nude woman, exerting over the female body an aesthetic control that parallels the taming of the warrior woman in popular balladry. Liberty thus contains her contradictions: She is both a "dirty" revolutionary born of action and an other-worldly, idealized female subject born of a classical artistic inheritance and perhaps a new 19th-century definition of femininity.

It cannot be proven definitively that Delacroix saw the earlier graphic and used it as a model. But there is a great deal of circumstantial evidence to suggest that the allegory of piracy may have influenced Delacroix's greatest work. It is well known that Delacroix drew upon the experiences of real people in his rendition of *Liberty Leading the People,* including Marie Deschamps, who during the hottest of the July days in 1789 seized the musket of a recently killed citizen and fired it against the SwissGuards, and "a poor laundry-girl" remembered as Anne-Charlotte D., who was said to have killed nine Swiss soldiers in avenging her brother's death. These real women, like Anne Bonny and Mary Read, were bound to appeal to the romantic imagination.

Moreover, Delacroix himself noted that he often studied engravings, woodcuts, and popular prints as he conceptualized his paintings and sought to solve compositional problems. Finally, and most important, it can be established that piracy was on Delacroix's mind at the very moment he was painting *Liberty.* The English romantic poet Lord Byron was an endless inspiration to Delacroix, who engaged the poet's work intensely during the 1820s, exhibiting three major paintings on Byronic subjects in 1827 and executing several others on the Greek civil war, in which Byron ultimately lost his life. More crucially still, Delacroix was reading Byron's poem, "The Corsair"—about piracy—as he was painting *Liberty* between October and December 1830. At the very same salon at which he exhibited his greatest painting in 1831, Delacroix also entered a watercolor based on Byron's poem.

The image of piracy (1725) preceded the image of liberty (1830) by more than a century, and the two pirates who inspired that image were by then long since dead. Read died in prison of what was probably typhus soon after her trial; Bonny was eventually reprieved and released, but what became of her after that is lost to history. Yet it seems that the pirate's liberty seized by Anne Bonny and Mary Read may have taken a strange and crooked path from the rolling deck of a ship in the Caribbean to the wall of an art salon in Paris—a peculiar and perhaps fitting testament to two very exceptional women.

The French Revolution in the Minds of Men

Maurice Cranston

Maurice Cranston, a former Wilson Center Guest Scholar, is professor of political science at the London School of Economics. Born in London, he was educated at St. Catherine's College and Oxford University. His books include John Stuart Mill *(1965),* Jean-Jacques: The Early Life and Work of Jean-Jacques Rousseau, 1712–54 *1982, and* John Locke: A Biography *(1985).*

On July 14, 1989—Bastille Day—political and cultural leaders of every ideological persuasion assembled in Paris to celebrate the bicentennial of the French Revolution. Was there something strange about their unanimous applause? All subsequent major revolutions, such as those that took place in Russia and China, remain controversial today. But the French Revolution, which served as the direct or indirect model for these later upheavals, now passes for an innocuous occasion which anyone, Marxist or monarchist, can join in celebrating.

Was this proof only of the anaesthetizing power of time, that two centuries could turn the French Revolution into a museum piece, an exhibition acceptable to all viewers, even to a descendent of the old Bourbon monarchs? Or is there something about the French Revolution itself that, from its beginning, sets it apart from later revolutions?

The *tricouleur,* the *Marseillaise,* the monumental paintings of David—all celebrate a series of connected events, alternately joyous and grim, which make up the real, historical French Revolution. But there is another French Revolution, one which emerged only after the tumultuous days were over and the events and deeds became inflated or distorted in the minds of later partisans. This is the French Revolution as myth, and it is in many ways the more important of the two.

It is so, one could argue, because the myth, and not the reality, inspired the scores of revolutions that were to come. The actors of the French Revolution, announcing their principles on behalf of all mankind, clearly intended their deeds to have a mythic dimension. They wanted to inspire others to follow their example. Consider the Declaration of the Rights of Man, passed in August of 1789. At no point does it refer to the specific conditions or laws of France. Instead, it speaks in grand universals, as if it were the voice of mankind itself. Replete with terms like citizen, liberty, the sacred rights of man, the common good, the document provides the lexicon for all future revolutions.

By contrast, the earlier revolutionary models which stirred the French in 1789 to act—the English Revolution of 1688 and the American Revolution of 1776—had been essentially political events, limited in scope and conservative in objectives. The English revolutionists claimed to restore the liberty that the despotic James II had destroyed; the American revolutionaries made the kindred claim that they were only defending their rights against tyrannical measures introduced by George III. Neither revolution sought to change society.

The French Revolution, however, sought to do exactly that. Indeed, to many of the more zealous French revolutionaries, the central aim was the creation of a new man—or at least the liberation of pristine man, in all his natural goodness and simplicity, from the cruel and corrupting prison of the traditional social order.

It is easy to see how this grandiose vision of the Revolution's purpose went hand-in-hand with the emergence of Romanticism. The great Romantic poets and philosophers encouraged people throughout the West to believe that imagination could triumph over custom and tradition, that everything was possible given the will to achieve it. In the early 1790s, the young William Wordsworth expressed the common enthusiasm for the seemingly brave and limitless new world of the Revolution:

> France standing on the top of golden hours, And human nature seeming born again.

Here we encounter one of the many differences between reality and myth. The reality of the French Revolution, as

Tocqueville maintained, was prepared by the rationalist philosophers of the 18th-century Enlightenment, by Voltaire, Diderot, Helvétius, d'Alembert, and Holbach no less than by Rousseau. Its myth, however, was perpetuated during the 19th century by Romantic poets such as Byron, Victor Hugo and Hölderlin. Byron in his life and in his poetry bore witness to that romanticized revolutionary idealism, fighting and then dying as he did to help the Greeks throw off the Turkish yoke and set up a free state of their own.

The grandeur of its lofty aims made the French Revolution all the more attractive to succeeding generations of revolutionaries, real and would-be; the violence added theatrical glamor. The guillotine—itself an invention of gruesome fascination—together with the exalted status of its victims, many of them royal, noble, or political celebrities, made the Terror as thrilling as it was alarming. The wars which broke out in 1793, when France declared war on Great Britain, Holland, and Spain, were fought not by professional soldiers but by conscripts, ordinary men who were expected to "know what they fought for and love what they know." These wars were thought of as wars of liberation. It hardly mattered that Napoleon turned out to be an imperialist conqueror no better than Alexander or Caesar; he was still a *people's* emperor.

If historians of the French Revolution are unanimous about any one point, it is this: that the Revolution brought the people into French political life. To say that it introduced "democracy" would be to say too much. Although popular suffrage in varying degrees was instituted as the revolution unfolded, no fully democratic system was set up. But popular support came to be recognized as the only basis for legitimating the national government. Even the new despotism of Napoleon had to rest on a plebiscitary authority. These plebiscites, which allowed voters only to ratify decisions already made, denied popular sovereignty in fact while paying tribute to it in theory. (The vote for the Constitution which made Napoleon emperor in 1804—3,500,000 *for* versus 2,500 *against*—hardly suggests a vigorous democracy.)

But if Napoleon's government was not democratic, it was obviously populistic. The people did not rule themselves, but they approved of the man who ruled them. The end of Napoleon's empire in 1815, which was also in a sense the end of the historical French Revolution, could only be brought about by the intervention of foreign armies.

Those foreign armies could place a king on the throne of France, as they did with Louis XVIII in 1815, but they could not restore the principle of royal sovereignty in the hearts of the French people. They simply put a lid on forces which would break out in another revolution 15 years later, this time not only in France but in other parts of the Western world.

The French Revolution had turned the French into a republican people. Even when they chose a king—Louis-Philippe—to lead that revolution of 1830, he was more of a republican prince than a royal sovereign in the traditional mold. Louis-Philippe, the "Citizen King," had to recognize, as part of his office, "the sovereignty of the nation." And what kind of sovereign is it, one may ask, who has to submit to the sovereignty of the nation? The answer must clearly be, one who is king neither by grace of God nor birth nor lawful inheritance but only through the will of the people, who are thus his electors and not his subjects.

The "sovereignty of the nation" was a new and powerful idea, a revolutionary idea, in the 19th century. At the philosophical level, it is usually ascribed, with some justification, to the teaching of Jean-Jacques Rousseau, whom Edmund Burke, Alexis de Tocqueville, and many lesser commentators considered the ideologue of the French Revolution. What Rousseau did was to separate the concept of *sovereignty,* which he said should be kept by the people in their own hands, from the concept of *government,* which he urged the people to entrust to carefully chosen elites, their moral and intellectual superiors. Rousseau held that neither hereditary kings nor aristocrats could be considered superiors of this kind. Rousseau was uncompromisingly republican. To him a republic could be based only on the collective will of citizens who contracted to live together under laws that they themselves enacted. "My argument," Rousseau wrote in *The Social Contract,* "is that sovereignty, being nothing other than the exercise of the general will, can never be alienated; and the sovereign, which is simply a collective being, cannot be represented by anyone but itself—power may be delegated, but the will cannot be."

The American Revolution's principles were universalized and served as a model for the French Revolution.

The sheer size of France, however, with a population in 1789 of some 26 million people, precluded the transformation of the French kingdom into the sort of direct democracy that Rousseau—a native Swiss—envisaged. Still, the Americans had very recently proved that a nation need not be as small as a city-state for a republican constitution to work. And as an inspiration to the average Frenchman, the American Revolution was no less important than the writings of Rousseau.

The American Revolution thus became a model for France, despite its conservative elements. Moreover, the American Revolution later served as a model for others largely because its principles were "translated" and universalized by the French Revolution. In Latin America, the Spanish and Portuguese colonies could not directly follow the American example and indict their monarchs for unlawfully violating their rights; Spain and Portugal, unlike England, recognized no such rights. But following the example of the French Revolution, Latin Americans like Simón Bolivar and José de San Martin were able to appeal to abstract or universal principles. To describe Bolivia's new constitution in 1826, Simón Bolivar used the same universal and idealistic catchwords which the French had patented 37 years before: "In this constitution," Bolivar announced, "you will find united all the guarantees of permanency and liberty, of equality and order." If the South American republics sometimes seemed to run short on republican liberty and equality, the concept of royal or imperial sovereignty was nonetheless banished forever from American shores. The short reign of Maximilian of Austria as Emperor of Mexico (1864–1867) provided a brief and melancholy epilogue to such ideas of sovereignty in the New World.

Even in the Old World, royal and aristocratic governments were on the defensive. In 1815, the Congress of Vienna, under Prince Metternich of Austria's guidance, attempted to erase the memory of the Revolution and restore Europe to what it had been before 1789. Yet only five years after the Congress, Metternich wrote to the Russian tsar, Alexander I, admitting, "The governments, having lost their balance, are frightened, intimidated, and thrown into confusion."

The French Revolution had permanently destroyed the mystique on which traditional regimes were based. No king could indisputably claim that he ruled by divine right; nor could lords and bishops assume that their own interests and the national interests coincided. After the French Revolution, commoners, the hitherto silent majority of ordinary underprivileged people, asserted the right to have opinions of their own—and to make them known. For once the ideas of liberty, democracy, and the rights of men had been extracted from philosophers' treatises and put on the agenda of political action—which is what the French Revolution with its "universal principles" did—there could be no security for any regime which set itself against those ideals.

In old history textbooks one can still find the interpretation of the French Revolution first advanced by Jules Michelet and Jean Jaurès and other left-wing historians who explained the Revolution as one abolishing feudalism and advancing bourgeois capitalist society. While few historians still view the Revolution this way, the Michelet interpretation was widespread during the 19th century, and its currency prompted many an aspiring Robespierre to "complete" the revolution.

Completing the revolution meant overthrowing the bourgeoisie in favor of the working class, just as the bourgeoisie had supposedly overthrown the feudal aristocracy in 1789. The convulsive year of 1848 was marked in Europe by several revolutions which attempted to complete the work of 1789. Their leaders all looked back to the French Revolution for their "historic justification." Tocqueville observed of these revolutionaries that their "imitation [of 1789] was so manifest that it concealed the terrible originality of the facts; I continually had the impression they were engaged in play-acting the French Revolution far more than continuing it."

If the 19th century was, as many historians describe it, the "century of revolutions," it was so largely because the French Revolution had provided the model. As it turns out, the existence of a proper model has proved to be a more decisive prod to revolution than economic crisis, political unrest, or even the agitations of young revolutionaries.

Indeed, the role of professional revolutionaries seems negligible in the preparation of most revolutions. Revolutionaries often watched and analyzed the political and social disintegration around them, but they were seldom in a position to direct it. Usually, as Hannah Arendt observed, "revolution broke out and liberated, as it were, the professional revolutionists from wherever they happened to be—from jail, or from the coffee house, or from the library." Tocqueville made a similar observation about the revolutionaries of 1848: The French monarchy fell "before rather than beneath the blows of the victors, who were as astonished at their triumph as were the vanquished at their defeat."

Disturbances which during the 18th century would hardly have proven so incendiary ignited one revolution after another during the 19th century. They did so because now there existed a revolutionary model for responding to crises. During the 1790s, revolutionaries outside of France such as Toussaint L'Ouverture in Haiti and Wolfe Tone in Ireland tried simply to import the French Revolution, with its ideals of nationalism, equality and republicanism, and adapt it to local conditions. And well into the 19th century, most revolutionaries continued to focus their eyes not on the future but on the past—on what the French during the 1790s had done in roughly similar circumstances.

To be sure, the French Revolution possessed different and even contradictory meanings, differences which reflect the various stages of the historical Revolution. The ideals and leaders of each stage inspired a particular type of later revolutionary. The revolutionary men of 1789-91, including the Marquis de Lafayette, inspired liberal and aristocratic revolutionaries. Their ideal was a quasi-British constitutional monarchy and suffrage based on property qualifications. The revolutionaries of 1830-32 realized this liberal vision in France and Belgium.

The Girondins and moderate Jacobins of 1792-93 became the model for lower-middle-class and intellectual revolutionaries whose political goal was a democratic republic and usually some form of a "welfare state." The French Revolution of 1848, with its emphasis on universal manhood suffrage, and the state's obligation to provide jobs for all citizens, initially embodied their vision of society.

A third type of revolutionary, the extremists of 1793-94 such as Robespierre and Gracchus Babeuf, inspired later working-class and socialist revolutionaries.

A reactionary such as Prince Metternich would hardly have distinguished among these three types of revolutionaries. But a later observer, Karl Marx, did. Seeing that the nationalist revolutions of his time ignored the socialist-radical strain of the French Revolution, he came to deplore its influence on later revolutionaries.

World War I put revolutionary socialism back on the agenda, and Lenin used this to persuade the world that the French Revolution could be repeated as a communist revolution in Russia.

Marx, who by 1848 was already active in communist politics, condemned what he considered the confusion of understanding in most of these revolutionary movements. An emotional yearning to reenact the dramas of 1789-1815 seemed to him to stand in the way of a successful revolutionary strategy. In a letter to a friend in September, 1870, Marx wrote: "The tragedy of the French, and of the working class as a whole, is that they are trapped in their memories of momentous events. We need to see an end, once and for all, to this reactionary cult of the past."

Vladimir Ilyich Lenin had no such reservations. He passed up no rhetorical opportunity to present his Russian Bolsheviks as the heirs of the French revolutionary tradition and the Russian Revolution of 1917 as a reenactment of France's Revolution of 1789. Lenin went so far as to call his Bolshevik faction "the Jacobins of contemporary Social-Democracy."

It is not difficult to understand Lenin's motives. Throughout the 19th century, most of the successful revolutions in Europe and Latin America had been nationalist revolutions. (Indeed, when the revolutionary German liberals of 1848 issued their Declaration of Rights, they ascribed those rights to German *Volk* as a whole and not to private persons.) But the example of the French Revolution suggested that a revolution could be more than just a matter of nationalism. Taking the example of the French Revolution under the fanatical Robespierre, one could argue, as Lenin did, that the true goal of revolution was to alter the way people lived together, socially and economically.

Yet, as we know, Lenin looked back upon a century when attempts at radical social revolutions had been ultimately and uniformly abortive. The French Revolution of 1848, which removed the "liberal" King Louis-Philippe, briefly gave greater power to the working class. During its most promising days, the anarchist Pierre-Joseph Proudhon (1809–1865) even accepted a seat in the legislative chamber. But the coup d'état of Napoleon III in 1851 soon brought an end to all this. The communist movement, which Marx described as a specter haunting Europe, produced no more tangible results than most specters do. Before World War I, Marx was notably less influential as a theoretician than were the champions of "revolutionary socialism" such as Proudhon and Ferdinand Lassalle (1825–1864) who persuaded the workers that their interests would be better served by reform and democratic process than by revolution.

It was World War I which put revolutionary socialism back on the agenda again. The "war to end all wars" gave Lenin the opportunity to persuade the world that the French Revolution could be repeated as a communist revolution in, of all places, Russia. Not only did the upheavals of war play into his hands but the ideology and propaganda adopted by the Allied powers in World War I did so as well. When their early military campaigns went badly, the Allies attempted to make the war more popular, and the enormous casualties more tolerable, by declaring their cause to be a war for "liberty." In the name of liberty, Great Britain, France, and the United States encouraged the subject nations of the German, Austrian and Turkish empires to throw off the imperial yoke.

But in championing national liberty, the Allies were guilty of hypocrisy. Neither Great Britain nor France had any intention of permitting nationalist revolutions within their own empires or those of any neutral power. But Lenin was able to catch them in the trap of their own contradictions.

By declaring to the world that the Bolshevik seizure of power in 1917 was a reenactment of the French Revolution, he was able to attach to his regime all those strong, if mixed, emotions which the French Revolution had kindled in the outside world from 1789 on. In symbolic ways, both large and small—such as naming one of their first naval ships *Marat,* after the French revolutionary leader—the early Soviets underscored their connection with the earlier revolution. The attempts of the Allied powers to send in troops to save Tsarist Russia from the Bolsheviks was immediately seen by a war-weary world as a reactionary, counter-revolutionary "White Terror," and public opinion soon put an end to that intervention.

After 1917, the Soviet Union's self-image became less that of a revolutionary regime and more that of a well-established socialist empire. This transition unexpectedly enabled its adherents at last to obey Marx's injunction to abolish the cult of the revolutionary past and to fix their eyes on the present. The idea of revolution thus passed from the left to the ultra-left, to Stalin and Trotsky and, later, to Mao Zedong and his Cultural Revolution in China.

Yet even during the extreme phase of the Cultural Revolution, Mao still evinced his debt to the French Revolution, a debt which he shares with the later "Third World" revolutionaries. Whenever a revolutionary leader, from Ho Chi Minh and Frantz Fanon to Fidel Castro and Daniel Ortega, speaks of a new man, or of restructuring a whole society, or of creating a new human order, one hears again the ideas and assumptions first sounded on the political stage during the French Revolution.

In fact, there can be no doubt that a "cultural revolution" is what Robespierre set afoot in France, and what, if he had lived, he would have tried to bring to completion. As a disciple of Rousseau, he truly believed that existing culture had corrupted modern man in all classes of society, and that an entirely new culture was necessary if men were to recover their natural goodness. The new religious institutions which Robespierre introduced—the cult of the Supreme Being and the worship of Truth at the altar of Reason, as well as the new patriotic festivals to replace the religious holidays—were all intended to be part of what can only be called a cultural revolution. Robespierre did not believe that political, social, and economic changes alone, however radical, would enable men to achieve their full humanity.

But while the ideals and the language of the cultural revolution sound nobler than those of the political revolution, such elevation of thought seems only to authorize greater cruelty in action. Robespierre's domination of the French Revolution lasted for only a short period, from April 1793 until July 1794, when he himself died under the same guillotine which he had used to execute his former friends and supposed enemies. Moderation was restored to the French Revolution after his execution by the least idealistic of its participants—a cynical Talleyrand, pusillanimous Sieyès, and a crudely ambitious Napoleon. Likewise, moderation was restored to the Chinese Revolution by the Chinese admirers of Richard Nixon. Yet while moderation had been restored to the real historical French Revolution, the inevitability of the return to "normalcy" was often conveniently ignored by later revolutionaries.

And what of France itself? At first glance, all the major subsequent "dates" of French history seem to be in a revolutionary tradition or at least of revolutionary magnitude—1830 (Louis-Philippe); 1848 (the Second Republic); 1852 (the Second Empire); 1871 (the Third Republic); 1940 (the Vichy French State); 1945 (the Fourth Republic); 1958 (the Fifth Republic). Yet these headline dates, all suggesting recurrent tumult, may be misleading: France has not been wracked by major upheavals nor by social earthquakes that left the structure of society unrecognizable, as Russia and China were after their revolutions. Continuity may be the most striking feature in French life. Robert and Barbara Anderson's *Bus Stop to Paris* (1965) showed how a village not more than 10 miles from Paris remained unaffected year after year by all the great rumblings in the capital. Are we dealing with a revolution whose myth is all out of proportion to the facts?

Tocqueville, that most dependable of all political analysts, offers an answer:

The major change effected by the Bourbon kings during the 17th and 18th centuries was the increasing centralization of France and the creation of a strong bureaucracy to administer it. This bureaucracy, in effect, ruled France then and has continued to rule it through every social upheaval and behind every facade of constitutional change. This bureaucracy has provided stability and continuity through the ups and downs of political fortune. The French Revolution and Napoleon, far from making an abrupt break with the past, continued and even accelerated the tendency toward bureaucratic centralization.

Tocqueville almost broached saying that the French Revolution never happened, that the events not only looked theatrical but were theatrical: The French could afford to have as many revolutions as they pleased, because no matter what laws they enacted, or what persons they placed in their legislative and executive offices, the same civil servants, the functionaries, the members of *l'Administration,* would remain in command.

How many revolutions can the historian cite as having left the people better off at the end than they were at the beginning? Unfortunately the discrepancy between its myth and its reality may have made the French Revolution a deceptive model for other nations to imitate. The myth treated society like a neutral, ahistorical protoplasm from which old corrupt institutions could be extracted and into which new rules for human interaction could be inserted at will. The reality was that France, with its unusually strong state bureaucracy, could withstand the shocks and traumas of radical constitutional upheaval.

In modern history, revolution often seems a luxury that only privileged peoples such as the French and the Americans and the English can afford. Less fortunate peoples, from the Russians in 1918 to the Cambodians in 1975, on whom the burden of the established regimes weighed more cruelly, have often enacted their revolutions with catastrophic results. It is perhaps one of the harsher ironies of history that, since the defeat of Napoleon in 1815, the more a country appears to need a revolution, the less likely it will be able to accomplish one successfully.

The Passion of Antoine Lavoisier

With its revolution, France founded a rational republic and lost a great scientist

Stephen Jay Gould

Stephen Jay Gould teaches biology, geology, and the history of science at Harvard University.

Galileo and Lavoisier have more in common than their brilliance. Both men are focal points in a cardinal legend about the life of intellectuals—the conflict of lonely and revolutionary genius with state power. Both stories are apocryphal, however inspiring. Yet they only exaggerate, or encapsulate in the epitome of a bon mot, an essential theme in the history of thinking and its impact upon society.

Galileo, on his knees before the Inquisition, abjures his heretical belief that the earth revolves around a central sun. Yet, as he rises, brave Galileo, faithful to the highest truth of factuality, addresses a stage whisper to the world: *eppur se muove*—nevertheless, it does move. Lavoisier, before the revolutionary tribunal during the Reign of Terror in 1794, accepts the inevitable verdict of death, but asks for a week or two to finish some experiments. Coffinhal, the young judge who has sealed his doom, denies his request, stating, "La république n'a pas besoin de savants" (the Republic does not need scientists).

Coffinhal said no such thing, although the sentiments are not inconsistent with emotions unleashed in those frightening and all too frequent political episodes so well characterized by Marc Antony in his lamentation over Caesar: "O judgment! thou are fled to brutish beasts, And men have lost their reason." Lavoisier, who had been under arrest for months, was engaged in no experiments at the time. Moreover, as we shall see, the charges leading to his execution bore no relationship to his scientific work.

But if Coffinhal's chilling remark is apocryphal, the second most famous quotation surrounding the death of Lavoisier is accurate and well attested. The great mathematician Joseph Louis Lagrange, upon hearing the news about his friend Lavoisier, remarked bitterly: "It took them only an instant to cut off that head, but France may not produce another like it in a century."

I feel some need to participate in the worldwide outpouring of essays to commemorate the 200th anniversary of the French Revolution. Next month, on July 14, unparalleled displays of fireworks will mark the bicentenary of the fall of the Bastille. Nonetheless, and with no desire to put a damper on such pyrotechnics, I must write about the flip side of this initial liberation, the most troubling scientific story of the Revolution—the execution of Antoine Lavoisier in 1794.

The revolution had been born in hope and expansiveness. At the height of enthusiasm for new beginnings, the revolutionary government suppressed the old calendar, and started time all over again, with year I beginning on September 22, 1792, at the founding of the French republic. The months would no longer bear names of Roman gods or emperors, but would record the natural passage of seasons—as in *brumaire* (foggy), *ventose* (windy), *germinal* (budding), and to replace parts of July and August, originally named for two despotic Caesars, *thermidor.* Measures would be rationalized, decimalized, and based on earthly physics, with the meter defined as one ten-millionth of a quarter meridian from pole to equator. The metric system is our enduring legacy of this revolutionary spirit, and Lavoisier himself was the guiding force in devising the new weights and measures.

But initial optimism soon unraveled under the realities of internal dissension and external pressure (the powerful monarchists of Europe were, to say the least, concerned lest republican ideas spread by export or example). Governments tumbled one after the other, and Dr. Guillotin's machine, invented to make execution more humane, became a symbol of terror by sheer frequency of public use. Louis XVI was beheaded in January, 1793 (year one of the republic). Power shifted from the Girondins to the Montagnards, as the Terror reached its height and the war with Austria and Prussia continued. Finally, as so often happens, the architect of the terror, Robespierre himself, paid his visit to Dr. Guillotin's device, and the cycle played itself out. A few years later, in 1804, Napoleon was crowned as emperor, and the First Republic ended. Poor Lavoisier had been caught in the midst of the cycle, dying for his former role as tax collector on May 8, 1794, less than three months before the fall of Robespierre on July 27 (9 Thermidor, year II).

Old ideals often persist in vestigial forms of address and writing, long after their disappearance in practice. I was reminded of this phenomenon when I acquired, a few months ago, a copy of the opening and closing addresses for the course in zoology at the Muséum d'Histoire naturelle of Paris for 1801–2. The democratic fervor of the revolution had faded, and Napoleon had already staged his *coup d'etat* of 18 Brumaire (November 9, 1799), emerging as emperor de facto, although not crowned until 1804.

Reprinted with permission from *Natural History,* June 1989, pp. 16, 18, 20, 22-25.

Nonetheless, the author of these addresses, who would soon resume his full name Bernard-Germain-Etienne de la Ville-sur-Illon, comte de Lacépède, is identified on the title page only as C^en^ Lacépède (for *citoyen,* or "citizen"—the democratic form adopted by the revolution to abolish all distinctions of address). The long list of honors and memberships, printed in small type below Lacépède's name, is almost a parody on the ancient forms; for instead of the old affiliations that always included "member of the royal academy of this or that" and "counsellor to the king or count of here or there," Lacépède's titles are rigorously egalitarian—including "one of the professors at the museum of natural history," and member of the society of pharmacists of Paris, and of agriculture of Agen. As for the year of publication, we have to know the history detailed above—for the publisher's date is given, at the bottom, only as "l'an IX de la République."

Lacépède was one of the great natural historians in the golden age of French zoology during the late eighteenth and early nineteenth century. His name may be overshadowed in retrospect by the illustrious quartet of Buffon, Lamarck, Saint-Hilaire and Cuvier, but Lacépède—who was chosen by Buffon to complete his life's work, the multivolumed *Histoire naturelle*—deserves a place with these men, for all were *citoyens* of comparable merit. Although Lacépède supported the revolution in its moderate first phases, his noble title bred suspicion and he went into internal exile during the Terror. But the fall of Robespierre prompted his return to Paris, where his former colleagues persuaded the government to establish a special chair for him at the Muséum, as zoologist for reptiles and fishes.

By tradition, his opening and closing addresses for the zoology course at the Muséum were published in pamphlet form each year. The opening address for year IX, "Sur l'histoire des races ou principales variétés de l'espèce humaine" (On the history of races and principal varieties of the human species), is a typical statement of the liberality and optimism of Enlightenment thought. The races, we learn, may differ in current accomplishments, but all are capable of greater and equal achievement, and all can progress.

But the bloom of hope had been withered by the Terror. Progress, Lacépède asserts, is not guaranteed, but is possible only if untrammeled by the dark side of human venality. Memories of dire consequences for unpopular thoughts must have been fresh, for Lacépède cloaked his criticisms of revolutionary excesses in careful speech and foreign attribution. Ostensibly, he was only describing the evils of the Indian caste system in a passage that must be read as a lament about the Reign of Terror:

> Hypocritical ambition, . . . abusing the credibility of the multitude, has conserved the ferocity of the savage state in the midst of the virtues of civilization. . . . After having reigned by terror [*regné par la terreur*], submitting even monarchs to their authority, they reserved the domain of science and art to themselves [a reference, no doubt, to the suppression of the independent academies by the revolutionary government in 1793, when Lacépède lost his first post at the Muséum], and surrounded themselves with a veil of mystery that only they could lift.

At the end of his address, Lacépède returns to the familiar theme of political excesses and makes a point, by no means original of course, that I regard as the central structural tragedy of the nature of any complex system, including organisms and social institutions—the crushing asymmetry between the need for slow and painstaking construction and the potential for almost instantaneous destruction:

> Thus, the passage from the semisavage state to civilization occurs through a great number of insensible stages, and requires an immense amount of time. In moving slowly through these successive stages, man fights painfully against his habits; he also battles with nature as he climbs, with great effort, up the long and perilous path. But it is not the same with the loss of the civilized state; that is almost sudden. In this morbid fall, man is thrown down by all his ancient tendencies; he struggles no longer, he gives up, he does not battle obstacles, he abandons himself to the burdens that surround him. Centuries are needed to nurture the tree of science and make it grow, but one blow from the hatchet of destruction cuts it down.

The chilling final line, a gloss on Lagrange's famous statement about the death of Lavoisier, inspired me to write about the founder of modern chemistry, and to think a bit more about the tragic asymmetry of creation and destruction.

Antoine-Laurent Lavoisier, born in 1743, belonged to the nobility through a title purchased by his father (standard practice for boosting the royal treasury during the *ancien régime*). As a leading liberal and rationalist of the Enlightenment (a movement that attracted much of the nobility, including many wealthy intellectuals who had purchased their titles to rise from the bourgeoisie), Lavoisier fitted an astounding array of social and scientific services into a life cut short by the headsman at age fifty-one.

We know him best today as the chief founder of modern chemistry. The textbook one-liners describe him as the discoverer (or at least the namer) of oxygen, the man who (though anticipated by Henry Cavendish in England) recognized water as a compound of the gases hydrogen and oxygen, and who correctly described combustion, not as the liberation of a hypothetical substance called phlogiston, but as the combination of burning material with oxygen. But we can surely epitomize his contribution more accurately by stating that Lavoisier set the basis for modern chemistry by recognizing the nature of elements and compounds—by finally dethroning the ancient taxonomy of air, water, earth, and fire as indivisible elements; by identifying gas, liquid, and solid as states of aggregation for a single substance subjected to different degrees of heat; and by developing quantitative methods of defining and identifying true elements. Such a brief statement can only rank as a caricature of Lavoisier's scientific achievements, but this essay treats his other life in social service, and I must move on.

Lavoisier, no shrinking violet in the game of self-promotion, openly spoke of his new chemistry as "a revolution." He even published his major manifesto, *Traité élémentaire de chimie,* in 1789, starting date of the other revolution that would seal his fate.

Lavoisier, liberal child of the Enlightenment, was no opponent of the political revolution, at least in its early days. He supported the idea of a constitutional monarchy, and joined the most moderate of the revolutionary societies, the Club of '89. He served as an alternate delegate in the States General, took his turn as a *citoyen* at guard duty, and led several studies and commissions vital to the success of the revolution—including a long stint as *régisseur des poudres* (director of gunpowder, where his brilliant successes produced the best stock in Europe, thus providing substantial help in France's war against Austria and Prussia), work on financing the revolution by *assignats* (paper money backed largely by confiscated church lands), and service on the commission of weights and measures that formulated the metric system. Lavoisier rendered these services to all governments, including the most radical, right to his death, even hoping at the end that his crucial work on weights and measures might save his life. Why, then, did Lavoisier end up in two pieces on the *place de la Révolution* (long ago renamed, in pleasant newspeak, *place de la Concorde*)?

The fateful move had been made in 1768, when Lavoisier joined the infamous Ferme Générale, or Tax Farm. If you regard the IRS as a less than benevolent institution, just consider taxation under the *ancien régime* and count your blessings. Taxation was regressive with a vengeance, as the nobility and clergy were entirely exempt, and poor people supplied the bulk of the royal treasury through tariffs on the movement of goods across provincial boundaries, fees for entering the city of Paris, and taxes on such goods as tobacco and salt. (The hated *gabelle,* or "salt tax," was applied at iniquitously differing rates from region to region, and was levied not on actual consumption but on presumed usage—thus, in effect, forcing each family to buy a certain quantity of taxed salt each year.)

Moreover, the government did not collect taxes directly, They set the rates and then leased (for six-year periods) the privilege of collecting taxes to a private finance company, the Ferme Générale. The Tax Farm operated for profit like any other private business. If they managed to collect more than the government levy, they kept the balance; if they failed to reach the quota, they took the loss. The system was not only oppressive in principle; it was also corrupt. Several shares in the Tax Farm were paid for no work as favors or bribes; many courtiers, even the King himself, were direct beneficiaries. Nonetheless, Lavoisier chose this enterprise for the primary investment of his family fortune, and he became, as members of the firm were called, a *fermier-général,* or "farmer-general."

(Incidentally, since I first read the sad story of Lavoisier some twenty-five years ago, I have been amused by the term farmer-general, for it conjures up a pleasantly rustic image of a country yokel, dressed in his Osh Kosh b'Gosh overalls, and chewing on a stalk of hay while trying to collect the *gabelle.* But I have just learned from the *Oxford English Dictionary* that my image is not only wrong, but entirely backward. A farm, defined as a piece of agricultural land, is a derivative term. In usage dating to Chaucer, a farm, from the medieval Latin *firma,* "fixed payment," is "a fixed yearly sum accepted from a person as a composition for taxes or other moneys which he is empowered to collect." By extension, to farm is to lease anything for a fixed rent. Since most leases applied to land, agricultural plots become "farms," with the first use in this sense traced only to the sixteenth century; the leasers of such land then became "farmers." Thus, our modern phrase "farming out" records the original use, and has no agricultural connotation. And Lavoisier was a farmer-general in the true sense, with no mitigating image of bucolic innocence.)

I do not understand why Lavoisier chose the Ferme Générale for his investment, and then worked so assiduously in his role as tax farmer. He was surely among the most scrupulous and fair-minded of the farmers, and might be justifiably called a reformer. (He opposed the overwatering of tobacco, a monopoly product of the Ferme, and he did, at least in later years, advocate taxation upon all, including the radical idea that nobles might pay as well.) But he took his profits, and he provoked no extensive campaign for reform as the money rolled in. The standard biographies, all too hagiographical, tend to argue that he regarded the Ferme as an investment that would combine greatest safety and return with minimal expenditure of effort—all done to secure a maximum of time for his beloved scientific work. But I do not see how this explanation can hold. Lavoisier, with his characteristic energy, plunged into the work of the Ferme, traveling all over the country, for example, to inspect the tobacco industry. I rather suspect that Lavoisier, like most modern businessmen, simply jumped at a good and legal investment without asking too many ethical questions.

But the golden calf of one season becomes the shattered idol of another. The farmers-general were roundly hated, in part for genuine corruption and iniquity, in part because tax collectors are always scapegoated, especially when the national treasury is bankrupt and the people are starving. Lavoisier's position was particularly precarious. As a scheme to prevent the loss of taxes from widespread smuggling of goods into Paris, Lavoisier advocated the building of a wall around the city. Much to Lavoisier's distress, the project, financed largely (and involuntarily) through taxes levied upon the people of Paris, became something of a boondoggle, as millions were spent on fancy ornamental gates. Parisians blamed the wall for keeping in fetid air and spreading disease. The militant republican Jean-Paul Marat began a campaign of vilification against Lavoisier that only ended when Charlotte Corday stabbed him to death in his bath. Marat had written several works in science and had hoped for election to the Royal Academy, then run by Lavoisier. But Lavoisier had exposed the emptiness of Marat's work. Marat fumed, bided his time, and waited for the season when patriotism would become a good refuge for scoundrels. In January 1791, he launched his attack in *l'Ami du Peuple* (the Friend of the People):

> I denounce you, Coryphaeus of charlatans, Sieur Lavoisier [coryphaeus, meaning highest, is the leader of the chorus in a classical Greek drama] Farmer-general, Commissioner of Gunpowders. . . . Just to think that this contemptible little man who enjoys an income of forty thousand livres has no other claim to fame than that of having put Paris in prison with a wall costing the poor thirty millions. . . . Would to heaven he had been strung up to the nearest lamppost.

The breaching of the wall by the citizens of Paris on July 12, 1789, was the prelude to the fall of the Bastille two days later.

Lavoisier began to worry very early in the cycle. Less than seven months after the fall of the Bastille, he wrote to his old friend Benjamin Franklin:

> After telling you about what is happening in chemistry, it would be well to give you news of our Revolution. . . . Moderate-minded people, who have kept cool heads during the general excitement, think that events have carried us too far . . . we greatly regret your absence from France at this time;

you would have been our guide and you would have marked out for us the limits beyond which we ought not to go.

But these limits were breached, just as Lavoisier's wall had fallen, and he could read the handwriting on the remnants. The Ferme Générale was suppressed in 1791, and Lavoisier played no further role in the complex sorting out of the farmers' accounts. He tried to keep his nose clean with socially useful work on weights and measures and public education. But time was running out for the farmers-general. The treasury was bankrupt, and many thought (quite incorrectly) that the iniquitously hoarded wealth of the farmers-general could replenish the nation. The farmers were too good a scapegoat to resist; they were arrested en masse in November 1793, commanded to put their accounts in order and to reimburse the nation for any ill-gotten gains.

The presumed offenses of the farmers-general were not capital under revolutionary law, and they hoped initially to win their personal freedom, even though their wealth and possessions might be confiscated. But they had the misfortune to be in the wrong place (jail) at the worst time (as the Terror intensified). Eventually, capital charges of counter-revolutionary activities were drummed up, and in a mock trial lasting only part of a day, the farmers-general were condemned to the guillotine.

Lavoisier's influential friends might have saved him, but none dared (or cared) to speak. The Terror was not so inexorable and efficient as tradition holds. Fourteen of the farmers-general managed to evade arrest, and one was saved as a result of the intervention of Robespierre. Madame Lavoisier, who lived to a ripe old age, marrying and divorcing Count Rumford, and reestablishing one of the liveliest salons in Paris, never allowed any of these men over her doorstep again. One courageous (but uninfluential) group offered brave support in Lavoisier's last hours. A deputation from the Lycée des Arts came to the prison to honor Lavoisier and crown him with a wreath. We read in the minutes of that organization: "Brought to Lavoisier in irons, the consolation of friendship . . . to crown the head about to go under the ax."

It is a peculiar attribute of human courage that when no option remains but death, criteria of judgment shift to the manner of dying. Chronicles of the revolution are filled with stories about who died with dignity—and who went screaming to the knife. Antoine Lavoisier died well. He wrote a last letter to his cousin, in apparent calm, not without humor, and with an intellectual's faith in the supreme importance of mind.

I have had a fairly long life, above all a very happy one, and I think that I shall be remembered with some regrets and perhaps leave some reputation behind me. What more could I ask? The events in which I am involved will probably save me from the troubles of old age. I shall die in full possession of my faculties.

Lavoisier's rehabilitation came almost as quickly as his death. In 1795, the Lycée des Arts held a first public memorial service, with Lagrange himself offering the eulogy and unveiling a bust of Lavoisier inscribed with the words: "Victim of tyranny, respected friend of the arts, he continues to live; through genius he still serves humanity." Lavoisier's spirit continued to inspire, but his head, once filled with great thoughts as numerous as the unwritten symphonies of Mozart, lay severed in a common grave.

Many people try to put a happy interpretation upon Lagrange's observation about the asymmetry of painstaking creation and instantaneous destruction. The collapse of systems, they argue, may be a prerequisite to any future episode of creativity—and the antidote, therefore, to stagnation. Taking the longest view, for example, mass extinctions do break up stable ecosystems and provoke episodes of novelty further down the evolutionary road. We would not be here today if the death of dinosaurs had not cleared some space for the burgeoning of mammals.

I have no objection to this argument in its proper temporal perspective. If you choose a telescope and wish to peer into an evolutionary future millions of years away, then a current episode of destruction may be read as an ultimate spur. But if you care for the here and now, which is (after all) the only time we feel and have, then massive extinction is only a sadness and an opportunity lost forever. I have heard people argue that our current wave of extinctions should not inspire concern because the earth will eventually recover, as so oft before, and perhaps with pleasant novelty. But what can a conjecture about ten million years from now possibly mean to our lives—especially since we have the power to blow our planet up long before then, and rather little prospect, in any case, of surviving so long ourselves (since few vertebrate species live for ten million years).

The argument of the "long view" may be correct in some meaninglessly abstract sense, but it represents a fundamental mistake in categories and time scales. Our only legitimate long view extends to our children and our children's children's children—hundreds or a few thousands of years down the road. If we let the slaughter continue, they will share a bleak world with rats, dogs, cockroaches, pigeons, and mosquitoes. A potential recovery millions of years later has no meaning at our appropriate scale. Similarly, others could do the unfinished work of Lavoisier, if not so elegantly; and political revolution did spur science into some interesting channels. But how can this mitigate the tragedy of Lavoisier? He was one of the most brilliant men ever to grace our history, and he died at the height of his powers and health. He had work to do, and he was not guilty.

My title, "The Passion of Antoine Lavoisier," is a double-entendre. The modern meaning of *passion,* "overmastering zeal or enthusiasm," is a latecomer. The word entered our language from the Latin verb for suffering, particularly for suffering physical pain. The Saint Matthew and Saint John Passions of J. S. Bach are musical dramas about the suffering of Jesus on the cross. This essay, therefore, focuses upon the final and literal passion of Lavoisier. (Anyone who has ever been disappointed in love—that is, all of us—will understand the intimate connection between the two meanings of passion.)

But I also wanted to emphasize Lavoisier's passion in the modern meaning. For this supremely organized man—farmer-general; commissioner of gunpowder; wall builder; reformer of prisons, hospitals, and schools; legislative representative for the nobility of Blois; father of the metric system; servant on a hundred government committees—really had but one passion amidst this burden of activities for a thousand lifetimes. Lavoisier loved science more than anything else. He awoke at six in the morning and worked on science until eight, then again at night from seven until ten. He devoted one full day a week to scientific experiments and called it his *jour de bonheur* (day of happiness). The letters and reports of his last year are painful to read, for Lavoisier never abandoned his passion—his conviction that reason and science must guide any just and effective social order. But those who received his pleas, and held power over him, had heard the different drummer of despotism.

Lavoisier was right in the deepest, almost holy, way. His passion harnessed feeling to the service of reason; another kind of passion was the price. Reason cannot save us and can even persecute us in the wrong hands; but we have no hope of salvation without reason. The world is too complex, too intransigent; we cannot bend it to our simple will. Bernard Lacépède was probably thinking of Lavoisier when he wrote a closing flourish following his passage on the great asymmetry of slow creation and sudden destruction:

> Ah! Never forget that we can only stave off that fatal degradation if we unite the liberal arts, which embody the sacred fire of sensibility, with the sciences and the useful arts, without which the celestial light of reason will disappear.

The Republic needs scientists.

Napoleon Takes Charge

Two hundred years ago, the hero of Toulon was a destitute officer without a command. Then duty suddenly called again—in the streets of Paris, as France's revolutionary Convention came under attack.

James W. Shosenberg

James W. Shosenberg is a writer who lives in Oshawa, Ontario, Canada. For further reading, he recommends: Napoleon, *by André Castelot; or, if you read French,* Bonaparte *by the same author. For everything you ever wanted to know about the* Jeunesse Dorée, *he recommends* The Gilded Youth of Thermidor, *by François Gendron.*

It was raining heavily in Paris on the morning of the 12th *Vendemaire,* in the fourth year of the French Republic—or October 4, 1795, as that date was acknowledged to be in the rest of Europe—when the door of the shabby hotel Au Cadran Bleu swung open and a young man stepped into the rain-lashed Rue de la Huchette. He was not an impressive sight. According to a contemporary observer, "he was very careless of his personal appearance . . .his hair was ill-combed and ill-powdered, giving him the look of a sloven." He was thin to the point of emaciation. His boots were badly made and carelessly blackened. He was without gloves, believing they were a useless luxury. Around his waist was tied the sash of a *Général de Brigade de l'Artillerie.*

The young general, Napoleon Bonaparte, was on half pay and almost destitute. He had spent the past five months knocking on every door in Paris in an attempt to evade an order from the Committee of Public Safety assigning him to assume an infantry command with the Army of the West; Bonaparte wanted an artillery command with the Army of Italy. Now, with every option exhausted, he spent his days wandering the city, hoping that in the ever-changing chaos of national politics something would turn up. He could not know that his career was about to change forever.

Bonaparte crossed the Seine and walked briskly through the downpour until he arrived at a small house in the Chaussée d'Antin, the home of a Madame Permon. It was the general's daily custom to visit the widow Permon, who was a friend of the Bonaparte family. Here, the young Corsican officer found an atmosphere that reminded him of his family, now living in faraway Marseille.

Bonaparte entered the house and prevailed upon the maid to brush his dirty boots before leaving the foyer. One of the things for which Madame Permon had a particular dislike was the smell of wet, dirty boots put to the fire to dry. Her daughter recorded that "to her this smell was so unpleasant that she frequently left the room, and did not return till the boots had been thoroughly dried and removed from the fire." His boots clean, Bonaparte entered the salon, where he ate a bunch of grapes and drank a big cup of coffee with Madame and her daughter Laure, age 10.

"I had a late breakfast," he told them. "There was so much talk of politics that I couldn't stand any more of it. I'm going out to pick up some news. If I find out anything interesting, I'll come back and tell you."

Outside, there was plenty to see. The rain had slackened to a drizzle, and the streets were crowded with excited people. Young men with their hair cut long à la Victoire (in the "Victory" style) and wearing capes with the colors of the ultraroyalist *Comte* d'Artois were running about the streets shouting "Down with the Two-Thirds." The people had much to be excited about. The previous day, the royalist section of Le Peletier and 15 other Paris sections had declared themselves to be in a state of rebellion against the National Convention. Their presidents had ordered a muster of the National Guard and appointed *Général* Danican, described by one observer as "a versatile but vain personage," to command the sectionary forces.

How had royalist plotters managed to undermine the young French Republic? For an answer, one must follow events since the fall of Maximilien François de Robespierre on the 10th *Thermidor* of the previous year (July 28, 1794). Since Robespierre and his Jacobin party had been overthrown and sent to the guillotine, the government of France had been in the hands of a group of deputies of the National Convention. To sustain themselves in power against the *sans-culottes,* the lower-class radicals who had been Robespierre's main support, the deputies had turned to a group of young men called *Jeunesse Dorée* (gilded youth). Although some members of the Convention, notably Stanislas Fréron, Jean-Lambert Tallien and Joseph Fouché, were openly sympathetic to the activities of the *Jeunesse Dorée,* the majority would come to disown its methods.

The *Jeunesse Dorée* had begun to appear on the streets shortly after *Thermidor.* Most of its members came from the middle class of minor officials and small shopkeepers. Many were either avoiding conscription or were outright deserters from the French armies. Now, with the unspoken protection of the National Convention, members of the group roamed about in gangs, ostentatiously displaying their bizarre "uniforms." The men wore a tight coat of either bottle green or brown over close-fitting knee breeches. On their heads they wore wigs

From *Military History,* December 1995, pp. 34-41.

under huge bicorne hats. They rounded out their costume with gigantic monocles and boots that were waxed to a high gloss. Their female companions were equally provocative, strolling about almost naked in sheaths of transparent gauze. Both sexes affected a lisp, dropping their r's in a manner thought to be English. Their choice of clothes gave rise to the name "*les Incroyables*" (the incredibles); their choice of musk as a scent was the source of another label, "*Muscadins.*" The *Jeunesse Dorée* were openly nostalgic for the monarchy. Around their necks they wore rust-colored muslins and black collars, mourning the death of Louis XVI. But while their dress might have made them look ludicrous, they were dangerous. The *Muscadins* carried leadweighted clubs they called "rogue-beaters," or "executive power," in a derisory reference to the revolutionary regime—and they were willing to use them.

The 2,000 to 3,000 men that comprised the *Jeunesse Dorée* constituted a large enough force for the Convention to count on for protection—and to set against the surviving Jacobins. With the Convention's tacit approval, members of the *Jeunesse Dorée* hounded the Jacobins in the streets and cafes of French cities; they forced the Convention to decree the closure of Jacobin clubs and purged *sans-cullote* influence from government administration. But by September 1795, the Convention—having freed itself from the domination of the Jacobins—began to realize that it had survived only to fall under the control of the *Jeunesse Dorée.* In the southwest of France, *Muscadins* were conducting a "white terror" campaign against republicans. In Paris, the right wing royalists actually had control of the majority of the city's 48 sections.

By now, the National Convention had become so ineffective that the French economy was in ruins. The cash value of the national currency, the *assignat,* had plummeted 68 percent since December 1794. A bushel of flour, which in 1790 had cost 2 livres, now cost 225, and a decent hat, formerly 14 livres, was now 500. France was starving.

The remedy, decided the Convention, was to reorganize the government. The deputies decided that France needed a two-chamber government and—to prevent the excesses committed by the old Committee of Public Safety—a strong, separate executive organ to be composed of five directors. But in the manner of politicians, the deputies wanted to ensure that their own positions were secure. Therefore, their new constitution called for two-thirds of the members of the new chambers, the Council of Five Hundred and the Council of the Ancients, to be chosen from among the current deputies.

On September 23, 1795, a national plebiscite approved the new constitution, but so many voters abstained that the result was suspect. Royalist-spread rumors that the results of the plebiscite were falsified began to sweep across France. Soon posters began to appear on the walls of Paris, exhorting the French people to "take their religion and their King back to their hearts in order to have peace and bread." By October 4, the country was on the verge of anarchy. What no one could foresee, however, was how the events of that day and the next would alter the future of France and, in particular, that of an unknown, unemployed 26-year-old general of artillery.

On the evening of the 4th, Bonaparte—still on the streets—walked through the rain to the Feydeau Theater to see a sentimental play, *Le Bon Fils.* Everywhere, he could see rebellious blue-coated National Guardsmen beating their drums, calling the people to arms against the Convention. Despite the rain and the biting west wind, angry and armed crowds were gathering in the streets of Paris.

At the Tuileries Palace, meanwhile, the Convention was in an uproar over the behavior of the commander in chief of its forces, *Général* Baron Jacques Menou. Whether due to royalist sympathies or simple incompetence, Menou had seriously compromised the Convention's position. The deputies had just learned that earlier that evening, instead of sealing all the streets leading to the rebellious sections, Menou had advanced by the Rue Vivienne only, crowding all his troops into a single street. Worse still, he had parleyed with the rebels instead of taking decisive action. Finally, acting on a simple promise on the part of the insurgents that they would disperse, he had withdrawn his troops and marched them back to the Place de la Révolution (today, the Place de la Concorde), where they were now bivouacked. Far from disbanding, however, the sections were arming themselves for an attack on the Tuileries.

Bonaparte recorded what happened next: "I . . . was at the Feydeau theater, when I heard of the extraordinary scene that was passing so near me. I felt curious to observe all its circumstances. Seeing the Convention's troops repulsed, I hastened to the tribunes of the Convention to witness the effect of this news, and observe the character and coloring which it would receive. The Convention was in the greatest agitation. The representatives deputed to the army, wishing to exculpate themselves, eagerly accused Menou, attributing [to] treachery what arose from unskillfulness alone. Menou was put under arrest. Different representatives then appeared at the tribune, stating the extent of the danger, the magnitude of which was but to be clearly proved by the news which arrived every moment from the sections."

From the gallery Bonaparte watched as the panicky deputies named *Député* Paul Barras the new commanding general of the Army of the Interior. To contain an armed mob, however, the Convention would need more than handsome, sensual Paul François Jean Nicholas Barras. Despite his lofty military rank, Barras had little practical experience—in seven years he had never risen above second lieutenant in Louis XVI's colonial troops. If the Convention was to defend itself, Barras would need experts to help him.

There are two versions of the events that followed. The first suggests that, following Barras' speech, *Député* Fréron had a few words with Bonaparte and asked him to come with him to Barras' headquarters at the Carrousel. Barras recognized Bonaparte, whom he had known at the siege of Toulon, and offered him a position as his second-in-command, giving Bonaparte just three minutes to make his decision. The second version is less dramatic. Jean Tulard records that "neither the minutes of the proceedings, nor *Le Moniteur,* the official government newspaper, mention Bonaparte's name at all. In likelihood, the Convention simply called upon Bonaparte to serve along with other unemployed officers."

Barras himself records: "When Menou gave way in our hands, and the Committee of Public Safety was at its wits' end, I said: 'There is nothing easier than to replace Menou. I have the man you want: a little Corsican officer who will be less finicking. . . .' The committee, at my suggestion, at once decreed to place

Bonaparte on the active list. . . .But that day, the 12th, when he ought to have been attending me with other soldiers and patriots, I had not had a glimpse of him all morning. As there was still no sign of him when I had secured approval of his appointment, I sent to his lodging. He was not there, nor at any of his usual cafés or eating houses. It was almost 9 o'clock when he finally appeared at the Carrousel, which I had made my headquarters. I upbraided him for being so slow. Every day till then he had been making me such eager, and even fulsome offers of service against the enemies of the Republic!"

Whatever the truth, Bonaparte found himself at Barras' headquarters, where there was a job open for him. "What post," he asked Barras, "have you actually assigned to me in this struggle?" Barras replied: "All my positions are commanded by the officers who got here first. You will be one of my aides-de-camp." In spite of that inauspicious beginning, Bonaparte quickly made himself invaluable. He realized that the key to the defense of the Tiuleries was to prevent the insurgents from concentrating their forces under the palace windows. To win, he advised Barras, the Convention must deploy its forces to block all the avenues leading to the palace, and for that purpose, artillery was essential.

But to their chagrin, Barras and Bonaparte soon discovered that the Convention's forces were mediocre—just 5,000–6,000 men, scattered about the terraces and squares around the Tuileries. Opposing them, the rebellious sections could muster five times that many insurgents. What was worse, the all-important artillery was nonexistent. Menou admitted he had left all of the artillery—40 guns—at the camp at Sablons, six miles away. Undeterred, Bonaparte immediately called for the commanding officer of the nearest available cavalry force. This turned out to be the *21ème Chasseurs à cheval*—thanks to Menou—now conveniently encamped in the Tuileries courtyard just down the staircase.

Within a few minutes, a handsome young officer names Joachim Murat, uniformed in the green and gold of a *chef d'escadron* (major) *de Chasseurs*, snapped to attention before Barras and Bonaparte. Bonaparte ordered him to take 300 horsemen, ride to the Place de Sablons, and bring back the guns and the ammunition. Murat bounded down the stairs of the Tuileries to the bivouac in the courtyard. Putting himself at the head of 150 *chasseurs* and 150 troopers of the *3ème Régiment de Dragons*, also stationed nearby, he set off at a brisk trot through the narrow dark streets of Paris.

Meanwhile, Barras and Bonaparte collected the Convention's scattered forces and redeployed them in the avenues and streets around the Tuileries. The *séctionnaires* numbered 30,000. Against them the Convention could muster only 5,000 regular troops, 1,500 *gendarmes* (military and civilian police), and 1,500 men expelled from the rebellious sections who formed a battalion called either *Le Batalion Sacré des Patriotes de 1789* (Sacred Battalion of the Patriots of '89) or "the Terrorist Battalion," according to one's point of view. Fréron, whose nerve knew no bounds, went to the Faubourg Antoine to ask the *Quinze Vingts* section for reinforcements, and returned with a contingent of 250 men. Then they waited for Murat.

At 6 a.m. on 13 *Vendemaire* (October 5), as the gray dawn rose above Paris, the rainstorm dwindled to an unrelenting drizzle, whipped by the wind against the gray facade of the Tuileries. In the salon reserved for the Military Committee, a sleepless Bonaparte paced. Suddenly the cobblestones of the Tuileries courtyard groaned under the rumble of heavy wheels. Bonaparte strode to a window. Below him, guns defiled one by one under the gateway of the Louvre, some drawn by requisitioned horses, others dragged by cavalry with ropes. At their head was the swashbuckling Murat, now returned from Sablons, where he had beaten the insurgents to the guns by only moments.

The first light of dawn had been breaking through the rain as Murat's troopers filed into the Place de Sablons. Through the drizzle Murat had seen the head of a column of National Guards marching into the Place from the opposite side. It was the *Battalion de la Section La Pelletier*, arriving to secure the artillery. *"Enbataille,"* he had ordered, and his two squadrons wheeled into a line behind him. *"En evant,"* he then ordered. When the National Guardsmen had caught sight of a 200-meter line of resolute horsemen advancing with sabers drawn, they had recoiled, then scattered. Murat had secured the guns, and then he and his men had galloped back from Sablons scattering people, vehicles, and animals as they passed.

Bonaparte expected the main rebel attack to come from the north. Approach from the east was out of the question because the narrow streets and passages led only to the Carrousel courtyard, where the rebels could be cut off and destroyed. The only approach to the Tuileries from the south, or left bank of the Seine, was across the Pont Royal, which could be easily defended. If the rebels attacked from the west—from the direction of the Rue Royal, the Place de la Révolution, or the Champs Elysées—the wide streets and squares would allow the Convention to attack them with its cavalry and cut them down. By dawn on October 5, Bonaparte had guns emplaced to cover all the approaches to the Tuileries, "confiding the guarding of them," as he put it, "to officers of known fidelity." He had guns trained on the Louis XVI bridge (now the Pont de la Concorde), the Pont Royal, and the Rues de St. Florentin and St. Honoré. Other guns he sited at the Rue de la Convention, which runs south from the Rue St.-Honoré, then the main street of Paris, directly to the palace gardens. The whole mass of buildings making up the Louvre and the Tuileries were held by the Convention's troops.

Although very serious, the situation was not without humor. That morning, Barras had received a report from an adjutant general who had been informed by "some rather indiscreet young men" that the attack on the Convention would start at 4 p.m. "Why not 4 in the morning?" jokes Barras, to which the reply was that "no doubt the estimable bourgeois of Paris . . .[are] incapable of changing their hours."

All morning the *sectionnaires* gathered in increasing thousands along the Rue St. Honoré and around the Church of St. Roch, where they had their headquarters. In places, the Convention's posts were not more than 10 to 15 paces away from the royalist revolutionaries. "The *sectionnaires*," recorded Bonaparte, "sent women to corrupt the soldiers; even the leaders presented themselves several times, unarmed, and waving their hats, to fraternize, they said!"

At 2 o'clock in the afternoon, several columns of insurgents joined in the Place Dauphin, near the Pont Neuf. *Général* Carteaux, who was stationed on the Pont Neuf with 400 men and four guns with orders to defend the two sides of the bridge, fell back to the Louvre. An hour later, *Général* Danican sent a flag of truce to summon the Convention to remove the troops that threatened the people, and to disarm the Terrorists. The Convention refused.

As the day wore on, however, the danger increased. Night was coming on, and with it the probability that the *sectionnaries* would use the darkness to climb from house to house to reach the Tuileries. Bonaparte recorded: "I had 800 muskets, belts and cartridge boxes brought into the hall of the Convention, to arm the members themselves and the clerks, as a corps of reserve. This measure alarmed several of them, who then began to comprehend the extent of the danger."

At 4 o'clock, however, muskets were fired from the houses near St. Roch, and some balls fell on the steps of the Tuileries, wounding a woman who was going into the garden. At the same time, a column of insurgents could be seen forming ranks at the head of the Rue de la Convention. A few moments later, a huge cheer went up from the insurgents, their drums beat the *pas de charge,* and the great mass of *sectionnaries* boiled forward down the Rue St. Roch into the Rue de la Convention.

At the Tuileries, President Louis Legendre exclaimed, "Let us die with a courage fitting for the friends of liberty!" And, trembling somewhat, the deputies of the National Convention charged their muskets with powder and ball. After the insurgents, with muskets blazing and bayonets fixed, broke through the barricades across the Rue de la Convention, one of Bonaparte's 8-pounders fired as a signal. Every gun opened up on the insurgents. For 15 minutes, a cloud of gun smoke billowed above the street as both sides fired and reloaded as fast as they could. Then, step by step, the rebels began to give way and retreated sullenly up the street to the steps of St. Roch.

Capitaine Paul Thiébault, a staff officer with the Convention's forces, recounted what happened next: "When, in this way, the cannons had overthrown or removed all that was in sight, 1,000 men of the Patriot Battalion emerged from the cul-de-sac and attacked the *sectionnaires* who were still in front of the church door and occupied the Rue Saint-Honoré. The collision was violent, and the fighting was hand-to-hand, but our troops gained ground; six guns were at once brought into action and completed the rout of the *sectionnaries,* who withdrew in all haste toward the Place Vendôme and the Palais-Royal. . . ."

A weak attack led by Lafond from across the Seine by the Pont Royal was dispersed in the same manner, Bonaparte reporting that "Lafond's column, taken in front and flank by the artillery placed on the quay even with the wickets of the Louvre, and at the head of the Pont Royal, was routed. . . ."

By 6 p.m. the rebellion was over. Lying in the streets were 400 dead and dying men, many with green and black collars. But it had not been a bloodless victory for the Convention. The vestibule and the ground floor of the Tuileries were full of wounded men stretched out on straw. Many of the deputies' wives had come to the palace either to share the fate of their husbands or in flight from the fury of the *sectionnaries.* "Of this number," Paul Thiébault reported, "the oldest served as nurses while the youngest shredded linen. Thus it was at once a senate, a government, a headquarters, a hospital, a camp, and a bivouac."

At 2 a.m., a triumphant Napoleon Bonaparte wrote to his elder brother, Joseph: "At last all is over. My first impulse is to think of you and to tell you my news. The royalists, organized in their sections, became every day more insolent. The Convention ordered the Section Lepelletier to be disarmed. It repulsed the troops. Menou, who was in command, is said to have betrayed us. He was instantly superceded. The Convention appointed Barras to the command [of] the military force; the committee appointed me second-in-command. We made our dispositions; the enemy marched to attack us in the Tuileries. We killed many of them; they killed 30 of our men and wounded 60. We have the sections and all is quiet. As usual, I was not wounded."

There was no question that it was Bonaparte who was responsible for the Convention's victory. "From the first," recorded *Capitaine* Thiébault, "his activity was astonishing; he seemed to be everywhere at once, or rather he vanished at one point to reappear instantly. He surprised people further by his laconic, clear and prompt orders, imperative to the last degree. Everyone was struck with the vigor of his arrangements and passed from admiration to confidence, from confidence to enthusiasm."

On October 11, a grateful Convention appointed Napoleon Bonaparte second-in-command of the Army of the Interior and, five days later, promoted him to the rank of *Général de Division* (major general). On October 26, the Convention held its last sitting, and the next day the Directory began. For his services to the Convention, Barras was chosen to be one of the new directors. He resigned his command of the Army of the Interior. It was decided that someone expert with guns should succeed him. And so, at age 26, Naploeon Bonaparte found himself in command of the Army of the Interior, and was later to get what he wanted—command of the Army of Italy. He was embarked on a remarkable career.

The First Feminist

In 1792 Mary Wollstonecraft wrote a book to prove that her sex was as intelligent as the other: thus did feminism come into the world. Right on, Ms. Mary!

Shirley Tomkievicz

The first person—male or female—to speak at any length and to any effect about woman's rights was Mary Wollstonecraft. In 1792, when her *Vindication of the Rights of Woman* appeared, Mary was a beautiful spinster of thirty-three who had made a successful career for herself in the publishing world of London. This accomplishment was rare enough for a woman in that day. Her manifesto, at once impassioned and learned, was an achievement of real originality. The book electrified the reading public and made Mary famous. The core of its argument is simple: "I wish to see women neither heroines nor brutes; but reasonable creatures," Mary wrote. This ancestress of the Women's Liberation Movement did not demand day-care centers or an end to women's traditional role as wife and mother, nor did she call anyone a chauvinist pig. The happiest period of Mary's own life was when she was married and awaiting the birth of her second child. And the greatest delight she ever knew was in her first child, an illegitimate daughter. Mary's feminism may not appear today to be the hard-core revolutionary variety, but she did live, for a time, a scandalous and unconventional life—"emancipated," it is called by those who have never tried it. The essence of her thought, however, is simply that a woman's mind is as good as a man's.

Not many intelligent men could be found to dispute this proposition today, at least not in mixed company. In Mary's time, to speak of *anybody's* rights, let alone woman's rights, was a radical act. In England, as in other nations, "rights" were an entity belonging to the government. The common run of mankind had little access to what we now call "human rights." As an example of British justice in the late eighteenth century, the law cited two hundred different capital crimes, among them shoplifting. An accused man was not entitled to counsel. A child could be tried and hanged as soon as an adult. The right to vote existed, certainly, but because of unjust apportionment, it had come to mean little. In the United States some of these abuses had been corrected—but the rights of man did not extend past the color bar and the masculine gender was intentional. In the land of Washington and Jefferson, as in the land of George III, human rights were a new idea and woman's rights were not even an issue.

In France, in 1792, a Revolution in the name of equality was in full course, and woman's rights had at least been alluded to. The Revolutionary government drew up plans for female education—to the age of eight. "The education of the women should always be relative to the men," Rousseau had written in *Emile*. "To please, to be useful to us, to make us love and esteem them, to educate us when young, and take care of us when grown up, to advise, to console us, to render our lives easy and agreeable; these are the duties of women at all times, and what they should be taught in their infancy." And, less prettily, "Women have, or ought to have, but little liberty."

Rousseau would have found little cause for complaint in eighteenth-century England. An Englishwoman had almost the same civil status as an American slave. Thomas Hardy, a hundred years hence, was to base a novel on the idea of a man casually selling his wife and daughter at public auction. Obviously this was not a common occurrence, but neither is it wholly implausible. In 1792, and later, a woman could not own property, nor keep any earned wages. All that she possessed belonged to her husband. She could not divorce him, but he could divorce her and take her children. There was no law to say she could not grow up illiterate or be beaten every day.

Such was the legal and moral climate in which Mary Wollstonecraft lived. She was born in London in the spring of 1759, the second child and first daughter of Edward Wollstonecraft, a prosperous weaver. Two more daughters and two more sons were eventually born into the family, making six children in all. Before they had all arrived, Mr. Wollstonecraft came into an inheritance and decided to move his family to the country and become a gentleman farmer. But this plan failed. His money dwindled, and he began drinking heavily. His wife turned into a terrified wraith whose only interest was her eldest son, Edward. Only he escaped the beatings and abuse that his father dealt out regularly to every other household member, from Mrs. Wollstonecraft to the family dog. As often happens in large and disordered families, the eldest sister had to assume the role of mother and scullery maid. Mary was a bright, strong child, determined not to be broken, and she undertook her task energetically, defying her father when he was violent and keeping her younger brothers and sisters in hand. Clearly, Mary held the household together, and in so doing forfeited her own childhood. This experience left her with an everlasting gloomy streak, and was a strong factor in making her a reformer.

At some point in Mary's childhood, another injustice was visited upon her, though so commonplace for the time that she can hardly have felt the sting. Her elder brother was sent away to be educated, and the younger children were left to learn their letters as best they could. The family now frequently changed lodgings, but from her ninth to her fifteenth year Mary went to a day school, where she had the only formal training of her life. Fortunately, this included French and composition, and somewhere Mary learned to read critically and widely. These skills, together with her curiosity and determination, were really all she needed. The *Vindication* is in some parts long-winded, ill-punctuated, and simply full of hot air, but it is the work of a well-informed mind.

Feminists—and Mary would gladly have claimed the title—inevitably, even deservedly, get bad notices. The term calls up an image of relentless battle-axes: "thin college ladies with eyeglasses, no-nonsense features, mouths thin as bologna slicers, a babe in one arm, a hatchet in the other, grey eyes bright with balefire," as Norman Mailer feelingly envisions his antagonists in the Women's Liberation Movement. He has conjured up all the horrid elements: the lips with a cutting edge, the baby immaculately conceived (one is forced to conclude), the lethal weapon tightly clutched, the desiccating college degree, the joylessness. Hanging miasmally over the tableau is the suspicion of a deformed sexuality. Are these girls man-haters, or worse? Mary Wollstonecraft, as the first of her line, has had each of these scarlet letters (except the B.A.) stitched upon her bosom. Yet she conformed very little to the hateful stereotype. In at least one respect, however, she would have chilled Mailer's bones. Having spent her childhood as an adult, Mary reached the age of nineteen in a state of complete joylessness. She was later to quit the role, but for now she wore the garb of a martyr.

Her early twenties were spent in this elderly frame of mind. First she went out as companion to an old lady living at Bath, and was released from this servitude only by a call to nurse the dying Mrs. Wollstonecraft. Then the family broke up entirely, though the younger sisters continued off and on to be dependent on Mary. The family of Mary's dearest friend, Fanny Blood, invited her to come and stay with them; the two girls made a small living doing sewing and handicrafts, and Mary dreamed of starting a primary school. Eventually, in a pleasant village called Newington Green, this plan materialized and prospered. But Fanny Blood in the meantime had married and moved to Lisbon. She wanted Mary to come and nurse her through the birth of her first child. Mary reached Lisbon just in time to see her friend die of childbed fever, and returned home just in time to find that her sisters, in whose care the flourishing little school had been left, had lost all but two pupils.

Mary made up her mind to die. "My constitution is impaired, I hope I shan't live long," she wrote to a friend in February, 1786. Under this almost habitual grief, however, Mary was gaining some new sense of herself. Newington Green, apart from offering her a brief success as a schoolmistress, had brought her some acquaintance in the world of letters, most important among them, Joseph Johnson, an intelligent and successful London publisher in search of new writers. Debt-ridden and penniless, Mary set aside her impaired constitution and wrote her first book, probably in the space of a week. Johnson bought it for ten guineas and published it. Called *Thoughts on the Education of Daughters,* it went unnoticed, and the ten guineas was soon spent. Mary had to find work. She accepted a position as governess in the house of Lord and Lady Kingsborough in the north of Ireland.

Mary's letters from Ireland to her sisters and to Joseph Johnson are so filled with Gothic gloom, so stained with tears, that one cannot keep from laughing at them. "I entered the great gates with the same kind of feeling I should have if I was going to the Bastille," she wrote upon entering Kingsborough Castle in the fall of 1786. Mary was now twenty-seven. Her most recent biographer, Margaret George, believes that Mary was not really suffering so much as she was having literary fantasies. In private she was furiously at work on a novel entitled, not very artfully, *Mary, A Fiction.* This is the story of a young lady of immense sensibilities who closely resembles Mary except that she has wealthy parents, a neglectful bridegroom, and an attractive lover. The title and fantasizing contents are precisely what a scribbler of thirteen might secretly concoct. Somehow Mary was embarking on her adolescence—with all its daydreams—fifteen years after the usual date. Mary's experience in Kingsborough Castle was a fruitful one, for all her complaints. In the summer of 1787 she lost her post as governess and set off for London with her novel. Not only did Johnson accept it for publication, he offered her a regular job as editor and translator and helped her find a place to live.

Thus, aged twenty-eight, Mary put aside her doleful persona as the martyred, set-upon elder sister. How different she is now, jauntily writing from London to her sisters: "Mr. Johnson . . . assures me that if I exert my talents in writing I may support myself in a comfortable way. I am then going to be the first of a new genus . . ." Now Mary discovered the sweetness of financial independence earned by interesting work. She had her own apartment. She was often invited to Mr. Johnson's dinner parties, usually as the only female guest among all the most interesting men in London: Joseph Priestley, Thomas Paine, Henry Fuseli, William Blake, Thomas Christie, William Godwin—all of them up-and-coming scientists or poets or painters or philosophers, bound together by left-wing political views. Moreover, Mary was successful in her own writing as well as in editorial work. Her *Original Stories for Children* went into three editions and was illustrated by Blake. Johnson and his friend Thomas Christie had started a magazine called the *Analytical Review,* to which Mary became a regular contributor.

But—lest anyone imagine an elegantly dressed Mary presiding flirtatiously at Johnson's dinner table—her social accomplishments were rather behind her professional ones. Johnson's circle looked upon her as one of the boys. "Wollstonecraft" is what William Godwin calls her in his diary. One of her later detractors reported that she was at this time a "philosophic sloven," in a dreadful old dress and beaver hat, "with her hair hanging lank about her shoulders." Mary had yet to arrive at her final incarnation, but the new identity was imminent, if achieved by an odd route. Edmund Burke had recently published his *Reflections on the Revolution in France,* and the book had enraged Mary. The statesman who so readily supported the quest for liberty in the American colonies had his doubts about events in France.

Mary's reply to Burke, *A Vindication of the Rights of Men,* astounded London, partly because she was hitherto unknown, partly because it was good. Mary proved to be an excellent polemicist, and she had written in anger. She accused Burke, the erstwhile champion of liberty, of being "the champion of property." "Man preys on man," said she, "and you mourn for the idle tapestry that decorated a gothic pile and the dronish bell that summoned the fat priest to prayer." The book sold well. Mary moved into a better apartment and bought some pretty dresses—no farthingales, of course, but some of the revolutionary new "classical" gowns. She put her auburn hair up in a loose knot. Her days as a philosophic sloven were over.

Vindication of the Rights of Woman was her next work. In its current edition it runs to 250-odd pages; Mary wrote it in six weeks. *Vindication* is no prose masterpiece, but it has never failed to arouse its audience, in one way or another. Horace Walpole unintentionally set the style for the book's foes. Writing to his friend Hannah More in August, 1792, he referred to Thomas Paine and to Mary as "philosophizing serpents" and was "glad to hear you have not read the tract of the last mentioned writer. I would not look at it." Neither would many another of Mary's assailants, the most virulent of whom, Ferdinand Lundberg, surfaced at the late date of 1947 with a tract of his own, *Modern Woman, the Lost Sex.* Savagely misogynistic as it is, this book was hailed in its time as "the best book yet to be written about women." Lundberg calls Mary the Karl Marx of the feminist movement, and the *Vindication* a "fateful book," to which "the tenets of feminism, which have undergone no change to our day, may be traced." Very well, but then, recounting Mary's life with the maximum possible number of errors per line, he warns us that she was "an extreme neurotic of a compulsive type" who "wanted to turn on men and injure them." In one respect, at least, Mr. Lundberg hits the mark: he blames Mary for starting women in the pernicious habit of wanting an education. In the nineteenth century, he relates, English and American feminists were hard at work. "Following Mary Wollstonecraft's prescription, they made a considerable point about acquiring a higher education." This is precisely Mary's prescription, and the most dangerous idea in her fateful book.

"Men complain and with reason, of the follies and caprices of our Sex," she writes in Chapter 1. "Behold, I should answer, the natural effect of ignorance." Women, she thinks, are usually so mindless as to be scarcely fit for their roles as wives and mothers. Nevertheless, she believes this state not to be part of the feminine nature, but the result of an equally mindless oppression, as demoralizing for men as for women. If a woman's basic mission is as a wife and mother, need she be an illiterate slave for this?

The heart of the work is Mary's attack on Rousseau. In *Emile* Rousseau had set forth some refreshing new ideas for the education of little boys. But women, he decreed, are tools for pleasure, creatures too base for moral or political or educational privilege. Mary recognized that this view was destined to shut half the human race out of all hope for political freedom. *Vindication* is a plea that the "rights of men" ought to mean the "rights of humanity." The human right that she held highest was the right to have a mind and think with it. Virginia Woolf, who lived through a time of feminist activity, thought that the *Vindication* was a work so true "as to seem to contain nothing new." Its originality, she wrote, rather too optimistically, had become a commonplace.

Vindication went quickly into a second edition. Mary's name was soon known all over Europe. But as she savored her fame—and she did savor it—she found that the edge was wearing off and that she was rather lonely. So far as anyone knows, Mary had reached this point in her life without ever having had a love affair. Johnson was the only man she was close to, and he was, as she wrote him, "A father, or a brother—you have been both to me." Mary was often now in the company of the Swiss painter Henry Fuseli, and suddenly she developed what she thought was a Platonic passion in his direction. He rebuffed her, and in the winter of 1792 she went to Paris, partly to escape her embarrassment but also because she wanted to observe the workings of the Revolution firsthand.

Soon after her arrival, as she collected notes for the history of the Revolution she hoped to write, Mary saw Louis XVI, "sitting in a hackney coach . . . going to meet death." Back in her room that evening, she wrote to Mr. Johnson of seeing "eyes glare through a glass door opposite my chair and bloody hands shook at me . . . I am going to bed and for the first time in my life, I cannot put out the candle." As the weeks went on, Edmund Burke's implacable critic began to lose her faith in the brave new world. "The aristocracy of birth is levelled to the ground, only to make room for that of riches," she wrote. By February France and England were at war, and British subjects classified as enemy aliens.

Though many Englishmen were arrested, Mary and a large English colony stayed on. One day in spring, some friends presented her to an attractive American, newly arrived in Paris, Gilbert Imlay. Probably about four years Mary's senior, Imlay, a former officer in the Continental Army, was an explorer and adventurer. He came to France seeking to finance a scheme for seizing Spanish lands in the Mississippi valley. This "natural and unaffected creature," as Mary was later to describe him, was probably the social lion of the moment, for he was also the author of a best-selling novel called *The Emigrants,* a farfetched account of life and love in the American wilderness. He and Mary soon became lovers. They were a seemingly perfect pair. Imlay must have been pleased with his famous catch, and—dear, liberated girl that she was—Mary did not insist upon marriage. Rather the contrary. But fearing that she was in danger as an Englishwoman, he registered her at the American embassy as his wife.

Blood was literally running in the Paris streets now, so Mary settled down by herself in a cottage at Neuilly. Imlay spent his days in town, working out various plans. The Mississippi expedition came to nothing, and he decided to stay in France and go into the import-export business, part of his imports being gunpowder and other war goods run from Scandinavia through the English blockade. In the evenings he would ride out to the cottage. By now it was summer, and Mary, who spent the days writing, would often stroll up the road to meet him, carrying a basket of freshly-gathered grapes.

A note she wrote Imlay that summer shows exactly what her feelings for him were: "You can scarcely imagine with what pleasure I anticipate the day when we are to begin almost to live together; and you would smile to hear how many plans of employment I have in my head, now that I am confident that my heart has found peace . . ." Soon she was pregnant. She and Imlay moved into Paris. He promised to take her to America, where they would settle down on a farm and raise six children. But business called Imlay to Le Havre, and his stay lengthened ominously into weeks.

Imlay's letters to Mary have not survived, and without them it is hard to gauge what sort of man he was and what he really thought of his adoring mistress. Her biographers like to make him out a cad, a philistine, not half good enough for Mary. Perhaps; yet the two must have had something in common. His novel, unreadable though it is now, shows that he shared her political views, including her feminist ones. He may never have been serious about the farm in America, but he was a miserably long time deciding to leave Mary alone. Though they were separated during the early months of her pregnancy, he finally did bring her to Le Havre, and continued to live with her there until the child was born and for some six months afterward. The baby arrived in May, 1794, a healthy little girl, whom Mary named Fanny after her old friend. Mary was proud that her delivery had been easy, and as for Fanny, Mary loved her instantly. "My little Girl," she wrote to a friend, "begins to suck so manfully that her father reckons saucily on her writing the second part of the Rights of Woman." Mary's joy in this child illuminates almost every letter she wrote henceforth.

Fanny's father was the chief recipient of these letters with all the details of the baby's life. To Mary's despair, she and Imlay hardly ever lived together again. A year went by; Imlay was now in London and Mary in France. She offered to break it off, but mysteriously, he could not let go. In the last bitter phase of their involvement, after she had joined him in London at his behest, he even sent her—as "Mrs. Imlay"—on a complicated business errand to the Scandinavian countries. Returning to London, Mary discovered that he was living with another woman. By now half crazy with humiliation, Mary chose a dark night and threw herself in the Thames. She was nearly dead when two rivermen pulled her from the water.

Though this desperate incident was almost the end of Mary, at least it was the end of the Imlay episode. He sent a doctor to care for her, but they rarely met again. Since Mary had no money, she set about providing for herself and Fanny in the way she knew. The faithful Johnson had already brought out Volume I of her history of the French Revolution. Now she set to work editing and revising her *Letters Written during a Short Residence in Sweden, Norway, and Denmark,* a kind of thoughtful travelogue. The book was well received and widely translated.

And it also revived the memory of Mary Wollstonecraft in the mind of an old acquaintance, William Godwin. As the author of the treatise *Political Justice,* he was now as famous a philosophizing serpent as Mary and was widely admired and hated as a "freethinker." He came to call on Mary. They became friends and then lovers. Early in 1797 Mary was again pregnant. William Godwin was an avowed atheist who had publicly denounced the very institution of marriage. On March 29, 1797, he nevertheless went peaceably to church with Mary and made her his wife.

The Godwins were happy together, however William's theories may have been outraged. He adored his small stepdaughter and took pride in his brilliant wife. Awaiting the birth of her child throughout the summer, Mary worked on a new novel and made plans for a book on "the management of infants"—it would have been the first "Dr. Spock." She expected to have another easy delivery and promised to come downstairs to dinner the day following. But when labor began, on August 30, it proved to be long and agonizing. A daughter, named Mary Wollstonecraft, was born; ten days later, the mother died.

Occasionally, when a gifted writer dies young, one can feel, as in the example of Shelley, that perhaps he had at any rate accomplished his best work. But so recently had Mary come into her full intellectual and emotional growth that her death at the age of thirty-eight is bleak indeed. There is no knowing what Mary might have accomplished now that she enjoyed domestic stability. Perhaps she might have achieved little or nothing further as a writer. But she might have been able to protect her daughters from some part of the sadness that overtook them; for as things turned out, both Fanny and Mary were to sacrifice themselves.

Fanny grew up to be a shy young girl, required to feel grateful for the roof over her head, overshadowed by her prettier half sister, Mary. Godwin in due course married a formidable widow named Mrs. Clairmont, who brought her own daughter into the house—the Claire Clairmont who grew up to become Byron's mistress and the mother of his daughter Allegra. Over the years Godwin turned into a hypocrite and a miser who nevertheless continued to pose as the great liberal of the day. Percy Bysshe Shelley, born the same year that the *Vindication of the Rights of Woman* was published, came to be a devoted admirer of Mary Wollstonecraft's writing. As a young man he therefore came with his wife to call upon Godwin. What he really sought, however, were Mary's daughters—because they were her daughters. First he approached Fanny, but later changed his mind. Mary Godwin was then sixteen, the perfect potential soul mate for a man whose needs for soul mates knew no bounds. They conducted their courtship in the most up-to-the-minute romantic style: beneath a tree near her mother's grave they read aloud to each other from the *Vindication.* Soon they eloped, having pledged their "troth" in the cemetery. Godwin, the celebrated freethinker, was enraged. To make matters worse, Claire Clairmont had run off to Switzerland with them.

Not long afterward Fanny, too, ran away. She went to an inn in a distant town and drank a fatal dose of laudanum. It has traditionally been said that unrequited love for Shelley drove her to this pass, but there is no evidence one way or the other. One suicide that can more justly be laid at Shelley's door is that of his first wife, which occurred a month after Fanny's and which at any rate left him free to wed his mistress, Mary Godwin. Wife or mistress, she had to endure poverty, ostracism, and Percy's constant infidelities. But now at last her father could, and did, boast to his relations that he was father-in-law to a baronet's son. "Oh, philosophy!" as Mary Godwin Shelley remarked.

If in practice Shelley was merely a womanizer, on paper he was a convinced feminist. He had learned this creed from Mary Wollstonecraft. Through his verse Mary's ideas began to be disseminated. They were one part of that vast tidal wave of political, social, and artistic revolution that arose in the late eighteenth century, the romantic movement. But because of Mary's unconventional way of life, her name fell into disrepute during the nineteenth century, and her book failed to exert its rightful influence on the development of feminism. Emma Willard and other pioneers of the early Victorian period indignantly refused to claim Mary as their forebear. Elizabeth Cady Stanton and Lucretia Mott were mercifully less strait-laced on the subject. In 1889, when Mrs. Stanton and Susan B. Anthony published their *History of Woman Suffrage,* they dedicated the book to Mary. Though Mary Wollstonecraft can in no sense be said to have founded the woman's rights movement, she was, by the late nineteenth century, recognized as its inspiration, and the *Vindication* was vindicated for the highly original work it was, a landmark in the history of society.

Industry, Ideology, Nation-Building, and Imperialism: The Nineteenth Century

The early years of the nineteenth century were marked by the interplay of powerful countervailing forces. The French Revolution and industrialization provided the impetus for political, economic, and social changes in Western civilization. The ideals of the French Revolution remained alive in France and inspired political movements in other parts of Europe as well. Industrialization brought material progress for millions, particularly the burgeoning middle class, but often at the expense of the great mass of unskilled workers who were victims of the low-paying, impersonal factory system. Shifting demographic patterns created additional pressures for change. It had taken all of Europe's history to have reached a population of 180 million in 1800. Then, in the nineteenth century, Europe's population doubled, causing major migrations on the continent, typically from the countryside to the cities, and sending waves of emigrants to America, Australia, and elsewhere. By 1919 about 200 million Europeans had settled elsewhere.

But forces of continuity were at work also. Notwithstanding the impact of industrialism, much of Europe remained agrarian, dependent upon the labor of peasants. Christianity remained the dominant religion and, for the moment, the institution of monarchy retained the loyalty of those who wanted to preserve an orderly society. In addition, millions of Europeans, having experienced more than enough turbulence during the French Revolution and Napoleonic era, were willing to embrace even the most reactionary regimes if they could guarantee peace and stability.

The interplay of tradition and change raised vital new issues and generated fundamental conflicts in politics and thought. Of necessity the terms of political discourse were redefined. The century was an age of ideologies: conservatism, with its distrust of untested innovations and its deep commitment to order and tradition; liberalism, with its faith in reason, technique, and progress (usually measured in material terms); various forms of socialism, from revolutionary to utopian, each with its promise of equality and economic justice for the downtrodden working class; and nationalism, with its stirring demand, at once unifying and divisive, that the nationalities of the world should be autonomous. Even Darwinism, the great scientific paradigm of the era, was misappropriated for political purposes. Transformed into Social Darwinism, it was used to justify the domination of Western nations over their colonies. Popular misconceptions of evolution also reinforced prevailing notions of male supremacy.

In sum, the nineteenth century, for those who enjoyed economic and political status, was the epitome of human progress. For the rest, many of whom shared the materialist outlook of their "betters," it was a time to struggle for a fair share of the fruits of progress.

Several articles in this unit explore the dynamics of change in the nineteenth century. Economic forces and related ideologies are covered in "Engels in Manchester: Inventing the Proletariat" and "Samuel Smiles: The Gospel of Self-Help." The effects of liberalism could be discerned even in autocratic Germany, as "Justice Seen, Justice Done? Abolishing Public Executions in 19th Century-Germany" attests. Nineteenth-century social change did not always bring opportunities for women, even those who were educated and from relatively well-off families, but the article on Sarah Bernhardt illustrates what a talented, willful woman could accomplish in the relatively open sphere of the theatre. "The Life and Resurrection of Alexandre Dumas" gives us an unlikely nineteenth-century success story. Denis Mack Smith's profile of Giuseppe Garibaldi offers some insights on nation-building in Italy. James Fallows's article about Matthew Perry's 1853 expedition to Japan reminds us that nineteenth-century imperialism was not confined to Africa.

Looking Ahead: Challenge Questions

Samuel Smiles and Friedrich Engels were eminent Victorians, yet their perceptions of nineteenth-century En-

UNIT 3

gland varied greatly. What were their responses to the great issues of their age and how can we account for the differences?

What, if anything, does the career of Sarah Bernhardt reveal about the place of women in France during the nineteenth century?

Define Giuseppe Garibaldi's contributions to the unification of Italy.

What were the consequences, short-term and long-term, of Matthew Perry's expedition to Japan?

Explain the arguments for and against public executions in nineteenth-century Germany.

Engels in Manchester

Inventing the Proletariat

Gertrude Himmelfarb

Gertrude Himmelfarb is Distinguished Professor of History at the Graduate School of the City University of New York. She is the author of several books, including On Liberty and Liberalism: The Case of John Stuart Mill. *This essay is adapted from her volume,* The Idea of Poverty: England in the Early Industrial Age, *published by Knopf.*

Friedrich Engels, writing in 1845, described Chartism as only one manifestation of the "social war" that was being waged in England, a war that was bound to issue in a full-scale revolution. And this not in the remote future but within a few years, following the economic crisis he predicted for 1846–47, or the one after that in 1852–53.

> The proletarians, driven to despair, will seize the torch which Stephens [the Chartist] has preached to them; the vengeance of the people will come down with a wrath of which the rage of 1793 gives no true idea. The war of the poor against the rich will be the bloodiest ever waged. Even the union of a part of the bourgeoisie with the proletariat, even a general reform of the bourgeoisie, would not help matters. . . . The revolution must come; it is already too late to bring about a peaceful solution.

Nothing could now prevent the revolution. All that could be hoped for was some mitigation of the violence, and that would depend on the "development" of the proletariat. "In proportion, as the proletariat absorbs socialistic and communistic elements, will the revolution diminish in bloodshed, revenge, and savagery," noted Engels.

In most commentaries on Engels's book, *The Condition of the Working Class in England,* this scenario of revolution has been dismissed as a *folie de jeunesse,* a youthful excess of zeal that was surely mistaken, at least in its timing, but that did not seriously affect the substance of the book or the subject denoted by the title. Engels himself was so little discomfited by the patent failure of this prediction that, in supervising the English edition almost half a century later, he let stand the whole of this passage (and others to the same effect), noting only that he had been right in predicting the repeal of the Corn Laws.

Questions have been raised about the accuracy of Engels's citation of documents and the accuracy of the documents themselves, about the bias in his selection of sources and the bias in the sources themselves, about the representativeness of his examples and the validity of his generalizations. But there is another question that is no less important. To what extent was his account of the condition of the English working class shaped by his prognosis of social war and revolution? He himself claimed that the class struggle and revolution were the logical, necessary consequences of the total impoverishment of the proletariat—its "immiseration" in the language of later Marxism. One may well be wary of an ostensibly descriptive or empirical account of the condition of the English working class that so neatly confirmed Engels's ideological predispositions. This does not necessarily invalidate his account; it may be that his ideology was firmly rooted in the actuality. It does, however, mean that the whole of the historical record has to be examined: the reports, articles, and books cited by Engels, his personal observations and reflections, and another set of sources he did not cite or make explicit—the ideas he brought with him to his study of the English working class. To raise this issue is not to subject him to any special or invidious kind of examination. It is only to take seriously ideas he himself took seriously. In the preface to the English edition written many years later, he observed that the book revealed the "stamp of his youth," "traces of the descent of modern Socialism from one of its ancestors, Germany philosophy"—by which he meant that he had not yet emancipated himself from the philosophy and politics of Young Hegelianism.

Die Lage der arbeitenden Klasse in England was published in Leipzig in 1845; the first English language edition appeared in 1887 in America, and in 1892 in England, under the title *The Condition of the Working Class in England in 1844.* The date in the English title reminds us that almost half a century intervened between the book's original publication and its first appearance in England, a period during which the book was known only in Germany (and mainly in the German radical movement) and not at all in the country that was the object of its concern (except perhaps among the small group of German émigrés in London). Whatever else may be said about it—as social reportage, ideological polemic, literary text, psycho-biographical revelation, or "semiotic" exercise—Engels's book was not, in the context of early Victorian England, a contemporary document in the way that Carlyle's or Cobbett's writings were. It was contemporary in the sense of being contemporaneous with the period it was describing. But it had no public resonance, no echoes in public opinion, no part in the shaping of the public consciousness. Later, to be sure, the book did enter the public domain, at a time, not by accident, when English socialism finally emerged as an important force. It has since become so much a part of the historical record, of the consciousness of historians if not of contemporaries, that it has been accused of unduly dominating

From *The American Scholar,* Autumn 1983, pp. 479-496.

that record. For this reason as well as its intrinsic interest—as a picture of the English working classes seen through the eyes of a German radical newly resident in England—*The Condition of the Working Class in England* is a fascinating historical document.

Engels was twenty-two years old when he arrived in Manchester in November 1842 to join a textile firm in which his father was a partner. He remained in England for twenty-one months and started his book after his return to Germany in September 1844; it was completed by March and published in May. These bare facts are suggestive enough, although they hardly begin to tell the story. By the time the young man came to England, he had been initiated into the various factions of German radicalism known collectively as Young (or Left) Hegelianism, had met the leading figures in that movement (Wilhelm Weitling, Moses Hess, Bruno and Heinrich Bauer, Arnold Ruge, and Karl Marx), had published articles on various subjects (including an attack on the mill owners of his own town, of which his father was one), and had become a regular contributor to the radical journal, the *Rheinische Zeitung.* Before leaving for England he paid two visits to Cologne to meet with the staff of the *Zeitung.* On one occasion he was coolly received by the newly appointed editor, Karl Marx, who disapproved of his association with the "Freien" sect in Berlin, the extremist faction led by the Bauers and Ruge. Another editor, Moses Hess, befriended him and engaged him in long discussions. "We spoke about current questions," Hess wrote to a friend several months later, "and he, an Anno I revolutionary, departed from me an enthusiastic communist." Those "current questions" must have included England, for Hess had just published his book, *Die europäische Triarchie,* describing the three stages in the history of human emancipation: the German Reformation that he identified with religious freedom, the French Revolution with political freedom, and a future English revolution with social freedom.

When Engels arrived in England it was as a confirmed communist and an avowed revolutionary. His first weeks were spent in London, and either then or on a subsequent visit he met the German colony of exiled revolutionaries, members of the League of the Just who had been implicated in the Blanquist uprising in Paris in 1839; they were, he later explained, the first "proletarian revolutionaries" he had met. During his first week in London he wrote three articles for the *Rheinische Zeitung,* one of which assured his German readers that the inherent "contradictions" in the English economy could be resolved only by revolution. No sooner had he installed himself in Manchester than he sent off an article entitled "The Condition of the Working Class in England," which opened by asserting that that condition was becoming "daily more precarious, in spite of the fact that unemployment had recently decreased and the English worker was generally in a far better state than the German or French worker.

> The worker there (in Germany and France) earns just enough to allow him to live on bread and potatoes; he is lucky if he can buy meat once a week. Here he eats beef every day and gets a more nourishing joint for his money than the richest man in Germany. He drinks tea twice a day and still has enough money left over to be able to drink a glass of porter at midday and brandy and water in the evening. This is how most of the Manchester workers live who work a twelve-hour day.

This affluence, however, was temporary for the smallest fluctuation of trade would throw thousands out of work, and a major depression was in the offing.

In the following months, in the spare time left him from business, Engels managed to write a series of articles for a German émigré magazine in Zurich (the *Rheinische Zeitung* having ceased publication), other articles for the Owenite *New Moral World* and the Chartist *Northern Star,* and a long essay, "Outlines of a Critique of Political Economy," for the *Deutsch-Französische Jahrbücher* edited by Marx and Ruge in Paris. When the Soviet translator of the "Critique" later commented on the lingering traces of "ethical 'philosophical' communism" and "abstract principles of universal morals and humaneness," he had in mind such passages as that on the private ownership of land: "To make land an object of huckstering . . . was the last step towards making oneself an object of huckstering. It was and is to this very day an immorality surpassed only by the immorality of self-alienation." For the most part, however, the "Critique" was an impassioned but not notably "philosophical" or moralistic analysis, using the language and concepts of political economy—wealth, value, price, capital, rent, wages—to criticize the system of private property that the political economists took for granted. That system, Engels argued, was destined to collapse as a result of its inherent contradictions. Competition would lead to monopoly and the centralization of property; economic crises would become more acute and widespread; the world would be divided into capitalists and workers and eventually with the impoverishment of the small capitalists, into millionaires and paupers; wages would decline to the point where the worker received "only the very barest necessities, the mere means of subsistence"; and the final crisis would result in the abolition of private property and the "total transformation of social conditions." (Fifteen years later Marx, in his own *Critique of Political Economy,* paid tribute to Engels's "brilliant outline" that anticipated his own in so many respects.)

The final words of Engels's essay read like an advertisement for *The Condition of the Working Class in England.* Having raised the question of machinery and the factory system, Engels explained that that subject was beyond the scope of the present essay. "Besides," he added, "I hope to have an early opportunity to expound in detail the despicable immorality of this system, and to expose mercilessly the economist's hypocrisy which here appears in all its brazenness." The allusion was to the book he was planning on the political and economic state of England, with a chapter or two on the working class. He published two articles on that subject in yet another German émigré magazine in the summer of 1844. That same summer, returning from England, Engels stopped off in Paris to meet the exiled revolutionaries assembled there, including Karl Marx. That visit marked the beginning of a lifelong friendship and collaboration between the two men. It may also have been then, perhaps on the advice of Marx, that Engels decided to devote the whole of his forthcoming book to the English working class.

Returning to his home in Barmen in the Rhineland, Engels immersed himself in the books and newspapers he had brought with him from England—not, however, to the exclusion of political activities. He joined Hess in founding a new radical periodical, helped organize a working-class society, addressed two public meetings in which he explained why the continued expansion and impoverishment of the proletariat would lead to a social revolution "in a very short time," continued to write for the *New Moral World* and various German radical publications, and contributed his small part to *The Holy Family* (Marx's polemic against the Bauers and Stirner)—all this during the six or seven months in which he also wrote the 300-odd-page *Condition of the Working Class in England.* It was a prodigious accomplishment, testifying to his extraordinary intellectual vitality and his total political commitment.

Even if one were unaware of the ideological background of *The Condition of the Working Class in England,* one could not fail to see in it a good deal more than a descriptive account of that "condition." At the very least it included an analysis of the system responsible for that condition, a moral critique of both the condition and the system, and a prognosis of the development of the system and its eventual destruction by those who suffered so grievously under it. In a letter to Marx written soon after he started work on the book, Engels explained that he was drawing up a "bill of indictment" against the English bourgeoisie and, by the same token, against the German bourgeoisie.

> I shall present the English with a fine bill of indictment. I accuse the English bourgeoisie before the entire world of murder, robbery and all sorts of other crimes on a mass scale, and am writing an English preface which I shall have printed separately and shall send to the English party leaders, literary men and Members of Parliament. Those fellows will have to remember me. Moreover, it is a matter of course that while I hit the bay I also mean to strike the donkey, namely the German bourgeoisie, of whom I say clearly enough that it is just as bad as the English, only not so courageous, consistent and adept in sweat-shop methods.

In the book itself Engels was entirely candid about his purpose, at least in respect to the English. In the preface addressed to "the Working Classes of Great Britain," he identified himself with the workers in the struggle against their "oppressors," and throughout the book he spoke of the middle classes as "murderers," the social order as a systematic form of "social murder," and the class struggle as a form of "social war."

The bill of indictment consisted of descriptions, episodes, and statistics culled from parliamentary reports, newspapers, books, and pamphlets, supplemented by Engels's own observations and judgments. The effect was a picture of desperate, hopeless misery: workers dying of starvation or so malnourished and enfeebled as to be on the verge of death, fifty thousand homeless people wandering the streets of London and millions more crowded into the meanest, foulest slums, all of them clothed in rags, exposed to the damp and cold, their bodies sickly, crippled, stunted, deformed. The moral state of these unfortunates was no less appalling, as they drowned their sorrows in drink, vented their rage in crime and violence, and lost themselves in the only indulgence left to them, sexual licentiousness. As misery and vice was the refrain of Malthus's work, so degradation and demoralization was the refrain of Engels's.

Occasionally, Engels raised the issue that has exercised his critics: Was the condition he described the extreme or the average condition of the working class? What part of the working class was in that state of destitution, degradation, and demoralization? In the course of one chapter, caustically entitled "The Great Towns," he estimated that one-tenth of the workers were utterly degraded, that 12 percent lived in the foulest cellars, and that "the average is much nearer the worst cases than the best"—the "worst" having just been described as "bitter want, reaching even homelessness and death by starvation." Potentially every worker was in that worst condition. "Every proletarian, everyone, without exception, is exposed to a similar fate without any fault of his own and in spite of every possible effort."

It could be said that Engels's portrait was so stark because the reality itself was stark. He had arrived in Manchester, the worst of all industrial towns—"the shock city of the age," as Asa Briggs has aptly called it—at the worst of all times, in the midst of the most severe economic depression in half a century. Even then, however, as he himself reported in the first of his newspaper articles from Manchester, less than 10 percent of the workers were unemployed, and those who were employed could afford a quantity and quality of meat and drink that would have been the envy of the German or French worker. Engels did not reproduce that passage, or anything like it, in his book, but he could have done so without any logical inconsistency (although it would have detracted from the prevailing impression of gloom). For the point was not so much the actual, existential condition of the worker as his essential and potential condition, the condition that was his simply by virtue of his being a "proletarian," a member of the propertyless class. It was this state of propertylessness that doomed the worker to the "worst" condition even if, for the moment, he seemed to be in a "better" or "best" condition. In this sense the question of percentages and averages was irrelevant, since it was the extreme, not the average, that was the essential condition of the whole of the working class.

In the same sense, every aspect of the worker's being, his moral and intellectual as much as his economic and physical condition, was in that extreme state. One might have expected a bourgeois reformer like Edwin Chadwick to speak of the working class as a "race" so thoroughly degraded and demoralized that it "must really have reached the lowest stage of humanity," or to describe dwellings in which "only a physically degenerate race, robbed of all humanity degraded, reduced morally and intellectually to bestiality could feel comfortable and at home." It was, in fact, from Chadwick and his kind—J. P. Kay (later Kay-Shuttleworth), Peter Gaskell, Nassau Senior, and other "bourgeois" reformers, critics, and investigators—that Engels took his material. He went further than they did, however, because his purpose was different. They wanted to arouse the consciousness and conscience (and perhaps the fears as well) of the middle classes in order to promote specific reforms. Engels wanted to portray the workers in that condition of destitution and degradation which was a prelude not to reform but to revolution, a revolution to restore the humanity that the present system denied to them.

There was no hidden agenda here, no secret strategy. Engels was quite explicit about the revolutionary implications of his account. Again and again he interrupted his description of the vile state of the workers to hold out the promise of redemption, the redemption that would come, not as the result of rebellion, but in the very act of rebellion. The impulse to rebel was the saving grace, the one glimmer of humanity in an otherwise dehumanized race.

> There is, therefore, no cause for surprise if the workers, treated as brutes, actually become such; or if they can

> maintain their consciousness of manhood only by cherishing the most glowing hatred, the most unbroken inward rebellion against the bourgeoisie in power. They are men so long only as they burn with wrath against the reigning class. They become brutes the moment they bend in patience under the yoke, and merely strive to make life endurable while abandoning the effort to break the yoke.
> . . . How can such a sentence [to the division of labor] help degrading a human being to the level of a brute? Once more the worker must choose, must either surrender himself to his fate, become a "good" workman, heed "faithfully" the interest of the bourgeoisie, in which case he most certainly becomes a brute, or else he must rebel, fight for his manhood to the last, and this he can only do in the fight against the bourgeoisie.

To every point the same message came through: the condition of brutality was the precondition for change, the only kind of change that was of any consequence—revolution. "The Great Towns" opened with a memorable description of hordes of people crowded together, streaming past one another, yet brutally indifferent to and entirely separated from one another. It was an altogether repulsive sight, repugnant to human nature itself. "This isolation of the individual, this narrow self-seeking, is the fundamental principle of our society elsewhere, [and] it is nowhere so shamelessly barefaced, so self-conscious as just there in the crowding of the great city." The "dissolution of mankind into nomads" reminded Engels of the recent book by Max Stirner, the most anarchistic of the Young Hegelians, who described all of society and capitalist society preeminently as a "war of each against all." In this atomistic, ferociously competitive world, everyone looked upon everyone else as an object to be used and exploited, and the capitalists, being the strongest, were able to seize everything for themselves, leaving the mass of the poor with the barest means of existence. But these same cities, the breeding places of misery and vice, were also—and here Engels parted from Stirner—the "birthplaces of the labor movements." Were it not for the cities, the workers, isolated and exploited as individuals, would have been slower in coming to a consciousness of their oppression, of their class interests and class identity. Thus the cities aggravated the social problem and, by aggravating it, helped solve it; they were the disease and the remedy. "The great cities have transformed the disease of the social body, which appears in chronic form in the country into an acute one, and so made manifest its real nature and the means of curing it."

Industrialism had the same dual aspect. It stupefied the worker by limiting him to a single process in the division of labor, enslaved him by the tyrannical discipline of the factory, dehumanized him by reducing him to a machine, a "chattel" to be used and discarded as his employer saw fit—but it was also the means of his salvation. The most highly industrialized part of the economy produced the most intelligent and energetic workers who were in the forefront of the labor movement and of the class struggle. Even those workers who were not so intelligent, whose "mental state" was as enfeebled as their physical condition, who were more ignorant than the working classes of Spain and Italy—even they, by sheer force of "necessity," came to know their own interests and to know them to be implacably opposed to the bourgeoisie. Similarly the immigration from Ireland, which had the immediate effect of degrading and barbarizing the English workers, also "deepened the chasm between workers and bourgeoisie, and hastened the approaching crisis."

In each case the disease contained within itself its own antidote. Since the antidote matured only as the disease did, the disease had to run its course before the antidote became effective. As in a grave sickness where the fate of the patient was determined by the final, violent crisis, so the social disease had to await its crisis. The only difference was that the English nation, unlike an individual patient, could not die. "And as the English nation cannot succumb under the final crisis, but must go forth from it, born again, rejuvenated, we can but rejoice over everything which accelerates the course of the disease." (This was later to be known as the "worse is better" principle, the principle that makes reactionaries preferable to reformers—"reformists," as Marxists called them—and, in one famous instance, Nazis preferable to Social Democrats.)

When Engels authorized the translation and publication of *The Condition of the Working Class in England* in 1887, in the midst of another economic crisis, he believed the book to be as relevant and urgent as ever. The timing of the revolution may have been inexplicably delayed, but the revolution itself was still on the agenda of history. From the perspective of "mature Marxism," Engels's work was a case study of capitalism *in extremis,* the existential confirmation of the scenario outlined in the *Communist Manifesto* and elaborated in *Capital.*

To be sure, there were deviations, some traces of "German philosophy," which gave it the "stamp of his youth." Engels's own example of that vestigial idealistic philosophy was the passage: "Communism is a question of humanity and not of the workers alone. . . . Communism stands above the strife between bourgeoisie and proletariat." He might also have cited the image of the city as the "dissolution of mankind"; or the portrait of the worker deprived of his "humanity" and "manhood," forced to rebel in order to assert himself as a "human being"; or the Feuerbachian "generic" or "species" man in the preface addressed to the "Working Classes of Great Britain":

> I found you to be more than mere *Englishmen,* members of a single isolated nation, I found you to be *Men,* members of the great and universal family of Mankind, who know their interest and that of all the human race to be the same. And as such, as members of this Family of "One and Indivisible" Mankind, as Human Beings in the most emphatical meaning of the word, as such I, and many others on the Continent, hail your progress in every direction and wish you speedy success.

Apart from these occasional idealistic effusions, as he later thought them, and some unfortunate predictions, Engels had good reason to be pleased with the *Condition,* for it gave every appearance of corroborating the *Manifesto* both in its general thesis and in its details. The pauperization of the English working class appeared here, as in the *Manifesto,* as the necessary precondition for the historical process that would inevitably lead to revolution. And in the *Condition,* again as in the *Manifesto,* material impoverishment was accompanied by a moral degradation that ensured the total alienation of the working class. Although the word "alienation" did not appear in the *Condition* (or for that matter in the *Manifesto,* except to deride the "True Socialists" who still talked of the "alienation of humanity"), it was a thoroughly alienated working class Engels described, a class alienated from "generic" humanity as well as from bourgeois society and culture.

Like the proletariat in the *Manifesto,* which was utterly divorced from bourgeois family relations, national character, law, morality and religion, the English working class in the *Condition* was a "race wholly apart" in just these respects. "The workers speak other dialects, have other thoughts and ideals, other customs and moral principles, a different religion and other politics than those of the bourgeoisie." In some ways the workers were more humane than the bourgeoisie, friendlier, more generous, less greedy, less bigoted. But it was their less agreeable traits Engels dwelt on at much greater length and in starker detail: drunkenness, brutality, licentiousness, and criminality. To be sure, there was an explanation for each of these. They drank themselves into a state of bestiality and engaged in hideous sexual practices because these were the only pleasures they had. They stole and committed crimes because they were starving and desperate. They were irreligious for the same reason that they were illiterate, because the bourgeoisie totally ignored their education save for the futile attempt to inculcate the incomprehensible dogmas of conventional religion. Their families were destroyed by the factories and by filthy, crowded homes devoid of any domestic comfort. Where the family was not "wholly dissolved," it was "turned upside down," with the wife working and the unemployed husband at home, a situation that "unsexes the man and takes from the woman all womanliness." In addition to the sexual promiscuity among the workers themselves, the women were at the mercy of their employers, who enjoyed the traditional privilege of the master over the slave, the *jus primae noctis*—except that the employer could choose to exercise that right at any time.

The working class and the bourgeoisie were thus "two radically dissimilar nations, as unlike as difference of race could make them." They were different as much by will as by circumstance. The rejection by the working class of bourgeois morality and culture was an expression of defiance, a conscious or unconscious act of rebellion. Crime was a form of "social war," a war that the bourgeoisie had been waging against the proletariat and that the proletariat was now turning against their exploiters. Stealing was more than a means of staving off hunger, it was a "primitive form of protest," a denial of the "sacredness of property," an assertion by the worker of "contempt for the existing social order" and of opposition to the "whole conditions of his life." The "surplus population" that roamed the streets, begging, stealing, and murdering, was engaged in the same social war: "He among the 'surplus' who has courage and passion enough openly to resist society to reply with declared war upon the bourgeoisie to the disguised war which the bourgeoisie wages against him, goes forth to rob, plunder, murder, and burn!" These violations of the law were the evidence of a society "already in a state of visible dissolution," the prelude to that "universal outburst" whose symptoms were ordinary crimes. Atheism was another form of that social war. Echoing Marx's essay "On the Jewish Question" published the previous year, Engels equated religion with the worship of money. "Money is the god of this world; the bourgeois takes the proletarian's money from him and so makes a practical atheist of him." That atheism announced to the world that the proletariat no longer respected the "sacredness and power of the earthly God" and was prepared to "disregard all social order."

If the working class and bourgeoisie were "radically dissimilar," so were the modern working class and the preindustrial workers. Engels's account of the latter recalls the ambiguous passage in the *Manifesto* about the "feudal, patriarchal, idyllic relations" that had been "pitilessly torn asunder," leaving nothing but "naked self-interest" and "callous 'cash-payment.' " The *Condition* enlarged upon that idyllic preindustrial state.

> So the workers vegetated throughout a passably comfortable existence, leading a righteous and peaceful life in all piety and probity; and their material position was far better than that of their successors. They did not need to overwork; they did no more than they chose to do, and yet earned what they needed. They had leisure for healthful work in garden or field, work which, in itself, was recreation for them, and they could take part besides in the recreations and games of their neighbours, and all these games—bowling, cricket, football, etc., contributed to their physical health and vigour. They were, for the most part, strong, well-built people, in whose physique little or no difference from that of their peasant neighbours was discoverable. Their children grew up in the fresh country air, and, if they could help their parents at work, it was only occasionally; while of eight or twelve hours of work for them there was no question.

Engels continued in this vein, rhapsodizing about those "respectable" workers who had a "stake in the country," who were good husbands and fathers, drank no more than was good for them, mingled happily with the yeomanry and had a comfortable "patriarchal relation" with their "natural superior," the squire. Their children enjoyed the same natural relationship with their fathers; working at home, and raised in "obedience and the fear of God," they grew up in "idyllic simplicity and intimacy with their playmates." (This moral regimen did not preclude the practice of premarital intercourse, but since it was invariably followed by marriage, that "made everything good.")

The idyll went on for several hundred words before the fatal flaw emerged. Just as in the *Manifesto* where the "feudal, patriarchal, idyllic relations" were shortly exposed as the "idiocy of rural life," so in the *Condition* that comfortable, respectable, patriarchal existence suddenly appeared, in mid-paragraph, to be a life "not worthy of human beings." Spared the violent fluctuations of the industrial cycle, the workers were also spared all mental and political activity. "Comfortable in their silent vegetation," they were intellectually dead, aware only of their petty, private concerns, and ignorant of the "mighty movement which, beyond their horizons, was sweeping through mankind." In truth, they were not human beings; they were merely "toiling machines in the service of the few aristocrats who had guided history down to that time." It was only when the industrial revolution roused them out of that happy life, making them "machines pure and simple," that they were forced to "think and demand a position worthy of men," and thus were drawn into the "whirl of history."

This portrait of the happy, healthy, moral, if mentally torpid preindustrial worker has been criticized by some historians as the familiar myth of the Golden Age, and defended by others on the ground that that age was indeed golden compared with that which followed. The controversy, however important in its own terms, is largely irrelevant to Engels. For here, even more than in the rest of his book, he was concerned not so much with the actual condition of the preindustrial workers as with their role in his historical schema; and in that schema these workers had no role. If Engels's account of them seems mythical and unhistorical, it is because they themselves were unhistorical, which is to say prehistorical—prehistorical from the perspective of the revolution that would bring them on the stage of history and make them the leading actors in history, the agents of the "dissolution" of society and the "transformation" of mankind.

It is no accident that the *Condition* was one of the first occasions when the phrase "industrial revolution" was used, not once but repeatedly, and with the full force of a revolutionary event. The industrial revolution was for Engels the decisive "historical moment," the beginning of the expansion and concentration of the means of production which led to contradictions and crises. It was also then that the working class started its descent into pauperism and degradation which left it no choice but to rebel. The preindustrial workers, by contrast, were not "ripe for revolution" because the economy was not ripe for revolution. Spared the misery that was a precondition of revolution, they were healthy, happy, and comfortable; spared the self-consciousness that would have made them rebellious, they were apathetic and torpid. They had precisely the qualities required of them in a drama in which their only role was to exist and survive. Like a nation without a history, they were happy—and boring.

In the preface to the German edition of his book, Engels explained that a "knowledge of proletarian conditions" was necessary to provide a "solid ground for socialist theories," and that only in England did these conditions exist "in their classical form and in their perfection." *The Condition of the Working Class in England* was meant to give that solid, empirical "ground" for Marxist theory. All the essential ingredients were there: the preindustrial workers in a comfortable, unconscious, unrevolutionary state; the modern proletariat pauperized and degraded, reduced to a "slavery" worse than the serfdom of old, totally alienated from bourgeois morality and culture; the "lower middle class" impoverished and forced down into the ranks of the proletariat; society divided into two irreconcilable classes; the bourgeoisie, the "ruling class," exercising the "power of the State"; the increasing concentration of industry, wealth, property, and population; the increasing intensity of economic crises, misery, and "social war"; and finally the "violent revolution, which cannot fail to take place." Although no one of these propositions was novel in England at the time, the totality was. And it was the totality that added up to an ideology significantly different from the prevalent modes of English radicalism and significantly similar to that of the *Communist Manifesto.*

A distinctive and crucial part of this ideology was its vocabulary—"proletariat" most notably. The word was not invented by Marx or Engels. Derived from the Latin *proles* (offspring), it originally referred to the lowest class of Roman citizen who served the state only by producing children. In one variation or another (as an adjective, or in the French form of *prolétaires*), it was used in England from at least the seventeenth century to describe either the ancient populace or the contemporary "rabble." In its modern meaning, applied to the working classes as a whole, it began to appear in Germany in the mid-1830s and was popularized in 1840 by Pierre Joseph Proudhon's *Qu'est-ce que la propriété?* and in 1842 by Lorenz von Stein's *Der Sozialismus und Communismus des heutigen Frankreichs.* (Unlike Proudhon, Stein was a conservative who was as wary of the proletariat as of socialism or communism.) By the time Engels wrote the *Condition,* "proletariat" was part of the vocabulary of French and German Socialists—but not of English radicals.

Engels himself was fully aware of the alien connotation of "proletariat." The original preface to the *Condition,* written in English and intended for distribution to members of parliament and English literary men, was couched in the familiar English vocabulary. It was entitled "To the Working Classes of Great Britain," its salutation read "Working Men!" and the text itself referred to "working men." The German preface, however, which followed the English one, started by speaking of the condition of the "working class," went on in the next sentence to "proletarian conditions," and in the following paragraph to the "English proletariat"—all on the first page—and concluded with some comments on terminology.

> I have used the word *Mittelklasse* all along in the sense of the English word *middle-class* (or *middle-classes,* as is said almost always). . . . Similarly, I have continually used the expressions working men (*Arbeiter*) and proletarians, working class, propertyless class and proletariat as equivalents.

The opening words of the book established the significance of the term. "The history of the proletariat in England," Engels explained, dated from the second half of the eighteenth century with the invention of the steam engine and textile machinery. These inventions gave rise to an "industrial revolution, a revolution which altered the whole civil society." England was the "classic soil" of this revolution and, therefore, "the classic land of its chief product also, the proletariat." The preindustrial worker, the handweaver working at home, had been "no proletarian." With the appearance of the spinning jenny the class of farm weavers merged with the new class of weavers who lived entirely upon wages, had no property and so became "working men, proletarians." At the same time, the propertyless, wage-earning agricultural laborers became an "agricultural proletariat." The proletariat was fully developed only in England because only there were both industry and agriculture transformed by the industrial revolution. "The industrial revolution is of the same importance for England as the political revolution for France, and the philosophical revolution for Germany." It was decisive for the development of the economy and even more for the development of the proletariat. "The mightiest result of this industrial transformation is the English proletariat."

Engels prided himself on the fact that his was the first book to deal with "*all* the workers." And so it did, all workers being subsumed under the category of the proletariat. The "industrial proletariat," the "mining proletariat," and the "agricultural proletariat" shared the crucial characteristic of being propertyless. By the same token, the propertied classes—the middle class and landed aristocracy—belonged to the single class of the "bourgeoisie": "In speaking of the bourgeoisie I include the so-called aristocracy."

This condition of propertylessness proletarianized the workers and then, by the logic of capitalist development, pauperized them. Contemporaries (and historians) might object that not all workers were impoverished, that the navvy or artisan was in a far better state than the agricultural laborer, and the factory worker better off than the handloom weaver. Engels recognized these differences but regarded them as ultimately inconsequential. If some workers were not actually currently impoverished, they were so essentially and potentially. They were a single class characterized by a single condition; the propertylessness that defined them as the proletariat pauperized them and revolutionized them. That single "class" and "condition" were reflected in the singular title. It was probably out of deference to English usage that Engels chose to call his book *The Condition of the Working Class* rather than *The Condition of the Proletariat.* But he could not have adopted the more familiar "working classes," "poor," or "people" without doing violence to his thesis.

The idea of poverty that emerged from the book was implicit in the word "proletariat." It was total, unrelieved poverty, a poverty that extended itself to every realm of life—cultural, moral, and intellectual as much as material—a poverty that created a class so different as to constitute a different "race." The poverty of the proletariat was quantitatively different from the poverty of the old poor: the preindustrial poor were less impoverished, less hardworking, less miserable. And it was qualitatively different, creating a new consciousness, a new identity and a new historical role. This is what impressed Lenin when he read the *Condition:* "Engels was the *first* to say that the proletariat is *not only* a suffering class; that it is, in fact, the disgraceful economic condition of the proletariat that drives it irresistibly forward and compels it to fight for its ultimate emancipation. And the fighting proletariat *will help itself.*"

Engels was not, in fact, the first to say that. Stein made it the crucial difference between the "proletariat" and the "poor." There had always been poor, he said. What was new and dangerous, was the proletariat: "dangerous in respect of its numbers and its often tested courage; dangerous in respect of its consciousness of unity; dangerous in respect of its feeling that only through revolution can its aims be reached, its plans accomplished." This dangerousness, which made the proletariat so perilous to Stein, was a source of pride and hope to the Young Hegelians. When they distinguished between the proletariat and the poor, it was precisely the size and courage of the new class, its unity, self-consciousness, and above all, revolutionary character that made it superior to the old poor, that made it a historical class endowed with the highest historical mission.

In his "Introduction to the Critique of Hegel's *Philosophy of Right,*" published early in 1844, Marx described the proletariat (in a passage now regarded as the classic expression of Feuerbachian "humanism") as "a class of civil society which is not a class of civil society, an estate which is the dissolution of all estates, a sphere which has a universal character by its universal suffering." Less well known but equally notable was the next paragraph in which the "artificially *impoverished*" proletariat was contrasted to the "*naturally arising* poor"; the latter, impoverished by nature and natural circumstances, would be gradually absorbed into the larger class that was impoverished by the artificial institution of private property. In *The Holy Family,* the following year, the proletariat retained some of that generic, humanistic character—"the abstraction of all humanity"—while acquiring a more historical, deterministic character, for it was driven to revolt against the inhuman conditions of its life by "absolutely imperative *need*—the practical expression of necessity," the necessity to abolish private property in order to "abolish" itself. "It is not a question of what this or that proletarian, or even the whole proletariat, at the moment *regards* as its aim. It is a question of what the *proletariat* is, and what, in accordance with this *being,* it will historically be compelled to do." By 1847 Marx was attacking Proudhon, who had been one of the first to popularize the idea of the proletariat as well as the idea of property as "theft," for not appreciating the revolutionary nature of poverty, for seeing "in poverty nothing but poverty, without seeing in it the revolutionary subversive side, which will overthrow the old society." At the same time Engels, in the credo he drew up for the Communist League (parts of which were incorporated in the *Communist Manifesto*), explained the difference between the old poor and the new proletariat.

> Poor folk and working classes have always existed. The working classes have also for the most part been poor. But such poor, such workers as are living under conditions indicated above, hence proletarians, have not always existed, any more than free and unbridled competition has always existed.

It was this new idea of poverty that pervaded the *Condition*—a poverty qualitatively different from the old, just as the proletariat was qualitatively different from the poor. In his commentary on Engels's book, Steven Marcus has suggested a psychoanalytic distinction between poor, on the one hand, and "working class" or "proletariat," on the other. Inspired by Erik Erikson's observation that young Gandhi's interest in "the poor" rather than in "labor" was a symptom of what Gandhi himself had called his "mother complex," Marcus applied this distinction to Engels.

> As a boy, he [Engels] had often given his little savings to "the poor." As a young man, he has now decided in more ways than one actively to throw his lot in with labor, with the working class or proletariat. The difference between an identification with "the poor" and an identification with the "working class" represents, among many other things, the measure in which an idealistic and rebellious young man could appreciate for himself a traditional historical masculine identity and maintain that identity even in the role of insurrection against the world in which it was grounded.

Whatever credibility one assigns to this feminine–masculine dichotomy, it is interesting that "poor" should be taken to connote an attitude of passivity or acquiescence, and "working class" or "proletariat" an attitude of rebelliousness. This much, at least, is consistent with the Marxist interpretation.

What was unique about the *Condition,* distinguishing it from everything else Marx and Engels wrote at this time or later, was the fact that here the proletariat was something more than a historical abstraction, a logical category subsumed under a larger historical schema, a "world-historical" class furthering the "world-historical" movement of communism. Instead of the usual abstract, universal proletariat, Engels described a specifically English proletariat, located in real towns and villages, living in real cottages and cellars, working at real jobs, participating in real events, suffering real hardships, and indulging in real vices. All this was attested to by real newspapers, books, parliamentary reports, and personal observations. Contemporaries may not have known Engels's proletariat under that name and might have disputed his descriptions, generalizations, and predictions. But they would have recognized the names of the towns and villages, the views of back streets and houses, the scenes of riots and demonstrations, the titles of newspapers and royal commissions, the identities of politicians and writers. And they would have responded (as readers still respond) to the emotive force of the book, the dramatic evocation of misery and the powerful sense of outrage. Almost twenty years later, rereading the *Condition* in preparation for the writing of *Capital,* Marx confessed to Engels that it made him feel his advancing years.

> How freshly and passionately, with what bold anticipations and no learned and scientific doubts, the thing is still dealt with here! And the very illusion that the result itself will leap into the daylight of history tomorrow or the day after gives the whole thing a warmth and jovial humour—compared to which the later "gray in gray" makes a damned unpleasant contrast.

That passion and boldness, the illusion that his predictions would "leap into the daylight of history tomorrow or the day after," came in no small part from the powerful ideology Engels imposed on the actuality of history. His English proletariat was the "world-historical" proletariat writ small, a miniature version of the universal phenomenon. If the English working classes never carried out Engels's prediction of revolution, it was for the same reason that they resisted the label "proletariat"—resisted in fact the whole of the historical schema that would have made them what Lenin was pleased to call a "fighting proletariat."

Samuel Smiles: The Gospel of Self-Help

Victorian Britain's prophet of honest toil was far from being the crudely complacent reactionary, as he has sometimes been caricatured.

Asa Briggs

Asa Briggs is Provost of Worcester College, Oxford, and author of The BBC, The First Fifty Years *(Oxford University Press, 1985).*

Self-help was one of the favourite mid-Victorian virtues. Relying on yourself was preferred morally—and economically—to depending on others. It was an expression of character even when it did not ensure—even, indeed, when it did not offer—a means of success. It also had social implications of a general kind. The progressive development of society ultimately depended, it was argued, not on collective action or on parliamentary legislation but on the prevalence of practices of self-help.

All these points were made succinctly and eloquently, but none of them originally or exclusively, by Samuel Smiles whose *Self-Help* appeared in one of the golden years of mid-Victorian Britain, 1859, the year that also saw the publication of John Stuart Mill's *Essay on Liberty* and Charles Darwin's *The Origin of Species.* Mill examined the attractions of individuality as well as the restraints on individualism: Darwin explored struggle as well as evolution, or rather explained evolution in terms of struggle. Neither thinker escaped attack. Smiles by contrast was not looking for argument and counter-argument. He believed that he was expounding not something that was new or controversial but something that was old and profoundly true, a gospel, not a thesis; and that behind that gospel was a still more basic gospel, the gospel of work.

Smiles did not claim that all his contemporaries practised self-help. He rather extolled the virtues of self-help as part of an 'old fashioned' but 'wholesome' lesson in morality. It was more 'natural,' he admitted, to be 'prodigal' than to be thrifty, more easy to be dependent than independent. What he was saying had been said by the wisest of men before him: it reflected 'experience, example and foresight'. 'Heaven helps them who help themselves.'

As far as individuals were concerned, Smiles was anxious to insist on the value of perseverance, a favourite word of one of his heroes, George Stephenson. 'Nothing that is of real worth,' he insisted, 'can be achieved without courageous working. Man owes his growth chiefly to that active striving of the will, that encounter with difficulty, which he calls effort; and it is astonishing to find how often results apparently impracticable are then made possible.' As far as society was concerned, 'national progress was the sum of individual industry, energy and uprightness' as 'national decay' was of 'individual idleness, selfishness and vice. What we are accustomed to decry as great social evils will, for the most part, be found to be but the outgrowth of man's perverted life.' 'The spirit of self-help is the root of all genuine growth in the individual; and exhibited in the lives of many, it constitutes the true source of national vigour and strength. Help from without is often enfeebling in its effects, but help from within invariably invigorates. Whatever is done for men and classes to a certain extent takes away the stimulus and necessity of doing for themselves; and where men are subjected to over-guidance and over-government, the inevitable tendency is to render them comparatively helpless.'

Smiles adopted the phrase *Self-Help,* which proved to be very difficult to translate into other languages, from a lecture by the American reformer and prophet, R. W. Emerson, delivered in 1841; and while Smiles' own book first appeared in 1859, its contents had first been delivered by Smiles in lectures to Leeds working men fourteen years before—one year, indeed, before the passing of the repeal of the corn laws. While the book belonged unmistakably to mid-Victorian Britain, the message, therefore, was an early-Victorian transatlantic message, delivered in years not of relative social harmony in Britain but of social conflict. The point is of crucial importance in any discussion of Victorian values in the 1980s. Smiles emerged not from a conservative but from a radical background, the background of Chartism, and the Anti-Corn Law League. He was not encouraging Leeds working men to be quiescent or deferential but to be active and informed. Richard Cobden was one of his heroes. Another was the radical Joseph Hume, and both figured prominently in *Self-Help.* Smiles knew them both personally, and in a letter to Cobden in 1841 he had described the extension of the suffrage as 'the key to all great changes, whose object is to elevate the condition of the masses.'

Smiles' direct political involvement was limited, however, after the 1840s, and he settled down during the next decade to the more complacent view, which he expressed in 1852, that 'as men grow older and wiser they find a little of good in everything . . . they begin to find out that truth and patriotism are not confined to any particular cliques or parties or factions.' Indeed, he moved well to the right of Cobden, and by the late-Victorian years, when new political causes, radical or socialist of which he disapproved were being canvassed, what he had had to say had come to sound 'conservative', as it has done to late-twentieth-century defenders of 'Victorian values'.

Yet there is a difference in the response. Whereas late-Victorian rebels attacked Smiles for his cheerful economics, claiming—unfairly—that he was interested only in individual advancement reflected in material success, late-twentieth-century defenders have praised him primarily for his hard economic realism. In particular, Sir Keith Joseph, himself writing from a Leeds vantage point, in the introduction to a new and abridged edition of *Self-Help* (1986), has set out to rehabilitate Smilesian trust in the *entrepreneur* and 'the virtues that make him what he is'. While describing *Self-Help* as 'deeply expressive of the spirit of its own times', he does not note that these were changing times and that modes of economic organisation and responses to 'entrepreneurship' were very different by 1904, the year when Smiles died, from what they had been when *Self-Help* was published.

Smiles was born not in Leeds but in Haddington, a few miles east of Edinburgh, seven years before the birth of Queen Victoria, and he took a medical degree from Edinburgh University. His first book was called *Physical Education: or the Nurture and Management of Children,* and was published in 1838, the year he moved to Leeds. There is an evident Scottish strain in his writing before and after, although curiously it is less apparent in *Physical Education* than in some of his other work. It was, after all, Robert Bruce who had had attributed to him the motto 'if at first you don't succeed, try, try, try again', and Calvin who had provided Scotsmen with a religion which made the most of austerity and vocation.

In more modern times Thomas Carlyle, born seventeen years before Smiles, had described life as 'a scene of toil, of effort, of appointed work', and had extolled 'the man who works' in the warmest language: 'welcome, thou art ours; our care shall be of thee'. The mill-owner economist, W. R. Greg, writing one year after the publication of *Self-Help,* praised Carlyle above all others for 'preaching

Upward mobility — this 1861 cartoon shows a 'Lancashire working-man living rent free in his own home', the fruits of diligence and temperance.

upon the duty and dignity of work, with an eloquence which has often made the idle shake off their idleness and the frivolous feel ashamed of their frivolity. He has proclaimed, in tones that have stirred many hearts, that in toil, however humble, if honest and hearty, lies our true worth and felicity here below'.

Smiles himself took as one of his examples of perseverance in *Self-Help* Carlyle's prodigious effort to rewrite the first volume of his *French Revolution* after a maid had used the manuscript to light the kitchen and parlour fires: 'he had no draft, and was compelled to rake up from his memory facts, ideas and expressions, which had long been dismissed'. No one could have appreciated this experience more than Smiles who was a prodigious writer who followed up *Self-Help* with many volumes, including three related works *Character* (1871), *Thrift* (1875) and *Duty* (1880). He also produced a history of his publisher, John Murray and 'his friends' in 1891.

Self-Help was full of anecdotes. Essentially it was a case-book drawing its material, including some of its most apposite quotations, from personal biographies. 'Our great forefathers still live among us in the records of our lives', he claimed, again very much as Carlyle had always claimed. 'They still sit by us at table, and hold us by the hand'. There was more than a touch of Victorian hero worship here. Yet Smiles always broadened the range to include the humble as well as the great, extending the range as far as he possibly could in his *Life and Labour* (1887). Biographies offered demonstrations of 'what men can be, and what they can do' whatever their station. 'A book containing the life of a true man is full of precious seed. It is still a living voice'. And much as he made his own living out of books, Smiles maintained that living examples were far more potent as influences than examples on paper. His book *Thrift* took as its motto a phrase from Carlyle 'Not what I have, but what I do is my kingdom'. He might have chosen instead Emerson's motto, 'The importance of man as man . . . is the highest truth'.

Smiles himself was a lively phrasemaker, interlacing his anecdotes, which by themselves were memorable and well set out, with short phrases that linger in the mind—'he who never made a mistake never made a discovery'; 'the tortoise in the right road will beat a racer in the wrong'; 'the nation comes from the nursery'. Such phrases bind together the whole text of *Self-Help* which is far more readable—as it is pertinent—today than the verse of Martin Tupper's *Proverbial Philosophy* (1838), the popularity of which (on both sides of the Atlantic) reached its peak during the 1850s. It is far more readable too than most of the many other Victorian books designed to inspire young men like the anonymous *Success in Life* (1852), the original idea of which had been suggested by 'an American publication', perhaps John Todd's *Hints Addressed to the Young Men of the United States* (1845), which included one chapter on 'industry and economy' and another on 'self-government and the heart'. Smiles himself acknowledged a debt to G. L. Craik's *Pursuit of Knowledge under Difficulties* (1831), published by Charles Knight who specialised in diffusing knowledge. Indeed, he had been so inspired by it, Smiles wrote, that he learnt some of its key passages by heart.

The transatlantic element in the self-help literature demands a study of differences as well as of influences. There were to be many American 'success' books aiming, as Smiles aimed, at large audiences, some of the first of which were influenced, as Smiles was, by the cult of phrenology. The later line of descent can be traced through books, which move from phrenology to popular psychology, like J. C. Ransom's *The Successful Man in his Manifold Relations with Life* (1887), A. E. Lyon's *The Self-Starter* (1924), Dale Carnegie's *How to Win Friends and Influence People* (1936), C. E. Poppleston's *Every Man a Winner* (1936) and Norman Vincent Peale's *The Power of Positive Thinking* (1955). Yet many of these authors are slick where Smiles was sturdy, and consoling where he was inspiring. Few would have had much sympathy either with Smiles' attack on 'smatter knowledge'. Such 'short-cuts', he explained, as learning French or Latin in 'twelve lessons' or 'without a master', were 'good for nothing'. The would-be learner was more to blame than the teacher, for he resembled 'the lady of fashion who engaged a master to teach her on condition that he did not plague her with verbs and particles'.

One American with whom Smiles has sometimes been compared is Horatio Alger (1832–99) after whom a twentieth-century American business award was named. In his own lifetime Alger's sales were spectacular, though his books took the form of stories rather than biographies or homilies. *Ragged Dick* was one title, *Upward and Onward* another. The *genre* has been well described as 'rags to riches stories', although the twentieth-century award was endowed more generally to honour a person who had 'climbed the ladder of success through toil and diligence and responsible applications of his talents to whatever tasks were his'.

There are as many myths about 'Holy Horatio' as Alger himself propounded. In fact, he allowed a far bigger place to luck (sponsors appearing by magic at the right time and place) than Smiles ever could have done, and he grossly simplified the nineteenth-century social context, particularly the city context, in which poor people found or failed to find their chances. As the late-nineteenth-century American institutional economist, Richard T. Ely, put it neatly, 'if you tell a single concrete workman on the Baltimore and Ohio Railroad that he may get to be president of the company, it is not demonstrable that you have told him what is not true, although it is within bounds to say that he is far more likely to be killed by a stroke of lightning.'

Smiles was less concerned with social 'mobility' than with mental and physical 'effort', but he, too, could be accused of living in a land of myth when he exclaimed that 'energy accomplishes more than genius'. It was a favourite mid-Victorian statement, however, which implied a contrast between what was happening then and what had happened before, and between what was happening in Britain and what was happening elsewhere. By stating it so simply Smiles actually did influence *entrepreneurs,* few of whom depended on great intellects or on deep and systematic study. William Lever, for example, fittingly born in 1851, was given a copy of *Self-Help* by his father on his sixteenth birthday, and treasured it so much that he in turn gave copies to young men he employed in his works at Port Sunlight. On the front page of one such copy the words are inscribed, 'It is impossible for me to say how much I owe to the fact that in my early youth I obtained a copy of Smiles' *Self-Help.*'

Andrew Carnegie (1835–1919) would have made no such comment. Yet his own biography not only proclaimed many Smilesian virtues, but might well have provided the basis for an Alger true story. Carnegie was born in a tiny weaver's cottage at Dunfermline, and he had his first real break in life when he became a messenger boy in a Pittsburgh telegraph office at a salary of $2.50 a week. In 1901, when he had sold his steel business for $480 million, he became the richest man in the world. 'It's a God's mercy I was born a Scotsman,' he declared in a remark that might have appealed to Smiles, 'for I do not see how I could ever have been contented to be anything else.'

The testimonials Smiles himself received from readers of his books often came from people very differently placed from Lever or Carnegie. Thus, a working man in Exeter told him that his books had 'instructed and helped him greatly' and that he wished 'every working man would read them through and through and ponder them well'; a surgeon in Blackheath declared that *Self-Help* had given 'fresh energy and hopefulness to his career'; and an emigrant to New Zealand exclaimed that self-help had 'been the cause of an entire alteration in my life, and I thank God that I read it. I am now devoted to study and hard work, and I mean to rise, both as regards my moral and intellectual life. I only wish I could see the man who wrote the book and thank him from my heart'.

There was at least one late-Victorian socialist, a man who was himself capable of inspiring 'the millions', who was deeply impressed by Smiles. Robert Blatchford, pioneer of *Merrie England,* wrote an essay on *Self-Help* after Smiles' popularity had passed its peak in which he condemned fellow-socialists who spoke mockingly of Smiles as 'an arch-Philistine' and of his books as 'the apotheosis of respectability, gigmanity and selfish grab'. Blatchford himself considered Smiles 'a most charming and honest writer', and thought *Self-Help* 'one of the most delightful and invigorating books it has been my happy fortune to meet with'. He paid tribute to Smiles' indifference to worldly titles, honour and wealth, and declared that the perusal of *Self-Help* had often forced him 'to industry, for very shame'.

The prolific rationalist writer Grant Allen, a leading spokesman of the late-Victorian revolt, took a very similar view. In a little book published in 1884 called *Biographies of Working Men* he asserted his debt to Smiles and made explicit what many of Smiles' critics then and since failed to see in Smiles' work. 'It is the object of this volume', Grant Allen began, 'to set forth the lives of working men, who through industry, perseverance and high principle, have raised themselves by their own exertions from humble beginnings. Raised themselves! Yes, but to what? Not merely, let us hope, to wealth and position, nor merely to worldly respect and high office, but to some conspicuous field of real usefulness to their fellow men.' Smiles made the same point in *Self-Help.* He would not have shared Allen's view, however, which brings out clearly the difference between the mood of the 1850s and the 1880s, that 'so long as our present social arrangements exist . . . the vast mass of men will necessarily remain workers to the last, [and] no attempt to raise individual working men above their own class into the professional or mercantile classes can ever greatly benefit the working classes as a whole'.

Nonetheless, on certain social matters, Smiles had often expressed radical views. Like many people trained as doctors he was deeply concerned with public health. As Mary Mack has pointed out, Jeremy Bentham had used medicine as a source of *analogy* for the understanding of morals and legislation, and Smiles, who as a young man met Edwin Chadwick and Dr Southwood Smith, Bentham's disciples, never believed that the environment should be left uncontrolled if it threatened the private health not only of the deprived but of people and power and influence. Smiles supported measures, too, to deal with the adulteration of food. Drawing a distinction between economic and social *laissez-faire*—and he was not alone in this—he was fully aware of the presence in mid-Victorian society not only of Adam Smith's beneficent invisible hand but of a 'terrible Nobody'. Indeed, Charles Dickens could not have written more forcefully than Smiles did:

> When typhus or cholera breaks out, they tell us that Nobody is to blame. That terrible Nobody! How much he has to answer for. More mischief is done by Nobody than by all the world besides. Nobody adulterates our food. Nobody poisons us with bad drink . . . Nobody leaves towns undrained. Nobody fills jails, penitentiaries, and convict stations. Nobody makes poachers, thieves, and drunkards. Nobody has a theory too—a dreadful theory. It is embodied in two words: laissez-faire—let alone. When people are poisoned with plaster of Paris mixed with flour, 'let alone' is the remedy . . . Let those who can, find out when they are

A 'Punch' cartoon of 1858 attacking the adulteration of food — one of the areas where Smiles decidedly did not believe in the principle of laissez-faire.

cheated: *caveat emptor.* When people live in foul dwellings, let them alone, let wretchedness do its work; do not interfere with death.

Like many other believers in economic *laissez-faire* Smiles was prepared to use the machinery of the law to provide a framework for dealing with abuses:

> Laws may do too much . . . but the abuse of a thing is no proper argument against its use in cases where its employment is urgently called for.

Throughout the whole of his life Smiles was far too active a Victorian to believe that *vis inertiae* was the same thing as *laissez-faire.* Nor was he ever tempted, as many Americans were, into the entanglements of social Darwinism. There is no reference to Herbert Spencer in his *Autobiography,* which appeared in 1905, one year after his death, and only one reference to Darwin. One of the lecturers he had heard at Edinburgh, he observed *en passant,* had already expounded very similar views 'or at all events had heralded his approach'.

There was another subject which fascinated Smiles and which he believed required very positive state intervention—national education. He had forcefully urged the need for a national system in Leeds in 1850, and he paid tribute in his *Autobiography* to W. E. Forster, MP for neighbouring Bradford, who 'by a rare union of tact, wisdom and commonsense, introduced and carried his measure [the 1870 Education Act] for the long-wished education of the English people. It embodied nearly all that the National Public School Association had so fruitlessly demanded years before'.

In pressing for nationally provided primary education in Leeds in 1850 and later, Smiles had been drawn into controversy with Edward Baines, editor of the *Leeds Mercury* and one of the most vociferous advocates, then and in 1870, of education managed by voluntary agencies and not by the state. In the course of a continuing controversy Smiles had no doubts about his own position. There were no analogies between education and free trade in commodities, he pointed out:

> The classes who the most require education are precisely those who do not seek it. It is amongst the utterly uneducated that the least demand exists. In the case of bread it is very different. The consumer wants it, knows he wants it, and will give every present consideration for it.

A further false analogy, he thought, was that between education and the freedom of the press:

> Nobody proposes to establish newspapers for everybody, supported by the government, and the want of such a Press is not felt. But let it be shown that it is of as much importance to the interests of society that everybody should have a newspaper as that everybody should be educated, and then the analogy may be admitted . . . but not till then.

It was through his philosophy of education that Smiles blurred any divisions that others might have made between 'self-help' for the individual and 'mutual self-help' for the group. He always attached even more importance to adult—or continuing—education than to school education, necessary though the latter was. The process which started at school had to be followed through: 'the highest culture is not obtained from teacher when at school or college, so much as by our ever diligent self-education when we have become men.' Such education could be fostered in groups like the group of young working men he had addressed in Leeds. There were possibilities of other forms of 'mutual self-help' also, for example friendly societies. Indeed, in *Thrift* Smiles made as much as he could of the mutual insurance principle. He could never have been accused of neglecting 'welfare', provided that it did not lead to dependence.

The Smiles message was not merely a transatlantic one. It made its way round the world, sometimes to the most unlikely places. It was translated into Dutch and French, Danish and German, Arabic and Turkish, 'several of the native languages of India' (in the words of a happy publisher) and Japanese. Victorian values, it was implied, were universal values, and there was confidence in their power to change societies. The Japanese, in particular, treasured it, and many of them continue to treasure it. 'The English work forms an octavo of moderate size,' *The Times* wrote; 'in Japanese it is expanded into a book of fifteen hundred pages.' This was no handicap to its sale, for it seemed as useful as looms and steam engines. In Latin America the Mayor of Buenos Aires is said to have compared Smiles with Rousseau and to

The doctrine of 'honest toil' could have a radical cutting-edge, as in this 1858 'Punch' cartoon of the working man 'enlightening' the 'superior' (but idle) classes.

have added 'Alexander the Great slept with his Homer, Demosthenes and Thucydides, and every notable man of the times should have at hand the social gospel'.

The universalism was restricted, however, although it went with the universalism of steam power and railways, in particular. Smiles had become secretary of a railway company in 1845 and he wrote *The Life of George Stephenson* two years before *Self-Help.* Nonetheless, he ended *Self-Help* with a chapter which introduced a word which was at least as difficult to translate from English into other languages as 'self-help' itself—the word 'gentleman'. Hippolyte Taine, convinced that the three syllables 'gentleman' summed up the whole history of English society, felt that the syllables expressed all the distinctive features of the English upper-class—a large private income, a considerable household of servants, habits of ease and luxury and good manners, but it also implied qualities of heart and character. Smiles, however, felt that:

> For Englishmen a real 'gentleman' is a truly noble man, a man worthy to command, a disinterested man of integrity, capable of exposing, even sacrificing himself for those he leads; not only a man of honour, but a conscientious man, in whom generous instincts have been confirmed by right thinking and who, acting rightly by nature, acts even more rightly from good principles.

Taine's reference to Mrs Craik's novel *John Halifax, Gentleman* (1856) is a practical illustration of the extension of the old ideal of the gentleman in a new nineteenth-century society. He might have referred instead to the last pages of *Self-Help,* where Smiles chose a 'grand old name' to express the kind of character he most wanted to see in action. Smiles drew out the 'grand old name' of the gentleman from its upper-class context. It had no connection with riches and rank, he argued, but with moral worth.

The equipoise of society rested on such ideological balances as well as on the balance of interests. From the 1870s onwards, however, both kinds of balance broke down. Britain was never again the same.

FOR FURTHER READING:

Samuel Smiles, *Self-Help* (first edition 1853, Penguin Books with an introduction by Keith Joseph, 1986); Asa Briggs, *Victorian People* (Penguin Books, 1985); Grant Allen, *Biographies of Working men* (1884); J. Burnett, editor, *Useful Toil: Autobiographies of Working people from the 1820s–1920s* (Penguin Books, 1974); T. Travers, *Samuel Smiles and the Pursuit of Success in Victorian Britain* (Canadian Historical Association, 1971); M. D. Stephens and G. W. Roderick, *Samuel Smiles and Nineteenth-Century Self-Help in Education* (Nottingham Studies, 1983).

Giuseppe Garibaldi

Infrequently does a historian acquire the reputation of synonymity with the history of the country he or she has studied, but* Denis Mack Smith *has accomplished this fact with his work and writing on Italy. This is a portrait of Italy's hero of the risorgimento in which the author deftly combines an assessment of the achievement with all the colour of Garibaldi's personal idiosyncracies.

Tough cookie; a heroic image of Garibaldi at Caprera, the remote island to which he eventually retired, having played a major role in steering Italy towards unification.

Denis Mack Smith

Giuseppe Garibaldi is one of the great men of the nineteenth century. He was a remarkably successful admiral and general. He was the very prototype of patriotic hero, but also a great internationalist, and later in life one of the pioneers of Italian socialism. Connecting all his activities was the fact that he was a liberator by profession, a man who spent his life fighting for oppressed peoples wherever he found them, however naive his analysis of oppression. Whatever he did, moreover, was done always with passionate conviction and boundless enthusiasm, and this makes his character the more striking and attractive.

Garibaldi's career was dazzlingly full of colour and incident; but behind the public personality was someone of simple good nature and amiability, a lovable and fascinating person of transparent honesty whom men would obey unhesitatingly and for whom many were glad to die. In his time he was probably the most widely known and loved figure in the world. He appealed directly to the common people, just because he himself was the embodiment of the common man: as a radical democrat and humanitarian he believed above all else in liberty and social justice. Yet, at the same time, he was quite exceptional in character, a real individual and non-conformist, whether in his religion, his clothes, his personal habits, or in the events of his extraordinary life.

This article first appeared in *History Today,* August 1991, pp. 20-26.

Garibaldi lived from 1807 to 1882. He was born in Napoleonic France, and all his life, like Cavour, spoke Italian imperfectly. By trade he followed his father and became a sea-captain. He knew the Black Sea and also the China seas. He served in ships of Italy and France, and also of the United States and Peru, and even for a time with the Bey of Tunis; and he also captained the first screw-propelled steamer to fly the Italian flag. Twice in his life he was a schoolmaster, at Constantinople and Montevideo. Once at least he was a commercial traveller, and once he worked in a candle factory on Staten Island. He married three times. For several years he was engaged to a wealthy and talented Englishwoman, and subsequently he proposed unsuccessfully to another. In the course of his various wanderings he claimed British as well as United States citizenship; sat as an elected deputy in the French assembly; and was offered a command by Lincoln in the American civil war. In sum, it was a more than ordinarily variegated and dramatic life, and this provided a fitting back-cloth for his flamboyant character.

Garibaldi first became a household name with his defence of Rome in 1849. Before then, however, and this is most important for understanding his temperament and influence, he had been for half his adult life a guerrilla leader in the political bear-garden of Brazil and Argentina. When he returned from South America to Europe he brought back a novel and successful type of warfare. A few irregulars, by breaking the accepted conventions of war, could acquire a high nuisance-value in foreign-occupied Italy.

The South American influence is seen in the gaucho costume that Garibaldi carried to the end of his life—the cloak or poncho, and the red shirt which came from the slaughter houses of Buenos Aires. Following the gaucho example, his Italian armies were able to live in hostile territory by lassoing stray animals and barbecueing them in the open. The hard democracy of the pampas, furthermore, had taught Garibaldi to treat all men as equals, and many Italians were subsequently to learn through him a new freedom of behaviour, to give up obsequious habits of hand-kissing and caste apparel and deferential forms of speech. Italy also learnt by the same means a dangerous praxis of government, one not without analogues in Italian history but which had been developed to a fine art in a land where the caudillo and the pronunciamento were accepted as normal.

Garibaldi came back to Europe with a confirmed love of fighting. He never was able to resist the call of battle, especially where honour was to be plucked or people delivered. All too easily he convinced himself that he was fighting for humanity and liberty in general. From earliest boyhood his actions and daydreams show his fixation on becoming a hero and making the world a freer and healthier place. Surprisingly unambitious himself, he offered his services alternately to king and republic, to one caudillo after another, even on one occasion to the Pope. Such a simple soul inevitably became the catspaw of more selfish and less idealistic factions, in Italy as in Uruguay and the Rio Grande. Himself a man of complete integrity, he was also credulously quixotic, a romantic Arthurian knight who rushed in to support some causes which later he had reason to regret.

Garibaldi's importance in the history of Italy is firstly as a soldier, and secondly as a patriotic legend. At a time when statesmen were silent and impotent, he, with a single-minded and simple-minded belief in victory, had the brute courage to act; and it was the kind of action that ennobled his country, publicised her grievances and potentialities, and cheered and emboldened the laggards and the sceptics among his countrymen.

For example, in 1848, with only a few score men, he dared to take on the might of Austria in a private war. In 1849 his defence of the Roman republic kept liberal Europe breathless with admiration, and proved that some Italians at least knew what to fight for and loved what they knew. His retreat from Rome subsequently furnished an abundance of martyrs to feed the cult of patriotism, and gave Italy her one risorgimento heroine in the South American creole, Anita. These feats were enough to make him celebrated. But eleven years later, in 1860, Garibaldi on his own initiative set off with a thousand men for Sicily, and in a few months conquered almost half of Italy; only to hand it over without fuss to his great enemy Cavour, and return voluntarily, a king-maker, into humble private life.

Compared with this quite extraordinary achievement, his other military exploits were not so momentous. It is true that in the Austrian wars of 1859 and 1866, though very poorly equipped by the government, he proved himself the only Italian general who had enough skill and character to earn the respect of his opponents. But he failed in three separate attempts at a march on Rome, and the jealousy of the regular army, coupled with the strong personal and political dislike of almost all Italian statesmen, contrived to make him henceforward an isolated figure.

When present politics merged into past history, Garibaldi's importance in the risorgimento was to be deliberately played down by the Establishment. The army disliked him for his outstanding military success, the Church for his heresies, Cavour and the deputies for his political insubordination, the middle classes for his threat of social revolution. Even Mazzini broke with him over his obstinate disobedience and individualism. The official historians of Italy, therefore, in their subsequent effort to develop a justification for the triumph of Piedmont and conservatism, made him out to be unserious as a character, and merely marginal in his contribution to victory.

Nor did he himself leave much reliable documentary evidence in his wake for the benefit of later historians. His several versions of autobiography were fanciful—one was written in hendecasyllabic verse—and sometimes even contradictory. There were no close disciples to annotate his every movement, and his letters were those of an extrovert who obstinately spoke of other things than his own mental processes. The guerrilla armies upon whom his fame depended inevitably melted away and left no archives; and, in any case, his battles had been mostly impromptu combinations without any prearranged plan that could be re-created. Hence the romantic legends on the one hand, and official denigration on the other, both equally untrustworthy.

Yet Garibaldi it was, along with Mazzini, who succeeded in accustoming the rest of Europe to the idea of an Italian nation, and he it was who forced Cavour to go faster and further than seemed possible or desirable on any rational analysis. It was his uncritical and unshakeable confidence in unification that finally converted the sceptical statesmen in Turin, and his constant refusal to count the cost brought about almost the only military victories in the saga of national rebirth. He had discovered the secret of inspiring untrained volunteers with an enthusiasm that moved mountains and frontiers. Along with Gordon he is the supreme leader of irregulars in partisan warfare. Through him the common people were won over to a cause that might otherwise have seemed in their eyes remote and profitless; or at least he helped to obscure their vision of what was happening until they were too late to intervene and stop it.

If Garibaldi was mistrusted by the new ruling classes of Italy whom he had helped into power, it was partly because he remained this type of popular hero. His main backers, apart from certain radical financiers such as Adriano Lemmi and the armament firm of Ansaldo, were not politicians but ordinary people whose imagination was fired by his panache and his genuine altruism. The illiterates who voted uncomprehendingly for Italy in the plebiscites often did so because told that this was to support 'Don Peppino' or 'Galubardu'. The concept of Italy for these people was at best a vague abstraction, at worst a meaningless word.

The risorgimento, like all revolutions, was the work of a small, perhaps very small, minority. Again and again Garibaldi had to lament that Neapolitans, Venetians and Romans in turn stirred hardly a finger to 'liberate' themselves from 'foreign' or priestly rule. His volunteers were mostly made up of townsmen from the north, with a nucleus of simple adventurers; they were chiefly professional men and students hoping to avoid their examinations. Often he bewailed this unpromisingly narrow basis of recruitment. The peasants who formed the great majority of Italians, though personally moved by his heroism in adversity, were usually neutral or hostile. His army was sometimes treated as a band of brigands. Villages could bar their gates against him; the local inhabitants often refused him information while acting as unofficial spies for the Austrian soldiery; and he even found some who made no concealment of welcoming a return to Austrian rule.

The fact was that admiration for Garibaldi's person seldom went with any desire to share the hardships which he undertook on the nation's behalf. 'The Italians have too much individual egoism and too little love of their country,' he complained:—'this hermaphrodite generation of Italians whom I have so often tried to ennoble, little though they deserve it.' Patriotism certainly existed, but it was really strong only among remarkable individuals. Usually it was a generalised, rhetorical feeling, skin-deep, and falsified by other sentiments. Noisy patriotic demonstrations could thus be a compensation, making amends for earlier frigidity. In particular, the widespread—but quite exceptional—popular insurrection in Sicily was partly a mere grudge-war against the Neapolitan overlords, partly a peasants' revolt that cut across politics and had nothing to do with patriotic feeling.

As soon as Garibaldi was in retirement, and once he too, like the separatists and peasants in Sicily, was in opposition to the new Italy which they had together helped into existence, he became the natural focus of many of these same discontents, the natural outlet and expression of a general disillusionment. When the romantic cult of Garibaldi grew up in the collective subconscious, it was in part a boost for national morale during a period of disappointment. His exploits were to be sometimes exaggerated in compensation for the dreary

Two *Punch* cartoons satirise Garibaldi's dealings with Victor Emmanuel and Pope Pius IX. Preferring royal dictatorship to a parliamentary system, Garibaldi in his relationship with the monarch, showed none of the hostility he felt towards the Catholic faith.

showing made by the national army between 1848 and 1866. A legend appeared, compounded by romantic story-tellers such as Dumas who liked a good tale as much as the truth.

In this phase of his life Garibaldi became a kind of idealised symbol of the millennium, a sanctified representative of that different and more glorious national revolution which should have taken place but had not. In Naples and Sicily he had been credited with magic powers; and in the more sober north women held up their children for him to bless, even for him to baptise. Garibaldi's image replaced that of God in many a humble peasant's cabin, and his haircut *alla nazzarena* helped this illusion. Prostrate with arthritis, he was carried in solemn procession through the streets of Milan and Palermo, and it seemed like the catafalque of a miracle-working saint.

Abroad, too, he was the object of an extravagant adulation. When injured by a bullet in 1862, twenty-three surgeons from all over the world were sent to see him by zealous enthusiasts. Passionate love-letters arrived secretly from wives of members of both House of Commons and House of Lords, and Cavour knew what he was doing when he slyly sent authenticated locks of the hero's hair to London for distribution to the faithful. Garibaldi's daughter religiously kept even his nail clippings, and a host of relics was preserved for the edification of those who came on pilgrimage in the weekly packet-boat to Caprera.

The 1860s found this ex-dictator of the Two Sicilies in more or less continual opposition, and this did much to weaken popular allegiance to the state and so store up dangers for the future. Naturally he resented that his project for an Italian revolution had been obstructed by the politicians and then captured and drastically watered down. As long ago as the 1830s he had fled into exile after being condemned to death by the king's government. Again, after his retreat from Rome, he had been arrested and exiled for another four years. Three times subsequently did the national army move against him to stop his conquest of Rome, and in one engagement they crippled him for life. But this made him only yet more of a popular hero, and unprecedented mass ovations misled his not very subtle or critical mind into dangerous deeds of insubordination. Laconic communiques were issued from Caprera criticising various aspects of government policy. Parliament he condemned as the seat of corruption and gerrymandering, as a rubber stamp for ministerial autocracy, a fraud designed by the clever lawyers who specialised in oratorical dexterity and corridor intrigue. 'Give us battles, not liberties,' was his cry to the king; for behind 'liberties' he discerned a contrivance by parliament to prefer an oligarchy of wealth and intellect at the expense of the common people.

What made this attitude particularly dangerous was that Garibaldi understood from the king that he might rely on royal support in subverting the normal constitutional government of the country. Sometimes he was even positively encouraged to rebel, and this led directly to his tragic wounding at Aspromonte. Victor Emanuel engaged in private political activity behind the backs of all of his successive Prime Ministers, just as he commonly appointed or dismissed them without any reference to parliament; and in such monarchical irresponsibility is the key to many involved moments in modern Italian history.

For example, the king came to blows frequently with Cavour over the morals and politics of the Court; whereas on the other hand, Garibaldi was someone he could appreciate—a bluff, frank, soldierly man, with a firm sense of loyalty and without the subtle finesse and secondary aims of a politician. Garibaldi was always genuine, and what he said rang true, even if it was silly; whereas Cavour and his successors were guileful and dissembling almost from habit. Moreover, they used parliament to control the king, while Garibaldi on the contrary preferred a royal dictatorship over parliament. Cavour was not only too much a civilian for Victor Emmanuel, who liked people in uniform; he was also too clever; and the king had his own reasons for preferring character to intelligence.

This secret royal favour, when combined with Garibaldi's own lack of brains, his recklessness, his urge towards action and his great popular following, made him a person of great but irresponsible power. The United States Minister wrote back to his government in 1861 that, 'though but a solitary and private individual, he is at this moment, in and of himself, one of the great Powers of the world.' Garibaldi's political views are therefore of peculiar interest.

The first point to be made is that he was too simple and guileless to understand more than the surface of politics. Florence Nightingale, one of his great admirers, was shocked on meeting him to find that he understood very little indeed of the causes he so ardently professed. He was a convinced republican, but also fought for the monarchy; he believed in dictatorship, but all his life fought for freedom and against despotism; he was a bellicose patriot, but also adhered to a pacifist internationalism.

And yet in some convictions he never wavered, for instance in his antipathy to the Catholic faith and his attachment to democracy. He always believed in a wider suffrage and in free and universal education. Unlike the twentieth-century Garibaldians, he thought it criminal folly for a poor country such as Italy to acquire overseas colonies and spend so much on armaments. Repeatedly he addressed memoranda to the Great Powers on the abolition of war and on the means of creating through international arbitration a United States of Europe. For he was a patriot with a difference. 'If Italy ever in her turn threatened the independence of neighbour states, I should regretfully but surely be on the side of the oppressed.' Such a statement would have astonished some of his later disciples.

Garibaldi's combination of idealism and simple good sense can also be traced in his notions on social reform; for here he spoke with genuine knowledge and feeling. By heredity, environment and temperament, he understood the masses as Cavour and Mazzini never did, and if others had shared his understanding, Italy might have been a more stable and tranquil place today. He believed prophetically that 'the great future of Italy lies with her working classes,' and hence that their emancipation and education was an urgent task. Proudly he called himself a socialist; but his socialism was of the heart not of the head; it was based not on class-war but on easing the tension between capital and labour. Though disapproved of by Marx, this sentiment nevertheless was to become an important strand within the Italian socialist movement.

Another trend inside the Italian Left has been towards authoritarianism, and this too goes back to Garibaldi. His own favourite type of warfare had accustomed him to the need for quick and unchallenged decisions, and his preference for autocratic methods became instinctive. Among his volunteers the penalty for disobedience was instant death; and we are told that he would shoot a man without stopping to take the cigar from his mouth.

In politics his aim was always freedom, but people might have to be forced to be free. Whenever he possessed civil authority he chose to be a dictator, and he was hailed as *Duce* by the mob when he appeared on numberless balconies. Too unambitious, unintelligent and uncorrupted to play the Mussolini himself, he advocated a royal dictatorship. Government needed the *fasces*—he employed the very word. And the deputies should be packed off home as a corrupting and disabling element; for Cavour seemed to be setting up a pseudo-constitutional government like that of Louis Napoleon, in which liberty was only a sham. Garibaldi's impatience here with Italian parliamentarism was excessive. He sensed the disease, but was not the man to devise an adequate remedy. Yet in partial explanation it may be remembered that, in 1922, many of the liberals who claimed to inherit from Cavour were also to invoke the *fasces* against a corrupt and anarchical parliamentary regime.

G. M. Trevelyan admirably describes that great moment when the hero of two worlds stepped down from his autocratic position at Naples and retired to a lonely island off Sardinia. For a long time he had been an admirer of Robinson Crusoe, and at Caprera he too could exist free from the intrigue and misgovernment that he thought were ruining his country. Caprera was a barren granite outcrop where he could live a simple life independent of the social obligations and political involvements he so much disliked; and there, not far from that other romantic island of Montecristo, he spent most of his declining days, surrounded by his legitimate and illegitimate children.

With difficulty he built up a farm in this unlikely spot, helped by heavy subventions from his admirers all over the world. His affairs were always entangled, for he was a bad administrator and the farm was singularly unprofitable. But his needs were few. He himself, when in health, would milk the cows. He washed his own shirts, and rarely possessed more than one change of clothing. He had trained himself to cut a coat and trousers by eye. For food he was self-sufficient. Increasingly he became a vegetarian, though to go shooting and spearing fish remained almost his favourite pastime.

He also read books—his small library included Shakespeare, Byron, Plutarch, La Fontaine, Voltaire, Arthur Young on agriculture, and other English books on navigation, agriculture and the art of war. And he wrote too, partly to try to earn his living, partly to stir up the younger generation to emulation of great deeds. The three novels he wrote are dull and absurd to a degree, and his poems are often embarrassing; but he had a genuine love of roughly improvised verse such as may still be found here and there among the Italian peasantry.

Garibaldi died at Caprera in 1882. Always unconventional, he had enjoined his wife to place his body on a pyre of aromatic wood, and to burn him under the open sky in the same pagan, hygienic way he had lived. But the dignitaries of Rome, whom he had always execrated alive, would not be done out of a good funeral, and were revenged on him dead. They argued, as an added touch of irony, that burning would offend people's religious sensibilities. So he was incongruously buried in the presence of dukes and ministers. The world had the last word against him.

His own last word was a Political Testament. To his children and friends he bequeathed his love for liberty and truth. He explicitly condemned the Catholic priesthood and the Mazzinians as the great national enemies. And again he recommended his countrymen to select the most honest man in Italy and make him a temporary dictator. Only when Italians were more educated to liberty, and their country was less threatened from outside and in, should dictatorial rule give way to a regular republican government. Here, in brief, was a neat abstract of the lessons learnt by a simple-minded but strong-hearted soldier during a lifetime of devotion to an ideal.

After Centuries of Japanese Isolation, a Fateful Meeting of East and West

When Japan's rulers finally let in Yankee trade and technology, they changed the history of their country and of the world

James Fallows

James Fallows, Washington editor of the Atlantic Monthly, *has published* Looking at the Sun, *a Study of Japanese and East Asian economic systems.*

From the deck of the USS *Susquehanna* the sailors watched the sea around them fill with little boats. The *Susquehanna* and its sister ships—the *Mississippi,* the *Saratoga,* the *Powhatan*—had been traveling for more than half a year. From Norfolk, Virginia, they had sailed in the late fall of 1852 across the Atlantic, then down around Capetown, and across the Indian Ocean to the South China Sea. Through the spring of 1853 they labored northward past Macao, Hong Hong, Okinawa and the Bonin island chain—Iwo Jima and Chichi Jima—toward the main islands of Japan.

On the evening of July 8, 1853, they rounded a promontory and came to the entrance of the Uraga Channel, itself the entrance to Edo Wan, now known as Tokyo Bay. At the head of the bay, less than a day's sail away, lay Edo itself, Japan's largest city, insulated from foreign contact for nearly 250 years.

The Japanese guard boats that teemed around the American flotilla in the Uraga Channel were made of wood, with sharply angled prows. Sweating oarsmen propelled the boats through the ocean chop. Above the rowers' heads flapped the geometric- or floral-patterned standards of the Tokugawa shoguns who ruled Japan. The American sailors could not understand the shouts that came to them in Japanese. Yet every crew member knew that in the past, uninvited visitors to Japan had often been jailed, tortured or decapitated.

As the lead guard boat approached the *Susquehanna,* the Americans peering down from the deck found, with relief, that they could make out a few familiar characters from the Roman alphabet, rather than the gracefully swirling *hiragana* of Japanese phonetic writing or the intricate *kanji* ideograms the Japanese had adapted from written Chinese. As the guard boat drew closer still, sharp-eyed crewmen sounded out the first word: *"Départez!"* The entire message was in French, not English. It said, "Depart immediately and dare not anchor!" The two nations that would become the main Pacific powers made their first significant contact in a language neither really understood.

THE LENGTHENED SHADOWS OF TWO MEN

Japan's rulers had not in any way invited the encounter; indeed, the more imminent it had become, the more it filled them with dread. America forced the encounter on Japan for a confused tangle of reasons, many of which the American instigators did not honestly discuss among themselves. Yet the aftereffects of this moment prepared Japan for the most impressive feat in its history, and one of the most surprising in the history of any nation. At the same time American interests were more shrewdly advanced by the man who sat hidden in his cabin on the *Susquehanna* than by other American leaders almost any time in U.S. history. Ninety years afterward, Japan and America would be at war, but that was not the fault of the two men who guided this encounter on a hot summer day in 1853; Masahiro Abe, in the shogun's council at Edo, and Matthew Calbraith Perry, in command of the vessels known today in Japan as *kurofune,* "black ships."

Matthew Perry, bearing the title not of Commodore but of "Commander in Chief, United States Naval Forces Stationed in the East India, China, and Japan Seas," was 59 years old when his fleet reached Uraga. For the era, that was old—especially for a man undertaking a prolonged voyage to an essentially unknown destination. Perry suffered from arthritis and other maladies that confined him to his cabin during much of the long trip. Even at age 25 he had been remarked on for his gravitas; as he grew older he took on the air of a mandarin. This demeanor proved a great asset. Like Douglas MacArthur, another American too regal to fit easily into his home culture, Matthew Perry was well prepared by training and temperament for negotiations in Japan. An aw-shucks, unassuming manner might be an asset on the American frontier, but not surrounded by little boats in Tokyo Bay.

Perry's career, indeed his whole life, was devoted to the expansion of the U.S. Navy. His older brother, Oliver Hazard

Library of Congress

Perry, had become a hero at the Battle of Lake Erie before Matthew was out of his teens. Matthew, by contrast, spent his early career in a peacetime navy "where members of a small clique of senior officers scrambled for the limited command opportunities, where feuding, backbiting, and even dueling were a way of life," as Peter Booth Wiley puts it in *Yankees in the Land of the Gods.* "During the navy's first fifty years, thirty-three officers were killed in duels." Perry's first important mission, in 1819, was to transport freed slaves to Africa during the founding of Liberia. He did not see combat until he was in his 50s, at the Battle of Veracruz in the Mexican War, as the nation kept expanding westward toward a second sea frontier on the Pacific.

One great struggle over America's maritime future turned on the relative future roles of clipper ships versus steam-powered vessels. By the 1850s the fast and graceful clippers had given America the lead in the shipping trade. But the British were outbuilding America in steamships, and by the 1840s, Britain's steam-powered Cunard line was winning the battle for passengers and valuable freight on the transatlantic route.

Steam power required coal, and at the time no ship was large enough to carry all the coal it needed to cross the vast Pacific. Clipper ships had to choose routes to China on the basis of favorable winds, but steamers could be more deliberate, following a "great circle" route up toward Alaska and then down the Japanese archipelago. With coaling stations along the way, the great circle route would be possible, and in 1851 Americans learned that Japan had deposits of coal. "The moment is near when the last link in the chain of oceanic steam navigation is to be formed," said Senator Daniel Webster of New Hampshire, not stinting on rhetoric, as he endorsed an American expedition to Japan. The point of this link would not be to buy from the Japanese their own handicrafts and manufactures but to obtain a "gift of Providence, deposited, by the Creator of all things, in the depths of the Japanese islands for the benefit of the human family"—that is, Japan's coal.

The desire to expand a coal-using, steam-powered navy was not the only reason for the expedition to Japan. Beyond lay China, where Americans hoped to find markets to develop and souls to convert. For a century before the age of steamships, American whalers had worked the waters of the North Pacific surrounding Japan. Frequently the ships did not come home. American sailors stranded by typhoon or shipwreck had washed ashore in Japan since the late 1700s. Often they were executed; usually they were jailed; a few were forced to perform ritual disrespect to Christian symbols, for instance by walking on a portrait of the Virgin Mary.

GETTING THE JUMP ON DUTCH, FRENCH AND ENGLISH

These icons of the Blessed Virgin were leftovers from Portuguese Jesuits, who had proselytized in Japan for nearly a century before being driven out in the early 1600s. The shipwrecked Americans, mainly Protestants, found this ordeal less excruciating than the Japanese expected, yet news of such episodes, especially one involving the whaler *Lagoda,* filtered back to America, where at a minimum they stirred a passion for better protection for whalers, and among some people a desire to make the "pagans" atone. "If that double-bolted land, Japan, is ever to become hospitable, it is the whale-ship alone to whom the credit will be due," Herman Melville wrote in *Moby-Dick* in 1851.

The British had won their Opium Wars against China. From the north came Russian vessels. Swarming around were the French and the Dutch. The expansionist U.S. Government watched these plans with care. Finally, to establish America's presence first, the Administration of Millard Fillmore, in by far its most consequential step, commissioned the Japan Expedition and convinced Matthew Perry to command it. For nearly two and a half centuries, since the great warlord Hideyoshi took steps that led to the policies known as *sakoku,* or "closed country," Japan's officials had isolated themselves from the world-and wondered apprehensively when the isolation might end.

In 1549 a Portuguese Jesuit, Francis Xavier, had come ashore on the island of Kyushu. Initially tolerated, even supported by some local noblemen, the Jesuits had in the next 50 years made tens of thousands of Japanese converts. By the end of the century Hideyoshi, weakened by a costly and failed attempt to conquer Korea, and chastened to learn that savage conquistadors had often followed the cross in Latin America, had expelled all missionaries. Soon, the Tokugawa shogunate launched its radical policy of seclusion. As far as possible, Japan and its leaders would function as if there were no world beyond Japan's seacoast. "So long as the Sun shall warm the earth, let no Christian dare to come to Japan," said the shogun's expulsion order of 1638. If contact with foreigners was unavoidable, it would be handled through an enclave of Dutch traders, concentrated in an island ghetto called Deshima, near Nagasaki in the far southern extreme of the country—hundreds of miles from the great, protected centers of Kyoto and Edo.

The sakoku policy worked for a while—indeed, for as many years as the United States has now existed as an independent country. Yet in the early 1800s, as Japan began its third century of near-total isolation, the strains were evident. "In 1642, the year Isaac Newton was born, the last Japanese priest had been crucified and Japan had closed like an oyster," one American historian has written. But the leaders who made the decision "could hardly guess that Japan, which went into seclusion as one of the two or three strongest nations on the globe, would emerge from it, centuries later, as a distinctly second-class power."

The same whalers and fishermen who were inconvenient when washed onto Japanese shores inevitably brought news of the Industrial Revolution and other advancements outside Japan. A young Japanese fisherman named Manjiro Nakajima was himself shipwrecked and picked up by an American whaler in 1841. Under Japan's seclusion law, it was a capital offense to leave the country—or to come back, if one had escaped. But after spending a decade in New England, under the name John Mung, Manjiro decided to risk returning to Japan.

The *daimyo,* or lord, of the southern province of Satsuma realized, as Samuel Eliot Morison puts it, that decapitating Manjiro would not only sever his head but also "would cut off an important source of information." Instead, the daimyo sent him to Nagasaki, "where officials pumped Manjiro dry of everything he knew about the United States." Among the facts Manjiro revealed (as Walter McDougall wrote in *Let the Sea Make a Noise . . .*) was that Americans were lewd by nature, and that in their country "toilets are placed over holes in the ground. It is customary to read books in them."

Officially, the Japanese rulers faced news of foreign developments with redoubled sternness. In 1825, as whaling traffic increased, the shogun issued an edict forbidding any foreign ship to land. When a foreign ship came into view, the order read, it was crucial to shoot at it first and ask questions later. "Have no compunctions about firing on [the Dutch] by mistake," the order went on. "When in doubt, drive the ship away without hesitation. Never be caught off guard."

Behind this bravado was a debate, based on very little information but heated because the Japanese felt the very survival of the nation was at stake. In the town of Mito, a day's walk to the northeast of Edo, the "Mito School" of theorists said that an increased threat required increased determination to resist. Japan must shore up its coastal defenses, girding itself for the inevitable battle to the death that would keep the foreigners away. "Today the alien barbarians of the West, the lowly organs of the legs and feet of the world, are . . . trampling other countries underfoot, and daring, with their squinting eyes and limping feet, to override the noble nations," one such scholar wrote in 1825. With such a foe, no compromise could be possible.

COULD JAPAN BEND WITHOUT BREAKING?

In the other camp were the Rangakusha, or "masters of Dutch learning," so called after Holland's role during the closed-country years as the vehicle for all learning from overseas. A realistic assessment of the circumstances, said members of this camp, required Japan to bend so as to avoid being broken. They had evidence of weakness inside the country. Taxes, levied in rice, were becoming oppressive. In several centuries of peace the samurai class had grown large and dependent; in 1850 Edo alone supported some 17,000 bureaucrats, compared with 1,500 in Washington, D.C.

Evidence of the strength of potential invaders was even more dramatic. In 1846, seven years before Matthew Perry's arrival, Commodore James Biddle of the U.S. Navy had reached the mouth of the Uraga Channel. He had retreated with humiliating loss of face, after letting Japanese sightseers and officials inspect every inch of his ship and after accepting a letter from the shogun telling him never to return. Yet the shrewder Japanese officials of the era carefully noted the size and power of his ships, and of the American guns. Biddle's vessels represented destructive potential of a sort Japan had barely imagined.

Most of all the Japanese realists noticed what had happened to China—noticed, and were appalled. China was not just another country but the Middle Kingdom, the Central Country. Its emperor had historically referred to Japan's emperor as "your little king." A new China had been carved up by Westerners, debauched by opium and left totally unprotected by either the Ch'ing dynasty or armed force. If the British and French could polish off China, what hope was there for little Japan—against Britain, France, Russia and the United States? Japan could try to enforce its seclusion law, said one of its very shrewdest leaders after the Biddle affair, but if "the foreigners retaliated, it would be a hopeless contest, and it would be a worse disgrace for Japan."

This leader was Masahiro Abe, the senior counselor for the shogun's government. As the shogun was the power that ruled Japan in the emperor's name, so Abe was the strategist who made plans on behalf of the weakened shogun, Tokugawa Ieyoshi, who was in place when Perry arrived. Abe was a generation younger than Perry, only 34 years old as Perry's flotilla of Black Ships neared Edo. Raised in a scholar's family, he had through force of intellect made himself one of the shogun's most influential advisers while still in his 20s.

In the split between the hard-liners and compromisers in the shogun's court, Abe sided initially with the hard-liners. But after extensive consultation among the daimyos of Japan, he and his allies came up with a brilliant compromise. Japan would open itself to the Western traders—but only for a time—placating them just long enough to learn how to rebuild its own navies and arsenals. Naosuke Ii, the most influential of all the daimyos, reminded the shogun that, even as Japan had earlier used Dutch traders as its bridge to the outside world, it was time to use the Americans and other foreigners as another, broader bridge. Across this bridge new discoveries could flow into Japan—providing the country, in the long run, with means to rearm itself, learn from outside technology, and ultimately "gain a complete victory" over the foreigners.

United States Naval Academy Museum, Annapolis

Of gifts given, those from Japanese were more decorative, while Perry's aimed to impress Japan with industrial might. Baby steam engine was biggest hit, but offerings included plow, scythe, grindstone.

Some of the American politicians promoting the Japan Expedition had cast it in missionary terms, a chance to open the Orient to faith and flag. "I am sure that the Japanese policy of seclusion is not according to God's plan of bringing the nations of the earth to a knowledge of the truth," Samuel Wells Williams, a missionary traveling with Perry as cultural expert and interpreter, wrote in his journal as the expedition neared Edo. Perry himself, pious enough, never described his duties in these terms. Instead he concentrated on how to deploy his men, his ships and himself for maximum effect. Before the trip began, Perry foresaw that his fleet's substantial armament "would do more to command their fears, and secure their friendship, than all that the diplomatic missions have accomplished in the last one hundred years." In a set of "Instructions" for the voyage, Perry said that the Commander "will be careful to do nothing that may [compromise] his own dignity or that of the country. He will, on the contrary, do every thing to impress them with a just sense of the power and greatness of this country, and to satisfy them that its past forbearance has been the result, not of timidity, but of a desire to be on friendly terms with them."

GIFTS TO SHOW A NATION'S STRENGTH

Like Masahiro Abe, Perry had studied the sad history of Commodore Biddle, who had been forced out of Edo Bay in 1846. In Perry's view, Biddle never recovered from setting his first foot wrong with the Japanese: rather than insisting on retaining a mysterious distance, he had let them climb onto his ship and, in effect, imprison it with guard boats. Speaking of himself in the third person, in his memoir of the voyage Perry said, "The Commodore . . . was well aware that the more exclusive he should make himself, and the more unyielding he might be in adhering to his declared intentions, the more respect these people of forms and ceremonies would be disposed to award him." He would meet only with officials of "the highest rank" in Japan. He would make a threat only when he was absolutely certain he could carry it out.

Power could be demonstrated through generosity as well as reserve. Perry had prepared gifts to demonstrate the range of strengths his nation possessed. Editions of Audubon's *Birds of America* and *Quadrupeds of America* that had cost $1,000 apiece—a decade's earnings for an average American family at the time. Champagne, perfume and mirrors. Whisky, liqueurs, and small weapons from the Colt factory. And, most important, American machines: plows, a telegraph, a crude camera, even a nifty little quarter-scale steam-powered railroad train.

This was the man who appeared in the Uraga Channel in July 1853. He was not one to be driven away by instructions to *"Départez!"* Sweating alone in his cabin, unwilling to present himself prematurely to the crowd of Japanese, he issued his orders. The *Susquehanna* and sister ships were to repel, with all necessary force, any Japanese who attempted to board the boats. They would proceed up the channel, toward Edo, until their wish to meet a truly senior official, one who could speak for the ruler, was fulfilled. After the failure of the French message, a Japanese official had neared the *Susquehanna* and yelled out, in English, "I can speak Dutch!" To him the Americans conveyed their wish to meet someone truly in command.

Throughout Edo, news of the Black Ships' arrival created near-panic. Some citizens fled, carrying their possessions to the countryside, fearing pillage and war. The shogun's council met to consider bleak-seeming alternatives. The usual reflexive responses to outside pressure—asking the foreigners to come back again in a few years, telling them to go on to Nagasaki, the only site where Japan had done business with foreign representatives through the sakoku years—seemed to have lost their potency. The Americans would not retreat—in fact, they kept sending surveying ships farther up the bay, ignoring Japanese assertions that this violated local law and saying that they needed to be sure about anchorages, for "the next time."

As the governing council quarreled, Abe pushed them toward a decision: the Americans must be placated, at least for now. Perry had been asking to meet the emperor; that was out of the question, of course. Indeed, to this point the Americans were not even aware that a real emperor existed, hidden in Kyoto. When they said "emperor," they were referring to the shogun; their official goal was to present him with letters from President Fillmore.

Clearly some meeting was essential, and so on July 14, after elaborate arguments over protocol, Matthew Perry himself came ashore at the town of Kurihama.

In retrospect this result seems inevitable. America was a country on the rise. Japan could not wall itself off eternally. Each party had a stake in negotiating reasonably with the other: Perry, because he was outnumbered on the scene; the Japanese, because other Americans could come back and exact retribution if anything went wrong. But at the time it was very much touch and go. More than once Perry's men came to the brink of violent confrontation. Crewmen on the *Mississippi* had to level a loaded musket at a Japanese official's chest to keep him from climbing aboard. A small American survey boat, commanded by Lieut. Silas Bent, found itself surrounded by three dozen Japanese guard boats. Bent prepared for hand-to-hand combat, instructing his small crew to fix bayonets—until the mighty *Mississippi* steamed into view and the Japanese retreated.

And so, on the night before Perry's scheduled landing in Kurihama, his crew members watched apprehensively from their decks as more and more Japanese troops filled the shore. Perry considered the possibility that the proposed meeting was really an ambush. After his surveyors reported that Kurihama's harbor was deep enough, Perry ordered his gunboats brought in close to shore, where they could bombard the Japanese if anything went wrong. On the long night before the meeting, 250 American sailors were chosen by lot for the dangerous mission of accompanying their commander ashore. The Japanese worked through the night to prepare a pavilion for the meeting—and to increase the boats guarding the entrance to Edo Bay, in case the Americans were planning a sudden, treacherous assault.

On the morning of July 14, the American boats drew near to shore. Members of the landing party, dressed in their formal uniforms, were issued 20 rounds of ammunition apiece and carefully loaded their muskets and pistols. On the shore they saw three new pavilions, covered with the bright flags and standards of Japanese officialdom. Surrounding the pavilions were files and files of soldiers, armed with swords, bows and arrows, and a few antique firearms.

At 10 o'clock barges full of Americans began arriving on the shore. Miscalculations at this moment might have had historic consequences; long after the event, one of the Japanese commanders revealed that ten swordsmen had been hiding under the floor of a pavilion, with orders to leap out and slaughter the foreigners if they made the slightest aggressive move.

As their numbers grew on the beach, Perry's men formed a double line, through which their commander, arriving at last, marched toward the waiting Japanese. Ahead of Perry was a Marine officer walking with sword in hand. On either side of him were two of the largest men from his ship, both black stewards, loaded with all the weapons they could carry and towering over every other person on the beach. Once Perry was safe ashore, tension eased a bit. He was met by two Japanese governors, to whom the stewards presented large rosewood boxes. Inside were small solid-gold cases, which in turn contained Millard Fillmore's letters requesting that Japan open itself to the world. The governors, in return, presented Perry with a letter said to be from Japan's ruler. When translated, it turned out to contain warnings that the Americans had broken Japanese law by landing in Kurihama and must not come back. Perry said that, with his mission accomplished, he was leaving Japan—but he would be back the next year to hear the Japanese government's response. With quite as many ships? the interpreter asked. "All of them," Perry replied. "And probably more, as these are only a portion of the squadron."

After the meeting in Kurihama, Perry had compounded Japan's sense of threat by sending surveying parties even deeper into Edo Bay. Then his departing fleet retraced the route it had taken toward Japan, visiting Okinawa and the Bonin Islands before stopping for repairs and refitting in Macao. He studiously ignored suggestions from Washington that he wait and assemble a much larger force before his return trip. Perry knew that French and Russian missions would soon be heading to Japan. He was suffering terribly from arthritis; a winter passage back to Edo would be dangerous and unpleasant. Yet to forestall all other navies and force action from the Japanese, Perry set sail northward from Macao in the middle of January 1854.

Back in Edo everything was till uncertain. What did the Americans really want? What compromise would be enough to make their warships go away? Suppose the shogun's government offered to give the Americans half the trading rights now monopolized by the Dutch? Or dragged out the negotiations themselves over five or ten years; after which time the Americans might lose interest or Japan might come up with a new plan?

FIGHT IT OUT OR FACE UP TO PROGRESS

Masahiro Abe had ordered Japan's coastal defenses fortified as soon as Perry's flotilla headed south after its first visit. He engineered the repeal of a law—enacted at the start of the sakoku era—that prohibited Japanese citizens from building seagoing vessels, and he opened negotiations with the Dutch about buying some steam-powered warships from them. All factions in Japan agreed that negotiations should be strung out as long as possible. Yet when the moment of choice arose, should Japan fight to the death, as influential figures like Tokugawa Nariaki, daimyo of Mito, were advocating? Or should it bow to the reality of superior force and instead plan for long-term survival, and future revenge?

The issue was forced in the middle of February, when American ships arrived once more in the Uraga Channel. This time Perry's flotilla numbered three steam-powered frigates, seven ships under sail, and combined crews totaling more than 1,500 men. Overcoming bitter accusations that he was betraying Japan, Abe at last forced through a decision. Japan would greet the Americans with conciliation. It would accept a code of conduct for shipwrecked whalers and seamen. It would let the Americans obtain coal in Shimoda, near Edo, and trade with them at sites other than the traditional foreigner's ghetto in Nagasaki. It asked only for a transition period of a few years before the full agreement came into effect.

There were still points of detail to be negotiated—how many ports would be open to trade, what tariff the Japanese could impose. But under Abe's guidance Japan had given in. Matthew Perry, confined by disease and dignity to his Black Ship cabin, was ready by early March to deal face-to-face with his Japanese counterparts. On March 8 he came ashore at Yokohama for a detailed, though still touchy, negotiating session.

On March 13 Perry went ashore once again for the first gift-exchanging ceremony. One by one he gave away the marvels of artistry and engineering he had stowed aboard his ships nearly two years before. The Japanese onlookers were entranced by the scale-model locomotive pulling a train. The passenger coach, complete with interior benches and curtains, was too small for human passengers, but samurai and shogun's officials took rides sitting on top of the train. In their turn, the Japanese offered gifts. But because they thought that valuable gifts might be insulting—suggesting the possibility of a bribe or the need to reply in kind—their gifts were modest, though artistic and of fine workmanship. Perry regarded them as trifling. More impressive were their mammoth sumo wrestlers. Perry watched as the *sumotori* strode in, heavy sacks of rice atop their heads. One of the wrestlers approached Perry, who accepted the invitation to punch the immense stomach and feel its strength. Samuel Wells Williams, "Perry's missionary-interpreter, who was generally quite admiring of Japan and who despaired of his crewmates' insensitivity to foreign ways, nonetheless wrote in his diary that the spectacle demonstrated the clash of two cultures: the "success of science and enterprise" on the American side, the "brute animal force" on Japan's.

A final disagreement arose over Perry's desire to walk the streets of the capital city. Here the Japanese held firm: Perry could, if he chose, view Edo from the deck of his ship, but must not come ashore. Perry accepted, sailed to the top of Edo Bay for a look, and then, on April 14, headed south again.

Negotiations between Japan and the United States were just beginning. For most of the next decade an American counsel, Townsend Harris, would accuse Japanese officials of backsliding, dissembling and attempting to evade the treaty's terms. More than a century later in the debate over trading issues, Japanese and American officials have assumed roles very similar to those first played in Uraga and Kurihama, with the Japanese debating the merits of acquiescence or defiance, and the Americans, far less powerful now, attempting to display impressive and intimidating force.

Perry's role in Japan was complete. It was to be a profound role and, though deeply unwished for by the Japanese, in the long run it had quite positive effects. Although Japan had been forced to make concessions and accept "unequal treaties," it had avoided outright defeat—and had prepared for the rapid modernization that began with the Meiji Restoration of 1868. For this progress Japan could, with mixed emotions, thank Perry and the shock he delivered with the Black Ships.

Perry thought he would be lionized by his countrymen on his return, but he was not, in part because his countrymen were preoccupied with tensions over slavery that would lead to the Civil War. Retiring to his town house in New York, the Commodore worked methodically on his *Narrative of the Expedition,* which he submitted to the publisher at the end of 1857. Masahiro Abe, who had skillfully guided Japan through its greatest challenge of the 19th century, died while still in his 30s, a few months before Perry completed the manuscript. On March 4, 1858, shortly before his 64th birthday, Matthew Perry died at home, of rheumatism and heart failure. His cortege was led down Fifth Avenue by the men with whom he had sailed to Japan—the men, that is to say, with whom he had changed history.

Justice Seen, Justice Done? Abolishing Public Executions in 19th-Century Germany

The ritual execution in public of wrongdoers has been seen by historians as part of a regime of ceremonial retribution regarded as essential to maintain order in early modern Europe. But what was the nature of such proceedings and how far did the intellectual pressure of movements like the Enlightenment actually influence a process of removing executions from the public eye? Richard Evans looks at what actually happened and the reasons for it in Germany during the nineteenth century.

Richard J. Evans

Richard J. Evans is Professor of History at Birkbeck College, University of London, and the author of Rituals of Retribution.

One of the most striking changes in the nature of penal policy in nineteenth-century Europe was the abolition of public executions in many major states. Even where this did not formally take place, as in France, public participation was severely curtailed by a series of reforms carried out at roughly the same time as the removal of executions behind prison walls elsewhere.

It used simply to be assumed that this change was no more than a step in the direction of a civilised and humanitarian administration of the law. This view is still taken by those who, like the Dutch historian Pieter Spierenburg, follow the great German sociologist Norbert Elias in discerning a 'civilising process' at work here, as in other aspects of European society at this time. The rise of the modern state, in this view, depended on people restraining the kind of vengeful and sadistic emotions which had found expression in the violence and ribaldry of crowd behaviour during public executions. Aggression was sublimated in the impersonal operation of the law, and a process of 'conscience formation' began in which the citizen developed a kind of human identification with other citizens which led to an increasing revulsion against the open display of physical mutilation and annihilation which public executions involved.

Others, however, following the lead taken by the French philosopher-historian Michel Foucault, have taken a far more critical view of this process, arguing that public punishments were abolished not because they were inhumane, but because they were ineffective. Governments became increasingly alarmed at the behaviour of execution crowds, who treated the occasion as a kind of carnival, an opportunity to make fun of the whole process, to mock the authorities and to turn the criminal on the scaffold into a kind of hero. Such exemplary and demonstrative punishments were replaced in the course of the nineteenth century by an increasingly elaborate and effective system of policing and surveillance, and instead of attempting merely to restore the integrity of violated authority in a symbolic and exemplary fashion by desecrating and destroying the offender's body, punishment undertook to discipline society by imposing a prison regime of penal labour, solitary confinement, secrecy and silence designed to remould the offender's mind. It was not surprising, therefore, that in this new penal regime, executions were taken out of the public domain.

More recently still, Victor Gatrell has argued, in a path-breaking study of capital punishment in England, that early Victorian élites abolished public executions not because they were afraid of the

This article first appeared in *History Today,* April 1996, pp. 20-25.

violent emotions of the crowd, but because they wished to conceal and deny these same emotions in themselves. They projected their own darker impulses onto the spectators at public hangings and repressed them by abolishing the opportunity for their display. What they were not prepared to do, of course, was to confront them directly, since it was widely agreed long after the ending of the 'Bloody Code' in the 1830s that the maintenance of order continued to require the exercise of the death penalty. The abolition of public executions in England was thus a means of securing and strengthening capital punishment by making its operation less disquieting to the conscience of the political and administrative élite.

None of these three explanations of the ending of public executions is really tied to the history of any one European country, since none of them deals with national specificities in any explicit way. This should not be surprising, since, as we have already seen, the ending of public punishments, including executions, was a widespread European phenomenon. At the same time, however, none of these explanations is actually based on a serious examination of the actual process by which public executions were brought to an end. They all concentrate instead on the analysis and description of public executions themselves, and assume rather than demonstrate that they were abolished for the reasons they claim. There is room, therefore, for a study of this process, taking one particular country as an example. Germany is especially useful in this regard because at the time of the abolition of public executions it was not yet united, but consisted of a number of independent states, so that it provides not one example of the decision-making process, but many.

A public execution in eighteenth- or early nineteenth-century Germany was an elaborate and highly ritualised affair. Its usually began with a public sentencing ceremony on the main square of the town where it was to be carried out. This provided the crowd with the first opportunity to see the condemned offender, since trials in most parts of Germany were not held before a jury or carried out in public. The condemned then set off, surrounded by troops and public officials of various kinds, for the scaffold, which was generally outside the town walls. The order of the procession was carefully laid down, and representatives of the local guilds, so vital to the political economy of the urban community in Germany, were very prominent. More ceremonies were held at the scaffold, before the execution itself took place.

Decapitation was the method of execution most commonly used, except in Austria, where hanging was preferred, and it was carried out by a variety of methods, largely according to tradition: the guillotine in areas influenced by French tradition, such as the Rhineland or the south-west, the sword in conservative states such as Hanover and Bavaria, the hand-held axe in east-Elbian Prussia and most of the north. In addition, for much of the eighteenth century, and in Prussia up to the end of the 1830s, particularly serious offenders—usually murderers who had killed their victim in the course of a robbery—were 'broken on the wheel': they were spread-eagled on the scaffold and their limbs smashed by a heavy cartwheel wielded by the executioner (in practice, they were usually silently garrotted immediately before undergoing this punishment). Up to the beginning of the nineteenth century, their bodies were dismembered and left on the gallows to rot.

The execution ritual was not simply a display of state power, but a religious ceremony as well and involved a high level of popular and communal participation. As well as the guilds, there were priests present in the procession and on the scaffold, intoning prayers and reading out Biblical quotations, and choirboys too, singing hymns and dirges for the dead. In Catholic areas the condemned confessed his sins immediately before the execution and was given a crucifix to hold during the proceedings. In Protestant districts, an element of popular folk-religion presented itself, as epileptics came up at the end of the execution, equipped with glasses and mugs to catch the offender's blood as it spurted from the severed neck, and drank it as a cure for their affliction.

In all cases, the ceremony ended with a sermon from the officiating priest or pastor, admonishing the crowd to heed the moral lesson of what they had just witnessed. All this had the function not only of imparting Divine approval to the proceedings, but also of involving the whole community in an act of collective expiation, whereby they reassured themselves that the person whom they were killing would be absolved of his sins and go straight to Heaven. It was indeed the 'holy' character of the condemned which lent his blood the healing quality so prized by sufferers from epilepsy, which popular culture still widely attributed, even in the nineteenth century, to demonic possession. Popular ballads and broadsheets printed and distributed at executions underlined the sacral nature of the proceedings and the redemption and salvation of the condemned.

Examples of crowd riot and rebellion at executions in eighteenth-century Germany were extremely rare. Faced with a return to the dungeons for a fresh round of torture if they recanted, as well as the prospect of eternal damnation held out to them by the clergy, most offenders were content to confess their sins and co-operate fully in the proceedings from beginning to end. There was nothing carnivalesque about any of this: on the contrary, public executions were an affirmation of official hierarchies and values, asserted in the replication of the social order in the procession and the repetition of official secular and religious dogma at the public sentencing ceremony and on the scaffold.

The relative absence of the kind of crowd hostility which was so characteristic of eighteenth-century executions in England, and to a lesser extent *ancien régime* France, reflected the fact that from the penal reforms of the mid-century Enlightenment onwards, execution for theft was extremely rare. In England you could be hanged for stealing a sheep as late as the 1830s, but in Germany for most of the previous century, it was only homicide that brought you to the gallows, a crime which aroused more popular disapproval than any other. There was a degree of popular sympathy for the offender discernible in the case of infanticide, but executions for this crime were extremely rare from the 1770s onwards. The relatively low priority given to property crimes in comparison with capitalist England, and the existence of policing arrangements which made it unnecessary to use the death penalty as a threat to deter thieves, ensured that the vast majority of executions in Germany were of offenders who had earned the strong disapproval of popular opinion by their crimes.

By the beginning of the nineteenth century, however, this situation was beginning to change. 'Enlightened' authorities objected to the religious elements in the execution ceremony, which they thought glorified the offender instead of making him an object of revulsion. So they cut them down to a perfunctory minimum. This policy failed to stop crowds from articulating magico-religious beliefs at executions, and examples of blood-drinking can still be found as late as the 1850s, but it did reduce the ceremonial and consensual aspects of public punishment. Released from the pressure to confess and repent previously brought to bear on them by the continual ministrations of the clergy, and freed from the threat of torture, abolished everywhere in Germany by the 1820s, the condemned felt more able to rebel against their fate, and increasingly did so.

Moreover, the breakdown of traditional urban community hierarchies under the impact of industrialisation and the earlier decline of the guilds gradually untied the social knots that bound the execution crowd together in a fixed hierarchical structure. Finally, executioners began to make more mistakes as the number of executions declined and they became increasingly out of practice at wielding the sword or the axe. A botched job was almost bound to lead to a riot, in which the executioner was stoned by the crowd. Together with the violation of guild privileges through the simplification of the execution ritual, such occasions led to a growing number of crowd disturbances from the beginning of the century onwards.

None of this was evidence of growing sympathy for the condemned on the part of either officialdom or populace. As far as the authorities were concerned, the problem from the eighteenth century onwards was that execution crowds were rather too sympathetic to the offender on the scaffold, and that the nature of the public execution ritual tended to reinforce this sympathy rather than undermine it. As far as popular opinion was concerned, on the other hand, the gradual secularisation of the execution ceremony tended to reduce their identification with the offender rather than reinforce it. Traces of a 'civilising process' can perhaps be seen in the decision of most German states to cease the practice of displaying the remains of executed criminals in public places earlier in the century, since this was in part a response to complaints from officials and ordinary citizens who were clearly finding the sight and smell of rotting corpses on the open highway increasingly offensive. But 'conscience formation', if any such thing did indeed take place, had no role in the abolition of public executions itself.

Nor, when we come to examine the actual process by which this took place, is there much more plausibility in the idea that public executions were brought to an end merely because the élites and the authorities wanted to make capital punishment more effective. The timing of the reforms is particularly significant. Apart from the small Thuringian state of Saxe-Altenburg, which abolished public executions in 1841, no German state took this crucial step until the 1850s: Prussia in 1851, Württemberg and Upper Hesse in 1853, Hamburg and Brunswick in 1854, Saxony in 1855, Baden in 1855, Bavaria in 1861, Rhenish Hesse in 1863.

This was the period of reaction and retrenchment after the failure of the liberal Revolution of 1848, when governments all over Germany were obsessed with the restoration and maintenance of public order. And it was this issue above all others that led them to put capital punishment behind closed doors. In Prussia the authorities justified this step by referring to the 'coarse behaviour' of the 'mob' and the 'excesses' to which this allegedly gave rise; in Bavaria the government condemned the 'demonstrations and excesses' of the crowd in similar terms; in Baden the ending of public executions was justified by reference to the 'general excitement' of the crowd and the 'troubles' to which this led. Everywhere, it was above all fear of the potential public order consequences of an uncontrolled assembly of thousands of emotionally charged people which provided the stimulus for the crucial step.

There was no hint in any of this of a projection onto the crowd of élite embarrassment at the principle of capital punishment itself. On the contrary, the authorities who introduced this measure, whether as an administrative order or a legislative act, took careful steps to ensure that the élites themselves would still be able to go to executions if they wished. As far as they were concerned, executions did not cease to be public at all, for although they were now to be held inside prisons rather than in the open, they could still be attended by means of obtaining an entry card. In succeeding decades, well into the Weimar Republic of the 1920s, it was normal for anything between 60 and 200 people to be admitted to a German execution wherever it took place. What was new was that the 'public' who attended could now be vetted and selected: these were 'honourable citizens', the top-hatted and frock-coated gentlemen (no ladies were ever given entry cards) who formed the bourgeois 'public' of late nineteenth- and early twentieth-century Germany—doctors, lawyers, civil servants, clerks, businessmen, teachers, manufacturers and artisans. Their keenness to obtain entry cards spoke little for any process of 'conscience formation' or identification with the sufferings of the condemned. Often enough, indeed, many more requests for cards were received than could practicably be granted.

What this signified was a good deal of approval among elements of the German middle classes for the principle as well as the practice of capital punishment. In the 1850s, indeed, the ending of public executions had been part of a wider package of reforms that had aimed to restore public order and provide a guarantee against the renewal of revolutionary violence (the liberals of 1848 had failed partly because of their fear of the 'mob'). This meant that the 'reactionary' measures characteristic of the 1850s were by no means merely backward-looking. In Prussia, the fact that the Criminal Code of 1851 introduced trial in open court, with the equivalent of a jury or the presence of lay assessors, was an important concession to liberal opinion. Elsewhere too, the introduction of public trials went together with the abolition of public executions, since the public demonstration of the guilt of the accused, one of the main functions of the public execution under the old order, could now be shifted from the latter to the former.

The ending of public executions was thus not so much an act of penal policy as a measure of public order. In a wider sense, too, capital punishment in Germany had more to do with politics than with crime prevention. In 1848, liberals in the Frankfurt Parliament had voted for its abolition by a substantial though not an overwhelming majority, as a means of symbolising the commitment of Germany's proposed new, united liberal state with the ideals of human rights and human dignity they were so characteristically concerned to proclaim. Abolished as a consequence by a number of German states, it was reintroduced everywhere as the failure of the revolutions became clear. Reaction, everywhere in the ascendant in the 1850s, gave way in the following decade to a renewal of liberalism, and with this came the revival of the campaign for the ending of capital punishment altogether. So powerful was the principle of abolition in liberal public opinion that while few German states actually took the step of outlawing the death penalty in law, almost all of them ceased applying it in practice. There were no executions at all in Prussia between 1868 and 1878, and in the entire territory of the German Reich, founded in 1871, there were no executions in 1870, 1871 or 1872 and only twenty in the remaining years of the decade.

It was only with Bismarck's insistence on the execution of Hödel, the young radical who had attempted to assassinate Wilhelm I in 1878, that capital punishment regained a secure footing in Germany, and only with the anarchist scares of the 1880s that bourgeois opinion in Germany swung over in its majority to the support of the death penalty, with the abandonment by the National Liberal Party of its previous abolitionism. What this suggests is that the experience of Germany was indeed different to that of Britain or France in some crucial respects. Although, surprisingly perhaps, not a great deal seems to be known about the history of British debates on the death penalty between the mid-nineteenth century and the mid-twentieth, opposition to capital punishment in principle appears to have been very muted after the ending of public executions in 1868. In France, the allegiance of the left to the principles of the French Revolution precluded open hostility to the guillotine.

Only in Germany did the abolition of the death penalty become identified, above all through the experience of 1848, as a central tenet of political liberalism and democracy. Only in Germany did the retention of capital punishment, correspondingly, come to serve so powerfully as a symbol of sovereignty, authority and the rejection of liberal beliefs such as tolerance, participation and the freedom of the individual. As a consequence, the rise and fall of the number and frequency of executions came to reflect precisely the varying fortunes of liberalism and authoritarianism in modern German history, since it reflected the operation not of court verdicts and sentences, but of the power of clemency, which was almost always wielded, whether by monarchs or by republican heads of state, as a manifestation of political intention and will.

Given this politicisation of the issue, it was hardly surprising that the advent of Hitler's Third Reich in 1933 was immediately followed by an increase of executions and of overt state violence against political opponents and ordinary criminals which far outweighed anything the nineteenth century ever witnessed.

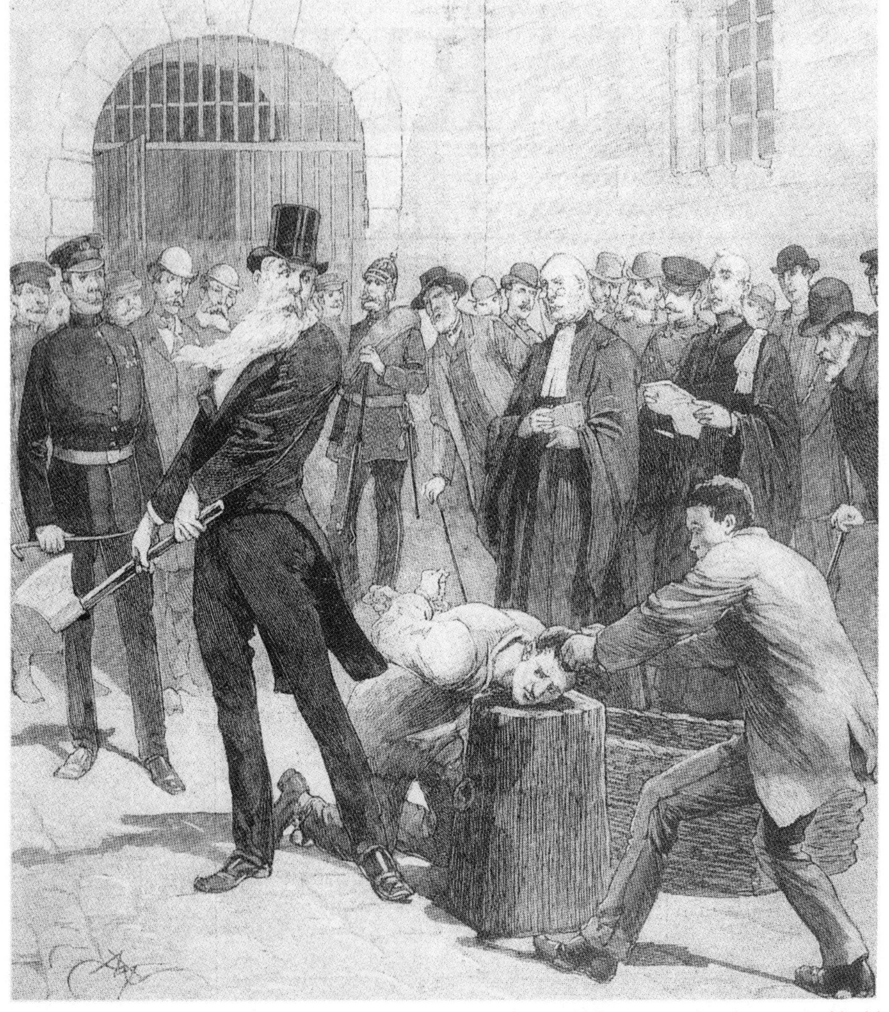

Other popular European media showed garish fascination with German executions, as with this illustration from *Le Petit Parisien* of the infamous executioner Reindel demonstrating his skill in Berlin Prison, 1891.

FOR FURTHER READING:

Richard J. Evans, *Rituals of Retribution: Capital Punishment in Germany 1600–1987* (Oxford University Press. 1996); Michel Foucault, *Discipline and Punish: The Birth of the Prison* (Penguin, 1977); V. A. C. Gatrell, *The Hanging Tree: Execution and the English People 1770–1868* (Oxford University Press, 1994); Pieter Spierenburg, *The Spectacle of Suffering: Executions and the Evolution of Repression: From a Preindustrial Metropolis to the European Experience* (Cambridge University Press, 1984).

The Life and Resurrection of Alexandre Dumas

The grandson of a Haitian slave, he became the most famous author in France; now, his rousing Romantic novels are enjoying renewed popularity.

Victoria Foote-Greenwell

Victoria Foote-Greenwell, who lives and works in Paris, writes on travel and culture for Time *magazine.*

When Alexandre Dumas built his estate in Port Marly in 1846, he didn't cover his Gothic cottage in wisteria but in words: 88 titles of his works. The titles carved in stone proved an unnecessary safeguard against oblivion: 150 years later they abound both in print and on screen. Though many today know his works, few know that Dumas, the most successful author of 19th-century France and one of the greatest storytellers of all time, was the grandson of a Haitian slave.

Dumas (known as Dumas *père* to distinguish him from his son, Alexandre, or Dumas *fils*) had to confront poverty, lack of education, censorship and slander, and the insidious wear and tear of 19th-century racism. Mademoiselle Mars, the leading lady at the Comédie-Française, once yelped as the gangly, young playwright departed, "Open the windows. It smells of Negro!" And yet, Dumas would eventually befriend princes, help the cause of three revolutions and have a French magazine today trumpet one of his novels as "the most read book after the Bible."

For a long time Dumas was treated with condescension by academia as a mere plebeian entertainer. More recently his reputation has been hampered by the 20th-century credo that endorses spare, analytical writing and minute psychological revelation. Dumas's skills run in quite the opposite direction: instinctive heroes, voluptuous atmosphere, a galloping narrative and breakneck dialogue. But in the past few years academic scholars have shown a renewed interest in the writer. They point out that before he was 35, Dumas contributed to French literature by laying the foundations of bourgeois drama, and helping to popularize history and create a new kind of Romantic novel.

Dumas's popular bequest is profoundly anchored. His books, translated into nearly a hundred languages, are selling briskly. In 1993, there were 140 million copies of his works sold in the former Soviet Union. In 1994, French publishers printed 17 new editions, including 8 alone of *Queen Margot,* on the French best-seller list that summer and reissued in the United States because of the screen version starring Isabelle Adjani. Twenty-two new editions of his stories were released in France in 1995, and nine never-before-published texts, stories and essays are scheduled for release this fall. Next year, *The Count of Monte Cristo,* which has already generated some 50 films, is expected to appear on French television with international screen star Gérard Depardieu in the title role. *The Three Musketeers* has been fodder for at least 60 films and spinoffs, including a 1993 Walt Disney remake of the same title, and *D'Artagnan's Daughter,* a faithfully imagined romp released in 1994 in France and 1995 in England.

The magical estate that Alexandre Dumas created outside Paris is now fully restored and open to the public. The neo-Renaissance chateau, just paces down the hill from the Gothic pavilion where he worked, is wreathed with his initials and sculpted with portrait medallions of his favorite authors, from Homer to Sir Walter Scott. Above the front door is a medallion of Dumas himself.

Recent studies have begun to dismiss the longstanding view of Dumas as the naive bon vivant. Instead, a more complicated image emerges, of a man who triumphed in spite of a society that rewarded him for his talent while expressing its disdain for him.

The prejudice Dumas encountered was usually more subtle than overt, but enemies could be baldly bigoted at times. A gentleman once began to make racist remarks within earshot, and when he finally said, "Mr. Dumas probably knows a thing or two about Negroes, since so much black blood runs in his veins," Dumas coolly responded, "Yes, of course. My father was a mulatto, my grandfather was a Negro, and my great-grandfather was an ape. You see, sir, my family began where yours left off."

His family tree began in the Caribbean island of Santo Domingo. Dumas's father, Thomas-Alexandre, was born in

1762 to a beautiful black house slave, Cessette Dumas, and to her owner, the Marquis de la Pailleterie, who had left Normandy to seek his fortune as a sugar planter. The marquis returned to Europe in 1775, though not before selling off his four children, a practice not uncommon at the time. He later bought back his 14-year-old illegitimate son and had him brought to France. The young man eventually broke off ties, took his deceased mother's name and entered the army. Promotion to lieutenant colonel was the carte blanche that allowed the handsome mulatto to marry an innkeeper's daughter, and his rapid climb up the ranks continued.

At 31 he became a general and soon began serving under Napoleon Bonaparte. The feats he performed and the wrongs he suffered read like scenes from a Dumas novel: he held a bridge alone against a squadron of men, cutting them down as they came two and three abreast toward him, sustaining three wounds and seven bullet holes in his cloak as he halted their advance. They named him "the black devil."

Soon he and Napoleon fell out, and thereafter Napoleon referred to him as "that Negro Dumas." Still, the general served honorably, seizing a treasure worth millions and sending it to Napoleon with a note: "Should I be killed or die . . . remember I have left behind me in France a wife and child."

But when the general left the ranks for France, he was captured, imprisoned and poisoned by the enemy, resulting in ulcers, partial paralysis and blindness in one eye. Freed after an 1801 armistice, he was denied back pay and a military pension by Napoleon.

A year after his return, in Villers-Cotterêts, Madame Dumas gave birth to a boy christened Alexandre. The general died penniless in 1806 but not before instilling in his son a sense of the heroic. Alexandre's frugal childhood was spent hunting in the nearby woods. He had his first brush with social outcasting by the local nobility when he was insulted at a ball for wearing his undersized communion suit. At 13 Dumas felt the first tingling of ambition. An older friend, Auguste Lafarge, wrote a witty epigram revenging himself on the girl who had jilted him, and soon the whole county was reciting the stanza. Noted Dumas: "I must admit that all the brouhaha around his name . . . made my head spin. I wanted the glory of having others speak of me even when I wasn't there." The youngster must have been equally impressed by the power of the pen to settle a score.

In 1822 Dumas visited Paris for the first time. Once back home he happened to play billiards and traded his winnings—600 glasses of absinthe—for 12 round-trip tickets by coach to the capital. Within a year he took the trip to Paris one way. He realized he had nothing to barter for room and board but his wits, an elephantine memory and graceful handwriting. This last landed him a modest job as a copyist for the duc d'Orleans. Before long Dumas was attending the theater nightly and staying up until dawn reading Corneille, Milton and Schiller. He soon began writing poems, short stories and maudlin melodramas.

Dumas won a place at the dinner parties of Charles Nodier, a central figure in the French Romantic movement, and in time he became friends with Victor Hugo, Lamartine and George Sand. Dumas made his name and set off a Romantic revolution in theater with *Henry III and His Court,* the first in a series of historical plays and novels that featured the hapless 16th-century king and his conniving mother, Catherine de Médicis. After the February 1829 premiere at the Comédie-Française, the young partisans of Dumas's drama chanted "Down with Racine, down with Voltaire!" and tried to heave the marble busts of classical authors out the foyer windows. In several hundred lines Dumas had liberated theater from the shackles of restraint, verse and the sacrosanct unities of place and time. He also showed on stage the physical brutality that traditionally happened off: the duc de Guise, trying to force a confession from his wife that she has a lover, crushes her hand in his iron gauntlet.

Dumas also anticipated modern social drama. He was one of the first French playwrights to depict characters in contemporary costumes and settings, and to conclude a play on a spine-tingling note. In 1831 *Antony* wowed the crowds when the illegitimate hero, in an effort to protect the honor of his dead mistress, tells her husband in the final curtain line: "She resisted me so I killed her!"

The amorous Dumas often courted his actresses and tallied up 28 mistresses in his lifetime. He had three children: a son born in 1824 that he legally wrested seven years later from the child's mother, a dressmaker; a daughter born to actress Belle Krelsamer in 1831; and another daughter born in 1860 whom he adored in old age. He was married briefly to mediocre actress Ida Ferrier in the 1840s.

A revolution in the way newspapers were sold provided the next jump up in Dumas's flourishing career. In 1836, when newspapers were bought by yearly subscription only, the newly launched *La Presse* sold cheaply and by the issue. To lure readers and to keep them, a new formula proposed: "Next episode in tomorrow's edition." With his *Countess of Salisbury,* set in the 14th century, Dumas helped develop the *roman-feuilleton,* or serial novel, and his run-on stories were soon highly sought after by the public.

As his star rose and his fortunes with it, Dumas became a target for newspaper satirists and salon squatters, resulting in a succession of duels and lawsuits. Mostly he was criticized for his prodigious output and for using ghostwriters. He openly admitted to collaborating with other writers, a practice in wide use at the time. He was also attacked for playing fast and loose with historical facts. When accused of raping history, he responded, "Yes, but look how beautiful the children are."

In a period of savage caricature, Dumas was a moving target for cartoons. *"Mon fouilli tropical"* ("my tropical tangle"), as he called his hair, was grist for dozens of drawings.

A lesser man might have buckled under so many offenses, but Dumas found productive ways to fight back. His works confront not only society's stigmas against illegitimacy and divorce, but also the horrors society inflicts because of race. In *Georges,* Dumas describes the insurmountable prejudice encountered by the wealthy son of a mulatto planter on the island of Mauritius. The hero's struggle is interwoven with plans for a slave revolt and set against a background of imperialist French and English forces vying for control of the island.

In addition to *Georges,* Dumas wrote *Ingénue,* a novel of the French Revolution published in 1853, in which he gives a gut-wrenching account of the slave trade and an impassioned plea for abolition.

Dumas was ardent about all forms of social injustice and, to the end of his life, was a true political activist. In July 1830 the barricades went up all over Paris to finally protest the reign of the conservative Bourbon king, Charles X. Dumas grabbed two pistols and went down into the street to help. He commandeered a coach for the town of Soissons, where he ordered the local commander to turn over a supposed store of 200 pounds of gunpowder. With a battle-ax Dumas broke down the wooden doors and stumbled onto a mother lode: a ton and a half of explosives. He and anti-Bourbon rebels escorted the powder back to Paris where they were congratulated for their efforts. In 1860 Dumas used his 78-ton schooner *Emma* to personally run guns to the Italian Republican patriot Garibaldi.

Dumas seemed to find opportunity and adventure in even the worst of situations. When an initial need to flee emotional entanglements and problems with creditors led him to travel through France and other European countries, North Africa and Russia, he churned out sprightly travelogues, which became fodder for future fiction. During a trip to the island of Saint-Marguerite he took notes on the man in the iron mask, the mysterious figure unfairly imprisoned for 40 years. This tale of inequity would resonate for Dumas and inspire the plot of *The Viscount of Bragelonne,* the last book in his Musketeer trilogy.

Dumas's recourse from society's pressures was to write, and the theme of arbitrary injustice and subsequent redemption would bubble to the surface of many of his works. In 1848 Dumas asserted that he had written for 20 years at an average of ten hours a day. He wrote a full-length play in three-and-a-half days, a one-act play in an afternoon. His published works, including novels, novellas, dramas, memoirs and travel books, total about 300. He also published eight newspapers and was the only writer for some of them.

But as Dumas wrote in 1857: "As always I search in my work for a distraction from my distress." This was his cure also for physical ailments. One night his son, Alexandre Dumas *fils,* found the elder Dumas awake. "Can't you sleep?" he asked.

"No, I've been walking."

"You don't feel good?"

"My stomach aches. When I get that, I walk. When it gets worse, I read."

"And what about when it gets too painful to read?"

"I work."

If his work provided solace, it also yielded considerable riches. In 1840 the average worker's salary was 3 francs a day; one line from Dumas's pen was worth 3 francs. He earned 80,000 francs in a single year and was not yet at the height of his success.

In the 1840s he bought up nearly 13 acres of forest and fields overlooking the Seine Valley. Though he initially wanted a small country house as a retreat from Paris, Dumas got carried away and pushed his architect, Hippolyte Durand, to ever more fanciful designs. Construction began in 1845. When it was finished the initial budget of 48,000 francs had ballooned to more than 200,000 francs. The worldly writer Balzac clucked over the price of what he called "one of the most delicious follies ever built."

Dumas was entranced with what he called his "paradise on earth in miniature." In the summer of 1847 he invited 50 people to his sumptuous housewarming; instead 600 turned up to see the house that was the talk of Paris. Thereafter Dumas would write in his moated pavilion while the beau monde, including strangers, milled in the chateau with his mistresses and friends, his children, dogs, cats and a pet vulture. One of his detractors wrote: "Everywhere ostentation and lack of taste . . . morals of a most extravagant nature were the rule here."

In less than a year the estate had swallowed up more than half a million francs, and Dumas went bankrupt. Pressed by his creditors, Dumas eventually had to sell the house for a seventh of what it had cost.

The one house Dumas was able to call home was slated for demolition in 1970. But an appeal by French historian Alain Decaux prompted thousands of letters of protest, and Monte-Cristo was bought by the local townships.

Today the public can see the park as it once was, a meandering tract of rock gardens and roses, bridges and waterfalls, man-made pools and grottoes that lead the way to the author's Gothic pavilion, which is still guarded by a stone dog asleep in a stone doghouse. The motto over the door of the chateau itself succinctly captures the duality of Dumas's nature, his generosity and his narcissistic delight in adulation: *"J'aime qui m'aime"* ("I love those who love me"). Inside, the rooms trace Dumas's life and heritage, beginning with his grandfather's chateau in Normandy and ending with his son, Alexandre Dumas *fils,* who would go on to write the celebrated *La Dame aux Camélias,* later adapted in Verdi's *La Traviata.*

The French have a hardheaded saying: "Revenge is a platter best tasted cold," and Dumas's sweetest of desserts is his enduring success. Dumas *fils* went on to be a guiding force of modern drama. Unlike his father, but to the elder's delight, he was inducted into the hallowed Académie Française. As for the offspring of Dumas's imagination, they are alive and well today in the bookstore, on the college syllabus and on the marquee.

All this even though the novels are clearly books of their time. Consider the best known of them, *The Three Musketeers.* Long, theatrical, at times preposterous, its pages are filled with improbable coincidence and dialogue worthy of a modern-day bodice-ripper: "Buckingham seized her hand and kissed it passionately. Then he got to his feet and said: If I escape alive I shall see you again before six months have passed, even if I have to set the world ablaze to reach you."

But the book, awash with derring-do and sly comedy, is also great fun to read. The Musketeers twirl their mustaches, clank their swords, and dispatch with aplomb the minions of the villainous Cardinal Richelieu. The hot-blooded young d'Artagnan—"our hero"—has an "I'm as good as you are and tell me I'm not" air about him, and manages to get himself into—and out of—one scrape after another. Fresh from the country on his second morning in Paris, he manages in separate encounters to offend Athos, Porthos and Aramis, and challenges each to a duel. The three master swordsmen all turn up at the appointed time and place, and are astonished to find themselves facing the same bumptious youth. Providentially, a squad of the Cardinal's henchmen appears, d'Artagnan joins the Musketeers in routing them, and the four are henceforth as brothers.

Scenes like these, of course, make Dumas's books a treasure trove for celluloid. His novels and plays have generated more than 200 films and spin-offs, as well as innumerable shorts and cartoons.

In a recent best-selling literary whodunit, *The Dumas Club* by the Spaniard Arturo Perez-Reverte, the Dumasian scholar-narrator declares in vivid apologia: "*The Three Musketeers* has lost none of its freshness, in spite of the evolution in taste and the stupid discredit in which action has fallen. Ever since Joyce, we are forced to resign ourselves to Molly Bloom. . . ." Certainly modern literature has run out of stories, and worse yet, has also run out of heroes. Camus and Beckett gelded their heroes, the self-obsessed stranger diddling with his second thoughts, the two tramps waiting morosely for Godot. America had its cowboys and Superman. Luckily, France has d'Artagnan and his triumvirate: the earthy Porthos, the spiritual Aramis and the noble Athos. The tale has guided generations who learned their moral standards from the Musketeers: to behave well, or to misbehave in style.

Undying friendship and loyalty is a dicey proposition anywhere but on a printed page. With their succinct motto ("All for one, one for all"), d'Artagnan and the Musketeers offer us the best of male bonding, dispensing in one sword sweep with the more anguishing issues of ambivalence and the Other.

In *The Count of Monte Cristo* the hero, Dantes, is now being viewed as a Promethean figure, even a Nietzschean superman. "Farewell to all feelings that warm the heart," says Dantes, as he leaves Marseilles after coming to the aid of a friend. "I have been Heaven's substitute to recompense the good. Now let the God of vengeance yield me the power to punish the wicked!" Omniscient and omnipotent, Dantes systematically ferrets out his old enemies and avenges himself on them. The story is a fantasy of justice and divine retribution, in a cantilevered universe oblivious to such moral order.

On his deathbed Dumas asked his son, "Will I be remembered?" Dumas was an old man by then, had toted the weary load in exemplary fashion and can thus be forgiven for asking such a question. Against all social odds Alexandre Dumas joins the immortal pantheon of the great men of letters.

Sarah Bernhardt's Paris

Christopher Hibbert

Christopher Hibbert is a prize-winning British author of more than 30 books of history, military history and biography. They include The Days of the French Revolution; The Great Mutiny: India 1857; Versailles; The Court of St. James's; The House of the Medici; Disraeli and His World; *and biographies of Charles I, George IV and Edward VII.*

In the summer of 1862 an astonishingly thin young girl with a pale face, frizzy reddish hair, intense blue eyes and a prominent nose stood on the corner of the Rue Duphet and the Rue St. Honore in Paris looking at the yellow playbills which were pasted up to advertise forthcoming productions at the Theatre Francais. *Iphigenie by Jean Racine,* one of these playbills announced, *For the Debut of Mademoiselle Sarah Bernhardt.* "I have no idea how long I stood there, fascinated by the letters of my name," she recorded years later. "But I remember that it seemed to me as though every person who stopped to read the poster looked at me afterwards."

Sarah Bernhardt was then just eighteen. Her mother, a beautiful woman of Jewish Dutch descent, had once been a milliner and was now a highly successful courtesan with an apartment in the Rue St. Honore where, so it was said, attractive women of her calling could command a hundred thousand francs a month and enjoy the use of two carriages and the services of a footman and a chef. Certainly Julie Bernhardt lived well, and in her comfortable apartment received a succession of generous friends, protectors and lovers, bankers and noblemen, musicians and writers. They included the Italian composer Gioacchino Rossini, who had settled in Paris some years before, Alexandre Dumas, the prodigal, exuberant author of *The Three Musketeers,* who believed that in fiction as in life the two most important ingredients were "*l'action et l'amour,*" and Charles Auguste-Louis-Joseph, Duc de Morny, the half-brother of the Emperor Napoleon III whose *coup d'etat* he had helped to engineer.

Napoleon III had been born in Paris in 1808, the third son of a younger brother of Napoleon I. Adventurer and idealist—though with his waxed moustache and half-closed eyes, looking, as Theophile Gautier said, "more like a ringmaster who has been sacked for getting drunk"—he believed himself to be a man of destiny, bound to follow his star. After the overthrow of the Orleans monarchy in 1848 he was elected Prince President of the Second Republic, and four years later, following the *coup d'etat* by which he forcibly dissolved the *Assemblee Nationale Legislative,* he was proclaimed Emperor. Since then, with the help of Baron Haussmannn, Prefet de la Seine, he had been transforming Paris, intent not only upon freeing the fine monuments of the past from the jumble of buildings that enclosed them on every side, and upon creating a modern dazzling *ville lumiere* with wide, gaslit boulevards and magnificent perspectives, but also upon ensuring that it became a capital city which artillery could overawe with clear fields of fire against revolutionary mobs.

Under Haussmann's ruthless direction pavements were torn up and narrow streets demolished; grandiose apartment blocks took the place of huddled houses whose poor occupants were forced out into the suburbs. Five hundred miles of water mains were laid, over 200 miles of sewers; more than 30,000 gas lamps replaced the ancient lanterns; railway stations were constructed close to the heart of the city. Imposing new thoroughfares were driven through the gardens of the Luxembourg Palace; the Boulevard de Sebastopol made its way through a populous district beside the cast-iron and glass food markets known as Les Halles; the Boulevard Haussmann pushed east from the Place de l'Etoile; the Boulevards Saint-Germain and St. Michel and the Rue de Rennes appeared on the Left Bank. The Ile de la Cite was transformed and its greatest pride, Notre-Dame, restored under the direction of Eugene-Emmanuel Violet-le-Duc. The Tuileries and the Cour Carree were joined by a new gallery along a lengthened Rue de Rivoli. The Bois de Boulogne was laid out with artificial lakes and carriage drives. In 1861 the foundation stone of a vast opera house, which was to occupy almost three acres, was laid to the north of the Boulevard des Italiens; and here, after fourteen years' work, Charles Garnier's extravagant edifice, decorated with 33 varieties of marble and the works of 73 sculptors, was opened at last, a fitting tribute to the pomp and opulent display of the Second Empire.

In this prosperous and rapidly changing city of 1,825,000 people, the cosmopolitan capital of the world, the working day of the poor began as those more fortunate were going to bed after a night of pleasure. Before dawn *chiffonniers* appeared with lanterns and forks and with baskets on their backs to poke through the piles of rubbish which had been thrown out into the streets, searching for rags and bones, bottles and jars, hoping to find, and sometimes finding, an article more valuable before the rubbish wagons trundled along to cart the mounds away. And then, as the sun came up, bootblacks came out with scissors as well as brushes for they were as expert at clipping poodles as they were at polishing shoes; women who sold sweetmeats in the streets prepared their trays of cakes and chocolates, while soup and coffee vendors took up their places on the Pont Notre-Dame; *marchands de coco,* relics of the time of King Louis Philippe, wearing cocked hats and little bells, chopped up lemons and sticks of licorice to flavor

From *Mankind,* October 1982. © 1982 by *Mankind,* the magazine of popular history. Reprinted by permission.

the water they carried on their backs in highly polished ornamental tanks to offer for sale in goblets to thirsty passers-by; mechanics greased the wheels of the roundabouts in the Champs Elysees where gardeners watered the exotic flowers; and waiters scattered damp sand under the tables of cafes where clerks and laborers called for coffee and croisettes, brandy plums, absinthe or cheap Orleans wine as they streamed down on their way to work from the heights of Montmartre and La Chapelle, smoking clay pipes, toolbags slung on their backs and loaves of bread under their arms—masons in white jackets, locksmiths in blue overalls, tilers in blouses and small round caps, painters in long smocks swinging their pots, bricklayers with hods on their shoulders, chimney-sweepers harnessed to their barrows of soot.

After their *petit dejeuner* visitors from the country and foreign tourists emerged from their hotels, from the Hotel de Helder; the Hotel Louvre in the Place du Palais Royal which the enterprising Pereire brothers, Emile and Isaac, had built for the Paris Exhibition of 1855; from the even larger Grand Hotel on the Boulevard des Capucines which, with its 750 rooms was the largest in Europe; and from the Ambassade, the Ritz, and the Bristol which, patronized by the Prince of Wales who stayed there, ineffectively incognito, as the Duke of Lancaster, was to become the most fashionable of all.

The doors of the shops now opened, of the smaller, smarter boutiques whose prices varied in accordance with the apparent wealth or gullibility of their customers; of Denton's bookshop in the Palais-Royal where 6,000 copies of the Goncourt brothers' *La Lorette* had been sold in a single week in 1853; and of those recent phenomena, the large department stores, the Maison du Bon Marche, which had been founded by Norman Boucicaut in 1852, Chaucard's Louvre in the Rue de Rivoli and Jaluzot's Au Printemps on the Boulevard Haussmann. Their shopping done, mothers and nurses took their children and charges out to play with hoops and balls and wooden horses on wheels by the sparkling fountains in the gardens of the Tuileries, wearing billowing, brilliantly colored and intricately embroidered crinolines and flowered hats, while men walked past on their way to the Jockey Club, the Club de L'Union or Le Cercle Agricole, resplendent in shining silk hats, long, narrow-waisted coats, elaborate cravats and tight trousers with buttons down the seams.

By midday the boulevards were crowded with horse-drawn *imperiale* omnibuses, with phaetons and *voitures a laquais,* cockaded coachmen and footmen sitting on the boxes. Smaller equipages, fiacres, traps, landaus and tandems rattled down the Champs Elysees towards the Bois de Boulogne to parade around the lakes and along the Allee des Poteaux. Soon the green iron chairs beneath the striped awnings of the cafes and restaurants were occupied; and familiar faces could be seen at the Cafe de Cardinal on the corner of the Rue Richelieu, at Tortoni's on the Boulevard des Italiens, next door to the Restaurant de la Maison Doree, at the Cafe de Paris which was the favorite haunt of Eugene Sue, Heinrich Heine and Balzac, and at the Moulin Rouge, a smart restaurant on the Champs Elysees where "at the bottom of the garden, at all the windows on every floor, in the lighted depths of private rooms, just as in boxes at the theater, women's heads could be seen nodding left and right to former companions of their nights." In the evenings, as guests set out for fancy dress balls and private dinner parties and the cafe-concerts and the theaters began to fill, crowds collected outside the Theatre Francais to watch the fashionable and famous go into the House of Moliere.

Here it was that Sarah Bernhardt had decided to become an actress. She had been taken by her mother and three of her mother's friends—Regis Lavolie, a rich banker, Dumas and the Duc de Morny—to see a performance of Racine's *Britannicus.* She had found it so moving that she had burst into tears and then into sobs so loud that her mother blushed scarlet in embarrassment, other members of the audience had turned round calling "*Sh! Sh!*" and Lavolie had stalked out of the box in disgust, slamming the door behind him.

On their return to Julie Bernhardt's apartment, Sarah had been sent to bed in disgrace. But Dumas had kindly gone up with her and kissing her at her door, had whispered in her ear, "Goodnight, little star." Her chance of being a star had come in 1862 with her performance of *Iphigenie.* She had worked hard for the opportunity. With the influential help of the Duc de Morny, she had been granted an audience at the Conservatoire; then, having attended the classes there with enthusiastic assiduity, she had been taken on as a *pensionnaire* by the Comedie Francaise.

Overcome by stage fright, she gabbled her words throughout the first act, and although she recovered her confidence later on, neither audience nor critics were favorably impressed. Her subsequent performances were equally disappointing, and it was widely felt that the Comedie Francaise had been ill-advised to take her on in the first place. There was little regret when, after breaking her parasol over the head of the stage doorkeeper for some imagined slight and punching an elderly actress in the face during a violent quarrel, she was told to resign from the company. At least she could comfort herself with the thought that she had made a name for herself. Caricatures and stories about her appeared in the newspapers; and her mother's friend, Lavolie, had little difficulty in persuading the directors of the Gymnase, a theater which specialized in popular comedies, to give the now notorious young actress another chance. She did not flourish at the Gymnase either, though, and after one particularly disastrous performance, which reduced her to thoughts of suicide, she decided to follow Dumas' advice and go abroad for a time. According to her own account she went to Spain. But, since her own accounts were always flavored by a reckless indifference to truth, she may well have gone no further than Brussels. Certainly she returned to Paris pregnant by a Belgian aristocrat, the paternity of whose child she ascribed at various times to Leon Gambetta, Victor Hugo, General Boulanger and even to the infant Duke of Clarence who was, in fact, born a fortnight before his alleged progeny.

Within a few weeks of Maurice Bernhardt's birth, his mother went back to work, this time at the Porte-Saint-Martin, a theater renowned for its melodramas and *vaudevilles feeriques.* Here yet again she proved a disappointment. And it was not until—once more with the help of one of her mother's friends—she signed a contract at the Odeon, a national theater on the Left Bank near the Jardin du Luxembourg, that she made her mark at last. Here, in the leading female role in a revival of Dumas' *Kean,* she enjoyed her first unalloyed success. Thereafter triumph followed triumph. Her name on the playbills was sure to fill the theater. She became the darling of the Left Bank. After her portrayal of the minstrel boy

Zanetto in Francois Coppee's *Le Passant* in 1868, the Emperor's cousin, Princess Mathilde, arranged for a command performance at the Tuileries where she so impressed the Emperor himself that he gave her a splendid brooch blazing with diamonds. She moved into a large apartment in the Rue Auber; and here, in an untidy clutter of furniture and ornaments, over which turtles with gold-plated shells crawled to escape from barking dogs, she received an assortment of friends and lovers even more varied and distinguished than those who had paid court to her mother.

She entertained Leon Gambetta, then a young barrister and leading member of the political opposition, who was one day to become President of the Chamber of Deputies. She welcomed Princess Mathilde's brother, Prince Napoleon, like his sister a patron of literature and the arts, and a patron, too, of Cora Pearl, the saucy, irresistible English courtesan who was known to have presented herself to her admirers wearing nothing but a sprig of parsley. Sarah Bernhardt also welcomed Theophile Gautier, "*le bon Theo,*" whose praise of her art had done much to further her career. And, with particular pleasure, she opened her arms to Gautier's friend, George Sand, who, many years before, had left her husband, Baron Dudevant, to lead an independent, unconventional life in Paris, writing novels, wearing trousers, smoking incessantly, nursing Alfred de Musset through an illness before deserting him for his doctor, then going to live with Chopin. She was in her mid-sixties now, but working as hard as ever: Sarah Bernhardt appeared in two of her plays and grew to admire and to love her.

Both Gautier and George Sand were members of that coterie of writers and artists who, during these final years of the Second Empire, met regularly at Magny's, the restaurant in the Rue Contrescarpe-Dauphine which was run by Modeste Magny, an exceptionally gifted restaurateur from the Marne. George Sand had been one of his earliest customers, preferring his restaurant to the Pinson in the Rue de l'Ancienne-Comedie which she had previously patronized, despite the row made next door to Magny's by the performers and spectators at Aublin's *Les Folies Dauphine,* a *boui-boui* or music-hall known more familiarly as *Le Beuglant* because of the bellowing sounds that burst from its windows.

George Sand had not, however, been present at the inauguration of the dining club at Magny's on November 22, 1862. On this Saturday evening among those present had been the once lively but now rather morose lithographer and caricaturist Gavarni, whose sketches of Parisian life had been one of the most notable features in the satirical paper, *Le Charivari;* Gavarni's friends and future biographers, the two inseparable brothers, Edmond and Jules de Goncourt, novelists, social historians, diarists and men of letters, who spoke alternately, the one elaborating, complementing and developing the remarks of the other; and the great critic, Sainte-Beuve, an ugly, fat little man with a black skull-cap on his bald head, now nearing the end of his life but seeming to enjoy it as much as in those earlier days when he had been the lover of Victor Hugo's wife and had dined in a private room every Saturday night at Magny's with other women friends. On later occasions these four had been joined by Gustave Flaubert, the robust though syphilitic author of *Madame Bovary* and *Salammbo;* by the philogist and historian, Ernest Renan whose influential and controversial *Vie de Jesus* cost him the professorship of Hebrew at the College de France; the towering, bearded Ivan Turgenev, out of favor with the rulers of his native Russia; and Hippolyte Taine, critic and philosopher, whose *Histoire de la litterature anglaise* had appeared in three volumes in 1862.

They dined in one of the seven private rooms on the first floor, served by the head waiter Charles Labran, who was to remain at Magny's until his master's death. And, as the Goncourts wrote in their journal after their first dinner there, they enjoyed "an exquisite meal, perfect in every respect, a meal such as [they] had thought impossible to obtain in a Paris restaurant." The *specialites de la maison* were *tournedos Rossini, chateaubriand, petites marmites, puree Magny* and *becasses a la Charles,* all of which the proprietor had contrived himself. Also exquisitely cooked at Magny's were *pieds de mouton a la poulette,* and *ecrevisses a la Bordelaise* which, as one customer said, "once you had begun eating there was no reason to stop, and you didn't stop either, unless there was a revolution or an earthquake."

With such dishes Magny gained for himself a special commendation in Adolphe Joanne's guide to the restaurants of Paris which, dividing them all into six categories, considered only a few worthy of being listed in the first class. Apart from Magny's and Philippe's in the Rue Montorqueil, the knowledgeable *bon viveur* recommend Brebant's, haunt of the racing people from Longchamps and Chantilly; Vefour's for Rhenish carp, baked and stuffed and surrounded by soft roe; Ledoyen's for salmon with a green sauce the secret of which was unknown to other establishments; Aux Trois Freres Provencaux for cod with garlic; the Cafe Riche for *sole aux crevettes;* the Maison Doree for fillet steak, braised with tomatoes and mushrooms and served with "a veritable gravy of truffles"; and Bignon's for *barbue au vin rouge* and *filet Richelieu.* But though there were so few restaurants which Joanne could recommend without reserve, he calculated that there were 4,000 pot-houses which were "frequented only by workmen and coachmen." And even in these cheaper places the food was generally good and the service excellent, for in a city where prosperity had created an apparently insatiable demand for pleasure, those in search of it had learned to be discriminating.

"Civility appears to be the motive power of his life," an English visitor wrote of the Parisian waiter. "That wonderful fleetness with which he dashes through the cafe into the open air, and threads his way through rows of lounging customers at the green tables, carrying on the tops of his four fingers and thumb an immense pile of cups, liqueur glasses, bottles of iced water, and lumps of sugar . . . appears to be the noble effort of a chivalrous nature. Ask him for a light and he produces lucifers from any pocket. Although people are calling him or hissing to him in various directions, he finds time to light two or three lucifers and even to hold them till the fumes of the sulphur have passed away before he presents them to you . . . He is free with you; he has a light retort for any attempted joke; but he is never familiar—never rude . . . The reader who wishes to study the Parisian waiter in perfection, should choose a fine summer's night, and take his seat outside the rotunda in the Palais Royal about eight o'clock, in the midst of about 300 people, served by about eight waiters, who caper, loaded with crockery and newspapers with an activity that any Harlequin might envy."

There were numerous cafes in the Palais Royal, but mostly expensive and respectable. But for those who preferred less decorous establishments there were even more of these elsewhere. Paris, indeed, was a very *embarras de richesse* of cafes, cafe-concerts, taverns, *bouillons, cremeries, brasseries, pensions bourgeoises, assommoirs* and *estaminets* as well as brothels, *cabinets particuliers* and licentious dance-halls. One of the best known brothels was Farcy's where, in the drawing-room sprawling on red velvet divans around the floral-papered walls, the girls smiled and cooed and asked for drinks. One of the most expensive *cabinets particuliers* was the Grand Seize, an exotic private room at the Cafe Anglais hung with red wallpaper and gold hieroglyphics, furnished with gilt chairs and a crimson sofa, where Sarah Bernhardt was herself to be entertained by the Prince of Wales. And one of the most lively and wanton dance-halls was Mabille's in the Allee des Veuves where an orchestra of 50 played in a Chinese pavilion surrounded by artificial palm trees with gas globes hanging from the leaves; where, as a guidebook warned, "the limits of propriety [were] frequently passed"; and where parlormaids, *grisettes* and milliners could find men willing to pay them twenty francs for a night of pleasure, more than they could otherwise earn in a month.

In the summer of 1870 the carefree frivolity of the Second Empire came suddenly to a close. Napoleon III declared war on Prussia, and a few weeks later his army was crushingly defeated at Sedan. The confidence of the Parisians, who had never believed in the remotest possibility of such a catastrophe, was shattered overnight.

"Who can describe the consternation written on every face," wrote Edmond de Goncourt as his fellow citizens pondered on the consequences of the fall of the imperial government, "the sound of aimless steps pacing the streets at random, the anxious conversations of shopkeepers and *concierges* on their doorsteps, the crowds collecting at street-corners, the siege of the newspaper kiosks, the triple line of readers gathering around every gaslamp."

At news of the German army's approach, preparations for the expected siege of Paris gathered momentum. Mines were laid, woods chopped down, road blocks thrown up, road and river approaches obstructed, monuments protected by sandbags and boarding; and the capital's extensive defensive system of bastions, walls, moats and forts—which Adolphe Thiers had had constructed in 1840 but which had subsequently been neglected—was hastily restored and strengthened. Railway stations were converted into balloon factories or cannon-foundries, theaters into hospitals; couturiers' workshops began to make military uniforms, the Louvre to turn out armaments. Regular troops, marines and sailors marched into the city; conscripts and volunteers paraded through the streets; thousands of heavy guns were dragged out to the forest, while herds of cattle and sheep were driven into the Bois de Boulogne.

In the excitement of all this activity the morale of the Parisians rose. On September 13, a few days before the last mail-train left the city and the one remaining telegraph line to the west was cut, a review of the defenders was held by General Louis-Jules Trochu, president of the newly formed Government of National Defense, who galloped onto the scene to the rattle of drums and to shouts of *"Vive la France! Vive la Republique! Vive Trochu!"* Tens of thousands of soldiers lined the boulevards from the Place de la Bastille to the Arc de Triomphe. The National Guard, some in frock-coats, others in workmen's smocks, marched past to the strains of the *Marseillaise,* their rifles decorated with flowers and ribbons, children holding their fathers' hands.

Poets declaimed their verses; journalists issued proclamations; politicians harangued the crowds; priests preached sermons. Adelaide de Montgolfier, daughter of the great balloonist, watched the *Neptune,* the first postal balloon to leave Paris, soar into the sky above the Place Saint-Pierre in Montmartre, shouts of *"Vive la Republique!"* ringing in her ears, proud to think that her "dear father's invention [was] now proving of such great value to his country."

Enthusiasm was not matched, though, by achievement. Outside the city the French troops proved no match for the German invaders. Dejected and dispirited soldiers returned disconsolately from the front to the streets of Paris where already long queues were to be seen outside the butchers' shops as early as two o'clock in the morning and the restaurants started to serve beef that looked suspiciously like horse flesh. Looking for scapegoats, the Parisians turned on foreigners, particularly on the English residents who were believed to share their Queen's sympathetic attitude towards Germany: *Les Nouvelles* proposed that the best way to settle the question as to whether the British were spies or not was to shoot the lot of them. "Anyone who did not speak French with purity was arrested," commented Trochu's aide-de-camp, Maurice d'Herisson. "Englishmen, Americans, Swedes, Spaniards and Alsatians were arrested alike. A similar fate befell all those who, either in dress or manner, betrayed anything unusual. Stammerers were arrested because they tried to speak too quickly; dumb people because they did not speak at all; and the deaf because they did not seem to understand what was said to them. The sewermen who emerged from the sewers were arrested because they spoke Piedmontese."

The people turned, too, on Trochu and his government whom they accused of not facing the crisis with sufficient determination. Demonstrations were held in the Place de la Concorde; marches made to the Hotel de Ville; demands presented for a *levee en masse* and a *sortie en masse,* the election of a Municipal Commune, the formation of a corps of Amazons, the manufacture of "guns, more guns and still more guns." At the end of October news reached the capital that Marshal Bazaine had surrendered Metz to the enemy and that Le Bourget, a village north of Paris which had been captured by the Prussians, had been retaken by them. There were also rumors that Leon Gambetta, who, with a basket of homing pigeons, had left Paris by balloon at the beginning of the month to join the elderly members of the Delegation of Tours, was inclining to their view that surrender was inevitable.

Incensed by all this, a crowd of about 15,000 demonstrators advanced on the Hotel de Ville, shouting "No armistice!" and "The Commune forever!" Several hundred of them burst inside the building, demanding the resignation of all the members of the Government of National Defense and calling out the names of men whom they wished to replace them. Their leaders—with Gustave Flourens, a revolutionary member of the National Guard, well to the fore—climbed onto the baize-covered table of the council-chamber and strode along it, trampling on papers and notebooks, knocking over inkstands and sandboxes, crushing pens and pencils, their voices lost in the clangor of shouts, drums and trumpets, while General Trochu calmly smoked his cigar.

Trochu's apparent indifference to these agitators was justified: an energetic colleague, Ernest Picard, called upon the more constructive leaders of the National Guard for help, and a bourgeois battalion marched to the Government's rescue. While Flourens went into hiding, Parisians were asked to answer the following question in a plebiscite: "Does the population of Paris wish to maintain the powers of the Government of National Defense? *Out ou Non?*" Overwhelmingly the answer was yes.

So Trochu continued in office; his forces remained on the defensive; and Paris grew more and more to resemble a beleaguered city. Many shops put up their shutters, having nothing to sell; others filled their windows with telescopes, knives, revolvers and brandy-flasks. Fashionable clothes were no longer conspicuous on the boulevards: men wore makeshift uniforms, women their oldest dresses or nurses' aprons.

As Henry Labouchere, Paris correspondent of the London *Daily News,* recorded on November 15, Paris' mood now veered wildly "from the lowest depths of despair to the wildest confidence. Yesterday afternoon a pigeon arrived covered with blood, bearing on his tail a despatch from Gambetta, announcing that the Prussians had been driven out of Orleans . . . The despatch was read at the Mairies to large crowds, and in the cafes by enthusiasts who got up on the tables. I was in a shop when a person came in with it. Shopkeepers, assistants and customers immediately performed a war dance round a stove."

This festive mood was short-lived. People were soon complaining again about the National Guard, who performed very confidently on parade but showed little inclination to fight the enemy, and about General Trochu who, so one junior officer said, had associated so much with lawyers that he had become to resemble one himself: "He has dipped his pen in his scabbard and his sword in his inkstand, and when he finally attempts to draw the sword, he'll unsheath a penholder." Hopes were raised at the end of November by rumors of a great sortie involving 150,000 men who were to cross the Marne and occupy the enemy's positions at Champigny. But these hopes were dashed when the crowds, which had gathered at Pont d'Austerlitz and along the Avenue du Trone, learned that the sortie had ended in tragic failure. Hard upon this reverse came news of the defeat of the Army of the Loire and the recapture of Orleans. Less than a fortnight later the spirits of the people were revived again by an optimistic message from Gambetta published in the *Journal Officiel,* only to be dampened soon afterwards by the failure of another sortie.

In common with most other theaters and many hotels, the Odeon was converted into a hospital. Assuming the responsibility for organizing it, Sarah Bernhardt rushed from one admirer to another, asking for supplies, obtaining brandy from Baron Rothschild, chocolate from Meunier, sardines from the rich grocer, Felix Potin, outside whose store in the Boulevard de Strasbourg long queues stood throughout the night. Acting as nurse as well as storekeeper, she dressed wounds, assisted at operations, carried food to the helpless and brandy to the dying; and as the weeks passed and the supplies of food grew ever more depleted, often went without meals herself so that the patients might be fed.

By the end of the year the shortage of food in Paris had become acute. Beef and mutton, at first severely rationed, now disappeared from the shops altogether. Cab-horses and race-horses were sold by the butchers instead, then cats, rats and dogs. Eels and gudgeons from the Seine fetched their weight in silver.

> "People talk of nothing but what is eaten, can be eaten, or is there to be eaten [wrote Edmond de Goncourt]. Conversation has come down to this:
>
> " 'You know, a fresh egg costs twenty-five sous.'
>
> " 'It appears there's a fellow who buys up all the candles he can find, adds some coloring, and produces that fat which sells at such a price.'
>
> " 'Mind you don't buy any coconut butter. It stinks a house out for three days at least.'
>
> " 'I've had some dog chops, and found them really very tasty: they look just like mutton chops.'
>
> " 'Who was it who told me he had eaten some kangaroo?' "

As well as kangaroo, the director of the zoo sold all manner of animals for slaughter—buffaloes and zebras, reindeer and camels, yaks and elephants. But these animals were soon consumed. And "failing meat," one commentator observed, "you cannot fall back on vegetables: a little turnip costs eight sous and you have to pay seven francs for a pound of onions. Nobody talks about butter any more, and every other sort of fat except candle-fat and axle-grease has disappeared too. As for the two staple items of the diet of the poor—potatoes and cheese—cheese is just a memory, and you have to have friends in high places to obtain potatoes at twenty francs a bushel. The greater part of Paris is living on coffee, wine and bread." And even bread, a hard black substance made principally of bran, rice and starch, was scarce.

Hunger was not the only privation. By the end of the year the temperature had fallen to twelve degrees below zero. While sentries froze to death, orders were given for the felling of six square miles of trees in the Bois de Boulogne and the Bois de Vincennes and along the city's boulevards. But the people could not wait: fences, trellises, benches and telegraph poles were cut up as well and dragged away to their homes.

To cold and hunger and the attendant sickness and disease was added the horror of bombardment. At first it was only the forts that were shelled. But at the beginning of January 1871, shells began also to burst in the city itself, mainly on the poorer houses on the Left Bank where the people bore the cannonade with stoic courage. "On every doorstep, women and children stand, half frightened, half inquisitive," wrote Edmond de Goncourt, "watching the medical orderlies going by, dressed in white smocks with red crosses on their arms and carrying stretchers, mattresses and pillows."

Before long most people grew quite accustomed to the bombing. Children, hearing an explosion, would say, "That was a shell," and then calmly continue with their game. And street urchins on seeing a well dressed person walk by, so Henry Labouchere observed, would cry out, "Flat! Flat! A shell—a shell—*a plat ventre!* Down on your faces!" "The man, gorgeous in fur, falls flat on the ground—perhaps in the gutter—and the Parisian urchin rejoices with exceeding great joy."

Despite all the hardships, Labouchere continued, the Parisians behaved with remarkable resignation. They criticized Trochu and the government endlessly, denouncing their mistakes and blunders; but, they made "no complaint about their miseries," accepting them "with an unpretending fortitude which no people in the world could surpass." By the end of January, however, it was clear that resistance could not much longer be maintained. Men and women were falling down dead in food queues; the death rate rose to almost 4,500 a week, many of these being children. "At every step," one survivor wrote, "you met an undertaker carrying a little deal coffin."

Edmond de Goncourt was struck by the deathly silence that had fallen over the city. You could no longer hear Paris living, he noted in his journal. Every face looked like that of a sick person or convalescent. You saw "nothing but thin, pallid features, faces as pale and yellow as horseflesh." One day a prostitute, splashing along behind him in the Rue Saint-Nicholas, called out pathetically, "Monsieur, will you come up to my room, for a piece of bread?"

On January 23, Jules Favre, the Foreign Minister, left Paris for the German headquarters at Versailles to open negotiations for surrender. "A tall, thin, stooping, miserable-looking lawyer," as his secretary described him, "with his wrinkled frock-coat and his white hair falling over his collar," he seemed no match for Count Bismarck, the robust, broad-chested Iron Chancellor, who received Favre in the tight, white tunic and yellow-banded cap of the White Cuirassiers. Yet Favre's apparent weakness, real dignity and "good old French manners" worked to his advantage. "It is very difficult for me to be as hard with him as I have to be," Bismarck told his wife. "The rascals know this, and consequently push him forward." The terms imposed upon them were, therefore, not as hard as the French had feared they might be. But they were nevertheless obliged to agree to the German army's ceremonial march into the capital. So, on Wednesday, March 1, German troops escorted by blaring bands and by cavalry with drawn swords, paraded through the Arc de Triomphe and down the Champs Elysees.

Parisians, their houses shuttered and their shops closed, were now in a bitter mood, harboring resentment not only against the Germans but also against the Government and the generals who, they felt, had failed them, as well as against the rich who, during the siege, had been able to pay for the food and warmth denied to others and who, now that it was over, had left for the country. There was resentment, too, against the provinces which, having escaped most of the horrors of the war, chose to elect a predominantly royalist assembly. In protest a *Federation Republicaine de la Garde Nationale* was formed; and insurgents established the Commune of Paris.

Civil war was now inevitable. On the orders of Adolphe Thiers, soon to be President of the Third Republic, an army of regulars was collected at Versailles under General MacMahon and marched into Paris. The subsequent slaughter was fearful. Prisoners taken by the Versailles forces were shot out of hand; in retaliation the Commune seized hostages, including the Archbishop of Paris and the Presiding Judge of the Court of Appeals, and executed them. In the Rue Haxo scores of other hostages, among them several priests, were shot by a frenzied crowd of men and women. Street battles raged and the pavements ran with blood; numerous public buildings were destroyed. The Palais des Tuileries and the Hotel de Ville, the Palais Royal and the Louvre, the Ministry of Finance and the Prefecture de Police were all set on fire. By the time the last defenders of the Commune had been shot down in the Pere Lachaise cemetery nearly 20,000 people, men, women and children, had lost their lives—more than the total number who had perished in the whole of France throughout the six years of the Revolution of 1789–95.

During the days of the Commune Bernhardt had left Paris to escape from the vindictive Prefect of Police whom she had much offended in the past by contemptuously returning to him a play he had written which she had said was "unworthy to touch let alone to read." But as soon as the troubles were over she returned to her apartment over which she splashed bottles full of her favorite scent to disperse the smell of smoke from the hill smoldering buildings on every side. Victor Hugo had also returned from exile in Guernsey to what he himself described as "an indescribable welcome" from fellow republicans who elected him a senator. Although he was now in his seventies his career as poet, novelist and dramatist was far from over; but it was in a play which he had written over 30 years before, *Ruy Blas,* that Bernhardt, as the Queen of Spain, was to achieve the greatest triumph she had yet enjoyed. After the first night Hugo knelt before her to kiss her hand; cheering crowds filled the Rue Vaugirard; and a band of admiring young men unharnessed the horse of her carriage to drag it back themselves to her apartment, excitedly shouting "Make way for our Sarah!"

A few weeks later she was invited to return to the Theatre Francais. And here, in *Britannicus,* in Voltaire's *Zaire,* above all in Racine's *Phedre,* which some critics thought she played even more movingly than Rachel, she established herself as the most powerful dramatic actress of her time, mesmerizing her audiences, as Arthur Symons thought, "awakening the sense and sending the intelligence to sleep," interpreting her parts instinctively rather than intellectually with a kind of hypnotic fervor, and speaking in a voice in which, as Lytton Strachey said, "there was more than gold, there was thunder and lightning, there was heaven and hell."

As well as a great actress, Bernhardt also became known as a most outlandishly eccentric showman about whom stories—many invented, others that were not, yet seemed so—filled column after column in newspapers and magazines. Her apartment in the Rue de Rome and the house she later built on the corner of the Rue Fortury and the Avenue de Villiers, were furnished and decorated in the most bizarre manner, with a satin-lined rosewood coffin in which she sometimes slept and a canopied fur-strewn divan prominent amidst the medley of ill-matched chairs, tables, cupboards, carpets, a stuffed vulture, a leering skeleton and works of art of extraordinarily uneven quality. Visitors were likely to be accosted by an alarming variety of strange animals, wild cats, hawks, a baby tigress, a puma that ate Dumas *fils*' straw boater and a boa constrictor that devoured its owner's cushions.

They were also likely to meet many of the most famous and notorious people in Paris, from actors and actresses such as the lovable comedian Constant Coquelin whose creation of *Cyrano de Bergerac* was to become legendary, Sophie Croizette in whose company Bernhardt used to stuff herself with cakes and chocolates in Chiboust's *patisserie,* and the alluring Jean Mounet-Sully, to exotic aesthetes like Robert de Montesquiou and Oscar Wilde, the composer Gounod, Ferdinand de Lesseps and Louis Pasteur. She would hold court on her divan, Persian hangings and the leaves of jungle plants framing her intense, pale, quizzically seductive face, a vast Russian wolfhound sprawled by the fur hem of a dress raised slightly to reveal a pretty, provocative white-stockinged ankle. It was in this pose that one of her numerous lovers, the painter Georges Clairin, portrayed her in a picture which was the principal talking-point of the Academy's 1876 exhibition in the Salon d'Apollon in the Louvre.

Those interested more in art than in iconography, however, were discussing another exhibition that year, the second held by the so-called Impressionists. The growing dissatisfaction of these artists with academic teaching had been brought to a head in 1863 when an exhibition of works rejected by the Salon, including Manet's *Dejeuner sur l'herbe,* was ridiculed by traditionalists. Four of them, Renoir, Sisley, Bazille and Monet were fellow-students at the studio of Marc Charles Gabriel Gleyre. They remained friends after leaving Gleyre's studio and used to meet regularly at the Cafe de la Nouvelle-Athenes in Montmartre, where they were often joined by Pisarro, Cezanne, Degas, Manet and Berthe Morisot. In 1873, after works by several of these artists were turned away by the Salon, they decided to hold an exhibition of their own; and the next year they did so in the studio of Nadar, the aeronaut, caricaturist and photographer. One of the pictures shown was Manet's *Impression, soleil levant* which led a mocking journalist from *Le Charivari* to deride the whole movement as Impressionism, a term which the artists themselves accepted as applying to them all. For, although their school was never a homogeneous one with a jointly recognized purpose, they did share a common belief that painting and its techniques should not be restricted in the way that the Salon seemed to prescribe. "One does not paint a landscape, a seascape, a figure," Manet declared in a summary of the Impressionists' view: "one paints the impression of one hour of the day in a landscape, in a seascape, upon a figure." The Impressionists' exhibition of 1876 was followed by six others in which Caillebotte, Forain and the American exile, Mary Cassatt, also showed their work.

But none of them aroused any interest in Sarah Bernhardt. She far preferred the traditional style of Georges Clairin and the sweetly Romantic pictures of her Lesbian friend, Louise Abbema; and in her own watercolors and facile sculptures, which she occasionally exhibited at the Salon, she displayed no sign of willingness to depart from the accepted Academy style. Discerning critics did not take her work seriously, agreeing with Rodin—whose masterpiece of 1877, *The Age of Bronze,* was condemned by Academicians as scandalous—that it was nothing but "old-fashioned tripe." Bernhardt, however, had one powerful apologist, a moody art critic, the first of whose great cycle of twenty *naturaliste* novels, *Les Rougon-Macquart,* had just been published. This was Emile Zola.

The Paris which Zola described in some of these novels was a far cry from the fashionable restaurants of the Boulevard des Italiens. It was a Paris where life was hard and the working day long, the Paris of the poor as depicted by Honore Daumier, a sad contrast to that of the elegant dandy as sketched by Constantin Guys. Here, in those mean streets northwest of the Gare du Nord, streets of crumbling, leaking tenement buildings and lodging-houses with rotting, rain-sodden shutters, scraggy hens scratched for worms between the pavements; colored streams of water poured from dye-works; butchers in bloodstained aprons stood before the doors of slaughter-houses; men dragged beds and mattresses to pawnshops from which they emerged to get drunk in wine shops, to eat six-sous meals in *bistingos* or to take home paper bags of chipped potatoes or cans of mussels; and, as the factory bells summoned their husbands to work, women carried their dirty clothes to the wash-house where, in steamy air, smelling of sweat and soda and bleach, they banged shirts and trousers against their washboards, their red arms bare to the shoulders, their skirts caught up to reveal darned stockings and heavy laced boots, shouting to each other above the din. This is the world of *L'Assommoir,* of Coupeau, the roofer, and Gervaise, the laundry-woman, and of their daughter, Nana, whose career Zola later unfolded in his great novel of 1880.

The year before *Nana* was published Bernhardt left Paris for the first of those foreign tours which were to make her as celebrated abroad as she was at home. She returned from America in 1881 at the age of 36 to find Zola the most discussed and widely read author in France. She also found herself far from popular with her fellow Parisians who were resentful of her having abandoned their theaters for more lucrative appearances overseas and who were assured by various hostile journalists that she was becoming a prima donna of the most selfish, pretentious and avaricious kind. Her electrifying recitation of the *Marseillaise* at the end of a gala performance of the Opera on the glorious 14th of July, however, followed by a magnificent performance in Victorien Sardou's *Fedora*—whom she portrayed, in Maurice Baring's words, with "such tigerish passion and feline seduction which, whether it be good or bad art, nobody has been able to match since"—restored her to her former pre-eminence. She followed her Fedora with other equally brilliant performances—as Marguerite Gauthier in Dumas *fils' La Dame aux camelias,* as the Empress in Sardou's even more melodramatic *Theodora,* and as the heroine of Sardou's *Tosca.*

There were failures, too, though, and her private life was unhappy. Her sister, whom she loved dearly and had helped to bring up, died a drug addict. The Greek diplomat and would-be actor, the arrogant, selfish, compulsively satyric Aristide Damala, whom she found sexually enchanting and married, also became a morphine and cocaine addict, shamelessly injecting himself through his trouser leg in front of her friends, and further humiliating her by spending the money she gave him on other women before dying at the age of 34. Her former friend and colleague, Marie Colombier, of whom Manet painted a delightful portrait, revenged herself upon her for a professional slight by writing an obscene and libelous book, *The Memoirs of Sarah Barnum* which induced Bernhardt to burst upon the author in her apartment, brandishing a dagger in one hand and a riding crop in the other, committing a violent assault which furnished journalists and caricaturists with irresistible copy. Finally, Bernhardt's beloved son, as costly an expense as her husband, quarreled bitterly with his mother over the Dreyfus case and took himself off with his wife and daughter to the South of France where he remained for over a year, refusing to communicate with her.

Captain Alfred Dreyfus, a Jewish officer of unsullied reputation, was court-martialled in December 1894, found guilty of having passed military secrets to the German Embassy, and sentenced to life imprisonment on Devil's Island. It later appeared that the German's informant was not Dreyfus but another officer, Major Esterhazy. But the War Office suppressed this damaging discovery;

and, when Esterhazy was himself court-martialled, he was acquitted. The resultant uproar divided France into rival factions of furiously antagonistic *Dreyfusards* and *anti-Dreyfusards.* Sarah Bernhardt was as violent a champion of Dreyfus as her son was a denigrator of the "Jewish traitor." It is said that it was she who approached her friend Zola and persuaded him to write the celebrated letter, *J'Accuse,* to the President, denouncing the Army's disgraceful behavior. Certainly she proclaimed her sympathies loudly and publicly; professed her horror when Dreyfus, despite all the evidence, was found guilty after a fresh trial; and rejoiced when at last he was pardoned.

The quarrels over the Dreyfus affair were still raging when Bernhardt appeared as the Duc de Reichstadt in Edmond Rostand's *L'Aiglon* which night after night filled the large theater in the Place Chatelet that she had recently taken over at the age of 55 on a 25-year lease, restored and redecorated at immense expense, and renamed the Theatre Sarah Bernhardt. The play opened in March 1900 and was still running to packed houses in the summer when the Great Exhibition of that year filled Paris with visitors from all over the world.

This Exhibition was one of several which Paris had seen in Sarah Bernhardt's lifetime. The first had been in 1855 when a huge Palais de l'Industrie had been built beside the Champs Elysees and when Gustave Courbet had defiantly held a private exhibition of his work, entitled *Le Realisme,* immediately opposite the Palais des Beaux Arts where the more respectable paintings of Delacroix, Ingres, Vernet and Winterhalter had been shown. The next had been in 1867 when, in an immense brown and gold palace covering 40 acres on the Champ de Mars, the pictures of Jean Francois Millet had been displayed together with numerous marvels of modern science.

"A day at the Exhibition seems a mere hour," wrote Ludovic Halevy, who with Henri Meilhac wrote the libretto for Offenbach's *La Grande-Duchesse de Gerolstein* in which Hortense Schneider appeared at Varietes during the Exhibition's course. "How many things there are to see! . . . There are two miles or so of cafes and restaurants . . . You can eat and drink in every language . . . And the park round the palace, the houses from every land, the factories for glass-blowing and diamond-cutting, the bakery, the machine for making hats, and the machine for making shoes, and the machine for making soap . . . They make everything, these damned machines. I looked everywhere for the machines that turned out plays and novels. They are the only ones that are missing. They will be there at the next Exhibition."

The next Exhibition, the Universal Exhibition, had been held in 1878 to celebrate Paris' quick recovery from the horrors of the Commune. Another Palais de l'Industrie had appeared on the Champ de Mars, and Davioud's ornate palace on the Trocadero; and electric light had illuminated the Avenue de l'Opera. Eleven years later, another Universal Exhibition was held on the anniversary of the Revolution. And in that year visitors to Paris had their first sight of what was to become one of Paris' most familiar landmarks, the 300-meters-high iron tower constructed to the designs of Gustave Eiffel. And then in 1900 this new Universal Exhibition attracted over 50,000,000 visitors who visited the fine art shows in the new cast-iron halls by the Pont Alexandre III, who went for rides on the vast great wheel, and admired the immense metal bouquet glittering with electric lights near the Ecole Militaire.

Paris was now a modern city. Horse-drawn vehicles still trotted down the busy streets, but motor cars and electric trams were also to be seen, and the underground metropolitan railway was spreading fast beneath the pavements. *Haute couture* had become a large and thriving industry, enormously expanded since the days when the rich, following the example of the beautiful Empress Eugenie, had gone to the rooms in the Rue de la Paix where the Englishman, Charles Frederick Worth, held sway as the acknowledged arbiter of fashion. Now the firm founded by the banker Isadore Paquin and his wife alone employed nearly 3,000 people. Yet, for all the city's change and growth, its traditional pleasures remained unaltered. The essence of that Paris, to which King Edward VII made his famous and triumphant state visit in 1903, was the same as it had been when he was first captivated by its charm half a century earlier. The cafes of Montmartre, where Paul Verlaine had sat in slippered feet drinking hard until his death in 1896, were little different from those that the Goncourts had known a generation before; the performers at the Moulin Rouge, where La Goulue, plump and lascivious, and the pale, thin-legged Jane Avril kicked out their legs in the can-can, were as lively and exciting as Rigolette and Mogador and those other polka dancers at the Mabille in the days of Bernhardt's childhood. The brothels of the Rue des Moulins and Rue d'Amboise, where the ugly, crippled Comte de Toulouse-Lautrec sat closely observing the naked women through his pince-nez and portraying them with realistic sincerity, were much the same as those that Baudelaire had known at the time of the Second Empire.

When Toulouse-Lautrec died in 1901, Bernhardt was approaching her 57th birthday. But age meant nothing to her. She dismissed all thoughts of retirement, putting on play after play, some successful, others not, choosing them for the roles they offered her genius. In 1904 she was still "highly triumphant over time," in the words of Max Beerbohm, who was a professed "lover of Sarah's incomparable art," though he had derided her Hamlet which had made him wonder if she would next play Othello opposite the booming voiced Mounet-Sully as Desdemona. So little regard did Bernhardt pay to her age, in fact, that when she was 65 she took the leading role in Emile Moreau's *Proces de Jeanne d'Arc* in which she turned with serene confidence to the audience, when the Grand Inquisitor asked Joan her age, to answer in her still beautifully clear, silvery voice, "*Dix-neuf ans*" (19). Night after night the audience broke into rapturous applause.

Not long after the finish of this play's run the Great War broke out. Bernhardt announced her intention of remaining in Paris as she had done in 1870; but she was persuaded to leave by Clemenceau himself who told her that, as she was likely to be on a list of possible hostages, the Government did not want to be responsible for her safety.

She asked to be taken to the station by way of the Champs Elysees which she feared she might never see again. And as she drove into it she was amazed to come upon long lines of taxis, nose to tail and packed with soldiers, stretching as far as the eye could reach. These were the famous *Taxis de la Marne,* rushing troops to the front to reinforce the French 5th and 6th Armies which were making what was to prove a successful counterattack against the German forces on the River Marne.

Bernhardt had left Paris with her right leg in a plaster cast. She had injured it some time before, and by the time she reached the villa in the Bay of Arcachon where she was to stay, gangrene had set in. In February 1915 the leg was amputated in a hospital in Bordeaux. Yet even this did not destroy her determination to continue on the stage. By the end of the year she was back in Paris, appearing in Eugene Moraud's patriotic piece *Les Cathedrales,* balancing on one leg as she supported herself on the arm of a chair. She protested that she would carry on thus until she died, having herself strapped to the scenery if necessary. "Madame," she said to Queen Mary during a visit to England, "I shall die on the stage. It is my battlefield."

The prediction was almost fulfilled. On the night of a dress rehearsal of a play in which she was to appear with her old friend Lucien Guitry, his son Sacha and his daughter-in-law, Yvonne Printemps, she collapsed in a coma. Some weeks later, on May 26, 1923, her doctor opened a window of her house in the Boulevard Pereire and announced to the crowds below, "Messieurs, Madame Bernhardt is dead."

"Bernhardt is dead" one Parisian said, passing on the sad news to another. "How dark it seems all of a sudden."

Modernism, Statism, and Total War: The Twentieth Century

The nineteenth century ended with high hopes for the future of Western civilization. Popular novelists foresaw air travel, television, visual telephones, sound recordings, interplanetary travel, and even the construction of a new continent in the Pacific. Technology would liberate those living in the twentieth century from most of their burdens, or so argued the futurists of the day. There were skeptics, of course: Mark Twain punctured the pious hypocrisies of

UNIT 4

fellow Occidentals who presumed that their Christianity and their technology demonstrated their superiority over the benighted heathens of the non-Western world. And a few observers questioned whether humankind would be any happier, even with all the material benefits the future promised.

Even before this glittering future could be realized, turn-of-the century artists and thinkers brought forth an alternative vision of far greater originality. They set in motion a period of unprecedented cultural innovation and artistic experimentation, out of which emerged modern music, modern theater, modern literature, modern art, and modern architecture. Never before had there been so many cultural manifestos: Fauvism, Cubism, Futurism, and other avant-garde movements proclaimed themselves. In "When Cubism Met the Decorative Arts in France," Paul Trachtman traces the lasting influence of one such movement. In philosophy it was the age of pragmatism, positivism, and Bergsonism. On another intellectual frontier, Alfred Binet, Ivan Pavlov, and Sigmund Freud reformulated the premises of psychology. Advanced work in experimental science concentrated on rays, radioactivity, and the atom, setting the stage for Albert Einstein's abstract but unsettling theories.

Thus, in the years before the Great War, the West was able to point to unrivaled accomplishments. Aristocrats and the middle class were confident of the future because they were eminently satisfied with the present. Their general sense of well-being was captured by author Osbert Sitwell in his autobiography:

> Never has Europe been so prosperous and so gay. Never had the world gone so well for all classes of the community. . . . I remember from my childhood, what must have been a common experience with members of my generation, reading the Bible, and books of Greek, Roman, and English history, and reflecting how wonderful it was to think that, with the growth of commerce and civilization, mass captivities and executions were things of the rabid past, and that never again would man be liable to persecution for his political or religious opinions. This belief, inculcated in the majority, led to an infinite sweetness in the air we breathed. (*Great Morning*, London: Macmillan, 1957)

In light of subsequent events, all this seems a great illusion. We can see now how such illusions blinded Europeans to the impending war. Millions of lives were lost in World War I, which was a showcase for the destructive force of Europe's vaunted technology. The war dashed the hopes of an entire generation and contributed to revolution in Russia, the fall of the Hohenzollern and Habsburg dynasties, the breakup of the Ottoman Empire, the collapse of the international economy, and the emergence of totalitarian dictatorships. It finally played itself out in a second, even more devastating conflict.

The essay "1918" demonstrates how World War I influenced twentieth century notions of world order. "How the Modern Middle East Map Came to Be Drawn" traces many current problems to the geopolitics of the World War I settlement. The articles by Charles Delzell and Matthew Stibbe explore fascism in Italy and Germany. In "The Commanders," Stephen Ambrose assesses the significance of the D-Day invasion. "How The Bomb Saved Soviet Physics" tells how the Soviet Union ended the U.S. atomic weapons monopoly, while "The Future That Never Came" explains why the U.S.-Soviet rivalry did not produce a nuclear war. In their reports, Raymond Garthoff and John Lukacs offer perspectives on the cold war and other major political and ideological conflicts of our century. "The Other Camus" explores the difficulties of being a man of conscience in the intellectual climate of the twentieth century.

Looking Ahead: Challenge Questions

Why was the year 1918 so important?

What were the major consequences of the two major wars of this century? Who were the real winners and losers?

Describe the roles of German women in World War II.

Why do you think Italians turned to Mussolini and Fascism?

Why did the U.S.-Soviet atomic rivalry never lead to a nuclear war?

How does your assessment of the twentieth century compare to that of John Lukacs?

When Cubism Met the Decorative Arts in France

From side tables to the dazzling dress designs of Sonia Delaunay, a new exhibition at the Portland Museum in Maine surveys the scene

Paul Trachtman

Paul Trachtman's most recent SMITHSONIAN *article was about the computer artist Charles Csuri (February 1995). He writes from New Mexico.*

"When we invented Cubism, we had no intention whatsoever of inventing Cubism," said Pablo Picasso, many years later. "We wanted simply to express what was in us." What was in Picasso and his contemporaries was a voracious, if not violent, appetite for new forms of intellectual, cultural and industrial life that were shaping a nascent 20th century. The decorative and flowing Art Nouveau, along with the vibrant and emotional expressiveness of the Impressionist painters—a last flowering of 19th-century Romanticism—was cast aside for the new ideas of Freud and Einstein, stripping bare the human psyche and the physical universe. When a prominent collector objected to Picasso's use of house paint in some 1912 paintings, the artist told his Paris dealer, "Perhaps we shall succeed in disgusting everyone, and we haven't said everything yet."

At first, there wasn't much of a public to disgust. Early critical responses to the new Cubist art ranged from "ugly" to "grotesque," but only a few people actually looked at it, even in Paris. Gertrude Stein, an American writer in Paris who was doing away with grammar as Picasso did away with perspective and anatomy, recorded the young painter's ire at his critics: "Picasso said to me once with a good deal of bitterness, they say I can draw better than Raphael and probably they are right, perhaps I do draw better but if I can draw as well as Raphael I have at least the right to choose my way and they should recognize it, that right, but no, they say no."

Yet, despite its early limited influence, the new style spread from the artists' studios to the salons and then into popular culture in a relatively short time. By the 1920s, about the same time that the Spanish philosopher José Ortega y Gasset was declaring modern art "antipopular" and predicting that it "will always have the masses against it," a modern geometric style of decorative arts, drawn partly from Cubism, was inspiring French designers of clothing, furniture, lamps, clocks, dinnerware, even architecture. By the mid-1920s, the new Art Deco style had spread into almost every aspect of popular life. Its influence would soon be seen in the United States as well, in the sleek geometric facades of movie palaces, roadside diners and gas stations, and the stripped-down fashions of the flapper era. By 1925, when an international exposition of decorative and industrial arts was staged in Paris, a critic could see Cubism's influence in epochal terms, writing: "With the Exposition des Arts Décoratifs a new style is established to take its place with the historic periods. To the Renaissance, the Jacobean, the Georgian, the Rococo and the Colonial is added the Modern."

The popularity of Cubism in the decorative arts caught the attention of Kenneth Wayne, a young curator at the Portland Museum of Art in Maine, who went on to organize the museum's current show "Picasso, Braque, Léger and the Cubist Spirit, 1919–1939," which runs through October 20. One part of the show sets the objects of Art Deco design alongside paintings and sculptures of the Cubists from the years between the two world wars. And in doing so, it offers a rare chance to see the Cubists from a different angle, a fresh perspective.

The first Cubist brushstrokes appeared in Picasso's historic painting *Les Demoiselles d'Avignon,* made in 1907. A composition that combines elements of realism, primitive form and geometric abstraction, it depicts five nude figures gathered around a small arrangement of fruits. It was not yet Cubism but certainly pointed the way with faces inspired by African masks or broken down into geometric forms, with breasts and torsos represented by diamonds, rectangles and triangles along with more natural orbs and curves. Perspective was diminished in the flat planes of the painting, and the background fractured, as if the scene were reflected in a broken mirror. What was indeed reflected in this painting was the legacy of Paul Cézanne (SMITHSONIAN, April 1996), his flattened landscapes and still lifes expressing the elemental forms and planes of nature.

Georges Braque met Picasso around this time, and in 1909 they began a col-

From *Smithsonian,* July 1996, pp. 45-51. © 1996 by Paul Trachtman. Reprinted by permission of the author.

laboration that could be called the invention of Cubism. Henri Matisse, seeing some Braques the year before, rather scornfully coined the term "Cubism." For the next few years, Braque and Picasso maintained a close but private relationship, showing each other their new paintings and constructions. These works were part of their visual dialogue, and it was often hard to tell which artist painted which. They rarely exhibited in the Paris salons, but other artists, visiting their studios and glimpsing their work, were converted to the new style.

Fernand Léger, fascinated with the machines and designs of industrial society, found in Cubism an ideal technique to express his own vision of modern life. Juan Gris, more intrigued with the landscape of his own mind than the outer world, gave Cubism its purest, most mathematical form, using a compass and ruler to plot out his paintings. Others, including Matisse and the young Mexican painter Diego Rivera, who came to Paris in 1912, had brief flirtations with the Cubist style. The sculptor Jacques Lipchitz cast Cubist images in bronze. "What began as a rarefied pictorial style," says Kenneth Wayne, "became a popular language." To understand this language, it helps to clear away the layers of interpretation that have been added over the years. "Mathematics, trigonometry, chemistry, psychoanalysis, music and whatnot have been related to Cubism to give it an easier interpretation," Picasso once complained. "All this has been pure literature, not to say nonsense, which brought bad results, blinding people with theories."

The show Wayne has put together includes more than 100 paintings, sculptures, prints and decorative objects made in the two decades after World War I, when Picasso and Braque emerged from their hermetic, prewar collaborations into a Cubism that could delight the senses. Among the paintings in the show one finds two Braque still lifes with a bright, decorative air: his *Pipe and Basket* of 1919 and 1927's *Still Life with Pears, Lemons and Almonds*. The later work seems an almost playful throwback to the still lifes of Cézanne, with the table slightly tilted and everything just about to slip off. There is also Picasso's *Harlequin Musician* of 1924, a vibrant play of form and color in a figure that may represent the artist himself. "Picasso identified with the harlequin figure," one critic observed, "because it's an entertainer, a trickster, a figure on the fringes of society, and that's how he saw himself."

One of the most striking paintings in the show is Fernand Léger's *Two Women*, made in 1922 when the artist turned to human rather than purely industrial forms in the hope of coming closer to life, albeit life with a metallic sheen. He was seeking a Cubism the working class could understand, his wife recalled.

The decorative objects in the show are displayed in two large alcoves, where one can clearly see the influence of the artists on popular style and fashion. A vivid example of this influence is the ceramic vase made by Robert Lallemant in the late '20s; its jagged edges and geometric motifs use the same Cubist vocabulary as the canvases on the walls near it. A folding screen by decorator Jean Dunand and a pair of side tables by Pierre Chareau exhibit a Cubist play of planes, as if blurring the distinction between flat and three-dimensional space.

The bold, geometric clothing designs of Sonia Delaunay, a painter who once collaborated on fashions with Coco Chanel, are another highlight of the Portland Museum show. Delaunay, like Picasso, designed costumes for Diaghilev's avant-garde Ballet Russes, but her successes in the world of textiles and fashion took Cubism off the stage and into the streets, ready to wear.

In its emphasis on geometric forms, Cubism was often mistaken as a rejection of nature and the landscape altogether. But Picasso declared, "One cannot go against nature, it is stronger than the strongest man."

Her dresses first appeared in Paris just before the war, in 1913–14, when she wore them to the Bal Bullier, a popular dance hall where artists and poets tried out new dances like the fox-trot and the tango. Delaunay's dresses were made from geometric scraps of various fabrics, combining taffeta and tulle, flannel and silk, in bright, contrasting colors, from violet and green to scarlet and blue. She dressed her husband, Robert, also a painter, with similar style. One account describes him as wearing "a red oat with blue collar, a green jacket, sky-blue waistcoat, a tiny red tie, black pants, red socks, black-and-yellow shoes." By the war's end, Delaunay could sell her designs from her own Paris boutique and attract such famous customers as the Hollywood actress Gloria Swanson. By 1923 her geometric patterns were being printed by a French silk manufacturer. Soon after, her garments could be found in London and New York department stores.

The Portland show is significant not only for its content but for its location as well. Small and medium-sized museums around the country are becoming more important to our cultural life at a time when great blockbuster shows are ever more costly and difficult to mount. "There will always be the blockbusters," says Wayne, "but the smaller museums are doing interesting things that draw on their own strengths." Wayne arrived at the Portland Museum of Art only a year ago, fresh out of Stanford graduate school, and was asked to organize a major exhibition for this summer. "I've been sprinting ever since," he says.

The show at the Portland Museum is an invitation to take another look at what the Cubists were up to. It was a sociable world where Cubists and other young artists rubbed shoulders. Picasso went horseback riding with Matisse; Modigliani sketched Picasso in a restaurant; and avant-garde writers, composers and painters all gathered together at cafés, salons and dinner tables.

Even the lines between fine art and the decorative arts were in question. Duchamp hung hardware on gallery walls. Sonia Dulaunay made Cubist-inspired dresses. Le Cordusier painted still lifes and also designed houses, which he defined as machines for living in. Léger saw machines as objects of beauty.

The Cubists and their friends were taking their cues from their environment: from the landscape, the streets, the materials of everyday life. "When one crosses a landscape by automobile or express train, it becomes fragmented," Léger said. "A modern man registers a hundred times more sensory impressions than an eighteenth-century artist. . . . The compression of the modern picture, its variety, its breaking up of forms, are the result of all this." Painting, he declared, "has never been so truly realistic, so firmly attached to its own period as it is today." To claim realism for the geometic Cubist compositions may seem like a bit of avant-garde hyperbole, but Léger was being quite literal. "We live in a geometic world," he asserted. The Cubists were painting their experience of the world, a world in which "rupture and change crop up unexpectedly."

In its emphasis on geometic forms, Cubism was often mistaken as a rejection of nature and the landscape altogether. Ortega y Gasset described the modern painter as willfully blind to nature: "He shuts his eyes to the outer world and concentrates upon the subjective images in his own mind." But this is hardly what Léger or Picasso had in mind. On one of the rare occasions when he really spoke about his art, Picasso declared, "One cannot go against nature, it is stronger than the strongest man." Gertrude Stein recalled his bringing back some early Cubist paintings of a Spanish village after a trip to Spain in 1909: "Picasso had by chance taken some photographs of the village that he had painted and it always amused me when every one protested the fantasy of the pictures . . . [he wanted to show them] that the pictures were almost exactly like the photographs." It was as if Picasso saw Cubism out of one eye, reality with the other.

It was not the details but the emotions, the feeling of life and nature that Picasso was after. "The painter goes through states of fullness and evacuation," he said. "That is the whole secret of art. I go for a walk in the forest of Fontainebleau. I get 'green' indigestion. I must get rid of this sensation into a picture. Green rules it. A painter paints to unload himself of feelings and visions."

Léger sometimes seemed to doubt that he could ever paint with the vividness of the real machinery all around him. Once recalling a showing of his paintings at an annual Paris exhibition, the Salon d'Automne, he wrote: "I had the advantage of being next to the Aviation Show, which was about to open. I jumped over the barrier, and never had such a stark contrast assailed my eyes. I left vast surfaces, dismal and gray, pretentious in their frames, for beautiful, metallic objects, hard, permanent, and useful, in pure local colors; infinite varieties of steel surfaces at play next to vermilions and blues. The power of geometic forms dominated it all."

Cubism was not the only new art movement that flourished in the avant-garde movement. There were the Futurists, the Surrealists, the Dadaists, and there was Matisse who ignored them all.

The vividness Léger found in the Aviation Show had its match in the life of the Paris avant-garde. Looking back, we tend to think of the Cubists only in terms of their art, as though they were making their painting in a vacuum. But they were living in an exciting milieu, and the artists and their lives often provided the raw material of Cubism. A few anecdotes, like old snapshots, give only a faded impression of the time: Gertrude Stein observed that Picasso often got new ideas from writers, not from other painters. Jean Cocteau was one of those writers. Soon after they met, Picasso asked Cocteau to pose for him. In turn, Cocteau invited Picasso to join him and the composer Erik Satie in collaborating on costumes and sets for the ballet *Parade.* "Picasso was the great encounter for me," Cocteau wrote of his visits to the painter's studio. "How my heart pounded as I hurried up those stairs." Marcel Duchamp, who made his second sale of a painting to the dancer Isadora Duncan, knew the writers, too. "The amusing thing about the literary people of that time," he recalled, "was that, when you met two authors, you couldn't get a word in edgewise. . . . One was torn between a sort of anguish and an insane laughter."

Like Gertrude Stein, the young American writer Ernest Hemingway was in Paris and became intrigued by the painters. Hemingway claimed that he studied the Cézannes at the Louvre to improve his writing style and said he could see Cubist images in the nightlife of a Paris street. There were no sewers, and at night tank wagons pumped out the cesspools of the old apartment buildings. "The tank wagons were painted brown and saffron color," he wrote, "and in the moonlight when they worked the rue Cardinal Lemoine their wheeled, horsedrawn cylinders looked like Braque paintings."

Cubism was not the only new art movement that flourished in this avant-garde hothouse. There were the Futurists, the Surrealists, the Dadaists, and there was Matisse who ignored them all. But it was Cubism that had the greatest impact on the popular mind, producing a new visual consciousness.

The Cubists' view of things became more understandable as the world was fractured by World War I. In fact, the war was a kind of alchemy through which a modern consciousness was formed from its elements. As the French mobilized, Gertrude Stein was with Picasso at a telling moment. "I very well remember at the beginning of the war being with Picasso on the boulevard Raspail when the first camouflaged truck passed," she wrote. "It was at night, we had heard of camouflage but we had not yet seen it and Picasso amazed looked at it and then cried out, yet it is we who made it, that is Cubism."

It wasn't only the camouflage that was Cubist. The French novelist Louis-Ferdinand Céline portrayed the war, as seen by a young soldier, in images a Cubist well might have painted. When Picasso described his pictures as "a sum of destructions," he was talking about esthetics, not war. "I do a picture—then I destroy it," he said. "In the end, though, nothing is lost: the red I took away from one place turns up somewhere else." But a Cubist esthetic that defined the creative process in terms of destructions seemed less strange after the shock of World War I. Céline's soldier, and many others, saw both armies as madmen "shut up on earth as if it were a looney bin, ready to demolish everything on it, Germany, France, whole continents, everything that breathes, destroy, destroy. . . ." As Gertrude Stein saw it, people "were forced by the war to recognize Cubism."

As the war ended, French designers did more than recognize it. They helped to popularize it. Their "capricious geometry" was set in concrete mansions, embodied in tubular steel furniture, printed onto wallpaper and textiles, even embroidered into women's shoes. One innovation of the Cubist painters, the arresting surface textures and odd materials in some of their canvases and collages, was seized on with gusto by the designers. Braque had painted still lifes with oils and sand on canvas, for example, and Picasso produced collages with dishcloth fabric, pins and nails. Then the designers rushed in, adding exciting new contrasts and materials as well as new forms to popular decor and fashion.

Sonia Delaunay's postwar couture sometimes combined fur, wool and silk. Le Corbusier introduced a leather and metal chaise longue molded to fit the human body. Interior designer Marcel Guillemard dreamed up a Cubist cabinet and bar made of metal tubing and square panels stacked in pivoting sections that could swing out at various angles; it would fit right in with the plastic cubes and sectional furniture found in today's shopping malls. Others achieved their effects with new and sometimes improbable juxtapositions of materials. Jacques Le Chevallier designed a desk lamp of aluminum and plastic, cut into trapezoids and rectangles, with adjustable metal flaps for the shade. And Pierre Legrain's faceted, geometric clock was made of metal and sharkskin.

When Picasso painted a portrait, he wanted us to see a face not as God created it but as Picasso created it. He rearranged it so we would see what he had made.

The Cubists kept on painting after the war, although heading in different directions. While Braque mostly stuck to his still lifes and Léger began to explore biomorphic forms, Picasso pursued several other styles along with Cubism, including Neoclassicism and Surrealism, and sometimes put them all into the same painting. By then the Cubist spirit was alive and well in the world, and the original Cubists knew that they had been seen, if not always understood. And that was what they were really after. When Picasso painted a portrait, for example, he wanted us to see a face not as God created it but as Picasso created it. He rearranged it so we would see what he had made. As he quipped about one of his Cubist portraits, "I had to make the nose crooked so they would see it was a nose."

1918

Seventy-five years after the guns fell silent along the Western Front, the work they did there remains of incalculable importance to the age we inhabit and the people we are

John Lukacs

John Lukacs's book, The End of the Twentieth Century, *is issued by Ticknor & Fields.*

In many ways 1918 is closer to us than we are inclined to think.

Look at Fifth Avenue in New York (or Regent Street in London, or the Champs-Elysées). Most of their present buildings were there seventy-five years ago. Automobiles, telephones, elevators, electric power, electric lights, specks of droning airplanes in the sky—there they were in 1918. Now count back seventy-five years from 1918. That was 1843, when just about everything looked different. Everything *was* different: the cities, their buildings, the lives of the men and women outside and inside their houses, as well as the furniture of their minds. But many of the ideas current in 1918 are still current in 1993: Making the World Safe for Democracy; the Self-Determination of Peoples; the Emancipation of Women; International Organizations; a World Community of Nations; "Progress." Seventy-five years is a long time; but then, the twentieth century was a short century, also exactly seventy-five years long, having burst forth in 1914, formed and marked by two world wars and the Cold War, ending in 1989.

In many ways 1918 is farther from us than we are inclined to think. After taking comfort—and, more important, pleasure—from a picture of Fifth Avenue in 1918 (I am thinking of that splendid painting by Childe Hassam, with all those Allied flags waving, dramatic poppies in a wheat-colored field of sun-bleached architecture), look closer; lean downward; try to look inside. The people are different from us, and I do not mean only the difference of two or three generations: They look different, because their composition and their clothes and their manners and their attitudes and aspirations are different. So are the interiors of those still-standing buildings, what there is and what goes on inside them: their furnishings, in most cases not only their inhabitants but the functions of their rooms. Yes, Fifth Avenue is different, New York is different, America is different, the world is different. The twentieth century is over.

It was—and in many ways it still is—the American century. In 1898 the United States became a world power—not because of some kind of geopolitical constellation, not because of the size of its armed forces, but because that was what the American government and the majority of the American people wanted. Before 1898 the United States was the greatest power in the Western Hemisphere. Twenty years later the United States chose to enter the greatest of European wars (the very term *world war* was an American invention, circa 1915). In 1918 it decided the outcome of the war. By Armistice Day the United States was more than a World Power; it was the greatest power in the world.

That was more than a milestone in the history of the United States. It was a turning point: the greatest turning point in its history since the Civil War and perhaps the greatest turning point since its very establishment. For more than three centuries the colonists and Americans were moving westward, away from Europe. The trickle, and later the flow, of immigrants moved westward too, across the Atlantic, away from Europe. When foreign armies crossed the Atlantic, it was westward, from the Old World to the New. Now, for the first time in history, this was reversed. Two million American soldiers were sent eastward through the Atlantic, to help decide a great war in Europe.

That was an event far more important—and decisive—than was the Russian Revolution in 1917, both in the short and in the long run. In early 1918 Russia dropped out of the war. The United States entered it. Russia abandoned its European allies. The United States came in to join them. In 1918 the Allies were able to defeat Germany and win the war, even without Russia (something that would not be possible in another world war). The presence of an American army on the battlefield proved to be more decisive than the absence of the Russians. In the long run, too, the twentieth century turned out to be the American century, on all levels, ranging from world politics to popular democracy and mass culture. Compared with this, the influence of communism and the emulation of the Soviet Union were minimal. The exaggeration of the importance of communism blinded, willfully, not only many intellectuals but many Americans, pro-Communists and anti-Communists, developing into a popular ideological view of the world. In 1967 I was astonished to find how here, in America, article after article, book after book was devoted to commemorating and analyzing the importance of the Russian Communist Revolution on its fiftieth anniversary, while hardly any notice was paid to the commemoration of the American entry into World War I in 1917.

For a long time Americans believed that the destiny of their country was to differ from the Old World. Beginning in the 1890s, and culminating in 1918, this fundamental creed changed subtly. Many

Americans were now inclined to believe that it was the destiny of the United States to provide a model for the Old World. For a while these two essentially contradictory beliefs resided together in many American minds. In 1918 the second belief had temporarily overcome the first. This was the result of a revolution of American attitudes that—on the popular, rather than on the political, level—still awaits a profound treatment by a masterful historian. In 1914 not one American in a thousand thought that the United States would, or should, intervene in the great European war. In less than three years that changed. By 1917 most Americans were willing—and many were eager—to go Over There, to decide and win a war through the employment of American muscle, American practices, American ideas.

After that the tide of American confidence rose, and in November 1918 came the moment of victory. All over the world, but especially in Europe, admiration and gratitude and hope in the United States were suddenly at their zenith—a powerful ray of a faraway sunbeam breaking through those grayest of leaden skies in November 1918. Unlike after 1945, there was no trace of radical, or intellectual, anti-Americanism. The youngest and one of the most promising and most avant-garde of French writers, Raymond Radiguet, wrote about a romantic rendezvous in the spring of 1917 in "an American Bar in the rue Daunou." His lover "went into ecstasies, like a schoolgirl, over the barman's white jacket, the grace with which he shook the silver goblets and the poetic and bizarre names of the concoctions." An old goateed French academician, Henri Lavedan, wrote about President Wilson, "He will remain one of the legends of history . . . he will appear in the poetry of coming ages, like that Dante whom he resembles in profile." Lavedan needed better glasses than his pince-nez, but that is beside the point. "Future generations will see him guiding through the dangers of the infernal world that white-robed Beatrice whom we call Peace. . . ." Whether Dante or Beatrice, when Woodrow Wilson landed in France, little girls in white frocks threw rose petals from baskets at his large feet. Harold Nicolson, then a young British diplomat and budding aesthete, had the highest hopes for Wilson and his new ideas—although they would vanish soon. The hope that Wilson and the United States would dominate and design the coming settlement of peace, with principles vastly superior to the petty and vengeful practices of European statesmanship in the past, existed not only in France and Britain but also in Germany, Austria, Hungary. In Vienna and Budapest governments and peoples welcomed the presence of American officers, members of the Allied military missions, some of whom were to distinguish themselves by their impartiality and humaneness. A great Hungarian writer, Gyula Krúdy, found it remarkable how the hapless and ephemeral president of the new Hungarian Republic, Count Károlyi, kept pronouncing—oddly—Wilson's name to his anxious entourage, again and again: "Uilson! Uilson!" Of all the foreign officers, the Americans were the smartest, in their well-cut uniforms, with their Sam Browne belts and superb boots. In France a war-worn, tired population had thronged the streets when the first American troops, fresh, grinning, confident, arrived in their villages and towns. They looked modern. They *were* modern—a wondrous adjective then, though it has lost much of its shine since.

Soon the high tide of enthusiasm receded—and the neap tide of disillusion came in: disillusion with Wilson abroad, disillusion among Americans themselves. The reaction to the war, to peacemaking, to Wilsonianism has been recorded often since. Even about 1918 some questions remain. Was the American intervention decisive? Yes, but the British and the French armies, weary and torn as they were, had halted the great German spring offensive by June 1918, before the mass of the Americans moved up to combat. The training and the transporting and the provisioning and the disposition of the American army had taken very long—almost too long. They did not go into battle until about fifteen months after the American declaration of war. It is arguable that their first great battle in Belleau Wood may have been a mistake, costing too many American lives, misestimating its tactical value. General Pershing had virtues, but he was not a great general, occasionally hardly better than some of his British colleagues, whose generalship was often famously poor. Still—the freshness and the courage of the American soldier in 1918 remain unarguable.

The trouble was with their President, about whom his Postmaster General once wrote that Woodrow Wilson was "a man of high ideals but no principles." That, too, is arguable, but then so many of his ideals were to be proved wrong—again, in both the short and the long runs. In the short run—that is, 1918 and 1919—during that extraordinary chapter in the history of the American Presidency, his absence from Washington for long months in Paris showed up many of his weaknesses. "Open diplomacy" was one thing that men such as Harold Nicolson admired, but Nicholson was abashed to learn that there was no such thing in Paris. Before Versailles Wilson made compromise after compromise involving his principles or his ideas, whatever we call them. He was no match for Clemenceau or Lloyd George, and the result was one of the worst botched peace treaties in modern history. As Chesterson once wrote, the best things are lost in victory and not in defeat. That would dawn on the American people only later. That was not why their elected representatives repudiated him in late 1919 and 1920. But Wilson's failure to bring the United States into the League of Nations was not that important in the long run. Had he had his way at home, had the United States entered the League, it would have made some difference, but not much. The source of the Second World War (and of Adolf Hitler's career) was not American nonparticipation in the League of Nations. It was Versailles, for which Wilson was as responsible as for the former. He also bequeathed to the American people a philosophy of internationalism (enthusiastically espoused by such different Americans as Herbert Hoover and Eleanor Roosevelt, Richard Nixon and Dean Rusk, Jimmy Carter and Ronald Reagan) that, because of its legalistic (and therefore insubstantial) moralism, including its promotion of National Self-Determination, has been rather disastrous. But that is another story.

One year after the armistice, American influence in Europe was receding fast. Within the United States, too, a great national hangover set in—in part a reaction to some of the exaggerations and fever of the earlier war propaganda. It was a return of sorts—but neither to innocence nor to "normalcy" (a word coined by Warren

Gamaliel Harding). There followed a decade or more of American isolationism (in regard to Europe, though not to the Caribbean or the Pacific), together with the self-righteous belief, expressed in one of Barton W. Currie's editorials in *The Ladies' Home Journal:* "There is only one first-class civilization in the world today. It's right here in the United States. . . . Europe is hardly second-class." For the first time in American history a very restrictive Immigration Act was passed. It had something to do with the obsession with communism (from which the Republican party knew how to profit, from Harding to Reagan), though there was more to it. Many people, too, forgot that while one out of every one thousand Americans died in World War I, thirty-five of every one thousand Frenchmen died. The French did not forget. Those memories maimed them. They fell out of World War II in the summer of 1940. Soon after that Americans were beginning to ready themselves to enter it and to help liberate France again.

This brings me to a last question that I, and presumably many others, have pondered often. Which was the zenith year of the American century, 1918 or 1945? Perhaps it was 1918—when the United States did not have to share the victory with Russia (although it had to share it with Britain and France, Italy, Japan). Perhaps it was 1945—when the United States, alone among the Great Powers, could wage a war on two vast fronts and conclude it victoriously, across the Atlantic and Pacific alike. In 1918 the Western democracies had all the cards—the ace, the king, the queen, and the jack, with Germany defeated and Russia down and out. In 1945 the United States had the ace (and what an ace!), but Stalin had at least the king. Yet in 1918 America and its Allies played their cards badly and lost the peace almost immediately afterward. In 1945 they let Stalin cash in his winnings, but further than that they did not let him go. The world order (or disorder) shaping up in 1945 was more lasting than that in 1918. The effect of World War II was greater. It transformed the structure of American government and much of American life. A few years after 1918 the American military presence in Europe was gone. After 1945 it remained there. No American general of World War I became a permanent national figure or President. After World War II there was Eisenhower—and also Patton and MacArthur and Kennedy and Bush, whose impressive war records helped form their popular images. Yet there was more enthusiasm in 1918 than in 1945. There was no popular song in World War II comparable to "Over There." Sergeant York was a real soldier, unlike John Wayne. Harry Truman fought in the Argonne, not in Hollywood. Perhaps, if only for a moment, 1918 may have been the highest point, with all of that new American presence in Europe, with all of those great expectations.

And now, [over] seventy-five years later, the United States is the only superpower left in the world, but everything else is different.

How the Modern Middle East Map Came to be Drawn

When the Ottoman Empire collapsed in 1918, the British created new borders (and rulers) to keep the peace and protect their interests

David Fromkin

Lawyer-historian David Fromkin is the author of a prizewinning book entitled A Peace to End All Peace.

The dictator of Iraq claimed—falsely—that until 1914 Kuwait had been administered from Iraq, that historically Kuwait was a part of Iraq, that the separation of Kuwait from Iraq was an arbitrary decision of Great Britain's after World War I. The year was 1961; the Iraqi dictator was Abdul-Karim Qasim; and the dispatch of British troops averted a threatened invasion.

Iraq, claiming that it had never recognized the British-drawn frontier with Kuwait, demanded full access to the Persian Gulf; and when Kuwait failed to agree, Iraqi tanks and infantry attacked Kuwait. The year was 1973; the Iraqi dictator was Ahmad Hasan al-Bakr; when other Arab states came to Kuwait's support, a deal was struck, Kuwait made a payment of money to Iraq, and the troops withdrew.

August 2, 1990. At 2 A.M. Iraqi forces swept across the Kuwaiti frontier. Iraq's dictator, Saddam Hussein, declared that the frontier between Iraq and Kuwait was invalid, a creation of the British after World War I, and that Kuwait really belonged to Iraq.

It was, of course, true, as one Iraqi dictator after another claimed, that the exact Iraq-Kuwait frontier was a line drawn on an empty map by a British civil servant in the early 1920s. But Kuwait began to emerge as an independent entity in the early 1700s—two centuries before Britain invented Iraq. Moreover, most other frontiers between states of the Middle East were also creations of the British (or the French). The map of the Arab Middle East was drawn by the victorious Allies when they took over these lands from the Ottoman Empire after World War I. By proposing to nullify that map, Saddam Hussein at a minimum was trying to turn the clock back by almost a century.

A hundred years ago, when Ottoman governors in Basra were futilely attempting to assert authority over the autonomous sheikdom of Kuwait, most of the Arabic-speaking Middle East was at least nominally part of the Ottoman Empire. It had been so for hundreds of years and would remain so until the end of World War I.

The Ottomans, a dynasty, not a nationality, were originally a band of Turkish warriors who first galloped onto the stage of history in the 13th century. By the early 20th century the Ottoman Empire, which once had stretched to the gates of Vienna, was shrinking rapidly, though it still ruled perhaps 20 million to 25 million people in the Middle East and elsewhere, comprising perhaps a dozen or more different nationalities. It was a ramshackle Muslim empire, held together by the glue of Islam, and the lot of its non-Muslim population (perhaps 5 million) was often unhappy and sometimes tragic.

In the year 1900, if you traveled from the United States to the Middle East, you might have landed in Egypt, part of the Ottoman Empire in name but in fact governed by British "advisers." The Egyptian Army was commanded by an English general, and the real ruler of the country was the British Agent and Consul-General—a position to which the crusty Horatio Herbert Kitchener was appointed in 1911.

The center of your social life in all likelihood would have been the British enclave in Cairo, which possessed (wrote one of Lord Kitchener's aides) "all the narrowness and provincialism of an English garrison town." The social schedule of British officials and their families revolved around the balls given at each of the leading hotels in turn, six nights out of seven, and before dark, around the Turf Club and the Sporting Club on the island of El Gezira. Throughout Egypt, Turkish officials, Turkish police and a Turkish army were conspicuous by their absence. Outside British confines you found yourself not in a Turkish-speaking country but in an Arabic-speaking one. Following the advice of the *Baedeker,* you'd likely engage a dragoman—a translator and guide—of whom there were about 90 in Cairo ("all more or less intelligent and able, but scarcely a half of the number are trustworthy").

On leaving Egypt, if you turned north through the Holy Land and the Levant toward Anatolia, you finally would have encountered the reality of Ottoman government, however corrupt and inefficient, though many cities—Jerusalem (mostly Jewish), Damascus (mostly Arab) and Smyrna, now Izmir (mostly Greek)—were not at all Turkish in character or population.

Heading south by steamer down the Red Sea and around the enormous Arabian Peninsula was a very different matter. Nominally Ottoman, Arabia was in large part a vast, ungoverned desert wilderness through which roamed bedouin tribes knowing no law but their own. In those days Abdul Aziz ibn Saud, the youthful scion of deposed lords of most of the peninsula, was living in exile, dreaming of a return to reclaim his rights and establish his dominion. In the port towns on the Persian Gulf, ruling sheiks paid lip service to Ottoman rule but in fact their sheikdoms were protectorates of Great Britain. Not long after you passed Kuwait (see map) you reached Basra, in what is now Iraq, up a river formed by the union of the great Tigris and Euphrates.

A muddy, unhealthy port of heterogeneous population, Basra was then the capital of a province, largely Shiite Arab, ruled by an Ottoman governor. Well north of it, celebrated for archaeological sites like Babylon and Nippur, which drew tourists, lay Baghdad, then a heavily Jewish city (along with Jerusalem, one of the two great Jewish cities of Asia). Baghdad was the administrative center of an Ottoman province that was in large part Sunni Arab. Farther north still was a third Ottoman province, with a large population of Kurds. Taken together, the three roughly equaled the present area of Iraq.

Ottoman rule in some parts of the Middle East clearly was more imaginary than real. And even in those portions of the empire that Turkish governors did govern, the population was often too diverse to be governed effectively by a single regime. Yet the hold of the Turkish sultan on the empire's peoples lingered on. Indeed, had World War I not intervened, the Ottoman Empire might well have lasted many decades more.

In its origins, the war that would change the map of the Middle East had nothing to do with that region. How the Ottoman Empire came to be involved in the war at all—and lost it—and how the triumphant Allies found themselves in a position to redesign the Middle Eastern lands the Turks had ruled, is one of the most fascinating stories of the 20th century, rich in consequences that we are still struggling with today.

The story begins with one man, a tiny, vain, strutting man addicted to dramatic gestures and uniforms. He was Enver Pasha, and he mistook himself for a sort of Napoleon. Of modest origins, Enver, as a junior officer in the Ottoman Army, joined the Young Turks, a secret society that was plotting against the Ottoman regime. In 1913, Enver led a Young Turk raiding party that overthrew the government and killed the Minister of War. In 1914, at the age of 31, he became the Ottoman Minister of War himself, married the niece of the sultan and moved into a palace.

As a new political figure Enver scored a major, instant success. The Young Turks for years had urgently sought a European ally that would promise to protect the Ottoman Empire against other European powers. Britain, France and Russia had each been approached and had refused; but on August 1, 1914, just as Germany was about to invade Belgium to begin World War I, Enver wangled a secret treaty with the kaiser pledging to protect the Ottoman domains.

Unaware of Enver's coup, and with war added to the equation, Britain and France began wooing Turkey too, while the Turks played off one side against the other. By autumn the German Army's plan to knock France out of the war in six weeks had failed. Needing help, Germany urged the Ottoman Empire to join the war by attacking Russia.

Though Enver's colleagues in the Turkish government were opposed to war, Enver had a different idea. To him the time seemed ripe: in the first month of the war German armies overwhelmingly turned back a Russian attack on East Prussia, and a collapse of the czar's armies appeared imminent. Seeing a chance to share in the spoils of a likely German victory over Russia, Enver entered into a private conspiracy with the German admiral commanding the powerful warship *Goeben* and its companion vessel, the *Breslau,* which had taken refuge in Turkish waters at the outset of hostilities.

For years the real ruler of Egypt was Lord Kitchener, a general, whose main concern was for the Suez Canal.

Though he was blamed for Gallipoli, Winston Churchill was put in charge of reorganizing the entire Middle East.

During the last week of October, Enver secretly arranged for the *Goeben* and the *Breslau* to escape into the Black Sea and steam toward Russia. Flying the Ottoman flag, the Germans then opened fire on the Russian coast. Thinking themselves attacked by Turks, the Russians declared war. Russia's allies, Britain and France, thus found themselves at war with the Ottoman Empire too. By needlessly plunging the empire into war, Enver had put everything in the Middle East up for grabs. In that sense, he was the father of the modern Middle East. Had Enver never existed, the Turkish flag might even yet be flying—if only in some confederal way—over Beirut and Damascus, Baghdad and Jerusalem.

Great Britain had propped up the Ottoman Empire for generations as a buffer against Russian expansionism. Now, with Russia as Britain's shaky ally, once the war had been won and the Ottomans overthrown, the Allies would be able to reshape the entire Middle East. It would be one of those magic moments in history when fresh starts beckon and dreams become realities.

"What is to prevent the Jews having Palestine and restoring a real Judaea?" asked H. G. Wells, the British novelist, essayist and prophet of a rational future for mankind. The Greeks, the French and the Italians also had claims to Middle East territory. And naturally, in Cairo, Lord Kitchener's aides soon began to contemplate a future plan for an Arab world to be ruled by Egypt, which in turn would continue to be controlled by themselves.

At the time, the Allies already had their hands full with war against Germany on the Western Front. They resolved not to be distracted by the Middle East until later. The issues and ambitions there were too divisive. Hardly had the Ottoman Empire entered the war, however, when Enver stirred the pot again. He took personal command of the Ottoman Third Army on the Caucasus frontier and, in the dead of winter, launched a foolhardy attack against fortified positions on high ground. His offensive was hopeless, since it was both amateurishly planned and executed, but the czar's generals panicked anyway. The Russian government begged Lord Kitchener (now serving in London as Secretary of State for War) to stage a more or less instant diversionary action. The result was the Allied attack on the Dardanelles, the strait that eventually leads to Constantinople (now Istanbul).

Enver soon lost about 86,000 of his 100,000 men; the few, bloodied survivors straggled back through icy mountain passes. A German observer noted that Enver's army had "suffered a disaster which for rapidity and completeness is without parallel in military history." But nobody in the Russian government or high command bothered to tell the British that mounting a Dardanelles naval attack was no longer necessary. So on the morning of February 19, 1915, British ships fired the opening shots in what became a tragic campaign.

Initially, the British Navy seemed poised to take Constantinople, and Russia panicked again. What if the British, having occupied Constantinople, were to hold onto it? The 50 percent of Russia's export trade flowing through the strait would then do so only with British permission. Czar Nicholas II demanded immediate assurance that Constantinople would be Russia's in the postwar world. Fearing Russia might withdraw from the war, Britain and France agreed. In return, Russia offered to support British and French claims in other parts of the Middle East.

With that in mind, on April 8, 1915, the British Prime Minister appointed a committee to define Britain's postwar goals in the Middle East. It was a committee dominated by Lord Kitchener through his personal representative, 36-year-old Sir Mark Sykes, one of many remarkable characters, including Winston Churchill and T. E. Lawrence, to be involved in the remaking (and remapping) of the Middle East.

British camel unit jogs down the Jordan Valley; Prince Faisal and T. E. Lawrence often used camels in guerrilla raids on Turks.

A restless soul who had moved from school to school as a child, Sykes left college without graduating, and thereafter never liked to stay long in one spot. A Tory Member of Parliament, before the war he had traveled widely in Asiatic Turkey, publishing accounts of his journeys. Sykes' views tended to be passionate but changeable, and his talent for clever exaggeration sometimes carried over into his politics.

As a traditional Tory he had regarded the sultan's domains as a useful buffer protecting Britain's road to India against Britain's imperial rivals, the czar chief among them. Only 15 months earlier, Sykes was warning the House of Commons that "the disappearance of the Ottoman Empire must be the first step towards the disappearance of our own." Yet between 1915 and 1919, he busily planned the dismantling of the Ottoman Empire.

The Allied attack on the Dardanelles ended with Gallipoli, a disaster told and retold in books and films. Neither that defeat, nor the darkest days of 1916–17, when it looked for a while as though the Allies might lose the war, stopped British planning about how to cut up the Turkish Middle East. Steadily but secretly Sykes worked on. As the fight to overthrow the Ottoman Empire grew more intense, the elements he had to take into account grew more complex.

It was clear that the British needed to maintain control over the Suez Canal, and all the rest of the route to their prized colonial possession, India. They needed to keep the Russians and Germans and Italians and French in check. Especially the French, who had claims on Syria. But with millions of men committed to trench warfare in Europe, they could not drain off forces for the Middle East. Instead, units of the British Indian Army along with other Commonwealth forces attacked in the east in what are now Iraq and Iran, occupying Basra, Baghdad and eventually Mosul. Meanwhile, Allied liaison officers, including notably T. E. Lawrence, began encouraging the smallish group of Arabian tribesmen following Emir (later King) Hussein of the Hejaz, who had rebelled against the Turks, to fight a guerrilla campaign against Turkish forces.

Throughout 1917, in and near the Hejaz area of Arabia (see map), the Arabs attacked the railway line that supported Turkish troops in Medina. The "Arab Revolt" had little military effect on the outcome of the war, yet the fighting brought to the fore, as British clients and potential Arab leaders, not only Hussein of the Hejaz, but two of his sons, Faisal and Abdullah. Both were deadly rivals of Ibn Saud, who by then had become a rising power in Arabia and a client of the British too.

British officials in Cairo deluded themselves and others into believing that the whole of the Arabic-speaking half of the Ottoman Empire might rise up and come over to the Allied side. When the time came, the Arab world did not follow the lead of Hussein, Abdullah and Faisal. But Arab aspirations and British gratitude began to loom large in British, and Arab, plans for the future. Sykes now felt he had to take Arab ambitions into account in his future planning, though he neglected those of Ibn Saud (father of today's Saudi king), who also deserved well of Britain.

By 1917 Sykes was also convinced that it was vital for the British war effort to win Jewish support against Germany, and that pledging support for Zionism could win it. That year his efforts and those of others resulted in the publication of a statement by Arthur James Balfour, the British Foreign Secretary, expressing Britain's support for the establishment of a Jewish national home in Palestine.

The year 1917 proved to be a turning point. In the wake of its revolution Russia pulled out of the war, but the entrance by the United States on the Allied side insured the Allies a victory—if they could hold on long enough for U.S. troops to arrive in force. In the Middle East, as British India consolidated its hold on areas that are now part of Iraq, Gen. Edmund Allenby's Egyptian-based British army began fighting its way north from Suez to Damascus. Lawrence and a force of Arab raiders captured the Red Sea port of Aqaba (near the point where Israel and Jordan now meet). Then, still other Arabs, with Faisal in command, moved north to harass the Turkish flank.

By October 1918, Allenby had taken Syria and Lebanon, and was poised to invade what is now Turkey. But there was no need to do so, because on October 31 the Ottoman Empire surrendered.

As the Peace Conference convened in Paris, in February 1919, Sykes, who had been rethinking Britain's design for the Middle East, suddenly fell ill and died. At first there was nobody to take his place as the British government's overall Middle East planner. Prime Minister David Lloyd George took personal charge in many Middle East matters. But more and more, as the months went by, Winston Churchill had begun to play a major role, gradually superseding the others.

Accordingly, early that year the ambitious 45-year-old politician was asked by the Prime Minister to serve as both War Minister and Air Minister. ("Of course," Lloyd George wrote Churchill, "there will be but one salary!") Maintaining the peace in the captured—and now occupied—Arab Middle East was among Churchill's new responsibilities.

Cheerful, controversial and belligerent, Churchill was not yet the revered figure who would so inspire his countrymen and the world in 1940. Haunted by the specter of a brilliant father, he had won fame and high office early, but was widely distrusted, in part for having switched political parties. Churchill's foresighted administration of the Admiralty in the summer of 1914 won universal praise, but then the botched Dardanelles campaign, perhaps unfairly, was blamed on him. As a Conservative newspaper put it, "we have watched his brilliant and erratic course in the confident expectation that sooner or later he would make a mess of anything he undertook." In making Churchill minister of both War and Air in 1919, Lloyd George was giving his protégé a try at a political comeback.

By the end of the war, everyone was so used to the bickering among the Allies about who was going to get what in the postwar Middle East that the alternative—nobody taking anything—simply didn't enter into the equation. Churchill was perhaps the only statesman to consider that possibility. He foresaw that many problems would arise from trying to impose a new political design on so troubled a region, and thought it unwise to make the attempt. Churchill argued, in fact, for simply retaining a reformed version of the Ottoman Empire. Nobody took him seriously.

After the war, a British army of a million men, the only cohesive military force in the region, briefly occupied the Middle East. Even as his real work began, however, Churchill was confronted with demands that the army, exhausted from years of war, be demobilized. He understood what meeting those demands meant. Relying on that army, Prime Minister Lloyd George had decided to keep the whole Arab Middle East under British influence; in the words he once used about Palestine: "We shall be there by conquest and shall remain." Now Churchill repeatedly warned that once British troops were withdrawn, Britain would not be able to impose its terms.

Lloyd George had predicted that it would take about a week to agree on the terms of peace to be imposed on the defeated Ottoman Empire. Instead it took nearly two years. By then, in Churchill's words, the British army of occupation had long since "melted

After the final surrender of the Turks, on October 31, 1918, the question was: How to administer the remains of the Ottoman Empire?

away," with the dire consequences he predicted.

In Egypt, demonstrations, strikes and riots broke out. In Arabia, Ibn Saud, though himself a British client, defeated and threatened to destroy Britain's protégé Hussein. In Turkey, the defeated Enver had long since fled the country to find refuge in Berlin. From there he journeyed to Russia, assumed leadership of Bukhara (in what is now the Uzbek Republic of the USSR) in its struggle for independence from Moscow, and was killed in battle against the Red Army of the Soviet Union in 1922. Turkish nationalists under the great Ottoman general Mustafa Kemal (later known as Kemal Ataturk) rebelled against the Allied-imposed treaty and later proclaimed the national state that is modern Turkey.

In Palestine, Arabs rioted against Jews. In what is now Saddam Hussein's Iraq, armed revolts by the tribes, sparked in the first instance by the imposition of taxes, caused thousands of casualties. "How much longer," the outraged London *Times* asked, "are valuable lives to be sacrificed in the vain endeavour to impose upon the Arab population an elaborate and expensive administration which they never asked for and do not want?"

By the end of 1920, Lloyd George's Middle East policy was under attack from all sides. Churchill, who had warned all along that peacetime Britain, in the grip of an economic collapse, had neither the money, the troops, nor the will to coerce the Middle East, was proved right—and placed even more directly in charge. On New Year's Day 1921 he was appointed Colonial Secretary, and soon began to expand his powers, consolidating within his new department responsibility for all Britain's domains in Arabic-speaking Asia.

He assembled his staff by combing the government for its ablest and most experienced officials. The one offbeat appointment was T. E. Lawrence. A young American journalist and promoter named Lowell Thomas, roaming the Middle East in search of a story, had found Lawrence dressed in Arab robes, and proceeded to make him world-famous as "Lawrence of Arabia." A complex personality, Lawrence was chronically insubordinate, but Churchill admired all the wonderful stories he'd heard of Lawrence's wartime exploits.

Seeking to forge a working consensus among his staff in London and his men in the field, Churchill invited them all to a conference that opened in Cairo on March 12, 1921. During the ten-day session held in the Semiramis Hotel, about 40 experts were in attendance. "Everybody Middle East is here," wrote Lawrence.

Egypt was not on the agenda. Its fate was being settled separately by its new British proconsul, Lord Allenby. In 1922 he established it as an independent kingdom, still largely subject to British control under terms of a unilateral proclamation that neither Egypt's politicians nor its new king, Fuad, accepted.

Prime Minister Lloyd George (right) sought full control of the Middle East.

All Britain's other wartime conquests—the lands now called Israel, the West Bank, Jordan and Iraq—were very much on the agenda, while the fate of Syria and Lebanon, which Britain had also conquered, was on everybody's mind. In the immediate aftermath of the war, it was control of Syria that had caused the most problems, as Lloyd George tried to keep it for Britain by placing it under the rule of Lawrence's comrade-in-arms, Prince Faisal, son of Hussein. After Syria declared its independence, the French fought back. Occupying all of Syria-Lebanon, they drove Faisal into exile. The French also devised a new frontier for Lebanon that invited eventual disaster, as would become evident in the 1970s and '80s. They refused to see that the Muslim population was deeply hostile to their rule.

Early planning for postwar Middle East fell to Sir Mark Sykes, whose work grew in complexity as rival Allied and Arab claims evolved.

Churchill, meanwhile, was confronted by constant Arab disturbances in Palestine. West of the Jordan River, where the Jewish population lived, Arabs fought against Jewish immigration, claiming—wrongly, as the future was to show—that the country was too barren to support more than its existing 600,000 inhabitants. Churchill rejected that view, and dealt with the Arab objections to a Jewish homeland by keeping—though redefining—Britain's commitment to Zionism. As he saw it, there was to be a

Jewish homeland in Palestine, but other homelands could exist there as well.

The 75 percent of Palestine east of the Jordan River (Transjordan, as it was called, until it became Jordan in 1950) was lawless. Lacking the troops to police it and wanting to avert additional causes of strife, Churchill decided to forbid Jews from settling there, temporarily at least.

Fittingly while still War and Air Minister, Churchill had devised a strategy for controlling the Middle East with a minimum number of British troops by using an economical combination of airpower and armored cars. But it would take time for the necessary units to be put in place. Meanwhile tribal fighting had to be contained somehow. As the Cairo conference met, news arrived that Abdullah, Faisal's brother, claiming to need "a change of air for his health," had left Arabia with a retinue of bedouin warriors and entered Transjordan. The British feared that Abdullah would attack French Syria and so give the French an excuse to invade Transjordan, as a first step toward taking over all Palestine.

As a temporary expedient Churchill appointed Abdullah as governor of a Transjordan to be administratively detached from the rest of Palestine. He charged him with keeping order by his prestige and with his own bedouin followers—at least until Britain's aircraft and armored cars were in place. This provisional solution has lasted for seven decades and so have the borders of Transjordan, now ruled over by Abdullah's grandson, Hussein, the Hashemite King of Jordan.

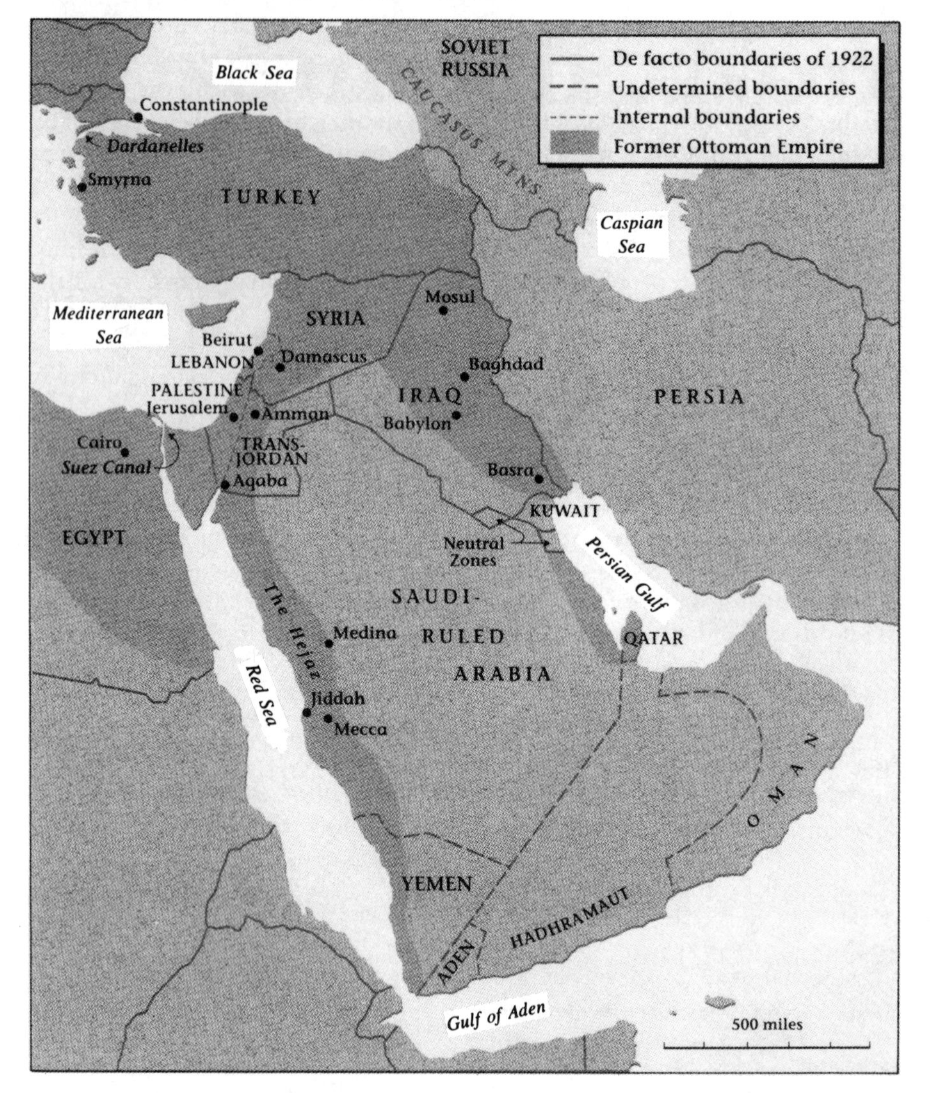

Map shows the Middle East redrawn by the British as of 1922. Iraq has just been created out of three more or less incompatible Ottoman provinces. Part of Palestine has become Transjordan (today's Jordan), which is still ruled by one of Abdullah's descendants.

The appointment of Abdullah seemed to accomplish several objectives at once. It went partway toward paying what Lawrence and others told Churchill was Britain's wartime debt to the family of King Hussein, though Hussein himself was beyond help. Too stubborn to accept British advice, he was losing the battle for Arabia to his blood rival, Ibn Saud. Meanwhile Prince Faisal, Britain's preferred Arab ruler, remained in idle exile.

Other chief items on the Cairo agenda were the Ottoman territories running from the Persian Gulf to Turkey along the border of Persia, which make up present-day Iraq. Including what were suspected—but not proved—to be vast oil reserves, at a time when the value of oil was beginning to be understood, these territories had been the scene of the bloodiest postwar Arab uprisings against British rule. They caused so many difficulties of every sort that Churchill flirted with the idea of abandoning them entirely, but Lloyd George would have none of it. If the British left, the Prime Minister warned, in a year or two they might find that they had "handed over to the French and Americans some of the richest oil fields in the world."

As a matter of convenience, the British administered this troubled region as a unit, though it was composed of the three separate Ottoman provinces—Mosul, Baghdad and Basra, with their incompatible Kurdish, Assyrian Christian, Jewish, Sunni Muslim, and Shiite populations. In making it into a country, Churchill and his colleagues found it convenient to continue treating it as a single unit. (One British planner was warned by an American missionary, "You are flying in the face of four millenniums of history . . .") The country was called Iraq—"the well-rooted country"—in order to give it a name that was Arabic. Faisal was placed on the throne by the British, and like his brother Abdullah in Transjordan, he was supposed to keep Iraq quiet until the British were ready to police it with aircraft and armored cars.

One of the leftover problems in 1921 was just how to protect Transjordan's new governor, Abdullah, and Iraq's new king, Faisal, against the fierce warriors of Ibn Saud. In August 1922 Ibn Saud's camel-cavalry forces invading Transjordan were stopped outside Amman by British airplanes and armored cars. Earlier that year, the British forced Ibn Saud to accept a settlement aimed at protecting Iraq. With this in mind, the British drew a frontier line that awarded Iraq a substantial amount of territory claimed by Ibn Saud for Arabia: all the land (in what is now Iraq) west of the Euphrates River, all the way to the Syrian frontier. To compensate Ibn Saud's kingdom (later known as Saudi Arabia) the British transferred to it rights to two-thirds of the territory of Kuwait, which had been essentially independent for about two centuries. These were valuable grazing lands, in which oil might exist too.

It is this frontier line between Iraq, Kuwait and Arabia, drawn by a British civil servant in 1922 to protect Iraq at the expense of Kuwait, that Iraq's Saddam Hussein denounced as invalid when he invaded.

In 1922, Churchill succeeded in mapping out the Arab Middle East along lines suitable to the needs of the British civilian and military administrations. T. E. Lawrence would later brag that he, Churchill and a few others had designed the modern Middle East over dinner. Seventy years later, in the tense deliberations and confrontations of half the world over the same area, the question is whether the peoples of the Middle East are willing or able to continue living with that design.

Remembering Mussolini

Charles F. Delzell

Charles F. Delzell, 68, is professor of history at Vanderbilt University. Born in Klamath Falls, Oregon, he received a B.S. from the University of Oregon (1941) and an M.A. (1943) and a Ph.D. (1951) from Stanford University. He is the author of Mussolini's Enemies: The Italian Anti-Fascist Resistance *(1961),* Italy in Modern Times *(1964), and* Italy in the 20th Century *(1980).*

After meeting Benito Mussolini in Rome in 1927, Winston Churchill, then a Conservative member of Parliament, said that had he been an Italian, he would have "wholeheartedly" supported the Fascist leader's "triumphant struggle against the bestial appetites and passions of Leninism." In 1940, however, when he was prime minister of an embattled Britain, Churchill called the *Duce* a "jackal," and blamed this "one man alone" for dragging Italy into World War II and disaster.

There have been few, if any, dictators of the Right or Left in our century whose rise to power owed more to the myopia of democratic statesmen and plain citizens. Mussolini's fall from power was as dramatic as his ascent, and the Fascist era merits our reflections today.

Many younger Americans may think of Mussolini only as actor Jack Oakie portrayed him in Charlie Chaplin's classic 1940 film, *The Great Dictator*: a rotund, strutting clown, who struck pompous poses from his Roman balcony and tried to upstage Adolf Hitler when they first met, in Venice in 1934.

Yet the caricature should not blind us to history. Perhaps the most sobering aspect of Benito Mussolini's career was how much applause he once enjoyed from highly respected intellectuals, journalists, and politicians, abroad and at home. Exasperated by Italy's fragile, fractious parliamentary democracy, worried about increasing popular unrest, and fearful of the Socialists' rising popularity, statesmen such as the Liberal Party leader Giovanni Giolitti and King Victor Emmanuel III welcomed Mussolini's advent to power in 1922. And the King supported him during most of the 21 years that the *Duce* ruled in Rome.

Mussolini's strong-man appeal—and that of the Fascism he espoused—grew out of the postwar disorder and economic hardship which reigned in Italy and much of Europe. It also stemmed in some measure from the fact that during the late 19th and early 20th centuries, Italy had been governed by squabbling legislators. By 1883, the year Mussolini was born, the various kingdoms and duchies on the Italian peninsula had only recently been unified under Victor Emmanuel II, King of Sardinia-Piedmont. "The patriotism of the Italians," as the 19th-century Neapolitan historian Luigi Blanch has observed, "is the love of a single town, not of a country; it is the feeling of a tribe, not of a nation."

Indeed, Italy was heir to long-embedded regional differences; these were aggravated by poor transportation and great disparities in education, wealth, and class. During the early 20th century, the church was powerful almost everywhere. And every corner of the country had its own traditions, customs, and dialect. The north-south contrasts were striking: At the turn of the century, for example, there were no primary schools in the south; in fact nearly 80 percent of all southerners were illiterate. Many peasants lived in a kind of Third World poverty, subject to drought, malaria, and the vagaries of absentee landlords.

The nation was politically fragmented too. In rural Italy, especially in the central "Red" Romagna region where Mussolini was born, anarchist-socialist ideas had spread rapidly. By the 1890s, a Marxist brand of socialism won favor among workers in northern Italy's new "industrial triangle." By 1919 Italy's Socialist Party—"revolutionary" and "revisionist" factions—held more seats than any other single party (though still not a majority) in the Parliament, thanks to the introduction of universal manhood suffrage and proportional representation. The Roman Catholic Church, meanwhile, was at odds not only with the Socialists but also with the kingdom of Italy itself. The kingdom had annexed the papal states of Rome and central Italy between 1861 and 1870, prompting Pope Pius IX to proclaim himself a "prisoner of the Vatican."

In the eyes of his early Fascist supporters, Benito Mussolini was the man who was restoring order and establishing national unity.

His origins were no more auspicious than Hitler's or Stalin's. He was born on July 29, 1883, into a poor but politically active household. His father, Alessandro Mussolini, was a blacksmith and an anarchist-socialist who helped organize a local group of the Socialist International, and who read aloud parts of *Das Kapital* to his family. Benito's mother, Rosa, was a pious Catholic schoolteacher who insisted that the family speak high Italian, rather than the Romagna dialect. Benito lived with his parents and a younger brother and sister in two rooms on the second floor of a small, shabby building outside of Predappio, about 50 miles southeast of Bologna. Two pictures hung on a wall in the parents' bedroom: one of the Virgin Mary and one of the Italian nationalist and anticlerical agitator Giuseppe Garibaldi. The parents named their eldest son not after a saint but after Benito Juarez, the Mexican revolutionary who had helped overthrow Santa Anna's dictatorship in 1855.

In his youth, Benito was moody at home and a bully at the Catholic boarding school he attended in nearby Faenza. Indeed, he was expelled after stabbing a fellow student with a knife and assaulting a priest who tried to discipline him. Benito was, nevertheless, an academic achiever; in 1901 he got his diploma from another school, in Forlimpopoli, and later became a part-time schoolteacher. At age 19, Mussolini left Italy for Switzerland ("that republic of sausages"), partly to avoid compulsory military service. "I was a bohemian in those days,"

From *The Wilson Quarterly,* Spring 1988, pp. 118-135.

he later wrote. "I made my own rules and I did not keep even them."

CHANGING TUNES

At first, Mussolini lived a vagabond's life in Switzerland—moving from town to town, doing odd jobs to survive, sometimes sleeping in public lavatories and parks. But the young man's interest soon turned to politics. In 1903 Mussolini took up residence in Bern; he began contributing articles to socialist journals, organized a strike of masons, and fought a (harmless) pistol duel with a fellow socialist.

After wandering through Switzerland, France, and Germany, Mussolini returned to Italy to do his military service. In 1909 he decided to move to Italian-speaking Trento in Austria-Hungary. There he edited a weekly socialist newspaper, *L'Avvenire del Lavoratore* ("The Workers' Future"). Later, in Forlì, Italy, he edited another socialist weekly, *La Lotta di Classe* ("The Class Struggle"), and translated Pyotr Kropotkin's *Great French Revolution.* By 1910, displaying a natural talent, he was one of Italy's best-known socialist journalist-polemicists. That year he also began to live with Rachele Guidi, the 17-year-old daughter of a widow with whom Benito's father had lived after the death of his wife. Their civil marriage would not take place until 1915.

Mussolini's early commitment to socialism, or to any other *ism,* should not be taken too seriously, despite his passionate rhetoric. Mussolini would repeatedly demonstrate his willingness to change his political stance whenever it advanced his prospects. As a young man he read the works of Niccolò Machiavelli, Friedrich Nietzsche, Georges Sorel, and others. But he was mostly interested in ideas that he could appropriate for his own use. Like other Italian socialists, Mussolini at first condemned World War I as an "imperialist war." His country's involvement, he said, would constitute an "unpardonable crime." But after France's amazing survival at the Marne in September 1914, he reversed his position. In *Avanta!*, the Socialist Party newspaper that he then edited in Milan, he urged that Italy enter the conflict on the side of Britain and France. The Socialists promptly expelled him as a traitor.

FASCI DI COMBATTIMENTO

Now a maverick "national" socialist, Mussolini quickly founded his own newspaper in Milan, *Il Popolo d'Italia* ("The People of Italy"). The paper was financed, in part, by local industrialists. Slogans on the paper's masthead read: "Whoever has steel has bread" (from the French revolutionary Auguste Blanqui) and "The Revolution is an idea which has found bayonets!" (from Napoleon). When the government declared war on Austria-Hungary in May 1915, Mussolini hailed the event as "Italy's baptism as a great power" and "a culminating point in world history."

Mussolini's own role in the conflict—he was drafted in August 1915 and served in the Alps—would provide him with a lode of (mostly imaginary) stories about his heroics in combat. Never involved in any major battles, the young sergeant was injured on February 22, 1917, when a mortar accidentally exploded in his trench, spraying his backside with 44 pieces of shrapnel. After recovering, Mussolini returned to *Il Popolo,* where he pounded out fiery editorials in favor of the war effort and against bolshevism. He considered Lenin a "man of straw" and observed that "only a Tartar and Mongolian people could fall for such a program as his."

As time went on, Mussolini became increasingly nationalistic. Insisting upon Italy's "great imperial destiny," he demanded the annexation of the Austro-Hungarian territories where Italian was spoken, such as the port of Trieste, the Italian Tyrol, and most of Dalmatia. With strong business support, Mussolini changed the subtitle of *Il Popolo d'Italia* from "a socialist newspaper" to "the newspaper of combatants and producers." And in a speech in Rome in February 1918, Mussolini declared that Italy needed "a man who is ferocious and energetic enough to make a clean sweep, with the courage to punish without hesitation, particularly when the culprits are in high places."

Although Italy emerged as a victor in World War I, the conflict had wreaked havoc on Italian society. Some 650,000 soldiers had perished. Returning veterans swelled the ranks of the unemployed; nearly two million Italians found themselves out of work by the end of 1919. A wave of industrial strikes broke out in the north. Some workers, stirred by the news of the Bolshevik Revolution in Russia, urged a "dictatorship of the proletariat" for Italy. Meanwhile, in Rome, one feeble Liberal Party coalition government after another tried vainly to restore stability.

With the Great War at an end, and the fear of bolshevism widespread, Mussolini cast about for a new nationalist cause to lead. On March 23, 1919, he founded Italy's Fascist movement in a businessmen's club off Milan's Piazza San Sepolcro. His *Fasci di Combattimento* ("Fighting Fasces") took their name from the bundle of rods with protruding axe-blades that had been the symbol of authority and discipline in ancient Rome. About 120 people were present at the Milan meeting, including veterans of the *arditi,* a group of wartime shock troops. "We, the survivors who have returned," Mussolini wrote, "demand the right of governing Italy." The Fascists chose as their uniform the same black shirt Romagna laborers had favored.

Though Mussolini's Fascist movement was always anti-Marxist, anti-Liberal, and virulently nationalistic, it would endorse (and quickly drop) many causes. At first Mussolini called for a republic and universal suffrage, and criticized the Roman Catholic Church. Later, he would endorse the monarchy, render elections meaningless, and cozy up to the church. The Fascist movement attracted unemployed youths, frightened members of the bourgeoisie, industrialists, landowners, and, especially, war veterans who believed that Italy, at the 1919 Paris peace conference, had not gained all of the territories she was due.

"When I came back from the war," Italo Balbo, a noted Fascist, would later recall, "I, like so many others, hated politics and politicians, who, it seemed to me, had betrayed the hopes of the fighting men and had inflicted on Italy a shameful peace. . . . Struggle, fight to return the country to Giolitti who had bartered every ideal? No. Better [to] deny everything, destroy everything in order to build everything up again from the bottom."

CUDGELS AND CASTOR OIL

The Fascist movement's ability to straddle, however awkwardly, Italy's conventional political divisions between Right and Left proved to be one of its greatest initial strengths. During the "Fascism of the First Hour," Mussolini's program did not differ much from that of the Socialists, except that the Fascists had favored Italy's wartime role and still praised it. But when the Fascist movement failed to elect even one of its candidates to Parliament in the November 1919 election, Mussolini decided to shift to the Right.

To win more support from Catholics, he muted his anticlerical rhetoric and said that Rome should subsidize churches and religious schools. The Liberal government's decision to withdraw troops from Albania, which they had occupied since 1914, Mussolini said, represented a "disgusting exhibition of national cowardice." Above all, Mussolini intensified his anti-Socialist rhetoric and berated the Liberal government for "doing nothing" when, in September 1920, metal workers in the north forcibly occupied the factories and set up Soviet-style workers' councils. The Fascists, Mussolini promised, would restore "law and order."

Mussolini's message won over many employers, who believed that the Fascists could keep militant labor at bay. Bands of Fascist thugs, known as *squadristi,* launched "punitive expeditions" against Socialist and Catholic leagues of laborers and farmworkers. They beat some members with cudgels and forced castor oil down their throats. By official count, the Fascists destroyed 120 labor union offices and murdered 243 persons between January and May of 1921.

The ruling Liberals were happy to look the other way. Local police officers even supplied the Blackshirt militias with weapons. And when Prime Minister Giovanni Giolitti called for new elections, to take place on May 15, 1921, he proposed to the Fascists that, following the election, they should join his constitutional bloc in Parliament. This time, Mussolini's Fascist Party would win 35 seats.

By 1922, Mussolini was impatient to seize power in what seemed more and more like a political vacuum. In October of that year, the Fascist party held a congress in Naples, where Mussolini and his colleagues drew up plans for a "March on Rome." Under the plan, Fascist militias would lead the march while Mussolini prudently remained close to the Swiss border in case the attempted coup d'état failed. "Either we are allowed to govern," Mussolini warned in a speech to the Fascist militiamen, "or we will seize power by marching on Rome" to "take by the throat the miserable political class that governs us."

TAKING POWER

The weak coalition government led by Luigi Facta knew that Mussolini was planning a coup, but at first the prime minister did not take the Fascists' intentions seriously. "I believe that the prospect of a March on Rome has faded away," Facta told the King. Nor were all of the Socialists eager to confront the Fascist threat. Indeed, some radical Marxists hoped that Mussolini's "reactionary buffoonery" would destroy both the Socialists and the Liberals, thus preparing the way for a genuine Communist revolution. For their part, the Liberals worried most about the Socialists, because of their anticapitalist ideology. Indeed, Liberals and Socialists were "as anxious to scuttle each other," as historian Denis Mack Smith has observed, "as to prevent a Fascist revolution."

The Fascists initiated the "March on Rome" on the night of October 27–28, 1922. The militias began taking over telephone exchanges and government offices. Luigi Facta wanted the King to declare a state of siege, but in the end no showdown occurred. Unconvinced that the army could or would defend Rome from the Fascists, or that the Liberals could provide effective leadership, Victor Emmanuel refused to sign a formal decree declaring a state of emergency. Instead, he telegraphed Mussolini, asking him to come to Rome to form a new government.

Boarding a train in Milan, Mussolini informed the stationmaster that he wanted to depart "exactly on time [because] from now on everything must function perfectly"—thereby giving rise to the myth that he made Italy's trains run on time. Upon his arrival in Rome, the *Duce* proceeded at once to the Palazzo del Quirinale. Still wearing a black shirt, he told the 53-year-old monarch (who had expected him to appear in formal dress): "I have come from the battlefield."

Thus, on October 31, 1922, at age 39, Mussolini became the youngest prime minister in Italy's short parliamentary history. With the Fascists holding only 35 seats in the 510-member Chamber of Deputies, he headed a cabinet of "national concentration" composed mostly of Liberals, socialist Democrats, and Catholic *Popolari.* In his first speech to the deputies, who gave him an overwhelming vote of confidence, he boasted: "I could have transformed this drab hall into a bivouac for my squads . . . I could have formed a government exclusively of Fascists, but I chose not to, at least not for the present."

Despite the *Duce*'s threats, many veteran politicians in Rome thought that, in time, they could co-opt Mussolini. Even Giovanni Giolitti and Antonio Salandra, the two senior members of the Liberal Party establishment favored Mussolini's ascension to power. Luigi Albertini, the editor of Milan's *Corriere della Sera* voiced his delight that Fascism had, above all, "saved Italy from the danger of Socialism."

Others were pleased that, finally, Italy enjoyed strong leadership, of whatever kind. "The heart of Fascism is the love of Italy," observed the Liberal senator and philosopher Benedetto Croce in January 1924. "Fascism is overcoming the traditional indifference of Italians to politics . . . and I value so highly the cure which Italy is undergoing from it that I rather hope the patient will not get up too soon from his bed and risk some grave relapse."

In Britain, France, and the United States, many conservatives also gave their blessings. The *New York Tribune* remarked that "the Fascisti movement is—in essentials—a reaction against degeneration through socialistic internationalism. It is rough in its methods, but the aims which it professes are tonic." Even the *New York Times* suggested that Mussolini's coup was of a "peculiar and relatively harmless type."

THE MATTEOTTI CRISIS

Now at the center of power, Mussolini increasingly became a solitary figure. During his first five years in office, the *Duce* lived alone in a small rented apartment; his wife Rachele remained in Milan, where she cared for their five children. He lived austerely, dined on vegetarian meals, and, partly to avoid irritating a gastric ulcer, eschewed alcohol and tobacco. (He once bragged of his "utter contempt for the lure of money.") An inveterate womanizer, Mussolini evinced little genuine affection for the opposite sex, or for people in general. "I have no friends," he once admitted to the German publicist Emil Ludwig, "first of all because of my temperament; secondly because of my views of human beings. That is why I avoid both intimacy and discussion."

Mussolini managed to project a more congenial image to the outside world. He contrived frequent "photo opportunities," posing at the controls of an airplane, grinning behind the wheel of a sports car, or taming a lion cub in its cage at the zoo. Many Americans saw him as an Italian Teddy Roosevelt—a stout-hearted advocate of the strenuous life.

But "image" was not enough. Eager to put more Fascists in Parliament, Mussolini called for an election, to take place on April 6, 1924. During the campaign and voting, the *squadristi* engaged in widespread intimidation. "When it is a matter of the Fatherland or of Fascism," Mussolini said on January 28, 1924, "we are ready to kill and die."

In the election, the Fascists claimed to have won 64.9 percent of the votes. But on May 30, Giacomo Matteotti, the widely respected leader of the Unitary Socialist Party, courageously stood up in Parliament to read a list of incidents in which Blackshirts had threatened voters and tampered with the ballot boxes. Fascist deputies, now in the majority, taunted him, yelling "Hireling!", "Traitor!", "Demagogue!". Ten days later, Fascist toughs who were closely linked to Mussolini's press office kidnapped Matteotti near his home in Rome, stabbed him, and then half buried his corpse in a grove outside the capital.

The assassination precipitated the most serious crisis of Mussolini's early days in power. Many Italians, after all, believed that Mussolini had at least incited, if not ordered, the murder. The anti-Fascist opposition—Socialists, Catholic *Popolari,* Republicans, and Constitutional Democrats—boycotted the Parliament, forming the "Aventine Secession." It was time for the King, they believed, to dismiss Mussolini and call for new elections.

But the ever-timid King, who was weary of the governments of the past, refused to intervene. Nor did the Vatican support the oppositionists. Pope Pius XI himself warned Italians against "cooperation with evil" (i.e. the Socialists) for "whatever reason of public welfare."

In a fit of wishful thinking, many foreign commentators did not blame Mussolini for the murder. They preferred to cite certain "gangster elements" among the Fascists. "The Matteotti incident," lamented the *New York Times* "is of a kind that may kill a movement by depriving it at one stroke of its moral content."

In Rome, Mussolini taunted his hapless, divided opponents during a speech in Parliament:

> But after all, gentlemen, what butterflies are we looking for under the arch of Titus? Well, I declare here before this assembly, before the Italian people, that I assume, I alone, the political, moral, historical responsibility for everything that has happened. . . .

By failing to oust Mussolini during the Matteotti crisis, his foes effectively entrenched the *Duce* as Italy's all-powerful leader.

On January 3, 1925, Mussolini launched a counter-offensive, announcing in an impassioned half-hour speech to Parliament that "force" was the "only solution" to the threat of disorder. Under a series of "exceptional decrees," Mussolini censored the press and outlawed all opposition parties, including the Socialists and Liberals. He replaced labor unions with Fascist syndicates. His Special Tribunal for the Defense of the State sentenced thousands of opposition activists (especially Communists and anarchists) either to long prison terms or to internal exile in the south. Youngsters were recruited by Fascist youth organizations—a future model for Germany's Hitler Youth—which stressed indoctrination and discipline, and exhorted them to "Believe! Obey! Fight!"

All the while, Mussolini continued to garner praise abroad. "Mussolini's dictatorship," observed the *Washington Post* in August, 1926, "evidently appeals to the Italian people. They needed a leader, and having found him they gladly confer power upon him."

GIVING ITALY BACK TO GOD

Mussolini called his regime the Totalitarian State: "Everything in the State, Nothing outside the State, Nothing Against the State!" But his "totalitarianism," harsh and noisy as it often was, was far less brutal than that of Stalin's Russia or Hitler's Germany—partly because the King retained control of the Italian Army and the right to dismiss the prime minister. Not until 1938 did the regime begin to discriminate against the nation's roughly 40,000 Jews; many would lose their jobs in government and academia. But Mussolini did not seek a "final solution" to Italy's "Jewish problem"—as the Germans did after they occupied northern Italy in September 1943.

On the economic front, Mussolini's "Corporative State" tried to foster "class conciliation." The regime set up parallel Fascist syndicates of employers and workers in various sectors of the economy. Labor courts settled disputes under a system of compulsory arbitration.

In 1933, the regime established the Institute for Industrial Reconstruction (IRI) as a holding company to shore up failing industries. State-subsidized (or "parastate") industrial organizations would soon furnish about 17 percent of all goods and services. To stimulate the economy, Mussolini built roads, sports stadiums,and government buildings. The government launched numerous programs for mothers and children and developed a land reclamation scheme, which was responsible for draining the Pontine Marshes near Rome. Mussolini initiated a much-publicized "battle for grain"; newsreel cameramen filmed him pitching straw, bare from the waist up. Perhaps most significantly, the *Duce* began an ill-fated effort to rebuild the nation's army, navy, and air force.

Despite Mussolini's promise to restore "the Augustan Empire," he generally failed to push Italy's backward economy forward. The regime's cartels sometimes hindered economic advance by discouraging innovation and modernization. The *Duce* demoralized workers by cutting wages, raising taxes, and banning strikes and other forms of protest. Even as the government took over industries and prepared for war, unemployment remained high. Fully half of those who did work were employed in agriculture. Italian families, meanwhile, were spending 50 percent of their incomes on food.

Mussolini, however, sought (and gained) amicable relations with the Catholic church by signing the Lateran Pacts with the Vatican in February 1929. The pacts created the State of Vatican City, within which the Pope would be sovereign. They established Roman Catholicism as Italy's state religion, bestowing on it extensive privileges and immunities. The *Duce*'s star soared throughout the Catholic world; devout Italian peasants flocked to church to pray for the man who had "given back God to Italy and Italy to God." Ignoring the suppression of civil liberties, Pope Pius XI referred to Mussolini as "a man whom Providence has caused to meet us" and sprinkled him with holy water.

GRABBING ETHIOPIA

By the late 1920s, the *Duce* had solidified support for his regime, both in Rome and abroad. Soon after entering the White House in 1933, Franklin D. Roosevelt wrote that he was "deeply impressed" by this "admirable Italian gentleman," who seemed intent upon "restoring Italy and seeking to prevent general European trouble."

Indeed, until the mid-1930s, Mussolini stayed (for the most part) out of foreign ventures. But great nations, Mussolini believed, could not be content with achievements at home. "For Fascism," as he wrote in the *Enciclopedia Italiana* in 1932, "the growth of empire . . . is an essential manifestation of vitality, and its opposite a sign of decadence. Peoples which are rising, or rising again after a period of decadence, are always imperialist: any renunciation is a sign of decay and death."

Mussolini would become increasingly obsessed with foreign conquests after January 1933, when Adolf Hitler became chancellor of Germany and soon won dictatorial powers. Although Mussolini and Hitler, as fellow Fascists, admired each other, their alliance would be marked by periodic fits of jealousy on the *Duce*'s part. Hitler, as biographer Joachim C. Fest has written, "aroused in Mussolini an inferiority complex for which he thereafter tried to compensate more and more by posturings, imperial actions, or the invoking of a vanished past."

Mussolini's first major "imperial action" would occur in Africa. The *Duce* had long coveted Emperor Haile Selassie's Ethiopia, which an Italian army had failed to conquer in 1896. On the morning of October 2, 1935, as 100,000 troops began moving across the Eritrea-Ethiopia border, Mussolini announced that "A great hour in the history of our country has struck . . . forty million Italians, a sworn community, will not let themselves be robbed of their place in the sun!"

Paralyzed by economic depression and public antiwar sentiment, Britain's Prime Minister Stanley Baldwin refused to intervene, despite the inherent threat to British colonies in Africa. The League of Nations denounced the Fascist aggression. However, lacking any coherent leadership or U.S. support, the League stopped short of closing the Suez Canal or imposing an oil embargo on Italy. Either action, Mussolini said later, would have inflicted "an inconceivable disaster."

The barefooted Ethiopian levies were no match for Italy's Savoia bombers and mustard gas. The *Duce*'s pilot son, Vittorio, told journalists in Africa that the Ethiopian soldiers, when hit from the air, "exploded like red roses." Addis Ababa fell in May 1936. With this victory, Mussolini reached the pinnacle of his popularity at home. Speaking to an enormous crowd from his Palazzo Venezia balcony, the *Duce* declared that his "triumph over 50 nations" meant the "reappearance of the Empire upon the fated hills of Rome." Signs everywhere proclaimed *Il Duce ha sempre ragione* ("The leader is always right").

Emboldened by his Ethiopian success, Mussolini began to intervene elsewhere. He dispatched aircraft and some 70,000 "volunteers" to help Generalissimo Francisco Franco's Falangist insurgents in the Spanish Civil War. He pulled Italy out of the League of Nations and decided to line up with Hitler's Germany, which had already quit the League. Thus, in June 1936, Mussolini's 33-year-old foreign minister and son-in-law, Count Galeazzo Ciano, negotiated the Rome-Berlin Axis, which was expanded into a full-fledged military alliance, the "Pact of Steel," in May 1939. Both countries also established links with Japan through the Anti-Comintern pact. The *Duce* now belonged to what he called the "most formidable political and military combination that has ever existed."

HUMILIATIONS IN THE DESERT

Mussolini's military forces, however, could not be described as formidable. Lacking coal, iron, oil, and sufficient heavy industry, Italy's economy could not support a major war effort. The *Duce,* who spoke of "eight million bayonets," proved a better propagandist than military planner. On the eve of World War II, the Italian Army owned 1.3 million outdated rifles and even fewer bayonets; its tanks and artillery were obsolete. By June 1940, the Italian Navy boasted fast battleships and Western Europe's largest fleet of submarines. But it sadly lacked radar, echo-sounding equipment, and other new technologies. And Mussolini's admirals and generals were better known for their political loyalty than for professional competence.

When Hitler quickly annexed Austria in March 1938, and Czechoslovakia in March 1939, Mussolini complained to Count Ciano: "The Italians will laugh at me. Every time Hitler occupies a country, he sends me a message." The *Duce,* ignoring Catholic sensibilities, ordered the invasion of Albania on Good Friday, April 7, 1939, bringing that backward Adriatic country into his empire.

When Germany invaded Poland on September 1, 1939, thereby launching World War II, Mussolini knew that Italy was not ready to fight. He initially adopted a position of "non-belligerency." The list of needed war supplies that the *Duce* requested from Berlin, noted Count Ciano, "is long enough to kill a bull." But as Hitler's Blitzkrieg brought Denmark, Norway, the Low Countries, and France to their knees in 1940, Mussolini decided he had little to lose, and perhaps some spoils to gain.

On June 10, 1940, without consulting either his cabinet or the Fascist Grand Council, Mussolini declared war on both France and Britain. In joining the conflict, Mussolini inadvertently let Hitler become the master of Italy's fate.

The Italian people soon felt the pain. The battlefield performance of Mussolini's armed forces reflected the home-front's lack of zeal. One debacle after another ensued. Under Field Marshal Rodolfo Graziani, Italy's much-touted armored brigades in Libya attacked the British in Egypt, hoping to capture the Suez Canal. But in the seesaw battles across the desert, as well as in naval engagements in the Mediterranean, the outnumbered British inflicted repeated humiliations on the Italians, who had to beg the Germans for help. By the end of 1941, the British had also shorn Mussolini of Italian Eritrea and Somalia, as well as Ethiopia, reinstating Haile Selassie as emperor.

THE KING SAYS GOOD-BYE

Italy's invasion of Greece, launched from Albania on October 28, 1940, did not fare much better. Saying he was "tired of acting as Hitler's tail-light," Mussolini launched the attack without notifying Berlin. The war against the Greeks, the *Duce* predicted would be little more than a "military promenade." But the Italians were bogged down in the mountains for months, until Hitler's spring 1941 invasion of the Balkans rescued Mussolini's lackluster legions. And

Italy's participation in Germany's 1941 invasion of the Soviet Union yielded few triumphs. Mussolini dispatched three infantry divisions and one cavalry division. At least half of the 240,000 Italian soldiers sent to the Eastern front never returned.

For Italy, the beginning of the end came on December 7, 1941, when the Japanese bombed Pearl Harbor, bringing the United States into the war against the Axis powers. Although Mussolini seemed delighted to be fighting "a country of Negroes and Jews," he knew that his regime was now in deep trouble.

Across the Mediterranean, in November 1942, General Dwight Eisenhower put Allied forces ashore in Morocco and Algeria. He began a push to meet Field Marshal Bernard Montgomery's British Eighth Army, which had already broken through Axis defenses at el-Alamein. The German *Afrika Korps* fought a tough delaying action. But when the North Africa campaign ended in May 1943, some 200,000 Italians had been taken prisoner; few had fought the Allies with much enthusiasm.

New bases in North Africa enabled Allied airmen to step up the bombing of Italian cities and rail centers, which left the nation's already hard-pressed economy in tatters. Tardily, the regime rationed food supplies and restricted the consumption of gas and coal. Despite wage and price controls, inflation soared, and a black market flourished. Ordinary Italians began to demonstrate their disaffection. In early 1943, public employees in Turin and Fiat workers in Milan went on strike. "In Italy," Mussolini would later write, "the oral repercussions of the American landing in Algiers were immediate and profound. Every enemy of Fascism promptly reared his ugly head. . . ."

By the time the Allies invaded Sicily on July 10, 1943, even those Italian politicians who had long enjoyed privileges and perquisites were fed up; plots were being hatched in Rome to oust Mussolini and turn over political power to King Victor Emmanuel. All this came to a head on the night of July 24–25, when the Fascist Grand Council met at the Palazzo Venezia to decide Mussolini's fate. Some Fascist councillors criticized the shaken dictator to his face for being too indecisive; others berated him for not ridding the government of incompetents. Nothing was working, they said, and the Germans in Italy, coping with Anglo-American advances, regarded their sagging ally with contempt.

In a two-hour monologue, the *Duce* tried to defend himself saying that "this is the moment to tighten the reins and to assume the necessary responsibility. I shall have no difficulty in replacing men, in turning the screw, in bringing forces to bear not yet engaged." But the council adopted a resolution, which had been supported by Count Ciano, calling upon the King to take over the leadership of the nation.

The next afternoon, Mussolini went to the King's villa, hoping to bluff his way through the crisis. But the King had decided, at last, to separate himself from the Fascist regime. He quickly informed Mussolini that he had decided to set up a royal military government under the 71-year-old Army Marshal, Pietro Badoglio. "Then everything is finished," the *Duce* murmured. As the ex-dictator left the Villa Savoia, a *Carabiniere* officer motioned him into an ambulance, pretending this was necessary to avoid "a hostile crowd."

Mussolini was taken to a police barracks, unaware that he was under arrest. At 10:45 a government spokesman announced over the radio the formation of the new regime by the King and Badoglio. Jubilant crowds rushed into the streets to celebrate. But they were dismayed by Badoglio's statement that "the war continues"—a statement made to ward off German retaliation.

RESCUING THE DUCE

Marshal Badoglio placed the former *Duce* under guard. Later, he was transferred to a ski resort atop Gran Sasso, the tallest peak in central Italy. He remained there for almost a fortnight, while the new regime secretly negotiated an armistice with the Allies. The armistice was announced on September 8—even as American and British troops landed against stiff German resistance at Salerno, near Naples.

Thereafter, events moved swiftly.

Anticipating Italy's' about-face, Hitler had dispatched strong *Wehrmacht* reinforcements across the Alps; the Germans were able quickly to disarm and intern the badly confused Italian troops. Fearing capture, the King and Badoglio fled Rome before dawn on September 9 to join the Allied forces in the south. Six weeks later the Badoglio government, now installed in Bríndisi, declared war on Germany.

On September 12, 1943, Captain Otto Skorzeny, leading 90 German commandos in eight gliders and a small plane, landed outside the mountaintop hotel on Gran Sasso where the sickly *Duce* was still being kept. Skorzeny's men brushed aside the Italian guards, and took Mussolini to Munich, where Hitler met him. Henceforth, the *Duce* would be one of Hitler's lackeys, a "brutal friendship" as Mussolini put it.

The *Führer* ordered Mussolini to head up the new pro-Nazi Italian Social Republic (RSI) at Salò, in German-occupied northern Italy. The Italian Fascists would help the Nazis deport, and later exterminate, over 8,000 Jews. From Munich, Mussolini appealed by radio to his "faithful Blackshirts" to renew Axis solidarity, and purge the "royalist betrayers" of the regime.

But few Italians willingly backed the "Salò Republic." Instead, most hoped for a swift Allied victory. A determined minority even joined the partisans—the armed anti-German and anti-Fascist resistance—in northern Italy. But Mussolini did manage to punish the "traitors of July 25." In Verona, a special Fascist tribunal put on trial Mussolini's son-in-law, Count Ciano, and others in his party who had voted for "the elimination of its *Duce.*" Rejecting the pleas of his daughter Edda, Mussolini decreed that Ciano and his co-conspirators be shot to death, and so they were, on January 11, 1944.

At last, in April 1945, the grinding Allied offensive, having reached northern Italy, overwhelmed the Germans, whose homeland was already collapsing under attack from East and West. At this point, Mussolini tried to save himself by negotiating with anti-Fascist resistance leaders in Milan. but when he learned that they insisted on an "unconditional surrender," he fled with several dozen companions to Lake Como, where he was joined by his mistress, Clara Petacci. From there, they planned to escape to Switzerland.

PER NECESSITÀ FAMILIALE

Unable to cross the border, Mussolini and his band decided to join a German truck convoy that was retreating toward Switzerland through the Italian Alps. But Italian partisans halted the convoy near Dongo. Ever the actor, Mussolini donned a German corporal's overcoat, a swastika-marked helmet, and dark glasses, and climbed into one of the trucks. But the partisans identified Mussolini, arrested him and his companions, and let the Germans proceed unmolested.

The next day, Walter Audisio, a Communist resistance chief from Milan, arrived, claiming he had orders to execute the *Duce* and 15 other Fascist fugitives. He summarily shot Mussolini and his mistress at the village of Giulino di Mezzegra on April 28. Their corpses were taken to Milan and strung up by the heels in Piazzale Loreto, where an infuriated mob repeatedly kicked and spat on the swinging cadavers.

Looking back on Mussolini's career, it might be said that he changed Italy more than he changed the Italians. Indeed, the *Duce* left behind a network of paved roads, reclamation projects, and a vast centralized bureaucracy. The IRI holding company and other para-state corporations that Mussolini founded still exist today; they account for the most inefficient 20 percent of the nation's economy.

But Mussolini convinced few Italians for long that Fascism was the wave of the future. To be sure, many had supported the *Duce* enthusiastically, especially from the time his regime signed the concordat with the Pope (1929) through the easy conquest of Ethiopia (1936). And a small neo-Fascist party, the *Movimento Sociale Italiano* (MSI), still wins roughly five percent of the popular vote in national elections today.

Most Italians quietly turned their backs on Mussolini once it became clear that he had engaged the nation in costly ventures that could not succeed. (More than 400,000 Italians lost their lives in World War II.) During the *Duce*'s foolish expeditions against the Greeks, the British, and the Soviets, many Italians considered themselves to be "half-Fascists," who had taken out their Fascist Party membership cards only *per necessità familiale* (for the good of the family).

On June 2, 1946, the first time that Italians got a chance to vote in a postwar election, they chose to oust the monarchy. They could not forgive King Victor Emmanuel for inviting Mussolini to take power, and for supporting the *Duce*'s imperial ambitions—even if they forgave themselves. The voters elected a constituent assembly, which drafted a new constitution for the republic, providing for a prime minister, a bicameral parliament, and a system of 20 regional governments.

Mussolini and his ideology proved influential beyond Italy's borders. As the world's first and perhaps most popular Fascist leader, he provided the model for other aspiring authoritarian rulers in Europe and Latin America who, for a time, would make fascism seem an attractive alternative to socialism, communism, or anarchy.

In Germany, Adolf Hitler called Mussolini's 1922 March on Rome "one of the turning points of history." The mere idea that such a march could be attempted, he said, "gave [Germany's National Socialists] an impetus." When Nazis did their outstretched arm salutes, or when Spanish Falangists cried "Franco! Franco! Franco!", they were mimicking their counterparts in Italy. Juan Perón, Argentina's president (1946–1955), echoed the sentiments of many another ambitious Latin strongman when he called Mussolini "the greatest man of our century."

Just before Mussolini came to power, Italians, like citizens of several troubled European societies after World War I, faced a choice—either muddling through disorder and economic disarray under often inept, yet essentially benevolent democratic regimes, or falling in line behind a decisive but brutal dictatorship. Italians chose the latter. They embraced the strong man's notions of a grand New Age. But Mussolini's intoxicating vision of Italy as a great power, they eventually discovered, was a disastrous delusion.

The Fascist era serves to remind Italians and others of something important: that national well-being may not come from charismatic leadership, revolutionary zeal, or military might. Indeed, Italy's peculiar greatness today may lie in its citizens' tolerance of regional and economic differences, in their ability to cope with the inefficiencies of democratic government, in their pragmatic acceptance of human foibles—and, most of all, in their appreciation of the rich texture of everyday life.

Women and the Nazi State

Hitler may have thought that women were there for cooking, children and church, but recent research has shown that female attitudes to, and involvement in, the apparatus of the Third Reich was much more significant, argues **Matthew Stibbe.**

Matthew Stibbe

Matthew Stibbe is a research student at Sussex University doing an MA in European history.

Since the 1960s gender-based research in a wide variety of areas has increasingly rectified distortions produced by a process of historical enquiry based exclusively on men and records kept by men. At first sight, however, the Third Reich would appear to be an area in which the importance of women as actors in history could not easily be demonstrated. After all, Nazism was the most reactionary and repressive of all modern ideologies, and one which from the outset totally excluded women from holding any leading positions of power and responsibility. Indeed, much early work on National Socialism, reflecting a traditional male bias, tended either to ignore the importance of gender or else reinforce a stereotype of women as the passive and innocent victims of a male-dominated movement. Nevertheless, as historians are increasingly coming to recognise, the success of Nazism depended not on one single all-embracing factor but on its ability to enforce a dynamic integration of a variety of conflicting interests, not least those of women, who at the time constituted over half of the German population. For example, although the male vote for the Nazis during the Weimar Republic was always higher than the female, the difference did narrow in the early 1930s and in some Protestant areas was even reversed. In particular, it seems likely that many younger women who had not voted before cast their first ballot for Nazi candidates, which suggests that there was something in the party programme which positively attracted them.

It is now well established that the Nazis anti-feminism was related in significant ways to their racist ideology as a whole. Like the Jew, the modern 'emancipated' woman was seen as an agent of degeneracy and national decline, bringing in her wake the 'destructive' forces of Bolshevism, democracy and parliamentarianism. German women, it was frequently claimed, were being lured by Jews and Marxists into rational thinking and an 'unhealthy' preoccupation with sexuality, whilst the advocates of female emancipation were accused of working for no less than the complete destruction of 'Christian-Germanic' existence and family life.

The Nazis promised to restore the traditional balance between the sexes by inducing women to celebrate their 'natural' domestic roles as mothers and housewives. 'Equal rights for women', Hitler declared, 'means that they receive the esteem they deserve in the sphere nature has assigned to them'. In particular, women were to become the focus of the Nazis' drive to boost the birth rate. At least in the early years of the regime they were systematically directed away from the idea of a full-time career towards starting or extending a family, and to this end a generous system of marriage loans was introduced. Similarly, in education policy the emphasis was away from developing 'unnatural' qualities, such as academic ability and independence, in favour of training for future maternal roles through compulsory courses in domestic science and biology.

Women were also discouraged from using cosmetics and wearing 'decadent' foreign modes of dress: sex appeal was considered to be 'Jewish cosmopolitanism', whilst slimming cures were frowned upon as counter to the birth drive. Attempts were made to create a new 'Germanic style' through a German Fashion Bureau, set up in 1933 under the honorary presidency of Magda Goebbels, in order to combat clothes considered decadent or slavish imitations of men's styles. There was also an increased emphasis on physical fitness: women were encouraged to achieve the Reich Sport Medal, and smoking, especially whilst pregnant, was strictly condemned.

In marriage, the principle of love was replaced by the principle of *Rassegefühl* or racial awareness, and couples intending to apply for the marriage loan were forced to go through a demanding medical examination, leading to a great fear of revealing hereditary defects and to a lucrative black market in documents proving Aryan ancestry. The future wives of SS men were subject to a particularly rigorous procedure, and had to attend special *Bräuteschule* or bride schools to prepare them for motherhood.

Those considered to be racially or socially unsuitable for motherhood were denied the relative benefits afforded to 'racially desirable' women. According to one estimate, 27,958 'undesirable' women had been forcibly sterilised by the end of 1934, with 5 per cent of these cases resulting in death. Jewish women in particular were victimised, not only on account of their race, but because of their sex, which placed them on a lower scale even than Jewish men. Aryan men who had married Jewish women were encouraged to divorce them, and in such cases any offspring were often removed from the mother. And in 1939 it was announced that the strict prohibition on abortion did not apply to Jewish women.

Non-Jewish women who chose not to get married and have children, or who for reasons beyond their control were unable to do so, were subject to a different kind of harassment and discrimination. For one woman the pressure to bear children became so great that she resorted to kidnapping. Another complained in an open letter to Hitler: 'We see our daughters growing up in stupid aimlessness, living only in the vague hope of getting a husband and having children. If they do not succeed, their lives will be thwarted'. Indeed, the Nazi state showed little interest in the fate of single women beyond child-bearing age, who were often forced to seek the lowest paid and most monotonous work. Perhaps the clearest indication of this can be seen in Article 3 of the Nuremburg race laws of 1935, which banned Aryan women from serving as maids in Jewish houses except for those over forty-five, who were considered to be out of danger of violation by their Jewish employers.

These facts were well-documented by female opponents of the regime at the time that they were happening (for a good example see Katherine Thomas' *Women in Nazi Germany,* London, 1943) and have long been known to historians. However, the first serious attempts at a gender-based analysis of Nazism in the 1960s and 1970s produced findings which challenged the conventional view that a complete transformation of the position of German women for the worse had taken place after 1933. Jill Stephenson, for instance (*Women in Nazi Society,* Croom Helm, 1975) has pointed out that the Nazis' reactionary policies towards women were in line with a more general European trend in the inter-war years. Measures designed to curb abortions and contraception, and a pre-occupation with reversing the declining birth rate among 'healthy' sections of the community were common to dictatorships of the right and the left, as well as to democracies. France, for instance, had even more reason than Germany to be worried by the decline in her birth rate, and it was here, in 1920, that the practice of giving awards to prolific mothers, later taken up by the Nazis, was first introduced. In 1939, the *Code de la Famille* increased the penalties for contraception and abortion, the latter becoming a capital offence under the wartime Vichy regime in 1942.

Similarly, campaigns to remove married women from the labour market in order to make way for unemployed males were a typical European-wide response to the world recession of the early 1930s. In Germany itself, such policies were already being pursued by Chancellor Brüning's government between 1930 and 1932, and enjoyed the support of large sections of public opinion, including conservatives, and churches and even some trade unionists and members of the women's movement, whilst in 1933 the Dolfuss regime in Austria enacted measures to remove married women from the civil service which were very similar to those brought in by the Nazis in the same year. Throughout the inter-war years restrictions on women's eligibility for professional positions remained in force in many European countries, including France, Belgium, Italy, Bulgaria, Greece, the Netherlands, and until 1938, Norway. In Britain, married women were largely excluded from the teaching profession until the 1944 Butler Education Act, and it was only in the mid-1950s that the principle of equal pay was introduced in the civil service.

Meanwhile, Stephenson argues, the most significant break in the regime's stance towards women came after 1936, when unemployment had been brought down to acceptable levels and the Nazis began to reverse their previous policies in line with the requirements of rearmament and an expanding economy. The increased demand for female labour, she asserts, meant that whatever the long-term ideological goals of the Nazis may have been, in the intermediate term they could only discriminate against women to a very limited extent. Indeed, she turns the conventional picture almost completely on its head: women under Nazism benefited both from a rise in the status and benefits afforded to mothers and housewives, whilst at the same time consolidating their position in employment outside the home, including the professions.

A few years earlier David Schönbaum (*Hitler's Social Revolution. Class and Status in Nazi Germany 1933–1939,* Weidenfeld and Nicolson, 1967) had already noted how economic pressures helped to improve the competitive position of women in the labour market, so that the gap between men and women's wages actually decreased during the Third Reich (differentials remained nonetheless, and the average unskilled male worker, for instance, could still expect to be paid more than the average skilled female worker). The most significant area in which the Nazis were able to uphold their ideological insistence on the 'natural inferiority' of the female sex, he argues, was in their total exclusion of women from positions of political power and responsibility within the party and state apparatus. Nevertheless, Schönbaum also claims that this loss of political status was to a large extent offset by increased job opportunities and rising wage rates, as well as improved maternity benefits and services. Overall, he concludes, 'the pressures of the totalitarian state combined with those of an industrialising and industrial society to produce for women . . . a new status of relative if unconventional equality'.

Such work has helped to shed light on the reasons why some leading figures in the pre-1933 women's movements, most notably Gertrud Bäumer of the Federation of German Women's Associations, were willing to come to a rapprochement with the regime and even to praise some of its policies, such as the introduction of Labour service for young women in 1937, as a step towards greater equality for women within their own gender-conditioned spheres of activity. The Nazi regime itself, meanwhile, was able to produce a number of its own high-profile female personalities, such as the fashion-conscious, Magda Goebbels, the screen-idol turned film producer, Leni Riefenstahl, the air pilot, Hannah Reitsch, and above all the *Frauenführerin,* (Women's Leader) Gertrude Scholtz-Klink, who managed to combine her leadership of the six to eight million members of the Nazi Women's Bureau with her responsibilities as a mother of four.

On a broader level too there has been a move away from the stereotype image of women as passive victims in the Third Reich towards women as actors in their own right. This in turn has opened up new controversies surrounding the issue of female consent to Nazism. Claudia Koonz, for instance, (*Mothers in the Fatherland, Women, the Family and Nazi Politics,* Jonathan Cape, 1987) has revealed the existence of women who actively supported the movement during its rise to power. Such 'Nazi feminists', if indeed they can be described as such, typically sought to distinguish themselves from their religious, bourgeois and socialist counterparts in their outright rejection of emancipation as a hoax: equal rights for women, they argued, had merely meant 'equal rights to be exploited'. Paula Sieber, a Nazi activist in Düsseldorf, wrote to her local paper in 1934:

> The women's movement of yesterday led thirty-six parliamentarians and hundred of thousands of women out onto the streets of our great cities. It made one woman a high-ranking civil servant and hundreds of thousands wage-slaves of the capitalist economic order.

More conservative figures such as Guida Diehl were to praise the efforts of National Socialism in restoring women to their lost dignity as defenders of 'German-Christian' spiritual values and family life. Others emphasised the opportunities which Nazism seemed to offer to forge a radically new public role for women within their own separate sphere of child care, education and welfare work. Indeed, Koonz's research reveals that those women who were actively involved in the Nazi movement during its rise to power typically expressed satisfaction in having 'broken free' both from the alienation of the modern rationalised world and from the rigid class divisions which had hitherto divided the women's movement.

In particular, members of the League of Young German Maidens nurtured a strong sense of peer group solidarity in the face of parental disapproval and the snobbery of the 'bluestockings' in the older, more respectable women's organisations. Another common theme was the sense of pride many of these women felt in being able to make a contribution, however small, to the process of national renewal. Nazi leaders themselves were often at pains to stress that women were *nicht gleichartig sondern gleichwertig*—'different, but not inferior'—to men, and made frequent comparisons between the 'honour' of men in performing military service and the 'honour' of women in their battle as the bearers of the next generation.

In reality women came to exercise very little control in the Third Reich, even in the separate sphere assigned to them. After 1933 the male-dominated Nazi leadership preferred to recruit more passive women who would be content to implement policies handed down from above. Gertrude Scholtz-Klink, eventually appointed as head of the Women's Bureau in 1934, was typical in this respect. With her classic Aryan looks and her four children she represented the ideal 'Gretchen' type, displaying those simple womanly virtues—comradeship, self-sacrifice and devotion to family—which the Nazis were attempting to encourage. Her guiding principle was always that women should campaign not against men, but alongside them, and as *Frauenführerin* she sought to maintain the illusion that she had created considerable autonomy for women within their own sphere of activity. In reality however, she was excluded from all high level discussions, even when these affected areas which directly concerned women, such as plans to mobilise female labour during the war. In 1942, for instance, when she suggested that the benefits of child subsidies be extended to women factory workers, she was told by the director of the Labour Front, Robert Ley, that *volksbiologisch,* or racial-biological considerations must be put before the needs of the war economy.

Meanwhile, the known promiscuity of top political leaders, the divorce reform act of 1938, leading to a steady increase in the number of legal separations, the official encouragement given to children who informed on their parents, and conscription forcing more and more men to live away from home, increasingly exposed the contradictions in Nazi pro-family rhetoric. Scholtz-Klink and her social workers were expected to play an active role in ideological indoctrination and the promotion of eugenics and 'racial awareness' among the women in their care, whilst collecting the names of those deemed fit for sterilisation or the euthanasia programme. The introduction of the *Lebensborn* programme, whereby specially selected women were encouraged to 'donate a baby to the Führer' by having illegitimate children by SS officers, also represented a radical departure from traditional family values with no parallels either in the German past or in contemporaneous fascist movements.

Koonz, however, takes her argument one stage further. By surrendering their political rights in return for the honour and prestige bestowed on them as mothers in the fatherland, she argues, German women ultimately played an equal role in helping to make war and genocide possible. Whilst Nazi men launched their racially-charged war of conquest in the east, Nazi women were equally busy creating their own domestic *Lebensraum* (living space) in the form of a private retreat from the outside world. In particular, she claims, the Nazis made efforts to select men from 'good family backgrounds' to oversee the mass killings in the concentration camps. The role of their wives was to preserve 'an illusion of love in an environment of hatred', and 'a place of contact with the more humane self', which provided a kind of 'ersatz sanity' for those who worked daily with mass murder.

Controversial as Koonz's conclusion may be, her work has undoubtedly been of major importance in demonstrating the importance of women's history in examining all historical issues, even when this might put women themselves in a bad light. As she herself argues, it is only by examining the everyday banality of evil that we can begin to appreciate the true horrors of the holocaust.

However, German women were by no means always predetermined to act in the way Koonz's work suggests, and there are other, equally important ways in which they can be seen as actors in the Third Reich. Whilst, undoubtedly, many women did play their part in making life unbearable for 'racially undesirable' citizens, those directly involved in implementing Nazi policies were at best a small minority. Rather, as an earlier study by Tim Mason ('Women in Germany 1925–1940. Family, Welfare and Work', *History Workshop Journal,* Part 1 Spring 1976, Part 2 Autumn 1976) reveals, the most significant trend in Nazi family life was towards the ideal of the small suburban middle class family. This he sees as a specific reaction to the demands made on women's lives by increasing industrialisation and bureaucratisation, which was not just peculiar to Nazi Germany, but is very much a part of contemporary Western life. It explains the popularity of the Nazi Marriage Loan scheme, which enabled many young women to escape the boredom of routine work by getting married and setting up home, but significantly, it also led to resistance towards the Nazi drive to increase the birth rate, and later toward the regime's efforts to encourage women to leave their domesticity for war work. Overall, as Mason notes, the mobilisation of women for war production was strikingly inefficient when compared to that of wartime Britain. Even after Hitler's ideological objections to the conscription of married women were finally overcome after the reversal of Stalingrad in 1943, many women continued to find ways of avoiding it, some of them ironically by deliberately getting pregnant.

Much early work on resistance explicitly excludes this struggle by women against the encroachments of a rational-bureaucratic state on their private sphere and proceeds from the conventional view that resistance was only possible among those who were committed anti-Nazis before 1933. Even Mason is content to argue that:

> The low level of women's participation in the resistance groups of all political persuasions, in particular the conservative resistance, also points in the direction of a high degree of passive acceptance of the regime by women.

However, recent women's studies of the resistance have shown how women themselves were able to develop strategies for political activism within the context of their everyday lives, for instance, by extending their roles as housewives to feeding and sheltering the victims of Nazism and active members of the resistance, or by exploiting opportunities arising from their employment as secretaries to providing the resistance with distribution services, false papers or intelligence. Similarly, those working with the sick and mentally-handicapped, often members of religious orders, rather than party members, were not predestined to collaboration in Nazi sterilisation and euthanasia programmes, but were also frequently presented with opportunities to save at least some of their charges by, for instance, altering reports, hiding patients from the authorities, or sending them back to their parents and warning them of the imminent dangers. During the war itself even providing food to foreign deportees or addressing them in their own language became a punishable offence, and thus by definition an act of resistance.

Indeed, Koonz herself recognises that in certain contexts motherhood could take on a different meaning from the one which informs the main part of her book. In her chapter on Jewish women, she notes that: 'Whilst men did their best to cope with the hostile world of business, profession and bureaucracy, women struggled to preserve their families as a refuge from a menacing world outside'. In the concentration camps people used to form themselves into little groups of 'ersatz families' as a source of private comfort from the sheer terror and madness of reality. In both these instances women can be found doing exactly what Koonz attacks German women in general for doing—providing a private sphere of love in an environment of hatred—and yet here the contrast between love and terror takes on an entirely different meaning. The family unit, often headed by the woman in cases where the husband had been killed or taken prisoner, also remained for a long time after the war the only institution left which could provide the Germans with a measure of sanity as they picked through the ruins of the 'thousand-year Reich'.

One of the major themes, then, which emerges from an analysis of women as actors in the Third Reich is the essential ambiguity of their position as mothers in the fatherland. Claudia Koonz is correct to suggest that the promise of greater autonomy within the traditional sphere of female activity persuaded significant numbers of women in the early 1930s to acquiesce in the removal of their (only recently won) political rights. However, her attempt to link this to a collective female responsibility for the crimes of Nazism breaks down because of its failure to do justice to the wide variety of strategies employed by women in the struggle to define their own *Lebenstraum.* This struggle did not simply cease after 1933, but increasingly provided women with the means of creating their own opportunities for political action along a broad spectrum of activity, from defence of their own private 'space' against the intrusion of a totalitarian state, to a more conscious and active resistance to Nazism.

The Commanders

Eisenhower's canniness, Rommel's absence, Hitler's sleeping habits—all combined to open way for Europe's reconquest

Stephen E. Ambrose

Stephen E. Ambrose, the author of multivolume biographies of Dwight Eisenhower and Richard Nixon, is director of the Eisenhower Center at the University of New Orleans.

Adolf Hitler had learned the lesson of World War I—that Germany could not win a war of attrition. In the first two years of World War II, his policy was blitzkrieg. But in the late fall of 1941, his lightning-war strategy foundered in Russia and he made the most incomprehensible of his many mistakes. He declared war on the United States in the same week that the Red Army launched its counteroffensive outside Moscow. In the summer of 1942, the Wehrmacht tried blitzkrieg against the Red Army again, on a much-reduced scale, only to fail once more when the snow began to fall. At the end of January 1943, nearly a quarter of a million German troops in Stalingrad surrendered. That July the Wehrmacht launched its last offensive on the eastern front, at Kursk. The Red Army stopped it cold, inflicting horrendous casualties and denying Hitler any chance of victory against the Soviet Union.

Hitler's only hope was to negotiate a new division of Eastern Europe between the Nazi and Soviet empires, akin to what existed from August 1939 to June 1941. That meant persuading Stalin that the Wehrmacht was still a serious threat and that the Allies could not be depended on. To do that, Hitler had to hurl Allied forces back into the sea when they made their inevitable attack in the west. "Once defeated, the enemy will never again try to invade," Hitler told his principal commanders in the west. "They would need months to organize a fresh attempt. And an invasion failure would also deliver a crushing blow to British and American morale. For one thing, it would prevent Roosevelt from being re-elected—with any luck he'd finish up in jail somewhere! For another, war weariness would grip Britain even faster, and Churchill, already a sick old man with his influence waning, wouldn't be able to carry through a new invasion operation."

But how to hurl the coming invasion back into the sea? Germany was overextended far more than in World War I. On the eastern front, Hitler's troops were stretched over more than 1,200 miles; on the Mediterranean front, where the line ran from southern Greece through Yugoslavia, then across Italy and southern France, his troops were defending a line of some 1,800 miles; on the western front, his troops had to defend 3,700 miles of coastline from Holland to the southern end of the Bay of Biscay. And actually, there was a fourth front, at home. The Allied air offensive against German cities had driven the Luftwaffe out of France, forcing it to stay home patrolling its own skies.

Hitler hated the defensive. It stuck in his craw so bad that it led him to make strategic and technological blunders of the greatest magnitude. In May 1943, Prof. Willi Messerschmitt had an ME-262 twin-jet fighter ready for serial production. Its cruise speed was 520 miles per hour, more than 120 miles an hour better than any plane the Allies could send against it. Hitler was impressed, but he wanted a bomber to hit London, not a fighter to defend Germany. Demanding that the plane be made into a bomber, which was impossible, he thwarted Reichsmarschall Hermann Goering's plans to produce the jet fighters, and only in the final weeks of the war, when Germany was past saving from defeat, did the Luftwaffe get as many as 100 jets into the air at one time. They dramatically outperformed Allied aircraft, knocking them out of the sky even when outnumbered 100 to 1. A report prepared for General Eisenhower concluded that if the Germans had been able to deploy the jets in force on D-Day, "they could have denied us air superiority and frustrated the Normandy landings and might even have compelled us to work our way up into Europe via the Italian route."

Ike and Erwin. Second only to Hitler in the imprint they would leave on D-Day—for good or for ill—were Dwight Eisenhower and Erwin Rommel. On the battlefield, Rommel was an aggressive risk taker, Eisenhower a cautious calculator. Rommel won battles through brilliant maneuvering, Eisenhower by overwhelming the enemy. As Rommel always commanded forces inferior in numbers and firepower, his method was appropriate; as Eisenhower always commanded forces that were superior, so was his.

Born in 1890, Eisenhower was one year older than Rommel. His father was a mechanic, Rommel's a schoolteacher. Both fathers were classic Germanic parents who imposed a harsh discipline on their sons, enforced by physical punishment. Both boys were avid athletes. Although neither family had a military tradition, each boy went to military school; in 1910 Rommel entered the Royal Officer Cadet School in Danzig; Eisenhower in 1911 went to West Point.

Their careers diverged in World War I. Rommel was a combat leader in France and Italy, highly decorated (Iron Cross, first and second class; the coveted Pourle Mérite). Eisenhower was stuck in the States as a training commander, a bitter blow from which he feared he would never recover. Still, as junior offi-

From *U.S. News & World Report*, May 23, 1994, pp. 62-70. Adapted from *D-Day, June 6, 1994: The Climactic Battle of World War II* by Stephen E. Ambrose.

cers, both showed remarkable leadership ability.

In the interwar years, Rommel remained a line officer, while Eisenhower was a staff officer. Rommel's regimental commander wrote of him in 1934: "Head and shoulders above the average battalion commander in every respect." That same year, Eisenhower's superior, Chief of Staff Douglas MacArthur, wrote of him: "This is the best officer in the Army. When the next war comes, he should go right to the top."

The war brought both men out of obscurity. Rommel made his reputation first of all as commander of the panzer division that led the way through France in 1940; he added enormous luster to it and became a world figure as commander of the Afrika Korps in the eastern North African desert in 1941–42. Eisenhower became a world figure in November 1942 in the North African desert, as commander of the Allied forces.

Yet, after Rommel lost the Battle of El Alamein in the late fall of 1942, he became what Hitler called a defeatist, what others would call a realist. On November 20, when he learned that of the 50 transport planes bringing fuel for his tanks, 45 had been shot down, Rommel went for a walk in the desert with one of his battalion commanders, Major Hans von Luck. Rommel said: "Supplies will not be forthcoming. Hitler's HQ has already written off this theater of war. All he requires now is that 'the German soldier stands or dies.' . . . Luck, the war is lost!"

First blood. The Americans, coming from the western desert, were waiting for the Afrika Korps in Tunisia. There, in February 1943, Rommel and Eisenhower first clashed, in the Battle of Kasserine Pass. Through surprise and audacity, Rommel scored impressive initial gains against the untried and inadequately trained Americans, who were led by untried and ill-prepared generals—including Eisenhower, who was fighting his first real battle. Eisenhower made many mistakes but recovered from them, used his logistical and firepower superiority effectively and eventually won the battle.

By this time Rommel was suffering from high blood pressure (so was Eisenhower), violent headaches, nervous exhaustion and rheumatism. With surrender in North Africa imminent, Hitler ordered Rommel home, after promoting him to field marshal. He spent most of the rest of 1943 without a command.

In late October 1943, Gen. Alfred Jodl, chief of operations at Oberkommando der Wehrmacht (OKW), suggested to Hitler that Rommel be given tactical command in the west, under Field Marshal Gerd von Rundstedt, who was commander in chief, west. Rundstedt was Germany's senior serving field marshal, at 69 too old to command in battle. He was short of energy and short of supplies, so although he had been charged with building an impregnable Atlantic wall, almost nothing had been done except around Pas de Calais, where the English Channel was narrowest. The Germans thought the invasion most likely to come there. Jodl's idea was that Rommel would provide the badly needed energy and drive to get on with the work. In August 1942, Hitler had decreed that fortress construction in France should proceed with *fanatismus* (fanatic energy) to create a continuous belt of interlocking fire emanating from bombproof concrete structures. He wanted 15,000 concrete strongpoints occupied by 300,000 men.

Hitler's passion for detail was astonishing. He often spent hours studying the maps showing installations along the Atlantic wall. He demanded reports on building progress, the thickness of concrete, the kind of concrete used, the system used to put in the steel reinforcement. Then, after demanding creation of the greatest fortification in history, not once did he bother to inspect any part of it. He did not give Rommel tactical command for the invasion battle, but he ordered him to make an inspection of the Atlantic wall and report back to him. Rommel was shocked by what he saw. He denounced the Atlantic wall as a farce, "a figment of Hitler's *wokenkuckucksheim* [cloud-cuckoo-land] . . . an enormous bluff . . . more for the German people than for the enemy . . . and the enemy, through his agents, knows more about it than we do."

"I want mines." Rommel believed Allied control of the air would prevent the movement of German reinforcement to the battle area, so "our only possible chance will be at the beaches—that's where the enemy is always weakest." As a start on building a genuine Atlantic wall, he said, "I want antipersonnel mines, antitank mines, antiparatroop mines. I want mines to sink ships and mines to sink landing craft." But he felt that no matter how many millions of mines were laid, fixed defenses could only hold up the assault, not turn it back; it would take a rapid counterattack on D-Day itself by mobile infantry and panzer divisions to do that. Those units had to be moved close to the coast to be in a position to deliver the decisive counterattack.

On the critical issue, Rundstedt disagreed. He wanted to let the Allies move inland, then fight the decisive battle in the interior of France, well out of range of the heavy guns of the British and American battleships and cruisers. This fundamental disagreement would persist to plague the German high command right through D-Day and beyond. Strategically, the German generals never learned the plain lesson that the Red Army could have taught them had they studied Red Army strategy—that a flexible defense that can give under pressure

King George's D-Day Mission

Winston Churchill visited Dwight Eisenhower shortly before D-Day to beg a favor: He wanted to go along on the invasion on HMS Belfast. Eisenhower told him it was out of the question; he was worth too much to the Allied cause.

As Eisenhower related the story, the prime minister said, "You have operational command of all forces, but you are not responsible administratively for the makeup of the crews." When Eisenhower agreed that this was so, the 69-year-old Churchill said, "Well, then, I can sign on as a member of the crew of one of His Majesty's ships, and there's nothing you can do about it."

"That's correct. But, Prime Minister, you will make my burden a lot heavier if you do it."

Churchill said he was going to do it anyway. Eisenhower had his chief of staff, Gen. Walter Bedell Smith, call King George VI to explain the problem. The king told Smith, "You boys leave Winston to me." He called Churchill to say, "As long as you feel that it is desirable to go along, I think it is my duty to go along with you." Churchill gave up.

and strike back when the attacker is overextended best suited the conditions of World War II. Despite their disagreement, Rommel and Rundstedt got on well together. Rundstedt urged that Rommel's Army Group B headquarters be given command of the 15th and 7th armies, stretching from Holland to the Loire River in southern Brittany. Hitler agreed. Rommel assumed his new command on Jan. 15, 1944.

On that very day, Eisenhower took up his duties as supreme commander for the Allied Expeditionary Force. Franklin Roosevelt had wanted Army Chief of Staff George Marshall to lead the invasion of France, but he decided that he could not sleep at night with Marshall out of the country. There were manifold reasons for Eisenhower's selection. He had commanded three successful invasions, all joint operations involving the British. He got on well with the British, and they with him. Gen. Bernard Montgomery, already selected as commander of the ground forces committed to Overlord, said of Eisenhower: "He has merely to smile at you, and you trust him at once."

Eisenhower found that having Overlord headquarters in London was too distracting. Within two weeks he moved it to Bushy Park, outside the city. His staff, with much grumbling, moved into tents. He moved into the two-bedroom Telegraph Cottage, making do with the least pretentious home of any general in England. Rommel, likewise, found Paris a Babel. He wanted his headquarters elsewhere. His staff, with much grumbling, left the City of Light and moved 37 miles down the Seine River to the sleepy village of La Roche Guyon. Eisenhower wanted a dog for a companion. Aides found him a scottie puppy. Rommel wanted a dog for a companion. Aides found him a dachshund puppy. The dogs slept in their masters' bedrooms.

Each general galloped into action, setting a pace that exhausted other men in their early 50s. Where there had been hesitation and drift, there was now conviction and movement. "I'm going to throw myself into this new job with everything I've got," Rommel wrote to his wife, "and I'm going to see it turns out a success." Eisenhower said on arrival, "We are approaching a tremendous crisis with stakes incalculable." Each general was typically on the road by 6 each morning, inspecting, driving, training, preparing his men. They ate on the run—field rations or a sandwich and a cup of coffee. Eisenhower averaged four hours' sleep per night. Rommel hardly more.

'The Man Who Won the War'

Andrew Higgins was hot tempered, loudmouthed and given to drinking a bottle of whisky a day. He was also a self-taught genius in small-boat design whom Dwight Eisenhower called "the man who won the war for us." Higgins produced the landing craft that carried infantry ashore in the Mediterranean, in the Pacific and at Normandy. The cigar-shaped LCVP—36 feet long and 10½ feet wide with plywood sides and stern and a metal ramp up front—could bring a platoon to the water line, discharge it and then go back to the mother ship for another load.

To make 20,000 LCVPs by the war's end, Higgins rapidly expanded his fly-by-night New Orleans company into vast assembly lines employing 30,000 workers at peak production. He inspired his workers the way a general tries to inspire his troops. A huge sign above the work floor announced: "The Man Who Relaxes Is Helping the Axis." In his factories' bathrooms, Higgins displayed pictures of Hitler, Mussolini and Hirohito sitting on toilets. "Come on in, brother," the caption read. "Take it easy. Every minute you loaf here helps us plenty."

Power games. Rommel was cursed with a confused command structure. Hitler ran the armed services as he ran the government, by the principle of divide and rule. Rommel did not have control over the Luftwaffe in France, nor of the Navy. He did not have administrative control of the Waffen SS units in France, nor of the paratrooper or anti-aircraft units (they belonged to the Luftwaffe). It was never clear whether Rommel or Rundstedt would control the battle. Worst of all, Hitler wanted to command the panzer divisions himself. They could be committed to the battle only on his orders—and his headquarters was more than 600 miles from the scene—and those were the divisions Rommel was depending on for a first-day counterattack! Eisenhower had no such problems. His command was clear-cut, absolute.

Another profound difference: Eisenhower believed with all his heart in the cause he was fighting for. He hated the Nazis and all they represented. Rommel was no Nazi—although at times he had been a toady to Hitler. And Rommel faced a battle against an enemy he never hated and indeed respected.

On June 3, 1944, Rommel drove to Paris to buy shoes for his wife, Lucie, whose birthday, fatefully, fell on June 6. In Paris, he conferred with Rundstedt, who agreed with him that "there is still no sign that the invasion is imminent." The tides in the Strait of Dover would not be suitable for an invasion until mid-June. The weather report indicated increasing clouds, high winds, rain. He decided to go to his home in Herrlingen for Lucie's birthday, then to Berchtesgaden to beg Hitler for reinforcements. He wanted more panzer divisions and control of all the tanks. He wrote in his diary, "The most urgent problem is to win the *führer* over by personal conversation."

Although Rommel had half or less of what he calculated he required in men, guns, mines, beach obstacles and fixed emplacements, he exuded confidence. Morale was apparently high all along the Atlantic wall, or so the German leaders told themselves. That was Rommel's achievement. He had managed to persuade many of his officers and some of his troops that not only did they have a chance, they would prevail.

History on hold. Eisenhower had set D-Day for June 5. On June 4, at a predawn meeting, as ships began forming into convoys, he was told that the weather the next day would be overcast and stormy. He decided to postpone for at least one day. At 6 a.m. he gave his orders to put everything on hold. At just that moment, Rommel began his long journey east, away from the coast, to see his wife and his *führer*. As he departed, in a light drizzle, he remarked, "There's not going to *be* an invasion. And if there is, then they won't even get off the beaches!" Rommel spent the day on the road, arriving in Herrlingen in time to walk in the twilight with Lucie. She tried out her new shoes.

That evening, Eisenhower met in the mess room of Southwick House with his top commanders and other aides. At 9:30 p.m. came the latest weather report. It was good news: The rain that was then pouring down would stop before daybreak. There would be 36 hours of more or less clear weather. The bombers and fighters ought to be able to operate on Monday night, June5–6, although they would be hampered by scattered clouds. Eisenhower began pacing, head down, chin on his chest, hands clasped behind his back. Suddenly, he shot his chin out at his chief of staff, Gen. Walter Bedell Smith: "What do you think?" Smith replied: "It's a helluva gamble, but it's the best possible gamble."

Eisenhower polled the high command. It was split. Only he could decide. The only sounds in the room were the rattling of the french doors and the rain. It hardly seemed possible an amphibious attack could be launched in such weather. At 9:45, he gave his decision: "I am quite positive the order must be given." By midnight, the convoys again were forming. Eisenhower woke at 3:30 a.m, June 5. The wind was shaking his trailer. The rain seemed to travel in horizontal streaks. According to the forecast, it should have been letting up. He dressed and drove through a mile of mud to Southwick House for the last weather meeting. It was not too late to call off the operation, to have the fleet return and try again on June 19, the next time the tides would be favorable—and if the storm kept up, that would have to be done.

The forecast was even firmer than five hours earlier that the storm would break before dawn. But the good weather was only likely through Tuesday; Wednesday could be rough again. That raised the danger that the first waves would get ashore but the follow-up units would not.

Eisenhower asked for opinions, pacing, shooting out his chin. Montgomery still wanted to go. Adm. Bertram Ramsay was concerned about proper spotting for naval gunfire but thought the risk worth taking. Air Marshal Arthur Tedder was reluctant. Air Vice Marshal Trafford Leigh-Mallory still thought air conditions were below the acceptable minimum. Eisenhower reviewed in his mind the alternatives. If the weather forecast was wrong, at best he would be landing seasick men without air cover or an accurate naval bombardment. Yet, the men had been briefed; they could not be held on their transports and landing craft for two weeks; the risk that the Germans would penetrate the secret of Overlord was very high.

Forward march. He stopped pacing, faced his subordinates, then said quietly but clearly, "OK, let's go." Cheers rang through Southwick House. The commanders dashed outside to get to their command posts. Within 30 seconds, the mess room was empty, except for Eisenhower. His isolation was symbolic, for, having given the order, he was now powerless. Later that day, Eisenhower scrawled a press release on a pad of paper, to be used if necessary: "Our landings . . . have failed and I have withdrawn the troops. My decision to attack at this time and place was based upon the best information available. The troops, the air and the Navy all did all that bravery and devotion to duty could do. If any blame or fault attaches to the attempt, it is mine alone." Rommel was spending a quiet June 5 with Lucie. He gathered wildflowers for a birthday bouquet.

At about 7 p.m., Eisenhower visited the 101st Airborne Division at Greenham Common, where he told a group of enlisted men not to worry, that they had the best equipment and leaders in the world, with a vast force coming in behind them. A sergeant from Texas piped up, "Hell, we ain't worried, General. It's the Krauts that ought to be worrying now." With one group, Eisenhower asked whether anyone was from Kansas, and Pvt. Sherman Oyler of Topeka said he was. "What's your name, son?" Oyler was so stricken by being addressed by the supreme commander that he froze up and forgot his name. After an embarrassing pause, his buddies shouted, "Tell him your name, Oyler." Eisenhower gave him a thumbs up and said, "Go get'em, Kansas." Several hours later, Eisenhower stood on the runway and watched as the paratroopers departed, the C-47s taking off at 1-second intervals. When the last plane roared off, he turned to his driver, Kay Summersby. She saw tears in his eyes, "Well," he said quietly, "it's on."

There was no German counterattack. Rommel's plans for fighting the D-Day battle were not put into motion. Without air reconnaissance, with Allied airborne troops dropping here, there and everywhere, with their telephone lines cut by the Resistance, with their army, corps, division and some regimental commanders at the war game in Rennes, the Germans were all but blind and leaderless. The commander missed most was Rommel, who spent the day on the road driving back to La Roche Guyon—another price the Germans paid for having lost control of the air; Rommel dared not fly.

As early as 6:15 a.m., Gen. Max Pemsel, chief of staff of the 7th Army, informed Rommel's headquarters at La Roche Guyon of the Allies' massive air and naval bombardment; a half-hour later he reported to Rundstedt's headquarters that the landings were beginning—but he added that the 7th Army would be able to cope with the situation from its own resources. With that news, Gen. Hans von Salmuth, commanding the 15th Army, went back to bed. So did most of Rommel's staff at La Roche Guyon. They believed the Allied landings were a diversion; the "real" attack would come at Pas de Calais.

Percy Hobart's Gadget Glory

D-Day was a theater of British technological inventiveness. In March 1943, Gen. Percy Hobart of the 79th Armoured Division had been given the task of figuring out how to get armored support onto and over the beaches, to breach the concrete and minefields of the Atlantic wall. He came up with swimming tanks. Duplex Drive, they were called, after their twin propellers working off the main engine. They had a waterproof, air-filled canvas screen all around the hull, giving them the appearance of a baby carriage. The inflatable screen was dropped when the tank reached shore. Another of "Hobart's funnies" carried a 40-foot box-girder bridge for crossing tank ditches. Still another, the Crab, had a rotating drum in front of the tank that safely detonated any mines in its path.

Even more astonishing were the prefabricated ports towed across the English Channel. The floating piers, or Mulberries, allowed the platform to slide up and down with the tide on posts resting on the sea floor. The Mulberries were sheltered by instant breakwaters sunk off the French coast on D-Day Plus 1.

Late sleeper. The only high-command officer who responded correctly was Rundstedt, an old man scorned by Hitler and Oberkommando der Wehrmacht. He tried to get two panzer divisions moving toward the action immediately, but they were not under his command. Jodl informed Rundstedt that the two divisions could not be committed until Hitler gave the order, and the *führer* was still sleeping. He refused to wake Hitler, who slept until noon. The two panzer divisions spent the morning waiting. There was a heavy overcast; they could have moved out free from serious interference from Allied aircraft. It was 4 p.m. when Hitler at last gave his approval. By then, the clouds had broken up and Allied fighters and bombers ranged the skies over Normandy, smashing anything that moved. The panzers had to crawl into roadside woods and wait until dark.

"The news couldn't be better," Hitler said when he was first informed that D-Day was here. "As long as they were in Britain, we couldn't get at them. Now we have them where we can destroy them." Later, Hitler spread a map of France and told Goering. "They are landing here—and here: just where we expected them!" Goering did not correct this palpable lie.

It had been galling to the Nazis that the Allies had been able to build their strength in England, untouched by the Luftwaffe or the Wehrmacht. Now they had come within range of German guns. But Hitler was still more eager to hit London than to fight a defensive war. He had a weapon to do it with, the V-1. It had first been flown successfully on Christmas Eve 1943; by June 1944, it was almost ready to go to work. The V-1 was a jet-powered plane carrying a 1-ton warhead. It was wildly inaccurate but flew more than 400 miles per hour, too fast for aircraft or antiaircraft to shoot it down. On the afternoon of June 6, Hitler ordered the V-1 attacks on London to begin. As was so often the case, he was giving an order that could not be carried out. It took six days to bring the heavy steel catapult rigs to the channel coast. The attack did not begin until June 12, and it was a fiasco: Of 10 V-1s launched, four crashed at once, two vanished without trace, one demolished a railroad bridge in London and three hit open fields.

Fortunately for the Allies, Hitler had picked the wrong target. Haphazard bombing of London could cause sleepless nights and induce terror, but it could not have a direct military effect. Had Hitler sent the V-1s against the beaches and artificial harbors of Normandy, by June 12 jammed with men, machines and ships, the "vengeance weapons" might have made a difference. On D-Day, Hitler misused his sole potential strategic weapon, just as he misused his tactical counterattack force. His interference with his commanders on the scene stands in sharp contrast to Churchill and Roosevelt, who made no attempt at all to tell their generals and admirals what to do on D-Day, and to Eisenhower, who also left the decision making to his subordinates.

On June 6, Eisenhower wrote a brief message to Marshall informing the chief of staff that everything seemed to be going well. He called a few members of the press into his canvas-roofed, pine-walled quarters and answered questions. For the rest of the day he paced, his mood alternating as he received news of the situation on the British and Canadian beaches and on Omaha and Utah. He retired early to get a good night's sleep. On D-Day itself, the supreme commander gave not one command.

Looking Back: The Cold War in Retrospect

Raymond L. Garthoff

Raymond L. Garthoff, senior fellow in the Brookings Foreign Policy Studies program, is the author of The Great Transition: American-Soviet Relations and the End of the Cold War *(Brookings, 1994), from which this article is drawn. An earlier version of the article also appeared in the spring 1992 issue of* Diplomatic History.

The Soviet Union and the United States waged the Cold War in the belief that confrontation was unavoidable, that it was imposed by history. Soviet leaders were convinced that communism would ultimately triumph in the world and that the Soviet Union was the vanguard socialist-communist state. They were also convinced that the Western "imperialist" powers were historically bound to pursue a hostile course against them. For their part, American and other Western leaders assumed that the Soviet Union was determined to enhance its power and to pursue expansionist policies by all expedient means to achieve a Soviet-led communist world. Each side thought that it was compelled by the very existence of the other to engage in zero-sum competition, and each saw the unfolding history of the Cold War as confirming its views.

The prevailing Western view was wrong in attributing a master plan to the Kremlin, in believing that communist ideology impelled Soviet leaders to expand their power, in exaggerating communist abilities to subvert a Free World, and in thinking that Soviet officials viewed military power as an ultimate recourse. But the West was not wrong in believing that Soviet leaders were committed to a historically driven struggle between two worlds until, in the end, theirs would triumph. To be sure, other motivations and interests, including national aims, institutional interests, and even personal psychological considerations, played a part. These influences, however, tended to enhance the ideological framework rather than weaken it. Moreover, the actions of each side were sufficiently consistent with the ideological expectations of the other side to sustain their respective worldviews for many years.

IDEOLOGY AND GEOPOLITICS

Within that ideological framework, the Americans and the Soviets carried on the Cold War as a geopolitical struggle, based more realistically on traditional balance-of-power politics than on world-class struggle or global containment and deterrence theory. If ideology alone had driven the superpowers, the Cold War would be seen as arising from the October Revolution of 1917 rather than from the ashes of World War II. But in 1917 and during the next 25 years the Soviet Union was relatively weak and only one of several great powers in a multipolar world. By the end of World War II, however, Germany and Japan had been crushed, Britain, France, and China were weakened, and the Soviet Union, even though much weaker than the United States, seemed to pose an unprecedented threat by virtue of its massive armies and their presence deep in Central Europe. Under these circumstances, Josef Stalin's reassertion in 1946 and 1947 of the division of the world into two contending camps seemed more valid and more threatening than ever before.

Thus charged by geopolitical circumstances, a Manichean communist worldview spawned a Manichean anticommunist worldview. Each side imputed unlimited objectives, ultimately world domination, to the other. Each side looked to realize its ambitions (or its historical destiny) over the long term and thus posited an indefinite period of conflict. But even though both sides envisioned a conflict of indefinite duration, and even though policy decisions were pragmatic and based on calculation of risk, cost, and gain, the hazard of a miscalculation always existed. And that could be fatally dangerous, given the historical coincidence of the Cold War and the first half-century of the nuclear age. Nuclear weapons, by threatening the existence of world civilization, added significantly to the tension of the epoch; the stakes were

From *The Brookings Review,* Summer 1994, pp. 10, 12-13.

utterly without precedent and beyond full comprehension.

Nuclear weapons also helped to keep the Cold War cold, to prevent a third world war in the 20th century. Nonetheless, in the final analysis and despite their awesome power, nuclear weapons did not cause, prevent, or end the Cold War, which would have been waged even had such weapons never existed. The arms race and other aspects of the superpower rivalry were, however, driven in part by ideological assumptions. As a result, while the Cold War and the nuclear arms race could be attentuated when opportunities or constraints led both sides to favor relaxing tensions, neither could be ended until the ideological underpinnings of the confrontation had fallen. And fall they did—under the leadership of Mikhail Gorbachev, who set in motion a fundamental reevaluation of the processes at work in the real world, a basic reassessment of threats, and finally a deep revision of Moscow's aims and political objectives. The United States and the West in general were cautious but eventually recognized this fundamental change and reciprocated.

DETERRENCE: REDUNDANT BUT REASSURING

The West did not, as is widely believed, win the Cold War through geopolitical containment and military deterrence. Still less was the Cold War won by the Reagan military buildup and the Reagan Doctrine, as some have suggested. Instead, "victory" came when a new generation of Soviet leaders realized how badly their system at home and their policies abroad had failed. What containment did do was to preclude any temptations on the part of Moscow to advance Soviet hegemony by military means. It is doubtful that any postwar Soviet leadership would have deliberately resorted to war. That was not, however, so clear to many at the time. Deterrence may have been redundant, but at the least it was highly successful in providing reassurance to the peoples of Western Europe. For four decades it performed the historic function of holding Soviet power in check, or being prepared to do so, until the internal seeds of destruction in the Soviet Union and its empire could mature. At that point, however, Gorbachev transformed Soviet policy and brought the Cold War to an end.

Despite important differences among them, all Soviet leaders before Gorbachev had shared a belief in an ineluctable conflict between socialism and capitalism. Although Gorbachev remained a socialist, and in his own terms even a communist, he renounced the Marxist-Leninist-Stalinist idea of inevitable world conflict. His avowed acceptance of the interdependence of the world, of the priority of human values over class values, and of the indivisibility of common security marked a revolutionary ideological change. That change, which Gorbachev publicly declared as early as February 1986 (though it was then insufficiently noted), manifested itself in many ways during the next five years, in deeds as well as words, including policies reflecting a drastically reduced Soviet perception of the Western threat and actions to reduce the Western perception of a Soviet threat.

In 1986, for example, Gorbachev made clear his readiness to ban all nuclear weapons. In 1987 he signed the Intermediate-range Nuclear Forces Treaty, eliminating not only the Soviet and U.S. missiles deployed since the late 1970s but also the whole of the Soviet strategic theater missile forces that had faced Europe and Asia for three decades. What is more, the treaty instituted an intrusive and extensive verification system. In 1988 Gorbachev proposed conventional arms reductions in Europe under a plan that would abandon the Soviet Union's numerical superiority, and he launched a substantial unilateral force reduction. In 1988–89 he withdrew all Soviet forces from Afghanistan. At about the same time, he encouraged the ouster of the old communist leadership in Eastern Europe and accepted the transition of the former Soviet-allied states into noncommunist neutral states. By 1990 he had signed the Conventional Forces in Europe Treaty accepting Soviet conventional arms levels much lower than NATO's. By that time he had not only accepted Germany's reunification but also the membership of a united Germany in NATO. Within another year he had jettisoned the Warsaw Pact and the socialist bloc and agreed, in the Strategic Arms Reduction Treaty, to verified deep cuts in strategic nuclear forces.

A NEW CONCEPT OF SECURITY

Although Gorbachev had not expected the complete collapse of communism (and Soviet influence) in Eastern Europe that took place in 1989 and 1990, he had made clear to the 27th Congress of the Soviet Communist Party as early as February 1986 that a new conception of security had to replace the previous one, and that the confrontation of the Cold War had to end. No longer speaking in Leninist terms of contending socialist and capitalist worlds, Gorbachev spoke instead of one world, an "interdependent and in many ways integral world." He denied that any country could find security in military power, either for defense or deterrence. Security, he said, could be found only through political means and only on a mutual basis. The goal, he asserted, should be the "creation of a comprehensive system of international security" that embraced economic, ecological, and humanitarian, as well as political and military, elements. Hence, the Soviet decision to give new support to the United Nations, including collective peacekeeping, and to join the world economic system. Hence, the cooperative Soviet efforts to

Although Gorbachev remained a socialist, and in his own terms even a communist . . . he renounced the Marxist-Leninist-Stalinist idea of inevitable world conflict.

resolve regional conflicts in Central America, Southern Africa, the Horn of Africa, Cambodia, Afghanistan, and the Middle East, not to mention the Soviet Union's support for the collective UN–endorsed action against Iraq in 1991. And hence Moscow's willingness to countenance the dissolution of the Eastern European alliance and socialist commonwealth, which had been fashioned to meet security requirements and ideological imperatives that had now been abandoned.

In the final analysis, because the Cold War rested on Marxist-Leninist assumptions of inevitable world conflict, only a Soviet leader could have ended it. And Gorbachev set out deliberately to do just that. Although earlier Soviet leaders had understood the impermissibility of war in the nuclear age, Gorbachev was the first to recognize that reciprocal political accommodation, rather than military power for deterrence or "counterdeterrence," was the defining core of the Soviet Union's relationship with the rest of the world. He accepted the idea of building relations on the basis of a "balance of interests" among nations, rather than trying to maximize the power of one state or bloc on the basis of a "correlation of forces," a balance of power. The conclusions that Gorbachev drew from this recognition, and consequent Soviet actions, finally permitted the Iron Curtain to be dismantled and the global confrontation of the Cold War to end.

Gorbachev, to be sure, seriously underestimated the task of changing the Soviet Union, and his miscalculation led to policy errors that contributed to the failure of his program for transforming Soviet society and polity. His vision of a resurrected socialism built on the foundation of successful *perestroika* and *demokratizatsiya* was never a realistic possibility. He knew deep economic reform was necessary, and he tried; he did not find the solution. A revitalized Soviet political union was perhaps beyond realization as well. The reasons for Gorbachev's failure were primarily objective, not subjective; that is, they were real obstacles he was unable to overcome—internal opposition, powerful inertia, intractable problems of economic transformation, and the politically charged problem of redefining a democratic relationship between a traditional imperial center and the rest of the country—*not* unwillingness or inability to give up or modify his ideological presuppositions and predispositions.

In the external political arena, however, Gorbachev both understood and successfully charted the course that led to the end of the Cold War, even though in this area, too, at first he had an exaggerated expectation of the capacity for reform on the part of the communist governments in Eastern Europe.

AMERICAN IMPERIALISM?

The American role in ending the Cold War was necessary but, naturally, not primary. How could it be when the American worldview was derivative of the communist worldview? Containment was hollow without an expansionist power to contain. In this sense, it was the Soviet threat, partly real and partly imagined, that generated the American dedication to waging the Cold War, regardless of what revisionist American historians have to say. These historians point to Washington's atomic diplomacy and to its various overt and covert political, economic, paramilitary, and military campaigns. Supposedly designed to counter a Soviet threat, they argue, these initiatives actually entailed an expansion of American influence and dominion.

The revisionist interpretation errs in attributing imperial initiative and design to American diplomacy, but it is not entirely wrong. American policymakers were guilty of accepting far too much of the communist worldview in constructing an anticommunist antipode, and of being too ready to fight fire with fire. Indeed, once the Cold War became the dominant factor in global politics (and above all in American and Soviet perceptions), each side viewed every development around the world in terms of its relationship to that great struggle, and each was inclined to act according to a self-fulfilling prophecy. The Americans, for example, often viewed local and regional conflicts of indigenous origins as Cold War battles and acted on that assumption. Like the Soviets, they distrusted the neutral and nonaligned nations and were always more comfortable when countries were either their allies or the satellites and surrogates of the other side. Thus, many traditional diplomatic relationships not essentially attendant on the superpower rivalry were swept into the vortex of the Cold War, at least in the eyes of the protagonists—and partly in fact as a result of their actions.

True, the Cold War led in some instances to constructive American involvements. The Marshall Plan is a prime example, not to mention American support for some democratic political movements and for the Congress for Cultural Freedom and the liberal journal *Encounter.* But overt and covert involvements were more frequently less constructive, and often subversive, of real liberalism and democracy. Apart from the loss of American lives and treasure in such misplaced ventures as the Vietnam War and in the massive oven-investment in weaponry, one of the worst effects of forcing all world developments onto the procrustean bed of the Cold War was the distortion of America's understanding and values. By dividing the globe into a communist Evil Empire controlled by Moscow and a Free World led by Washington, American policymakers promoted numerous antidemocratic regimes into membership in the Free World as long as they were anticommunist (or even rhetorically so). Washington also used the exigencies of the Cold War to justify assassination plots, to negotiate deals with war lords, drug lords, and terrorists, and to transform anticommunist insurgents, however corrupt or antidemocratic, into "freedom fighters." Alliance ties, military basing rights, and support for insurgencies were routinely given priority over such other American objectives as promoting nuclear nonproliferation, economic development, human rights, and democracy.

Parallel Soviet sins were at least as great. While Soviet foreign assistance to socialist and "progressive" countries was sometimes constructive (building the Aswan Dam, for example, or providing economic assistance to India), it was also skewed by the ideological expectation of moving the world toward communism and by expectations of Soviet geopolitical advantage in the Cold War. Often dictatorial regimes, "Marxist" or "socialist" only according to the cynical claims of their leaders, provided the basis for Soviet support, as with Siad Barre in Somalia, for example, or Mengistu in Ethiopia. The Soviet Union also engaged in many covert political operations and lent support to national liberation movements (some authentic, others less so) that sometimes included elements engaged in terrorism. On both sides, then, ideological beliefs combined with geopolitical considerations to fuel a Cold War struggle that left many victims in its wake.

REALITY CHECK

Although the decisive factor in the end of the Cold War was a change in these beliefs, it is worth repeating that the Soviet leaders could discard a long-encrusted and familiar ideology only because of a powerful transformation in the way Gorbachev and some colleagues perceived reality, and because they were ready to adapt domestic and foreign policies to the new perception. Over time, the extent and depth of these changes became inescapable and their validity compelling, bringing the Cold War to an end. The critical culminating event was the Revolution of '89.

The year between the destruction of the Berlin Wall in November 1989 and the European conference in Paris in November 1990 saw the removal of the most important manifestation of the Cold War: the division of Germany and Europe. The division of Europe had symbolized the global battle between the two ideological and geopolitical camps in the years immediately after World War II. When that division came to an end, the consequences for the international balance of power were so substantial that even the most hardened cold warriors in the West were forced to acknowledge that the Cold War had ended—even before the collapse of communist rule in the Soviet Union or of the Soviet Union itself. Moreover, the Revolution of '89 in Eastern Europe was decisive not only in demonstrating that the ideological underpinnings of the Cold War had been removed but also in shifting the actual balance of power. The removal of Soviet military power from Eastern Europe dissolved the threat to Western Europe and also restored a reunified Europe to the center of the world political stage. Russia and even the United States have now become less central. American-Russian relations nonetheless remain of great importance in the post–Cold War world.

How the Bomb Saved Soviet Physics

Stalin didn't mind if people starved in the name of Marxist science; but he had to have the bomb.

David Holloway

David Holloway is a professor of political science and co-director of the Center for International Security and Arms Control at Stanford University in California.

PHOTOS (UNLESS OTHERWISE NOTED) COURTESY OF DAVID HOLLOWAY AND YALE UNIVERSITY PRESS

Bomb physicists Igor Kurchatov and Yuli Khariton after the 1953 thermonuclear test in Central Asia.

At the end of World War II, Josef Stalin believed that postwar international relations would resemble those of the interwar period. Germany and Japan would rise from defeat. World capitalism would run into crisis, and sharp contradictions would emerge between the capitalist states. These contradictions would lead inevitably to a new world war.

Despite Stalin's grim long-range assessment, he saw no immediate danger. Atomic diplomacy by the United States seemed to him to be the greater threat. Atomic bombs were "meant to frighten those with weak nerves," he told Alexander Werth, the London *Sunday Times* correspondent in Moscow, in September 1946. If the Soviet Union were to compete in the tit-for-tat world of atomic diplomacy, it would have to have its own atomic bombs.

Although an atomic bomb program was launched during the war, its urgency and scope were greatly increased after Hiroshima. Lavrenti Beria, the most feared man in the Soviet Union after Stalin, would direct it. Massive secret facilities eventually would be built in many locations. But the heart of the program was to be Igor Kurchatov's Laboratory No. 2, located on the outskirts of Moscow, and its offspring, Arzamas-16.

Klaus Fuchs, the Soviet spy at Los Alamos, had provided a detailed description of the plutonium implosion bomb in June 1945. But neither Kurchatov nor Yuli Khariton, Kurchatov's closest associate, could be sure that Fuchs's information was completely reliable. Khariton and his team were assigned the task of verifying everything.

Investigating the implosion method called for repeated experiments with high explosives, which could not be done at Laboratory No. 2 because of its proximity to the city. Kurchatov therefore decided to set up a branch of the laboratory in an isolated area, where work on the design and development of the bomb could take place in total secrecy. Khariton would be the scientific director of the new laboratory.

By the spring of 1946, a site near the settlement of Sarov, about 400 kilometers east of Moscow, was chosen. It was on the edge of a large forest preserve, which provided room for expansion; and it was a beautiful spot. The town—or rather the carefully guarded "zone," which included the town and the research and development establishments—became known as Arzamas-16, after the city of Arzamas 60 kilometers

From *The Bulletin of the Atomic Scientists,* November/December 1994, pp. 46-55. Adapted from *Stalin and the Bomb* by David Holloway.

to the north. But it was sometimes known as the "Volga office"—as well as "Los Arzamas."

Scientists in the "white archipelago" worked in secrecy but lived relatively well.

The physicist Lev Altshuler moved to Arzamas-16 in December 1946. There was a narrow-gauge railway line that ran from Arzamas to Sarov, but Altshuler made the last part of the journey by bus:

"We made this journey in a bus which had been thoughtfully provided with sheepskin coats. Past the windows flashed villages which recalled the settlements of pre-Petrine Russia.

"On our arrival at the place we caught sight of the monastery churches and farmsteads, the forest, the Finnish houses nestling in the woods, the small engineering plant, and the inevitable companions of that period—the 'zones' [prison camps] populated by representatives of all the regions of the country, all the nationalities. . . . The columns of prisoners passing through the settlement in the morning on their way to work and returning to the zones in the evening were a reality that hit you in the eyes. Lermontov's lines came to mind, about 'a land of slaves, a land of masters.' "

Arzamas-16 was, Altshuler notes, at the epicenter of the "white archipelago" of atomic institutes and plants scattered about the country.[1]

Unlike the inhabitants of the Gulag Archipelago, the scientists and engineers who lived in the "white archipelago" had privileged living conditions. They were protected as far as possible from the dreadful economic conditions of the war-torn country. Arzamas-16 was like paradise compared to half-starved Moscow, in Altshuler's view. Scientists and engineers "lived very well. Leading researchers were paid a very large salary for those times. Our families experienced no needs. And the supply of food and goods was quite different. So that all material questions were removed."[2] Lazar Kaganovich, a member of the Politburo, complained in 1953 that the atomic cities were like "health resorts."[3]

These conditions reflected Stalin's belief that Soviet scientists, if they were given the "proper help," would be able to overtake the achievements of foreign science. Privileged though they were, however, the nuclear scientists were surrounded by great secrecy and tight security. They could not talk to unauthorized people about their work, and nothing was published about the Soviet effort to build the atomic bomb.

"BERIA'S PEOPLE WERE EVERYWHERE"

Within the project, secrecy was very strictly maintained. Reports were written by hand because typists were not trusted. If documents were typed—as, for example, the technical requirements for the first atomic bomb—the key words were written in by hand. Code words were used instead of scientific terms in secret reports and laboratory notes; neutrons, for example, were called "zero points." Information was strictly compartmentalized.

During Andrei Sakharov's first visit to Arzamas-16 in 1949, Iakov Zeldovich told him, "There are secrets everywhere, and the less you know that doesn't concern you, the better off you'll be. Khariton has taken on the burden of knowing it all."[4] The need for secrecy was so deeply instilled that some people had recurrent nightmares about breaching security regulations, and at least one suicide was attributed to anxiety about misfiled documents.[5]

Secrecy was reinforced by rigid security. Arzamas-16 was cut off from the outside world. A zone of about 250 square kilometers was surrounded by barbed wire and guards, and it was difficult in the early years to obtain permission to leave.[6] Khariton was accompanied wherever he went by a bodyguard. (Kurchatov and Zeldovich—and later, Sakharov—also had bodyguards.)

The security services had informers in the project, and encouraged denunciations. "Beria's people were everywhere," Khariton later remarked.[7] Once, when Khariton visited Chelyabinsk-40 to see how work on the plutonium production reactor was progressing, he attended a dinner to mark Igor Kurchatov's birthday. After the dinner—and a few drinks—Beria's representative said to Khariton: "Yuli Borisovich, if only you knew how much they write against you." Although he added, "But I don't believe them," the point had been made: there were plenty of accusations for Beria to use if he wanted to.[8]

Stalin and Beria were suspicious of the scientists' attachment to "Western science."

As the date of the first atomic bomb test grew near, the political climate in the country became increasingly oppressive. In August 1948 Trofim Lysenko

Arzamas-16, also known as the "Volga office" and "Los Arzamas."

achieved his final victory over the geneticists, and in January 1949 a campaign was launched against "cosmopolitans"—a euphemism for Jews.

The number of denunciations increased. In Anatoli Aleksandrov's words, "A great number of 'inventors,' including scientists, were constantly trying to find mistakes, writing their 'observations' on this score, and their number increased, the closer we came to completing the task."[9] Such "observations" would not have been confined to technical matters. Mistaken technical choices were frequently explained in those days as the consequence of political error or disloyalty.

Kurchatov was open to the accusation that he had surrounded himself with colleagues who were Jewish, or who admired Western science too much, or had strong links with the West. Khariton was particularly vulnerable: he was Jewish, and he had spent two years in Cambridge where he had worked closely with James Chadwick, a key figure in the British nuclear project. Besides, both of his parents had left Soviet Russia. His father had been expelled by the Soviet authorities and had worked in Riga as a journalist until 1940, when the Red Army occupied Latvia. He was arrested by the NKVD and was sent to the camps or shot. Khariton's mother lived with her second husband in Germany in the 1920s; later she moved to Palestine.

Stalin and Beria wanted the atomic bomb as soon as possible, and they had to rely on Kurchatov and his colleagues to make it for them. They gave the scientists massive resources and privileged living conditions. Yet they harbored a nagging suspicion of the nuclear scientists. After all, if Soviet geneticists and plant breeders had tried to undermine Soviet agricultural policy as Lysenko said, might not the physicists sabotage nuclear policy?

Aleksandrov, who was the scientific director of the chemical separation plant at Chelyabinsk-40 in 1949, was coating the plutonium hemispheres with nickel when a group that included party official Mikhail G. Pervukhin, several generals, and the plant director, arrived. "They asked what I was doing," writes Aleksandrov:

"I explained, and then they asked a strange question: 'Why do you think it is plutonium?' I said that I knew the whole technical process for obtaining it and was therefore sure that it was plutonium and could not be anything else. 'But why are you sure that some piece of iron hasn't been substituted for it?' I held up a piece to the alpha-counter, and it began to crackle at once. 'Look,' I said, 'it's alpha-active.' 'But perhaps it has just been rubbed with plutonium on the outside and that is why it crackles,' said someone. I grew angry, took that piece and held it out to them: 'Feel it, it's hot!' One of them said that it did not take long to heat a piece of iron. Then I responded that he could sit and look till morning and check whether the plutonium remained hot. But I would go to bed. This apparently convinced them, and they went away."[10]

In the 1920s and 1930s, Abraham Ioffe's Physicotechnical Institute became, according to Soviet physicists, the "maternal nest," the "cradle," the "forge," the "alma mater" of Soviet physics. Here Ioffe (far right) conducts a seminar. Attendees included, at extreme left, Peter Kapitsa, Iakov Frenkel, and Nikolai Semenov.

Such episodes, according to Aleksandrov, were not unusual. Vasili Emelyanov recounts a similar incident. He once showed People's Commissar Avraami Zavenyagin a regulus of plutonium before the atomic test. "Are you sure that's plutonium?" Zavenyagin asked, looking at Emelyanov with fear. "Perhaps," he added anxiously, "it's something else, not plutonium.' "[11]

"AN IMPORTANT PATRIOTIC DUTY"

The scientists were aware that failure would cost them dear, and they knew that Beria had selected understudies to take over the leading positions in case of failure.[12] Terror was a key element in Beria's style of management as well as a pervasive factor in the Stalinist regime. But the scientists were not motivated by fear. Those who took part in the project believed that the Soviet Union needed its own bomb in order to defend itself, and they welcomed the challenge of proving the worth of Soviet science by building a Soviet bomb as quickly as possible.

According to Altshuler, "Our consent [to work on the bomb] was determined, first, by the fact that we were promised much better conditions for research and

Kurchatov in 1924.

second, by an inner feeling that our confrontation with a very powerful opponent had not ended with the defeat of Fascist Germany. The feeling of defenselessness increased particularly after Hiroshima and Nagasaki. For all who realized the realities of the new atomic era, the creation of our own atomic weapons, the restoration of equilibrium became a categorical imperative."[13]

Victor Adamsky, who worked in the theoretical department at Arzamas-16 in the late 1940s, has written that "all scientists held the conviction—and it now seems right for that time—that the state needed to possess atomic weapons, that one could not allow one country, especially the United States, to hold a monopoly on this weapon. To the consciousness of performing a most important patriotic duty was added the purely professional satisfaction and pride from work on a splendid task in physics—and not only in physics. Therefore we worked with enthusiasm, without taking account of time, selflessly."[14]

Andrei Sakharov, who began work on thermonuclear weapons in 1948 and moved to Arzamas-16 in 1950, has said that "we (and here I speak not only in my own behalf, for in such cases moral principles are formulated in a collective psychological way) believed that our work was absolutely necessary as a means of achieving a balance in the world."[15]

In spite of the presence of informers and the threat of repression, a spirit of cooperation and friendship existed at Arzamas-16. "It was necessary to secure the defense of the country," Khariton later said. "In the collective of scientists there was quiet and intense work. Close cohesion and friendship. . . . Although, of course, we had our sons of bitches."[16] V. A. Tsukerman and Z. M. Azarkh write that "in the first, most romantic years of our work in the institute a wonderful atmosphere of good will and support was created around the research. We worked selflessly, with great enthusiasm and the mobilization of all our spiritual and physical forces."[17]

"IF YOU WANT PEACE, PREPARE FOR WAR"

It is striking how the apparatus of the police state fused with the physics community to build the bomb. In the 1930s the physics community had enjoyed an unusual measure of intellectual autonomy, which was sustained by a set of social relationships. That autonomy was not destroyed by the creation of the nuclear project. It continued to exist within the administrative system that was set up to manage the project.

Before the war the nuclear scientists had paid close attention to research being done abroad and had striven to show themselves as good as their foreign colleagues. The American atomic bomb presented a formidable challenge to Soviet scientists and engineers, who now sought to prove their worth in this new competition. The fact that the Americans had already used the bomb may have lessened the sense of responsibility that Soviet scientists felt in making this destructive weapon. They were responding to the American challenge, not initiating the atomic competition. They believed the Soviet Union needed its own atomic bomb in response.

Individual scientists could refuse personally to work on the bomb, as Sakharov did until 1948, but open opposition to the project would have been fatal.

Discussion of moral qualms would of course have been dangerous; open opposition to the project, fatal. Terror encouraged people to put such questions aside and immerse themselves in their work. But the scientists did not have to work on the bomb; they could refuse to join the project, and some did, including Sakharov before 1948.

In his memoirs, Nikolai Dollezhal, the chief designer of the first reactor, discusses his own thoughts in 1946 when Kurchatov first drew him into the project. Dollezhal had regarded the bombing of Hiroshima as a "repulsive act of cynical antihumanism."[18] If that was so, did the Soviet Union have the right to make and use the same weapon? His answer was yes, on two grounds:

First, making the weapon was not the same as using it against peaceful cities. The military and political leadership would choose the targets. And although Dollezhal knew something of the terrible purge of 1947, "Those affairs were internal—domestic, so to speak."[19] The Soviet Union as far as he knew, did not contravene the laws of war: unlike the Germans, they had not destroyed the noncombatant population; unlike the Allies, they had not carpet-bombed German cities.

Dollezhal's second argument was that possession of the bomb did not mean it would be used. All the main combatants in the war had had chemical weapons, but no one had employed them. That was because they feared retaliation. The Soviet Union needed all the means of attack possessed by the aggressor if it wanted to prevent such weapons from being used.

After the war, writes Dollezhal, cracks appeared in the foundation of the wartime alliance with the United States. Things that had not been spoken of in the critical moments of the war were now brought to light with merciless clarity: "The two systems were completely alien to each other ideologically—more than that, they were antagonistic, and the political trust generated by the wartime alliance was not long-lived or solid." The United States might declare the Soviet Union an enemy at any time in the future:

"The security of the country and patriotic duty demanded that we create the atomic bomb. And these were not mere words. This was objective reality. Who would forgive the leadership of the country if it began to create the weapons only after the enemy had decided to attack? The ancients had a point when they coined the phrase 'If you want peace, prepare for war.' "

From this reasoning Dollezhal drew the conclusion that work on the bomb was morally justified. In his memoirs he writes that in a conversation early in 1946 he found that this was Kurchatov's position too.

Whether or not Dollezhal's memory is accurate—he may be reflecting conclusions he reached later on—his account is consistent with what other scientists have written about their general attitude to the project. Moreover, on two specific points Dollezhal's view was shared by other scientists at the time. It is apparent that others—Lev Artsimovich and Vitali G. Khlopin for example—were appalled by Hiroshima and

Nagasaki.[20] Although they knew of the terror and the slave labor camps, they were not aware of the full extent of Stalin and Beria's crimes. Altshuler later observed that "we knew nothing of those horrors of Stalinism which are today generally known. You can't jump out of your own time."[21]

The attitude of Soviet scientists was shaped, finally, by the war against Nazi Germany. The participants in the atomic project had either fought in the war or contributed to the war effort by designing or producing weapons. They had taken part in a bitter and destructive war to defend the Soviet Union and whatever they may have thought of Stalin's regime or his policies, they believed that their cause was just.

The war was hardly over before the atomic bomb posed a potential new threat. They had taken up arms against the German invader, and now they worked to provide their country with its own atomic bomb. The atomic project was in some psychological sense a continuation of the war with Germany. In his memoirs Sakharov writes that he understood the terrible and inhuman nature of the weapons he was helping to build. But World War II had also been an inhuman affair. He had not been a soldier in that war, but "I regarded myself as a soldier in this new scientific war." Kurchatov, he notes, used to say they were soldiers, and he sometimes signed his letters and memoranda "Soldier Kurchatov."[22]

The United States tested its plutonium bomb on July 16, 1945. On July 24, President Truman informed Stalin at the Potsdam Conference (shown here) that the United States "had a new weapon of unusual destructive force." He did not, however, say it was an atomic bomb. Although Stalin already knew of the bomb program through his spy network, he gave no indication that he knew what Truman meant.

"IDEOLOGICALLY HARMFUL" WORKS

During the war Vladimir Vernadski and Peter Kapitsa called for collaboration with Western scientists. It seemed as though their wish might be granted when Vyacheslav Molotov, during the Academy celebration in June 1945 promised the "most favorable conditions" for closer ties between Soviet and world science. The scientists' hopes were part of a broad desire among Soviet intellectuals for greater contact with the rest of the world.[23] They also reflected the widespread longing in the country for an easing of repression and a return to normal life. The war had restored the people's "pride and dignity," Sakharov wrote later. "We all believed—or at least hoped—that the postwar world would be decent and humane. How could it be otherwise?"[24]

Stalin, however, dealt a blow to hopes of a normal life in a speech of February 6, 1946, which signaled a return to prewar economic policies and pointed to a dangerous period of international relations ahead. Stalin soon made it clear that the relative intellectual tolerance of the war would be brought to an end. In August 1946 the Central Committee criticized the Leningrad journals *Zvezda* and *Leningrad* for publishing "ideologically harmful" works. The campaign for ideological orthodoxy gathered momentum and in the course of 1947 "discussions" were organized in philosophy, economics, and biology. Militant critics attacked more moderate scholars and officials for subservience to Western ideas and a lack of ideological vigilance.[25]

The ideological campaign is associated with the name of Andrei Zhdanov, the party secretary responsible for ideology, but it was Stalin who orchestrated it. The attack on Western ideas was part of Stalin's effort to tighten party control over the intelligentsia. In May 1947 Stalin told Konstantin Simonov and two other writers:

"If you take our middle intelligentsia, the scientific intelligentsia, professors, physicians, they have an insufficiently educated feeling of Soviet patriotism. They have an unjustified admiration of foreign culture. They all feel themselves to be still under age, not a hundred percent, they have got used to thinking of themselves as eternal students. This is an obsolete tradition, it comes from Peter. Peter had good ideas, but soon there were too many Germans, that was the period of admiration for Germans.... First the Germans, then the French, there was admiration for foreigners.... A simple peasant will not bow for nothing, take his cap off, but these people do not have enough dignity or patriotism, do not understand the role that Russia plays."[26]

Stalin showed the writers a soon-to-be published letter condemning two Soviet scientists for sending a manuscript on the treatment of cancer to an American publisher. The publication of this letter marked the beginning of a campaign against admiration for foreign culture.

The changing political climate had a profound effect on Soviet science. It offered Lysenko the opportunity to revive his fortunes. In the brief period of hope at the end of the war Lysenko's position had been weak—in 1946 one of his main opponents, the geneticist N. P. Dubinin, had been elected a corresponding member of the Soviet Academy of Science. But Lysenko managed to link his crusade against genetics to the campaign for ideological purity. By clever political maneuvering, in which he portrayed his opponents as politically disloyal and in

Party overseers: Left, Mikhail Pervukhin; center, Vyacheslav Malyshev; right, Avraami Zavenyagin.

thrall to foreign ideas, he managed to win Stalin's support.[27]

In July 1948 Lysenko was summoned to a conversation with Stalin. He promised great improvements in agricultural output if he was allowed to defeat his scientific opponents and prevent their interference with his work. Stalin accepted Lysenko's argument. A special session of the Lenin All-Union Academy of Agricultural Sciences was hurriedly convened to review the situation in biology.[28]

Lysenko's report to the meeting, which had been read and edited by Stalin himself, asserted that the science of genetics was incompatible with Marxism-Leninism, and that genetics was a bourgeois fabrication designed to undermine the true materialist theory of biological development.[29] Several speakers rejected Lysenko's claims, but Lysenko effectively silenced them by declaring, at the end of the conference, that "the Party Central Committee had examined my report and approved it."[30]

In other words, to challenge Lysenko was to challenge the party leadership. The party—and more particularly Stalin—claimed ultimate authority in science, the right to say what constituted scientific truth. Thousands of geneticists and plant biologists were removed from their teaching and research positions. Sergei Kaftanov, who had advised Stalin to start an atomic project in 1942 and was now Minister of Higher Education, took an active role in this purge.[31]

Lysenko's victory gave heart to those who wanted to do for other disciplines what he had done for biology. In the next two years conferences were organized in physiology, astronomy, chemistry, and ethnography to root out foreign ideological influences: "cosmopolitanism" was attacked, and often ludicrous claims made for the priority of Russian and Soviet scientists and engineers in discovery and invention.[32]

"THE STRUGGLE AGAINST KOWTOWING"

Physics too came under threat. Quantum mechanics and relativity theory had been attacked by philosophers in the 1930s. A new controversy broke out in 1947, following the publication of an article by Moisei A. Markov of the Physics Institute of the Academy of Sciences (FIAN) on epistemological problems in quantum mechanics.[33] Markov was attacked by the militant philosopher A. A. Maksimov for his stand on these issues, and especially for his espousal of Niels Bohr's concept of complementarity.[34] The editor of the journal in which Markov's article had appeared was removed from his post in 1948, and the Copenhagen school's interpretation of quantum mechanics was banished from the Soviet press for over a decade.[35]

Lysenko's triumph in August 1948 presented a far graver threat to physics than the ban on a particular interpretation of quantum mechanics. Within four months preparations were under way for an All-Union Conference of Physicists to discuss shortcomings in Soviet physics. The conference was to be organized by the Ministry of Higher Education, headed by Kaftanov, and by the Academy of Sciences, of which Sergei Vavilov was now president. On December 17 an organizing committee was set up with A. V. Topchiev, Deputy Minister of Higher Education, as chairman and Abram Ioffe as his deputy.[36]

In a letter to Deputy Premier Klimenti Voroshilov, Kaftanov outlined the shortcomings the conference was expected to remedy:

"Physics is taught in many educational establishments without any regard to dialectical materialism. . . . Instead of decisively unmasking trends which are inimical to Marxism-Leninism, some of our scientists frequently adopt idealist positions, which are making their way into higher educational establishments through physics. . . . The modern achievements of physics do not receive consistent exposition on the basis of dialectical materialism in Soviet physics textbooks. . . . The role of Russian and Soviet scientists in the development of physics is treated in a completely inadequate way in textbooks; the books abound in the names of foreign scientists."[37]

Six hundred physicists were to be invited to the Moscow "House of Scholars" for this conference—a kind of sequel to the 1936 conference on physics, which was now criticized for having paid too little attention to ideology.[38]

The organizing committee met 42 times between December 30, 1948 and March 16, 1949. The meetings were attended not only by members of the committee but also by invited guests. The discussions were often bitter.

Battle lines were not only drawn between physicists and philosophers: In the late 1940s the Soviet physics community was split into two groups—those from the Academy (FIAN) and those from Moscow University.[39] This split dated back to the mid-1930s when Vavilov began to build up FIAN as a powerful institute. As FIAN grew stronger, the situation at the university worsened. After B. M. Gessen, dean of the physics faculty, was arrested in 1936, the faculty was increasingly dominated by physicists who were willing to resort to appeals to political authority in their academic and administrative disputes. A number of physicists, including Peter Kapitsa and Abram Ioffe, wrote to Molotov in 1944 to express their concern about the quality of teaching at the university and to ask him to appoint one of the leading physicists (Ivan Obreimov, Mikhail Leontovich, or Vladimir Fok) as dean. Molotov did not take their advice, and the situation grew worse after Leonid Mandelshtam died in 1944.[40]

One by one members of Mandelshtam's school—Grigorii S. Landsberg, Igor Tamm, S. E. Khaikin, and Leontovich—

left the university, which was taken over by a varied group of mediocre physicists. The group included some serious physicists such as Dmitri Ivanenko and Aleksandr S. Predvoditelev, but also men like V. M. Kessenikh and V. F. Nozdrev, who made up for their lack of ability in physics with ideological vigilance.[41]

What united the university physicists was the belief that their work had not received the recognition they thought it deserved. They were also annoyed that, in spite of strenuous efforts, they had not been drawn into the atomic project. Some of them were willing to resort to political charges to settle scores with the Academy physicists. The campaign against cosmopolitanism provided political cover for their accusations.[42]

An all-Soviet conference on physics was planned to deal with ideological problems: Frenkel, for instance, had once declared dialectical materialism irrelevant to physics.

The organizing committee discussed the ten papers that were to be presented at the conference. Vavilov was to deliver a paper "On Contemporary Physics and the Tasks of Soviet Physicists," and Ioffe "On Measures to Improve the Teaching of Physics in Technical Schools"; others were to speak on textbooks and ways to improve physics education. But the discussion in the committee ranged far beyond these apparently innocuous topics. The university physicists and their philosopher allies went on the attack, accusing the Academy physicists of spreading cosmopolitanism and idealism, of not citing Russian scientists, of avoiding honest arguments, of refusing to develop fundamental physics, and of spying for Germany.

This last charge was leveled against Mandelshtam, who had died five years earlier. But living physicists were also criticized. Ioffe, Tamm, and Markov, all of whom took part in the committee meetings, were severely criticized. Iakov Frenkel was a particular target, and his 1931 position on the irrelevance of dialectical materialism to physics was brought up against him. The absent Kapitsa was also attacked.[43]

Vavilov was in a difficult position. As a physicist he understood the absurdity of the charges made by the university physicists and their allies. As president of the Academy, however, he had to take part in a campaign that had been approved by the political authorities. He tried to balance these competing responsibilities but failed to satisfy the university physicists.

The Academy physicists rejected the criticisms of quantum mechanics and relativity theory. They also rejected the criticisms of their attitude toward Western science. If they did not cite the works of the university physicists more often, said Tamm, it was because they did not think they were very good. Landsberg accused Ivanenko of making citation of his work and that of his students the touchstone of a Soviet physicist's patriotism. The Academy physicists were willing to make token criticisms of the idealist philosophical views of some Western physicists. Under intense criticism Frenkel admitted that he had explained the ideas of the creators of quantum mechanics without criticizing them. On the key issues, however, the Academy physicists stood their ground.

In spite of their resistance, it is clear from the draft resolution the conference was expected to adopt that the university physicists had official support. "For Soviet physics," the resolution said, "the struggle against kowtowing and groveling before the West, and the education of a feeling of national pride, of faith in the inexhaustible powers of the Soviet people, have special significance. It is necessary to root out mercilessly every hint of cosmopolitanism, which is Anglo-American imperialism's ideological weapon of diversion."

The draft resolution also criticized specific physicists. Lev Landau and Abram Ioffe were accused of "groveling before the West"; Peter Kapitsa of propagating "open cosmopolitanism"; Iakov Frenkel and Moisei Markov of "uncritically receiving Western physical theories and propagandizing them in our country." Textbooks by S. E. Khaikin, Landau and Evgenii Lifshits, Eduard Shpolski and Frenkel were condemned for popularizing foreign ideological concepts and for not citing Russian authors frequently enough.[44]

"WE CAN ALWAYS SHOOT THEM LATER"

It is hard to say what effect the conference might have had on Soviet physics. The draft resolution did not condemn quantum mechanics and relativity theory as such, so the conference might not have been as devastating to physics as the August 1948 meeting was to biology. But it would have strengthened the position of the Moscow university physicists who, as a group, were narrow-minded, chauvinistic, and less able than the Academy physicists. Physics would have been drawn further into the realm of ideology, and disagreements and disputes would have been conducted more frequently in the language of Stalinist politics. The role of the philosophers as ideological policemen would have been strengthened. All this would have created a dangerous situation for Soviet physics.

In the end, though, Stalin chose the bomb over ideological purity.

The conference failed to take place, however, and its possible effects must remain a matter of speculation. The last meeting of the organizing committee took place on March 16, 1949, and the conference was due to start on March 21. It was canceled between those two dates. Only Stalin could have taken this decision, and it appears that he canceled the conference because it might retard the atomic project.

According to Gen. V. A. Makhnev, head of the secretariat of the Special Committee on the Atomic Bomb, Beria asked Kurchatov whether it was true that quantum mechanics and relativity theory were idealist, in the sense of antimaterialist. Kurchatov replied that if relativity theory and quantum mechanics were rejected, the bomb would have to be rejected too. Beria was worried by this reply, and may have asked Stalin to call off the conference.[45]

A more circumstantial account, which does not contradict Makhnev's story, was given by Artsimovich, on the basis of a conversation with Beria after Stalin's death. According to Artsimovich, three leading physicists—Kurchatov may have been among them—approached Beria in mid-March 1949 and asked him to call off the conference on the grounds that it would harm Soviet physics and interfere with the atomic project. Beria replied that he could not make a decision on this himself, but that he would speak to Stalin. Stalin agreed to cancel the conference, saying of the physicists, according to Beria, "Leave them in peace. We can always shoot them later."[46]

It was the atomic bomb that saved Soviet physics in 1949. Stalin was not so concerned about the condition of agriculture—he tolerated, after all, a desperate famine in the Ukraine in 1947—and so it may not have mattered very much to him whether Lysenko was a charlatan or not. The nuclear project was more important, however, than the lives of Soviet citizens, so it was crucial to be sure that the scientists in the nuclear project were not frauds.

For Beria, who was answerable to Stalin for the success of the project, it was important that the scientists should be politically reliable. But it was even more important that they should not be charlatans. Beria wanted the project to succeed and, in spite of the atmosphere of menace he created, he did not arrest any of the senior people in the project. For the same reason it was in his interest to resist those who wanted to do for physics what Lysenko had done for genetics.

The same logic can be seen in an episode that took place in 1951. A commission came to examine the level of political education at Arzamas-16. When Altshuler told the commission that he did not think Lysenko was right in his attack on classical genetics, the commission recommended that Altshuler be dismissed. Sakharov and Zeldovich protested to Zavenyagin, who was visiting the installation, and Altshuler was allowed to remain. A year later the issue came up again. This time Khariton telephoned Beria, who asked, "Do you need him very much?" Khariton replied that he did, and that was the end of the matter.[47]

The cancellation of the March 1949 conference and the successful atomic test five months later were serious setbacks for the university physicists and the philosophers. But their criticism of cosmopolitanism and idealism did not stop, and physicists had to parry their attacks. Kurchatov was forthright in his views. Zeldovich recalled that he was sitting in Kurchatov's office in the early 1950s when a telephone call came from an editorial board in Moscow asking whether they should publish an article attacking the theory of relativity. "Well, if that article is right," replied Kurchatov, "we can close down our business."[48]

In 1952 some of the papers prepared for the aborted March 1949 conference were published. The editors, headed by Maksimov, complained that Soviet physicists lagged behind specialists in such fields as agrobiology and physiology—both of which had been thoroughly purged—in fighting against the survival of capitalism in their own consciousness.[49]

THE FIRST EXAMPLE OF NUCLEAR DETERRENCE

A disjunction now existed in Soviet policy. Stalin had given support to Lysenko's argument that there was a fundamental difference between socialist science and capitalist science; at the same time Soviet physicists were building the plutonium bomb on the basis of the American design. Stalin had launched a campaign against kowtowing to the West, and against the denigration of Russian and Soviet science and technology; but it was the party leadership that took Western technology as the model and distrusted Soviet scientists and engineers.

The Soviet Union was copying foreign technology in several areas (the atomic bomb, the V-2 missile, the B-29 bomber), but trying to hide the fact from its own people by trumpeting Soviet achievements.

The campaign against foreign influence helped to create a political situation in which genetics was destroyed and physics put at risk. The Stalinist regime gave great importance to technology, and especially to military technology, but, unlike a technocracy, the regime did not accept the authority or autonomy of technical expertise. The regime's fundamental logic was political: it claimed the right to say what constituted scientific truth and destroyed whole disciplines in the name of ideological orthodoxy.

In the end, Stalin did not destroy physics because physics was needed to enhance the power of the state. Landau has said that the survival of Soviet physics was the first example of successful nuclear deterrence. What the bomb saved was a small island of intellectual autonomy in a society where the state claimed control of intellectual life.

Besides, the physics community saw itself in some significant sense as part of a larger international community, and it was perhaps more closely linked with the West, in cultural terms, than any other part of Soviet society. Thus the atomic bomb, the most potent symbol of the hostility between the Soviet Union and the West, saved a community that constituted an important cultural and intellectual link between the West and the Soviet Union.

Notes

1. Lev Altshuler, "Tak my delali bombu," *Literaturnaya Gazeta,* June 6, 1990, p. 13.
2. Ibid.
3. "Delo Beria," *Izvestia TsK KPSS,* (1991) no. 2, p. 168.
4. Andrei Sakharov, *Memoirs* (New York: Alfred A. Knopf, 1990), p. 108.
5. Sakharov, *Memoirs,* pp. 112, 115, 119; Altshuler, "Tak my delali bombu"; Yuli Khariton and Yuri N. Smirnov, "O nekotorykh mifakh i legendakh vokrug sovetskikh atomnogo i vodorodnogo proektov," in *Materialy iubileinoi sessii uchenogo soveta tsentra 12 ianvaria 1993* g. (Moscow: Kurchatov Institute, 1993), p. 46.
6. Sakharov, *Memoirs,* p. 115; Altshuler, "Tak my delali bombu"; Khariton and Smirnov, pp. 36–37.
7. Yuli Khariton, in V. A. Gubarev, *Arzamas-16* (Moscow: Izdat, 1991) pp. 21–22.
8. Interview with Yuli Khariton, July 16, 1992.
9. Yuri Abyzov, *Russhoe pechathoe slovo V Latvii, 1917–1944 gg., Part IV* (Stanford: Stanford Slavic Studies, 1991), pp. 260–61.
10. Anatoli Aleksandrov, "Gody s Kurchatovym," *Nauka i zhizn,* 1983, no. 2, p. 23.
11. Vasili Emelyanov, *S chego nachinalos* (Moscow: Sovetskaya Rossiya, 1979), p. 233.
12. I. N. Golovin and Yuri N. Smirnov, *Eto nachinalos v zamoskvoreche* (Moscow: Kurchatov Institute, 1989), p. 9.
13. Altshuler, "Tak my delali bombu."
14. Victor B. Adamsky, "Becoming a Citizen," in *Andrei Sakharov: Facets of a Life* (Gif-Sur-Yvette: Editions Frontières, 1991), p. 27.
15. Andrei Sakharov, "Ia pytalsia byt na urovne svoei sudby," *Molodezh Estonii,* Oct. 11, 1988, p. 2.
16. Yuli Khariton in Gubarev, *Arzamas-16,* p. 14.

17. V. A. Tsukerman and Z. M. Azarkh, "Liudi i vzryvy," *Zvesda,* 1990, no. 10, p. 151.
18. Nikolai A. Dollezhal, *U istokov rukotvornogo mira* (Moscow: Znanie, 1989), p. 137.
19. Ibid, pp. 137–39.
20. Max Steenbeck, *Impulse und Virkungen* (Berlin: Verlag der Nation, 1977), pp. 174–75; M. G. Meshcheriakov, "Akademik V. G. Khlopin: Voskhozhdenie na posledniuiu vershinu," unpublished paper, 1992, p. 28.
21. Altshuler, "Tak my delali bombu"; interview with Andrei Sakharov, June 15, 1987.
22. Sakharov, *Memoirs,* p. 97.
23. Konstantin Simonov, *Glazami Cheloveka moego pokoleniia* (Moscow: izd. Pravda, 1990), p. 106.
24. Sakharov, *Memoirs,* p. 41.
25. Werner G. Hahn, *Postwar Soviet Politics* (Ithaca: Cornell University Press, 1982), pp. 58–59; 67–93.
26. Ibid., p. 126.
27. David Joravsky, *The Lysenko Affair* (Cambridge, Mass.: Harvard University Press, 1970), pp. 133–37; Zhores Medvedev, *The Rise and Fall of T. D. Lysenko* (New York: Columbia University Press, 1969), pp. 114–17; Valery Soyfer, "Gorkii plod," *Ogonyok,* 1988, nos. 1 and 2.
28. Soyfer, "Gorkii plod," no. 2, p. 5.
29. Joravsky, *The Lysenko Affair,* pp. 137–39; Medvedev, *The Rise and Fall of T. D. Lysenko,* pp. 117–23; Soyfer, "Gorky plod," no. 2, pp. 5–7.
30. *O polozhenii v biologicheskoi nauke. Stenograficheskii otchet sessi vsesoiuznoi akademii sel skokhoziaistvennykh nauk imeni V. I. Lenina 31 iiulia-7. augusta 1948.g.* (Moscow: Selkhozizdat, 1948), p. 512.
31. Joravsky, *The Lysenko Affair,* p. 141; Medvedev, *The Rise and Fall of T. D. Lysenko,* pp. 123–36; Soyfer, "Gorkii plod," no. 2, pp. 7, 31.
32. Alexander Vucinich, *Empire of Knowledge, The Academy of Sciences of the USSR, 1917–1970* (Berkeley: University of California Press, 1984), pp. 220–28.
33. M. A. Markov, "O prirode fizicheskogo znaniia," *Voprosy filosofi,* 1947, no. 2, pp. 140–76; Loren R. Graham, *Science and Philosophy in the Soviet Union* (New York: Alfred A. Knopf, 1972), pp. 74–81.
34. M. A. Maksimov, "Ob odnom filosofskom kentavre," *Literaturnaya Gazeta* (April 10), 1948, p. 3; Hahn, *Postwar Soviet Politics,* pp. 79–82.
35. Graham, *Science and Philosophy in the Soviet Union,* p. 79.
36. A. S. Sonin, "Soveshchanie, kotoroe ne sostoialos," *Priroda,* 1990, no. 3, p. 99.
37. Ibid., p. 98.
38. Ibid., p. 99.
39. See G. E. Gorelik, "Fizika universitetskaia i akademicheskaia," *Voprosy istorii estestvoznaniia i techniki,* 1991, no. 2, pp. 31–46.
40. Peter L. Kapitsa, *Pisma o nauke* (Moscow: Moskovskii rabochii, 1989), pp. 216–17.
41. In 1948, Ivanenko complained that the Smyth Report had contrived "to set forth the important results of a large number of Soviet works, without so much as saying a word about Soviet science and its role in the physical discoveries of our time!" Dmitiri D. Ivanenko, "K itogam diskussi po Knige B. M. Kedrova 'Engel's i estestvoznanie,' " *Bolshevik,* 1948, no. 8, p. 69.
42. Gorelik, "Fizika universitetskaia i akademicheskaia," p. 37, Sonin, "Soveshchanie, kotoroe ne sostoialos."
43. Sonin, "Soveshchanie, kotoroe ne sostoialos." p. 91.
44. Ibid., no. 5, pp. 98–99.
45. Ibid., p. 99.
46. Letter from I. Zorich, Priroda, 1990, no. 9, p. 106.
47. Altshuler, "Tak my delali bombu"; Sakharov, *Memoirs,* pp. 135–36; Khariton in Gubarev, *Arzamas-16,* p. 12.
48. Aleksandrov, "Gody s Kurchatovym," p. 85.
49. *Filosofski voprosy sovremennoi fiziki* (Moscow: idz. Akademii Nauk SSSR, 1952), p. 4.

The Other Camus

Among Paris's postwar intellectuals, Albert Camus stood apart—both for his independence and his compelling lucidity. Yet few of his admirers knew how different Camus was even from the persona that came through in his early, existential writings. As our author shows, the publication of Camus's last, uncompleted novel brings us closer to the man we barely knew.

Robert Royal

Robert Royal is vice president of the Ethics and Public Policy Center in Washington, D.C. He is the author of 1492 and All That *(1992) and writes widely on literary and cultural matters.*

> ***What they did not like in him was the Algerian.***
> —From *The First Man* (Notes and Sketches)

Albert Camus died in literature's most stunning car crash on January 4, 1960; he had lived in two very different worlds. One extended into the highest reaches of French intellectual and political life and brought him fame and honors, including the 1957 Nobel Prize for literature. The other was that of the lower-class European workers in the Belcourt quarter of Algiers where Camus was reared, a world of "poverty and sunlight."

Even the details of his death reflected his movement between these two worlds. Returning from a vacation in the south of France with Michel Gallimard, scion of the prestigious Parisian publishing family, Camus died instantly when Gallimard lost control of his Facel Vega and struck a tree. (Gallimard died several days later.) Camus's body, accompanied by only a few family members and close friends, was taken back to the cemetery at Lourmarin, a humble village in Provence where, in the last few years of his life, he liked to write.

Camus's deep loyalty to the worlds of high art and simple human existence may be sensed in almost everything he wrote, but nowhere more poignantly than in *The First Man,* the unfinished manuscript found in his briefcase near the scene of the crash. The Camus family allowed scholars to consult the text of *The First Man* after the author's death, but, because it was unpolished and incomplete, withheld it from publication. Destroying it was unthinkable, however. Camus's daughter, Catherine, finally decided to oversee its publication. An instant sensation when it appeared in France last year, the novel remained on the best-seller lists for months. In her note to the American edition, which came out in August, Catherine reminds us that her father "was a very reserved man and would no doubt have masked his own feelings far more in its final version." But she also points to one of the novel's more intriguing qualities: in it, Camus's voice sounds much as it did to those who knew him best.

Albert Camus, 1956

The First Man also reveals how Camus, throughout his career, was both shadowed and inspired by the voiceless mass of people who, like the Algerians of his youth, go through their lives leaving barely a trace of their existence. Many of his tensions as a writer may have had to do with, on the one hand, his fear of sterility, a falling back into the simple silence of those people, and, on the other, his will to express the truth and beauty of their existence to a wholly different world.

In the preface to a new edition of some of his early work that appeared shortly before his death, Camus remarked that a writer "keeps within himself a single source which nourishes during his lifetime what he is and what he says. As for myself, I know that my source is in . . . the poverty and sunlight I lived in for so long, whose memory still saves me from two opposing dangers that threaten every artist, resentment and self-satisfaction."

In its printed version, *The First Man* runs to more than 300 pages, an already large text for the usually succinct Camus. But there are many indications that he was embarking on

From *The Wilson Quarterly,* Autumn 1995, pp. 53-67. © 1995 by Robert Royal. Reprinted by permission of the author.

At his uncle's workshop in 1920, Camus sits in the center of the front row, wearing a black smock.

something even larger. *The First Man* was to have been, Camus said, "the novel of my maturity," a large-scale saga on the order of Tolstoy's *War and Peace,* encompassing the whole panorama of Algerian history from the 1830 French conquest and subsequent colonization down through the Nazi Occupation and the eventual Nazi defeat.

> "There was a mystery about this man, a mystery he wanted to clear up. But at the end there was nothing but the mystery of poverty that creates people without a name and without a past."
>
> —*The First Man* (Notes and Sketches)

It is impossible to say how the novel would have finally turned out, or even whether Camus could have done what he intended. But the man painting on that large a canvas with the full palette of colors is quite different from the Camus that American readers of *The Stranger* and *The Plague* may expect. *The First Man* is neither stark nor anguished. Instead, a naked exuberance and love animate its pages. Camus seems to have been working back toward the wellsprings of his genius: "A man's work is nothing but this slow trek to discover, through the detours of art, those two or three great and simple images in whose presence his heart first opened," he wrote in the late 1950s. "This is why, perhaps after working and producing for 20 years, I still live with the idea that my work has not even begun."

By the end of his short life (he was only 46 when he died), Camus seems to have been shifting into a new phase as an artist and thinker. We know from various sources, including his journals, that Camus had early on formulated a multiphase writing plan. The first phase consisted of a triad of works—the play *Caligula* (1938), the novel *The Stranger* (1940), and the book-length essay *The Myth of Sisyphus* (1941). In them, he set out to confront the absurd—the nihilism that seemed to have gripped modern Europe. Unfortunately, many readers in his lifetime, and some even today, identify Camus exclusively with this first stage. To Camus, the radical confrontation with the absurd was an absolute necessity in the 20th century, but only as a first step toward a fuller vision of human meaning and value.

Even before completing the first phase in 1941, Camus, who was then still in his late twenties, laid out the second. Having faced and rejected the existential abyss, he believed that values could be constructed out of rebellion against the human predicament. Another triad of works was projected and took a decade to complete: a play entitled *The Misunderstanding* (1944), a novel, *The Plague* (1947), and an essay, *The Rebel* (1951). The first two phases contain many of the works usually associated with Camus, but, as he remarked in his journals in 1949, he regarded these early works as a necessary depersonalization before speaking "in my own voice."

For a subsequent phase, he planned on another triad of works exploring the need for limits and measure, even in revolt: *The First Man, The System* (a long essay never written), and another play. Camus saw these various phases as falling under three mythological markers: Sisyphus, Prometheus, and Nemesis. To readers who think writers produce spontaneously, this scheme may appear calculated and surprisingly rigid. But for Camus it was necessary. He believed that an inborn tendency to anarchy, unless vigorously disciplined, would lead to a fatal dispersal of his powers.

In many ways, it is remarkable that a man like Camus ever conceived of such a scheme. He had grown up with few of the supports that normally provide direction and order. Less than a year after his birth on November 7, 1913, Camus lost his father—a victim of wounds received at the Battle of the Marne. The penniless youth from Belcourt, one of the poorer quarters of Algiers, went on to the lycée and university only because certain kind teachers convinced his grandmother, who dominated the Camus household, that it would profit the family if he continued studying rather than go directly to work. At 17, just out of the lycée, he came down with tuberculosis and might well have died had not one of his uncles, a butcher, taken him under his wing and kept him well fed. Even so, his prospects were not bright: the tuberculosis meant that Camus, though intellectually promising, could not pass the physical for the *agrégation,* the usual route to a teaching position in the French university system.

In the 1930s, while he worked on his thesis at the University of Algiers, Camus took various odd jobs. He tutored, directed a theater company, recorded weather data for a meteorological office, sold car parts, and finally became a journalist at the *Alger Républicain.* During the same period, he also was briefly an activist and member of the Communist Party and found time to write two collections of essays, his play *Caligula,* and part of two novels, *A Happy Death* and what would become *The Stranger.*

By 1940, when he gave up on job prospects in Algeria and took a job at *Paris-Soir* under Pascal Pia, his former editor at *Alger Républicain,* Camus was still unknown but had already accomplished some remarkable work. Despite the war, he continued writing, publishing both *The Stranger* and *The Myth of Sisyphus* in 1942. The following year, he began writing for the Resistance paper *Combat* and eventually became its director.

Camus emerged from this period an almost legendary figure. In addition to his fame as a novelist, he had won recognition as perhaps the most distinguished moral voice in Europe. No one else wrote more movingly, for example, of the spiritual resistance to Nazism. His *Letters to a German Friend,* which came out in the months before the liberation of Paris, are still worth reading not only for the testimony they give to the human spirit but for their lyrical invocation, even in the flush of victory, of a humanity that refuses to sink to the enemy's level: "It would not be enough for me to think that all the great shades of the West and that 30 nations were on our side; I could not do without the soil. And so I know that everything in Europe, both landscape and spirit, calmly negates you, without feeling any rash hatred, but with the calm strength of victory."

To many readers, Camus was the romantic model of the 20th-century French intellectual. Attractive, modest, irresistible to women, a talented actor and director, a voice of the Resistance, he exerted a strange fascination over a whole generation. As one commentator put it, "He was like Bogart but more exuberant." Susan Sontag says in her well-known but often misleading essay on Camus's *Notebooks,* "Kafka arouses pity and affection on the part of his readers, Joyce admiration, Proust and Gide respect, but no modern writer that I can think of, except Camus, has aroused love."

This is even more curious because of a certain *pudeur* in everything Camus wrote, a reserve and a distance evident even in his notes to himself. The journal entries from the 1940s, for example, barely acknowledge the world war and nowhere mention how the publication of *The Stranger* and *The Myth of Sisyphus* brought the talented but obscure French Algerian to the forefront of the Paris literary scene.

Camus is often called the French Orwell, a fair comparison if not pressed too far. Both men suffered from tuberculosis and derived wisdom from their proximity to death. Both championed the working class but were by nature incapable of the public exaggerations and mendacities required by partisan politics. Both recognized early on a truth to which George Orwell gave precise formulation: "The sin of nearly all left-wingers from 1933 onwards is that they have wanted to be anti-fascist without being anti-totalitarian." Both writers demand description as decent human beings who tried to promote justice and a clear public language at a time when most intellectuals were ideologically corrupt or obscurantist.

Camus found it impossible to follow most left-wing intellectuals in Paris, and he denounced the National Liberation Front's policy of indiscriminate violence against all Europeans in Algeria.

Camus's reputation continued to grow steadily in the late 1940s and early '50s. He was a nonpartisan, humane voice during the Cold War and Algerian conflicts, and a reliable commentator on Communist injustices, the invasion of Hungary in 1956, and various other crises. Though a man of the Left, he clashed repeatedly with the Parisian literary leftists—at no time more pointedly than when his essay *The Rebel* appeared in 1951.

From the book's opening sentence—"There are crimes of passion and crimes of logic"—to its lyrical conclusion about a measured brotherhood, *The Rebel* is a vibrant exposition of Camus's belief both in the need for rebellion and in the equally strong need for limits to it. Camus indicts radical revolt not only among 20th-century Marxists and fascists but also its

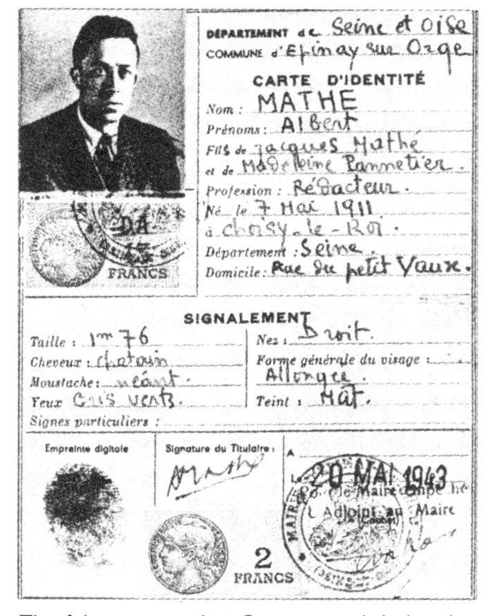
DÉPARTEMENT de Seine et Oise
COMMUNE d'Epinay sur Orge
CARTE D'IDENTITÉ
Nom : MATHE
Prénoms : Albert
Fils de Jacques Mathé
et de Madeleine Pannetier.
Profession : Rédacteur.
Né le 7 Mai 1911
à Choisy-le-Roi.
Département : Seine.
Domicile : Rue du petit Vaux.
FRANCS

SIGNALEMENT
Taille : 1m76
Nez : Droit.
Cheveux : Châtain
Forme générale du visage : Allongée.
Moustache : néant.
Yeux Gris verts.
Teint : Mat.
Signes particuliers :

Empreinte digitale
Signature du Titulaire : Mathé
A ... le 20 MAI 1943
Le Maire
L'Adjoint au Maire
2 FRANCS

The false papers that Camus used during the Occupation identified the Resistance worker as Albert Mathé.

expressions in the French Terror, de Sade, Hegel, Marx, portions of Nietzsche, the Russian anarchists, the French surrealists, and others.

To leftists, an appeal for limited rebellion always sounds like a defense of the status quo, and in fact Camus was disturbed to find that only French conservatives seemed to agree with him. But Camus was determined to present some third way that would not simply fall into the simplistic left-right dichotomies of the Cold War. Unfortunately, those very dichotomies shaped the early reactions to his argument.

Stung by Camus's criticism of their apologies for communist atrocities, Jean-Paul Sartre and other left-wing intellectuals savaged the essay in Sartre's magazine *Les Temps modernes.* They accused him, variously, of apologizing for capitalist exploitation, of misreading the historical record on several philosophers and literary figures, of having no political solutions, and of being in over his head. Though there was some truth to the latter charges, Camus was right on his main points—and his accuracy cost him his standing in Parisian literary circles for years to come.

The sharp intellectual criticism of *The Rebel* by Sartre and his circle seems to have shaken Camus's confidence during the early 1950s. Besides pointing to technical philosophical deficiencies, his critics had put their finger on a real problem: Camus had no concrete political program. That shortcoming became even more apparent in his agonized response to the growing conflict in Algeria. Camus found it impossible to follow most left-wing intellectuals in Paris, who blithely took the Arab side against their own government. In a famous remark, Camus denounced the National Liberation Front's policy of indiscriminate violence against all Europeans in Algeria, among other reasons because it would strike "my mother or my family." Unable to choose between the only available alternatives, Arab terrorism or France's repression, he lapsed into what he hoped was an eloquent silence: "When words lead men to dispose of other men's lives without a trace of remorse, silence is not a negative attitude."

The ferocity on both sides was something his instinctive moderation could not reach. When he went to Algiers in 1958, just two years before his death, to speak in favor of a just French-Arab society, he arrived as a hometown hero of the Resistance, a Nobel laureate, and a writer who commanded worldwide moral authority. Yet he was shouted down when he tried to speak at a political gathering and was threatened by both sides.

Personal as well as political tensions exacted a heavy emotional toll on Camus during the 1950s. He began having attacks of "claustrophobia" in restaurants and trains, he saw a psychiatrist, and extensive womanizing caused his second marriage to unravel, with Camus finally moving to a separate but nearby apartment in order to remain close to his two children.

The almost epic promiscuity that destroyed his marriage raises questions about Camus's relationships with women in general. In his early life, he was reserved, and Algerian friends teased him about his shyness. That changed after his short-lived marriage to Simone Hié in the early 1930s. A fellow French Algerian, wealthy, flamboyant, and beautiful, Hié knew how to manipulate men. She got together with Camus while her then-boyfriend Max-Pol Fouchet, one of Camus's best friends, was out of town. To make matters worse, Hié was also a morphine addict, who, if necessary, would seduce doctors for the drug. Discovering that the seductions were still going in 1935, a year after their marriage, Camus left her and almost never spoke of Hié again.

But the discovery deeply changed him. Camus became promiscuous, and something cold and strangely cynical in an otherwise remarkably uncynical man broke loose. It was five years before he married again, this time to a more proper French-Algerian beauty, Francine Faure. She was talented, attractive, and intelligent in her own right, but with a more stable nature that promised something Camus may have felt he needed: a regular family life.

Unfortunately for both of them, the war intervened. Faure came to Lyons in France for the wedding. But when she returned to Algeria for a visit, the Allied invasion of North Africa and the Nazi Occupation of the south of France separated her from Camus for the rest of the war. (In *The Plague,* an allegorical treatment of the Occupation, Camus writes of the effects of a similar separation caused by a medical quarantine.) When Camus moved to Paris during the Occupation, things took an even more tragic turn.

In the highly emotional atmosphere of the time, as he continued writing and producing plays, Camus met a passionate Spanish-French actress who would become the central romantic figure in his life, Maria Casarès. Camus valued the "Castilian pride" he had inherited from his mother's Spanish ancestors, and some strange harmony of passion, pride, and vulnerability united the two. Camus, whose reserve was legendary, could even be open with Casarès.

Until the liberation of Paris, they carried on a torrid affair. Both knew the relationship might end when the war did, and though Casarès wanted all or nothing, Camus could not make up his mind to divorce Francine. He split with Casarès, seemingly forever, in 1944, after a passionate struggle that she said "placed me at the center of life but left me completely vulnerable."

But the strange Castilian alchemy between them did not go away. Francine came to live in Paris and had twins after the liberation. Five years later, Camus and Casarès met by accident on the street and never separated again. Oddly, Camus continued to have many other affairs. His secretary had to keep a list of young women who were to be put right through to him at the Gallimard offices, and of others who were to be told he was unavailable. He and Casarès agreed that since they could not have everything, they would live by what they called the "75 percent rule." They existed mostly for each other, with some gaps. Ultimately, however, for Casarès, this meant that she could not even attend Camus's funeral.

> The Fall *seems to be Camus's best novel, and the stories show a life that* The Plague *and perhaps even* The Stranger *no longer have.*

Hard as this was for Casarès, Camus's irregularities were even harder on his wife. Unable either to leave Francine or curb his appetites, Camus finally drove her to a nervous breakdown. When he won the Nobel Prize in 1957, they went to Stockholm together for the sake of appearances, even though they were living apart. Camus was aware of his moral problem, even if many of his admirers were not, and it may have had something to do with his frequent confessions of weakness. In *The Fall* (1956), the protagonist makes a lengthy confession about all the women he seduced or harmed, one he may even have allowed to die, while appearing to the world to be an upright man. Though told humorously and with no little irony, the narrator's confessions may be Camus's as well.

It is in light of all of these political and psychological circumstances in the 1950s that we must read *The First Man.* What appears to be facile nostalgia floats over an immense abyss. Amid the Algerian apocalypse and personal troubles, Camus was trying to preserve an image of youthful innocence from total oblivion and perhaps make a statement as well. The critic Paul DeMan, writing without knowledge of *The First Man* and before his own past as a pro-Nazi writer was known, took Camus to task for believing that "he could shelter mankind from its own contingency merely by asserting the beauty of his own memories." DeMan wickedly went on to conclude that Camus the writer was like Camus the young man and soccer goalie: he did not enter the fray but merely defended a disappearing society from attacks against it. While the charge is unfair in many ways, DeMan had a point.

Yet the personal and political uncertainties and paralysis during the 1950s had some good effects for Camus. In an unforeseen divergence from his plan, he began writing the short stories that eventually were collected as *Exile and the Kingdom.* These powerful stories display a wider range of human life and emotion than appears in the earlier work. One story, "The Fall," grew into a long, intricate monologue that had to be published separately as a short novel. The speaker, Jean-Baptiste Clamence, a former Parisian lawyer living in Amsterdam, provides an anatomy of the moral hypocrisy of his time, and perhaps of Camus himself, in language that often becomes epigrammatic: "A single sentence will suffice for modern man: he fornicated and read the newspapers."

Simone Hié (upper left), Camus's first wife, was bright and beautiful, but suffered from a morphine addiction. Camus's second marriage, to Francine Faure, pictured here (lower left) with their two children, Jean and Catherine, lasted longer but was almost as tumultuous as the first. Although he had many mistresses, Camus's passion for the actress Maria Casarès (right), whom he met during the war, never subsided.

At first, these works were relatively neglected and disparaged, perhaps because they were so different from what Camus's readers had come to expect. Today, *The Fall* seems Camus's best novel, and the stories show a life that *The Plague* and perhaps even *The Stranger* no longer have. Some unanticipated impulse was making itself felt, an impulse that broke loose in 1958, when he began *The First Man.*

The First Man has been described as a book about a man in search of a father, and that is a central part of protagonist Jacques Cormery's story. The novel opens on the night of Cormery's birth, during a downpour, as his father, together with a sympathetic Arab, drives a wagon bearing Cormery's mother, already in labor, to their new home in Algeria. A note in the appendix may explain part of the significance of this scene: "At 40, he realizes he needs someone to show him the way and to give him censure or praise: a father. Authority and not power."

This strikes an unusual note in Camus, as does the whole novel, which is highly autobiographical and personal. Forty years after the death of his father, Camus (like Cormery in the novel) visited a military cemetery and discovered, with a shock that is physical as much as emotional, that his father died at 29. Until then, Camus had little interest in his unknown progenitor. But the silent graveyard confrontation with the fact of unfulfilled aspirations spurred Camus, as it does the fictional Cormery, to find out more about his family's Algerian past.

The larger saga of Algeria, the Tolstoyan dimension the author projected for *The First Man,* had not yet been sketched when Camus died. This is particularly unfortunate because Camus would have produced a balanced account of Algerian colonial experience; which, for all its moral ambiguities and outright horrors, had something heroic to it.

The manuscript of *The First Man* has been consulted by scholars in the years since Camus's death, and some parts of the story are fairly widely known. What is less known, and what alters our overall view of Camus, is the emphasis he gives to the aliterate, basically ahistorical silence of the people from whom he sprang. It is one of Camus's admirable qualities that his family, which knew nothing of civilizations, history, or wars other than their immediate effects on family members, never caused him shame or self-doubt. Those silent lives buffeted by nature and history were, for him, reasons for pride, not embarrassment. They were part of that great, wordless mass of humanity that, since the beginning of time, has had to face life without intellectual illusions. As Cormery says at one point, for all his travels and experience in a larger world, "they were greater than I am."

Prominent among these mute figures, almost to the point of obsession, is Camus's mother, Catherine. If much of *The First Man* involves the search for a father, some of the narrative and fragments at the end of the volume suggest that Camus intended to dedicate the book to his mother. In fact, he contemplated an unusual literary strategy: some scenes would be presented as they would appear to an average literate person, others as they would appear to a woman, like Camus's mother, whose everyday vocabulary ran to about 400 words. Dedicating the entire book to her, Camus explained, would add the irony that it would be an expression of love and admiration for a person, and a whole world, that could never understand it.

Though, like any writer, Camus changed, there is also much continuity in his emotional universe. For example, the very first entry in his

Returning to Belcourt

In this scene from The First Man, *we follow Jacques Cormery (Camus's fictional alter ego) as he returns from school to his apartment in a poor working-class neighborhood of Algiers.*

At seven o'clock came the rush out of the *lycée;* they ran in noisy groups the length of the rue Bab-Azoun, where all the stores were lit up and the sidewalk under the arcades was so crowded that some times they had to run in the street itself, between the rails, until a trolley came in sight and they had to dash back under the arcades; then at last the Place du Gouvernement opened up before them, its periphery illuminated by the stalls and stands of the Arab peddlers lit by acetylene lamps giving off a smell the children inhaled with delight. The red trolleys were waiting, already jammed—whereas in the morning there were fewer passengers—and sometimes they had to stand on the running board of a trailer car, which was both forbidden and tolerated, until some passengers got off at a stop, and then the two boys would press into the human mass, separated, unable in any case to chat, and limited to working their way slowly with elbows and bodies to get to one of the railings where they could see the dark port with its big streamers outlined by lights that seemed, in the night of the sea and the sky, like skeletons of burned-out buildings where the fire had left its embers. The big illuminated trolleys rode with a great racket over the water, then forged a bit inland and passed between poorer and poorer houses to the Belcourt district, where the children had to part company and Jacques climbed the never lighted stairs toward the circle of the kerosene lamp that lit the oilcloth table cover and the chairs around the table, leaving in the shadow the rest of the room, where Catherine Cormery was occupied at the buffet preparing to set the table, while his grandmother was in the kitchen reheating the stew from lunch and his older brother was at the corner of the table reading an adventure novel. Sometimes he had to go to the Mzabite grocer for the salt or quarter-pound of butter needed at the last minute, or go get Uncle Ernest, who was holding forth at Gaby's café. Dinner was at eight, in silence unless Uncle Ernest recounted an incomprehensible adventure that sent him into gales of laughter, but in any event there was no mention of the *lycée,* except if his grandmother would ask if he had gotten good grades, and he said yes and no one said any more about it, and his mother asked him nothing, shaking her head and gazing at him with her gentle eyes when he confessed to good grades, but always silent and a bit distracted; "Sit still," she would say to her mother, "I'll get the cheese," then nothing till the meal was over, when she stood up to clear the table. "Help your mother," his grandmother would say, because he had picked up *Pardaillan* and was avidly reading it. He helped out and came back to the lamp, putting the big volume that told of duels and courage on the slick bare surface of the oilcloth, while his mother, pulling a chair out of the lamplight, would seat herself by the window in winter, or in summer on the balcony, and watch the traffic of trolleys, cars, and passersby as it gradually diminished. It was, again, his grandmother who told Jacques he had to go to bed because he would get up at five-thirty the next morning, and he kissed her first, then his uncle, and last his mother, who gave him a tender, absentminded kiss, then assumed once more her motionless position, in the shadowy half-light, her gaze lost in the street and the current of life that flowed endlessly below the riverbank where she sat, endlessly, while her son, endlessly, watched her in the shadows with a lump in his throat, staring at her thin bent back, full of an obscure anxiety in the presence of a misfortune he could not understand.

His mother, Catherine Camus

first notebook, started in his early twenties, speaks of childhood poverty and the crucial importance of mothers: "The bizarre feeling that the son has for his mother constitutes *his whole sensibility.* The manifestations of that sensibility in the most diverse fields is adequately explained by hidden memory, material from his youth (a glue that sticks to the soul)." Read in isolation, this passage might appear to be either a truism or a confirmation of vaguely Freudian intuitions. But Camus's relationship to his mother has profound and particular echoes in his other work.

The mother who is dead before the action of *The Stranger* begins, it is now clear, belongs only to Camus's early "absurd" phase. And the indifference of her son, Meursault, is mostly an absurdist literary device. More normative is the presence of the mother in *The First Man,* who carries a startling, and almost defining, meaning for Camus's work and sensibility. Camus's mother was an odd type: illiterate, taciturn to the point of muteness, distant, and, to an outside eye, cold. (His grandmother was the more active presence in the household, and a violent one at that.) Most boys would have resented such a mother, but Camus made her a kind of ideal figure of rugged human love, a representative of the silent people who accept life and death with calm equanimity.

In terms of pure literary craftsmanship, Camus reveals himself here as a highly capable painter of scenes from life, whether they be set in the lycée, on the beach, in the streets, or at home. There is a great deal of color, taste, sound, and smell that is largely absent from the novels that were admired for their spareness and intellectual rigor. *The First Man* shows Camus's old genius for making fiction do the work of thought, but he is less concerned here to strip the story down to bare essentials. In fact, the story's main interest is its recreation of the lost life of Algiers, a world that nurtured the sensibility of the author and his fictional counterpart.

All his life, Camus pursued a kind of personal quest beyond or above politics, especially in his fiction. In some ways, the quest was philosophical. Although Camus received the *Diplôme d'études supérieures* in philosophy from the University of Algiers, both he and his professors knew that he would never make a proper academic philosopher. It was not that Camus was incapable: his essay *"On a Philosophy of Expression* by Brice Parain" shows philosophical gifts that could have been developed further, had he wished. But there was too much personal engagement in Camus's philosophizing and too little technical reasoning to satisfy the academic philosophers. A journal entry from 1935, just around the time he was finishing his university studies, expresses Camus's sense of his own path: "One only thinks through images. If you want to be a philosopher, write novels."

What kind of philosopher Camus became is difficult to specify. After their break with Camus, Sartre and his collaborators took him to task for the philosophical simplicity and second-hand knowledge in his work, especially *The Rebel.* But just as a standard political reading of Camus provides too narrow a focus, readers who approach him with the wrong philosophical expectations miss a crucial dimension of his work. Like Nietzsche, Camus valued the ancient Greeks, not the philosophers but the pre-Socratic thinkers and poets, as he construed them. Plato is too otherworldly for Camus, who always proclaimed loyalty to the earth and made a lucid recognition of the beauties and brutalities of the world—a joyful forgetting of death in the frank embrace of life—into a kind of personal ideal.

We might even think of Camus as a Stoic or Epicurean in the ancient sense of those terms. The original Stoics were not merely grim heroes; nor were the Epicureans pleasure addicts. Instead, both pursued a rational enjoyment of the world among friends, a resignation to inevitable evils, and a state of deep calm in the soul. Though much of that shared ethos harmonizes with the endurance of the simple people described in *The First Man,* Camus's love of beauty and the world was a bit too exuberant for either ancient school. Nevertheless, several entries in his notebooks show that he thought of himself as trying to find a kind of religious order: "The real problem, *even without God,* is the problem of psychological unity (the only problem really raised by the operation of the absurd is that of the metaphysical unity of the world and the mind) and inner peace. . . . Such peace is not possible without a discipline difficult to reconcile with the world. *That's where the problem lies.* It must indeed be reconciled with the world. It is a matter of achieving a *rule of conduct in secular life."*

Tolstoy's troubled pacifism and humanitarianism, his moral stature, and his irregular Christianity, and even his domestic problems, we now see, have striking parallels in the life and career of the later Camus.

This brings us to a crucial point. One of the more attractive features of Camus's thought and art to many readers is his sense of the sacred. By all accounts, his family in Algeria was only nominally Catholic and he made his First Communion at the insistence of his grandmother for social rather than religious reasons. Otherwise, the family seems to have been entirely non-practicing. Nothing conventionally religious appears in *The First Man.* In fact, a note states baldly: "Christ did not set foot in Algeria," perhaps echoing Carlo Levi's *Christ Stopped at Eboli.* In later years, Camus would describe religion as treason to the stoic endurance of his family. Yet something in Camus, even during his youth, suggested a deep religious sense to those who knew him.

Because of a certain tone and attitude in his work, it is often said that Camus might have become a Christian had he lived longer. But there is little reason to doubt his own words on the matter: "I feel closer to the values of the classical world than to those of Christianity. Unfortunately, I cannot go to Delphi to be initiated!"

Yet if Camus is pagan, he is also post-Christian, and Christian influences mark his work. He has a profound sense of the disunity of the human soul that parallels religious ideas such as original sin. Camus once described himself as an "independent Catholic" to his friend Paul Raffi and even allowed that a Christian reading of *The Fall* was legitimate. (Every element in the name of the single speaker in *The Fall,* Jean-Baptiste Clamence, has clear Christian overtones, as does the very title of the book.) Camus's highly successful stage adaptation of Faulkner's *Requiem for a Nun* in the late 1950s and several of the stories in *Exile and the Kingdom* involve dark and primitive spiritual themes. But in the final analysis, his was a pagan voice—though an unusual one. As he said in an interview shortly before he died, "I have a sense of the sacred and I don't believe in a future life, that's all."

"That's all," however, covers quite a bit of ground. Camus early became and remained a Nietzschean, of the rare sweet-tempered variety. In the same briefcase that held the unfinished manuscript of *The First Man,* there was also a copy of *The Gay Science.* Camus agreed with Nietzsche that Christianity had damaged the human race's image of itself. More seriously, he thought Christianity had inspired a neglect of justice and joy in this world in anticipation of happiness in the next. And like Nietzsche, Camus regarded the way back to real virtues as involving a confrontation with the abyss and a heroic response.

But Camus was not simply a blind disciple of Nietzsche. In Camus's work, there is no hint of the Nietzschean scorn for the great masses of people too hamstrung by Christianity and the usual human-herd instincts to pursue the heroic ideal. Camus was too aware of his own failings and too sympathetic to the human predicament for such arrogance.

And Camus had too great a love and reverence for the way of life and kinds of people who appear in *The First Man.*

Camus was powerfully attracted by the notion of a return to simple happiness after a plumbing of existential depths—for modern intellectuals. Whatever relationship this stance has to the truth about ancient Greece (probably very little), it was his task to make the simple greatness of his poor Algerians visible to the literate world. In the last analysis, it may be this Camus, the Camus of post-Christian pagan piety and the expansive energy emerging toward the end in *Exile and the Kingdom, The Fall,* and *The First Man,* that says the most to us in the post-Cold War world and that will endure. We may now also have to think about this Camus in unexpected company—that of Leo Tolstoy.

Such a pairing seems odd only if we insist on the spare, existential Camus as the essential man. The Camus of the first phase is certainly closer to Kafka and Dostoyevsky as one of the radical explorers of the modern predicament. By the 1950s, however, Camus said he preferred re-reading Tolstoy. Even earlier, in a note to himself, Camus revealed that the example of Tolstoy's life was much on his mind: "I must break with everything. If there is no desert at hand there is always the plague or Tolstoy's little railway station."

Tolstoy's troubled pacifism and humanitarianism, his moral stature and his irregular Christianity, and even his domestic problems, we now see, have striking parallels in the life and career of the later Camus. More pointedly, Tolstoy's descent into the confused wreckage of modern culture in search of "what men live by" unexpectedly anticipates Camus's own quest. Tolstoy saw in his Russian peasants and Camus in his *piednoirs* some simple virtue and calm hope that the intellectual and political world spurned. Tolstoy remains the much larger figure, of course. But we will never know how much closer their intellectual odysseys might have brought them had Michel Gallimard's car not strayed from the road that winter day, sending Camus to the grave at an age when Tolstoy had just reached the height of his powers.

The Future That Never Came

In August the world will solemnly mark the 50th anniversaries of Hiroshima and Nagasaki. Their devastation in 1945 inaugurated an age fraught with doomsday anxieties: the fear of Armageddon, of uncontrolled proliferation, and, more recently, of nuclear terrorism. Yet even before the Cold War began to fade, many countries were quietly retreating from the nuclear temptation. Mitchell Reiss explains why—and what can be done to encourage the trend.

Mitchell Reiss

Mitchell Reiss, a Wilson Center Guest Scholar, was special assistant to the U.S. national security advisor from 1988 to 1989. He is the author of Bridled Ambition: Why Countries Constrain Their Nuclear Capabilities, *published by the Woodrow Wilson Center Press and distributed by Johns Hopkins University Press. He is currently writing and consulting on the relationship between technology and foreign policy.*

Half a century ago, World War II ended in two blazing flashes of heat, light, and devastation. The radioactive clouds that rose over Hiroshima and Nagasaki on those two fateful days in August 1945 cast a dark shadow over what historian John Lewis Gaddis has called "the long peace" that followed. Within seven years, the United States tested a fusion device 1,000 times more powerful than the atomic explosive that flattened Hiroshima and killed more than 100,000 Japanese. By then, the Soviet Union also possessed its own atomic bomb and would soon explode a thermonuclear bomb. It seemed a foregone conclusion that many other countries, in the quest for national security and international military and technological prestige, would seek and, inevitably, obtain nuclear weapons.

During the darkest periods of these 50 years, there seemed to be only one question on many people's minds: when and where would the next Nagasaki occur? Few could have believed that every advanced country in the world would not want the bomb, and few would have imagined that such a "winning weapon" would not again be used in military conflict. Yet despite the wars and innumerable crises that have embroiled the nine countries known or believed to have acquired nuclear weapons (India, Israel, and Pakistan remain officially mute on the point), and despite the creation of nuclear warheads numbering in the tens of thousands, not one of these weapons has been used in war since Nagasaki. Never before in military history have countries exercised such restraint with the destructive power at their disposal.

Nor have nuclear arms proved to be the irresistible temptation that many feared they would be. Not only have nations such as Germany and Japan eschewed them, but some countries that possessed either the weapons or the means to build them have quietly (and without much fanfare in the press) retreated. Even North Korea, the greatest saber rattler of recent years, has avoided all-out confrontation on its suspected nuclear weapons program.

Instead of the dreaded global nuclear conflagration, the 50 years since Nagasaki have provided the world with an unexpected nuclear education. These weapons have proved much less useful and far more costly than anybody expected. The imperative now is to recognize these lessons and to apply them in the post–Cold War world.

To the nuclear physicists of the early 1940s, the future had an ominous cast. Scientists working on the wartime Manhattan Project quickly recognized the dangers of unbridled postwar competition in atomic arms. They knew far better than their political masters that science knows no borders and that the American nuclear monopoly could not last.

The Manhattan Project itself was a cooperative venture among the United States, the United Kingdom, Canada, and scientists from France. Its distinguished international cast, including Denmark's Niels Bohr, Germany's Hans Bethe, Hungary's Leo Szilard, and Italy's Enrico Fermi, was a living example of the cosmopolitan nature of scientific inquiry. The United States might keep its own atomic secrets (and even that proved impossible), but it was inevitable that other countries—perhaps many others—would eventually penetrate the mysteries of the atom on their own. The British physicist James Chadwick, whose experiments in the early 1930s revealed the inner structure of the atom, described his thoughts during the war: "I realized that a nuclear bomb was not only possible—it was inevitable.... Everybody would think about them before long, and some country would put them into action."

Even before the end of the war, these fears prompted Leo Szilard and other scientists working at the Metallurgical Laboratory of the University of Chicago, where history's first controlled-

From *The Wilson Quarterly*, Spring 1995, pp. 46-48, 50-66. © 1995 by Mitchell Reiss. Reprinted by permission of the author.

fission chain reaction took place in a squash court under Stagg Field in December 1942, to propose that the United States share its special knowledge with the world through a supranational organization. In return for receiving the peaceful benefits of the atom—chiefly, "energy too cheap to meter," in the phrase of the day—these nations would forgo autonomous nuclear research and development projects. The alternative was almost too horrifying to contemplate. Philip Morrison, a physicist who worked on the Manhattan project, wrote immediately after the war: "If we do not learn to live together so that science will be our help and not our hurt, there is only one sure future. The cities of men on earth will perish."

The first two decades of the nuclear age seemed to bear out some of the worst fears of the scientists. The poet W. H. Auden declared the postwar era an "age of anxiety." The bone-chilling prospect of a hundred Hiroshimas prompted policymakers to give serious thought to dispersing America's population to the countryside and even to building cities underground. The world-renowned British philosopher and pacifist, Bertrand Russell, was so alarmed by the nuclear peril that he recommended in 1946 that the United States launch an atomic attack against the Soviet Union if Moscow refused to help form a world government.

At first, hopes ran strong that atomic energy could be placed under international control. In a speech at the United Nations in June 1946, financier Bernard Baruch, the U.S. representative to the United Nations Atomic Energy Commission (UNAEC), proposed to transfer control of all the world's "dangerous" atomic activities, including fuel-production facilities, to just such a supranational authority. "Nondangerous" activities, such as the use of radioactive isotopes in medical research, would remain in national hands, monitored by the new agency. But only after these controls were in place would the United States relinquish the bomb. This plan, which now seems either hopelessly utopian or thoroughly cynical, was a serious attempt to prevent global disaster. "Let us not deceive ourselves: we must elect world peace or world destruction," Baruch declared.

The Baruch plan foundered on growing Soviet-American tensions. The Soviets offered a fundamentally different plan: the United States would eliminate its nuclear stockpile within three months, and an international control scheme would be developed in later negotiations. Two years of desultory political jousting followed before the UNAEC suspended its work in frustration. After Moscow exploded its first atomic device in August 1949, several years earlier than expected, most remaining enthusiasm for international control died, as did most talk in the U.S. scientific community of "one world or none."

Other countries, it was recognized, soon would be able to uncover the technological mysteries for themselves. As German physicist Werner Heisenberg warned in February 1947, the development of atomic bombs was "no longer a problem of science in any country, but a problem of engineering." In 1950, tens of millions of people around the world signed the Stockholm Appeal, a petition demanding that atomic bombs be outlawed as "weapons of terror and the mass destruction of whole populations." Audiences in the United States flocked to see *The Day The Earth Stood Still* (1951), a Hollywood Cold War fantasy in which a benevolent visitor from outer space lands a flying saucer in Washington to warn humanity of its peril: the human race will destroy itself and perhaps the universe if it does not bring an end to the arms race.

Great Britain became the third member of the atomic club in October 1952, detonating a bomb on board a ship near the Monte Bello Islands off the coast of Australia. (No Americans were invited to observe the test, in retaliation for Washington's curtailment of the flow of nuclear information to London after World War II. The test, declared the British defense minister, showed that Britain was "not merely a satellite of the United States.") Later that month, at Enewetak Atoll in the Pacific, the United States exploded the world's first hydrogen bomb. It was built despite the opposition of some top nuclear scientists, including Enrico Fermi and J. Robert Oppenheimer, who objected that such a "superbomb" could serve only as a weapon of genocide, not as a useful military device. "Mike," as it was called, gouged out a crater three miles wide and half a mile deep. Less than a year later, the Soviet Union exploded its own crude H-bomb. The arms race was on in earnest.

Inaugurating their famous "doomsday clock" in 1947, the scientist-editors of the *Bulletin of the Atomic Scientists* had set the minute hand at seven minutes to midnight; after the Mike test it edged five minutes closer. President Dwight D. Eisenhower, concerned about the growing cost of the U.S. defense effort and by the inability of the Western European countries to muster sufficient military forces to counter the Soviet threat, authorized in 1953 a "New Look" defense strategy. By emphasizing the use of battlefield (tactical) nuclear weapons to repel an attack, the New Look accelerated "vertical" proliferation: the enlargement of superpower arsenals. Now there would be nuclear artillery shells, demolition mines, and short-range missiles.

At the outset of Ike's presidency, 20 countries possessed independent nuclear-research projects that might allow them eventually to build the bomb. Eisenhower won worldwide applause in December 1953 when he announced his Atoms for Peace initiative before the United Nations. Coupling partial disarmament with the expansion of peaceful uses of the atom around the world, he proposed that the United States, Soviet Union, and United Kingdom "make joint contributions from their stockpiles of normal uranium and fissionable material to an International Atomic Energy Agency (IAEA)." This would have the effect of reducing the amount of material available for the manufacture of weapons—though it would handicap the Soviet Union more than the United States. The IAEA would act as a kind of nuclear-materials bank for countries with peaceful nuclear-energy programs.

By the time the IAEA came into existence in 1957, however, Eisenhower's original disarmament idea was all but forgotten. The IAEA, based in Vienna, was now designed to promote the peaceful uses of atomic energy and to act as a watchdog to ensure that nuclear technology was not diverted to military ends, an important function that it still performs today.

Another potential route to disarmament was a ban on nuclear testing. The idea gained impetus when American H-bomb tests at Bikini atoll in 1954 showered radioactive fallout over a broad swath of

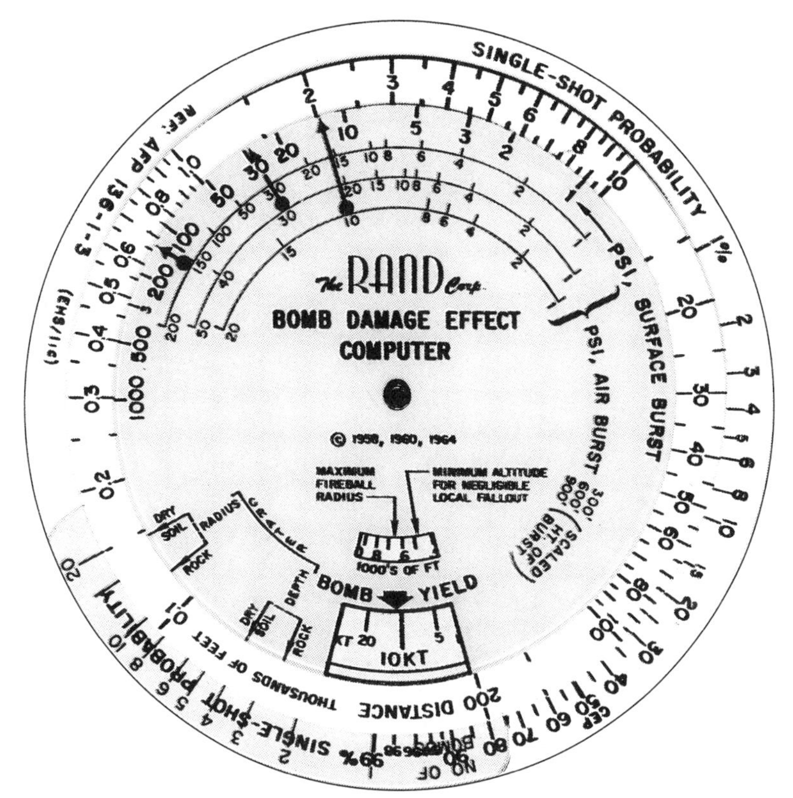

A Cold War artifact: defense specialists used the Bomb Damage Effect Computer to estimate such things as the extent of fallout and the size of fireballs produced by bombs of different sizes.

the Pacific, forcing the highly publicized evacuation of several islands. To the horror of the world, the crew of the *Lucky Dragon,* a Japanese tuna trawler that chanced to be nearby, contracted radiation sickness, and one of the men died. In Japan fear spread that fish, a staple of the national diet, had become contaminated. Forty million Japanese signed petitions calling for the abolition of nuclear weapons. Traces of fallout were later found in milk and other substances in the United States and elsewhere.

The public's sudden awareness of radioactivity raised a new kind of alarm, the threat of insidious nuclear contamination. The preoccupation with poisoning was reflected in such things as Nevil Shute's 1957 best seller *On the Beach,* with its eerie portrait of Australians carrying on as they await an invasion of deadly fallout produced by a world war that has destroyed the Northern Hemisphere.

Led by Indian prime minister Jawaharlal Nehru, the Non-Aligned Movement denounced the nuclear powers and demanded a total ban on nuclear testing. In January 1958, a petition signed by 11,000 scientists from around the world calling for an end to nuclear tests was presented to UN Secretary-General Dag Hammarskjöld. But the agreement that emerged five years later, the Limited Test Ban Treaty, prohibited tests only in the atmosphere, in outer space, and underwater. Because underground tests were still permitted, the treaty did little to slow either nuclear testing or the bomb's spread. The chief U.S. test-ban negotiator, Averell Harriman, later lamented that it was merely an environmental-protection measure.

Meanwhile, other hurdles to nuclear proliferation, such as scientific expertise and engineering competence, were being lowered; the global diffusion of civilian nuclear research and power reactors by the United States, Great Britain, France, and (with much tighter controls) the Soviet Union was another cause for concern.

Nuclear power plants have no direct use in bomb making, but possession of the technology allows a country to develop a cadre of trained scientists and engineers with the skills and knowledge to develop fuel reprocessing and other technologies needed to make a bomb. A 1958 American study, *1970 Without Arms Control,* predicted that "by 1970, most nations with appreciable military strength will have in their arsenals nuclear weapons—strategic, tactical, or both."

Two years later, in February 1960, an explosion in the Sahara made France the fourth member of the nuclear club. The British scientist and writer C. P. Snow predicted that "within, at the most, 10 years, some of these bombs are going off. . . . That is the certainty."

Speaking before the United Nations in 1963, President John F. Kennedy voiced the apprehension felt by many of his contemporaries: "I am haunted by the feeling that by 1970 . . . there may be 10 nuclear powers instead of four, and by 1975, 15 or 20. . . . I see the possibility in the 1970s of the president of the United States having to face a world in which 15 or 20 or 25 nations may have these weapons. I regard that as the greatest possible danger and hazard."

In 1964, China became the world's fifth nuclear power. By this time, every country that was technically competent to build nuclear arms, save Canada, had done so. China's test, the first by a member of the developing world, accelerated international efforts to halt the bomb's spread. New treaties restricting weapons in space and in Latin America were drawn up. In the United Nations, the Eighteen-Nation Disarmament Committee abandoned its work on comprehensive disarmament and turned instead to nonproliferation. Its efforts led to the Treaty on the Nonproliferation of Nuclear Weapons (NPT), signed by 61 countries in 1968.

Under the NPT, the non-nuclear states pledged to forswear nuclear weapons and to accept IAEA safeguards on their peaceful nuclear programs. The members of the nuclear club formally agreed not to help other countries to arm themselves. (China and France, however, did not sign the treaty until the 1990s.) In Article VI, they agreed to pursue negotiations on "cessation of the nuclear arms race at an early date, and to nuclear disarmament." The day the treaty was signed, July 1, 1968, the United States and Soviet Union announced the beginning of the Strategic Arms Limitations Talks (SALT).

But several countries that had no intention of swearing off the atom did not sign the NPT. With French help, Israel had developed a nuclear capability years earlier. In India, Prime Minister Lal Bahadoor Shastri had concluded in 1964 that China's nuclear blast left him no option but to permit research on "peaceful" nuclear explosives. On May 18, 1974, the Indians got their bomb. (Prime Minister Indira Gandhi received news of the successful test in code words: "the Buddha smiles.") From China and India, the chain reaction led to Pakistan. Prime Minister Zulfikar Ali Bhutto had already vowed that his country would acquire nuclear weapons if India did, even if his people had "to eat grass or leaves, even go hungry" to free up the necessary resources. New Delhi's nuclear test energized Pakistan's quest for an "Islamic bomb." South Africa decided that it too needed nuclear arms. The world appeared well on its way to fulfilling Kennedy's nightmare vision.

II.

The Cold War, however, ended not with the expected bang but a whimper—or at least a long, exhausted exhalation. Its passing has eased the world's most extreme anxieties about the nuclear age. Less than a decade ago, Armageddon seemed even more imminent to some than it had in Kennedy's day. "The world is moving inexorably toward the use of nuclear weapons," wrote a commentator in the *Journal of the American Medical Association* during the early 1980s, expressing a fairly common view. By 1984, the editors of the *Bulletin of the Atomic Scientists,* alarmed by the Reagan administration's military build-up and by the superpowers' increasingly bellicose rhetoric, had inched their famous minute hand to three minutes to midnight, as close to apocalypse as it had been since the early 1950s. Visions of "nuclear winter," a new nightmare scenario of how the world would slowly die in the aftermath of a nuclear war, terrified the public, much as *On the Beach* had 30 years before. Critics warned that the arms race was propelling the world toward disaster.

Then, suddenly, it was over.

The disintegration of communism and of the Soviet Union itself after the Berlin Wall fell in November 1989 brought the quickest imaginable end—short of war itself—to the old fears. True, there had been significant change before 1989. Modest arms-control agreements during the 1970s that placed ceilings on certain categories of nuclear systems were replaced in the latter half of the 1980s with ambitious agreements that cut deeply, such as the 1987 Intermediate-Range Nuclear Forces Treaty. But today the superpowers can't disarm fast enough to suit themselves.

In the fall of 1991, George Bush and Mikhail Gorbachev announced sweeping reciprocal unilateral reductions in deployed tactical nuclear weapons. The 1991 START I Treaty virtually halved the number of U.S. and Soviet strategic nuclear warheads. If START II is fully implemented, the superpowers will cut their strategic nuclear arsenals by more than 80 percent from their Cold War peak. The United States and Russia will dismantle more than 15,000 warheads. The chief drag on disarmament now is not military or political but technical: the limited number of U.S. and Russian facilities equipped to dismantle these warheads and safely and securely store the leftover nuclear material.

Yet there has scarcely been time to celebrate. From the allied victory in the Persian Gulf War, barely more than a year after the fall of the Berlin Wall, came the sobering discovery that Saddam Hussein's Iraq was well advanced on a secret project to build an atomic bomb. In late 1992, the IAEA uncovered (with the help of U.S. spy satellite imagery) another case of nuclear cheating, this time in communist North Korea. Earlier this year, news reports suggested that Iran was perhaps only five years away from developing a bomb, much closer than previously estimated. According to a 1988 study chaired by veteran military analysts Fred C. Iklé and Albert Wohlstetter, 40 countries will be able to produce nuclear weapons by 2000.

To borrow the metaphor used by R. James Woolsey, former director of the U.S. Central Intelligence Agency, the Soviet bear may be dead, but the forest is still full of poisonous snakes. The sprawling nuclear archipelago of the former Soviet Union, a complex of laboratories and factories employing almost one million physicists, chemists, metallurgists, engineers, and technicians, could well turn out to be a breeding ground for new nuclear snakes. Highly skilled scientists now earn less in a month than what an American teenager brings home after a day working the cash register at McDonald's. The temptations of going to work for a foreign power or even a terrorist group must be considerable.

Amid squalid military and deteriorating political conditions in Russia, there is also reason to worry about the safety and security of stockpiles of nuclear warheads and the fissile materials that can be used to make bombs. This is not an idle fear. To take one especially rich cache of bomb material out of circulation, operatives in a covert U.S. effort code-named "Project Sapphire" spirited 600 kilograms of highly enriched uranium (HEU), enough for perhaps 30 to 40 nuclear bombs, from a storage site in a remote and desolate corner of Kazakhstan. (However, 300 kilograms of HEU stored nearby was inexplicably left behind.) Nuclear smuggling from the former Soviet Union to the European black market is well documented. In one of the most alarming cases, police in the Czech Republic acting on an anonymous tip last year seized six pounds of highly enriched uranium, about one-sixth the amount needed for a bomb. Three men were arrested at the time, but who was behind the plot and where the uranium was bound remain a mystery.

But the great and still largely unrecognized surprise is that contrary to what scientists, statesmen, and ordinary people have assumed since Hiroshima and Nagasaki, the countries of the world have not rushed to arm themselves with nuclear weapons. Some have recognized the drawbacks and limitations of these weapons; others have gone so far as to conclude that they are a liability.

While the news media have focused with grim fascination on the new nuclear-nightmare scenarios of the post–Cold War world, several countries possessing nuclear weapons programs or harboring nuclear ambitions have, almost unnoticed, stepped back from the brink. They have slowed, halted, or even reversed their activities. Even North Korea, the most xenophobic and isolated country in the world, recently agreed to measures that promise over the course of 10 to 12 years to eliminate its ability to build nuclear weapons. These developments are without precedent in the nuclear age.

Very often people talk about the perils of proliferation as if nothing has changed during the course of the world's long experience with nuclear weapons.

The Nuclear World

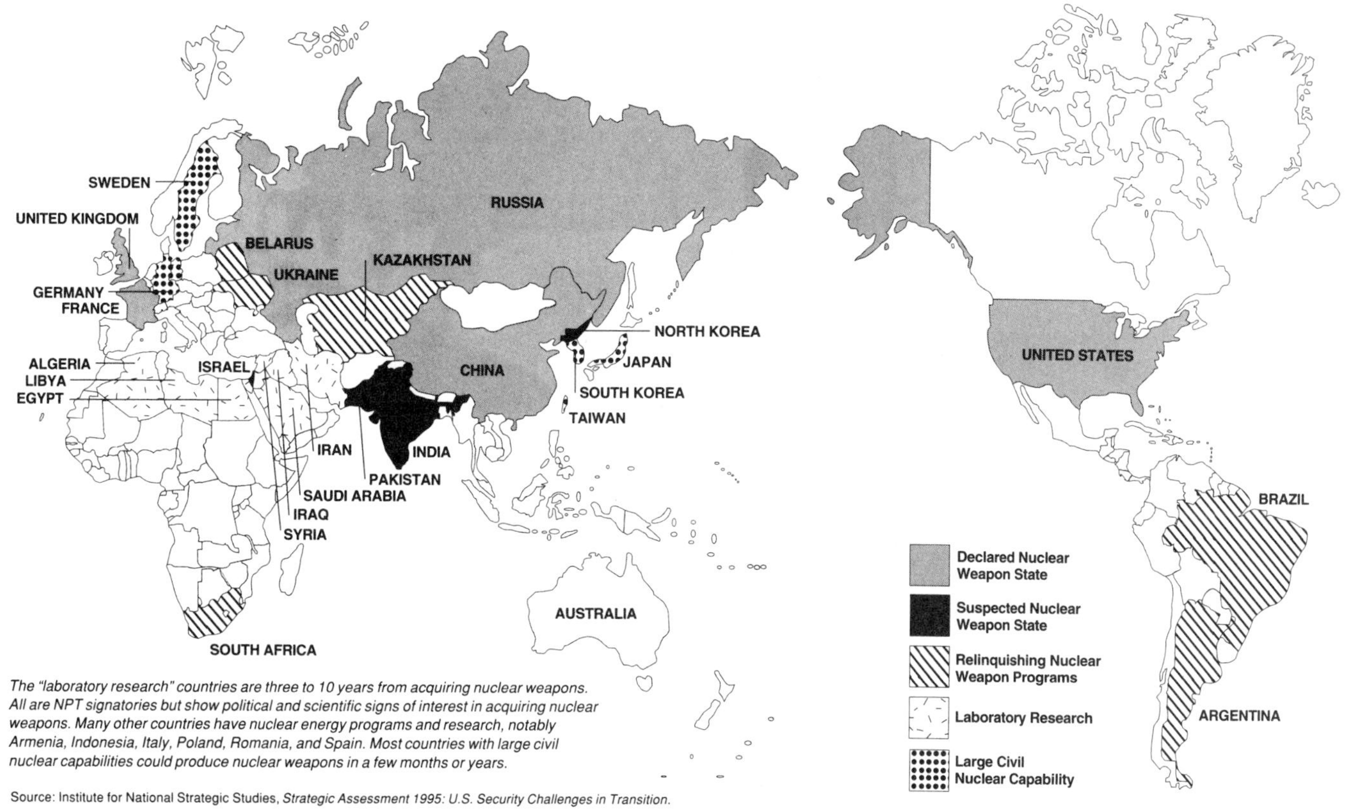

Declared Nuclear Weapon State
Suspected Nuclear Weapon State
Relinquishing Nuclear Weapon Programs
Laboratory Research
Large Civil Nuclear Capability

The "laboratory research" countries are three to 10 years from acquiring nuclear weapons. All are NPT signatories but show political and scientific signs of interest in acquiring nuclear weapons. Many other countries have nuclear energy programs and research, notably Armenia, Indonesia, Italy, Poland, Romania, and Spain. Most countries with large civil nuclear capabilities could produce nuclear weapons in a few months or years.

Source: Institute for National Strategic Studies, *Strategic Assessment 1995: U.S. Security Challenges in Transition.*

But this half-century of "mutual assured destruction" between the superpowers as well as nuclear crises in Cuba in 1962, the Middle East in 1973, and during the India-Pakistan clash of 1990 have provided the world with a profound nuclear education. The fact that an arsenal of some 30,000 strategic and tactical nuclear weapons could not preserve the Soviet Union, and may even have hastened its collapse, has raised new questions about the value of nuclear arms. The deep cuts scheduled by Moscow and Washington, moreover, have lowered the weapons' prestige value.

The stunningly large (and unexpected) bills that have started to fall due from the arms race also give other nations pause. The cost of dismantling nuclear weapons, storing excess plutonium and other dangerous materials, and repairing the environmental damage caused by more than 50 years of weapons research and production is huge. The United States will have to spend between $30 billion and $100 billion to clean up various installations, including production facilities at Rocky Flats, Colorado, Hanford, Washington, and Savannah River, South Carolina. In the former Soviet Union, the bill could reach $300 billion, although it is unlikely that anywhere near that amount will be found. And who knows what other costs of this radioactive legacy remain to be discovered? It is equally difficult to gauge the "opportunity costs" incurred by having generations of skilled scientists, engineers, and technicians devote their talents to building bombs instead of the gross national product.

All of these lessons have bred new attitudes toward nuclear weapons. In December 1991, when the Soviet Union was in its death throes, the world was confronted with the uncomfortable reality that three countries it had scarcely heard of—Ukraine, Belarus, and Kazakhstan—with leaders whom it hardly knew, now each possessed the means to devastate the United States, Europe, or any other target they chose. Thousands of Soviet tactical and strategic nuclear weapons were located on these three countries' soil. Yet each of them agreed to surrender these arms over the next few years.

Quickest to act was Belarus, site of more than 1,000 nuclear weapons. Stanislav Shushkevich, a physicist-turned-antinuclear activist after the 1986 Chernobyl disaster, used his largely ceremonial position as chairman of the Belarus Supreme Soviet to push a more rapid withdrawal than even Moscow wanted. In the West there was dread that the Muslim leaders of Kazakhstan might transfer some of its fearful nuclear inheritance—including 104 huge SS-18 intercontinental ballistic missiles, each code named "Satan"—to their radical coreligionists in the Middle East. Eager for U.S. aid and investment and wary of angering Moscow, Kazakhstan pledged in 1992 to return the SS-18s and other weapons to Russia.

Ukraine was a little more recalcitrant. The country's stolid president, former Communist Party ideology chief Leonid Kravchuk, understood that the weapons would not be terribly helpful in defending Ukraine or improving its appalling economic conditions. But they could be bartered for Ukrainian membership in useful international organizations such as the North Atlantic Treaty Organization's Partnership for Peace. Ukraine's assent was finally purchased in 1994 at the cost of hundreds of millions of dollars in U.S. denuclearization assistance and, among other things, Russian promises to forgive Ukraine's multibillion-dollar oil and gas debt and to provide fuel for the country's nuclear power plants.

For each of these three countries the nuances were slightly different, but the fundamental calculations were essentially the same. Their leaders recognized that nuclear weapons are largely irrelevant to the most pressing problems of the late 20th century: civil war, ethnic and tribal conflict, mass migration, AIDS, economic backwardness, and international terrorism. More and more, these weapons appear to be elaborate and expensive anachronisms. There is not even much scientific prestige to be gained by building a bomb—now, after all, a 50-year-old technique.

A nuclear arsenal rarely promotes domestic prosperity, fosters better relations with neighbors, enhances national security, or wins international prestige. Nuclear weapons programs are more likely to siphon off scarce scientific and engineering talent, trigger a costly nuclear arms race with a regional adversary, sow mistrust among allies, inhibit the transfer of sensitive technologies needed for economic development, and invite international ostracism. This "winning weapon," moreover, turns out to be almost too terrible to use.

That is one reason why the popular fear of nuclear terrorism, while not wholly unrealistic, is greatly exaggerated. Nuclear blackmail is a staple of international spy thrillers such as Dominique Lapierre and Larry Collins's *Fifth Horseman* (1980), in which Libya's Muammar Qaddafi tries to force the United States to support the establishment of a Palestinian state by threatening to blow up New York City. But terrorists and leaders of "rogue" nations face many of the same constraints limiting others who seek to promote a political agenda. Would a nuclear blast advance their cause, or would it unify a horrified international community against them? If one is bent on violence, isn't it far easier to strike at a symbolic target with conventional means? The terrorists who attacked the World Trade Center, after all, made their explosive from a mixture of fertilizer and diesel fuel. This is not to mention the still-daunting technical tasks of manufacturing and safely handling a nuclear bomb.

Only one country in history has unilaterally and voluntarily eliminated its own fully developed nuclear arsenal: South Africa. That it was done virtually without fanfare or international acclaim and headlines is regrettable, since South Africa's experience illustrates some of the new realities of nuclear weapons. Immediately after becoming president in September 1989, F. W. de Klerk ordered that the country's nuclear weapons program, including an arsenal of six nuclear devices that had taken a decade to build, be dismantled. By July 1991, the highly enriched uranium from the warheads had been removed and melted down and most of the non-nuclear components had been destroyed.

These extraordinary steps were part of a much larger design. The coming transfer of power to the black majority certainly helped sway de Klerk, but so did South Africa's growing sense of security from external threats following the negotiated removal of Cuban troops from Angola in December 1988 and the dwindling of Soviet influence in southern Africa. A nuclear arsenal, moreover, would hinder South Africa's efforts to become a respected member of the international community.

The power of international opinion is not merely a matter of rhetoric. Countries that insist on maintaining nuclear programs pay a price in the international arena. They are excluded from international organizations such as the IAEA. They may be denied loans and other assistance by the World Bank and other multilateral institutions, as well as the Japanese and some other aid givers. They are also subject to formal and informal embargoes on the transfer of a variety of sensitive technologies, ranging from supercomputers to civilian nuclear power plants to induction furnaces used in the fabrication of high-tech metals. Some countries (such as Belarus) now clearly hope that there may be as much prestige to be gained from forgoing nuclear weapons as from possessing them.

International standing was a powerful consideration in the slightly less dramatic December 1991 decision by two long-time rivals, Argentina and Brazil, to accept international safeguards on all their nuclear activities. During the 1980s, both countries seemed intent on producing nuclear bombs—more for prestige purposes, apparently, than because one posed any threat to the other. Although relations between the two countries improved in mid-decade, the breakthrough came in the late 1980s with the accession to power of two dynamic civilian leaders, Carlos Menem in Argentina and Fernando Collor in Brazil. The two presidents were eager to carve out larger roles on the international stage (and in the international economy) for their countries, and, not incidentally, for themselves. And that meant currying favor with the international community, especially the United States. Brazil, in addition, faced a threat from its long-time financial supporter, Germany, to cut off economic assistance by 1995 if Brasilia did not abandon its nuclear pretensions.

Whereas Argentina's Raul Alfonsín could declaim to popular approval in the mid-1980s that he would break before he would bend to the wishes of the United States and the industrialized West, his successor, Carlos Menem, stated that he would much prefer Argentina to be the last country in the First World rather than the first country in the Third World. (The Argentine foreign minister put the idea more colorfully when he declared that he wanted ties between Argentina and the United States as intimate as *"relaciones carnales."*) For Argentina and Brazil, the price of full admission to the international community was placing their nuclear programs under IAEA safeguards.

The United States had a hand in all of these success stories, directly cajoling, convincing, or coercing some countries and more indirectly influencing others through its support for international export controls, the NPT, and IAEA safeguards. But Washington probably played its most important role in May 1990, when the world may have come as close to nuclear war as it had since the 1962 Cuban missile crisis.

That spring, the explosive issue of Kashmir was again agitating India and Pakistan. Amid strikes, bombings, and assassinations by Muslim separatists and fundamentalists in the Indian state of Kashmir, Indian prime minister V. P. Singh ordered a crackdown. Singh's government accused the Pakistanis of aiding their Muslim brethren; there was an exchange of hot rhetoric and before long there were military maneuvers along the India-Pakistan border. In May, U.S. intelligence concluded that Pakistan had assembled nuclear bombs. President Bush instantly dispatched

Deputy National Security Advisor Robert Gates to mediate.

In Islamabad, Gates was blunt: "Our military has war-gamed every conceivable scenario between you and the Indians, and there isn't a single way you win," he informed Pakistan's leaders. Gates then visited New Delhi, where he warned that Indian air strikes against insurgent training camps in Pakistan-held Azad Kashmir might prompt Islamabad to use nuclear weapons immediately rather than as a last resort to save the regime. Gates was successful; both sides pulled their troops back.

In the annals of nonproliferation, however, the story of India and Pakistan must be counted a draw rather than a success. The two countries have not halted their nuclear programs, even though over the years they have exercised some self-restraint. India has not detonated a nuclear device since its first explosion more than 20 years ago. Pakistan has never conducted a nuclear test and reportedly stopped producing weapons-grade uranium in 1990 when President Bush cut off U.S. military and economic aid to Islamabad. Neither country has deployed nuclear weapons or ballistic missiles or even officially declared that it has nuclear weapons.

Nevertheless, the subcontinent remains a potential nuclear flash point. India can assemble 15 to 25 nuclear weapons on short notice and Pakistan can assemble six to eight, probably within a few days, according to U.S. government estimates. If nuclear war ever breaks out in the world, many defense analysts believe, the Indian subcontinent is the most likely location.

A more familiar "draw" is Israel, whose opaque nuclear posture was perfectly expressed by strategist Yigal Allon's remark in the mid-1960s: "Israel will not be the first to introduce nuclear weapons in the Middle East, but it will not be second either." Although widely suspected of having as many as 200 nuclear weapons, Israel has neither deployed nor detonated one, although some observers believe it was behind a mysterious flash in the South Atlantic detected by a U.S. satellite in September 1979.

Even nonproliferation success stories remain unfinished. Backsliding may yet occur; political commitments can be renounced and legal obligations can be flouted. Nuclear recidivism is a possibility, with North Korea the most likely candidate. A small number of countries will undoubtedly persevere in seeking to acquire nuclear arms or holding onto those they already have. Nuclear weapons are still thought by some to confer international status and enhance national security. For others, they remain useful tools for intimidating neighbors and regional rivals. These countries will pay the price of being hated in return for being feared.

There are military defenses against such transgressors—the United States, for example, is developing ballistic missile defenses. But nuclear weapons can be delivered by boat, truck, or several other means. Over the long term the most effective defenses are political.

III.

For four weeks this spring, delegates from 172 countries will meet in New York City to decide the fate of the Nuclear Nonproliferation Treaty. The conference can be seen, in effect, as a global referendum on the nature of the international system for the next century.

The absence of any solid security architecture to replace the Cold War's bipolar system has already contributed to a general unease in the world. Regional tensions have increased in many areas; ancient antagonisms, ethnic strife, and religious hatreds have resurfaced, literally with a vengeance in some cases. Without vigorous international regimes to control the spread of nuclear arms and other weapons of mass destruction, the world will certainly become an even more dangerous place.

Since it took effect in 1970, the NPT has been the most important means of easing nuclear anxieties around the world. It provides countries with reasonable assurances that their neighbors, potential rivals, and enemies are not arming themselves with the world's ultimate weapon.

Along with the inspection and verification system provided by IAEA safeguards (which would end with the NPT's demise), the treaty is a vital strand in a web of interlocking, overlapping, and mutually reinforcing political pledges and legal commitments. This web also includes strict export controls that deny sales of sensitive technologies, such as supercomputers, that can be helpful in building nuclear weapons; nuclear weapons-free zones, such as those established in Latin America and the South Pacific (and soon to be created in Africa); strong multilateral alliances; ballistic missile defenses to protect U.S. and allied forces; and "negative" and "positive" security assurances, which are vows by the nuclear powers that they will not use or threaten to use nuclear weapons against other countries and will come to their defense should they face nuclear aggression.

The NPT and the IAEA safeguards system are not panaceas and they are certainly not fail-safe. They do not *determine* decisions by countries on whether to acquire nuclear weapons. But this harsh truth overlooks the positive influence they do exert. Submitting to comprehensive IAEA safeguards and taking NPT membership are earnests of the intent not to develop nuclear weapons. Although the sincerity and durability of these pledges may be questioned in some cases, such as Iraq, Iran, and North Korea, they are an accurate barometer of the nuclear intentions of the vast majority of countries.

Many of the states not possessing nuclear weapons that will participate in this spring's conference complain that the nuclear powers have not kept their side of the original bargain, notably their promise to share the benefits of peaceful nuclear technology—chiefly nuclear power. They are threatening to block the treaty's renewal or extend it only for a limited period. They believe, as Ambassador Makarim Wibisono of Indonesia, the leader of the 77-member Non-Aligned Movement at the NPT conference, observes, that "efforts to combat the danger of proliferation have been used to preserve and promote a technological monopoly in the hands of nuclear supplier states and relegate the developing countries to a position of continued dependency." Some of the nonnuclear states also want speedier superpower disarmament, or even a firm target date for the total elimination of nuclear arsenals.

At the heart of all of these concerns is the worry that if the treaty is extended indefinitely and unconditionally this spring, the non-nuclear states will lose a valuable (and, for many countries, their only) means of leverage in their quest for wider technology transfer and nuclear disarmament. But the consequences of following through on their "nuclear extortion" would be very serious for these countries: without an NPT, their security would be at far greater risk than that of the states with nuclear weapons.

Anything less than the extension of the treaty indefinitely (or for a very long time) would be a failure. Even if the NPT is not canceled outright but only extended for a short period, countries such as South Korea, Japan, and Germany would be tempted to hedge their bets against the treaty's eventual collapse by increasing their ability to build bombs. Analysts at the RAND Corporation have dubbed this ratcheting up of nuclear potential "virtual proliferation."

Total collapse of the NPT would have more clear-cut results. Gradually but inexorably, the bomb would spread. Perhaps the treaty's demise would galvanize the leading states to devise new institutions and arrangements to halt proliferation. But a failure to agree on extension would itself suggest a breakdown in the global consensus against proliferation.

The stakes ultimately go beyond nuclear weapons. The treaty's demise would cripple efforts to restrain the spread of other weapons of mass destruction. Specialists warn that it could doom the Chemical Weapons Convention, which has been signed but not yet ratified by many countries, and vastly complicate efforts to strengthen the verification provisions of the Biological and Toxin Weapons Convention. (The Central Intelligence Agency estimates that 25 countries currently have programs to build nuclear, chemical, or biological weapons.) Even under the best of circumstances, controlling these weapons in the future will probably prove even more difficult than the regulation of nuclear arms. A world that cannot agree on the latter will be very unlikely to achieve the former.

Thinking about the Unthinkable, Again

Some U.S. analysts argue a new military strategy is needed to deal with nuclear threats in the post–Cold War world. In the National Interest *(Winter 1993–94),* **Eliot Cohen** *of the School for Advanced International Studies at Johns Hopkins University offers one such view.*

Three forces have come together to increase the danger of proliferation in the 1990s. First, over the decades technological know-how has diffused, putting nuclear potential within the range of a number of states. Second, the collapse of the Soviet Union has created a vast pool of scientists available for hire to work on such programs. It has also, in all likelihood, made nuclear material, including weapons, available for sale to potential proliferators. At the same time, the implosion of the Soviet state has removed from the world stage a major military power that had come to see the benefits of preventing nuclear proliferation. Third, and ironically, the Persian Gulf War has made it clear that no country can match the United States in a conventional conflict. To a hostile general staff, nuclear weapons look increasingly attractive as means of deterring either the Yankees or (more likely) their local clients, who provide the necessary bases from which American military power operates.

It is hard to see how any American strategy, no matter how clever the conception or assiduous the implementation, could do more than meliorate the fundamental problem. . . .

Of course it makes sense to pursue marginal remedies [such as anti-missile defenses and more aggressive efforts to help dismantle the Russian nuclear arsenal] as energetically as possible. . . . But both technically and politically they can achieve only limited success. The problem of detecting mobile missiles during the Gulf War offers a good example. Even if American pilots had received instantaneous warning of Scud launches (and some did, when they witnessed the actual firing of the missiles), they simply could not locate the launchers with sufficient accuracy to bring weapons to bear on them. . . . If ever the United States manages to defeat the ballistic missile, the low-flying (and soon, stealthy) cruise missile will prove a more difficult challenge yet. As for the talk of pre-emptive war, would that the United States were willing to engage in it, should the need arise. But really, who can imagine a president authorizing a large-scale, unilateral air and possibly ground attack against a country that has done no direct harm to the United States or its allies? The days of Osirak-type raids on a single, easily located and above-surface nuclear facility are over. Secrecy, camouflage, deception, and dispersion will make preemption a far more extensive and uncertain operation than ever before.

It is altogether proper to be gloomy about the proliferation problem. In addition to undertaking [other measures], the American government needs to prepare itself, materially, organizationally, and psychologically, for the day after the first nuclear weapon is used in anger. . . . The material preparation requires, among other things, a renewal of investment in the development of sophisticated nuclear weapons which the United States might use to destroy a nascent nuclear arsenal. It is technically feasible to develop nuclear weapons that could do useful work against such limited targets, without incinerating cities or blasting into the air large quantities of radioactive dust. The organizational preparation entails a kind of war planning unfamiliar to the armed forces in the recent past—crippling, punitive strikes against opponents whom the United States cannot disarm, or sudden, preemptive blows thrown at very short notice. The psychological preparation will prove the most difficult of all, however, for it will require a confession that none of the cleverly conceived arms-control efforts (export controls, buy-back plans, and international agreements) will do more than defer the dark day on which, for the first time since Nagasaki, a country uses an atomic bomb as a weapon of war.

IV.

In the early 1960s, a young physicist named Herman Kahn published a provocative book on thermonuclear war challenging the world to "think about the unthinkable." But it turned out that war, even with thermonuclear weapons, was easy to contemplate. The truly unthinkable challenge, as Kahn's critics noted, was to map out a realistic path toward a nuclear-free world. Until recently, this kind of thinking was casually dismissed, left to the liberal fringes of the peace and disarmament community. Hard-headed professional nuclear strategists, armed with their RAND Corporation "bomb wheels"—which allow them to estimate the size of the crater and the extent of the fallout from a blast of a given nuclear yield—preferred instead to discuss throw weights, MIRVs, and the seemingly ever-gaping "window of vulnerability."

Yet some especially visionary (or cynically calculating) politicians envisioned a different future. In January 1986, Mikhail Gorbachev called for a nuclear-free world by 2000. Nine months later at Reykjavík, Iceland, Ronald Reagan, the quintessential Cold Warrior, called for the elimination of all nuclear weapons (although his horrified advisers quickly qualified his statements). In 1988, Prime Minister Rajiv Gandhi of India proposed before the UN's Special Session on Disarmament a phased disarmament that would lead to a world without nuclear weapons by 2010. Recently a number of retired senior U.S. officials, including former secretary of defense Robert McNamara and General Andrew Goodpaster, former supreme allied commander in Europe, have urged that the United States dedicate itself to the elimination of all nuclear weapons.

In fact, under both domestic law and international treaty, the United States is already obligated to eliminate all of its nuclear weapons. The legislation that established the U.S. Arms Control and Disarmament Agency in 1961 and Article VI of the NPT both stipulate this goal. Is it really a desirable one?

Even among the dry policy analysts, there is serious discussion of moving toward a nuclear-free world. The end of the U.S.-Soviet rivalry, it is said, has vastly reduced the need for nuclear weapons. Their role in the Pentagon's war planning, for example, has greatly diminished. The United States, moreover, is highly unlikely ever to be the first to use these weapons in a conflict. Indeed, one former U.S. official argues that Washington would not likely use them even if the United States were attacked first. Nuclear weapons, in other words, are moving toward obsolescence.

At the other extreme, strategic analyst Kenneth N. Waltz of the University of California at Berkeley contends that "more might be better." The further spread of nuclear weapons to many countries might have a stabilizing influence on international life, he believes. Waltz's thinking is based on the Cold War experience of deterrence, the "balance of terror" that helped keep the peace between the United States and the Soviet Union. "The likelihood of war decreases as deterrent and defensive capabilities increase," Waltz argues. "New nuclear states will feel the constraints that present nuclear states have experienced."

Waltz's theory has been much discussed among academics during the past decade, and its flaws have been thoroughly vetted. It is not at all clear, for example, that other countries could reconstruct the same delicate balance of deterrence—and even the Soviet-American stand-off was full of perils. There are many other difficulties: a nuclear power might, for example, have an incentive to strike pre-emptively at a neighbor just developing a bomb. And as the number of nuclear powers rises, so does the chance of a classic "madman scenario" or, more likely, a fatal error in the more mundane command-and-control systems of the weapons.

Yet there is some wisdom in Waltz's argument, at least insofar as it applies to the *current* line-up of nuclear powers. Nuclear weapons do generally promote prudence and caution, in their possessors as well as in others. They deter others from using not only nuclear arms but perhaps chemical and biological weapons as well. Under some circumstances, they may even prevent conventional warfare among the states possessing nuclear weapons.

There are, in other words, benefits to be reaped from these ultimate weapons. But these benefits would survive even if the United States and other nuclear powers vastly reduced their arsenals. Borrowing a page from India and Pakistan, it may be possible to move to what specialists call "non-weaponized" deterrence. It is too late to "disinvent" the bomb, and impossible to lock its "secrets" away. But nuclear weapons can be taken off alert, deactivated, and disassembled. Such a step would greatly lengthen the "nuclear fuse." It would fall short of total nuclear disarmament. It could, however, be a significant way station on the long road toward a goal that seemed hopelessly utopian only a short while ago. Before it can be reached, we will need to reduce the role and number of nuclear weapons in international affairs and, ultimately, render them irrelevant to political life.

On this path to zero, perhaps the greatest danger is not from the spread of the weapons themselves but from our forgetting how very different they really are. For this reason, Harold Agnew, the former director of the Los Alamos National Laboratory, once suggested that a nuclear bomb be detonated in an isolated part of the ocean once each decade with world leaders in attendance. Then they would hear, see, and *feel* its awesome power. The danger is that as the echoes of Hiroshima and Nagasaki grow more distant with the passing of time, the devastation and unspeakable horror of those events may fade from our collective memories. We forget at our peril.

The End of the Twentieth Century

Historical reflections on a misunderstood epoch

John Lukacs

John Lukacs is the author of numerous books of history, among them Historical Consciousness: Or the Remembered Past; Budapest 1900; *and* The Duel: Ten May to Thirty-One July. *His new book, from which these reflections are drawn, is* The End of the Twentieth Century and the End of the Modern Age, *published by Ticknor & Fields.*

I. ON THE LENGTH OF CENTURIES

The twentieth century was a short century. It lasted seventy-five years—from 1914 to 1989. Its two main events were the two world wars. They were the enormous mountain ranges that dominated its entire landscape. The Russian Revolution, the atomic bomb, the end of the colonial empires, the establishment of Communist states, the dominion of the two world superpowers—the United States and the Soviet Union—the division of Europe and of Germany: all of these were the consequences of the two world wars, in the shadow of which we have been living. Until now.

The nineteenth century lasted ninety-nine years, from 1815 to 1914, from the end of Napoleon's wars to the start of the First World War. The eighteenth century lasted 126 years, from the beginning of the world wars between England and France (of which the American War of Independence was a part) until their end at Waterloo. The seventeenth century lasted 101 years, from the destruction of the Spanish Armada in 1588 (of which the establishment of a united France was one important consequence) to 1689, the year after the so-called Glorious Revolution in England, when the main threat to England became France and no longer Spain.

At that time, three hundred years ago, the very word "century" was hardly known. The Oxford English Dictionary notes its first usage, in English, in 1626. Before the middle of the seventeenth century, "century" meant a Roman military unit of one hundred men. Then it acquired another meaning, that of one hundred years.

That was one of the symptoms of the beginning of our modern historical consciousness. Another of its symptoms was the creation of the terms "ancient" and "modern." The three historical ages Ancient, Medieval, and Modern became accepted notions three hundred years ago. (One example: they appear in the texts of two second-rate German chroniclers, Hornius and Cellarius, in the 1680s.) So in 1689 some people thought that the Middle Ages were over, though no one thought then that the world order of the seventeenth century had ended. In 1815, too, no one knew that the end of the Atlantic world wars between England and France had come. Everyone, both enemies and sympathizers of the French Revolution, was concerned with the prospect of great revolutions erupting again. There were revolutions after 1815, but the entire history of the nineteenth century was marked by the absence of world wars for ninety-nine years. Its exceptional prosperity and progress were due largely to that.

We know that the twentieth century is over. We know this, at least in part, because of the evolution of our historical consciousness—which is something different from a widespread knowledge of history. That evolution may be the most essential ingredient of the history of our minds.

The twentieth century will end officially on the last day of the year 2000. But the true turning points (and turning points are different from milestones) in the lives of civilizations, of nations, of individuals, do not coincide with the decimal calendar. Also, history is not of one piece; the turning points are not absolute. So many violent symptoms of the cracking up of the Edwardian or Victorian order were present before 1914. So many of the habits, physical and mental, of the Middle Ages lived on after the seventeenth century. The end of the twentieth century is not wholly completed. The shadows of the two world wars have not yet disappeared. But they are retreating: they no longer dominate the historical landscape. *That* is why, by and large, the twentieth century *is* over.

II. ON THE BOLSHEVIK AND THE PRESBYTERIAN

I was born in 1924, ten days after Lenin had died and three days before Woodrow Wilson would die. The ideas, indeed the personalities, of these ephemeral protagonists of the early twentieth century belonged to the nineteenth. In 1914, by the time the twentieth century opened, their views of the world were already outdated. That their ideals seemed to triumph for a very short time, when they seemed to be two different and opposite architects of a new world, was not inconsequential; but they did not matter much in the long run. To think that the world could be made safe for democracy (or, more precisely, that democracy would make the world safe) was a shortsighted and self-serving idea. So was that of international Communism. That is obvious in the 1990s, at the end of the twentieth century; but it was already evident in 1914, at its very beginning.

Lenin, like Marx, believed that classes were more important than nations. The very opposite proved true

In 1914 Marxism suffered a huge blow from which it never really recovered. Marx and his followers and successors, including Lenin, believed that classes were more important realities than nations; that the economic motive determined what people thought and believed. The very opposite was true. In 1914 a German workingman had more in common with a German factory owner than with a French workingman. The same was true of French or British or American workingmen and their managers. In 1914 international Socialism melted away at once in the heat of nationalist enthusiasms, especially in Germany. But already two years before that, the young Mussolini had discovered that he was an Italian first and a Socialist only second. (He *was* a man of the twentieth century.) There was a Communist revolution in Russia in 1917, but what Lenin achieved was not an international revolution. To the contrary, it was Russia's withdrawal from Europe. To survive the civil war in Russia, Lenin had to let international Communism go by the board. After World War II, Communist states were erected in Eastern Europe, but not because of revolutions or because of the popular appeal of Communism. They were put there because of the national triumph of Russia over Germany, which resulted in the Russian occupation of most of Eastern Europe.

In 1914 Wilson too thought that the outbreak of the war in Europe was a reactionary event, a consequence of the outdated political and social order of the Old World. He was wrong: the carnage of that war became terrible because of nationalism and democracy. It was no longer a war between traditional armies of traditional states. Entire nations were rushing at each other, fighting to the end, making any kind of a compromise peace impossible. After the war Wilson was repudiated by the majority of his countrymen; years before his death he was, like Lenin, a broken man, not only physically, and his War to End All Wars as well as his idea of the League of Nations proved to be the sorriest of failures.

Yet—such is the irony of history—the ideas of this pale Presbyterian professor-president were more revolutionary than those of the Bolshevik radical from the middle Volga region. Wilson's propagation of the idea of national self-determination helped to bring about the destruction of entire empires in 1918. Seventy-five years later that idea of national self-determination is destroying some of the very states that Wilson helped to create: Yugoslavia and Czechoslovakia, for example. It has also destroyed the structure of the Soviet Union, that inheritor of the old Russian empire. Communism is dead, but national self-determination is very much alive.

This means—contrary to those who see the history of the twentieth century governed by the Cold War, by the struggle between Communism and democracy, incarnated, respectively, by the Soviet Union and the United States—that we are witnessing not only the end of the division of Europe that had been tacitly accepted at Yalta in 1945. We are beginning to witness changes in the political geography of Europe that was established in the first years of this century, in 1919 at Versailles.

III.
ON HITLER, THE CENTURY'S RADICAL

Nationalism, mass nationalism, was the main political and social phenomenon of the twentieth century. Its most radical incarnation was Hitler, whose unwillingness to compromise, whose ideas, and whose determination to carry out those ideas were more unyielding and radical than any other famous revolutionary leader, Lenin or Stalin or Mao.

Consider but this single, disturbing evidence: at the end of this century there are almost *no* believing Communists anywhere, not many even in the lands of the Soviet Union, where the remnant party men are merely nationalist bureaucrats. Yet there are Nazis still, admirers of Hitler, not only the remnants of an old generation but new adherents, young men and women, some open, others tight-lipped, in many countries of the world, not only in Germany and Austria.

We must not exaggerate their numbers or their influence. Still: if the mountain ranges dominating the landscape of the twentieth century were the two world wars, 1940–41 was the highest point of those mountain ranges. It was then that Hitler came very near to winning the Second World War—nearer than Germany had come in 1914 or in 1918. If he had done so, with what consequences! In a way, much of the twentieth century before 1940–41 led up to Hitler. And so much of the rest of the century, from 1941 on, was the consequence of the Second World War that he alone had begun and that was dominated by his presence until its end.

IV.
ON THE ORIGINS OF THE COLD WAR

By the time Hitler died, the division of Europe was accomplished. The upheaval at the end of the war was enormous, but there was nothing very revolutionary about that division. The eastern half (actually, one third) of Europe and of Germany was occupied and controlled by the Russians; it was to be ruled by them and by people who were subservient to them. In Western and Southern Europe, and in western Germany, the Anglo-American presence (after 1947 more and more American, less and less Anglo) helped to restore, or to establish, liberal and democratic governments. During the next forty-five years of the Cold War there would not be a single pro-Communist country in Western Europe and not a single anti-Communist country in Eastern Europe (except for Greece, which in 1944 was liberated not by the Russians but by the British).

Why, then, the Cold War at all? Because of a mutual—or, more precisely, reciprocal—misunderstanding. Soon after 1945 the Americans came to believe, and fear, that Stalin, having brutally forced Communist governments upon Eastern Europe, was ready and willing to push Communism farther into Western Europe (and western Germany). Conversely, Stalin believed, and feared, that the Americans, having established themselves in Western and Southern Europe, were willing and ready to challenge his rule in Eastern Europe. Both sides were wrong. The crude unscrupulousness of the Russians and of their Communist satellites—their obsessive propaganda and the brutality of their behavior—was a decisive contribution to these perceptions. But then so was the ideological appeal of anti-Communism, concentrating on Communism rather than on Russian national interests—and unable to recognize that precisely because of the weakness of the Communist appeal the iron curtain, that barbed-wire incarnation of the division of Europe, could not last.

There is one additional and important element that I must mention here. It involves some of the original perceptions of the Cold War's duration. In 1945 Roosevelt and the American government thought, and hoped, that the military situation at the end of the war would be temporary: that after the withdrawal of the occupying armies from most of Europe Stalin would be satisfied with the presence of pro-Russian, though not necessarily Communist, governments in Eastern Europe. That was not what Stalin wanted. He was well aware of the weakness of the Communist appeal outside the Soviet Union, which is why he preferred to have the states of Eastern Europe ruled by people whose inferior character was such that they were entirely, indeed abjectly, subservient to him. Very few Americans were aware of this inherent weakness, though Churchill was: as early as New Year's Day in 1953, when Stalin was still living and the dangerous tensions of the American-Russian Cold War were at their peak, Churchill told his secretary that if he (John Colville) lived his normal span he "should assuredly see Eastern Europe free of Communism." That meant the 1980s. Churchill's prediction was astonishingly precise. But it was long before the 1980s that the Cold War—its original character and its conditions—changed, and drastically, even though so many people were either unable or unwilling to recognize that.

V. ON THE END OF THE COLD WAR

How did the Cold War come to an end? Since 1956—perhaps even after 1953—it had been winding down. Yet the digestive problems of the Russians were insufficiently understood in the West, and especially misconstrued in the United States. From the Russians' bad table manners people concluded that their appetite was insatiable, whereas the opposite was rather true: their digestion was poor. And this condition no longer involved only political geography, the excessive quantity of their sphere; it involved, inevitably, the essence of Communism—that is, the quality of it. All over Europe, very much including Eastern Europe, and also in the Soviet Union, the remnant belief in Communism was evaporating until, in the 1980s, the realities of that evaporation became so obvious that even a Ronald Reagan could no longer ignore them. In Western Europe the Communist parties shrank year after year; in countries such as Italy and Spain they had become small-bourgeois capitalist parties, Communist in name only. *Mutatis mutandis,* the same thing happened in Eastern Europe. There a class of party members still formed the governments, but true Communist (or even Marxist) believers among them existed no longer. They were a new class of functionaries and bureaucrats, interested in nothing other than the maintenance and security of their power—for which, in a crisis, their only guarantee seemed to be the power of the Soviet Union. Some of them, like Ceauşescu in Romania, became extreme nationalists; that helped their popularity, at least for a while. By 1985–86 it became evident that while the United States no longer challenged their legitimacy, the Eastern European Communist leaders could not count on the unequivocal support of Moscow even when they were in trouble. In 1989 all of them gave up their power without risking, let alone firing, a shot. (The only exception was Romania, where there was some—not much but a little—fighting, since the security services of the Ceauşescu tribe were very large. They consisted not of Communists but of nationalist thugs serving the national dictator.)

Anti-Communists believed, and feared, that Stalin was ready to push into Western Europe. They were wrong

Much of this was true of the Soviet Union too, where, during the years of the decaying Brezhnev rule, it was increasingly obvious that the most corrupt and inefficient element in the government was the party itself. There the last believing Communists had dwindled to a small minority by the time Gorbachev appeared. His most ominous opponents were not former rock-ribbed Communists but nationalists, both without and within the Russian ethnic mass: military men and ideological nationalists, bitter as they witnessed the demolition not of Communist ideology but of the external and internal bulwarks of the Soviet state.

It is with the above in mind that we ought to consider the real nature of the occasional crises that punctuated Russian-American relations after 1956—hiccups in the digestion, delaying the winding down of the Cold War. In 1960 the Russians shot down an American spy plane, the U-2; but they shot it down over their own country, after having tolerated the crisscrossing flights of American spy planes over the Soviet Union for years. In 1961 came the Berlin Wall: but that monstrous thing was built to contain, not to expand; to keep tens of thousands of East Germans from filtering through to the West. In 1962 came the Cuban Missile Crisis: but that came about because the Russians had to do something for Castro, since they had been unwilling to guarantee him against an American invasion, which seemed to be more and more within John Kennedy's plans; and the evolution of the crisis showed that nothing was further from the Kremlin's purposes than to risk a war with the United States over Cuba. In 1968 Brezhnev sent troops into Czechoslovakia, but only after he had become sure that the Czechs would not put up a fight and that the Americans would not react; he overcame his reluctance to act when he began to worry that the disappearance of Communism in Czechoslovakia might spill over to its neighbors, including the Ukraine, which was part of the Soviet Union. In 1979 the Russians moved troops into Afghanistan, where one of its tribal chieftains, nominally a Communist, had been murdered by another nominally Communist tribal chieftain; but also because they—wrongly—feared that Jimmy Carter was about to invade the neighboring state of Iran. By that time Brezhnev's military advisers had built a large Russian war fleet, for the first time in Soviet history; but the presence of that fleet meant little or nothing in the Mediterranean. It was the American Sixth fleet that patrolled the Persian Gulf and the Lebanese coast, landing Marines there in 1982, 6,000 miles from Norfolk and only a few hundred miles from the state frontiers of the Soviet Union. The powerful Russian fleet stood by at a very respectable distance, doing nothing at all.

I wish not to be misunderstood. A bully, when feeling threatened, will act aggressively; he does not cease being a bully. The leaders of the Soviet Union were neither modest nor pacifist. But their most startling acts of intervention were made because of purposes that were defensive; they had more troubles of their own than people suspected or were willing to admit; their appetite for more foreign expansion and conquest was something quite different from being insatiable. With all the technological and analytical information at their disposal, people in charge of the enormous bureaucratic labyrinths in Washington—along with experts and, increasingly, intellectuals in high government positions—either did not see these things at all or surely not clearly enough. Worse: when people do not see something, this often means that they do not wish to see it—a condition that may be comfortable and profitable to them. That was true of many of our presidents during the Cold War, from Eisenhower to Reagan; of popular political figures, from Joe McCarthy to Oliver North; and of experts such as Henry Kissinger, who began his grand public career by touting the existence of a—as we now know, nonexistent—Missile Gap. Consequently, the Cold War lasted longer than it should have, and the United States became transformed into the very military-industrial state the prospect of which in 1960 a speechwriter put in one of Eisenhower's last public speeches—the end result being that while it is not now arguable that the Soviet Union lost the Cold War, it may be arguable whether the United States has won it.

VI. ON THE NATURE OF THE (SO-CALLED) THIRD WORLD REVOLUTIONS

One of the main reasons for the continuation of the Cold War—indeed, for some of its bloodiest episodes—was the unexpected appearance of Communist regimes in unexpected places around the globe. Until 1960 every Communist government, except for Yugoslavia and Albania, was a neighbor of either the Soviet Union or China (or, like East Germany, occupied by the Soviet army). From 1960 on, beginning with Cuba, Communist or pro-Communist governments came into being in the oddest places: Ethiopia, Angola, Suriname, Mozambique, Nicaragua, Afghanistan, Grenada. Some of these soon devolved into blood-encrusted tribal tyrannies—some of them *were* bloody tribal tyrannies from the beginning. Their self-invented "Communist" label confirmed the American

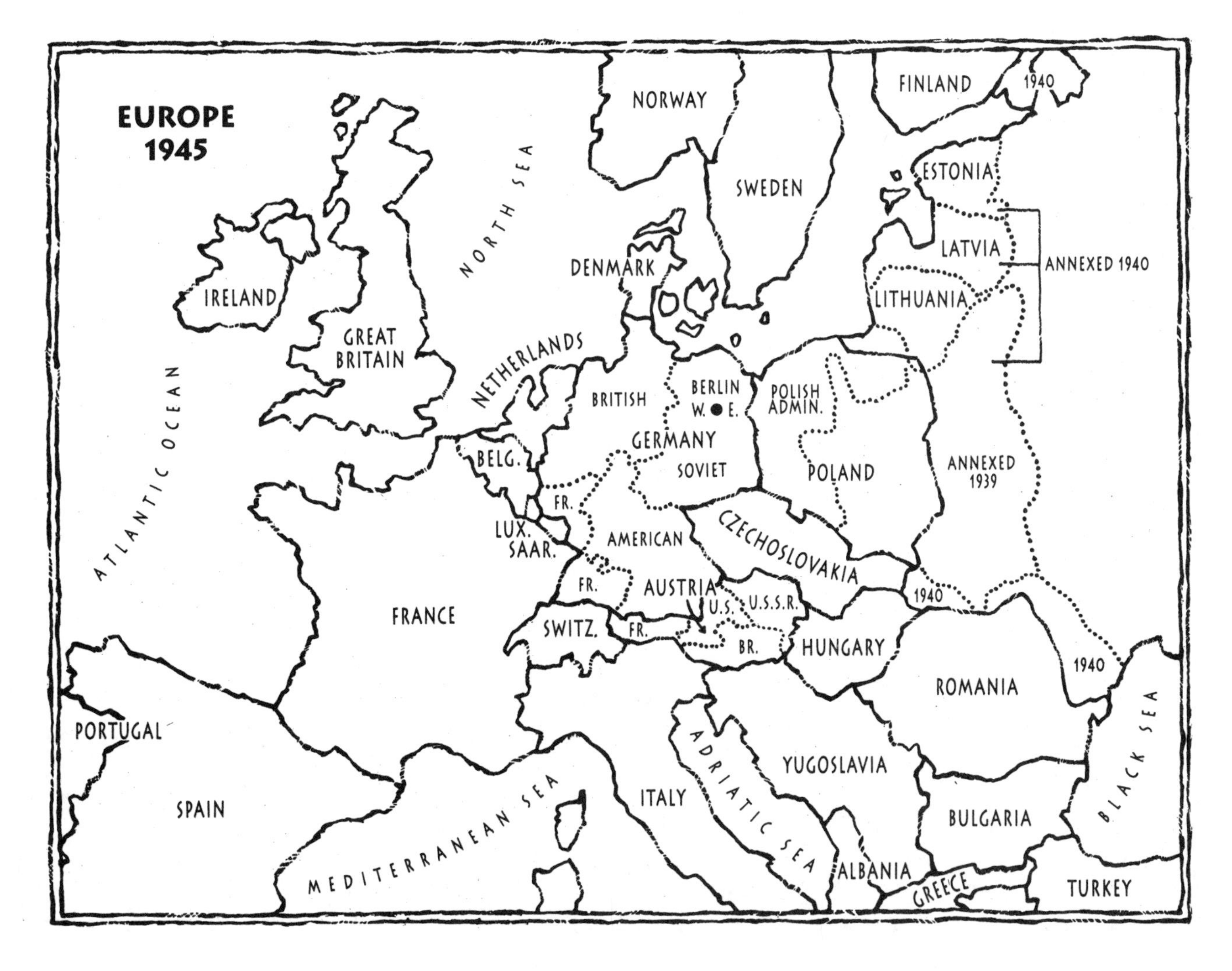

belief that the entire history of the twentieth century was marked by the titanic struggle of democracy versus Communism. Yet the Soviet Union had nothing to do with these "Communist" revolutions. Unlike the Russian-imposed Communist governments in Eastern Europe, these revolutions or coups were spontaneous, surprising Moscow as well as Washington. Often they were not even the results of local Communist agitation, of local Communist parties, of local Communist revolutionaries: Fidel Castro, for example, did not even know (or say) that he was a Communist until well after he had marched into Havana. He was a "Communist" because he was anti-American, not the reverse. (Had he arisen twenty years earlier, when the adversaries of the United States were Germany and Italy, Castro would have surely declared himself a "Fascist." Among other things, he was a great admirer of General Franco, at whose death in 1975 he declared three days of national mourning in Cuba.)

The leaders of the Soviet Union felt compelled to assist most of these newfangled allies—for a while. Yet the importance of their relationship with the United States had an absolute priority over their relations with their faraway supplicants. Russia did not have the slightest intention of establishing important Soviet bases in the Western Hemisphere or in Africa. During the last ten years, more of these "Marxist" governments gave up, except for Cuba, whose *líder maximo* had had his bitterest disappointments with the Soviet Union well before the 1980s.

Nearly two centuries ago, some thirty years after the American Revolution, some people in South America were sufficiently inspired by the example of North America to declare their own independence from the distant and weak Spanish motherland. One hundred and sixty years later few people in Washington were willing to recognize that the one common element in most of the revolutionary movements sputtering in the oddest places of the so-called Third World was a tribal hatred of foreign, in most cases white, power. That this kind of hatred was, in most instances, as unjustified as it was shortsighted is another matter. But I have to mention it here, since among other things it proves again that the ideas and the appeal of anti-colonialism (more precisely, tribal nationalism) have been more enduring than the idea of the proletarian revolution of the international working class; and that for two hundred years at least, the main agent of anti-colonialism has been the

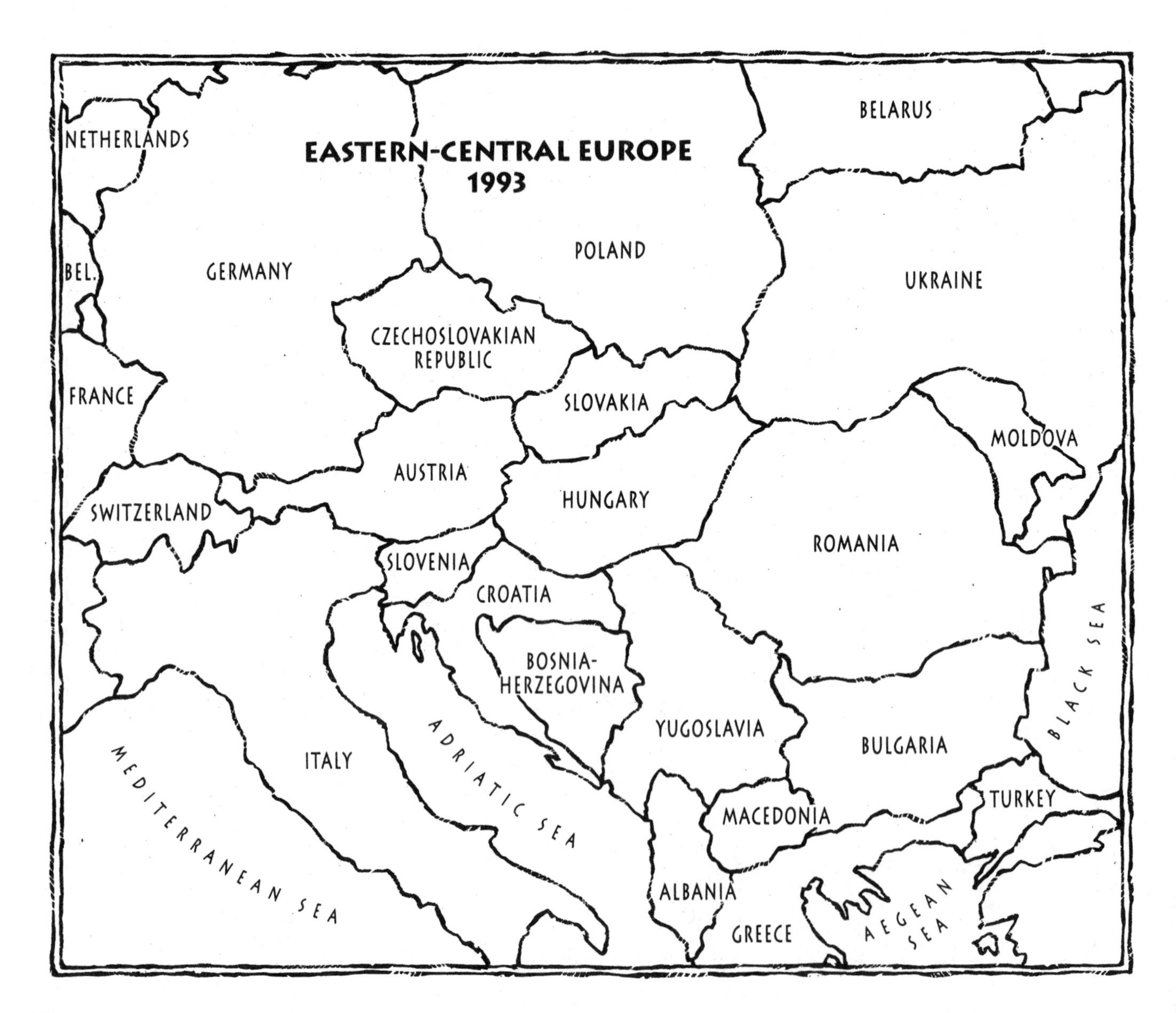

United States rather than Russia—in the twentieth century Wilson and Franklin Roosevelt rather than Lenin and Stalin.

VII. ON THE PSYCHOLOGY OF ANTI-COMMUNISM

"The insane fear of socialism throws the bourgeois headlong into the arms of despotism." Tocqueville wrote that in 1852, four years after he stood up against the socialist workers and the radical revolutionaries in the streets of Paris. A century later anti-Communism was due to more than insane fear, and it was not restricted to the bourgeois. Often it was most popular among the workers themselves, especially in the United States. (Marx ignored not only the nationalism of the proletariat—that antiquated word—but also their addiction to respectability.) Mussolini and Hitler and an endless host of demagogues could not have come to power without the popular appeal of anti-Communism. It is foolish to think that the mainspring of anti-Communism is the concern of people for their financial security. It has been far more popular and emotional than that.

The psychology of anti-Communism is a complex matter that has not yet received the attention it deserves. A dedication to truthfulness, a measure of honesty, and, yes, bravery (more precisely, a contempt for and a revulsion toward official and prevalent untruths) have been the qualities present in almost every private (or, rarely, public) expression opposed to Communism in countries and in places where Communists or their representatives have been in power. Where they have not been in power, a self-identification with anti-Communism has suggested a kind of self-satisfaction, the source of which has been, more than often, the desire for respectability, the wish to assert that one belongs within the mainstream of public opinion and within the authentic community of the nation. I have seen plenty of opportunistic Communist fellow travelers in my life (and not only in the twilight years of 1945–46 in Hungary, where I was born); I have, alas, seen even more opportunistic anti-Communists in the United States, many former leftists.

The ideology of anti-Communism contributed to the protracted nature of the Cold War. The identification of anti-Communism with American patriotism did, on occasion, damage traditional American liberties, and it contributed powerfully to the establishment of the American military-industrial state. The obsession with Communism obscured the main condition of the Cold War, which had little to do with Communism. That condition was the presence of Russian armed power where it did not belong. And now, when the Cold War is over, the temptations of many of these questionable patriots persist: unappeased by the Russian withdrawals, they go on with their propaganda to promote the dissolution of the traditional Russian state proper, trying to convince themselves and others that it is the prime interest—and task!—of the United States to propagate and impose its system of government and philosophy on most of the world, including Russia, half a globe away.

VIII. ON THE DISSOLUTION OF THE RUSSIAN EMPIRE

The historical consequences of the retreat and dissolution of empires are enormous. They last through centuries. The bankruptcy and decay of the Spanish empire led to the great Atlantic world wars between France and England. The emergence of the United States was a part of that vast chapter of history. The eighteenth-century world wars between England and France lasted 126 years; the decline and decay of the Spanish empire lasted more than 300 years, from the defeat of the Armada in 1588 to the Spanish-American War in 1898. (Eventually the United States inherited much of the Spanish empire, reaching as far as the Philippines—from which it is retreating now, as it will one day retreat from Puerto Rico.)

On the other edge of Europe the retreat and dissolution of the Turkish empire lasted a quarter millennium, from about 1683 to 1923. It led to what our ancestors called the Eastern Question (more correctly than their present successors, who keep calling the Near East the "Middle East"). The retreat and dissolution of the Turks led, among other things, to the outbreak of World War I. In the Balkans the Russians and the Austrians (and by 1914 even the Germans in Turkey) were asserting their interests; their support of their satellites led to many conflicts and small wars, threats of greater wars, and assassinations such as that of the Austrian archduke and heir in 1914. Farther to the east, the end of the Turkish empire led to many of the rational and irrational struggles that typify the Near East even now. (Were the Turks still in charge of Mesopotamia, were the Spanish still in charge of Cuba, were the British still in charge of India wouldn't we be better off? And wouldn't their subject peoples be better off? Now that is a historian's nostalgia.)

And now has come the dissolution of the Russian empire. It may be irreversible. What tremendous consequences may follow in that vastest landmass of the world, the Eurasian heartland of the globe about which geopoliticians have been speculating and scribbling since the beginning of the century?

Among the ruins of the former Soviet Union various states and statelets arise, including even some nationalities whose consciousness of their separate and distinct nationality is very recent, and who had never formed a national state, indeed any state, before. Others (Armenia and Georgia, for example) feed their minds and aspirations from long, and historically often dubious, memories of their medieval or even earlier "kingdoms," which they equate with "independence," "statehood." (Some of these Caucasian peoples had a surprising degree of economic, cultural, and political leeway even under Communist and Stalinist rule. Their tribal habits, including all kinds of illegal trading practices, were tolerated by the no less corrupt representatives of the Soviet bureaucracy in their midst.)

One great question is that of the Ukrainians. I find it difficult to believe that their sovereignty will ultimately be acceptable to the Russians, that the Russians will let them go entirely. There is the involved problem of millions of Russians living within Ukraine, as is the case also in the Baltic states. This mixture of nationalities is the main question in Yugoslavia too: were there no Serbs living within "Croatia," there would be no Yugoslav civil war now. One ought to berate the Serbs because of their violent nationalism; but the Croats ought to be berated, too, not only because of some of their misdeeds during World War II but also because it was they who wanted a Yugoslavia in 1918, just as the Slovaks wanted a Czechoslovakia then. (Both had been better off during the Hapsburg empire and state; but let that go.)

Among the ruins of the Soviet Union various states and statelets arise. Will the Russians let them go?

So many various new states and statelets arise before our eyes. They reflect the spontaneous desires of their peoples. But their promoters are ambitious politician-chieftains. While the impulse of nationalism, the desire for one's own independent national state, is one of the results of romanticism (and we are all romantics now, with the classicist rationalism of the eighteenth century gone), its promoters are political practitioners of power, attracted by their prospective emoluments, feeding their personal vanities, the perquisites of high state officialdom: the unexpected obeisances and comforts suddenly at their behest, bloated staffs, salutations, official travel.

IX.
ON THE CULTURAL WEAKNESS OF RUSSIAN COMMUNISM

If at the end of World War I (that is, at the beginning of the twentieth century) Communism had come to power in Germany, not in Russia, its influence would have been immeasurably greater. Russia and things Russian had no prestige, no attraction among Russia's neighbors. In Russia the Communist revolution succeeded; outside Russia it failed. Many of the social conditions of the peasantry and workers of the Baltic region and Poland were by and large not that different from conditions in the vast tracts of Russia; yet the local Communists, even when supported by the Red Russian armed forces, were routed in all of these countries in 1918–20. The opposite was true of Germany and things German. The German cultural influence was very large, even in those European nations that had been arrayed against Germany in the First World War. That cultural prestige, including the German system of education, was such that anything that was new and revolutionary in Germany—probably including an eventual German Communist regime—would have been emulated, whether consciously or unconsciously,

by ambitious people, radicals, revolutionaries, intellectuals. That was, after all, what happened with Hitler and German National Socialism. They had plenty of adherents and emulators in other countries (Romania, for example), where, on occasion, they were able to come to power without the presence of German armed force—something that the Russians could not count on, even at the time of or after their great military triumph in 1945.

Had a Communist system established itself in Germany, some of its achievements would probably have been impressive, especially for the workers in an industrial state. A Communist Germany would have been even more avant-garde than Weimar Germany, in many instances. Yet the fatal shortcomings and stupidities of Marxism—its materialism, its atheism, and, most of all, its shallow and insubstantial internationalism—would have weighed it down in the end.

X. THE END OF A DIVIDED GERMANY

The Russian-American division of Germany, at the center of Europe, is over. Its key date—it was the key date of the end of the Second World War, perhaps even more than the day of Hitler's suicide five days later or the official surrender of the German armed forces two weeks later—was April 25, 1945, when advancing units of the American and Russian armies met in the middle of Europe, along the Elbe River near the German town of Torgau. On the banks of that river, which carried the flooded wreckage of spring and war, American and Russian soldiers, fired with sentiments of friendship and with plenty of drink, celebrated late into the night. (That celebration was but a forerunner of a huge pro-American celebration in Moscow two weeks later.) Among the soldiers of the Fifty-eighth Russian Guards Division there may have been some whose home was Vladivostok, who came to the middle of Europe from the shores of the western Pacific. It is possible that among the soldiers of the U.S. Sixty-ninth Infantry Division there were some whose home was Seattle or San Francisco; they, too, had been sent to conquer halfway around the world. Their meeting took place not only in the middle of Germany but in the middle of European history; for Torgau is about midway between Wittenberg, where Luther's fire of great revolutions started, and Leipzig, where Napoleon's course of great victories ended. Less than fifty years have passed since then. Now the Russians are going, and the Americans will be going soon.

Sooner or later Americans will have to make another choice, a choice that has nothing to do with whether those already useless American garrisons and bases remain in Europe or not. In a few years we will see whether "Europe" becomes more "European" or more and more German-dominated—that is, whether the still largely powerless "European" institutions will develop sufficiently to assume a more definite character, capable of inspiring authentic loyalties, or whether German participation in those institutions in Brussels or Strasbourg will be not much more than formal and secondary when compared with an increasing reassertion of the primacy of German national and political interests. In the event of the latter—which, I think, is the more probable of these two alternatives—the United States and the American people may be faced with a choice between Germany and Britain.

A German-dominated Europe is a likelihood. Are the Germans immune to a revival of their nationalism?

That choice will reflect something deeper than strategic calculations. It will have emotional, cultural, and ethnic elements, as in 1914–17 and in 1939–41. Then, a decisive element was the presence and influence of a largely Anglo-Saxon, upper-class American elite, whose presence and influence have weakened greatly during the second half of the twentieth century. A reflection of that was the confrontation in the 1992 Republican Party primaries between the weak, unconvincing, and unconvinced representative of that former elite, George Bush, and the "America Firster" Pat Buchanan. Contrary to the accepted ideas—and to his own assertions—Buchanan is not really an isolationist (consider, for example—and it is a significant example—that this so-called isolationist is a strong advocate of American recognition of and support for Croatia, Slovenia, and Ukraine, as are all German and Austrian nationalists). But many of the America Firsters in 1940 were not really isolationists either. They were bitterly opposed to Roosevelt and to those Republicans who wished to engage the United States against the German Third Reich on the British side. In 1940 Hitler correctly called these Americans "radical nationalists." In that year the Anglophile internationalists among the Republicans were stronger than the radical nationalists; hence they engineered (by going around the primaries) the nomination of the anti-Fascist Willkie. In 1992 Buchanan was not the Republican nominee; but he and the nationalists may attempt to gain control of the Republican Party in the wake of George Bush's defeat. With some luck they may be able to achieve that. If that happens, their success will resound among the nationalists in many parts of the world, especially in Central and Eastern Europe.

XI. ON THE QUESTION OF GERMAN NATIONALISM

Are the Germans immune to the revival of their nationalism? Yes and no. Yes: because for most Germans the rejection of the Hitler past is not merely the result of a politic calculation. No: because that rejection is not necessarily identical with a rejection of German nationalism, including its memories. In the event of the surge of a populist nationalist party, people such as Kohl and others of his party will not be immune to the temptation to seek some kind of compromise, to adopt some of the rhetoric and some of the politics of the new nationalists of a younger generation. Again there will be more to that temptation than politic calculation. The official repudiation of the Hitler era will not cease. Nor will the cultivation of good German relations with Israel. But the time may come when at least some of the German memories of the Third Reich and of the Second World War will undergo a deeply felt revision, a matter of memory, which will be more than a matter of quarrel among historians. For, as Kierkegaard once said, we live forward but we can only think backward—and there is, of course, an inseparable connection between memory and knowledge, between a view of the past and a view of the future, between thinking and living.

XII. ON THE EUROPES, EAST AND WEST

The prevalent view of Eastern Europe in the West is wrong. According to this view, the deep crisis in Eastern Europe is economic; and its nations' uneven progress toward liberal democracy is a consequence of that. By and large—there are profound differences between, say, Albania and Hungary or, say, Serbia and Poland—the opposite of that *idée reçue* is true. The great and enduring problems are political, not economic. They involve the lust for power, not for money. (But then, this has been true of mankind ever since Adam and Eve, misunderstood by Adam Smith as well as by Karl Marx.)

The material problems (I prefer the word "material" to "economic") *are* serious. The universally accepted idea is that they are the result of forty-five years of Communist mismanagement. There is much truth to that, but it is not the entire truth. The material conditions in the lives of most Eastern European peoples are *less* different from those of the peoples of Western Europe than they were forty-five years ago (Romania may be in some respects an exception). In every Eastern European country the great majority were peasants forty-five years ago, whereas there is no country in Eastern Europe today (with the possible exception of Albania) where more than a minority are engaged in agricultural work. All over Eastern Europe people to whom such things were beyond the dreams of avarice forty-five years ago now possess their own automobiles, refrigerators, and television sets, with electricity at their disposal.

What remains true is that Communist governments delayed—and compromised—these developments considerably. Had there been no Communist regimes in these Eastern European countries, their populations would have reached their present material standards twenty-five or thirty-five years earlier. Yet even in that case they would not have reached the standards of everyday life in Finland or in Austria—the former mutilated and impoverished by the Second World War, and thereafter having to adjust its ideas of national interests to certain desiderata of Russian foreign policy; the latter partially occupied by Soviet troops until 1955. National conditions and, yes, national character remain as important as before, notwithstanding the uniformities declared by Communism. Yugoslavia pronounced its independence from the Soviet bloc in 1948, opened its borders soon thereafter, and began moving toward a mixed economy more than thirty years ago; yet even then Budapest was more of a Western city than Belgrade; and, of course, so it is now.

This brings me to the anomalies and contradictions in all economic "facts"—or, rather, in the categories defined by economists, which have scant relevance to the realities of everyday life, including its material realities. In Poland (alone in the Soviet bloc) agriculture was not collectivized; and agriculture in Poland is now worse off than in almost any other Eastern European country. Romania is the only Eastern European country whose foreign debts were wholly paid off; and material and financial conditions are worse in Romania than anywhere else in Eastern Europe. In Hungary material conditions are visibly improving, and the Hungarian national currency is now very close to Western standards of international convertibility, meaning worldwide acceptance; yet opinion polls as well as personal conversation show that Hungarians are among the most pessimistic peoples of Eastern Europe—a condition that has little to do with the Hungarian gross national product but much to do with the prosody of Magyar poetic diction, characterized by its ever falling tone.

This twentieth century is now over; and as we move into the twenty-first, Western and Eastern Europe will become more alike, as far as material conditions go. Foreign investments in Eastern Europe will assist in bringing this about; but—again, contrary to accepted ideas—they will not matter much in the long run for a number of reasons, one of them being that all foreign investors in Eastern Europe want to gather their profits in the short run. Their present advantage is the still low cost of labor in Eastern Europe, which, however, is bound to rise, sooner rather than later.

All over the world people tend to confuse international finance with economics. The former is—at least in the foreseeable future—truly international, with monies flowing rather freely across frontiers (in this respect Russia may remain an exception); but then capital has become increasingly abstract, and the more abstract money becomes, the less durable it is. Economics, on the other hand—in its proper, old, original meaning—refers to the husbanding of one's household assets, in the Greek and biblical (and also German: *Wirtschaft*) sense of the word. To believe that Slovaks or Bulgarians have now "entered" or "re-entered" the capitalist phase of their historical development is nonsense. Capitalism has grown slowly, with difficulty, in Western Europe during three hundred years, coming to its full development in the nineteenth century. That was the result of particular social, political, religious, and intellectual conditions that hardly existed in Eastern Europe then, as they do not exist now. Capitalism as well as parliamentary liberalism were nineteenth-century phenomena with little relevance to the twenty-first century, with its current material realities being obscured by an outdated vocabulary of economists.

XIII. ON THE QUESTION OF EASTERN EUROPEAN NATIONALISM

The main political reality in Eastern Europe—it is a reality and not a specter haunting it—is nationalism. The principal factor of the two world wars of the twentieth century was nationalism; and both of these wars broke out in Eastern Europe. In Eastern Europe nationalism is the only popular religion, by which I mean the only religion that still possesses a functional rhetoric. (That the traditional Western Christian religions no longer have much of a functional rhetoric may not necessarily be a loss—but only God knows about *that.*) When I say to an American nationalist that being a good American will not necessarily get one into heaven, he may be startled but he will understand, and presumably even agree. When I say to a Hungarian nationalist that just because someone is a good Hungarian he will not necessarily get into heaven, he is startled and may find it difficult to agree. Populist nationalism, as distinct from the now almost extinct variety of the liberal nationalisms of the nineteenth century, is a modern and democratic phenomenon. Populist nationalists are self-conscious rather than self-confident, extroverted, essentially aggressive, and humorless, suspicious of other people within the same nation who do not seem to agree with some of their populist and nationalist ideology. Hence they assign them to the status of minorities, suggesting—and at times emphasizing—that such minorities do not and cannot belong within the authentic body of the national people. This is, of course, yet another manifestation of the potential tyranny of a majority—which, as Tocqueville observed, is the great danger of democratic societies in democratic times.

When, in 1931, the king of Spain abdicated and a liberal parliamentary republic was proclaimed, Mussolini said that "this was going back to oil lamps in the age of electricity." He was right. Parliamentary liberalism belonged to the nineteenth century, not the twentieth. Indeed, in Spain it soon degenerated to a sorry mess, and after five years to civil war. But then came the Second World War and the demise of Hitler and Mussolini, reviving the prestige of Communism (which is now gone) and of American-type democracy, which is not gone yet. For that we must be thankful; and its effects must not be underestimated. It is because of the prestige of the West that populist nationalism and the tyranny of majorities in Eastern Europe will constrain themselves, within certain limits, for a foreseeable time. But this does not mean that parliamentary liberalism—including the habits of dialogue, compromise, and the sense of a certain community composed of the kind of people who make up the parliaments—is, or will be, the dominant political reality in Eastern Europe. Parliamentary liberalism, like capitalism, in the nineteenth century was the result not only of certain ideas but of a particular structure of society. That society was semi-aristocratic and bourgeois—bourgeois and not merely middle class—a class with a patrician tinge, a class from which most of its administrators, governors, professionals, and parliamentary representatives were drawn. Such societies, especially in Eastern Europe, do not now exist.

XIV. ON THE VARIETIES OF NATIONALISM

There is no first-rate book about the history of nationalism. (There are a few, though not many, usable books about its ingredients.) There are reasons for this. One of them is that nationalism may differ from country to country more than internationalism or socialism do. (That is why histories of the right are more interesting than those of the left.) This is not simply attributable to the different national characteristics of different peoples. Those characteristics, by themselves, have changed through history. Slovak nationalism differs from American nationalism, Latvian nationalism differs from Swedish nationalism, not only because Slovaks and Americans et al. are different but because the nationalism of the former is newer than that of the latter. An overall history of nationalism must necessarily proceed chapter by chapter, dealing with one country after another, which makes for dull reading. And while national feelings may be and indeed often are very old, nationalism as a political force is new. (The simple Slovak peasant of two hundred years ago may have been the ancestor of the half-baked Slovak nationalist intellectual of the twentieth century; yet their circumstances and their very characters, including not only the subjects but the functioning of their minds, were different.)

To think that nationalism is a reactionary phenomenon is a grave error. Now, at the beginning of the twenty-first century, the most powerful political force in the world is nationalism still. So it was in the beginning of the twentieth century, culminating in the two world wars. That, too, should make those who think that this century was dominated by the confrontation of democracy and Communism think twice. (They won't.) The twentieth century was marked not by the strength of classes and not even by a struggle of ideas. It was marked by the struggle of nations. Here and there it seems that wars among races might now succeed the wars of nations; but that awful prospect has not yet crystallized worldwide, and one hopes that it won't.

XV. ON THE WITHERING AWAY OF THE STATE

Above all other political matters, even in World War II, stood the relations of states. It was still a war fought primarily by states, not by classes, and not even by ideologies. It was a war fought by Germany and Poland and France and Britain and Italy and Russia and the United States and Japan; not by democracy and Communism and Fascism. Hitler, Mussolini, Stalin, Churchill, de Gaulle, Roosevelt, and Chiang were statesmen first of all. They subordinated their philosophical and political preferences to what they thought were the interests of their states. That primacy of state interests appears significantly in the history of the Soviet Union, a state that millions still consider to have been a party state, dedicated first and foremost to the utopian cause of world revolution. Stalin's real interest was security, not revolution; territory, not ideology. This tyrant cared not a fig for Communists abroad. Their activities in the interests of the Soviet Union, including espionage, were merely fringe benefits, secondary and unworthy of principal consideration. At times it was hardly more than a lunatic-fringe benefit, sometimes it was more than that; but Stalin knew that no one could pull the rug from under Hitler (or Churchill) by tugging at the fringe. In 1921 Lenin went through tortuous motions to isolate the handful of Americans who had gone to Russia in order to distribute large amounts of food during a famine. In 1941 Stalin asked Churchill to send British divisions to Russia under their own commanders: if the price for the survival of his state was the presence of foreign imperialist armies on its land, with all of the prospects of capitalist contamination, so be it.

At the beginning of the twenty-first century, there remains still the struggle not of ideas but of nations

Such were the facts of life. By 1939 the official Soviet vocabulary reflected this. Terms such as "state matters," "state relations," and "state interests" became sacrosanct, in a stiff parvenu sense. When Stalin or Molotov would employ them, it was instantly recognized that these were the matters of highest importance, while references to the class struggle or to the cause of the revolution belonged to an older category of Communist pieties.

Thus during the Second World War the authority of the state remained unquestionable and enormous. But during the last fifty years there has come a gradual, though often hardly visible, change everywhere. This may be due to the condition that the unquestionable and unquestioned respect for the sovereignty of states is essentially a monarchical and aristocratic phenomenon, surviving into the democratic age; but in a democratic world people will identify, or confuse, the nation with the state, and that unquestionable and unquestioned respect for the primary principle of the state will diminish.

We have seen that in the Soviet Union the very opposite of Marx's dictum was happening: Communist rule was unquestioned but the state did not wither away—quite the contrary. Thirty years after Stalin another phenomenon became apparent: the party, because of its corruptions, began to wither. Andropov and Gorbachev saw this. In order to reform the country, they wished to curtail and reduce the power of a corrupt and corroding party apparatus. Gorbachev's historical merits were, and remain, very great. Yet he not only failed to recognize the democratic and nationalist dangers to the authority of the state; he also failed to see the extent to which the authority of the state had been undermined during nearly seventy years because of its association with the party. Hence the final irony, a revelation of Lenin's dogmatic shortsightedness: the collapse of the Communist party preceding that of the state; the party withering away, and dragging the state with it.

Even now the monumental problem of the former Russian empire is not what kind of government will emerge there; it is, rather, what kind of state. That is the main problem for the peoples not only of the Russias but of our world at large, and not just because of the nuclear weapons scattered across their vast territories.

XVI.
ON THE END OF EUROPEAN STATES

The present devolution in Europe is without precedent in its history. Fifty or more years after the end of the European state system, the functioning, the authority, perhaps the very existence of the modern state that emerged in Europe five hundred years ago are weakening.

In Western Europe there is the movement toward an international or a supranational (these two things are not the same) bureaucratic organization. There is a common market, a European parliament, a European supreme court of sorts, a coordination of various economic, social, and financial regulations, including an agreement toward the creation of a common Western European currency by the end of the chronological century. But the most important matter is missing. A common market will not a state make. There is no European state and there are few signs that in the foreseeable future there will be one.

The states making up the present European "community" have agreed to relinquish some of the attributes of their sovereignty to this vague pudding of a Western European, and largely economic, community; but the pudding remains shapeless, having only a few, and these not altogether essential, attributes of a form that must be as real as it is solid. For one thing and it may be *the* essential thing—there is no authority, no instrument to enforce these agreements, laws, and regulations if one or another of the member states were to reject or refuse to abide by them. As long as the principle and practice of popular sovereignty are unquestioned and unquestionable, this possibility exists and will always exist, since every democratic government now depends on the will of its people expressed by its elected majorities.

Something new (and probably unexpected) will emerge in Western Europe during the next few decades. What this will be I do not know. What I do know is that *if* something like a united European state comes about, the nature and character and limits of its sovereignty—as defined, for instance, by its frontiers and by its army; that is, by the evidence of its authority—will be very different from the past and very different from what people are imagining now. (If they imagine anything at all. In recent months the enthusiasm of Frenchmen and Germans, not to speak of Englishmen and Englishwomen, for a new European union is fainter than before.)

In East-Central Europe, the sizzle and clangor of tribal wars have arisen because of tales told by nationalist idiots

---

Meanwhile in East-Central Europe, in the Caucasus, and elsewhere, the sizzle and clangor of tribal wars have arisen. The response of the Western powers and states is as ridiculous as it is fretful. They instantly "recognize" the "independence"—that is, the sovereign statehood—of Croatia and Bosnia-Herzegovina and Azerbaijan, as if that were a step in the right direction—which in most cases it isn't. It exacerbates problems, one of the reasons being that recognition, once given, is difficult to withdraw; recognition means approval, which is why in the past it was tendered only after considerable deliberation and experience, and thereby was an important instrument of influence, which is hardly the case now. At the same time, the European "community," or the Council of Europe, is incapable of exerting any authority over the civil war in Yugoslavia (nor is the Russian government capable of exerting authority over the tribal wars in the Caucasus). The thought occurs to me that perhaps this may work itself out for the—relative—best; that perhaps a new generation of Serbs, Croats, etc., may someday recognize some of the benefits of their interdependence as they find that the smoking rubble of their destroyed villages and towns came about because of tales told by nationalist idiots, full of sound and fury, fighting for an "independence" signifying nothing. But that is far from being certain.

XVII.
ON THE GROWTH OF THE AMERICAN STATE

During the last fifty years the power of the American state has been rising, beyond almost all American traditions and previous practices. Because of the Constitution and because of the older inclinations of American democracy, the clandestine and police powers of the national government, unlike in Europe, had been weak—indeed, for a long time they were almost nonexistent. The presidential Secret Service came into being only in 1901; the FBI, in its present form, in 1924; the CIA in 1947. However, it took only a few years for the modern FBI to become very popular. (Something of the same occurred with the CIA.) By 1940, J. Edgar Hoover was the most powerful policeman in the United States, with great political influence at his disposal, which he used on occasion rather freely, and without compunction. Still, his influence on the course of the American ship of state was small. But by 1955 Allen

Dulles was one of the chief officers, if not the chief pilot, on the bridge of that enormous American ship. Neither "national" nor "security" was a particularly venerated patriotic American term one hundred years ago. But during the second half of the twentieth century "national security," including its institutions, became an unassailable term. The national security establishment and the CIA became principal, and not merely secondary, instruments of the state. Those instruments of the American state—its defense establishments, its armaments and their contractors, its foreign intelligence and information services, together with its domestic governmental agencies—have grown enormous. At the same time, they have become ever more inefficient and vulnerable, mostly because of their bureaucratic (and politicized) character.

At the end of the twentieth century we see, almost everywhere, overextended and heavily bureaucratic governments vacillating atop societies whose cohesion is lessening visibly, with the former cement of civility, morals, common sense, and law and order dissolving in places, failing to hold them together. The size of the state increases along with the decrease of its authority, because of the decreasing respect and the decreasing efficiency of its powers.

XVIII. ON THE END OF THE AMERICAN CENTURY

The twentieth century was the American century. Shortly before its chronological beginning, the American people and their politicians decided that the United States must become a world power. They were no longer content with being the greatest power in the Americas. In 1898 the United States conquered Cuba and Puerto Rico and leapt across the Pacific. That was an isolated prelude to the First World War, but a prelude nonetheless. In 1917 the United States, allied with Britain and France, entered the First World War and helped to defeat Germany. Less than twenty-five years later the United States, allied with Britain and Russia, entered the Second World War and helped to conquer Germany, while conquering Japan almost alone. In 1945 the American flag, flying on American warships, ruled the seas from Tokyo Bay to the Bosporus. There followed the confrontation with Russia over the spoils of the Second World War. Here and there the leaders of the Soviet Union felt constrained to mitigate that confrontation, until in the 1980s they decided to abandon it altogether, giving up their European conquests.

The twentieth century was the American century not only because of the overwhelming power of the United States but also because of the overwhelming influence and prestige of things American. The American dollar became the universal standard of currency throughout the world. Many of the most valuable objects of European art and many of the greatest European artists came across the Atlantic to the United States. American universities became global centers of research and study. American customs, American practices, American music, and American popular culture were emulated in the farthest corners of the globe. As early as 1925, millions of people in Europe knew the names and faces of American movie stars while they knew not the name of their own prime minister. Much of this is still going on. Yet many of these movements—movements of power, of prestige, of presence—no longer carry the same force.

America's politicized and inefficient "national security" apparatus has grown, but not America's prestige

It seems that the twenty-first century will not be an American century. It must not be thought that the decline of American power came about only because of the decline of its once predominant ethnic component. The decline was probably preordained because of the decline of the age of superpowers, superstates. For more than one hundred years after the establishment of the United States most Americans saw themselves as representing something that was the opposite of the Old World and its sins. After about one hundred years this vision gradually transformed: the United States came to be seen as the advanced model of the Old World . . . and perhaps of the entire world. Neither of these visions is meaningful any longer. Will the American people have the inner strength to consolidate, and to sustain, the belief that their civilization is different not from the so-called Old World but from the so-called Third World, and not merely its advanced model? At the beginning of the third century of American independence, this is—or, rather, this ought to be—the question.

Conclusion: The Human Prospect

UNIT 5

From the perspective of the 1990s, the West contemplates the year 2000 and the turn of another century. This time the prospects for disillusionment seem slight, for there is little optimism about the current or future prospects of Western civilization. Indeed, with the development of nuclear weapons and intercontinental missiles, we are forced to consider the possibility that our civilization might destroy itself in an instant. Of course, like our ancestors a century ago, we can point to continued progress, particularly in science and technology. But, unlike our predecessors, we are attuned to the potential for the unforeseen disruptions and disasters that can accompany such innovation.

Our ambivalence about technology is paralleled by our growing recognition that we can no longer depend upon an unlimited upward spiral of economic growth. In the course of this century other dreams have eluded us, including the hope that we could create a just and equal society through drastic and rapid social reorganization. Most of the great revolutionary promises of the age have not been kept. Nor do we continue to believe very fervently that the elimination of repressive social and moral taboos will produce an era of freedom and self-realization. By now virtually all areas of human conduct have been demystified (and trivialized), but confusion rather than liberation seems to be the immediate result. Finally, modernism, that great artistic and intellectual movement of the century's early years, has exhausted itself. For decades avant-garde experimentation had challenged established styles and structures in art, music, and literature, creating an ever-changing "tradition of the new," to borrow Harold Rosenberg's phrase. Avant-gardism presumes the existence of cultural norms to be tested, but now we find ourselves in the so-called postmodern condition, "a kind of unregulated marketplace of realities in which all manner of belief systems are offered for public consumption." Old beliefs and new are in a continuous process of redefinition. Under the circumstances, as Walter Truett Anderson comments in *Reality Isn't What It Used to Be* (HarperCollins, 1992), our world cannot be defined by what it is, only by what it has just ceased to be.

These developments have contributed to an uncommon degree of self-consciousness in our culture. Seldom in any era have people been so apprehensive about the future of civilization and the prospects for humanity. The articles in this concluding section convey some current concerns. "Jihad vs. McWorld" focuses particularly on the widespread reversion to tribalization, a trend that is manifest in the ever-increasing conflicts that pit culture against culture, religion against religion, and ethnic group against ethnic group. These tensions are often aggravated by the unprecedented mass migrations of our time, a topic covered in the essay "Europe's Muslims." The unequal distribution of the world's wealth can also sow seeds of conflict. "The Poor and the Rich" surveys attempts to explain why some nations are richer than others. In "The *Real* Clash," James Kurth suggests that the West is in for a kind of cultural civil war between its traditional values and an emergent "post-Western" culture. Under the circumstances, many have raised doubts about the future of nation-states. That theme is taken up in the report "The Nation-State Is Dead. Long Live the Nation-State." "Technology and Its Discontents" takes up the pros and cons of the new information revolution. "A Golden Age of Discovery" reminds us that, despite the great explosion of knowledge in our century, there is still much to be learned about Earth itself. The volume concludes with Thomas Sowell's speculations about the prospects for Western civilization.

Looking Ahead: Challenge Questions

"Jihad vs. McWorld" outlines two possible scenarios for the world in the immediate future. Based on current developments in Western civilization and the world at large, which scenario seems most likely? Can you imagine (and defend with facts and trends) other scenarios?

What does James Kurth (see "The *Real* Clash") mean by "post-Western" culture?

Define the prospects for nation-states.

Explain why some nations are richer than others.

What exactly are the conflicts that exist between European and Muslim values? How do these conflicts affect the status of Muslims living in Europe?

What, according to Thomas Sowell (see "Whither Western Civilization?"), are Western civilization's major accomplishments and shortcomings? What, in his opinion, are its future prospects?

Jihad vs. McWorld

The two axial principles of our age—tribalism and globalism—clash at every point except one: they may both be threatening to democracy

Benjamin R. Barber

Benjamin R. Barber is the Whitman Professor of Political Science at Rutgers University. Barber's most recent books are Strong Democracy *(1984),* The Conquest of Politics *(1988), and* An Aristocracy of Everyone.

Just beyond the horizon of current events lie two possible political figures—both bleak, neither democratic. The first is a retribalization of large swaths of humankind by war and bloodshed: a threatened Lebanonization of national states in which culture is pitted against culture, people against people, tribe against tribe—a Jihad in the name of a hundred narrowly conceived faiths against every kind of interdependence, every kind of artificial social cooperation and civic mutuality. The second is being borne in on us by the onrush of economic and ecological forces that demand integration and uniformity and that mesmerize the world with fast music, fast computers, and fast food—with MTV, Macintosh, and McDonald's, pressing nations into one commercially homogenous global network: one McWorld tied together by technology, ecology, communications, and commerce. The planet is falling precipitantly apart and coming reluctantly together at the very same moment.

These two tendencies are sometimes visible in the same countries at the same instant: thus Yugoslavia, clamoring just recently to join the New Europe, is exploding into fragments; India is trying to live up to its reputation as the world's largest integral democracy while powerful new fundamentalist parties like the Hindu nationalist Bharatiya Janata Party, along with nationalist assassins, are imperiling its hard-won unity. States are breaking up or joining up: the Soviet Union has disappeared almost overnight, its parts forming new unions with one another or with like-minded nationalities in neighboring states. The old interwar national state based on territory and political sovereignty looks to be a mere transitional development.

The tendencies of what I am here calling the forces of Jihad and the forces of McWorld operate with equal strength in opposite directions, the one driven by parochial hatreds, the other by universalizing markets, the one re-creating ancient subnational and ethnic borders from within, the other making national borders porous from without. They have one thing in common: neither offers much hope to citizens looking for practical ways to govern themselves democratically. If the global future is to put Jihad's centrifugal whirlwind against McWorld's centripetal black hole, the outcome is unlikely to be democratic—or so I will argue.

MCWORLD, OR THE GLOBALIZATION OF POLITICS

Four imperatives make up the dynamic of McWorld: a market imperative, a resource imperative, an information-technology imperative, and an ecological imperative. By shrinking the world and diminishing the salience of national borders, these imperatives have in combination achieved a considerable victory over factiousness and particularism, and not least of all over their most virulent traditional form—nationalism. It is the realists who are now Europeans, the utopians who dream nostalgically of a resurgent England or Germany, perhaps even a resurgent Wales or Saxony. Yesterday's wishful cry for one world has yielded to the reality of McWorld.

The market imperative. Marxist and Leninist theories of imperialism assumed that the quest for ever-expanding markets would in time compel nation-based capitalist economies to push against national boundaries in search of an international economic imperium. Whatever else has happened to the scientistic predictions of Marxism, in this domain they have proved farsighted. All national economies are now vulnerable to the inroads of larger, transnational markets within which trade is free, currencies are convertible, access to banking is open, and contracts are enforceable under law. In Europe, Asia, Africa, the South Pacific, and the Americas such markets are eroding national sovereignty and giving rise to entities—international banks, trade associations, transnational lobbies like OPEC and Greenpeace, world news services like CNN and the BBC, and multinational corporations that increasingly lack a meaningful national identity—that neither reflect nor respect nationhood as an organizing or regulative principle.

The market imperative has also reinforced the quest for international peace and stability, requisites of an efficient international economy. Markets are enemies of parochialism, isolation, fractiousness, war. Market psychology attenuates the psychology of ideological and religious cleavages and assumes a concord among producers and consumers—categories that ill fit narrowly conceived national or religious cultures. Shopping has little tolerance for blue laws, whether dictated by pub-closing British paternalism, Sabbath-observing Jewish Orthodox fundamentalism, or no-Sunday-liquor-sales Massachusetts puritanism. In the context of common markets, international law ceases to be a vision of justice and becomes a workaday framework for getting things done—enforcing contracts, ensuring that governments abide by deals, regulating trade and currency relations, and so forth.

Common markets demand a common language, as well as a common currency, and they produce common behaviors of the kind bred by cosmopolitan city life everywhere. Commercial pilots, computer programmers, international bankers, media specialists, oil riggers, entertainment celebrities, ecology experts, demographers, accountants, professors, athletes—these compose a new breed of men and women for whom religion, culture, and nationality can seem only marginal elements in a working identity. Although sociologists of everyday life will no doubt continue to distinguish a Japanese from an American mode, shopping has a common signature throughout the world. Cynics might even say that some of the recent revolutions in Eastern Europe have had as their true goal not liberty and the right to vote but well-paying jobs and the right to shop (although the vote is proving easier to acquire than consumer goods). The market imperative is, then, plenty powerful; but, notwithstanding some of the claims made for "democratic capitalism," it is not identical with the democratic imperative.

The resource imperative. Democrats once dreamed of societies whose political autonomy rested firmly on economic independence. The Athenians idealized what they called autarky, and tried for a while to create a way of life simple and austere enough to make the polis genuinely self-sufficient. To be free meant to be independent of any other community or polis. Not even the Athenians were able to achieve autarky, however: human nature, it turns out, is dependency. By the time of Pericles, Athenian politics was inextricably bound up with a flowering empire held together by naval power and commerce—an empire that, even as it appeared to enhance Athenian might, ate away at Athenian independence and autarky. Master and slave, it turned out, were bound together by mutual insufficiency.

The dream of autarky briefly engrossed nineteenth-century America as well, for the underpopulated, endlessly bountiful land, the cornucopia of natural resources, and the natural barriers of a continent walled in by two great seas led many to believe that America could be a world unto itself. Given this past, it has been harder for Americans than for most to accept the inevitability of interdependence. But the rapid depletion of resources even in a country like ours, where they once seemed inexhaustible, and the maldistribution of arable soil and mineral resources on the planet, leave even the wealthiest societies ever more resource-dependent and many other nations in permanently desperate straits.

Every nation, it turns out, needs something another nation has; some nations have almost nothing they need.

The information-technology imperative. Enlightenment science and the technologies derived from it are inherently universalizing. They entail a quest for descriptive principles of general application, a search for universal solutions to particular problems, and an unswerving embrace of objectivity and impartiality.

Scientific progress embodies and depends on open communication, a common discourse rooted in rationality, collaboration, and an easy and regular flow and exchange of information. Such ideals can be hypocritical covers for power-mongering by elites, and they may be shown to be wanting in many other ways, but they are entailed by the very idea of science and they make science and globalization practical allies.

Business, banking, and commerce all depend on information flow and are facilitated by new communication technologies. The hardware of these technologies tends to be systemic and integrated—computer, television, cable, satellite, laser, fiber-optic, and microchip technologies combining to create a vast interactive communications and information network that can potentially give every person on earth access to every other person, and make every datum, every byte, available to every set of eyes. If the automobile was, as George Ball once said (when he gave his blessing to a Fiat factory in the Soviet Union during the Cold War), "an ideology on four wheels," then electronic telecommunication and information systems are an ideology at 186,000 miles per second—which makes for a very small planet in a very big hurry. Individual cultures speak particular languages; commerce and science increasingly speak English; the whole world speaks logarithms and binary mathematics.

Moreover, the pursuit of science and technology asks for, even compels, open societies. Satellite footprints do not respect national borders; telephone wires penetrate the most closed societies. With photocopying and then fax machines having infiltrated Soviet universities and *samizdat* literary circles in the eighties, and computer modems having multiplied like rabbits in communism's bureaucratic warrens thereafter, *glasnost* could not be far behind. In their social requisites, secrecy and science are enemies.

The new technology's software is perhaps even more globalizing than its hardware. The information arm of international commerce's sprawling body reaches out and touches distinct nations and parochial cultures, and gives them a common face chiseled in Hollywood, on Madison Avenue, and in Silicon Valley. Throughout the 1980s one of the most-watched television programs in South Africa was *The Cosby Show.* The demise of apartheid was already in production. Exhibitors at the 1991 Cannes film festival expressed growing anxiety over the "homogenization" and "Americanization" of the global film industry when, for the third year running, American films dominated the awards ceremonies. America has dominated the world's popular culture for much longer, and much more decisively. In November of 1991 Switzerland's once insular culture boasted best-seller lists featuring *Terminator 2* as the No. 1 movie, *Scarlett* as the No. 1 book, and Prince's *Diamonds and Pearls* as the No. 1 record album. No wonder the Japanese are buying Hollywood film studios even faster than Americans are buying Japanese television sets. This kind of software supremacy may in the long term be far more important than hardware superiority, because culture has become more potent than armaments. What is the power of the Pentagon compared with Disneyland? Can the Sixth Fleet keep up with CNN? McDonald's in Moscow and Coke in China will do more to create a global culture than military colonization ever could. It is less the goods than the brand names that do the work, for they convey life-style images that alter perception and challenge behavior. They make up the seductive software of McWorld's common (at times much too common) soul.

Yet in all this high-tech commercial world there is nothing that looks particularly democratic. It lends itself to surveillance as well as liberty, to new forms of manipulation and covert control as well as new kinds of participation, to skewed, unjust market outcomes as well as greater productivity. The consumer society and the open society are not quite synonymous. Capitalism and democracy have a relationship, but it is something less than a marriage. An efficient free market after all requires that consumers be free to vote their dollars on competing goods, not that citizens be free to vote their values and beliefs on competing political candidates and programs. The free market flourished in junta-run Chile, in military-governed Taiwan and Korea, and, earlier, in a variety of autocratic European empires as well as their colonial possessions.

The ecological imperative. The impact of globalization on ecology is a cliché even to world leaders who ignore it. We know well enough that the German forests can be destroyed by Swiss and Italians driving gas-guzzlers fueled by leaded gas. We also know that the planet can be asphyxiated by greenhouse gases because Brazilian farmers want to be part of the twentieth century and are burning down tropical rain forests to clear a little land to plough, and because Indonesians make a living out of converting their lush jungle into toothpicks for fastidious Japanese diners, upsetting the delicate oxygen balance and in effect puncturing our global lungs. Yet this ecological consciousness has meant not only greater awareness but also greater inequality, as modernized nations try to slam the door behind them, saying to developing nations, "The world cannot afford *your* modernization; ours has wrung it dry!"

Each of the four imperatives just cited is transnational, transideological, and transcultural. Each applies impartially to Catholics, Jews, Muslims, Hindus, and Buddhists; to democrats and totalitarians; to capitalists and socialists. The Enlightenment dream of a universal rational society has to a remarkable degree been realized—but in a form that is commercialized, homogenized, depoliticized, bureaucratized, and, of course, radically incomplete, for the movement toward McWorld is in competition with forces of global breakdown, national dissolution, and centrifugal corruption. These forces, working in the opposite direction, are the essence of what I call Jihad.

JIHAD, OR THE LEBANONIZATION OF THE WORLD

OPEC, the World Bank, the United Nations, the International Red Cross, the multinational corporation . . . there are scores of institutions that reflect globalization. But they often appear as ineffective reactors to the world's real actors: national states and, to an ever greater degree, subnational factions in permanent rebellion against uniformity and integration—even the kind represented by universal law and justice. The headlines feature these players regularly: they are cultures, not countries; parts, not wholes; sects, not religions; rebellious factions and dissenting minorities at war not just with globalism but with the traditional nation-state. Kurds, Basques, Puerto Ricans, Ossetians, East Timoreans, Quebecois, the Catholics of Northern Ireland, Abkhasians, Kurile Islander Japanese, the Zulus of Inkatha, Catalonians, Tamils, and, of course, Palestinians—people without countries, inhabiting nations not their own, seeking smaller worlds within borders that will seal them off from modernity.

A powerful irony is at work here. Nationalism was once a force of integration and unification, a movement aimed at bringing together disparate clans, tribes, and cultural fragments under new, assimilationist flags. But as Ortega y Gasset noted more than sixty years ago, having won its victories, nationalism changed its strategy. In the 1920s, and again today, it is more often a reactionary and divisive force, pulverizing the very nations it once helped cement together. The force that creates nations is "inclusive," Ortega wrote in *The Revolt of the Masses.* "In periods of consolidation, nationalism has a positive value, and is a lofty standard. But in Europe everything is more than consolidated, and nationalism is nothing but a mania. . . ."

This mania has left the post-Cold War world smoldering with hot wars; the international scene is little more unified than it was at the end of the Great War, in Ortega's own time. There were more than thirty wars in progress last year, most of them ethnic, racial, tribal, or religious in character, and the list of unsafe regions doesn't seem to be getting any shorter. Some new world order!

The aim of many of these small-scale wars is to redraw boundaries, to implode states and resecure parochial identities: to escape McWorld's dully insistent imperatives. The mood is that of Jihad: war not as an instrument of policy but as an emblem of identity, an expression of community, an end in itself. Even where there is no shooting war, there is fractiousness, secession, and the quest for ever smaller communities. Add to the list of dangerous countries those at risk: In Switzerland and Spain, Jurassian and Basque separatists still argue the virtues of ancient identities, sometimes in the language of bombs. Hyperdisintegration in the former Soviet Union may well continue unabated—not just a Ukraine independent from the Soviet Union but a Bessarabian Ukraine independent from the Ukrainian republic; not just Russia severed from the defunct union but Tatarstan severed from Russia. Yugoslavia makes even the disunited, ex-Soviet, nonsocialist republics that were once the Soviet Union look integrated, its sectarian fatherlands springing up within factional motherlands like weeds within weeds within weeds. Kurdish independence would threaten the territorial integrity of four Middle Eastern nations. Well before the current cataclysm Soviet Georgia made a claim for autonomy from the Soviet Union, only to be faced with its Ossetians (164,000 in a republic of 5.5 million) demanding their own self-determination within Georgia. The Abkhasian minority in Georgia has followed suit. Even the good will established by Canada's once promising Meech Lake protocols is in danger, with Francophone Quebec again threatening the dissolution of the federation. In South Africa the emergence from apartheid was hardly achieved when friction between Inkatha's Zulus and the African National Congress's tribally identified members threatened to replace Europeans' racism with an indigenous tribal war after thirty years of attempted integration using the colonial language (English) as a unifier, Nigeria is now playing with the idea of linguistic multiculturalism—which could mean the cultural breakup of the nation into hundreds of tribal fragments. Even Saddam Hussein has benefited from the threat of internal Jihad, having used renewed tribal and religious warfare to turn last season's mortal enemies into reluctant allies of an Iraqi nationhood that he nearly destroyed.

The passing of communism has torn away the thin veneer of internationalism (workers of the world unite!) to reveal ethnic prejudices that are not only ugly and deep-seated but increasingly murderous. Europe's old scourge, anti-Semitism, is back with a vengeance, but it is only one of many antagonisms. It appears all too easy to throw the historical gears into reverse and pass from a Communist dictatorship back into a tribal state.

Among the tribes, religion is also a battlefield. ("Jihad" is a rich word whose generic meaning is "struggle"—usually the struggle of the soul to avert evil. Strictly applied to religious war, it is used only in reference to battles where the faith is under assault, or battles against a government that denies the practice of Islam. My use here is rhetorical, but does follow both journalistic practice and history.) Remember the Thirty Years War? Whatever forms of Enlightenment universalism might once have come to grace such historically related forms of monotheism as Judaism, Christianity, and Islam, in many of their modern incarnations they are parochial rather than cosmopolitan, angry rather than loving, proselytizing rather than ecumenical, zealous rather than rationalist, sectarian rather than deistic, ethnocentric rather than universalizing. As a result, like the new forms of hypernationalism, the new expressions of religious fundamentalism are fractious and pulverizing, never integrating. This is religion as the Crusaders knew it: a battle to the death for souls that if not saved will be forever lost.

The atmospherics of Jihad have resulted in a breakdown of civility in the name of identity, of comity in the name of community. International relations have sometimes taken on the aspect of gang war—cultural turf battles featuring tribal factions that were supposed to be sublimated as integral parts of large national, economic, postcolonial, and constitutional entities.

THE DARKENING FUTURE OF DEMOCRACY

These rather melodramatic tableaux vivants do not tell the whole story, however. For all their defects, Jihad and McWorld have their attractions. Yet, to repeat and insist, the attractions are unrelated to democracy. Neither McWorld nor Jihad is remotely democratic in impulse. Neither needs democracy; neither promotes democracy.

McWorld does manage to look pretty seductive in a world obsessed with Jihad. It delivers peace, prosperity, and relative unity—if at the cost of independence, community, and identity (which is generally based on difference). The primary political values required by the global market are order and tranquillity, and freedom—as in the phrases "free trade," "free press," and "free love." Human rights are needed to a degree, but not citizenship or participation—and no more social justice and equality than are necessary to promote efficient economic production and consumption. Multinational corporations sometimes seem to prefer doing business with local oligarchs, inasmuch as they can take confidence from dealing with the boss on all crucial matters. Despots who slaughter their own populations are no problem, so long as they leave markets in place and refrain from making war on their neighbors (Saddam Hussein's fatal mistake). In trading partners, predictability is of more value than justice.

The Eastern European revolutions that seemed to arise out of concern for global democratic values quickly deteriorated into a stampede in the general direction of free markets and their ubiquitous, television-promoted shopping malls. East Germany's Neues Forum, that courageous gathering of intellectuals, students, and workers which overturned the Stalinist regime in Berlin in 1989, lasted only six months in Germany's mini-version of McWorld. Then it gave way to money and markets and monopolies from the West. By the time of the first all-German elections, it could scarcely manage to secure three percent of the vote. Elsewhere there is growing evidence that *glasnost* will go and *perestroika*—defined as privatization and an opening of markets to Western bidders—will stay. So understandably anxious are the new rulers of Eastern Europe and whatever entities are forged from the residues of the Soviet Union to gain access to credit and markets and technology—McWorld's flourishing new currencies—that they have shown themselves willing to trade away democratic prospects in pursuit of them: not just old totalitarian ideologies and command-economy production models but some possible indigenous experiments with a third way between capitalism and socialism, such as economic cooperatives and employee stock-ownership plans, both of which have their ardent supporters in the East.

Jihad delivers a different set of virtues: a vibrant local identity, a sense of community, solidarity among kinsmen, neighbors, and countrymen, narrowly conceived. But it also guarantees parochialism and is grounded in exclusion. Solidarity is secured through war against outsiders. And solidarity often means obedience to a hierarchy in governance, fanaticism in beliefs, and the obliteration of individual selves in the name of the group. Deference to leaders and intolerance toward outsiders (and toward "enemies within") are hallmarks of tribalism—hardly the attitudes required for the cultivation of new democratic women and men capable of governing themselves. Where new democratic experiments have been conducted in retribalizing societies, in both Europe and the Third World, the result has often been anarchy, repression, persecution, and the coming of new, noncommunist forms of very old kinds of despotism. During the past year, Havel's velvet revolution in Czechoslovakia was imperiled by partisans of "Czechland" and of Slovakia as independent entities. India seemed little less rent by Sikh, Hindu, Muslim, and Tamil infighting than it was immediately after the British pulled out, more than forty years ago.

To the extent that either McWorld or Jihad has a *natural* politics, it has turned out to be more of an antipolitics. For McWorld, it is the antipolitics of globalism: bureaucratic, technocratic, and meritocratic, focused (as Marx predicted it would be) on the administration of things—with people, however, among the chief things to be administered. In its politico-economic imperatives McWorld has been guided by laissez-faire market principles that privilege efficiency, productivity, and beneficence at the expense of civic liberty and self-government.

For Jihad, the antipolitics of tribalization has been explicitly antidemocratic: one-party dictatorship, government by military junta, theocratic fundamentalism—often associated with a version of the *Führerprinzip* that empowers an individual to rule on behalf of a people. Even the government of India, struggling for decades to model democracy for a people who will soon number a billion, longs for great leaders; and for every Mahatma Gandhi, Indira Gandhi, or Rajiv Gandhi taken from them by zealous assassins, the Indians appear to seek a replacement who will deliver them from the lengthy travail of their freedom.

THE CONFEDERAL OPTION

How can democracy be secured and spread in a world whose primary tendencies are at best indifferent to it (McWorld) and at worst deeply antithetical to it (Jihad)? My guess is that globalization will eventually vanquish retribalization. The ethos of material "civilization" has not yet encountered an obstacle it has been unable to thrust aside. Ortega may have grasped in the 1920s a clue to our own future in the coming millennium.

> Everyone sees the need of a new principle of life. But as always happens in similar crises—some people attempt to save the situation by an artificial intensification of the very principle which has led to decay. This is the meaning of the "nationalist" outburst of recent years. . . . things have always gone that way. The last flare, the longest; the last sigh, the deepest. On the very eve of their disappearance there is an intensification of frontiers—military and economic.

Jihad may be a last deep sigh before the eternal yawn of McWorld. On the other hand, Ortega was not exactly prescient; his prophecy of peace and internationalism came just before blitzkrieg, world war, and the Holocaust tore the old order to bits. Yet democracy is how we remonstrate with reality, the rebuke our aspirations offer to history. And if retribalization is inhospitable to democracy, there is nonetheless a form of democratic government that can accommodate parochialism and communitarianism, one that can even save them from their defects and make them more tolerant and participatory: decentralized participatory democracy. And if McWorld is indifferent to democracy, there is nonetheless a form of democratic government that suits global markets passably well—representative government in its federal or, better still, confederal variation.

With its concern for accountability, the protection of minorities, and the universal rule of law, a confederalized representative system would serve the political needs of McWorld as well as oligarchic bureaucratism or meritocratic elitism is currently doing. As we are already beginning to see, many nations may survive in the long term only as confederations that afford local regions smaller than "nations" extensive jurisdiction. Recommended reading for democrats of the twenty-first century is not the U.S. Constitution or the French Declaration of Rights of Man and Citizen but the Articles of Confederation, that suddenly pertinent document that stitched together the thirteen American colonies into what then seemed a too loose confederation of independent states but now appears a new form of political realism, as veterans of Yeltsin's new Russia and the new Europe created at Maastricht will attest.

By the same token, the participatory and direct form of democracy that engages citizens in civic activity and civic judgment and goes well beyond just voting and accountability—the system I have called "strong democracy"—suits the political needs of decentralized communities as well as theocratic and nationalist party dictatorships have done. Local neighborhoods need not be democratic, but they can be. Real democracy has flourished in diminutive settings: the spirit of liberty, Tocqueville said, is local. Participatory democracy, if not naturally apposite to tribalism, has an undeniable attractiveness under conditions of parochialism.

Democracy in any of these variations will, however, continue to be obstructed by the undemocratic and antidemocratic trends toward uniformitarian globalism and intolerant retribalization which I have portrayed here. For democracy to persist in our brave new McWorld, we will have to commit acts of conscious political will—a possibility, but hardly a probability, under these conditions. Political will requires much more than the quick fix of the transfer of institutions. Like technology transfer, institution transfer rests on foolish assumptions about a uniform world of the kind that once fired the imagination of colonial administrators. Spread English justice to the colonies by exporting wigs. Let an East Indian trading company act as the vanguard to Britain's free parliamentary institutions. Today's well-intentioned quick-fixers in the National Endowment for Democracy and the Kennedy School of Government, in the unions and foundations and universities zealously nurturing contacts in Eastern Europe and the Third World, are hoping to democratize by long distance. Post Bulgaria a parliament by first-class mail. Fed Ex the Bill of Rights to Sri Lanka. Cable Cambodia some common law.

Yet Eastern Europe has already demonstrated that importing free political parties, parliaments, and presses cannot establish a democratic civil society; imposing a free market may even have the opposite effect. Democracy grows from the bottom up and cannot be imposed from the top down. Civil society has to be built from the inside out. The institutional superstructure comes last. Poland may become democratic, but then again it may heed the Pope, and prefer to found its politics on its Catholicism, with uncertain consequences for democracy. Bulgaria may become democratic, but it may prefer tribal war. The former Soviet Union may become a democratic confederation, or it may just grow into an anarchic and weak conglomeration of markets for other nations' goods and services.

Democrats need to seek out indigenous democratic impulses. There is always a desire for self-government, always some expression of participation, accountability, consent, and representation, even in traditional hierarchical societies. These need to be identified, tapped, modified, and incorporated into new democratic practices with an indigenous flavor. The tortoises among the democratizers may ultimately outlive or outpace the hares, for they will have the time and patience to explore conditions along the way, and to adapt their gait to changing circumstances. Tragically, democracy in a hurry often looks something like France in 1794 or China in 1989.

It certainly seems possible that the most attractive democratic ideal in the face of the brutal realities of Jihad and the dull realities of McWorld will be a confederal union of semi-autonomous communities smaller than nation-states, tied together into regional economic associations and markets larger than nation-states—participatory and self-determining in local matters at the bottom, representative and accountable at the top. The nation-state would play a diminished role, and sovereignty would lose some of its political potency. The Green movement adage "Think globally, act locally" would actually come to describe the conduct of politics.

This vision reflects only an ideal, however—one that is not terribly likely to be realized. Freedom, Jean-Jacques Rousseau once wrote, is a food easy to eat but hard to digest. Still, democracy has always played itself out against the odds. And democracy remains both a form of coherence as binding as McWorld and a secular faith potentially as inspiriting as Jihad.

The *Real* Clash

James Kurth

James Kurth is professor of political science at Swarthmore College.

What will be the central conflicts of world politics in our future? That is the question that dominates the current debates about international affairs. The most comprehensive, and most controversial, answer has been given by Samuel Huntington, whose concept of "the clash of civilizations" has provoked its own major clash of authors.

I intend to engage in this clashing. I will first review the current clash of definitions over the nature of the new era in international affairs. I will then review Huntington's central argument bearing on potential conflicts between Western civilization and other ones, particularly between the West and a grand alliance of the Islamic and the Confucian civilizations. I will conclude, however, by arguing that the *real* clash of civilizations, the one most pregnant with significance, will not be between the West and the rest, but one that is already underway within the West itself, particularly within its central power, the United States. This is a clash between Western civilization and a different grand alliance, one composed of the multicultural and the feminist movements. It is, in short, a clash between Western and post-Western civilizations.

THE CLASH OF DEFINITIONS

In the first few years after the Second World War, it was common for people to refer to the time that they were living through as the post-war period. But a post-war or post-anything period cannot last long, and eventually an era will assume a characteristic name of its own. This began to happen as early as 1947 and was largely completed by 1949. The post-war period had become the Cold War era.

There has been no such development yet in our time of transition. Until recently, it was common to speak of the post–Cold-War era, but to continue to refer to the current period in this way—fully five years after the end of the Cold War—does seem to be stretching things a bit. To speak of the current period as the post-post-Cold-War era, however, clearly would sound ridiculous. And yet there is just as clearly no commonly accepted designation for this indisputably new era that we are now in. The lack of a common term for the era is an outer manifestation of the lack of a common interpretation of the international situation and a common basis for foreign policies, as is every day illustrated by the vacillating and reckless foreign policies of the Clinton administration, the first completely post-post-Cold-War presidency.

The problem is not that there are no reasonable contending definitions of the new era but rather that there are too many of them. Indeed, by 1993, there had developed at least four major candidates for the definition of the post–Cold War central axis of international conflict. Analogous to the war-centered definitions of past eras, these were: (1) trade wars, particularly between the United States, Japan, and Western Europe; (2) religious wars, particularly involving Islam; (3) ethnic wars, particularly within the former Soviet Union, the former Yugoslavia, and the "failed states" of Africa; and (4) renewed cold wars, particularly involving Russia or China. And then along came Samuel Huntington, who published a now-famous article, which in large measure subsumed the four different kinds of wars into "the clash of civilizations."[1]

Trade wars: In the immediate aftermath of the collapse of the Soviet Union and its communism, it was natural for some analysts to focus on the triumph of liberal capitalism and the spread of the global economy as the central features of the new era. But it was also natural to think, in continuity or analogy with past eras, that the major actors in international politics would be the great powers, except that they would now be what Richard Rosecrance has christened "trading states" rather than "military-political states." The great powers would be the great economies, i.e., the United States, Japan, and Western Europe, led by newly-united Germany. International conflict within the world would principally take the form of economic conflict or trade wars.

[1] Samuel P. Huntington, "The Clash of Civilizations?" *Foreign Affairs* (Summer 1993), pp. 22–49. The title included a question mark, which was both inconsistent with the article's strong assertions and with Huntington's customary style. A debate between Huntington and his critics followed in the next two issues of *Foreign Affairs.*

Religious wars: Other analysts found a different dimension of continuity or analogy with past eras, that of ideologies or world-views. With the collapse of communism, it was reasonable to think that there would be a new conflict with another radical ideology, or at least theology, that would take its place, i.e., Islamic fundamentalism. (The term Islamism is a better one, connoting the distinctive combination of traditional Islam and modern ideology.)

To become truly powerful in international politics, an ideology or world-view needs its "defender of the faith," an "idea-bearing state" that serves as its core country. For communism, that role had been performed principally by the Soviet Union. So too, for Islamism, the role of the core country or idea-bearing state would be taken, albeit imperfectly, by Iran. As it happened, however, it was Iran's much more secular adversary, Iraq, that stepped forward to briefly fill this role in 1990. Subsequently, however, Iran has again appeared as the core country of Islamism. With the growing strength of the Islamist movement in the Sudan, Algeria, and even Egypt, there appear to be good reasons to argue that conflicts involving Islamism will be the defining feature of the new era.

Ethnic wars: Some analysts focused upon the incidence of actual war itself, particularly on those associated with the resurgence of nationalist rivalries characteristic of pre–Cold War eras. The collapse of the Soviet Union was also the collapse of a multinational empire. The same was true of the collapse of Yugoslavia, which was in some ways a smaller version of the Soviet Union. The old communist regimes in the Soviet Union and Yugoslavia expired with remarkably little effort at violent repression. Once they were gone, however, there was violence aplenty among the ethnic groups left among the ruins of the multinational empires of communist parties, just as there had been at the end of the multinational empires of traditional dynasties, such as the Habsburgs and the Ottomans.[2] The Yugoslav conflicts in particular have seemed to many to define the nature of the new era.

Renewed cold wars: Other analysts have found a dimension of continuity or analogy in the military capabilities and political systems that had characterized the Cold War. The Soviet Union had been a threat because of its vast size, its military power, and its authoritarian regime. When the dust settled after the end of the Cold War, Russia was left with a population that was only half that of the former Soviet Union but that still made it the largest nation in Europe. It was also left with a territory that was three-fourths that of the Soviet Union and that still made it the largest country in the world. Most significantly, Russia was also left with twenty thousand nuclear warheads, that still made it the only state in the world that could destroy the United States. A renewed Cold War between Russia and the United States is a plausible prospect.

A variation on this theme of a renewed Cold War is represented by China. With its vast population and territory, its large army and nuclear weapons, its booming economy, and its still-communist regime, it has many capabilities that could be combined into a threat to the United States.

Thus, by 1993, there were four major contending definitions of the new era in international politics. Each was grounded, by continuity and analogy, in past concepts and experiences and each seemed to be supported by major events that had recently occurred in 1990–93. With so many reasonable contenders, there was no consensus on the nature of the new era or the focus for foreign policies. The Clinton Administration, in particular, has been torn between these contenders and has been unable to construct a coherent foreign policy.

ENTER HUNTINGTON

It was in this complex context that Samuel Huntington entered the debate. With his customary genius at discerning a common underlying pattern in a mass, and a mess, of disparate phenomena, Huntington argues that the central axis of conflict in the new era will be between cultures or civilizations. Although he does not directly address the four contending definitions that we have identified, his concept of civilizations deals with them all.

In regard to trade wars, Huntington implies that these might occur but that they will not be central. The United States and Western Europe are parts of the same Western civilization, and conflicts between them will be marginal and manageable. Japan is another matter, however, because, according to Huntington, Japan is its own distinct civilization. This is why, he observes, the economic conflict between the United States and Japan has been more acrimonious than that between the U.S. and Europe. Overall, however, Huntington sees Japan to be close enough in interests to the West to also make conflicts between them manageable.

Conversely, the conflict between the United States and Islamism becomes central and perennial in Huntington's view. It is the perfect example of a clash of civilizations.

Ethnic wars are also central in Huntington's scheme. He notes that the most prominent of these conflicts have occurred on the "fault lines" of civilizations. The most obvious is the conflict between Muslims, Serbs, and Croats in Yugoslavia, which represents a conflict between Islamic, Orthodox, and Western civilizations. Similarly, the conflicts within and among the successor states of the former Soviet Union have been not just between different ethnic groups but between different civilization groups, e.g., the Muslim Azeris and the Orthodox Armenians. Conversely, there has been almost no violence at all between different groups within the same Slavic-Orthodox civilization, e.g., Russians and Ukrainians.[3]

Finally, from the Huntington perspective, one would expect renewed conflict between the United States and Russia or between the United States and China. The United States represents Western civilization, Russia represents Orthodox civilization, and China represents Confucian civilization. The conflict will take different forms than it did during the Cold War, when the language was ideological. The language of the new conflicts will instead be cultural. But they will still be conflicts between great powers, and nuclear powers at that, who represent different world-views and different ways of life. And although Huntington does not himself say so, they conceivably would take the form of

[2]See my "Eastern Question, Western Answer," *The National Interest* (Winter 1993–94), pp. 96–101.

[3]There have, however, been violent clashes in Moldova, between Orthodox Slavs and Orthodox Rumanians. When the civilization is defined as Slavic-Orthodox alone, this anomaly can be overlooked.

a cold war, complete with those old and familiar features of nuclear deterrence and military alliances.

The Huntington vision not only subsumes each of the contending definitions of international conflict, it also orders the relations and the priorities between them. Given a civilizational perspective, one could see the axis of conflict to be between Western civilization, which is now dominant, and all the others, which are now subordinate—"the West and the Rest," as the title of Kishore Mahbubani's article had it *(The National Interest,* Summer 1992). Huntington, however, does not see it this way but rather sees the central conflict to be between the West and a sort of grand alliance between the Confucian and the Islamic civilizations, with the Confucian civilization strong in industrial power and military weaponry, and the Islamic civilization strong in oil reserves and geographical proximity to the West. Given a civilizational perspective, the long (really more than thirteen centuries) conflict between Islam and the West would indicate continuing conflict for a long time to come. On the other hand, although the conflict between the West and Confucian civilization is not long (really less than two centuries, or since the Opium War of 1840–42), it has frequently been extremely bitter. Furthermore, the booming economies of Confucian countries now give them the power to think about redressing the old and unequal balance between them and the West.

Conversely, Huntington does not see a central conflict between the West and the Orthodox civilization. He does not make an extended argument as to why not, but he does observe that Russia is a "torn country," the most important torn country in the world (others are Turkey and Mexico). Such a country is torn between two civilizations, perhaps with the elite and its policy drawn toward one, and the mass and its history drawn toward the other. Russia has been a torn country in this sense since Peter the Great or for almost three centuries—torn between "Westernizers and Slavophils," between Europe and Eurasia, between the Western and the Orthodox civilizations. Huntington seems to think that because there is so much of the West within Russia that a civilizational conflict will not develop between the two. One could just as easily conclude, however, that a civilizational conflict will develop within Russia itself and that the torn country will become a traumatized country, with a resulting rigidity and hostility in its relations with its repressed other self, the West.

Perhaps Huntington also found weighty two historical legacies. First, Orthodox civilization's most enduring and profound adversary has been Islamic civilization. Second, Russia's most traumatic sufferings were under the "Tartar yoke" of Genghis Khan and his successors—hardly Confucian "civilization" but, from a Russian perspective, much the same thing. If so, Huntington probably thinks that it would be a foolish West indeed that allowed its differences with Orthodox civilization to drive Russia into the arms of its most ancient adversaries. Rather, Russia should be a natural ally of the West against the grand alliance of Islamic and Confucian civilizations.

Similarly, but more simply, Huntington does not see a central conflict between the West and Japanese civilization. He explicitly states that the differences are largely economic and could be sensibly negotiated. It is also likely that he sees Japanese civilization as an isolated civilization, caught between Western and Confucian civilizations, and that a wise Western leadership can readily keep Japan as an ally rather than drive it into alliance with Confucian civilization. Indeed, a number of Huntington's critics in East Asia think that is precisely his purpose, to construct a way by which the West could once again divide and rule East Asia, this time by setting off an isolated and vulnerable Japanese civilization against a rising and threatening Confucian one. Alter all, on the face of it, there are good reasons and historical precedent to conclude that Japan is a part of Confucian civilization (or more accurately, that Confucian civilization is a part of Japan).

HUNTINGTON VERSUS HUNTINGTON

Huntington has had a long and exceptionally distinguished career as a political scientist. His distinctive contributions to political science have focused on political institutions, in particular the state, military organizations, and political parties. His books on these topics are seminal works that have made him one of the most read and respected political scientists in the world.[4] Yet political institutions are virtually absent from his essay on the clash of civilizations. In fact, however, the origins, spread, and persistence of civilizations have been intrinsically linked with political institutions, such as traditional dynastic empires and modern nation states, and with the power that they have wielded. But different civilizations have produced different kinds of political institutions, and this will make for different kinds of clashes and conflicts. A Huntingtonian attention to political institutions will cause us to amend the Huntingtonian analysis of civilizational clashes.

Islamic civilization: A legacy of weak states: Islamic civilization was created and spread by military prowess and political power. There were times when there was a leading Islamic power, most prominently the Ottoman empire (sometimes known as "the Ottoman Ruling Institution"). The Ottoman empire was a true civilization-bearing state. However, there was never a time when there was only one strong Islamic power. Even the Ottoman empire had to deal with other Islamic empires in Persia and in India. Since the Ottomans' collapse at the end of the First World War, the Islamic civilization has been fragmented into many conflicting states.

The closest approximation today to a core state for the Islamic civilization is Iran, but it is largely isolated from the rest of the Islamic world by either its Shi'ite theology or its Persian ethnicity (and, temporarily at least, also its dismal economy). It is virtually impossible for Iran to become the core state for the Islamic civilization; it is, however, also virtually impossible for any other state to become so. The other large states who might seem to be potential leaders (Egypt, Turkey, Pakistan, and Indonesia) are so different from, and so contemptuous of, each other that no concerted policy toward the West or toward the

[4]Especially *The Soldier and the State* (Cambridge, MA: Harvard University Press, 1957); *The Common Defense* (New York: Columbia University Press, 1961); *Political Order in Changing Societies* (New Haven: Yale University Press, 1968); and *American Politics: The Promise of Disharmony* (Cambridge, MA: Harvard University Press, 1981).

rest (e.g., Orthodox, Hindu, or Confucian civilizations) is possible. Islam will remain a civilization without an empire or even a core state to carry out a civilizational foreign policy. This means that the clash between the West and Islam is not likely to take place at the level of conventional or even nuclear wars between Western states and Islamic states. (The Gulf War is the exception that proves—and strengthens—the rule.) Rather, it will more likely take place between Western societies and Islamic groups, as a long series of terrorist actions, border skirmishes, and ethnic wars.

Confucian civilization—A legacy of a strong state: The story of Confucian civilization is precisely the opposite of that of Islam. Confucian civilization has been centered upon a core state for 2200 years, ever since the time of the Han dynasty. Whereas the history of Islamic civilization has been marked by long periods of fragmentation, punctuated by brief periods of unity, the history of Confucian civilization has been marked by long periods of unity (or at least deference to an imperial center), punctuated by brief periods of fragmentation.

Today, as in the past, Confucian civilization has only one contender for the role of core state, i.e., China. (Huntington may be wrong in holding that Japan is not Confucian enough to be a member of Confucian civilization, but he is right that it is not Confucian enough to be the leader of that civilization.) All of the other Confucian countries (and they are few and mostly small—Korea, Taiwan, Hong Kong, and Singapore) can be expected to revolve around, or at least defer to, China. The clash between Confucian civilization and the West (or the rest—i.e., Orthodox or Hindu civilizations) will really take the form of a clash between China and some other state (or states). This means that what happens to the Chinese state will be crucial to the direction, and the timing, of a clash of civilizations.

Two generations ago, almost no one thought that the Confucian form of statecraft had any value in the modern world. For all the differences between Western liberals and Chinese communists, they both agreed about this. For the past decade or more, however, there has been a broad consensus that the Confucian societies have created states that are outstanding at industrial development. These are South Korea, Taiwan, Singapore and (insofar as Confucianism rather than Shintoism or Buddhism should get the credit) Japan. They are the most successful trading states in the world.

The Chinese state must make the great transition from being a communist state to being a Confucian one. This is not going to be a smooth and easy process. The ideal Confucian state in the modern era has been the Singapore of Lee Kuan Yew. Its achievements have been extraordinarily great, but its size is extraordinarily small. (It is really a city-state, with a population of only 2.8 million.) The other successful Confucian states have also governed rather small countries, with the exception of only partly-Confucian Japan. So there is a crucial question: Will the modern Confucian state be able to govern 1.2 billion people?

There may indeed come a clash between Western and Confucian civilizations, but sometime soon there will intervene a clash between the communist past and the Confucian future in China itself. The nature of that internal clash will largely shape the nature and timing of the external one. A clash of civilizations that occurred after a long Chinese "time of troubles" would have different consequences than one that occurred in the near future.

In any event, the clash between the Western and Confucian civilizations, like the clash between Western and Islamic civilizations, is not likely to take place at the level of conventional or nuclear wars. Rather, it will more likely take place between Western-style or liberal capitalism and Confucian-style or state-guided capitalism, as a long series of economic conflicts, human-rights disputes with an economic dimension, and trade wars.

FROM CHRISTENDOM TO "THE WEST"

A closer look at Huntington's list of major civilizations will raise a fundamental question about the nature of civilizations and the differences between them. He identifies "Western, Confucian, Japanese, Islamic, Hindu, Slavic-Orthodox, Latin American, and possibly African civilization." This is, on the face of it, a motley collection of terms. Four clearly identify a civilization with a religion (in Toynbee's term, a universal church). However, the two civilizations with the most advanced economies—the Western and the Japanese—are identified in secular terms. We have already noted that Japanese civilization is a result of a synthesis of *three* religions—Confucianism, Shintoism, and Buddhism—so in its case the use of a national term rather than a religious one seems logical.

The real anomaly in Huntington's list is the most powerful and most pervasive civilization of them all—Western civilization, which is identified with a term that is only a geographical direction. Instead of connoting the profound essence of the civilization, the term Western connotes something bland and even insipid, with no content at all. And instead of connoting the global sway of the civilization, the term Western connotes a locus that is limited and confined, with no breadth at all.

The problematic quality of Western civilization goes deeper than an anomalous term, however. It reaches to the most fundamental character of the civilization, to its definition and its direction.

The fact of the matter is that Western civilization is the *only* civilization that is explicitly *non-religious* or post-religious. This is the radical difference of the West from the other civilizations. It helps to explain why there are new conflicts between the West and the rest. It predicts that these conflicts will become more intense in the future. And it also points to a possible fatal flaw within Western civilization itself.

Three hundred years ago, no one knew that there was a Western civilization, not even those that were living within it. The term then, and the one that would be parallel to Huntington's terms for the other civilizations, was Christendom. The story of how Christendom became Western civilization and how most other civilizations have retained a religious identity is crucial for understanding the clash of civilizations in the future.

Western civilization is, as Huntington notes, the product of a series of great cultural and historical movements. The featured tableaux in this grand parade are the Renaissance, the Reformation, the Counter Reformation, the Enlightenment, the French Revolution, and the Industrial Revolution. Huntington's own list does not include the Counter-Reformation. This may be natural enough for

Americans; Europeans, however, have good reasons to include it.

The Enlightenment brought about the secularization of much of the intellectual class, the idea-bearing class, of what hitherto had been called Christendom. The civilization was now no longer called that, even though much of its ordinary population remained Christian. The French Revolution and the Industrial Revolution spread Enlightenment ideas and secularization to important parts of this population, but the Christian churches continued to be a vital force within the civilization. But ever since the Enlightenment, it has not been possible to refer to the civilization as Christendom.

For a time in the late eighteenth and early nineteenth century, "Europe" became the preferred term for the civilization. But this was also the very time that saw the rise of European settlements in the New World to the status of independent nations. This soon made impossible the term "European civilization."

For a brief and exuberant time in the nineteenth century, when this civilization seemed to be the only dynamic and growing one and with all the others in manifest decline and decay, the preferred term was just "Civilization" itself, since this civilization seemed to be the only one around. But this term, too, could not be sustained.

It was only at the beginning of the twentieth century that the term "Western civilization" was invented. The term registered the awareness that this civilization, unlike others, did not place religion at its core. It also registered the awareness that this civilization was only one among many. It was a civilization past the enthusiasms of faith and also past the exuberance of being a civilization so blessed that it was in a class by itself. In short, the term Western civilization was the product of a high degree of intellectualism, perhaps even a sickly self-consciousness. The term was itself a sign of the first appearance of decline. It is no accident that, almost as soon as it was invented, it began to be used in this pessimistic context, as in Oswald Spengler's *The Decline of the West* (1918). Had the term been left in the hands, or rather the minds, of Europeans alone, it probably would have had only a short and unhappy life.

It was the New World that was called in to redress the pessimism of the Old. The Americans breathed a new meaning into the term Western civilization, first as they dealt with the European immigrants in America and then as they dealt with the European nations in Europe itself. For Americans then, and for Huntington now, Western civilization was the ideas of "individualism, liberalism, constitutionalism, human rights, equality, liberty, the rule of law, democracy, free markets, the separation of church and state."

The new content of Western civilization became the American creed. Conversely, the new context for the American creed became Western civilization. The combination of American energy and European imagery gave the idea of Western civilization both power and legitimacy. The power helped the United States win both the Second World War against Nazi Germany and the Cold War against the Soviet Union. The legitimacy helped it to order the long peace within Western Europe that was so much intertwined with that Cold War. The term Western civilization has experienced, therefore, its own heroic age.

That age, however, is now over. It is over partly because the term no longer provides the United States legitimacy among the Europeans. Even today, however, when there is no longer any obvious great power threatening Europe, the Europeans are often willing to defer to U.S. leadership (as the successive crises in the Persian Gulf, Bosnia, and Africa have illustrated in different ways). The main reason why the heroic age of the term is over is because it no longer provides any energy within the United States itself, and this is because it no longer has any legitimacy among Americans.

The decline of Western civilization is a tale that scholars have been telling ever since the *fin-de-siècle* of the nineteenth century. As I have argued, the rise of the term "Western civilization" was itself a sign of the first stage of that decline. Now, at the *fin-de-siècle* of the twentieth century, the decline of that term is a sign of a much more advanced decline. The tale of the decline of "Western civilization" as a term is part of the longer tale of the decline of Western civilization itself. This is connected with certain transformations within the West that have matured in the 1990s.

THE GREAT TRANSFORMATIONS

One big event of the 1990s, of course, has been the end of the Cold War. Many observers naturally see this development to be the most important one for international affairs, particularly those who focus on international security and the national interest (and who read *The National Interest).* But the 1990s have also seen the maturing of other major developments that will have major consequences for international security and the national interest, and that will shape the clash of civilizations: first, there has been the transformation of the most advanced countries from industrial to post-industrial economies, and their associated transformation from modern to post-modern societies; second, there has been the transformation of the international economy into a truly global one.

The transformation from industrial to post-industrial economy: At the most obvious level, this means the replacement of industrial production with service processes. These changes have been noted and discussed for more than a generation, at least since Daniel Bell published his seminal *The Coming of Post-Industrial Society* (1973). It will prove useful for our purposes, however, to emphasize one dimension of this transformation—that of gender.

The agricultural economy was one that employed both men and women. They were, it is true, employed at different tasks, but they worked at the same place, the farm, which was also the home. The industrial economy largely employed men. They worked both at different tasks from those of women and at a different place, the factory, which was away from the home. The service economy is like the agricultural economy in that it employs both men and women. But it employs them at much the same tasks and at the same place, the office. Like the industrial economy, that place is away from the home. These simple differences in tasks and place have had and will continue to have enormous consequences for society.

The greatest movement of the second half of the nineteenth century was the movement of men from the farm to the factory. Out of that movement arose many of the political movements that shaped the history of the time—socialism and anti-socialism, revolutions, and civil wars. The full consequences of this movement from the farm to the factory culminated in the first half of the twentieth century with the Communist revolution in Russia, the National Socialist reaction in Germany, and the Second World War that included the great struggle between the two.

The greatest movement of the second half of the twentieth century has been the movement of women from the home to the office. Out of that movement there have already arisen political movements that are beginning to shape the history of our own time. One is feminism, with its political demands ranging from equal opportunity to academic deconstructionism to abortion rights. Feminism has in turn produced a new form of conservatism. These new conservatives speak of "family values;" their adversaries call them "the religious right."

The full consequences of this movement from the home to the office will only culminate in the first half of the twenty-first century. They may not take the form of revolutions, civil wars, and world wars, as did the earlier movement of men from the farm to the factory. Feminists have constructed elaborate theories about how women are far less violent than men. But there are other factors at work.

The movement from farm to factory in large measure brought about the replacement of the extended family with the nuclear family. The movement from home to office is carrying this process one step further. It separates the parents from the children, as well as enabling the wife to separate herself from the husband. By splitting the nuclear family, it is helping to bring about the replacement of the nuclear family with the non-family ("non-traditional" family, as seen by feminists; no family at all, as seen by conservatives). The splitting of the family's nucleus, like the splitting of the atom's nucleus, will release an enormous amount of energy (which feminists see as liberating and conservatives see as simply destructive).

Some indication of that energy, and its direction, may be gleaned from the behavior of the children of split families or single-parent families, especially where they have reached a critical mass forming more than half the population, as in the large cities of America. In such locales, there is not much evidence of "Western civilization" or even of civility. For thousands of years, the city was the source of civilization. In contemporary America, however, it has become the source of barbarism.

The transformation of the international economy into a global one: At the most obvious level, this means the replacement of national production that is engaged in international trade with global production that is engaged in a world-wide market in trade, investment, and technology. These changes too have been noted and discussed for a generation, ever since Raymond Vernon published his seminal *Sovereignty at Bay* (1971). But their maturity has only come in the past decade, as Vernon has recently discussed in his *Defense and Dependence in the Global Economy* (1992). We will only note one of these aspects. The globalization of production means the relocation of industrial production from high-wage and high-skill advanced-industrial countries to low-wage but high-skill newly-industrial countries (NICs). This is the de-industrialization of the advanced countries, the dark half of the post-industrial transformation that we discussed above. The two transformations—from industrial to post-industrial and from international to global—are intimately connected.

The conjunction of two processes—the de-industrialization of the advanced countries and the industrialization of the less-advanced countries—means that the most advanced countries are becoming less modern (i.e. post-modern), while the less advanced countries are becoming more modern. Or, viewing it from a civilizational perspective, the West is becoming less modern and the rest, especially Confucian civilization, are becoming more modern.

AMERICANIZATION VS. MULTICULTURALISM

The most significant development for Western civilization, however, has occurred within its leading power, which was once its "defender of the faith." Increasingly, the political and intellectual elites of the United States no longer think of America as the leader, or even a member, of Western civilization. Western civilization means nothing to many of them. And in the academic world, Western civilization is seen as an oppressive hegemony that should be overturned.

The American political and intellectual class instead thinks of America as a multicultural society. The preferred cultures are those of African Americans, Latino Americans, and Asian Americans. These cultures are derived from the African, Latin American, Confucian, and Islamic civilizations rather than from the Western one. Together, they form a sort of series of beachheads or even colonies of these civilizations on the North American continent, and are now contesting the hegemony there of Western civilization.

The United States, however, has always had a large African American population, and it has long had a large Latino American one. Conversely, although the U.S. Asian American population has more than doubled since the changes brought by the immigration law of 1965, Asian Americans still represent only three percent of the U.S. population. The gross demographics of the United States are still much the same as they have been for decades. Something else had to be added to convert a long-existing multiracial demography into a multicultural ideology, establishing a multicultural society.

It is not merely the addition of large numbers of immigrants from different cultures in recent years. This is not the first time that the United States has experienced large numbers of immigrants from different cultures, with prospects for their acceptance of the dominant culture seemingly problematic. A similar condition existed a century ago, particularly from the 1880s to the 1920s, when the culture formed within the U.S. by Western Europeans (principally by those of British descent) had to confront large numbers of immigrants from Eastern and Southern Europe (principally Poles, Jews, and Italians). These immigrants were all from Western civilization, but this was no consolation to the Americans who were already here. Most of these "old-stock" Americans did not even know that they were part of Western civilization (the concept had hardly been invented yet), but rather thought of themselves in terms of religious, national, or (spurious) racial identities.

The reaction of the political and intellectual elites of that time to their multicultural reality was precisely the opposite of that of the political and intellectual elites of today. They did not rejoice in multicultural society and dedicate themselves to making it even more multicultural. Rather, they undertook a massive and systematic program of Americanization, imposing on the new immigrants and on their children the English language, Anglo-American history, and American civics (what Robert Bellah would later term the American "civil religion" and what Huntington has elsewhere termed the "American Creed"). The Anglo-American elite was aided in its grand project of Americanization by the booming U.S. economy during this period, which gave immigrants ample economic reasons to assimilate, and by the restrictive immigration law of 1924, which essentially halted immigration from Eastern and Southern Europe and allowed the Americanization process to operate upon and shape a settled mass.

This grand project of Americanization was relentless and even ruthless. Many individuals were oppressed and victimized by it, and many rich and meaningful cultural islands were swept away. But the achievements of that project were awesome, as well as awful. In particular, when the United States entered into its greatest struggles of the twentieth century, first the Second World War and then the Cold War, it did so as a national state, rather than as a multicultural society. (Hitler consistently underestimated the United States because he thought it was the latter rather than the former; he was thinking that the U.S. was still what it was at the time of the First World War.) It was because of the Americanization project that the United States could become the leader and the defender of Western civilization.

Indeed, one of the consequences of this grand project of Americanization was the spread within the American academic elite of the concept of the Western civilization. The political elite remained comfortable with Americanization of the mass population. The academic elite (particularly at Harvard, Yale, Columbia, and Princeton), however, was in the business of teaching the elite of the future. For this purpose, simple Americanization was too rough and primitive. Rather than imposing Americanization unilaterally on people who were in some sense both European and American, it would be better to find a new common denominator for both Europeans and Americans. This became "Western civilization." As we have seen, very little in this Western civilization happened to contradict the American creed. All of the elements that Huntington identifies as being the elements of Western civilization were in the American creed also.

DECONSTRUCTING THE WEST

The presence of African Americans, Latino Americans, and Asian Americans might have been sufficient to create a multicultural ideology in the 1980s and 1990s. But these three groups alone probably would not have been sufficient to have that ideology adopted by much of the American political and intellectual elites, or to have it translated into policies aimed at establishing a multicultural society. Even a grand coalition between them would not have been grand enough to take power and make policy. A truly grand coalition had to include, indeed had to have as its core, a group that was much closer in social and educational background to the existing elite and much more central to the emerging post-industrial economy. That group, which was not really a group but a majority, was women. We have already noted the importance of women in the post-industrial economy and the consequent importance of feminism in post-modern politics.

The feminist movement is central to the multicultural coalition and its project. It provides the numbers, having reached a central mass first in academia and now in the media and the law. It promotes the theories, such as deconstructionism and post-modernism. And it provides much of the energy, the leadership, and the political clout.

The multicultural coalition and its feminist core despise the European versions of Western civilization, which they see as the work of "dead white European males." They also despise the American version or the American creed, particularly liberalism, constitutionalism, the rule of law, and free markets. (They also in practice reject the separation of church and state, because they want to use the state against the church, especially to attack a male-dominated clergy as a violation of equal opportunity and to attack the refusal of church hospitals to perform abortions as a violation of women's rights.) The multicultural project has already succeeded in marginalizing Western civilization in its very intellectual core, the universities and the media of America.

THE REAL CLASH

The ideas of the Enlightenment were invented in Britain in the aftermath of the religious wars of the seventeenth century. They were then adopted by the intellectual elite of the greatest power of the eighteenth century, France, which then proceeded to spread them throughout Europe. The ideas of the post-Enlightenment were invented in France in the aftermath of the ideological wars of the mid-twentieth century. They were then adopted by the intellectual elite of the greatest power of the late twentieth-century, the United States, which is beginning to spread them throughout Western civilization.

The overthrow of the Enlightenment by the post-Enlightenment is also the overthrow of the modern by the post-modern and therefore of the Western by the post-Western. At the very moment of its greatest triumph, its defeat of the last great power opposing it, Western civilization is becoming non-Western. One reason is that it has become global and therefore extra-Western. But the real, and the fatal, reason is that it has become post-modern and therefore post-Western.

The real clash of civilizations will not be between the West and one or more of the Rest. It will be between the West and the post-West, within the West itself. This clash has already taken place within the brain of Western civilization, the American intellectual class. It is now spreading from that brain to the American body politic.

The 1990s have seen another great transformation, this time in the liberal and the conservative movements that have long defined American politics and that, whatever their differences, had both believed in the modern ideas represented by the American creed. Among liberals, the political energy is now found among multicultural activists. Liberalism is ceasing to be modern and is becoming post-modern. Among conservatives, the political energy is now found among religious believers. Conservatism is ceasing to be modern and is becoming pre-modern. Neither these liberals nor these conservatives are believers in Western civilization. The liberals identify with multicultural society or a post-Western civilization (such as it is). The conservatives identify with Christianity or a pre-Western civilization. A question thus arises about who, in the United States of the future, will still believe in Western civilization. Most practically, who will believe in it enough to fight, kill, and die for it in a clash of civilizations?

It is historically fitting that Samuel Huntington has issued a call to Western civilization and to Americans within it. In the seventeenth century, the first Huntingtons arrived in America, as Puritans and as founders of the Massachusetts Bay Colony. In the eighteenth century, Samuel Huntington of Connecticut was a signer of the Declaration of Independence and a lender to General George Washington of the funds necessary to sustain his army at Valley Forge. In the nineteenth century, Collis P. Huntington was a builder of the transcontinental railroad. In the twentieth century, Samuel P. Huntington has been, for more than forty years, the most consistently brilliant and creative political scientist in the United States. Huntingtons have been present at the creation for most of the great events of American history, which in turn have been linked up with great movements of Western civilization—the Reformation, the Enlightenment, the French Revolution, and the Industrial Revolution. It is fitting indeed that, in our century, Samuel Huntington has been not just an analyst of Western civilization but an exemplar of its creative intelligence.

The American intellectual class of our time is present at the deconstruction of Western civilization. When that civilization is in ruins, however, it will be its glories, and not multiculturalism's barbarities, that will be remembered. And when that intellectual class has also passed away, it will be the brilliant achievements of Samuel Huntington, and not the boring clichés of the deconstructionists, that will be remembered also.

Europe's Muslims

Anthony Hartley

Anthony Hartley is editor of Encounter.

During the weekend of July 14–15, 1990, a conference, called together by the Muslim Institute—a body representing some of the more fervent Muslims residing in Britain—met in London. The director, Dr. Kalim Siddiqui, a controversial figure, presented to the meeting a document entitled "The Muslim Manifesto—A Strategy for Survival." The purpose of this document was to provide "a common text defining the Muslim situation in Britain. It also seeks to provide a framework for a healthy growth of all parts of the community as well as a common Muslim identity and purpose." By implicitly describing Muslims in Britain as a threatened species, the subtitle of the Manifesto set its tone, and Dr. Siddiqui's speech introducing it was equally uncompromising:

> We are an autonomous community, capable of setting our own goals and priorities in domestic and foreign relationships.

And still more forcefully:

> We are sick and tired of headmasters and teachers discriminating against our children. We are sick and tired of being told to "free" our women from "slavery." Our women will never be available to become sex slaves of the West. Our message to our tormentors is short and simple—get off our backs.

The Manifesto exhorts British Muslims to practice their religion and obey its laws. It calls for the establishment of a Council and General Assembly of British Muslims and rejects the idea of integration into British society. Finally, it contains an "agenda" for British Muslims—a list of subjects likely to be of importance to them in the future. These include a new legal status for Islam in Britain, including an extension of the law on blasphemy, Islamic proselytism in Britain, Islamic schools, and the possibility of an Islamic university.

The Muslim Institute is believed to be under Iranian influence (indeed, Dr. Siddiqui has acknowledged his own "special relationship" with Iran), and it might be doubted whether its followers are the majority or even a considerable proportion of British Muslims. The Manifesto has been attacked by Dr. Hesham el Essawy, head of the Islamic Society for Religious Tolerance, as being likely to play into the hands of "racists." Moreover, its excitable rhetoric has to be taken with a pinch of salt. Does Dr. Siddiqui really want to give up his vote in British elections, which is what his attitude would seem to imply? Nonetheless, there is little doubt that some of the questions raised in the Manifesto accurately reflect areas of friction between Muslim immigrants and the society which they have adopted—particularly in matters concerning religious observance, education, and sexual morality. Muslim parents fear that their authority over their children will wane as their children encounter, at school or through the media, the norms of Western life. Undoubtedly, this is a potentially explosive sociological situation—Islam's religious content makes it that—and it is hardly surprising that it should lead to reactions that are over emotional or appear to bring British Muslims into conflict with society at large.

One such incident was brought about by the publication of Salman Rushdie's novel, *The Satanic Verses,* in which Islam and the Prophet were satirized in a manner offensive to Muslims. After the Ayatollah Khomeini's sentence *(fatwa)* condemning Rushdie to death and the burning of his book by Bradford Muslims, it was Dr. Siddiqui who, at a meeting of Muslims in Manchester, asked those of his audience who approved the *fatwa* to raise their hands. Most did so. The episode was followed by calls for Dr. Siddiqui's prosecution for incitement to violence, but the matter was allowed to drop.

The Rushdie affair, accompanied as it was by bombings of bookshops, drew the attention of the British political class and educated public to the problems and paradoxes accompanying the existence of a substantial Muslim minority in their midst. At the same time it began to be apparent that Britain was not alone in such difficulties. A steady flow of immigration from the Indian subcontinent, Malaysia, the Middle East, and Africa, both north and south of the Sahara, is affecting all European countries. This movement has been caused by the desire for a higher standard of living on the part of the immigrants and by Europe's need for cheap labor.

In the 1980s, however, with unemployment running at higher levels in Western Europe and the prospect of East Germans replacing Turkish *gastarbeiter* (migrant workers) in the Federal Republic of Germany, increasing restrictions have been placed on immigration and work permits. No doubt, however, this movement of population still continues, since control is hard to exercise and will probably become still more difficult when frontier checks between European Community states diminish further after 1992. (France, Germany, and Benelux have already abolished them.)[1]

THE MAIN CONCENTRATIONS

Muslim communities in European countries differ in numbers, countries of origin, and types of employment. Likewise their impact on the host societies has varied according to the traditions and the political and legal structures of the countries concerned. Different local situations have engendered diverging political and social aspirations. Institutions offer differing levels of opportunities for Muslims to fit into communities, and conflicts can arise over a wide range of issues.

In Britain, the number of Muslims is variously estimated as between 1 million and 1.5 million; though, in the absence of any religious census and the fact that many have arrived illegally, there is no accurate count. They come mostly from the Indian subcontinent (Bangladesh, India, and Pakistan), but there are also East African Asians, Arabs, Malaysians, and Nigerians. The majority have collected in the centers of northern industrial cities (Birmingham, Leeds, Bradford) and in the East End of London in the garment districts once occupied by Jewish immigrants. Their jobs are mostly unskilled, though, surprisingly, there is also a higher proportion of Muslims in professional occupations than is the case with the population as a whole: based on 1981 census figures, 15.4 percent of Muslim men had managerial jobs (national figure, 6.5 percent).

These communities are served by some 600 mosques, the most important of which have been built with donations from the Middle East. Saudi Arabia appears to be the largest donor and has also exercised considerable influence on the appointment of Imams (prayer leaders). The next largest donor is Libya. The mosques, in addition to their religious function, organize Koranic teaching for children (i.e., instruction in Arabic for Urdu-speaking Asians) and generally act as a center for the communities in which they are located.

One characteristic of the status of British Muslims, which is significantly different from what is to be found in other European countries, is the fact that, since most of them were originally immigrants from Commonwealth countries, they are citizens and have the right to vote in local and national elections. This has far-reaching consequences. Despite what "The Muslim Manifesto" may say, these Muslims are integrated into British political life, and a number of them hold political office—something that gives them considerable potential leverage to realize specific objectives. The practical results of this and the issues it raises for British politicians will be discussed later.

In France, as might be expected given its geographical position and historic ties with the Maghreb, there is a still larger Muslim population: estimated to be between 2.5 and 3 million. These are mostly Algerians, Moroccans, and Tunisians, but there are also some Turks and an increasing number of Muslim Africans from countries like Senegal, Mali, and Niger. The Muslim communities are concentrated in the industrial areas of France, particularly in the north and in the suburbs of Paris. There are well over a thousand mosques or "prayer rooms" where Islam is practiced. Around these, and often as part of the struggle to obtain a place of worship on housing estates or in factories, have grown Muslim groupings, whose general aim is to improve the immigrants' lot. Sometimes these have merged into wider social or political movements such as "SOS Racisme" or the "March of the *beurs* (Arabs)," whose effect has been to end temporarily the isolation of Muslim communities and bring them into French political life. Since many Muslims work in factories—especially in the big automobile plants around Paris—strikes in those industries have been accompanied by efforts on the part of the communist Confederation Générale du Travail to organize Muslim workers, while making accusations that the leaders of a rival "company" union had broken the Ramadan fast.

Most French Muslims do not have the right to vote, though this is changing as young people, born in France, grow up as French citizens. This gradual formation of a Muslim electorate will facilitate the acceptance of demands voiced by the Muslim community—as, for example, the letter sent by the Union islamique en France to headmasters asking for an end to mixed classes. But the integration of Muslims into French political life will be a slow process and one which must involve a greater degree of cultural integration than would be welcomed by many Muslims. The controversy about the three Muslim girls in the town of Creil who wore head-scarves to school, thereby offending against the cherished principles of the *école laïque,* shows how difficult it is for a secular state to deal with Islamic activism. (The controversy ended with the minister of education, Liónel Jespin, a Socialist, giving way—much to the dismay of partisans of secular education and a unitary state.)

French Muslims have looked with some envy toward Belgium, which has given its Muslim community a distinct legal status by creating a Supreme Council for the Muslim religion. Recently, France's interior minister, Pierre Joxe, took the first step toward a similar solution by establishing an advisory council whose task will be to prepare the regulations for a consultative council of the Muslim community. Such a body would at least help the French government ascertain what Muslims really want. At present, in a medley of competing sects and rival influences from Muslim states, their aspirations remain problematic.

In what was until recently West Germany, according to the *Islam-Archives-Deutschland,* there are 1.9 million Muslims. Of these the great majority are Turkish (1.4 million) with considerable numbers of Arabs (130,000) and Bosnian Muslims (100,000). They have at their disposal nearly 900 mosques. Again, most of them live in the industrial areas of big cities or in city centers—the Kreuzberg area of West Berlin is the best known of these districts of Turkish settlement. These immigrants have the status of migrant workers; they do heavy or menial manual work, and are, to a considerable degree, at the mercy of economic circumstances (which now include competition of labor from the East). Some of them by now have wives and families with them. There are also close ties with families in their homelands. Remittances back to Turkey ran at DM 3.35 billion a year between 1981 and 1984. Relations with immigrants in matters such as education and social services are the responsibility of the regions (*Länder*), which work out their own solutions to problems. The Senate of West Berlin, for example, agreed with the Turkish government to pay for two hours of Islamic instruction per week for Turkish children.[2]

The Muslim workers in Germany have no vote and little political power. Though some 50,000 of them have become German citizens, this process is only at its beginning and goes ahead slowly. A considerable part of the Muslim community is drawn together by the Islamic Council for the Federal Republic. Most political activity among German Muslims, however, reflects the political attitudes of their country of origin. In the liberal atmosphere of the Federal Republic, Turkish Islamic zealots can find more tolerance and freedom of expression for their views than exist in Turkey itself. The *süleymanci* movement, for instance, a politico-religious party arising from a mystical confraternity of a type familiar in Turkish Islam, thrives in Germany, but is frowned on by the Turkish state.

Italy is also a host country for many Muslims, most of them from the other side of the Mediterranean—Egypt, Libya, Morocco, and Tunisia. Since the great majority of these are illegal immigrants—the use of tourist visas to enter the country is widespread among intending immigrants—figures are uncertain, but the Italian authorities put the number at 1.7 million. Their installation does not seem to have caused much trouble, though there is a growing movement behind the slogan "Jobs for Italians first!" However, in southern Italy and Sicily there have always been interchanges with North Africa, and so far the only notable crisis—apart from the incidence of assassinations inseparable from the pursuit of Middle Eastern politics in European capitals—has been worry as to whether the building of a mosque in Rome infringed the Lateran Treaty. Apart from the four major concentrations, Belgium and the Netherlands also have significant Muslim minorities. In Belgium they number 200,000 North Africans and Turks; in the Netherlands, there are 285,000 Turks, Moroccans, and Surinamese.

MUSLIM DEMANDS

As this brief overview indicates, the considerable Muslim community in Western Europe contains much diversity—above all in countries of origin and political status—but its peculiar requirements, as it inserts itself into Western industrial society, and, hence, the difficulties that arise between it and its hosts, are not dissimilar. These concern the practice of Islam, the bringing up of families in the Islamic faith, and anxiety lest social conditions in Europe should undermine Muslim morality and separate child from parent.

All over Europe Muslims have demanded places to pray at work, in workers' hostels, and on housing estates; the provision of *Halal* food (food that accords with the prescriptions laid down in the Koran) in canteens and schools; time off to celebrate Muslim holidays (the two great festivals *Aid al kabir* and *Aid al saghir)*; and the right to attend the mosque on Friday.

Many of these requirements are not easy to meet. The Ramadan fast—which involves not eating from sunrise to sunset for a whole month—may diminish the physical capacity of workers doing heavy manual labor, and absences during the day to pray are not easily compatible with the rhythms of modern industrial production. Islamic burial, which requires a corpse to be laid on its side facing Mecca, is difficult to arrange in crowded urban cemeteries. Young Muslims, during their life in Western society, are liable to encounter—and perhaps even acquire a taste for—alcohol, tobacco, and "unclean" food. For religious Muslims, everyday life in European cities is full of temptations that can lure the young away from Islam.

This preoccupation with the possible secularization of young Muslims is, of course, at its most sensitive when it comes to public education. It is no accident that a clash between Muslims and the French state should have taken place in this precise area. The surrender by the French minister of education to the girls of Creil is highly significant, a breach in French educational doctrine which was never conceded to France's Catholics. Moreover, it was a recognition of the principle of female segregation which runs contrary to that of equality of the sexes, now so firmly and, one might say in some cases, so fanatically established in the Western consciousness and practice.

Demands about schools put forward by Muslim parents in Britain include the adoption of Islamic dress by girls, segregated swimming and physical education classes, *Halal* food to be provided at school meals, the availability of "prayer rooms," and time off for visits to the mosque and Islamic festivals. It is at the mosque that children will receive their Koranic instruction. There is also deep disquiet among Muslims about sex education in schools, particularly about homosexuality. Similar demands were contained in the letter to French headmasters mentioned previously.

However, the situations in Britain and France differ in an essential respect. In France such decisions depend on the minister of education who rules a centralized school system. In Britain they are the responsibility of the local authorities. Moreover, a new British education act has given parents greater power over schools and introduced the possibility, if they so desire, of a school "opting out" of the local authority system. In a heavily Muslim area, therefore, the possibility now exists of Muslim governors and parents controlling the school and changing its workings in accordance with their own needs and beliefs. Private Muslim schools have also appeared and are seeking government grants in the same way that Anglicans, Catholics, and Jews have done before them.

Such possibilities pose difficult questions of principle for any British government. How can Whitehall refuse to Muslim schools subsidies which it gives to other religious groups? Why should a Muslim private school not become "grant-aided"? In state schools with a majority of Muslim pupils what is to happen to the non-Muslim minority? The rise of a specifically Muslim educational sector would institutionalize and perpetuate a barrier between Muslim immigrants and the rest of society which government policy has hitherto sought to overcome. To which it could be, and has been, answered that the discipline inculcated by Islam is a valuable asset for a country and that it is better for Muslim youth to be subjected to traditional forces of social control than to be left to its own devices. If Muslims do not want to integrate into Western societies, should they be forced to do so?

Here the responses given in Britain and France might be very different, reflecting very different conceptions of the state and its functions. It is significant that, in its dealings with the Muslim community over education, the French state was forced to abandon a general principle. In Britain, on the other hand, a looser structure of administration creates dilemmas which, though acute, remain local. But, whatever the response of the host country, immigrants who, for religious reasons, wish to remain distinct from the mass of the population pose one particularly fundamental problem: that of allegiance.

LOYAL TO WHOM?

One aspect of the Muslim communities in Western Europe which must be disquieting to governments is the influence exercised on them by Muslim states and sects in Asia and Africa. This is more fundamental than a mere importation of murderous feuding onto the streets of European cities, though this admittedly gives a good deal of trouble to police forces. Religious and political movements originating in Islamic countries from Malaysia to the Maghreb are also reflected in Muslim communities in Europe. The channels through which such influences travel are not well known. New immigrants, broadcasts, films, books, newspapers, tapes, videos, Imams sent out to man newly constructed mosques—messages from the Islamic world come in a variety of guises. (Western security services, lacking Arabic- or Urdu-speaking officers, are, it appears, none too well informed even about the content of the addresses given in the mosques.) However these channels work, the existence of such ties seems certain, as the evolution of opinion and political events in the Muslim world have their repercussions in Europe.

Sometimes there is a clear institutional channel of influence. In France, for instance, the Great Mosque in Paris is now directly under the control of the Algerian government, following a long and complicated dispute about who should appoint its rector. For a long time after Algerian independence, the mosque had remained under the leadership of Si Hamza Boubakeur, a nominee of the French government in its imperial days. Now, however, he has been replaced by Cheikh Abbas, an official of the Algerian Ministry of Education. His tenure has seen a reconciliation between the Algerian state and the associations of *harkis* in France as well as the "re-islamization" of the latter.[3] Backed by a number of Muslim communities, the Great Mosque has intervened on numerous issues affecting Muslims in France: custody of children in divorce cases concerning mixed marriages, immigration laws, relations between young Muslims and the police, etc. In other words, as Gilles Kepel, the foremost authority on Muslims in France, points out in *Les Banlieu l'Islam,* an institution under the aegis of Algiers is playing a part in France's political life—a part that may become more considerable as more French Muslims attain French citizenship.

Similarly, in Great Britain, appointments to the Central London Mosque have been influenced by Saudi Arabia, with results that were felt during the Rushdie affair. In his book, *A Satanic Affair: Salman Rushdie and the Rage of Islam* , Malise Ruthven, a well-informed observer sympathetic to Islam, comments:

> Dr. al Ghamdi and his colleagues in the Union of Mosques Organisation and the Islamic Council of Europe simultaneously contrived to inflame Muslim opinion and to alienate important sections of the British public by their ill-informed and overheated response to Rushdie's book. Instead of explaining to the Muslim community that their decision to settle in Britain had placed them outside the "protection" of *Dar al Islam* and the writ of the *Shari'a* law, they lent their authority to a campaign which they and their British advisors ought to have known would lead nowhere, since Rushdie had broken no British law.

It is certainty a paradox that Muslim institutions should become a conduit for influence exercised by those who care little for civil order in Britain. Ruthven adds:

> Given that the Islamic community is now an established part of the British population, the wisdom of allowing British Muslim institutions to be run by foreign-funded appointees possessing inadequate knowledge of British culture, law or institutions must be questioned.

A rather different type of influence has been that exerted by the example of the Iranian Islamic Revolution. In France, this was followed by an intense agitation excited by followers of the Ayatollah Khomeini. Among Muslim students in the mosques and Koranic schools, work of missionary endeavor and proselytism has gone forward. According to Kepel, the appeal of the Iranian model to young Muslims is clear:

> . . . the humiliation inflicted on the "arrogant" American superpower is a sign: the Western dominance of the universe is not irreversible, battle "in the name of God" can end in tangible earthly success.

The effect of the Iranian Islamic Revolution has been a heightening of Muslim consciousness in Western countries, whose effects range from assassinations and demonstrations to the founding of youth movements and a new impetus given to the building of mosques and the preaching of the Prophet's message. The influence exercised by Saudi money has been replaced by the far more fiery message from Tehran. That message is anti-Western, hostile to modern industrial society in Europe and the United States, and opposed to the integration of Muslims into it.

In Britain, outside sectarian influences played a major part in the inception of the Rushdie affair. Muslims in the United Kingdom seem to have been alerted to the implications of *The Satanic Verses* when the book was banned in India in October 1988 because of the danger of intercommunal riots. In November, the chairman of the Council for Mosques in Bradford, Sher Azam, wrote to the prime minister to protest against the book's publication. Earlier, the Islamic Foundation of Leicester had published its own protest. In this case the impulsion seems to have come from Muslim activists of the Jamaat-i-Islami, a highly politicized reforming sect based in India with links to the Muslim brotherhood in the Middle East. British Muslim reactions to the Rushdie affair were also affected by other events in the Indian subcontinent: the tense state of Muslim opinion in India following a court decision allowing Hindus access to a shrine on whose site a mosque had been built, and feelings among strict Muslims in Pakistan following the choice of a woman, Benazir Bhutto, as prime minister. By the beginning of 1989 an agitation among British Muslims was already under way. This was to be symbolized and given wide publicity by the burning of Rushdie's book at a Bradford demonstration in January. It was only in February that the Ayatollah Khomeini issued his *fatwa* condemning Rushdie as well as those associated with the book's publication and distribution.

The effect of the *fatwa,* apart from putting Salman Rushdie's life in real danger, was to create an obstacle in the path of any reconciliation between Iran and Western countries, which was presumably the intention of the radicals who had submitted the case to the Ayatollah for his judgement. Thus what was to become a difficult political problem in Britain was affected by political opportunism in Iran and Pakistan, and by the reactions of the Muslim minority in India. At present, though relations between Britain and Iran appear to be improving, it looks as if Rushdie will remain a virtual prisoner for the foreseeable future, as the agitation against his book by British Muslims continues. In Mr. Ruthven's words, "The goal of social integration has become significantly more distant for a community whose thrift and industriousness had made it likely to prosper in the free market conditions created by Thatcherism."

THE MULTICULTURAL TRAP

Two series of consequences stemming from the presence of Muslim communities in Europe—the insertion of Islamic beliefs and mores into a modern industrial setting and the influence exercised by the Muslim world on European countries—converge in the Rushdie affair. Out of it, however, emerges another problem: the status of religion in a secular society. In the April–June 1990 issue of *Political Quarterly,* Tariq Modood, a Muslim writer, identifies this point as the most salient feature of the Rushdie case:

> The Rushdie affair is not about the life of Salman Rushdie nor freedom of expression, let alone Islamic fundamentalism or book-burning or Iranian interference in British affairs. The issue is of the rights of non-European religious and cultural minorities in the context of a secular hegemony.

For anyone brought up in an Erastian—not to say agnostic—Western tradition, however, such a statement begs more questions than it answers. In fact, it appears—as an attempt to obscure issues such as law and order and freedom of speech in an impenetrable smokescreen, in which the only discernible feature is the emotive reference to the "rights" of "non-European religious and cultural minorities." But do these include the right to pursue individual citizens with death threats? And is the evolution of European society toward tolerance over three hundred years to go for nothing? In the sixteenth century anyone taking part in a desecration of the sacraments, such as was recently performed by gay activists in the Catholic cathedral of New York, would have met a lingering and painful death. Nowadays, whatever disgust may be felt concerning such actions, no one is about to burn the perpetrators. In Britain the blasphemy law is a rusty instrument, one rarely used in recent years, and prosecutions under it would probably be thrown out by juries. Now, liberals, opposed to any restriction on the right to publish, find themselves faced with Muslim demands for an extension of that law to protect Islam from insult. Their reply has been to demand the removal of the blasphemy law from the statute book—but this would hardly satisfy Muslims, even though it would put them on an equal footing with their Christian brethren. Indeed, on this and other issues (including religious education in the schools) there have recently been signs of an incipient alliance between British Muslims and some fundamentalist Christians.[4]

Faced with such choices, British liberal opinion has split. Intellectuals are pulled one way by their traditional attachment to free speech and another by their more recently acquired belief in the virtues of a "multicultural" society. That those, toward whom they have done their best to recommend a rational tolerance, should suddenly display violently illiberal feelings strikes at the very heart of a meliorist tradition that descends from the Enlightenment. Of course, their favorable view of a "multicultural" society depended on picking and choosing among the cultural elements composing it. Such phenomena as the infliction of the death penalty for apostasy or the social subjection of women were not considered as being "rich" or "exciting," and it came as a shock to find that Islam had to be accepted as a whole. The Rushdie episode has been part of the dissolution of the liberal consensus in Britain, and it may have served a useful purpose if it brings home the message that "multiculturalism" is only possible if it means embracing the (to modern European eyes) bad features of alien cultures as well as the good. The phrase itself is a hypocritical way of avoiding this conclusion.

France and other European countries have not yet had their Rushdie. But sooner or later a similar incident will almost certainly set off much the same train of events. The problem of Muslim communities is now posed for European governments and peoples. Is Islam to be given a special status, which carries with it immunity from criticism, let alone satire? Are the children of Muslim immigrants to integrate fully into the societies which their parents have chosen? Clearly it must be the aim of religious leaders, taking the view they do of Western behavior, to prevent this, to guard their young people with a ring fence of prohibitions and exhortations. But can they reasonably expect that the secular states in which they find themselves will aid them in this task? Can they also expect that, if tensions continue—which seems probable—Western countries will go on allowing preachers in mosques to indulge themselves in violent and abusive rhetoric? Can Islam expect to be above the law or to apply its own laws in European societies?

For what the spokesmen for Islamic communities in Europe appear to be demanding are additional rights over and above those they receive as citizens of their adopted countries. Dr. Siddiqui, for example, does not contemplate abandoning his right to vote in British elections. Nonetheless he wants other privileges which express the separateness of his community as Muslims. The girls of Creil are not leaving France's school system; in effect they have imposed their own terms on it. But this claim to a "special position" in European society could cut both ways. If Muslims succeed in remaining "apart" in, say, the same way in which British merchants in India during the eighteenth century were "apart," then they will find that there will be positions in society to which their sons and daughters cannot aspire. One man's "apartness," after all, quickly evolves into another man's discrimination.

APPLY THE LAW

In fact, it is likely that, were they to be let alone, European Muslims would resolve the tensions between them and their hosts by practical compromises and the application of common sense as to what is acceptable under Western law and what is not. It might be thought that it is perfectly legitimate for Muslims to seek the right to pray during their work day, but that rioting and calls for the death of individuals in the name of Islam are not acceptable. After all, even "The Muslim Manifesto" acknowledges that Muslims must obey the laws of the non-Muslim state in which they live. But compromise is undermined by constant calls from outside bodies for a purer and more intransigent Islam and by the waves of fanaticism which arrive from the Middle East.

There are conclusions to be drawn from the present situation:

First, European countries already have considerable Muslim communities. These are likely to grow and to acquire greater political influence as immigrants and their children become citizens of the states in which they are domiciled.

Second, these communities, in so far as they can be judged by their political spokesmen, appear not to be taking the path of integration trodden by other types of immigrants. Their Islamic identity carries with it beliefs and practices that separate them from their adopted societies. Their demand, therefore, is for a special status, privileges additional to the ordinary rights of European citizens.

Third, European societies are finding it hard to resist such a demand. Indeed, there have already been occasions when host societies have had to abandon their prevailing social norms and defer to the customs of Islam, even when these run contrary to cherished beliefs (e.g., on the equality of women).

And fourth, these Muslim communities have also become a conduit through which movements of opinion in the Islamic world are conveyed into the host country. The governments of Muslim countries and the leaders of Islamic religious sects can, therefore, to a certain extent, exert influence on European societies.[5]

For the host governments in Europe, therefore, there is only one course to pursue. While displaying sympathy for Islam as a great religion and doing their best to ensure that Muslims find the conditions necessary for the practice of their faith, they must also insist that their laws be observed and that public order not be endangered by ecclesiastical oratory. The complexities of the Islamic settlement in Europe are, after all, not going to go away. Indeed, it is likely that the numbers of Muslim immigrants will increase as instability in the Middle East and poverty in Africa drive migrants across the Mediterranean. Nor will the ties between Europe and the heartlands of Islam be cut; it may be expected that the European Muslims will continue to be influenced by messages from their home countries for a long time to come. All this is a reaction to past and present humiliations. But European countries will not for long take on a penitential stance about their past imperial dealings with Islam, nor will they forever make allowances for wounded religious sensibilities. The application of law is their only answer to the paradoxes of Muslim expansion and renewal. If the European Muslims get no more and no less than that, they will not have done badly.

NOTES

1. It is interesting—and perhaps indicative of trouble to come—that France should recently have protested to Bonn about what seemed to be German encouragement for the emigration to France of surplus Turkish workers.

2. This agreement, however, has led to a paradoxical form of religious instruction. Since the teachers are supplied by the Turkish government and Kemalism has made Turkey a secular state, this course in Islamic studies largely consists of the repetition of phrases like "My fatherland is Turkey. I love Turkey more than my life." See Tomas Gerholm and Yngve Georg Lithman, eds., *The New Islamic Presence in Western Europe* (London: Mansell, 1988).

3. The *harkis* are Algerians who fought for France during the Algerian war and had to leave the country when it became independent.

4. See S. P. D. Green, "Beyond the Satanic Verses," *Encounter* (June, 1990).

5. The latest instance of this, which may serve as a postscript to this article, is the reaction of British Muslims to the annexation of Kuwait. Both the Muslim Institute and the more moderate Association of British Muslims have denounced the presence of American forces in Saudi Arabia as "blasphemy" and a "desecration of these holy places." It is true that some voices have also attacked the Iraqi invasion, but the United States has drawn the most fire from British Muslims. See the *Independent on Sunday,* August 19, 1990. A non-Muslim reaction has been an arson attempt at the Saddam Hussein Mosque in Birmingham.

The Nation-State Is Dead. Long Live the Nation-State

Readjust your expectations of the 21st century. Neither the age of superstates, nor the end of all states, is about to happen.

The nation-state is not what it used to be. Ignored by the global money markets, condescended to by great multinational corporations, at the mercy of intercontinental missiles, the poor thing can only look back with nostalgia to its days of glory, a century ago, when everybody knew what John Bull and Marianne and Germania and Uncle Sam stood for. It seems inconceivable that so diminished a creature can much longer continue to be the basic unit of international relations, the entity that signs treaties, joins alliances, defies enemies, goes to war. Surely the nation-state is in the process of being dissolved into something larger, more powerful, more capable of coping with the consequences of modern technology: something that will be the new, stronger, basic unit of tomorrow's world?

No, wait; hold on a minute. As Bertie Wooster said, in telling a tangled story it is fatal to begin by assuming that the customers know how matters got where they are. They will simply raise their eyebrows, and walk out on you. The current argument about the role of the nation-state in world affairs is an excellent example of the danger Bertie was pointing to.

WHY IT ISN'T WHAT IT WAS

For most people, the world is made up of 185 nation-states, on the current count of the United Nations: some huge, some tiny, some of them democracies, most of them not, but all equal in the eye of the world's law. In fact, a majority of these 185 places are not nation-states in the strict meaning of the term, but survivals of older, cruder forms of political life. Nevertheless, all 185 share two vital characteristics. They each cover separate portions of the earth's surface; and each has a government whose claim to speak for it is recognized by most governments of the other portions of the earth's surface. These are the basic units of geopolitics, the pieces on the international chessboard, the essential components of the fearsome game known as foreign policy.

The trouble is that, over the past half-century or so, these basic units have all, big or small, become less dominant, less independent and, in a way, less separate than they were in their prime. This is because of the arrival in the world of new forces, created by the technological discoveries of the 20th century, which have the power to move things visible and invisible from one part of the globe to another whether any nation-state likes it or not. These forces take three main forms, all of which have to some extent eroded the nation-state's autonomy.

In economics, the growing ease and cheapness of moving goods from one place to another has demolished any lingering belief in national self-sufficiency. Almost every country now buys from abroad a larger proportion of what it consumes than it did 50 years ago, and a far bigger share of the world's capital is owned by multinational companies operating freely across national borders. This process has been accelerated by what electronics has done to the movement of money. The markets' ability to transfer cash anywhere at the push of a button has changed the rules for policy-making, introducing what sometimes seems like a sort of direct international democracy: when a government makes a false move, markets vote against it with ruthless speed.

A more globalized economy is in many ways a more efficient one. Most people in most countries are richer now than their ancestors ever were; and the faster discipline of today's international financial markets makes national governments more careful in the handling of their economies. But, for this article's purpose, that is not the point. The point is that the rise of new global forces has noticeably tamed the nation-state's old feeling of confident independence.

In military matters the change has been even more dramatic. Until about 60 years ago, the only way in which one country could successfully use force to impose its will on another was to defeat its soldiers on the ground. Between two countries of even approximately equal strength, that could be a long and hazardous business.

The little Heinkels and Dorniers that flew slowly over the English Channel to drop their tiny bomb-loads on Britain in 1940 were the messengers of a radical change in the nature of war. The use of force was no longer two-dimensional; the third dimension had become available. Only a few years later, the means of imposing defeat from the air had moved from aeroplanes to missiles, and their cargo had changed from a bomb that would knock down a house to one that could obliterate a city.

For at least the first part of the coming century, very few countries—perhaps only America, plus anybody who can shelter under America's protection—will have even the remotest technological hope of acquiring anti-missile defenses that can ward off the missiles with nuclear (or chemical or bacteriological) warheads which an enemy can aim at you from anywhere in the globe. Otherwise, the nation-state will be naked to such attacks.

The third technology-based challenge to the old picture of the nation-state is the information revolution. People in different countries now have the means to know far more about each other. They can see on television how others entertain themselves, or argue about politics, or kill their neighbors; and on the Internet, or on ever-cheaper telephones, they can then exchange opinions about it all. Even if the number of people who make active use of the information revolution is still fairly small, as the sceptics claim, this is a startling contrast with what most Englishmen and Germans knew about each other in the 1930s, let alone most Frenchmen and Englishmen in the 1790s.

Like the new forces of global economics, the globalization of knowledge is in general an excellent thing. It is always better to know than to be ignorant. But, like those economic forces, this change blurs the sense of national separateness. The similarities between people, as well as the differences, become more apparent; the supposed distinctiveness of nations grows less sharp-edged; one day, perhaps, it may even become harder for tomorrow's equivalent of Serb politicians to persuade their people that tomorrow's Bosnian Muslims are an inferior breed.

Between them, these three challenges to the nation-state look pretty powerful. So is the nation-state, as the tongue-in-cheek first paragraph of this article suggested, inevitably about to be replaced as the basic unit of global politics? The answer is no, for two reasons. None of the possible replacements, when you take a closer look at them, seems to have much real solidity. And the nation-state may have more durability than people realize, because it is still the sole possessor of what is needed to be that basic unit. Take the two points in turn.

WHY THE ALTERNATIVES WON'T WORK

One dreamy successor to the nation-state is certainly not going to happen. The disappearance of communism has not opened the door to the emergence of a one-world system. Until the final failure of the "world community" in Bosnia in 1995, many people still clung to the belief that, after the cold war, the "end of history"—in Francis Fukuyama's misleading phrase—was at hand. Such people reckoned that most countries would no longer have any serious differences of opinion with each other about politics and economics; that they could therefore, seeing things in broadly the same way, use the United Nations as their instrument for solving minor disputes and so keeping the world tidy; and that in this way the foundations would be laid of an eventual system of global government.

It could not be. Countries have long quarrelled, and will continue to quarrel, about many things besides ideology. Anyway, the end of the cold war's particular clash of ideas was not the end of all ideological argument; consult any ardent Muslim, or any earnest exponent of "Asian values". The world remains explosively divided.

By the end of 1995, almost everybody has come to understand this. That fond post-cold-war illusion was the result of a failure to look clearly either at the lessons of history or at today's observable facts.

Ah, says a sharper-eyed band of optimists, but surely the past year's progress towards freer trade, under the aegis of the new World Trade Organization, shows that the nation-state can indeed be persuaded to obey a global set of rules. That is true; but only up to a clearly defined point.

Most countries accept the discipline of a free-trade system because they recognize that free trade is beneficial to everybody (which does not stop them bargaining ferociously over the distribution of those benefits). But, in general, countries draw the line between this pooling of economic autonomy and the pooling of political and military power. They want to hold on to the means of being able to decide for themselves, in the last resort, what suits them—including whether it suits them to go on obeying free-trade rules. That is why even the most miraculously smooth-running free-trade regime will not inevitably glide forward into a global political unity.

Nor is there much plausibility in a second suggested alternative to the nation-state. This is the idea that various groups of today's nation-states, wanting to belong to something stronger, will gather together into big new entities, each speaking for the culture or civilisation of its component parts. The most lucid and provocative version of the theory has been set out by Samuel Huntington of Harvard University, who has worryingly talked of a future "clash of civilisations".

This idea, unlike the one-world dream, does rest on a basis of observable fact. Countries that belong to the same "culture-area"—meaning that they have grown out of a shared body of religious or philosophical beliefs, and a shared experience of history—often behave in similar ways long after the event that originally shaped their culture has passed into history.

The ex-communist countries in the Orthodox Christian part of Europe, for instance, seem to find it harder to become free-market democracies than those in the Protestant-Catholic part, perhaps because the Orthodox area never fully digested the Reformation, that great shaper of western civilisation. And the advocates of "Asian values", with their special respect for authority, almost all come from the background of the Confucian culture. It may well be that, as the world works itself into a new, post-cold-war shape, these cultural connections will be the basis of some formidable alliances; and that the competition between these alliances will be a large element in the geopolitics of the 21st century.

But alliances are alliances, not single units of power. The problem with the civilisation-unit theory is not just that Mr Huntington's list of civilisations includes some rather implausible candidates—does Africa, or Latin America, really seem likely to become an actor on the world stage?—but that the component parts of even the more plausible ones are still profoundly reluctant to surrender their separate identities.

It is striking that the new wave of self-awareness in the Muslim world has not produced any serious move towards a merger of Muslim states. Even the Arab sub-section of the Muslim world, with the advantage of a common language, has, after a series of abortive "unification" schemes, come up with nothing grander than the reunion of the two Yemens. In the Orthodox Christian part of the world, another arguably distinct culture-zone, the recent tendency has been for things to fall apart, not come together; this area now contains more separate states than it did a decade ago.

All the other culture-zones look equally unpromising, with one possible exception. Only in Western Europe is there any seriously conceived plan to dissolve existing nation-states into something bigger—and even this European experiment may now be running into the sands. The world does not, in short, seem to be heading for that fearfulsounding "clash of civilisations."

The only other sort of glue that might bind nation-states together, if the cultural glue proves too weak, is ideology. That may seem an odd thing to say while the dust still swirls from the stunning collapse of the communist edifice. But communism's fall does not mean that ideology has ceased to exist. What demolished the communist idea was the superior strength of a rival body of ideas, free-market democracy, which was powerful enough to hold together the 16 countries of the West's alliance through all the alarms and rigours of the cold war.

Free-market democracy won that fight, but free-market democracy is in turn now challenged by two self-proclaimed rivals. One part of the back-to-basics movement that is sweeping through the Muslim world seems to accept the free-market bit, but believes that democracy is a denial of the principle that God decides what should happen in the world. And the East Asian politicians who talk about "Asian values", though they say they accept democracy, want to run it like a family—with themselves, naturally, as the firm but kindly father—so that it does not succumb to the anarchy they think is caused by too much western individualism.

It is not yet clear whether either of these challenges to the West's picture of the future will endure. The Muslim one is already under attack from more open-minded Islamic revivalists, who insist that there should be a democratic way of deciding what God wants for the world. Advocates of Asian values may come to be judged, by their fellow Asians, as just a bunch of politicians trying to hold on to the pleasures of power. But for now it is plain that arguments of ideology are still helping to shape the world. They pull people into rival camps, and give them more precise reasons for disagreeing with each other than the mere fact of belonging to different "civilisations".

Unfortunately, ideologies suffer from exactly the same difficulty as culture-zones when they offer themselves as a substitute for the nation-state. Nobody seems to want to join the proposed substitute.

The proponents of Asian values happily go on working inside their existing countries, because that is where they wield the authority they want to preserve. The Islamic antidemocrats in various Muslim countries have made no progress in breaking down the frontiers between those countries; indeed, they do not even seem to talk to each other very much. And, when the communist ideology collapsed, it became painfully clear that its component parts had been kept together by mere force, not by the vigour of an idea.

So the late 21st century's maps will not show a handful of sprawling super-states with names like Democratia, Islamia and Leekuanyewia. Their dotted lines will continue to reveal large numbers of those boringly familiar places, nation-states.

WHY IT STUMBLES ON

Why is the nation-state so durable, for all the battering it has taken from 20th-century technology? Partly because, in its true meaning, it is a pretty recent arrival on the political scene, and has the resilience of youth; but mostly because it is still the sole possessor of the magic formula without which it is hard, in today's world, to hold any sort of political structure together.

It was little more than 200 years ago, a blink of history's eye, that men invented the nation-state as a better way of organizing the business of government than anyway previously available. Before that, the state—a recognizable chunk of territory, recognizably under somebody's control—had generally been one or the other of two things. Call them the brute-force state, and the justification-by-good-works state.

A brute-force state came into existence when some tough took power by strength of arms and stayed in power by killing or otherwise silencing those who objected. That was how government began in most places, and the species is by no means extinct. You could hardly have a better example of such a state than Saddam Hussein's Iraq.

The trouble with relying on brute force, though, is that however ruthless the rule may be there will in the end usually be somebody angry and desperate enough to put a sword or a bullet through him. This most primitive form of state-system therefore evolved, except in the unluckiest places, into one in which those who controlled power sought to justify their control of it. The rulers did not ask the ruled for their consent to being ruled. But they did try to keep them happy—or just happy enough—by providing for some of their essential needs.

In the arid empires of the Old Testament world, from Babylon to Persia, one essential need was the provision of a reliable flow of water. Later the Romans, having built their empire by force, sought to justify it by providing the rule of law and a sense of order (the British did much the same in India 1,800 years later). By the Middle Ages, the implicit bargain between governors and governed had become a complicated network of mutual obligations between king, barons and the lower orders.

It was not perfect, but it was better than plain thuggery or chaos. Even now, the world contains many examples of this second system. The Chinese government still seeks to justify its one-party grip on power by a claim to have produced order and good economic statistics; so, less convincingly, do the rulers of assorted Arab countries.

What this system still lacks, of course, is any organic link between government and people. Even the most conscientious prince of the pre-nation-state era assumed power by right of inheritance, not by the will of those he governed. "I am the state", said Louis XIV, that most *de-haut-en-bas* specimen of the old order. A century later, the inventors of the nation-state set out to provide an alternative to the lofty arrogance of his first person singular. As they saw it, a government should be able to say: "The state gives us our authority".

A nation-state is a place where people feel a natural connection with each other because they share a language, a religion, or something else strong enough to bind them together and make them feel different from others: "we," not "they". The nation-state is the politics of the first person plural. Its government can speak for its people because it is part of the "we". It emerges out of the nation.

There can be arguments about how the government does its emerging, by election or by some more obscure process. At many times in the 200-year history of the nation-state ambitious or obsessed men—Hitler was the worst of all—have claimed the right to power because they said they knew better than anybody else what their nation wanted. But even they were different from Louis XIV. They claimed their authority, truthfully or not, from the will of their people. One way or another, in the past couple of centuries the connection between people and government has become organic. The concept of the nation-state shakes hands with the concept of government by consent.

The sense of being "we" can come from a shared language, as it unitingly does in most European countries, but divisively in places like Quebec; or from a shared religion, as in Ireland or Pakistan; or from the proud ownership of some special political idea, such as direct democracy in four-language Switzerland or the "American idea" in the multi-ethnic United States; or from the memory of a shared horror, as in Israel. Sometimes it comes from a mixture of these things. The hatreds of Bosnia are rooted both in differences of religion and in the memories of long-ago frontier wars between different culture-areas.

However it comes about, it is the necessary foundation for any durable political system. No government, unless it is prepared to rely entirely on brute force, can do its job properly in the modern world if the people it governs do not have a clear-cut sense of identity that they share with the government—unless, in other words, they are both part of the "we".

And it still seems that only the nation-state possesses this necessary sense of identity. It is nice to learn that you belong to such-and-such a civilisation, or are a believer in this ideology or that; but learning this is not enough, it appears, to pull people across the familiar boundaries of the nation-state and into the creation of some new, bigger sort of political entity.

This may not remain true forever. There was a time when Prussians and Bavarians did not smoothly think of themselves as "we Germans", or Tuscans and Sicilians as "we Italians"; but they got round to it in the end. Perhaps, in the end, Muslims will smoothly be able to think of themselves as citizens of a wider Islamic state; or Chinese-speakers will salute a neo-Confucian flag fluttering over Beijing or Singapore; or, who knows, some pan-African power may rise out of that continent's present rubble. But it is not happening yet; and, until and unless it does happen, nation-states will be the only pieces on the geopolitical chessboard.

SO WATCH EUROPE

The chief test of whether this might change will take place in Europe over the next few years. The countries of the European Union have come very close to the line that separates the pooling of their economic life from the merging of their politics. They will soon have to decide whether or not they want to cross that line. To cross it, they would need to be reasonably sure that the new Europe passes the first-person-plural test. They would have to be confident that its people now think of themselves in some serious way not chiefly as Germans or French, or whatever, but as "we Europeans".

Twice in history, Europe, or a large part of it, has felt itself to be such a single place; and on both occasions there were solid grounds for such a sense of identity. The first time was when the Roman empire hammered much of Europe into a single entity that shared the blessings of Roman law, the Latin language and the peace of the legions. This was unquestionably a culture-zone: to the first-person-plural question, its people could reply, *Cives Romani sumus.*

The second time began when Charlemagne was crowned as "Emperor of the Catholic Church of Europe" in Rome on Christmas Day 800. The political unity of the Europe created by Charlemagne did not long survive his death. Yet, for another six centuries after Charlemagne, Europeans went on believing, as Muslims believe today, that there ought in principle to be no distinction between God's business and man's business, and that politics should come under God's guidance; and for most of that time they kept in existence institutions which tried to put this principle into practice. This was an ideological Europe. To the question of what "we Europeans" stood for, Charlemagne's descendants would have replied, *Credimus in unum Deum.*

The problem for today's unifiers of Europe is not just that Germany, France and Britain want different things out of a European union. It is that none of their versions of a united Europe would be rooted in a distinctive ideology. The political and economic ideas by which Europe lives are much the same as America's, and indeed America was ahead of most of Europe in making itself a democracy. Nor would it be a unique culture-zone. Europe and America come from the same cultural background; they are, with minor variations, subdivisions of a single civilisation.

The underlying argument of those who now pursue a separate European unity is that Europe either does not want to be, or does not think it can be, part of a wider union with its cultural and ideological cousin across the Atlantic. This is an argument of geography, and a circular one at that. Its answer to the "we" question is: We are Europeans because we are Europeans.

That need not rule it out. Tuscans and Sicilians joined each other to become Italians even though the Italy they created 134 years ago had much in common with the rest of Europe. People sometimes band together simply to be stronger than they were separately. The desire to be strong is a powerful force in politics. But not as powerful as the feeling that "we" are different from "them". That is one reason why a growing question-mark floats over Europe.

The nation-state will last longer than most people had thought. Only in one part of the world, Europe, is there a possibility that it may give way to a bigger post-nation-state system; and even that possibility now looks fainter than it did a few years ago. Like the natural world, the world of geopolitics does not easily change its species. The coming century will still be the home of recognizable beasts: muscular lions and fearful deer, lumbering rhinos and cunning jackals. That may be a pity; but the inhabitants of the jungle have to live with it.

A Golden Age of Discovery

"Satellites have killed geographical exploration," a veteran wanderer moans. He is wrong. Exploration of the face of the earth has only just begun

Artificial satellites can read car number-plates. They can photograph pebbles on mountain-tops. They can gaze into hitherto unfathomed trenches bigger than the Grand Canyon in the bowels of the oceans. Loggers, mineral-seekers and road-builders are rolling back tropical rain forest like a floor rug and destroying the lives of the world's last "noble savages". Ice, mountain, sea and desert no longer resist the wiles of modern man and his machines.

The world has shriveled in the past two centuries. It was only in 1806 that two American explorers, the unsuitably named Meriwether Lewis and his friend William Clark, became the first people (you can bet that no pre-Columbian personage would have been so mad) to trudge across the North American continent. A hundred years ago vast swathes of Africa were still unknown to outsiders. It was only in 1909 and 1912 that *Homo* supposedly *sapiens* managed to stand on the North and South Poles. Even into the second half of this century, chunks of the world, even people, were unknown to inquisitive industrial man. After the second world war, unheard-of-peoples—one of them 60,000 strong—living in the highlands and valleys of Papua New Guinea were "contacted" by outsiders for the first time. Much *terra* was *incognita.*

In the past few decades, the world's remotest places and peoples have been visited, classified, charted, often desecrated. While vulnerable tribes have died out, backpackers can hitch a ride (not that easily, it is true) across the Sahara. Mount Everest, the world's highest peak, first scaled in 1952, has now been climbed at least 750 times—by 33 people, two years ago, on one day. Tourists have been flown to the North Pole. Eccentrics cross the Atlantic in—as a seriously record-breaking explorer, Sir Ranulph Fiennes, puts it—"ever tinier amphibious bottles of gin".

But hundreds, if not thousands, of peaks and mountain routes are still to be climbed. Numerous Arctic and Antarctic challenges are still to be met. The rain forests of the Amazon, parts of Africa, New Guinea (that huge island north of Australia made up of Irian Jaya, part of Indonesia, to the west, and Papua New Guinea to the east), all still bulge with mystery: whole ranges of flora, fauna and even groups of people are scantily known about within them.

More than 70% of the earth's surface is water: and the oceans, on some measures, are the richest of all places in biodiversity—but the least known. Only once has a person (or two people together, to be precise) plumbed the depths of the deepest ocean trench. On land and sea, 97% of the world's species have yet—by some recent calculations—to be "discovered." Yes, 97%.

Exploration means many things. One is finding places that have never felt the imprint of a human foot. Another is satisfying the yen of industrial man to seek out "new", isolated peoples, whose languages or way of life have barely been recorded or analysed—let alone understood. A third thing usually thought of as belonging with exploration is the feat of human skill or will-power among nature's elements, gauged not just by "first visits" to mountain tops or ocean bottoms but by novel or even tougher methods of getting there.

A fourth type of exploration is scientific. Earth science rather than anthropology or the personal challenges to a man's (and, increasingly, a woman's) mind and body against the elements is nowadays perhaps the biggest exploratory motor. To explore—defined in the Oxford dictionary as "to examine (a country, etc) by going through it" has become more of a "micro" business. These days, mere "going through" is not good enough. Exploration, to more and more people, means examination of whole eco-systems. In this respect, most of the world is still up for exploratory grabs.

THE VAIN, THE CURIOUS AND THE GREEDY

The old yardsticks still provide the vain, the philanthropic, the greedy, the religious, the curious, the intrepid and the simply crazy with thousands of challenges not yet met. Forget, for a moment, the perhaps 40m species of flora and fauna yet to be classified. Think of the places and even peoples that have never been "discovered", the human feats of travel waiting to be achieved.

Most of the world's extremities and most extremely remote places have been visited—but by no means all. Deserts have been pretty thoroughly tramped across—though it is surprising how many "firsts," even by car, are not yet in record books. Most of the world's forests have been, roughly speaking, visited and mapped. But many have not been scrutinized. At the simplest level numerous jungle patches have probably never been trodden by industrial man before. In Africa, places such as the Ndoki forest, on the border of Congo and Cameroon, or the dense strip of jungle between the Lualaba river (as the upper reaches of the Zaire river, once the Congo, are known) and one of its tributaries, the Lomami, are still virtually unexplored by outsiders. And challenges of survival and travel, especially if you eschew machinery, exist even in well-trodden Africa. It was only in 1986, for instance, that someone (a duo, actually—a similar solo trip has yet to be done) went from west to east by camel across the continent, bisecting the Sahara.

The forests of Borneo, Sarawak and New Guinea, though well traversed in

Reprinted with permission from *The Economist,* December 23, 1995–January 5, 1996, pp. 56-58.

the past two decades, contain pockets of sketchily charted territory. Indeed, all the great jungles of Asia, Africa and South America, though photographed from the sky, are full of unsolved mystery.

The satellite camera cannot peer under the rain forest's canopy, which guards the richest repositories of unknown plant and animal life on land. Only recently have scientists begun to use special cranes and inflatable rafts to snoop into and under the tapestry of the forest roof. Yet the Amazonian ecology is so diverse that some patches, even of an isolated acre or two, may contain species of plants, for instance, that grow nowhere else on the planet. And even when they glimpse the jungle from the sky, the satellites—and their human interpreters—are fallible. Some seemingly authoritative recent atlases, according to John Hemming, director of the Royal Geographical Society, still make "gross errors" in delineating rivers in Amazonia.

Much is not yet known about the earth's cold bits. As it is landless (though not iceless) for hundreds of miles around the North Pole, the Arctic is also more of a place for the old-fashioned beat-the-elements explorer. Only in 1968 did Wally Herbert, an Englishman, manage the first surface crossing of the Arctic Ocean, from land to land, by way of the North Pole. Nobody, alone, has ever traversed the whole Arctic Ocean, nor gone from one side of the Antarctic continent to the other single-handed, "unsupported" and without mechanical vehicles. Even the rim of Greenland, that large Danish-owned island, has never been circumnavigated—and when a British mountaineer, Chris Bonington, and a fellow explorer, Sir Robin Knox-Johnston, climbed what they thought was the tallest mountain in Greenland in 1991, it turned out that the map-makers had marked the wrong summit. Other exploratory inadequacies are equally revealing: the world's northernmost island, off Greenland, was not discovered until 1978.

The Antarctic is sometimes called the "last major unexplored region of the world". Half as big again as the United States, it is valued both for the challenge it still offers to the intrepid and for its trove of undisclosed knowledge sought by the scientist. After the tragi-heroic competition of 1911–12, when a Norwegian, Roald Amundsen, and his team with dogs beat Robert Scott and his five-man team from Britain (all of whom perished) to become the first men at the South Pole, numerous challenges remained to be met. Not until 1993 did a Norwegian, Erling Kagge, become the first person to reach the South Pole, solo, by land and "unsupported".

And whole ranges of Antarctic mountains have never been climbed. Mr Bonington is heading for one of them soon. One free-standing pinnacle, about 1,000 metres (3,300 feet) high, is probably the tallest such tower in the world—unclimbed, of course. "Very, very exciting," he says.

But scientists are equally excited by Antarctica's potential for clues to understanding, among other things, the world's climate. To that end, scientists at the European Project for Ice Coring in Antarctica (EPICA) are embarking on a five-year scheme based at a research station 1,000km (625 miles) from its nearest neighbour, where the average temperature is -45°C. The ice-crust they will investigate is about 3km thick.

A MOST DANGEROUS SPORT

Though seemingly less remote, because more relentlessly explored over many more years, mountains are a source of extraordinary attraction for explorers. Here, too, there is a good generation or so to go before anybody can say "everything has been done". Mountaineering is a bizarre activity, because it combines so many contradictory features of humanity: individualism and teamwork, a thirst for survival inspired by a thirst for danger, speed and muscle matched by canniness and steadiness, the practical rubbing against the poetic.

Two ways to tackle a mountain have been called "the anarchist's" and "the organiser's". Mountaineers, it hardly needs saying, plan in detail and with ever fancier tackle, how to thwart the elements. Yet many of the hardier ones, rightly in their terms, complain that modern practice is making such heights as Everest too easy. "Doing more with less", is the phrase that mountaineers such as Mr Bonington like to use. "Easy" here means "not quite so terrifyingly hard". No sport continues to lead so many of its top practitioners to their deaths. "Simple" Everest has killed at least 120 people in the past four decades.

Not until 1978 did Reinhold Messner, an Austrian who many think is the world's finest living mountaineer, climb Everest in a colleague's company without bottled oxygen. All in all, the most difficult mountain to climb is the world's second tallest, K2, at the western end of the Himalaya range. In 1986, 13 people were killed trying to get up (or down) it. Alison Hargreaves, a Briton who was the first woman up Everest on "normal" air, died on K2 last summer.

But any of the 14 Himalayan peaks which rise to more than 8,000 metres still offer fearsome challenges; once you have gone up the most straightforward way, new "lines", as mountaineers call their routes, are still to be sought out—though not too many are left. Only two climbers—Mr Messner was the first—have scaled all 14. The other, a Pole, has since been killed. "Any of those mountains", says Stephen Venables, the first Briton up Everest without extra oxygen, "involves difficult climbing—your mind and body are teetering on the edge of control." And some terrifying unclimbed routes beckon: the west face of K2, the east face of Kanchenjunga, the west face of Makalu (probably the stiffest challenge of the lot), several oxygenless ascents and a number of peak-to-peak ridge traverses.

Of the 400 or so peaks between 7,000 and 8,000 metres, more than 100 remain unclimbed. With dollar-desirous China opening its mountains to outsiders, vast new ranges are offering fresh challenges: south-east Tibet, for instance, has a range as long as the Alps (and much taller) where outside professionals have hardly trodden. And the Himalaya is by no means the only range to lure the would-be record-breaker. Some of the Tepui mountains, sheer slabs of unscaled sandstone rising out of the wilderness of southern Venezuela, are magnificently inaccessible.

Another sport that now offers one of the biggest array of possible "firsts" is speleology, better known as caving. One of the world's top cavers, Andrew Eavis, a Briton, reckons that even in Britain, two-thirds of the country's caves have never been penetrated—and across the sea in Ireland, the proportion, he thinks, is 90%. Especially where there is limestone, caves lure the daring and the curious. Aerial photography plus greater geological savvy can predict where they are likely to be. China and New Guinea are prime candidates for a burst of cavernous exploration.

In the densest tropical rain forest of the remote Gunung Mulu National Park in Sarawak (part of Malaysia), Mr Eavis and colleagues found what is the largest known cave in the world: 400 metres wide, 700 metres long, and in places 250 metres high. The Hollywood Bowl could fit inside. Often the caver's challenge is to dig to enter; sometimes you must swim under water through riverine entrances. Mr Eavis's world-beating Sarawak Chamber requires a kilometre-long swim and a waterfall ascent—all in helmet-borne torchlight—before you can reach it. "We are relatively normal people," he says of his fellow speleo-fans.

THE VASTY DEEP

As for the relatively unexplored sea, nobody till recently was able to get far down. Man without mechanical artifice can dip only about ten metres before destroying himself. Even with a "self-contained underwater breathing apparatus" (scuba), invented in the 1940s, going 50 metres deep pushes an expert's luck. Yet the seas are deeper than the mountains are high. The Mariana trench in mid-Pacific is more than 11,000 metres deep (Everest, by contrast, is 8,848 meters high). Only two men have ever been there, a Frenchman, Jacques Piccard, and an American, Don Walsh, in the *Trieste* bathyscope in 1960. Nobody but a Japanese team has been so deep again. Most scientists say they are not missing much. Only 3% of the ocean is under the 6,000-metre mark.

All the same, the ocean's average depth is 3,700 metres. And recent discoveries, often by means of remotely operated vehicles (ROVs) and autonomous underwater vehicles (AUVs), show that far more life exists in the deep than most people had guessed. In fact, the oceans almost certainly contain the greatest biodiversity on the planet's surface, whether water-covered or not. New types of bacteria and viruses, as well as an array of new plant and fish life, exist in fantastic abundance: newly discovered sea-worms, mussels, even a huge 20-metre-long squid. Amazingly high temperatures, of more than 400°C, have been measured thousands of metres down. Hydrothermal vents are blowing away more than 2,000 metres below sea-level. Sink another 1,300 metres, and the Pacific Ocean is carpeted with an array of manganese, cobalt and countless other mineral valuables. Little volcanoes like wobbly black factory chimneys, known as "black smokers", are down there belching out metal sulphides and chemicals.

Most scientists think it not hugely useful for people to be squinting in person at minerals or fish: robots' photographs will do. But for those seeking new minerals, working out how continents were formed (by plate-tectonics) or predicting climatic and atmospheric change, the ability to explore the depths of the ocean opens a staggering new scientific vista.

On dry land, exploring for new flora, fauna and even human life remains as exciting as ever—guess as you might that few or no unknown big animals, let alone peoples, are left. But you would be wrong there, too. In Vietnam a completely new species of large mammal, the vu kwang ox (which looks a bit like an oryx), has recently been identified; so has a kind of giant muntjak (something like a fallow deer); and recent whispers from Sumatra suggest a new type of primate may have been found. A leading British ethno-biologist thinks a megatherium, a sort of giant ground sloth which may stand as high as a giraffe, and was thought to have become extinct several milennia ago, may lurk in the fastnesses of the Amazon basin.

Though less likely, discovering "new people" is also possible. "First-contact" yarns peddled by fame-seekers have to be listened to warily. "New" people are often splinters from "old" ones. But in 1995, both in Irian Jaya and in the Brazilian forest, people previously uncontacted by outsiders may have been found. Over a period of two decades both in the Amazon basin (where 370 or so indigenous groups exist) and in New Guinea (where there are more than a thousand), people unknown to the outside world, some of whose languages were sometimes undeciphered even by their neighbours, have come to light. Study of many well-known peoples living in broadly preindustrial ways has been so patchy that social anthropologists have eons of research to do—besides which, the people they study never stop evolving into "different" people.

Even in Africa linguists occasionally discover languages never before identified. Defining a language is tricky. Many cover a seamless continuum. But of the 6,528 or so living languages listed by the Summer Institute of Linguistics in Britain, hundreds are not fully understood outside the group that speaks them. Even in Nigeria (with 420 languages indexed, out of Africa's 1,995) a tiny new one popped up two years ago. More worrying, for those who would resist global homogeneity, is languages' galloping disappearance: some linguists reckon that more than 95% may vanish within a century, leaving a shrinking core of some 300 living tongues. Many need to be caught on tape before they fly into oblivion.

DISCOVERING YOURSELF

"The possibilities for exploration and discovery are infinite", says Mr Hemming. "New species are evolving faster than man can extinguish old ones." Explorers, he believes, are entering "a new golden age of discovery". Although he has experienced hardship and danger (a close friend was killed by Amazonian Indians) during decades of exploration, Mr Hemming stresses the scientific and philanthropic side—and has fought hard to defend the rights, indeed the survival, of indigenous peoples threatened by modern man.

Science may now predominate in exploration, but romance, poetry, heroism still call. Even boffins and flea taxonomists may sometimes admit that exploration is also about peering into their souls and asking who they are. Mountaineers, in particular, are unabashed about their urge to compete, both against the horrifying hunks of rock they clamber and often die on, and against their fellow men. Mountaineering, says Mr Bonington, should not be made "safe, tame and boring . . . Man should not over-impose himself on the mountain." Mr Venables talks of the need to "give the mountain a chance".

Sir Wilfred Thesiger, 85, last of the old school of British explorers, admits even to competing against the indigenous people which whom he lived in the deserts. Among the Rashid of southern Arabia, he candidly admits: "I had to meet the challenge of the desert on equal terms with them. I could equal them physically; the real challenge was to live up to them mentally and morally. But they were the only people I couldn't compete with on a moral level—in honesty, generosity, loyalty, courage. They always thought they were superior to everyone else—and they were".

The Poor and the Rich

In recent years, researchers have moved closer to answering the most important question in economics: why are some countries richer than others?

Understanding growth is surely the most urgent task in economics. Across the world, poverty remains the single greatest cause of misery; and the surest remedy for poverty is economic growth. It is true that growth can create problems of its own (congestion and pollution, for instance), which may preoccupy many people in rich countries. But such ills pale in comparison with the harm caused by the economic backwardness of poor countries—that is, of the larger part of the world. The cost of this backwardness, measured in wasted lives and needless suffering, is truly vast.

To its shame, economics neglected the study of growth for many years. Theorists and empirical researchers alike chose to concentrate on other fields, notably on macroeconomic policy. Until the 1980s, with a few exceptions, the best brains in economics preferred not to focus on the most vital issue of all. But over the past ten years or so, this has changed. Stars such as Robert Lucas of the University of Chicago, who last year won the Nobel prize in economics, have started to concentrate on growth. As he says of the subject, "the consequences for human welfare . . . are simply staggering. Once one starts to think about them, it is hard to think of anything else."

Early economists certainly thought about them. Adam Smith's classic 1776 book was, after all, called an "Inquiry into the Nature of Causes of the Wealth of Nations". Many building-blocks for understanding growth derive from him. Smith reckoned that the engine of growth was to be found in the division of labour, in the accumulation of capital and in technological progress. He emphasised the importance of a stable legal framework, within which the invisible hand of the market could function, and he explained how an open trading system would allow poorer countries to catch up with richer ones. In the early 19th century, David Ricardo formalised another concept crucial for understanding growth—the notion of diminishing returns. He showed how additional investment in land tended to yield an ever lower return, implying that growth would eventually come to a halt—though trade could stave this off for a while.

The foundations of modern growth theory were laid in the 1950s by Robert Solow and Trevor Swan. Their models describe an economy of perfect competition, whose output grows in response to large inputs of capital (ie, physical assets of all kinds) and labour. This economy obeys the law of diminishing returns: each new bit of capital (given a fixed labour supply) yields a slightly lower return than the one before.

Together, these assumptions give the neoclassical growth model, as it is called, two crucial implications. First, as the stock of capital expands, growth slows, and eventually halts: to keep growing, the economy must benefit from continual infusions of technological progress. Yet this is a force that the model itself makes no attempt to explain: in the jargon, technological progress is, in the neoclassical theory, "exogenous" (ie, it arises outside the model). The second implication is that poorer countries should grow faster than rich ones. The reason is diminishing returns: since poor countries start with less capital, they should reap higher returns from each slice of new investment.

THEORY INTO PRACTICE

Do these theoretical implications accord with the real world? The short answer is no. The left-hand side of the chart on the next page shows average growth rates since 1870 of 16 rich countries for which good long-term data exist. Growth has indeed slowed since 1970. Even so, modern growth rates are well above their earlier long-run average. This appears to contradict the first implication, that growth will slow over time. It may be that an acceleration of technological progress accounts from this, but this should hardly console a neoclassical theorist, because it would mean that the main driving force of growth lies beyond the scope of growth theory.

What about the second implication—are poor countries catching up? The right-hand side of the chart plots, for

Reprinted with permission from *The Economist,* May 25, 1996, pp. 23-25.

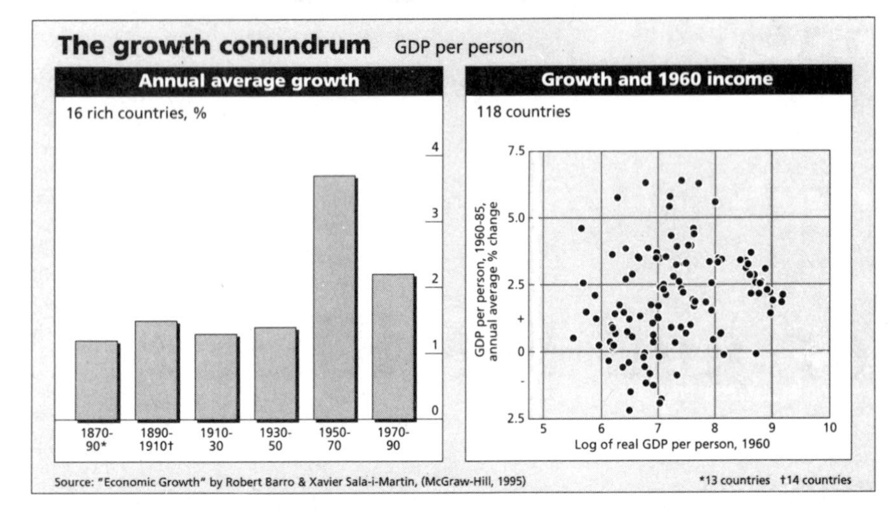

118 countries, growth rates between 1960 and 1985 against their initial 1960 level of GDP per person. If poor countries were catching up, the plots on the chart should follow a downward-sloping pattern: countries that were poorer in 1960 should have higher growth rates. They do not. Indeed, if there is any discernible pattern in the mass of dots, it is the opposite: poorer countries have tended to grow more slowly.

Having arrived at neoclassical growth theory, however, economics by and large forgot about the subject. It had a model that was theoretically plausible, but did not seem to fit the facts. How best to proceed was unclear. Then, after a pause of 30 years, along came "new growth theory".

This new school has questioned, among other things, the law of diminishing returns in the neoclassical model. If each extra bit of capital does not, in fact, yield a lower return than its predecessor, growth can continue indefinitely, even without technological progress. A seminal paper was published in 1986 by Paul Romer (see references at the end). It showed that if you broaden the idea of capital to include human capital (that is, the knowledge and skills embodied in the workforce), the law of diminishing returns may not apply. Suppose, for example, that a firm which invests in a new piece of equipment also learns how to use it more efficiently. Or suppose it becomes more innovative as a by-product of accumulating capital. In either case, there can be increasing, not decreasing, returns to investment.

In this and other ways, new growth theorists can explain how growth might persist in the absence of technological progress. But, they have gone on to ask, why assume away such progress? A second strand of new growth theory seeks to put technological progress explicitly into the model (making it "endogenous", in the jargon). This has obliged theorists to ask questions about innovation. Why, for instance, do companies invest in research and development? How do the innovations of one company affect the rest of the economy?

A further divergence from the neoclassical view follows. As a general rule, a firm will not bother to innovate unless it thinks it can steal a march on the competition and, for a while at least, earn higher profits. But this account is inconsistent with the neoclassical model's simplifying assumption of perfect competition, which rules out any "abnormal" profits. So the new growth theorists drop that assumption and suppose instead that competition is imperfect. Attention then shifts to the conditions under which firms will innovate most productively: how much protection should intellectual-property law give to an innovator, for instance? In this way, and not before time, technological progress has begun to occupy a central place in economists' thinking about growth.

In the latest resurgence of interest in growth theory, however, the original neoclassical approach has enjoyed something of a revival. Some economists are questioning whether the "new" theories really add much. For instance, the new theory emphasises human capital; arguably, this merely calls for a more subtle measure of labour than the ones used by early neoclassical theorists. More generally, it is argued that if factors of production (capital and labour) are properly measured and quality-adjusted, the neoclassical approach yields everything of value in the new theory, without its distracting bells and whistles. So it often proves in economics: the mainstream first takes affront at new ideas, then reluctantly draws on them, and eventually claims to have thought of them first.

THE MISSING LINK

To non-economists, however, both approaches seem curiously lacking in one crucial respect. Whereas in popular debate about growth, government policy is usually the main issue, in both neoclassical and new growth theory discussion of policy takes place largely off-stage. To the extent that government policy affects investment, for instance, either could trace out the effects on growth—but the connection between policy and growth is tenuous and indirect. Each approach may take a strong view about the role of diminishing returns, but both remain frustratingly uncommitted about the role of government.

An upsurge of empirical work on growth is helping to fill this hole—and, as a by-product, shedding further light on the relative merits of the new and neoclassical theories. The nuts and bolts of this work are huge statistical analyses. Vast sets of data now exist, containing information for more than 100 countries between 1960 and 1990 on growth rates, inflation rates, fertility rates, school enrollment, government spending, estimates of how good the rule of law is, and so on. Great effort has been devoted to analysing these numbers.

One key finding is "conditional convergence", a term coined by Robert Barro, a pioneer of the new empirical growth studies. His research has found that if one holds constant such factors as a country's fertility rate, its human capital (proxied by various measures of educational attainment) and its government policies (proxied by the share of current government spending in GDP), poorer countries tend to grow faster than richer ones. So the basic insight of the neoclassical growth model is, in fact, correct. But since, in reality, other factors are not constant (countries do not have the same level of human capital or the same government policies), absolute convergence does not hold.

Whether this is a depressing result for poor countries depends on what determines the "conditional" nature of the catch-up process. Are slow-growing countries held back by government policies that can be changed easily and quickly? Or are more fundamental forces at work?

Most empirical evidence points to the primacy of government choices. Countries that have pursued broadly free-market policies—in particular, trade liberalisation and the maintenance of secure property rights—have raised their growth rates. In a recent paper, Jeffrey Sachs and Andrew Warner divided a sample of 111 countries into "open" and "closed". The "open" economies showed strikingly faster growth and convergence than the "closed" ones. Smaller government also helps. Robert Barro, among others, has found that higher government spending tends to be associated with slower growth.

Human capital—education and skills—has also been found to matter. Various statistical analyses have shown that countries with lots of human capital relative to their physical capital are likely to grow faster than those with less. Many economists argue that this was a factor in East Asia's success: in the early 1960s the Asian tigers had relatively well-educated workforces and low levels of physical capital.

A more difficult issue is the importance of savings and investment. One implication of the neoclassical theory is that higher investment should mean faster growth (at least for a while). The empirical studies suggest that high investment is indeed associated with fast growth. But they also show that investment is not enough by itself. In fact the causality may run in the opposite direction: higher growth may, in a virtuous circle, encourage higher saving and investment. This makes sense: communist countries, for instance, had extraordinarily high investment but, burdened with bad policies in other respects, they failed to turn this into high growth.

The number-crunching continues; new growth-influencing variables keep being added to the list. High inflation is bad for growth; political stability counts; the results on democracy are mixed; and so on. The emerging conclusion is that the poorest countries can indeed catch up, and that their chances of doing so are maximised by policies that give a greater role to competition and incentives, at home and abroad.

But surely, you might think, this hides a contradiction? The new growth theory suggests that correct government policies can permanently raise growth rates. Empirical cross-country analysis, however, seems to show that less government is better—a conclusion that appeals to many neoclassical theorists. This tension is especially pronounced for the East Asian tigers. Advocates of free market point to East Asia's trade liberalisation in the 1960s, and its history of low government spending, as keys to the Asian miracle. Interventionists point to subsidies and other policies designed to promote investment.

Reflecting the present spirit of rapprochement between the growth models, it is now widely argued that this contradiction is more apparent than real. Work by Alwyn Young, popularised by Paul Krugman, has shown that much of the Asian tiger's success can be explained by the neoclassical model. It resulted from a rapid accumulation of capital (through high investment) and labour (through population growth and increased labour-force participation). On this view, there is nothing particularly miraculous about Asian growth: it is an example of "catch-up". Equally, however, the outlines of East Asian success fit the new growth model. Endogenous growth theory says that government policy to increase human capital or foster the right kinds of investment in physical capital can permanently raise economic growth.

The question is which aspect of East Asian policies was more important—which, up to a point, is the same as asking which growth model works best. Although debate continues, the evidence is less strong that micro-level encouragement of particular kinds of investment was crucial in Asia. Some economists dissent from that judgment, but they are a minority. Most agree that broader policies of encouraging education, opening the economy to foreign technologies, promoting trade and keeping taxes low mattered more.

ONE MORE HEAVE

There is no doubt that the neoclassical model of the 1950s, subsequently enhanced, together with the theories pioneered by Mr Romer, have greatly advanced economists' understanding of growth. Yet the earlier doubt remains. Both models, in their purest versions, treat the role of government only indirectly. The new empirical work on conditional convergence has set out to put this right. The fact remains that in the earlier theoretical debate between the neoclassical and the new schools, the question that matters most—what should governments do to promote growth?—was often forgotten.

A new paper by Mancur Olson makes this point in an intriguing way. The starting-point for today's empirical work is a striking fact: the world's fastest-growing economies are a small subgroup of exceptional performers among the poor countries. Viewed in the earlier theoretical perspective, this is actually rather awkward. Mr Romer's theories would lead you to expect that the richest economies would be the fastest growers: they are not. The basic neoclassical theory suggests that the poorest countries, on the whole, should do better than the richest: they do not. Neither approach, taken at face value, explains the most striking fact about growth in the world today.

Mr Olson argues that the simplest versions of both theories miss a crucial point. Both assume that, given the resources and technology at their disposal, countries are doing as well as they can. Despite their differences, both are theories about how changes in available resources affect output—that is, both implicitly assume that, if resources do not change, output cannot either. But suppose that poor countries simply waste lots of resources. Then the best way for them to achieve spectacular growth is not to set about accumulating more of the right kind of resources—but to waste less of those they already have.

Marshalling the evidence, Mr Olson shows that slow-growing poor countries are indeed hopelessly failing to make good use of their resources. Take labour, for instance. If poor countries were using labour as well as they could, large emigrations of labour from poor to rich countries (from Haiti to the United States, for instance) ought to raise the productivity of workers left behind (because each worker now has more capital, land and other resources to work with). But emigration does not have this effect.

Data on what happens to migrants in their new homes are likewise inconsistent with the two growth theories. Immigrants' incomes rise by far more than access to more capital and other resources would imply. It follows that labour (including its human capital, entrepreneurial spirit, cultural traits and the rest) was being squandered in its country of origin. When workers move, their incomes rise partly because there is more capital to work with—but also by a further large margin, which must represent the wastage incurred before. Mr Olson adduces similar evidence to show that capital and knowledge are being massively squandered in many poor countries.

This offers a rationale for the pattern of growth around the world—a rationale that, consistent with the recent work on conditional convergence, places economic policies and institutions at the very centre. According to this view, it is putting it mildly to say that catch-up is possible: the economic opportunities for poor countries are, as the tigers have shown, phenomenal. The problem is not so much a lack of resources, but an inability to use existing resources well. It is surely uncontroversial to say that this is the right way to judge the performance of communist countries (those exemplars of negative value-added) before 1989. Mr Olson's contention is that most of today's poor countries are making mistakes of an essentially similar kind.

The question still remains: what are the right policies? One must turn again to the empirical evidence. That seems a frustrating answer because, suggestive though recent work on conditional convergence may be, such findings will always be contested. Citizens of the world who sensibly keep an eye on what economists are up to can at least take pleasure in this: the profession has chosen for once to have one of its most vigorous debates about the right subject.

Main Papers Cited

"Increasing Returns and Long-Run Growth". By Paul Romer. Journal of Political Economy, 1986.

"Economic Reform and the Process of Global Integration". By Jeffrey Sachs and Andrew Warner. Brookings Papers on Economic Activity, 1995.

"The Tyranny of Numbers: Confronting the Statistical Realities of the East Asian Experience". By Alwyn Young. NBER working paper 4680, 1994.

"Big Bills Left on the Sidewalk: Why Some Nations Are Rich, and Others Poor". By Mancur Olson. Journal of Economic Perspectives, forthcoming.

Technology and Its Discontents

Our growing faith in computers raises a troubling question: Are we sacrificing reason on the sacred altar of information?

Reed Karaim

After covering the 1992 presidential campaign for Knight-Ridder Newspapers, Reed Karaim retired from 15 years of daily journalism to try his hand at fiction and magazine writing.

Early this winter Kirkpatrick Sale, co-founder in the 1980s of New York's short-lived Green Party, was among 26 "visionaries" gathered on the stage of Manhattan's Town Hall by *Utne Reader,* commonly referred to as the *Reader's Digest* of the counterculture. When Sale's turn came to share his vision with the audience, he was concise.

The 57-year-old activist and writer took a sledgehammer and, swinging it over his shoulder like a lumberjack, smashed a personal computer set up onstage. The first blow connected with the monitor; which bounced and exploded in a puff of shattered glass. The second crushed the keyboard into shards of plastic. "It turned out to be incredibly satisfying," Sale said afterward. "I was surprised, really, how good it felt."

Americans are told almost daily that we have entered the "information age" or even the "second industrial revolution," a time of endlessly unfolding technological wonder. *Newsweek,* in a recent special issue, went so far as to declare that we are in the midst of a kind of second Creation, the Big Bang followed by the "Bit Bang." From *Army Times* to MTV, the country is rushing to go on-line, digitize, dive down the virtual rabbit hole. But there is a little-noticed circle of social critics who beg to differ. Metaphorically at least, they are hammering away at our enthusiasm for the high-tech future.

This movement, if it can be granted the force of that word, ranges from neo-Luddites, like Sale, who see our souls trickling away every time a fluorescent light flickers on, to Internet jockeys who wish to raise a few caution flags about where we are headed. Neil Postman, a communications professor at New York University whose book *Technopoly* is one of the movement's touchstones, captures the ambivalence that characterizes many critics when he calls himself a "loving resistance fighter."

The technology-resistance movement clearly operates in occupied territory; but it may have more sympathizers than are apparent. When Bill Henderson, a New York publisher, wrote an Op-Ed piece in *The New York Times* last spring announcing the neo-Luddite "Lead Pencil Club," he received more than 600 letters of support.

Declaring his intention to "create a pothole on the Information Superhighway," Henderson took the pencil as a symbol of the virtues of old-fashioned communication and declared Thoreau the club's honorary founder. "I did it with a sense of humor," Henderson says. "But these letters I've gotten are impassioned. People are very upset, particularly by computers, the info net. They thought nobody else felt this way."

A sign of the pervasive triumph of technological culture is that most critics approach it gingerly. It's as if the PLO felt compelled to label itself "the Greater Israel Improvement Society" just to get people to listen. For what the resistance proposes is no less than a remaking of the map, a change in world view. It asks us to contemplate the possibility that we are shredding our society on the bright, shiny edge of our own cleverness.

The enigma of humankind's relationship to its machines has always been how much we are remade by the things we make. The Wright brothers, for example, gave birth not just to the airplane but also to the pilot and, finally, the bombardier. And so, is it fair to ask if the spark of imagination on which humanity takes wing ultimately lights the fires of Dresden?

The first response is that new technologies are simply tools, and whether they help or harm society depends on the wisdom of those who use them. The airplane leads no more inevitably to the firebombings of World War II than a hammer does to a bludgeoning. "Machines themselves are not good or bad, relationships between people are good or bad," says Phil Agre, a professor at the University of California, San Diego, whose on-line Internet news service, "The Red Rock Eater," examines issues central to the information age. "Technologies don't do things. People do things."

But in the eyes of the resistance, this is the fundamental error. Technology, they say, is *never* neutral. "Embedded in every tool is an ideological bias," writes Postman, "a predisposition to construct the world as one thing rather than another." He notes an old adage—"to a man with a hammer, everything looks like a nail" (apparently, even a key-

From *Civilization* magazine, May/June 1995, pp. 47-51.

board). He then adds, "To a man with a computer, everything looks like data."

The 20th century has been distinguished by transforming technologies: the automobile, the airplane, the atomic bomb, the television. The computer leads the way into uncharted ground. Voice-activated programming, robotics, artificial intelligence, mechanical implants, biotechnology—all of these "advances" blur the distinction between human and machine. Already our computers greet us with more courtesy than most salesclerks, have more facts on hand than our teachers and are more fan than half the people we meet at parties. On the other hand, it is not unknown for programmers to dream in computer code.

In this world, we have elevated the computer in status until it has become a kind of squared-off Buddha squatting at the center of our culture. It is the first machine that "thinks" and, until last year, when the Pentium chip unexpectedly proved unable to do certain calculations, was widely accepted as thinking flawlessly. "The computer doesn't make mistakes" has become an offhand way of comparing the rickety structure of human reasoning with the sleek precision of silicon-chip logic. Among artificial-intelligence engineers, consciousness is often considered to be only a particularly thorny software challenge. Once we can harness sufficient processing capability with the right program, it is assumed computers will quickly leave us behind. In the oft-quoted words of Ed Fredkin, an artificial-intelligence specialist formerly at M.I.T., "If we are lucky, they will keep us as pets."

How can the mind, a clumsy apparatus that forgets where it has left the car keys, hope to compete with a device that can regurgitate the complete works of Shakespeare? Theodore Roszak, a professor of history at California State University, argues that we have fallen into a trap in measuring ourselves by the machine, a trap exalting the limited, linear, data-processing capabilities of silicon chips over the intuitive nature of human consciousness.

In Roszak's view, human thought is a marvel of intuition and epiphany. The difference between man and machine, Roszak says, is understanding that "the mind thinks with ideas, not with information." In his book *The Cult of Information,* Roszak argues that the "data merchants" have endlessly hyped the significance of bits of information as they hurried us down the road to the new age. But "master ideas"—the religious and philosophical teachings at the center of our culture and consciousness—"are based on no information whatever." An example: "All men are created equal." This idea cannot be proved through the accumulation, addition or subtraction of data, but nonetheless millions have found it to be self-evident.

None of this has stopped educators from rushing to embrace computers as classroom tools, spurred on by manufacturers who have donated hardware to schools or sold it at greatly reduced prices. Roszak, however, notes that there is no empirical evidence that learning by computer is superior to learning through traditional methods. The computer is an excellent tool for rote memorization, but the essence of learning remains learning to *think.* Even as a tool for simple study, the computer cannot bypass the laborious process of mastering difficult subjects. As Princeton's Edward Tenner notes, "The trick isn't getting ancient Greek texts on-line, the trick is getting somebody to read ancient Greek."

Electronic databases have become common tools for academics, journalists and countless others who routinely sift through large amounts of information in their work. This reliance is also not without its problems. The most common are errors that refuse to die, rising like vampires from the grave to be reprinted in report after report. Still, electronic databases have made more information more accessible to a greater number of people. The Library of Congress's new on-line system, "THOMAS," for example, makes congressional data that used to be the province of Capitol Hill insiders available to anyone with access to the Internet. THOMAS, named for the Library's founder, Thomas Jefferson, provides the full text of bills, press releases and committee schedules in one location on the Net.

Remember the paperless office that was coming with the computer? Ever ponder how the push-button phone, which was supposed to speed up dialing, led to the automated systems that make simple calls last half a lifetime? (*... Dial 9 for more options... Dial 7 for accounts receivable... Please enter your account number now... Please hold... I'm sorry, the computer system is down... Thank you for calling Transworld MegaBank, your friendly neighhorhood bank...*)

The curious way the world has of getting even, defeating our best efforts to speed it up and otherwise improve it, has been termed "revenge effect" by Tenner, who has written extensively on our interaction with technology. Tenner believes that the failure of technology to solve problems can often be traced to the interaction between machine and man. Freeways, intended to speed travel, lead to suburbs, which end up spreading urban sprawl out instead of up, so commuting times climb. Computers make it remarkably easy to copy and print files, so many more files are copied and printed, and the paperless office fills up with paper.

The great problem of the 19th century was how to get more information . . . the new problem is information glut
—Neil Postman

New technology can also add extra layers of complication to what were simpler tasks. The automated phone system is only one example. Computers have allowed airlines to create fare systems so complicated that they cannot be understood without the aid of another computer. In *Harvard Magazine,* Tenner writes that the airline industry has recorded as many as 600,000 fare changes in 24 hours. This phenomenon, which Tenner calls "recomplicating," also explains why the clock on your VCR is blinking at 12:00 right now.

Now comes, at the heart of the information age, the on-line computer network, brought to you by your personal computer. The technologies are still awkward, but we can already shop, bank, read magazines, sample videos, make plane reservations and find a date through our computers. We can also "chat." The word has been remade to mean casual communication through typing.

Boy, can we chat. America Online, the country's most popular on-line service, with 2 million subscribers, resembles nothing so much as an electronic tower of babble. Log in and you can find electronic conversations rolling along about everything from comic books to Clinton. Television, sensing its reign over the electronic world threatened, is rushing to catch up. Soon, Vice President Gore and House Speaker Gingrich tell us with the enthusiasm of 16-year-olds contemplating the ultimate car stereo, we will be able to get 500 channels, many interactive.

But if 500 channels mean 300 *I Love Lucy* reruns, if interaction means home shopping and a chance to play Mortal Kombat head-to-head, are we really richer as a society? Librarian of Congress James H. Billington, describing the Library's plans for putting materials on the information superhighway (CIVILIZATION Jan.–Feb. 1995), offers a cautionary note: "Our democracy and, more than ever, our economic vitality depend on the kind of active mind that the print culture—the culture of the book and of the newspaper—has historically nurtured, and that television, feeding an essentially passive spectator habit, does not."

The benefits promised from the virtual world are virtually endless—more information, more entertainment, more choices. The on-line networks, supporters say, amount to a flowering of democracy, a million voices raised—*empowerment.* "On line it doesn't matter what color you are, how handsome you are, where you went to school," says Mike Godwin, an attorney who writes frequently about networks. "What matters is the quality of your ideas."

But what "revenge effect" will the virtual world have? The technology-resistance movement begins by pointing out that we are cobbling together virtual communities while our real cities crumble, at least partly because our sense of common purpose has frayed. Today, only about 5 percent of American households are on-line, but what happens, the critics wonder, when half the country is wired?

Will we escape the unpleasant complications of the world outside our locked doors by opting for communities in "cyberspace," where we can enjoy the company of people who share our interests and our views? Where the streets never need to be cleaned and you don't have to keep an eye on your neighbor's house? What happens if the sirens outside become too distracting? Will we simply buy insulated drapes?

"Prescribing greater mobility—whether automotive or electronic—as an antidote to society's fragmentation is like recommending champagne as a hangover remedy," says Tenner.

Richard Sclove, founder of the Loka Institute in Amherst, Massachusetts, which studies society's relationship with technology, has drawn fire from on-line enthusiasts by suggesting that we will need to find ways to temper the effects of virtual communities on everyday life. One possibility, Sclove says, is raising on-line access rates one night a week, levying a tax that would be used to promote genuine community activities. The idea is that Tuesday nights, for example, might become "community nights," when Americans unplug themselves and wander out goggle-eyed to vote, attend town meetings, relax and involve themselves in the things that need doing in the real world.

Smaller businesses, the neighborhood hardware and grocery stores already hurt by discount chains, may need similar help to fend off on-line shopping services, Sclove says. If not, "cyberspace will finish what Wal-Mart started."

The idea that on-line debate represents a flowering of democracy also comes under attack. Critics say we are mistaking the ability to voice an opinion for the ability to influence decisions. You can contact the White House through e-mail, but your message has no better chance of reaching the eyes of the president than it ever did.

"Everybody always talks about how [every advance in mass communication] is going to help the little guy," Tenner says. "But then the powers that be see how they can use the technology and they wind up using and controlling it quite well."

The *littlest* guy, the person at the bottom of the economic ladder, may simply be left out. The quality of your ideas doesn't matter very much if you can't get on-line. Tenner notes that the information "revolution" is unique in requiring an entrance fee of $1,200 or more for a computer. Godwin and others argue that you can buy a used system for much less. You can, but you'll find precious little software to run on it.

Those who see a flowering of democracy in computer networks generalize from their own middle- or upper-class experiences and assume the skills needed to go on-line are universal, observes Sonia Jarvis, a communications professor at George Washington University. She cites the finding of a Department of Education study that nearly half the U.S. adult population has difficulty dealing with complex information. In the poorest urban areas, she says, up to 25 percent of the homes do not even have phones. "How much sense does it make for the Speaker of the House to talk about putting lap-tops in the ghetto, when the rest of the infrastructure there makes that meaningless?" she asks. "When they can't read? When their schools are falling apart?"

So many images, words and other items are being cataloged and stored electronically that some librarians worry about our ability to retrieve what we need. "The great problem of the 19th century was how to get more information to more people fast and in diverse forms," says Postman. "The new problem is information glut." One imagines future explorers digging into long-forgotten databases the way archaeologists unearth lost cities, finding who knows what buried in the deepening sediment of the information age.

John R. Stilgoe, a professor of visual and environmental studies at Harvard, has noted the subtle degradation that occurs as information is microfilmed, digitized or moved on-line. The idea that something is preserved when it is transferred to the new technologies is an illusion, according to Stilgoe. What is preserved is a *facsimile.* The distinction can be minor if it is a piece of text but significant if it is an image or the reproduction of an object.

Stilgoe, who refuses to have a computer in his office because he says it inevitably ends up the center of attention, led a battle at Harvard against a plan to put much of the university library's archives of old magazines and other periodicals on microfilm. In his research, Stilgoe has examined old advertising to compare the fortunes of the automobile and railroad industries. There is a point in the early 20th century, he thinks, where advertising reveals the shift in the industries' fortunes—the train ads go from color to black and white while the automobile ads spring into glorious color for the first time.

"That tells you a tremendous amount," Stilgoe says. But it would have been lost with the transfer to microfilm, which records only in black and white. (Recognizing the legitimacy of the issue, Harvard decided to allow continued access to the original publications in storage.) The Library of Congress has moved to make its wealth of materials more broadly available through digitization. But Billington says the Library recognizes the distinctive value of the printed word and will continue to collect and make generally available books, magazines, newspapers and the rest. "Only a small fraction of humanity's vast paper record will be—or should be—digitized in the foreseeable future," he says.

The ability of computers to "enhance" images goes to the core of the resistance movement's objections to the virtual world. When we look at pictures of distant galaxies clarified by computer, are we looking into the far corners of the universe or the mind of the programmer? When we have redefined words such as *chat, community, visit* and *presence,* they ask, haven't we yielded some part of ourselves in the process?

Throughout history, there have been those who saw our doom approaching with every new contrivance, from the written alphabet to the television. When some cave dweller first lit his own fire, a guy dressed in skins sitting two rocks down probably turned to his buddy and said, "Oh man, I'm not sure *this* is a good idea."

The trick isn't getting Greek texts on-line, the trick is getting somebody to read ancient Greek
—Edward Tenner

Socrates worried that the written word might cripple learning. The medieval gristmill, the crossbow and the printing press were so threatening to the established order that political and religious leaders tried to ban or restrict their use. By the time the original Luddites came on the scene in the early 19th century, they were, at least indirectly, the inheritors of a tradition.

Kirkpatrick Sale, who happily smashed a computer in the opening of our story, has just had published *Rebels Against the Future,* a history of the Luddite movement and its relevance to today. The Luddites were a product of England's transformation into an industrial economy, which sharply lowered income and employment among the working class. The shift was particularly painful in cloth manufacturing, which had been a cottage industry until new mills and looms made it the business of factories. Suddenly, fewer weavers were required, and those who were working found themselves toiling in brutally primitive factories.

The people of England's industrial heartland reacted by breaking looms, burning factories and waging a war on the machine that lasted roughly from 1811 to 1816. They took their name from Ned Ludd, an early protester who was probably mythical. The British government responded by dispatching 14,000 troops to put down the protests and by making the act of destroying factory equipment a crime punishable by death.

"It seems so symbolic that the industrial revolution is won when the idea of killing a machine becomes a capital crime," Sale says. "There was only one voice raised against it in Parliament—George Gordon, Lord Byron . . . the great Romantic poet."

It ought to be noted that historians are divided about how much English workers suffered from the industrial revolution. There are those who argue that the cottage system of production has been falsely romanticized, and that life improved in modest ways for some workers who moved from the countryside to cities.

There have been no angry mobs taking hammers to the robots in auto plants, but the second industrial revolution has paralleled the first for many workers. Manufacturing jobs have fallen from about 30 percent to about 15 percent of the labor force. Job loss to computerized automation—the robot arms that toil tirelessly in many factories—has been estimated at roughly half a million a year from 1988 to 1994. Wassily Leontief, a Nobel Prize-winning economist, has suggested that people's role in manufacturing may go the way of the horse's in farming. Those of us too young to be put out to pasture will seek work in a changed world. Peter Drucker, a social scientist and writer, estimates that a third of us will be "knowledge workers." But for every software designer and laser surgeon, there be more waiters, janitors and nurse's aides toiling in lower-paying service industries.

James Gilbert, a historian at the University of Maryland who has studied utopian thought, says Luddite tradition within America has been of a different strain than the British model. Since at least the days of Emerson, there has been a current within American intellectual circles that exalts the beauty and solitude of nature over urban living. Thoreau contemplating the world in his cabin at Walden Pond and is the expression of this ideal.

America, however, is also a technologically obsessed society, the country of Franklin, Edison and Ford. Other nations have their counts and kings; we have captains of industry. And despite all predictions of doom, we have by traditional measures prospered. Our culture has its ills, but people live longer, enjoy better health and have more time to pursue their own interests than at any previous time in history. The country has survived the nuclear age and even, at least so far, television.

Why should today's alarms about our industrial, gadget-bewitched society be taken any more seriously than those of the past? The difference, say those in the technology resistance, is that never have we been so dependent on the products of our own ingenuity. The automobile determines where most of us travel. The television determines much of our leisure. Hidden technologies such as advertising and polling rule our political and corporate spheres. Postman calls the world we live in a "technopoly." Jerry Mander, an environmental activist whose book *In the Absence of the Sacred* is an evangelical text for many in the movement, calls our world a "technosphere."

"Technologies have organized themselves in relation to other technologies to create an interactive web, of which we're only one part," Mander says. "We feed it, and we serve it, and we interact with and we co-evolve with it, and we slowly become it. We're practicing a form of intra-species suicide."

We have now returned to the landscape of the unabashed neo-Luddites, a world where our only chance of survival is to abandon much of 20th-century technology to adopt a harmonious relationship with nature. The neo-Luddites have a particular distaste for television, which they view as a perverse addiction that dulls the mind into passivity while filling the body with unfocused anxiety.

It is tempting to write off the neo-Luddites and their grandiose suggestions that our first steps toward a saner society should be eliminating television and computers, as well as the chemical and power industries, which they think are befouling the environment. But the way our technology mediates and controls our daily existence *can* be unsettling, even in small and unexpected ways. For two months I have been "talking" with people in the technology-resistance movement. We have communicated by telephone, fax and e-mail. Many of those I have spoken to do not have computers. But they have been able to hear me typing on mine as we talk on the telephone, and most have fallen into the rhythm of the clicking keys, pacing their thoughts to my ability to input data on this machine. No one has even mentioned it.

Huddled in our homes amid neglected cities, our brains numbed into a stupor while our hearts race like engines popped into neutral because of television, turning late at night to the illusory companionship of strangers in electronic worlds where those who disagree with our prejudices can be dispatched with a keystroke, unable to relate to the leisurely reality of a sunset or trees creaking in the wind, surrounded by gadgets, yet more alone than ever—Is this really to be our future? There is a kind of apocalyptic, end-of-the-millennium gloom, a distaste for the world we have made, that permeates the thinking of the neo-Luddites. Maybe the world is being swallowed up by the technological spider, but it is also undeniably true that moose are drifting back into the Great Plains, most children are still amazed by a dandelion, and a good lightning storm can reduce even jaded urbanites to mute awe.

It seems clear that our machines and our technological society need to be remade to adhere more closely to the spirit of humanity. We should view with greater skepticism the latest electronic wonders paraded before our eyes. The rush to computerize our schools and our lives needs more debate. Smashing computers may be extreme, but turning one off can be good for the soul.

Still, we are tool-making creatures. It is hard to see, absent a neo-Luddite theocracy, how this can be changed. Or why we should deny the creative spirit that finds expression not only in Picasso but also in Edison. In his novel *Player Piano,* Kurt Vonnegut conjures up a future in which technology has left people useless and unemployed. The disenchanted rise up and destroy the machines. Yet in the last scene, some men come across a broken orange-drink machine and begin fiddling with it. "We'll fix that, won't we, Bud?" one of them says excitedly. And the strange, often troubling compulsion humanity has to make and remake its world sparks anew.

Whither Western Civilization?

Achievements and Prospects

Thomas Sowell

Mr. Sowell is a Senior Fellow at the Hoover Institution.

There are many reasons to enumerate and reflect upon the achievements of Western civilization, other than a parochial vanity. For several centuries now, Western civilization has been the dominant civilization on this planet, so that its fate is intertwined with the fate of human beings around the world, whether they live in Western or non-Western societies. The products of Western civilization, from the sophisticated technology of air travel to various flavors of carbonated drinks, can be found in the most remote and non-Western regions of the world. More important, the ideas and ideals of Western civilization are in the minds and hearts of people of non-Western races with non-Western traditions. Perhaps the most dramatic examples were the throngs of Chinese people who risked their lives in Tiananmen Square for Western concepts of freedom and democracy.

Unfortunately, even to speak of the achievements of Western civilization goes against the grain of the intellectual fashions of our time. Both Western and non-Western intellectuals tend to judge and condemn the West, not by comparison with the achievements and shortcomings of alternative cultures and traditions, but by comparison with standards of perfection which all things human must inevitably fail. Such attitudes of sweeping, corrosive, and incessant condemnation from within are among the principal dangers to the survival of Western civilization.

WESTERN CIVILIZATION AS GLOBAL CIVILIZATION

Western civilization today no longer means simply the civilization of Europe, where it originated. Transplants of this civilization in the Western Hemisphere, Australia, and New Zealand are among its most vigorous elements, and its leadership and survival in a nuclear age depend crucially on the United States of America. The cultural penumbra of Western civilization reaches even farther. Its science and technology are today also the science and technology of Japan. Its languages span the globe and provide a common medium of communication among peoples whose respective mother tongues are incomprehensible to one another. Pilots speak to control towers in English around the world, even if they are Japanese pilots speaking to an Egyptian control tower. English is spoken by a billion people of all races—more people than speak any other language.

Much of the global sweep of Western civilization today, as its critics are quick to point out, is a product of conquest over the past five centuries and of the enslavement of millions of human beings torn from their homelands. Tragically, the horrors of war, subjugation, enslavement, plunder, and devastation are the common heritage of all mankind, on every continent, and in *every* civilization—Western and non-Western. Conquerors and tyrants whose very names struck fear into every heart have come from every region of the globe and have come in every color and countenance found among the human species. What has been peculiar to the West has not been its participation in the common sins and agonies of the human race but its special ways of trying to cope with those sins and agonies—the philosophy, religion, and government of Western civilization, which provided the intellectual and moral foundation on which rise the benefits of freedom, of science, and the material well-being of hundreds of millions of humans around the world.

Western civilization has not always been in the forefront of world civilizations, though it clearly has been for the past two or three centuries. A thousand years ago, China was far more advanced than Europe. As late as the sixteenth century, China had the highest standard of living in the world. There were Chinese dynasties before there was a Roman Empire—indeed, before Rome itself was founded. Confucius had died before Plato and Socrates were born. The Chinese empire had cities of more than a million inhabitants each, at a time when the largest city in Europe contained only fifty thousand people. Even after the emergence of classical Greek and Roman civilization, the evolution of Christianity from its Judaic background, and the rise and fall of the Roman Empire over a period of several centuries, Western civilization was still just one of the great civilizations of the world—not yet preeminent. As late as the Middle Ages, Russian rulers were vassals of the Mongol conquerors, to whom they paid tribute. The Ottoman Empire also penetrated deep into Europe, conquering the Balkans and holding them in subjugation for centuries. As late as the sixteenth century, Ottoman armies were at the gates of Vienna. The organization, science, technology, and scholarship of the Ottoman Empire were comparable to those of Europe, and its military forces won victory after victory against European nations. But, from the seventeenth century on, the tide turned decisively in favor of Western civilization—technologically, militarily, economically, and politically. More than anything else, Western civilization became the free world.

Historically, freedom was a very long time developing in the West, though it developed here earlier and more fully than in any other mass civilization. It has been less than a thousand years since the Magna Charta, yet that document exem-

From *Current*, September 1991, pp. 18-25. Adapted from "Western Civilization: Achievements and Prospects" by Thomas Sowell, from *The World & I*, May 1991, pp. 585-603.

plified a crucially distinctive idea with deep roots in the Western tradition—the idea that the *law* is supreme and not the ruler. Whatever controversies may rage among scholars and polemicists as to the immediate effect or social bias of the Magna Charta, what has made it a landmark in the development of human freedom is that it established the supremacy of law—what has also been called "the rule of law" or "a government of laws and not of men."

THE RULE OF LAW

Like so many of the blessings of Western civilization that we so easily take for granted, the idea of the rule of law is radically different from the principles on which other great civilizations were founded. Even late in the twentieth century, many people in other cultures around the world found it incomprehensible that a president of the United States could be forced out of office on charges that he violated the law. Within Western civilization itself, it is little more than 300 years (not long as history is measured) since Louis XIV said, "I am the state." Yet, even then, the idea so conflicted with Western notions as to be worth remembering. Neither Genghis Khan nor Sultan Süleyman of the Ottoman Empire would have found it necessary to remind anyone that his *word* was the supreme law—and if anyone did need reminding, that reminder would be in blood and not in words. The West itself has of course also had rulers who were above any law—Hitler and Stalin being the most notorious examples, though unfortunately not the only examples. The West itself has not always lived up to Western ideals. The point here is that those ideals were distinct from the ideals of other great civilizations and, ultimately, they have made the West different in reality.

The rule of law—the principle that the law is supreme and that rulers are subject to it—goes far back into Roman times. The Emperor Julian once fined himself ten pounds of gold for a minor transgression and, in the words of Edward Gibbon, "embraced this public occasion of declaring to the world that he was subject, like the rest of his fellow-citizens, to the laws." Roman emperors in general were among the most flagrant violators of this principle, but the principle outlived the emperors and the empire—and ultimately the principle triumphed. The Magna Charta was only one landmark on the road to that triumph. The Constitution of the United States was another.

Other great civilizations might have traditions or religions to which the ruler was at least nominally subject, but no human being was authorized to disobey, oppose, or nullify the edicts of the ruler, as appellate courts under the U.S. Constitution can nullify the edicts of presidents or Congress. In the great Chinese dynasties, for example, as a scholar has noted:

> Chinese law was always merely an instrument of government; it was not thought to have divine sanction, nor was it considered an inviolable constitution. It was part of, and inseparable from, routine administration. There were no provisions limiting state authority, and there was no church or independent judiciary before which the state could legally be called to account.

In the Ottoman Empire, the supremacy of the ruler was likewise subject to no constraint. According to Lord Kinross' classic study of the Ottoman Empire, a fifteenth-century sultan "who was known to have ambivalent sexual tastes sent a Eunuch to the house of Notaras, demanding that he supply his good-looking fourteen-year-old son for the Sultan's pleasure." Notaras, a Christian, chose instead that he and his son would be beheaded—but that was the only alternative. There was no law higher than the sultan's command. The rule of law seems like such a mundane phrase, but without it, freedom and human dignity are in deadly peril. It is, perhaps, Western civilization's greatest gift to the world.

The rule of law, the supremacy of law, a government of laws and not of men—different ways of saying the same thing—is not a result of words written on pieces of paper. The Magna Charta was not accepted because King John thought it was a good idea but because the amount of military power lined up against him by his barons left him no choice. *Power offset by power* has remained the key to freedom through the rule of law. When the Constitution of the United States was crafted, the separation of powers was the heart and soul of it. The ability of each branch of government to impede or nullify the powers of the other branches means that there is no individual with supreme power.

What is to prevent whoever controls the military—the ultimate power of brute force—from imposing his will on the other branches of government and on the people at large? This has in fact happened in a number of Third World countries that received their independence after the Second World War, even though many of these countries copied the institutions of Western democracy—in some cases, right down to the powdered wigs of lawyers and judges in the British legal tradition. What they could not copy, however, were the centuries of history, distilled into the traditions that make free institutions viable. In a society where such traditions are deeply imbedded in the moral fiber of its people, no ruler can issue orders to violate the Constitution with any assurance that his officers or troops will obey—and if they do not obey, he may be facing not only the end of his power but imprisonment and disgrace as well. Behind the institutions of freedom are the traditions of freedom that give those institutions strength. Both are among the highest achievements of Western civilization.

SLAVERY AS AN INSTITUTION

Freedom has many dimensions and we so often take them all for granted that we find it almost inconceivable that other places and other times could have seen things so much differently. To virtually anyone raised in modern Western civilization, it is painful to realize that the evil and inhuman institution of slavery has existed in civilizations on every continent inhabited by human beings. Slavery existed for untold thousands of years in China. It existed in the Western Hemisphere long before Columbus' ships ever appeared on the horizon. Africa, Europe, the Middle East—it was virtually everywhere. The eastern European peoples known as Slavs were for centuries slaves—and their name provided the basis for the word. Ten million Africans were shipped as slaves to the Western Hemisphere but fourteen million were sent as slaves to the Islamic countries of the Middle East and North Africa. The sweeping scope and long history of slavery make it entirely possible that most of the peoples on this planet today are descendants of slaves, from one time or place or another.

What is even more incomprehensible to us today than the magnitude and endurance of slavery is that it aroused little, if any, moral concern in most parts of the world. A few offered moral apologies for it but in many places the institution was so widely accepted that no apologies were considered necessary. Only very late in the history of the world's great civilizations did a major moral revulsion against slavery begin. It began in the West.

Those who spearheaded the organized effort to abolish the slave trade were British evangelical Christians. The worldwide abolition of slavery was a long, arduous, and costly struggle—partly because of opposition within Western civilization but much more so because the non-Western world (Asia, Africa, and especially the Arab world) bitterly resisted abolition of this institution, around which their own economies were often built. For more than a half a century, British warships patrolled the waters off the coast of West Africa, capturing slave ships and setting the slaves free in Sierra Leone. It would be difficult, if not impossible, to find in history another example of a great nation committing such resources, for so many decades, for a cause which would gain it neither money nor territory.

The next phase of the struggle was to abolish slavery itself. This abolition first took place in the British Empire in 1834. Within sixty years, slavery was abolished in country after country, throughout the Western Hemisphere. A worldwide institution, untold thousands of years old, was gone from three of the five inhabited continents (North America, South America, and Europe)—all in less than a century. What doomed slavery was that all of Western civilization had finally turned against it.

Other civilizations still retained slavery for generations after it was abolished in Europe and in European offshoot societies around the world. In African societies where the enslavement of other Africans had been going on for centuries before the white man came, there was bitter resistance to the increasing pressures from European nations for an end to the slave trade and an end to slavery itself. Among the Arabs, opposition was the most determined. Even czarist Russia, a despotic government by Western standards, forced the abolition of slavery in Central Asia over the opposition of its Central Asian subjects, who evaded the prohibition, when they dared not defy it.

With slavery, as in other areas, the West has not been immune to the sins that have disgraced the human species around the world for centuries. But what was different about Western civilization was the way it attempted to cope with the sins that have plagued mankind. It is only the fact that the peoples of Western nations share all the shortcomings and evils of other peoples that makes their experience relevant to the rest of humanity and their example an encouragement to others. This is especially true of the United States, which has very few indigenous people and is populated by the peoples of other lands. It is the American traditions and American institutions that keep us free, not our individual virtues or our individual wisdom.

MATERIAL PROSPERITY

While freedom has been the highest achievement of Western civilization, material prosperity has been its most visible achievement. Stark as the contrast is today between an affluent, Western way of life and the grim poverty of many Third World countries, it has been just a few centuries since the masses of people in Europe lived on a level not very different from that found today among the masses in many parts of the Third World. In Scotland, at the beginning of the seventeenth century, people were still using farming implements as primitive as those in ancient Mesopotamia and it was common for ordinary people to live in unventilated, shantylike homes, homes shared with their animals and abounding with vermin. There were somewhat higher standards of living in England and on parts of the European continent but Ireland, southern Italy, and parts of eastern Europe were not better off. As late as the eighteenth century, visitors to Edinburgh found it worth mentioning that the inhabitants of that city no longer disposed of their sewage by throwing it out the windows—which had been a source of considerable unhappiness to passersby, even when warnings were shouted.

What changed all this? No great invention or discovery remade the economies of Europe or of European offshoot societies overseas. Instead, a gradual but persistent economic improvement continued over the years, with occasional setbacks, but building incrementally a new economic world of greater abundance. Here and there the wonders of science and technology gave Western civilization railroads, steamboats, electric lights, radio, and eventually the ability to fly. But the world did not stagnate between great inventions. Progress was virtually continuous and only cumulatively did it become dramatic. It was the wide diffusion of skills rather than the occasional outbursts of genius that was crucial. It was the spread of those skills from one Western nation to another that marked the rise of Western civilization to preeminence in the world, and the diffusion of its products that spread the benefits to non-Western regions of the globe as well.

England, for centuries lagging behind the economic and cultural progress of continental Europe, became in the eighteenth century the spearhead of economic development in Europe and the world. Englishmen introduced railroads to the world, not only by the example of railroad building in their own country, but also by themselves building and manning the first railroads in Germany, Argentina, India, Russia, Kenya, and Malaya—among other places. The steam engine was of course crucial to the railroad, and revolutionized industry and transport in general. For the first time in human history, man could *manufacture his own power* and was no longer dependent on his own muscles, or the muscles of animals, or on the spontaneous forces of nature (such as wind or water power) to get massive amounts of work done.

The modern technology of iron and steel making, on which a whole spectrum of industrial activities depends, also originated in the British Isles. Britain likewise spearheaded the development of the modern textile industry, supplying not only the major inventions but also initially the managers and skilled workers needed to train foreign workmen to operate British-made machinery in Russia, China, India, Mexico, and Brazil. In short, British know-how and British capital were transplanted and took root around the world—in Asia, Africa, and Latin America, as well as in such offshoots of British civilization as the United States, Canada, and Australia.

Once set loose in the world, the skills and technology acquired a life of their own, traveling unfettered, and flourishing wherever the social climate was favorable. While Englishmen had to install industrial equipment in Germany and teach the Germans how to use it, this knowledge was not merely absorbed but improved. By the last decade of the nineteenth century, Germany overtook Great Britain in the production of steel—

and by 1913 German steel output was double that of Britain. Across the Atlantic, the United States took the industrial technology in which the British had pioneered and developed it to become the leading industrial nation in the world. In 1870, Britain produced 32 percent of all the manufactured goods in the world, followed by the United States at 23 percent and Germany at 13 percent. By 1913, however, Britain's relative share of the world's growing supply of manufactured goods was down to 14 percent—exceeded by Germany at 16 percent and by the United States at 36 percent. Far away in Asia, Japan was already busy acquiring Western science and technology, though its own rise to prominence in the international economy was still decades away.

Why some countries and cultures seized upon the leading development in Western civilization and others did not is a question that may never be fully answered. It was certainly not due to "objective, material conditions" as some Marxist or other predestination theorists would have us believe. The industrial revolution did begin in a country (Britain) rich in coal and iron ore, among other natural resources used in industry. But one of the most spectacular current examples of high-technology industrialization is Japan, which is almost totally lacking in natural resources, while countries with rich natural resources (such as Mexico) are often lagging in economic and technological developments.

THE THIRD WORLD AND WESTERN CIVILIZATION

Different responses to the leading scientific, technological, political, and moral developments in the West have not been confined to those nations or cultures within Western civilization itself. Much of the ethnic strife within newly independent Third World countries is between groups who seized the benefits of Western civilization to differing degrees during the colonial era and achieved differing levels of progress and prosperity as a result. In Nigeria, for example, the Muslim northern region did not want Christian missionary schools established in their area. Therefore the majority of Nigerians, who lived in the northern region, did not receive the exposure to Western education received by the Yoruba and Ibo peoples of southern Nigeria. The Ibos, a weaker, poorer tribe in a less productive part of the country, were especially avid for Western education and Western ways. The net results, after two or three generations of British rule in Nigeria, were dramatic inequalities, now favoring southern Nigerians.

As of 1926, there were more than 138,000 Nigerian children in primary school, of whom only about five thousand were in northern Nigeria, where most Nigerians lived. In the middle of the twentieth century, as Nigeria was moving toward independence, there were a total of 160 physicians in the country—only one of whom was from the north. In the army, three-quarters of the riflemen were from the north but four-fifths of the commissioned officers were from the south. As late as 1965, half of the officer corps were from the Ibo minority. Within northern Nigeria itself, at one time most of the factory workers, merchants, and civil servants were from the south. The envy and resentments this generated—especially when inflamed by ambitious political leaders—led eventually to bloodbaths in the streets, in which thirty thousand Ibos were slaughtered by raging mobs in northern Nigeria. Surviving Ibos struggled back to their region of origin in southeastern Nigeria, which tried to secede from Nigeria to form the independent nation of Biafra. A million more lives were lost in the civil war that followed.

American missionary schools were established on the northern tip of the island of Ceylon, off the eastern coast of India, during the era of British colonial rule. This happened to be a region inhabited by the Tamil minority who, like the Ibos of Nigeria, lived in an agriculturally less productive part of the country and who were also eager to seize upon Western education as a way to improve their otherwise limited prospects in life.

By contrast, the Sinhalese majority, who had rich, fertile land, had no such sense of urgency about Western education and their Buddhist leaders were not anxious to see them attend schools run by Western Christian missionaries. With the passing years, the Tamil minority—about 15 percent of the population—became over-represented among those in the educated professions. By 1921, 44 percent of all doctors in Ceylon were Tamils, compared with 34 percent who were from the Sinhalese majority (the rest being members of other minority groups). Even in later years, after education became more widespread, the historical head start of the Tamils was evident in their continued over-representation in high-level professions. As of 1948, on the eve of Ceylon's becoming the independent nation of Sri Lanka, the Tamils were still 40 percent of all engineers and 46 percent of all accountants.

Until this time, Ceylon or Sri Lanka was widely known for having some of the most harmonious relations anywhere among its various ethnic, linguistic, and religious groups. Inequality alone was not enough to cause polarization—but all it needed was one skilled demagogue to whip up group against group. This happened in the 1956 election campaign and Sri Lanka has never been the same. Mob violence of Sinhalese against Tamils erupted again and again over the years, as a country once held up as a model of harmonious intergroup relations saw Sinhalese mobs capture Tamils at random and burn them alive in the streets.

Fortunately, not all intergroup inequalities among groups with differing exposure to Western culture have led to such dramatic and ghastly consequences. But such inequalities have been widespread, from India to Sierra Leone to Latin America. Those indigenous peoples who happened to be located where Western imperial powers established schools, colonial capitals, industry, or port facilities have tended to acquire decisive advantages over those in the hinterlands, and these advantages have persisted long after the Western powers have withdrawn and the former colony has become independent. There is a special irony to this pattern, for many intellectuals—both Western and non-Western—depict the Third World as exploited by the West, its poverty caused by the West, and Western prosperity as being extracted from the colonized nations. In reality, the poorest people in the Third World have typically been those with the least contact with Western civilization, while those who have achieved prosperity and leadership have been those most able and willing to absorb what Western civilization has had to offer.

Much has been said about the prospects of a decline of Western civilization, its eclipse by other, rising civilizations or its institutions and values succumbing to forces within the West with radically different ideas and goals. If there were some better world likely to be created by some new civilization replacing that of the West on the world stage, our fondness for what is familiar to us might have to compete for our loyalties with a broader concern for the happiness and progress of the whole human race. But no such conflict exists. There is no higher and nobler civilization standing in the wings. The alternative political and economic systems contending with Western democracy have little attractive power for the peoples of the world and in some cases have difficulty preventing their own citizens from fleeing to the West.

THE SURVIVAL OF WESTERN CIVILIZATION

With all its achievements, what are the prospects of survival for Western civilization? The external military danger is only one of the threats to the survival of Western civilization. Signs of internal degeneration are both numerous and dangerous: declining educational standards, the disintegration of families, drug addiction, and violent crimes are just some of the more obvious signs. Will such things alone destroy a society and a civilization? Perhaps not. But the internal and external threats are not wholly separate today, any more than they were in the days of the decline and fall of the Roman Empire. Internal demoralization of a free people cannot help affecting the confidence and zeal with which they are prepared to defend themselves—or the resignation with which some are willing to accept other systems that seem only marginally different from what they have.

In the Roman Empire, as in much of Western civilization today, there was a growing class of people who would not work but instead lived off the government. Today, healthy-looking young beggars are as common in Paris as they are in the streets of New York or San Francisco. The economic drain of such people may be overshadowed by the social demoralization they represent and which they contribute to in others.

THE TREASON OF INTELLECTUALS

Much more active agents of demoralization are the intelligentsia, including the media, schoolteachers, and academics. Despite some welcome exceptions, these classes tend generally to take an adversary stance toward Western civilization. Sins and tragedies common to the human race around the world are discussed as if they were peculiarities of "our society." Slavery is only one of these indictments of Western civilization. *Colonialism* or *imperialism* to the intelligentsia mean, almost exclusively, Western colonialism or Western imperialism, even though non-Western countries had empires long before the West and even though the West has been abandoning most of its former empires since World War II. The only empire that has expanded overseas in the postwar era is the Soviet empire, often using Cuban troops to suppress any uprising against unpopular communist regimes in Africa.

Double standards have become almost too common to notice. No matter how many billions of dollars Americans or other Westerners donate to humanitarian causes, at home or overseas, they are still called selfish and materialistic, while other countries are called spiritual and high-principled, on the strength of their words, unsupported by deeds. Representatives of foreign countries, where racial or ethnic clashes have killed more people in a week than such clashes have killed in the United States over the past half-century, nevertheless, lecture Americans on the subject.

Why intellectuals have so often repudiated their own country and civilization in the West is a large question on which there are many theories. Perhaps it is precisely the freedom of the common man—including his ability to ignore intellectuals and live as he chooses—that has made intellectuals look so favorably on so many foreign despotisms that impose a master blueprint from the top down. These despotisms to which many leading Western intellectuals gave praise have included both imperial Russia and China and communist Russia and China. Intellectuals have romanticized despots from Robespierre to Stalin and Castro. But they have not favored *all* despots; the principal difference between those despots who have been praised by intellectuals and those that have not been is that despots with a master plan to remake the common man in a predetermined image have had the intellectuals' support. Ordinary, garden-variety despots seeking power and money, but leaving the common man alone to live as he pleases, have not had the support of the intelligentsia. Intellectuals supported Castro but not Batista, though Castro was more of a despot. Similarly, they supported Mao Tse-tung but not Chiang Kaishek, Lenin but not Czar Nicholas. It is hard to deny Edmund Burke's observation, two hundred years ago, that intellectuals like theories more than people. And they support those who promote social theories. . . .

FREE MARKETS

The success of free market policies in the 1980s in the United States has spread the idea of free markets, not only to countries like Britain under Margaret Thatcher but also to left-wing and socialist governments in France, Australia, and New Zealand. Behind these practical political results have been a growing number of free market intellectuals. Friedrich Hayek once said that he was optimistic for the future because he was virtually alone when he wrote *The Road to Serfdom* in 1944. Now there are such intellectual giants as Milton Friedman and organizations—think tanks—springing up across the United States, in Britain, Jamaica, Hong Kong, Peru, Australia, and New Zealand. The political Left remains still dominant among intellectuals but today, at least, there is a struggle going on to save the basic values and institutions of Western civilization. Moreover, it is a struggle that can be won.

While millions of refugees from all parts of the world have flooded into Western democratic nations over the past half-century or more, some have come from totalitarian countries within Europe—first from Nazi Germany and its satellites and subjugated nations during the 1930s and 1940s, and now from the Soviet bloc. Russia has always been only partly a Western nation, whether under the czars or under the communists. It is not primarily a question of geography, though more of that country lies in Asia than in Europe. Nor is it a matter of racial composition, for people of European origin are about as high a proportion of the Soviet population as of the population of the United States. Russia has always been a fringe member of Western civilization in the deeper sense that the West's greatest achievements—freedom, democracy, and material prosperity—have come to the Russian empire (for that is what it still is) slowly, incompletely, and with a lag, if at all.

Nazi Germany likewise illustrates the fact that some of the greatest dangers to the survival of Western civilization can come from within Europe itself. Had

Hitler triumphed, nothing that we would recognize as Western civilization would have survived—not freedom, certainly not democracy, nor any of the other humane or spiritual achievements we call Western civilization. It is doubtful how long even material progress could have continued under suffocating economic controls by the Nazi state.

Western civilization today is endangered primarily from within the West—ideologically by Marxism, militarily by the Soviet bloc, morally and socially by degeneration within Western democratic nations. Let us look first at the external dangers and then at the internal dangers. Finally, let us console ourselves with a few hopeful signs that all may not be lost, though the hour is late and the outcome still uncertain.

Shortly after the end of the Second World War, Winston Churchill said: "There was never a war in all history easier to prevent than the war which has just desolated such great areas of the globe." How could the leaders of the Western democracies have failed to prevent a war that was preventable—a war in which forty million human beings lost their lives? They failed by operating on assumptions very much like our assumptions today and following policies very much like the policies of Western democracies in our time.

THE ILLUSION OF PACIFISM

One of the fundamental assumptions of the Western democracies throughout the period between the two world wars was that military weapons were the problem and that international treaties to reduce weapons were the answer. Strong pacifist movements and pacifist sentiments existed throughout the West, in the wake of the terrible carnage and devastation of the First World War. The shadow of that war hung over a whole generation, much as the grim shadow of Vietnam has hung over a generation of Americans. The determination to avoid another war is not only understandable but highly laudable. What was tragic was that the policies chosen led directly into another—and even worse—World War. At the heart of those policies was the assumption that disarmament treaties meant peace and that building a military deterrent meant war. Then, as now, maintaining and modernizing military forces sufficient to deter potential aggressors was called an "arms race"—something to be avoided at almost any cost.

If the theory that disarmament and international treaties mean peace were correct, there would never have been a Second World War. The two decades leading up to that war were filled with disarmament agreements and international peace treaties—perhaps more so than any other two decades in the history of the world. This long string of ineffective treaties began with the Treaty of Versailles that ended the First World War. That treaty severely limited the military forces Germany would be permitted to have, did not allow those forces to be stationed in Germany's Rhineland, and forbade the Germans from having military conscription. Those were the peace terms imposed by the victors on the vanquished.

Almost immediately after the war, new international disarmament agreements and treaties were signed among all the leading powers of the world, including not only large and small nations in Europe but also the United States and Japan. The 1920s saw the Washington Naval Agreement of 1922, the Kellog-Briand Pact, and the Locarno Pact, among others. The 1930s saw the Lausanne Conference of 1932, later an agreement between Britain and Germany limiting each side's naval forces, the Munich agreement of 1938, and the nonaggression pact of 1939 between Nazi Germany and the Soviet Union. Added to all this, and often part of the process, were repeated visits of heads of states, to establish "personal contacts" as British Prime Minister Neville Chamberlain repeatedly called them. Heads of state had met before to work out international agreements, as at Versailles in 1919 or at the Congress of Vienna in 1815. But now there were repeated, almost incessant meetings, supplemented by public exchanges of letters between heads of state. . . .

Why did all these efforts for peace end so tragically in war? Fundamentally, it was because international peace, like domestic freedom, depends on a *balance* between opposing forces. Both pacifist movements and disarmament treaties had completely asymmetrical effects on democratic nations and totalitarian powers. Pacifist movements operate freely and pacifist sentiments influence foreign policy only in democratic nations. They weaken the ability of democratic nations to maintain sufficient military forces to balance those of totalitarian nations. Disarmament treaties are likewise asymmetrical. It is much easier for a totalitarian government to maintain secrecy when it cheats on a disarmament treaty, even when the treaty itself is evenhanded. In addition, the political pressures are on democratic leaders to sign an agreement, which will be regarded as a "success," while returning home empty-handed from an international meeting will be considered a "failure." The actual specific terms of an agreement are likely to be known and their implications understood by far fewer people than those who measured "success" or "failure" by whether or not a treaty was signed. A totalitarian government, which does not have to meet the same pressures and potential public criticism at home, is in a much better position to hold out for favorable terms before signing. . . .

History need not inevitably repeat itself. Recent changes within the Soviet bloc may be matched by changes in their foreign policy as well. It is much too early to know how real or how lasting any of these changes are. But it is worth looking back at what preceded these changes. It was Ronald Reagan's insistence on matching the Soviet nuclear buildup in Europe with new American missiles in Europe, pointed at the Soviet Union. While many in the media decried the futility of a new "arms race," declaring that the Soviet Union would match everything we did, round after round, the Soviets themselves understood that they did not have the unlimited resources implied by that argument. In fact, the stresses of maintaining their existing military forces were being felt economically and politically.

Now that a show of strength and resolve has brought some pullbacks by the Soviets and some hope of better future relations, the cry is already heard, in Congress and elsewhere, that we should cut back our military forces, as they are no longer so necessary. This attitude is painfully similar to the attitude that developed after the discovery of a polio vaccine, which led to sharp reductions in the incidence of that disease. When there was less polio, fewer people felt a need to get vaccinated—with the result that more people were needlessly afflicted by polio. Now that military deterrence has produced beneficial results, unilateral cutbacks seem dangerously similar to the polio fallacy. Reductions in military forces on both sides can be mutually beneficial if they mean a balance of power—but *not* if they mean simply maintenance of Soviet military superiority at a price the Soviet bloc economies can afford.

Military superiority matters, even if a shot is never fired. "Power wins, not by being used but by being there," someone once said. The implicit threat of military power provides the framework within which all sorts of political and economic decisions are made, all over the world. The Soviets have not invested such huge resources in military weaponry for no reason—and certainly not for defensive reasons. Whether the current pause in their overseas expansionism will last probably depends on how long the resistance of the West will last.

Index

Credits/Acknowledgments

Cover design by Charles Vitelli

1. The Age of Power
Facing overview—Dover Pictorial Archives. 19, 20 (bottom), 21, 27, 29—Weidenfeld Archives. 20—(top) *History Today* Archives.

2. Rationalism, Enlightenment, and Revolution
Facing overview—National Gallery of Art. 44-45—Granger Collection. 57—Marcus Rediker.

3. Industry, Ideology, Nation-Building, and Imperialism
Facing overview—National Archives. 89, 94, 96—Mansell Collection. 91—*Punch*, November 1858. 92—*Punch*, October 1858. 108—Mary Evans Picture Library.

4. Modernism, Statism, and Total War
Facing overview—Library of Congress. 132—Bettman Archives. 133-134—Illustrated London News Picture Library. 135—UPI/Bettman. 136—Map by Bowring Cartographic. 167—© Henri Carter-Bresson/Magnum Photos, Inc. 168-172—*Album Camus*, edited by Robert Grenier. © 1982 by Editions Gallimard. 177—© 1964 Rand Corporation. 179—Map created by Easten & Associates, Washington, DC.

5. Conclusion
Facing overview—United Nations photo by Y. Nagata.

ANNUAL EDITIONS ARTICLE REVIEW FORM

■ NAME: ______________________________ DATE: ______________

■ TITLE AND NUMBER OF ARTICLE: ______________________________

■ BRIEFLY STATE THE MAIN IDEA OF THIS ARTICLE: ______________________________

____

■ LIST THREE IMPORTANT FACTS THAT THE AUTHOR USES TO SUPPORT THE MAIN IDEA:

____

____

____

____

____

■ WHAT INFORMATION OR IDEAS DISCUSSED IN THIS ARTICLE ARE ALSO DISCUSSED IN YOUR TEXTBOOK OR OTHER READINGS THAT YOU HAVE DONE? LIST THE TEXTBOOK CHAPTERS AND PAGE NUMBERS:

____

____

____

____

____

■ LIST ANY EXAMPLES OF BIAS OR FAULTY REASONING THAT YOU FOUND IN THE ARTICLE:

____

____

____

____

____

■ LIST ANY NEW TERMS/CONCEPTS THAT WERE DISCUSSED IN THE ARTICLE, AND WRITE A SHORT DEFINITION:

____

____

____

____

____

*Your instructor may require you to use this ANNUAL EDITIONS Article Review Form in any number of ways: for articles that are assigned, for extra credit, as a tool to assist in developing assigned papers, or simply for your own reference. Even if it is not required, we encourage you to photocopy and use this page; you will find that reflecting on the articles will greatly enhance the information from your text.

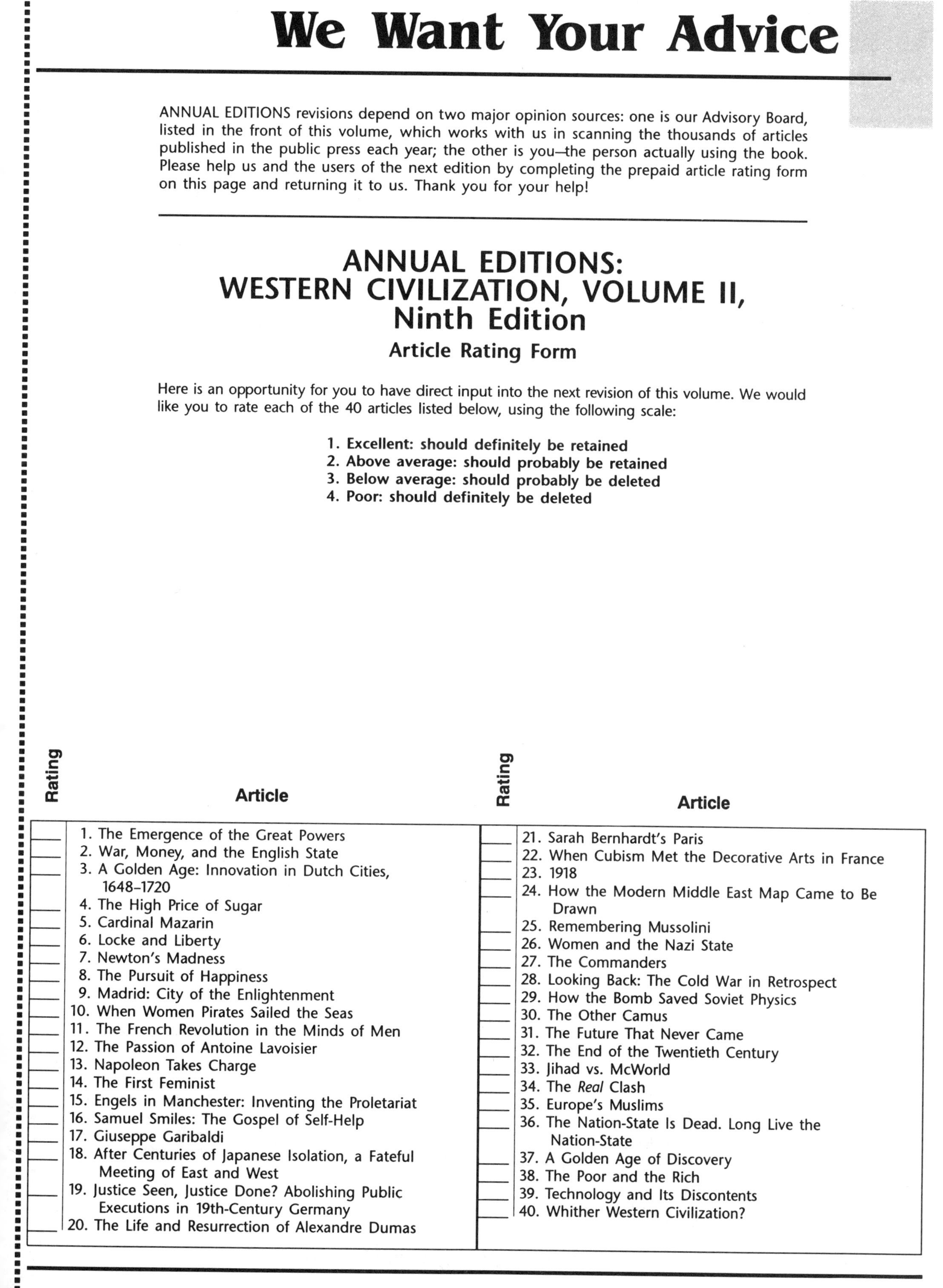

We Want Your Advice

ANNUAL EDITIONS revisions depend on two major opinion sources: one is our Advisory Board, listed in the front of this volume, which works with us in scanning the thousands of articles published in the public press each year; the other is you—the person actually using the book. Please help us and the users of the next edition by completing the prepaid article rating form on this page and returning it to us. Thank you for your help!

ANNUAL EDITIONS: WESTERN CIVILIZATION, VOLUME II, Ninth Edition

Article Rating Form

Here is an opportunity for you to have direct input into the next revision of this volume. We would like you to rate each of the 40 articles listed below, using the following scale:

1. **Excellent: should definitely be retained**
2. **Above average: should probably be retained**
3. **Below average: should probably be deleted**
4. **Poor: should definitely be deleted**

Rating	Article
____	1. The Emergence of the Great Powers
____	2. War, Money, and the English State
____	3. A Golden Age: Innovation in Dutch Cities, 1648–1720
____	4. The High Price of Sugar
____	5. Cardinal Mazarin
____	6. Locke and Liberty
____	7. Newton's Madness
____	8. The Pursuit of Happiness
____	9. Madrid: City of the Enlightenment
____	10. When Women Pirates Sailed the Seas
____	11. The French Revolution in the Minds of Men
____	12. The Passion of Antoine Lavoisier
____	13. Napoleon Takes Charge
____	14. The First Feminist
____	15. Engels in Manchester: Inventing the Proletariat
____	16. Samuel Smiles: The Gospel of Self-Help
____	17. Giuseppe Garibaldi
____	18. After Centuries of Japanese Isolation, a Fateful Meeting of East and West
____	19. Justice Seen, Justice Done? Abolishing Public Executions in 19th-Century Germany
____	20. The Life and Resurrection of Alexandre Dumas
____	21. Sarah Bernhardt's Paris
____	22. When Cubism Met the Decorative Arts in France
____	23. 1918
____	24. How the Modern Middle East Map Came to Be Drawn
____	25. Remembering Mussolini
____	26. Women and the Nazi State
____	27. The Commanders
____	28. Looking Back: The Cold War in Retrospect
____	29. How the Bomb Saved Soviet Physics
____	30. The Other Camus
____	31. The Future That Never Came
____	32. The End of the Twentieth Century
____	33. Jihad vs. McWorld
____	34. The *Real* Clash
____	35. Europe's Muslims
____	36. The Nation-State Is Dead. Long Live the Nation-State
____	37. A Golden Age of Discovery
____	38. The Poor and the Rich
____	39. Technology and Its Discontents
____	40. Whither Western Civilization?

(Continued on next page)

ABOUT YOU

Name ______________________________ Date ______________

Are you a teacher? ❑ Or a student? ❑

Your school name ______________________________

Department ______________________________

Address ______________________________

City ______________________ State ________ Zip ____________

School telephone # ______________________________

YOUR COMMENTS ARE IMPORTANT TO US!

Please fill in the following information:

For which course did you use this book? ______________________________

Did you use a text with this *ANNUAL EDITION*? ❑ yes ❑ no

What was the title of the text? ______________________________

What are your general reactions to the *Annual Editions* concept?

Have you read any particular articles recently that you think should be included in the next edition?

Are there any articles you feel should be replaced in the next edition? Why?

Are there other areas that you feel would utilize an *ANNUAL EDITION?*

May we contact you for editorial input?

May we quote you from above?

No Postage Necessary if Mailed in the United States

ANNUAL EDITIONS: WESTERN CIVILIZATION, VOLUME II, Ninth Edition

BUSINESS REPLY MAIL

First Class Permit No. 84 Guilford, CT

Postage will be paid by addressee

Dushkin Publishing Group/
Brown & Benchmark Publishers
Sluice Dock
Guilford, Connecticut 06437